17th Conference of the European Chapter of the Association for Computational Linguistics (EACL 2023)

System Demonstrations

Dubrovnik, Croatia
2-4 May 2023

ISBN: 978-1-7138-7377-8

Printed from e-media with permission by:

Curran Associates, Inc.
57 Morehouse Lane
Red Hook, NY 12571

Some format issues inherent in the e-media version may also appear in this print version.

Association for Computational Linguistics
209 N. Eighth Street
Stroudsburg, Pennsylvania 18360

Phone: 1-570-476-8006
Fax: 1-570-476-0860

acl@aclweb.org

Additional copies of this publication are available from:

Curran Associates, Inc.
57 Morehouse Lane
Red Hook, NY 12571 USA
Phone: 845-758-0400
Fax: 845-758-2633
Email: curran@proceedings.com
Web: www.proceedings.com

EACL 2023

The 17th Conference of the European Chapter of the Association for Computational Linguistics

Proceedings of System Demonstrations

May 2-4, 2023

The EACL organizers gratefully acknowledge the support from the following sponsors.

Diamond and Welcome Event

grammarly

Diamond

LIVEPERSON

Platinum and D&I Ally

amazon | science

Platinum

Bloomberg

Engineering

Silver

duolingo

Bronze

Adobe

Babelscape

Introduction

Welcome to the proceedings of the system demonstration track of the 17th Conference of the European Chapter of the Association for Computational Linguistics (EACL 2023) on May 2nd – May 4th, 2023. For the EACL 2022 system demonstration track, we received 56 submissions, of which 33 were selected for inclusion in the program (acceptance rate of 59%) after being reviewed by at least three members of the program committee. We would like to thank the members of the program committee for their timely help in reviewing the submissions. Lastly, we thank the many authors that submitted their work to the demonstrations track. As this year's EACL conference is a hybrid event, the demonstration papers will be presented through virtual presentations and also in person during the poster sessions. We appreciate the efforts made by all authors to showcase their work and contribute to the success of the conference.

Danlo Croce, Luca Soldaini
EACL 2023 System Demonstration Chairs

Program Committee

Chairs

Danilo Croce, University of Roma, Tor Vergata
Luca Soldaini, Allen Institute for AI

Program Committee

Abdalghani Abujabal, Amazon Alexa AI
Rodrigo Agerri, HiTZ Center - Ixa, University of the Basque Country UPV/EHU
Zeynep Akkalyoncu, University of Waterloo
Miguel A. Alonso, Universidade da Coruña
Rafael Anchiêta, Federal Institute of Piauí
Eleftherios Avramidis, German Research Center for Artificial Intelligence (DFKI)
Ioana Baldini, IBM Research
Gianni Barlacchi, Amazon Alexa
Mohaddeseh Bastan, Stony Brook University
Gábor Berend, University Of Szeged
Aljoscha Burchardt, DFKI
Daniel Campos, University of Illinois Urbana Champaign
Erion Çano, Research Group Data Mining, University of Vienna
Jiarun Cao, University of Manchester
Alberto Cetoli, Private
Chung-chi Chen, National Institute of Advanced Industrial Science and Technology
Guanyi Chen, Utrecht University
Jhih-jie Chen, National Tsing Hua University
Yagmur Gizem Cinar, Amazon
Marina Danilevsky, IBM Research
Thierry Declerck, DFKI GmbH
Shumin Deng, National University of Singapore
Michael Desmond, IBM Research
Joseph P. Dexter, Harvard University
Chenchen Ding, NICT
Carl Edwards, University of Illinois, Urbana-Champaign
Federico Fancellu, 3M
Paulo Fernandes, Merrimack College
Sudeep Gandhe, Google Inc
Andrew Gargett, The Open University
Xianpei Han, Institute of Software, Chinese Academy of Sciences
Ales Horak, Masaryk University
Claudiu Daniel Hromei, University of Rome, Tor Vergata Italy
Xiaodan Hu, University of Illinois at Urbana-Champaign
Ali Hürriyetoğlu, KNAW
Jeff Jacobs, Columbia University
Zhuoxuan Jiang, Tencent
Sudipta Kar, Amazon Alexa AI
Philipp Koehn, Johns Hopkins University
Mamoru Komachi, Tokyo Metropolitan University
Valia Kordoni, Humboldt-Universität zu Berlin

Philippe Laban, Salesforce Research
Tuan Lai, University of Illinois at Urbana-Champaign
Mark Last, Ben-Gurion University of the Negev
Dong-ho Lee, University of Southern California
Manling Li, UIUC
Xintong Li, Apple
Sha Li, University of Illinois Urbana-Champaign
Yanran Li, The Hong Kong Polytechnic University
Marina Litvak, Shamoon College of Engineering
Qian Liu, Sea AI Lab
Nitin Madnani, Educational Testing Service
Wolfgang Maier, Mercedes-Benz AG
Stella Markantonatou, ILSP/R.C. Athena"
Yoshitomo Matsubara, Amazon Alexa AI
Margot Mieskes, University of Applied Sciences, Darmstadt
Yusuke Miyao, University of Tokyo
Hamdy Mubarak, Qatar Computing Research Institute
Diane Napolitano, The Associated Press
Denis Newman-griffis, University of Pittsburgh
Tae-gil Noh, OMQ GmbH
Yusuke Oda, Inspired Cognition
Feifei Pan, Amazon
Alexandros Papangelis, Amazon Alexa AI
Xutan Peng, Huawei
Prokopis Prokopidis, ILSP/Athena RC
Yada Pruksachatkun, Alexa AI
Pablo Ruiz Fabo, LiLPa, Université de Strasbourg
Saurav Sahay, Intel Labs
Gözde Şahin, Koç University
Sashank Santhanam, University of North Carolina at Charlotte/ Apple
Michael Saxon, University of California, Santa Barbara
Sven Schmeier, Researcher
Jaydeep Sen, IBM Research AI
Liang-hsin Shen, National Taiwan University
Michal Shmueli-scheuer, IBM Research
Lei Shu, Google Research
Amy Siu, Berliner Hochschule für Technik
Yuanfeng Song, Hong Kong University of Science and Technology, WeBank Co., Ltd
Jacopo Staiano, University of Trento
Josef Steinberger, University of West Bohemia
Michael Stewart, The University of Western Australia
Carl Strathearn, Edinburgh Napier University
Jian Sun, China Mobile Research Institute
Chenkai Sun, University of Illinois at Urbana-Champaign
Natalia Vanetik, Shamoon College of Engineering
Rui Wang, Vipshop (China) Co., Ltd.
Qingyun Wang, University of Illinois at Urbana-Champaign
Zhenhailong Wang, University of Illinois at Urbana-Champaign
Jingjing Wang, Soochow University
Xianchao Wu, NVIDIA
Deyi Xiong, Tianjin University

Zhen Xu, Tencent PCG
Tae Yano, Expedia Group
Seid Muhie Yimam, Universität Hamburg
Dian Yu, Google
Qi Zeng, University of Illinois at Urbana-Champaign
Chengzhi Zhang, Nanjing University of Science and Technology
Zixuan Zhang, University of Illinois Urbana-Champaign
Qi Zhang, Fudan University
Cangqi Zhou, Nanjing University of Science and Technology
Guangyou Zhou, School of Computer Science, Central China Normal University

Table of Contents

Addressing Issues of Cross-Linguality in Open-Retrieval Question Answering Systems For Emergent Domains
Alon Albalak, Sharon Levy and William Yang Wang 1

CodeAnno: Extending WebAnno with Hierarchical Document Level Annotation and Automation
Florian Schneider, Seid Muhie Yimam, Fynn Petersen-frey, Gerret Von Nordheim, Katharina Kleinen-von Konigslow and Chris Biemann 11

NLP Workbench: Efficient and Extensible Integration of State-of-the-art Text Mining Tools
Peiran Yao, Matej Kosmajac, Abeer Waheed, Kostyantyn Guzhva, Natalie Hervieux and Denilson Barbosa 18

jTLEX: a Java Library for TimeLine EXtraction
Mustafa Ocal, Akul Singh, Jared Hummer, Antonela Radas and Mark Finlayson 27

CovRelex-SE: Adding Semantic Information for Relation Search via Sequence Embedding
Truong Do, Chau Nguyen, Vu Tran, Ken Satoh, Yuji Matsumoto and Minh Nguyen 35

ITMT: Interactive Topic Model Trainer
Lorena Calvo Bartolomé, José Antonio Espinosa Melchor and Jerónimo Arenas-garcía 43

FISH: A Financial Interactive System for Signal Highlighting
Ta-wei Huang, Jia-huei Ju, Yu-shiang Huang, Cheng-wei Lin, Yi-shyuan Chiang and Chuan-ju Wang 50

Yu Sheng: Human-in-Loop Classical Chinese Poetry Generation System
Jingkun Ma, Runzhe Zhan and Derek F. Wong 57

PANACEA: An Automated Misinformation Detection System on COVID-19
Runcong Zhao, Miguel Arana-catania, Lixing Zhu, Elena Kochkina, Lin Gui, Arkaitz Zubiaga, Rob Procter, Maria Liakata and Yulan He 67

NxPlain: A Web-based Tool for Discovery of Latent Concepts
Fahim Dalvi, Nadir Durrani, Hassan Sajjad, Tamim Jaban, Mus'ab Husaini and Ummar Abbas 75

Small-Text: Active Learning for Text Classification in Python
Christopher Schröder, Lydia Müller, Andreas Niekler and Martin Potthast 84

kogito: A Commonsense Knowledge Inference Toolkit
Mete Ismayilzada and Antoine Bosselut 96

Text-Blueprint: An Interactive Platform for Plan-based Conditional Generation
Fantine Huot, Joshua Maynez, Shashi Narayan, Reinald Kim Amplayo, Kuzman Ganchev, Annie Priyadarshini Louis, Anders Sandholm, Dipanjan Das and Mirella Lapata 105

ALAMBIC : Active Learning Automation Methods to Battle Inefficient Curation
Charlotte Nachtegael, Jacopo De Stefani and Tom Lenaerts 117

SPINDLE: Spinning Raw Text into Lambda Terms with Graph Attention
Konstantinos Kogkalidis, Michael Moortgat and Richard Moot 128

Linguistic Constructs Represent the Domain Model in Intelligent Language Tutoring
Anisia Katinskaia, Jue Hou, Anh-duc Vu and Roman Yangarber 136

GATE Teamware 2: An open-source tool for collaborative document classification annotation
David Wilby, Twin Karmakharm, Ian Roberts, Xingyi Song and Kalina Bontcheva 145

GameQA: Gamified Mobile App Platform for Building Multiple-Domain Question-Answering Datasets
Njall Skarphedinsson, Breki Gudmundsson, Steinar Smari, Marta Kristin Larusdottir, Hafsteinn Einarsson, Abuzar Khan, Eric Nyberg and Hrafn Loftsson 152

Towards Speech to Speech Machine Translation focusing on Indian Languages
Vandan Mujadia and Dipti Sharma 161

TextWorldExpress: Simulating Text Games at One Million Steps Per Second
Peter Jansen and Marc-alexandre Cote 169

TermoUD - a language-independent terminology extraction tool
Malgorzata Marciniak, Piotr Rychlik and Agnieszka Mykowiecka 178

INCOGNITUS: A Toolbox for Automated Clinical Notes Anonymization
Bruno Ribeiro, Vitor Rolla and Ricardo Santos 187

CoTEVer: Chain of Thought Prompting Annotation Toolkit for Explanation Verification
Seungone Kim, Se June Joo, Yul Jang, Hyungjoo Chae and Jinyoung Yeo 195

OLEA: Tool and Infrastructure for Offensive Language Error Analysis in English
Marie Grace, Jay Seabrum, Dananjay Srinivas and Alexis Palmer 209

TULAP - An Accessible and Sustainable Platform for Turkish Natural Language Processing Resources
Susan Uskudarli, Muhammet Şen, Furkan Akkurt, Merve Gürbüz, Onur Gungor, Arzucan Özgür and Tunga Güngör 219

ALANNO: An Active Learning Annotation System for Mortals
Josip Jukić, Fran Jelenić, Miroslav Bićanić and Jan Snajder 228

Automatically Summarizing Evidence from Clinical Trials: A Prototype Highlighting Current Challenges
Sanjana Ramprasad, Jered Mcinerney, Iain Marshall and Byron Wallace 236

Corpus Annotation Graph Builder (CAG): An Architectural Framework to Create and Annotate a Multi-source Graph
Roxanne El Baff, Tobias Hecking, Andreas Hamm, Jasper W. Korte and Sabine Bartsch 248

ferret: a Framework for Benchmarking Explainers on Transformers
Giuseppe Attanasio, Eliana Pastor, Chiara Di Bonaventura and Debora Nozza 256

Learn With Martian: A Tool For Creating Assignments That Can Write And Re-Write Themselves
Shriyash Upadhyay, Chris Callison-burch and Etan Ginsberg 267

EVALIGN: Visual Evaluation of Translation Alignment Models
Tariq Yousef, Gerhard Heyer and Stefan Jänicke 277

ALLECS: A Lightweight Language Error Correction System
Muhammad Reza Qorib, Geonsik Moon and Hwee Tou Ng 298

DAVE: Differential Diagnostic Analysis Automation and Visualization from Clinical Notes
Hadi Hamoud, Fadi Zaraket, Chadi Abou Chakra and Mira Dankar 307

Addressing Issues of Cross-Linguality in Open-Retrieval Question Answering Systems For Emergent Domains

Alon Albalak, Sharon Levy, William Yang Wang
University of California, Santa Barbara
{alon_albalak,sharonlevy,william}@cs.ucsb.edu

Abstract

Open-retrieval question answering systems are generally trained and tested on large datasets in well-established domains. However, low-resource settings such as new and emerging domains would especially benefit from reliable question answering systems. Furthermore, multilingual and cross-lingual resources in emergent domains are scarce, leading to few or no such systems. In this paper, we demonstrate a cross-lingual open-retrieval question answering system for the emergent domain of COVID-19. Our system adopts a corpus of scientific articles to ensure that retrieved documents are reliable. To address the scarcity of cross-lingual training data in emergent domains, we present a method utilizing automatic translation, alignment, and filtering to produce English-to-all datasets. We show that a deep semantic retriever greatly benefits from training on our English-to-all data and significantly outperforms a BM25 baseline in the cross-lingual setting. We illustrate the capabilities of our system with examples and release all code necessary to train and deploy such a system[1].

1 Introduction

One challenge of emergent domains is that the originating locality is unknown, leading to the need for reliable information to cross language barriers. However, it is unlikely that domain-specific information will be available across multiple languages for a new domain. Furthermore, information rapidly changes in emerging domains, compounding the challenge of accessing credible data.

An example of a prominent emergent domain is COVID-19, which has quickly spread across the globe. To combat the spread of misinformation about COVID-19, researchers have developed open-retrieval question answering (Chen and Yih, 2020) systems which use large collections of trusted documents. For example, Lee et al. (2020), Levy et al. (2021), and Esteva et al. (2021) all develop open-retrieval QA systems using large corpuses of scientific journal articles. However, because these systems focus on English, they leave a gap for implementation on emergent domains that do not originate in English-speaking locations.

To address the limitations of prior systems, we implement a cross-lingual open-retrieval question answering system that retrieves answers from a large collection of multilingual documents, where answers may be in a language different from the question (Asai et al., 2021).

In this work we take COVID-19 as an exemplar of an emergent domain and present our system, which addresses two main areas of importance:

- *Cross-linguality*: The locality of an emergent domain is unknown ahead of time, making cross-lingual QA essential. Additionally, because data can rapidly change in emerging domains, new information may develop in multiple languages, motivating the need for systems that work across many languages.
- *Scarcity of training data*: Data scarcity is an expected concern for emergent domains, but multilingual and cross-lingual data are even more limited. We demonstrate that by employing automatic translation, alignment, and filtering methods, this challenge can be overcome in low-resource open-retrieval QA.

This system demonstration provides in-depth technical descriptions of the individual components of our cross-lingual open-retrieval question answering system: cross-lingual retrieval and cross-lingual reading comprehension modules. Then, we describe how to combine the components along with document re-ranking into the complete system, shown in Figure 1, and present several examples taken from our system.

[1]Code is open-sourced on github (link). Short video demonstration provided on youtube (link).

Proceedings of the 17th Conference of the European Chapter of the Association for Computational Linguistics System Demonstrations, pages 1–10

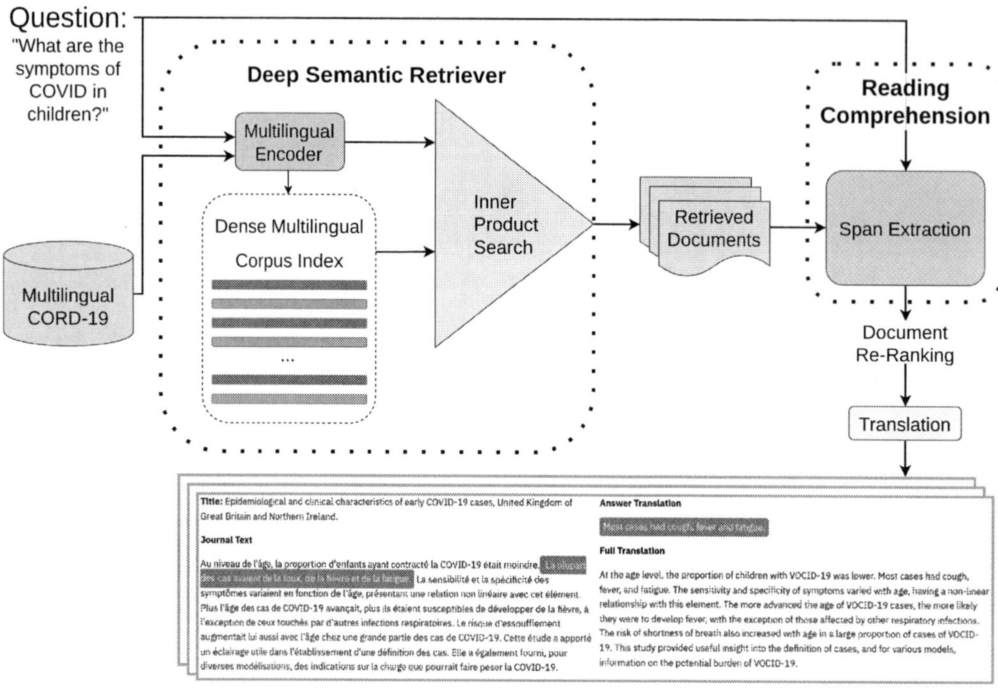

Figure 1: An overview of our cross-lingual COVID-19 open-retrieval question-answering system.

2 Cross-Lingual Dense Retrieval

Training a dense retriever is challenging in low-resource settings, such as emergent domains, due to the data-hungry nature of large language models. This challenge is compounded in the cross-lingual setting, where we aim to train a model to encode concepts from multiple languages into a similar location in the embedding space. In this section, we discuss how we overcome these challenges.

2.1 Data

Cross-lingual retrieval requires two datasets; a large-scale multilingual corpus of scientific articles from which to retrieve documents and a cross-lingual dataset for training the retriever. However, a very limited number of COVID-19 datasets have been released, few of which are multilingual and none of which are cross-lingual.

CORD-19 (Lu Wang et al., 2020) is a large-scale corpus of scientific papers on COVID-19, however a known limitation is that it contains only English articles. We draw inspiration from this work to address the lack of a large scale corpus of multilingual COVID-19 scientific articles. For our system, we use a manually collected corpus of English abstracts from PubMed, some of which have parallel abstracts in additional languages. The corpus is collected using the same query as described by Lu Wang et al. (2020) . We call this corpus multilingual CORD-19 (mCORD-19), and the language distribution can be found in Table 1.

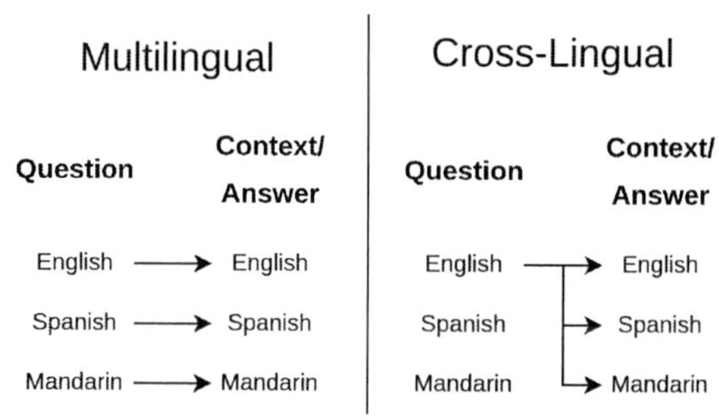

Figure 2: **Multilingual vs. cross-lingual question answering**: In the multilingual setting, QA pairs exist for multiple languages in a one-to-one mapping. On the other hand, in cross-lingual QA questions may have answers in any language, creating a one-to-many mapping.

To train our retriever we utilize the COUGH (Zhang et al., 2021) dataset, which is a multilingual FAQ retrieval dataset and consists of COVID-19 QA pairs. Although COUGH is multilingual, containing samples in 9 different languages, COUGH does not contain any cross-lingual QA pairs. The language distribution is shown in Table 1.

COUGH	9151 (en)	1077 (es)	778 (zh)	697 (fr)	573 (ja)	531 (ar)
mCORD-19	172977 (en)	1109 (es)	951 (zh)	711 (de)	614 (fr)	328 (pt)

Table 1: Top 6 languages by count for COUGH and the multilingual CORD-19 datasets. Language codes are the following: en-English, es-Spanish, zh-Chinese, fr-French, de-German, ja-Japanese, ar-Arabic, pt-Portuguese.

Answer Language	Spanish	Mandarin	French	Arabic	German	Russian	Vietnamese	Italian
En2All	8695	8441	8372	8231	8226	8156	8072	8003
Filtered En2All	6620	5869	5635	5808	5867	4137	531	6568

Table 2: QA pairs in our En2All and Filtered En2All variants of the COUGH dataset, where each question is in English, and the context and answer are in the language specified above.

2.2 Cross-lingual Data Generation

To address the lack of cross-lingual data in COUGH we introduce a modification of the dataset which we call English-to-all (En2All), where we convert the dataset from the multilingual to cross-lingual setting, as demonstrated in Figure 2. Because we are interested in a system which will find non-English answers to English questions, we create En2All through two translation processes. First, we translate the answer portion of every QA pair from COUGH into eight languages: Arabic, French, German, Italian, Mandarin, Russian, Spanish, and Vietnamese. Secondly, we translate the question portion of all QA pairs from any of the above languages into English[2].

As machine translation models do not perform perfectly, there may be instances within En2All that contain poor translations. To resolve this problem, we utilize LaBSE (Feng et al., 2020), an existing BERT-based sentence embedding model that encodes 109 languages into a shared embedding space. The model is utilized to compare the alignment of translations across different languages. We take the following steps to filter out any poor translations in the data:

1. We step through the current En2All and calculate similarity scores between translated answers and their original English answers. To do this, we have eight different comparisons for each translated English QA pair.

2. Once the similarity scores have been calculated, we remove translations that do not meet a threshold and are classified as poor translations.

After going through these steps, roughly one-third of the data samples from En2All are removed for poor translations.

2.3 Methodology: Deep Semantic Retriever

Our retrieval model is based on the dense passage retriever from Karpukhin et al. (2020). In contrast to their work, we train a unified encoder that encodes both query and corpus into a shared space. For the encoder, we train the multilingual BERT (mBERT) (Devlin et al., 2019) and XLM-RoBERTa (XLM-R) (Conneau et al., 2020) models. Both models have been pre-trained using a tokenizer which shares a vocabulary for over 100 languages, allowing the models to encode all languages into a shared space. We train these models on the FAQ retrieval task by maximizing the inner product of correct QA pairs and minimizing the inner product of within-batch incorrect pairs.

2.4 Cross-Lingual Retrieval Evaluation

To evaluate our models in the large-scale open-retrieval setting we utilize the questions from COUGH and En2All as our queries and the mCORD-19 dataset for our retrieval corpus. Because we have no ground truth labels for correct documents, and indeed there may be some unanswerable questions given this corpus, we measure model quality through a fuzzy matching metric, Fuzzy Match at top k documents (FM@k). FM@k utilizes the multilingual Sentence-BERT model from (Reimers and Gurevych, 2019)[3]. Each of the top k retrieved documents is split into it's component sentences and embedded using the sentence-BERT model. Next, each sentence is compared

[2]All translations are generated by the MarianNMT system (Junczys-Dowmunt et al., 2018) through the Huggingface Transformers (Wolf et al., 2020) library.

[3]We use the 'paraphrase-multilingual-mpnet-base-v2' variant

Model	COUGH (FM@5/100)	COUGH +En2All (FM@5/100)
BM25[4]	18.6/41.4	
mBERT$_{base}$	22.8/49.5	26.4/50.7
+ En2All	28.0/54.9	27.7/51.7
XLM-R$_{base}$	25.0/51.3	28.1/51.6
+ En2All	30.1/55.4	28.4/52.2
+ Filtered-En2All	**32.9/56.7**	**30.9/53.4**
XLM-R$_{large}$	30.5/56.6	29.8/53.2
+ En2All	32.1/56.4	29.6/52.9

Table 3: **Retrieval evaluation results**. All models are trained on COUGH and additional training data is denoted by "+". The middle column takes queries from COUGH, the right column from COUGH and En2All. For both columns, the retrieval corpus is mCORD. FM@5 and FM@100 are the fuzzy matching techniques proposed to determine open-retrieval accuracy described in section 2.4. Because BM25 is not cross-lingual, we translate it's queries into all languages in order to fairly compare against our cross-lingual models.

with the ground truth answer by calculating the cosine similarity with the reference answer embedding from COUGH. If any of the cosine similarities for that documents sentences are above a threshold, the document is evaluated as a positive retrieval.

The results for our models and a BM25 baseline[4] are found in Table 3. Since a multilingual BM25 cannot perform cross-lingual retrieval, in order to fairly compare against cross-lingual models, we translate all queries into every other language in the mCORD corpus and then perform BM25 retrieval.

BM25 drastically underperforms compared to encoder models and demonstrates the need for a dense retrieval model. Although encoder models outperform BM25 when trained on multilingual data (COUGH), they are further improved by training on cross-lingual data (En2All). Additionally, after filtering low quality translations from En2All, we see further improvement in performance.

3 Cross-Lingual Reading Comprehension

3.1 Data

To train our cross-lingual reading comprehension model, we would ideally use a cross-lingual covid-specific question answering dataset. However, similarly to cross-lingual retrieval no such dataset exists so we augment existing datasets.

[4]BM25 Implementation details found at https://github.com/alon-albalak/XOR-COVID/tree/master/bm25

Model	MCQA (EM/F1)	MCQA+En2All (EM/F1)
mBERT$_{base}$	20.0/57.5	19.6/55.4
+ XQuAD	21.2/57.7	20.5/55.6
+ En2All	19.3/56.1	19.2/55.8
XLM-R$_{base}$	25.1/60.0	24.4/58.9
+ XQuAD	26.7/61.6	26.1/61.3
+ En2All	24.0/58.8	23.9/58.3
XLM-R$_{large}$	26.5/**62.7**	26.4/**62.2**
+ XQuAD	**29.1**/62.1	**29.0**/61.7
+ En2All	26.3/61.1	26.6/60.8

Table 4: **Reading comprehension evaluation results**. All models are trained on MCQA, and additional training data is denoted by "+". The left column shows evaluation on a multilingual dataset where questions/contexts are always in the same language. The right column additionally evaluates on a cross-lingual dataset where questions are in english and context paragraphs may be in any language.

Artetxe et al. (2020) introduced XQuAD, a multilingual QA dataset composed of 240 paragraphs and 1190 QA pairs from SQuAD v1.1 which have been professionally translated into 10 languages. We utilize XQuAD as a pretraining dataset before performing any training on covid-specific datasets[5]. Möller et al. (2020) introduce Covid-QA, a covid-specific QA dataset consisting of 2019 question-answer pairs, however, it contains english-only data. We modify Covid-QA with translations from MarianMT (Junczys-Dowmunt et al., 2018) to generate two dataset variants based on the multilingual and cross-lingual settings shown in Figure 2: Multilingual Covid-QA (MCQA) and English-to-all (En2All). MCQA is a multilingual version of Covid-QA, created by translating all QA pairs into 9 languages to match those from XQuAD: Arabic, German, Greek, Spanish, Hindi, Mandarin, Romanian, Russian, and Vietnamese. En2All is our cross-lingual variation of Covid-QA, in a similar spirit to the cross-lingual variant of COUGH. Because Covid-QA is english-only, to generate En2All we translate all contexts/answers into the same 9 languages as MCQA.

3.2 Methodology: Span Extraction

Similar to our dense semantic retriever, we train mBERT and XLM-RoBERTa models for our reading comprehension task. We formulate reading comprehension as a span extraction task, where each model learns to find start and end tokens which represent the answer span in a document.

[5]We open-source our models pretrained on XQuAD at https://huggingface.co/alon-albalak

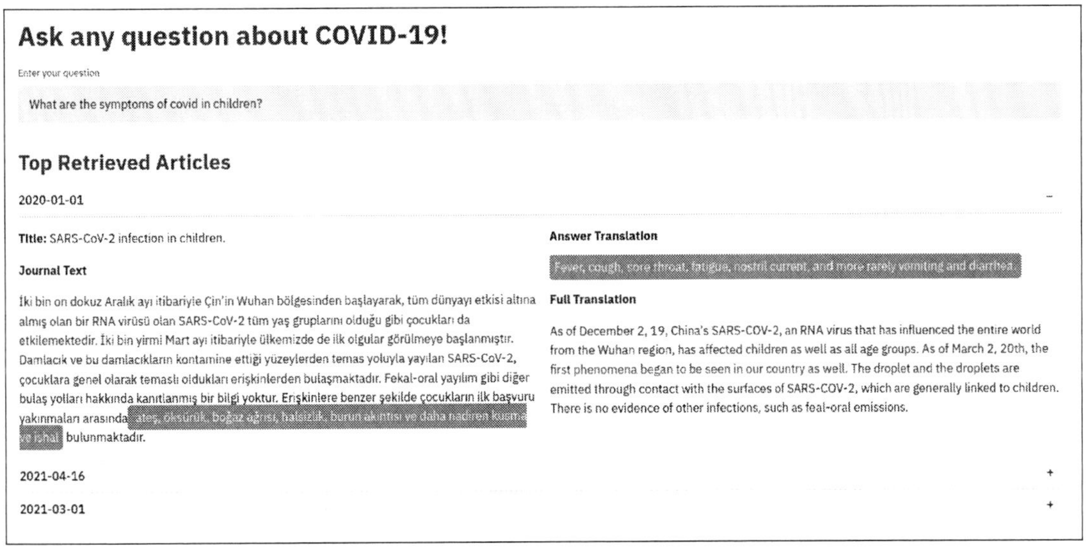

Figure 3: **The main interface of our system**. At the top is the search bar, where the current query is "What are the symptoms of covid in children?" Below the search bar are the three retrieved articles, ranked by relevance. In this example, the first retrieved document has been expanded to show the title and original text in Turkish, on the left. And on the right is the translation of the answer and the full document into English.

3.3 Cross-Lingual Reading Comprehension Evaluation

To evaluate our models in the reading comprehension task, we utilize the QA datasets described in Section 3.1. We evaluate our models based on exact match (EM) and F1 metrics by comparing the predicted answer spans with ground-truth answers.

The results for our models are found in Table 4. We train each of our models on MCQA and supplement it with data from XQuAD or En2All. Interestingly, we find that although En2All improved models in the retrieval setting, it only hurt model performance in QA. We also see that pretraining on XQuAD improves performance in all metrics for both base models, but leads to a slight decrease in F1 score for XLM-R_{large}. In our demo, we utilize XLM-R_{large} which was pretrained on XQuAD because it has only slightly worse F1 score, but significantly higher exact match compared to the next best model.

4 Cross-Lingual Open-Retrieval Question Answering

Our system is composed of the retrieval and reading comprehension modules described in sections 2 and 3. The full end-to-end system is shown in Figure 1. After the retriever has been trained, the mCORD-19 corpus is encoded and stored in the dense multilingual corpus index. When a question is posed to the system, the query is encoded, and a maximum inner product search is performed over the index to find documents most similar to the query. Answers are then extracted from the retrieved documents and the documents are re-ranked based on answer confidence from the span extraction model. Finally, the answer spans and full documents are translated into English and presented to the user with highlighted answers.

5 Demo

The demonstration retrieves documents from our mCORD-19 corpus, which has been encoded by the deep semantic retriever from section 2.3. We provide examples from the demo in Figures 4, 5, and 6.

5.1 Sidebar Interface

Our system has an options sidebar, shown in Figure 7, which gives the user several choices before entering a query. The user can determine how many documents they would like to see results from, they can select which languages the retrieved documents should be in, and they can specify a date range for the publications to search over. If there are no relevant documents in the desired date range, then the system will retrieve from any date range and displays a message to inform the user.

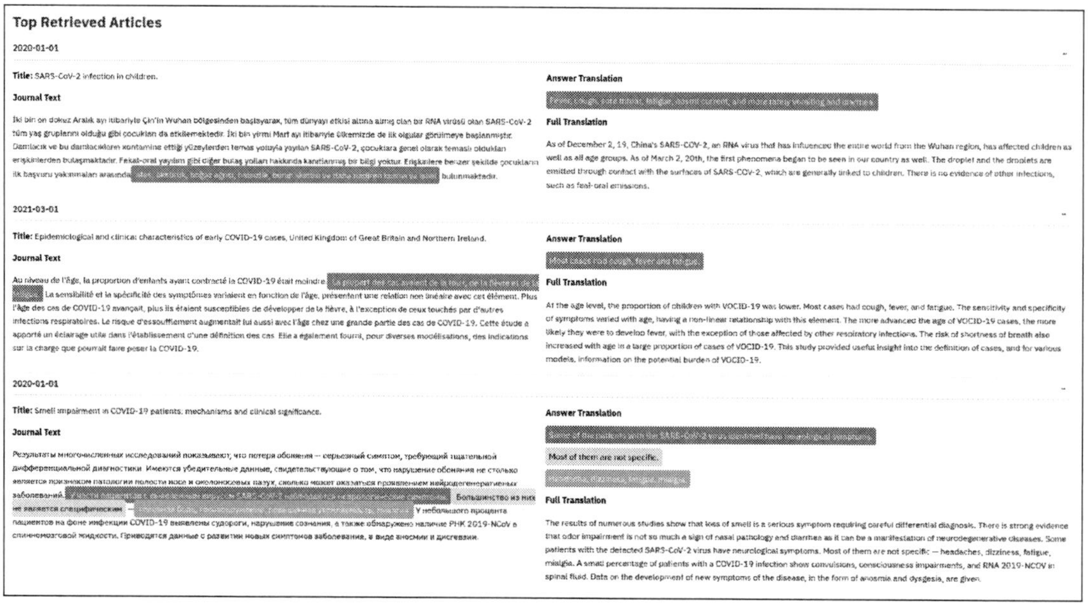

Figure 4: The top 3 non-English results for the query "What are the symptoms of covid in children?"

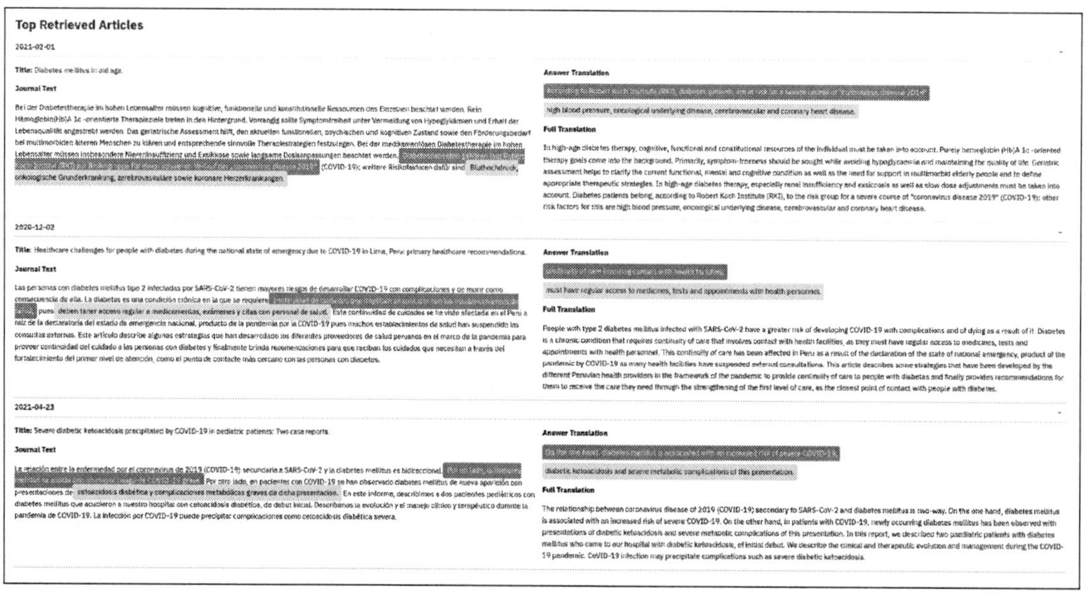

Figure 5: The top 3 non-english results for the query "What are the concerns of having covid and diabetes?"

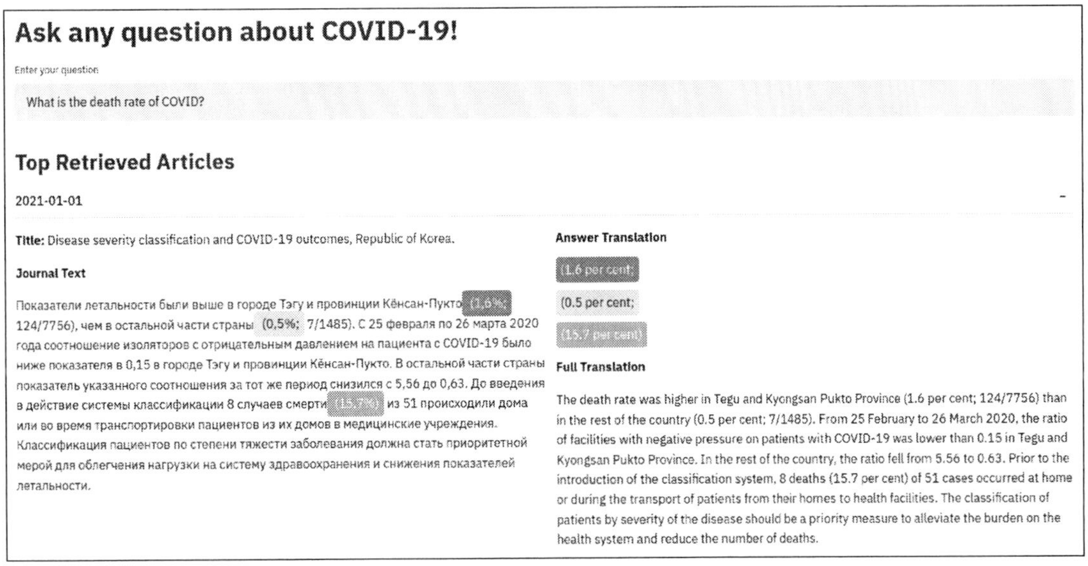

Figure 6: A retrieved document for the query "What is the death rate of COVID", which shows multiple correct answers corresponding to different provinces of South Korea.

Figure 7: The options sidebar for our demonstration system. The options include: number of articles to return, article languages to retrieve from, and publication date range. For visualization purposes we show all language options.

5.2 Main Interface

To query the system, a user simply selects the desired options from the sidebar and enters their question into the search bar, as seen in Figure 3. After the user enters their question, the system will encode the question using the trained deep semantic retriever and find the most relevant documents within the given language and date range constraints. Then, the reading comprehension model will extract the answer (or answers) most relevant to the query from each retrieved document. Additionally, for any non-English documents, the system translates both the retrieved article and extracted answers into English[6]. Finally, the retrieved documents will be re-ranked based on the confidence scores for the extracted answers.

The desired number of documents will be displayed to the user as a list of publication dates. Each item can be expanded to show the article title, original document with highlighted answers, translated answers, and the full article translation. If an article contains a single answer, it will be highlighted in red. If there are multiple answers, each answer will be highlighted with a different color to allow for easy alignment between original answers and their translations, demonstrated in Figure 6.

6 Conclusion

In this work, we tackled two challenging areas in open-retrieval QA: cross-linguality and data scarcity. We presented methods for generating cross-lingual data in an emergent domain, COVID-19. Then, we demonstrated that an open-retrieval QA system trained on our data significantly outperforms a BM25 baseline. We hope that the methods presented here allow for increased access to reliable information in future emergent domains.

[6]All translations are generated by MarianNMT (Junczys-Dowmunt et al., 2018) from the Huggingface Transformers library (Wolf et al., 2020).

7 Broader Impact and Limitations

Crucial to any open-retrieval question-answering system, the **credibility and truthfulness of the documents is paramount**, in particular when trying to prevent and combat misinformation that arises in emergent domains. Any question-answering system is limited by the corpus used. To this end, we do our best to ensure that any information included in our corpus is truthful by including only peer-reviewed scientific articles from PubMed[7].

Furthermore, there may be emergent domains without peer-reviewed scientific articles from which to draw answers. In these cases (and in fact in cases where peer-review does exist) it is imperative to include sources along with answers. This allows for users to judge the quality of information. In our system we present the title and date of publication for each returned article so that users can find the source content if desired.

Finally, **a known limitation** of dense-indexed open-retrieval systems is the static nature of the underlying database. This is a particularly important point for emerging domains, where current knowledge is quickly being updated. One disadvantage to the dense-index approach is that as new documents become available, the index may need to be recalculated if the new documents come from a significantly different distribution than the existing documents in the index. See here for further discussion and how to overcome these limitations.

References

Mikel Artetxe, Sebastian Ruder, and Dani Yogatama. 2020. On the cross-lingual transferability of monolingual representations. In *ACL*.

Akari Asai, Jungo Kasai, Jonathan H. Clark, Kenton Lee, Eunsol Choi, and Hannaneh Hajishirzi. 2021. XOR QA: Cross-lingual open-retrieval question answering. In *NAACL-HLT*.

Danqi Chen and Wen-tau Yih. 2020. Open-domain question answering. In *Proceedings of the 58th Annual Meeting of the Association for Computational Linguistics: Tutorial Abstracts*, pages 34–37, Online. Association for Computational Linguistics.

Alexis Conneau, Kartikay Khandelwal, Naman Goyal, Vishrav Chaudhary, Guillaume Wenzek, Francisco Guzmán, Edouard Grave, Myle Ott, Luke Zettlemoyer, and Veselin Stoyanov. 2020. Unsupervised cross-lingual representation learning at scale. In *Proceedings of the 58th Annual Meeting of the Association for Computational Linguistics*, pages 8440–8451, Online. Association for Computational Linguistics.

Jacob Devlin, Ming-Wei Chang, Kenton Lee, and Kristina Toutanova. 2019. BERT: Pre-training of deep bidirectional transformers for language understanding. In *Proceedings of the 2019 Conference of the North American Chapter of the Association for Computational Linguistics: Human Language Technologies, Volume 1 (Long and Short Papers)*, pages 4171–4186, Minneapolis, Minnesota. Association for Computational Linguistics.

Andre Esteva, Anuprit Kale, Romain Paulus, Kazuma Hashimoto, Wenpeng Yin, Dragomir Radev, and Richard Socher. 2021. Covid-19 information retrieval with deep-learning based semantic search, question answering, and abstractive summarization. *npj Digital Medicine*, 4(1):68.

Fangxiaoyu Feng, Yinfei Yang, Daniel Cer, Naveen Arivazhagan, and Wei Wang. 2020. Language-agnostic bert sentence embedding. *arXiv preprint arXiv:2007.01852*.

Marcin Junczys-Dowmunt, Roman Grundkiewicz, Tomasz Dwojak, Hieu Hoang, Kenneth Heafield, Tom Neckermann, Frank Seide, Ulrich Germann, Alham Fikri Aji, Nikolay Bogoychev, André F. T. Martins, and Alexandra Birch. 2018. Marian: Fast neural machine translation in C++. In *Proceedings of ACL 2018, System Demonstrations*, pages 116–121, Melbourne, Australia. Association for Computational Linguistics.

Vladimir Karpukhin, Barlas Oguz, Sewon Min, Patrick Lewis, Ledell Wu, Sergey Edunov, Danqi Chen, and Wen-tau Yih. 2020. Dense passage retrieval for open-domain question answering. In *Proceedings of the 2020 Conference on Empirical Methods in Natural Language Processing (EMNLP)*, pages 6769–6781, Online. Association for Computational Linguistics.

Jinhyuk Lee, Sean S. Yi, Minbyul Jeong, Mujeen Sung, WonJin Yoon, Yonghwa Choi, Miyoung Ko, and Jaewoo Kang. 2020. Answering questions on COVID-19 in real-time. In *Proceedings of the 1st Workshop on NLP for COVID-19 (Part 2) at EMNLP 2020*, Online. Association for Computational Linguistics.

Sharon Levy, Kevin Mo, Wenhan Xiong, and William Yang Wang. 2021. Open-Domain question-Answering for COVID-19 and other emergent domains. In *Proceedings of the 2021 Conference on Empirical Methods in Natural Language Processing: System Demonstrations*, pages 259–266, Online and Punta Cana, Dominican Republic. Association for Computational Linguistics.

Lucy Lu Wang, Kyle Lo, Yoganand Chandrasekhar, Russell Reas, Jiangjiang Yang, Darrin Eide, Kathryn Funk, Rodney Kinney, Ziyang Liu, William Merrill, Paul Mooney, Dewey Murdick, Devvret Rishi,

[7] https://pubmed.ncbi.nlm.nih.gov/

Jerry Sheehan, Zhihong Shen, Brandon Stilson, Alex D. Wade, Kuansan Wang, Chris Wilhelm, Boya Xie, Douglas Raymond, Daniel S. Weld, Oren Etzioni, and Sebastian Kohlmeier. 2020. Cord-19: The covid-19 open research dataset. *ArXiv*, page arXiv:2004.10706v2. 32510522[pmid].

Timo Möller, Anthony Reina, Raghavan Jayakumar, and Malte Pietsch. 2020. COVID-QA: A question answering dataset for COVID-19. In *Proceedings of the 1st Workshop on NLP for COVID-19 at ACL 2020*, Online. Association for Computational Linguistics.

Nils Reimers and Iryna Gurevych. 2019. Sentence-BERT: Sentence embeddings using Siamese BERT-networks. In *Proceedings of the 2019 Conference on Empirical Methods in Natural Language Processing and the 9th International Joint Conference on Natural Language Processing (EMNLP-IJCNLP)*, pages 3982–3992, Hong Kong, China. Association for Computational Linguistics.

Thomas Wolf, Lysandre Debut, Victor Sanh, Julien Chaumond, Clement Delangue, Anthony Moi, Pierric Cistac, Tim Rault, Rémi Louf, Morgan Funtowicz, Joe Davison, Sam Shleifer, Patrick von Platen, Clara Ma, Yacine Jernite, Julien Plu, Canwen Xu, Teven Le Scao, Sylvain Gugger, Mariama Drame, Quentin Lhoest, and Alexander M. Rush. 2020. Transformers: State-of-the-art natural language processing. In *Proceedings of the 2020 Conference on Empirical Methods in Natural Language Processing: System Demonstrations*, pages 38–45, Online. Association for Computational Linguistics.

Xinliang Frederick Zhang, Heming Sun, Xiang Yue, Simon Lin, and Huan Sun. 2021. COUGH: A challenge dataset and models for COVID-19 FAQ retrieval. In *Proceedings of the 2021 Conference on Empirical Methods in Natural Language Processing, EMNLP 2021*, pages 3759–3769.

A Additional Examples

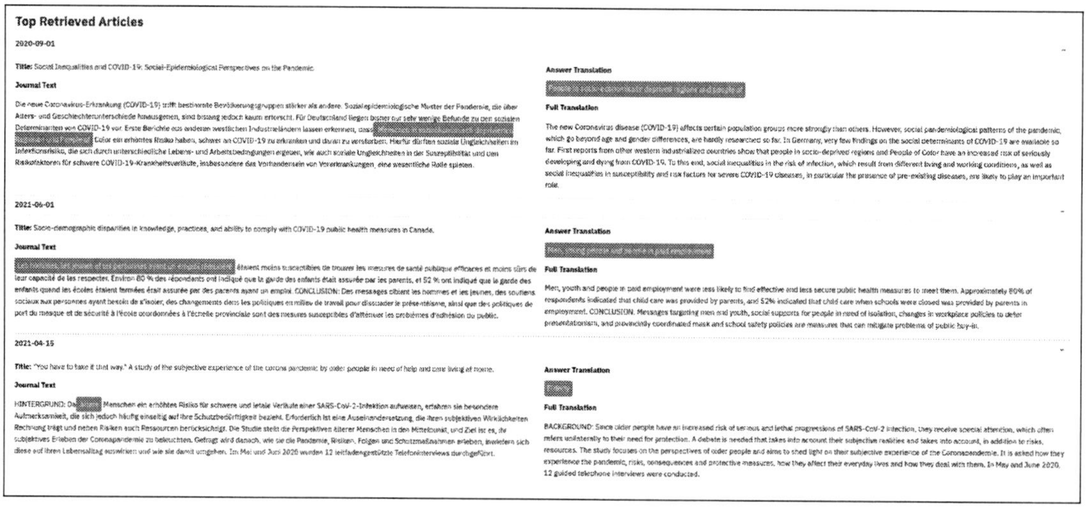

Figure 8: The top-3 non-english results for the query "Who is most vulnerable to covid?"

CodeAnno: Extending WebAnno with Hierarchical Document Level Annotation and Automation

Florian Schneider[†], **Seid Muhie Yimam**[†], **Fynn Petersen-Frey**[†]
Gerret von Nordheim[‡], **Katharina Kleinen-von Königslöw**[‡], **Chris Biemann**[†]
[†] Language Technology Group, Department of Informatics, Universität Hamburg, Germany
[‡] Institute of Journalism and Communication Studies, Universität Hamburg, Germany
{florian.schneider-1, seid.muhie.yimam, fynn.petersen-frey,
gerret.vonnordheim, katharina.kleinen, chris.biemann}@uni-hamburg.de

Abstract

WebAnno is one of the most popular annotation tools that supports generic annotation types and distributive annotation with multiple user roles. However, WebAnno focuses on annotating span-level mentions and relations among them, making document-level annotation complicated. When it comes to the annotation and analysis of social science materials, it usually involves the creation of codes to categorize a given document. The codes, which are known as **codebooks**, are typically hierarchical, which enables to code the document either with a general category or more fine-grained subcategories. **CodeAnno** is forked from WebAnno and designed to solve the coding problems faced by many social science researchers with the following main functionalities. 1) Creation of hierarchical codebooks, with functionality to move and sort categories in the hierarchy 2) an interactive UI for codebook annotation 3) import and export of annotations in CSV format, hence being compatible with existing annotations conducted using spreadsheet applications 4) integration of an external automation component to facilitate coding using machine learning 5) project templating that allows duplicating a project structure without copying the actual documents. We present different use-cases to demonstrate the capability of CodeAnno.

1 Introduction

When WebAnno was initiated, the main purpose was to address the missing functionalities from the annotation tools, particularly adding the distributive, web-based, generic, and customizable annotation layers behaviors (Yimam et al., 2013). Since then, WebAnno has been improved a lot, including the support for semantic annotation (Eckart de Castilho et al., 2016), support for automation functionality (Yimam et al., 2014), and adapted to the integrating knowledge-supported search 'INCEpTION' platform (Boullosa et al., 2018). The **Span** annotation type, which allows annotating tokens, sub-tokens, and phrases as well as the **Relation** type that connects two-span annotation types with relation value in WebAnno covers most of the linguistic and machine learning annotation tasks. The **Document** level annotation type is one of the most sought annotation types needed in WebAnno, which is also missed functionality from several annotation tools (Neves and Ševa, 2019). One of the workarounds in WebAnno was the **Zero-width spans**, which is not attached to any span but only to a specific sentence in a document. However, this still could not fully support document-level annotation, where the task is to label or classify a document based on a predefined category. The document-level annotation is particularly important for annotations in social science and digital humanities research. A typical example is document coding, where a researcher in communication science prepares a list of codes or tags known as **codebooks**. Journalists and media analysts prepare the codes for a given codebook but the annotation of content involves a lot of distraction, such as 1) preparing the code in a spreadsheet, 2) coding or annotating an article or media which is not linked with the codebook in the spreadsheet, 3) analyzing and interpreting the results from the coding.

CodeAnno is a fork and an extension to WebAnno, which enables coding based on hierarchical and fully customizable document-level annotations within WebAnno. CodeAnno facilitates the creation of codebooks and coding using the existing functionality from WebAnno such as curation, coding agreement, distributed annotation (annotating a single document by multiple coders or users), web-based annotation, and so on. As CodeAnno supports all existing functionalities of WebAnno, for example, span and relation annotation, one can easily connect the coding with the built-in WebAnno annotation support that can help to draw some conclusions.

The following are the main contributions of this

Proceedings of the 17th Conference of the European Chapter of the Association for Computational Linguistics
System Demonstrations, pages 11–17

work: 1) Support codebook creation and annotation (hierarchical and document-level annotation), 2) Importing and exporting annotations in comma-separated format, hence compatible with existing annotations conducted using spreadsheet applications, 3) Integration of an external automation component to facilitate media coding using machine learning models, 4) Project templating that allows duplicating a project structure without copying the actual documents.

In the remainder of this paper, we will first discuss the related works of document-level annotation in Section 2. In Section 3 and 4, the main components of CodeAnno and the automation functionalities are presented. Some use-cases showing the codebook annotation and automation components are presented in Section 5 while Section 6 highlighted the main contribution of this work.

2 Related Work

Most of the annotation tools support linguistic annotations such as POS tagging, dependency relation, named entity recognition and so on (Yimam et al., 2013; Neves and Ševa, 2019). Brat (Stenetorp et al., 2012), WebAnno (Yimam et al., 2013), Docanno (Nakayama et al., 2018), and LightTag (Perry, 2021) are some popular annotation tools. The survey by Neves and Ševa (2019) indicated that only 5 annotation tools out 78 have some kind of document level annotation supports. ActiveAnno (Wiechmann et al., 2021) is one of the latest annotation tools that support annotation and automation for document-level annotation tasks. ActiveAnno focuses on five central design goals, namely, efficiently creating annotations of high quality, supporting a broad range of use cases, responsive web application, open-source and APIs integration. While ActiveAnno has great support for document-level annotation, it does not natively support hierarchical annotation using codebooks. It also lacks the extensive generic annotation support from WebAnno, which can be used to link the document level annotation to span level annotations.

INCEpTION is another annotation platform, which integrates all the functionalities of WebAnno and focuses on corpus creation, annotation, and knowledge management. While INCEpTION extends the functionality of WebAnno to more advanced functionality, including the external recommender system and knowledge supported search, CodeAnno particularly focuses on the creation of document-level annotation with the hierarchical codebooks. Furthermore, CodeAnno uniquely supports importing/exporting documents in a spreadsheet format, which is the de facto annotation format in social science document coding. Project templating, external automation service, and document-level codebook agreements are additional specific functionalities in CodeAnno.

In social science, coding refers to the process of assigning descriptive or inferential labels to documents or parts of the document, that could help in developing a new concept or theory (Chen et al., 2018). Researchers usually take a sample of the data and apply manual coding. As the size of data increases, manually coding the entire dataset in detail is not feasible for social science researchers. Building a representative machine learning model is also becoming challenging (Chen et al., 2018). To address this issue, we have integrated an external automation component that could provide an initial suggestion of codes. The process is iterative and adaptive, where small portions of the document are labeled to train the external predictive model.

3 CodeAnno Features

CodeAnno extends WebAnno by introducing new functionalities in WebAnno. In WebAnno, "layers" are used for span, chain, or relation annotations on token, sentence, or paragraph level. CodeAnno introduces document-level annotations, referred to as Codebooks. The new functionality is seamlessly integrated into WebAnno, i.e., the backend is also based on Apache UIMA[1] while the frontend is based on Apache Wicket[2]. Besides the support for Codebooks, another main contribution of CodeAnno is the integration of an external machine-learning-based service to automate Codebook annotations.

Codebooks are hierarchical document-level annotations consisting of a name, optional parent and child Codebooks, and a list of Codebook Tags. The resulting Codebook structure is therefore best represented as a tree. Codebook Tags are the value of the respective Codebook annotation and can be predefined by the project organization or, if allowed, created ad-hoc by the annotator. Further, Codebooks and Codebook Tags can have a textual description so that the annotators know what they stand for and when or how to use them to ensure high coding quality.

[1] https://uima.apache.org/

[2] https://wicket.apache.org/

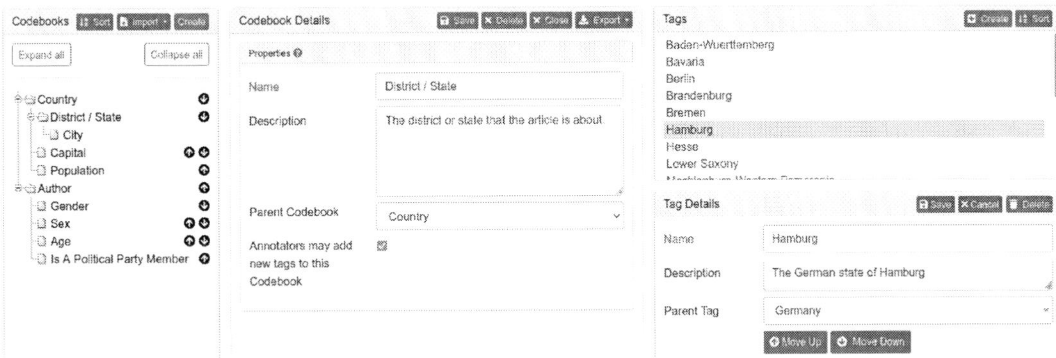

Figure 1: The Codebook settings UI in project settings to create and manage Codebooks and Codebook Tags.

Before the actual coding process starts, the project manager has to set up the Codebook structure that the coders will use to annotate the documents. This is done in the project settings with an intuitive and easy-to-use Codebook Editor shown in Figure 1. In the left part of the figure, a Codebook structure is displayed as a directory tree. The "Expand all" and "Collapse all" buttons are used to show or hide nodes in the Codebook tree. Codebooks can be moved up or down on the same level with the arrow buttons on the right. During creating a new Codebook, the project manager enters the Codebook properties in the middle part of Figure 1. To create a Codebook hierarchy, the parent Codebook can be selected from the drop-down list. If the Codebook is a root, none is selected. It is also possible to change the parent Codebook afterwards to update the tree structure. Further, if annotators should be allowed to enter custom Codebook Tags, the respective checkbox must be selected. Otherwise, only predefined Codebook Tags shown on the right side of Figure 1 can be chosen during the coding process.

In the "Tag Details" panel, that appears when a new Codebook Tag is created, its name, its description, and its parent tag will be recorded. The sort, move-up, and move-down buttons can be used to sort the list of Codebook Tags alphabetically or manually. When deleting a Codebook that is not a leaf node in the structure, all Codebooks in the subtree with their Codebook Tags also get deleted. Moreover, it is possible to import or export Codebook structures in human-readable JSON format. This is especially helpful when multiple coding projects with CodeAnno are planned.

3.1 Codebook Annotation

The WebAnno annotation interface is extended by a Codebook Editor panel that can be opened from the left sidebar to annotate documents with Codebooks. As shown in Figure 2, the classical WebAnno Layer Annotation editor can also be shown or hidden to enable span-level annotation at the same time. An example that shows the Codebook Editor with the configured Codebook structure from Figure 1 is shown in the left side of Figure 2. Each node in the tree represents a Codebook with its name in bold. The input for a Codebook combines a text input field and a dropdown selection. If enabled, annotators can enter any value to create a custom Codebook Tag or select a predefined tags from the dropdown list.

3.2 Codebook Curation and Agreement

Often, to ensure high-quality annotations, it is necessary that multiple users annotate the same document. However, since it can be subjective to decide which Codebook Tag fits best for the document, it can easily result in different Codebook annotations. This gives rise to the Codebook Curation feature, where project managers or curators can see how each user annotated the selected document in a separate UI. Based on this information, the curator chooses the "final" or correct Codebook Tag for each Codebook in the structure. An example of this UI is shown in Figure 3 – for space reasons, we cropped the image so that the document viewer, which would be on the right, is not shown. The Codebook structure is shown in a tree view similar to the annotation UI. The Codebook Tags of each user are shown in a list per Codebook. If all users agree on the same tag, the name of the respective Codebook is highlighted in green. Otherwise, it is highlighted in red. Below the list, the curation user can choose the correct Codebook Tag from a dropdown selection, where every tag is contained. If all users agree, the respective tag is preselected

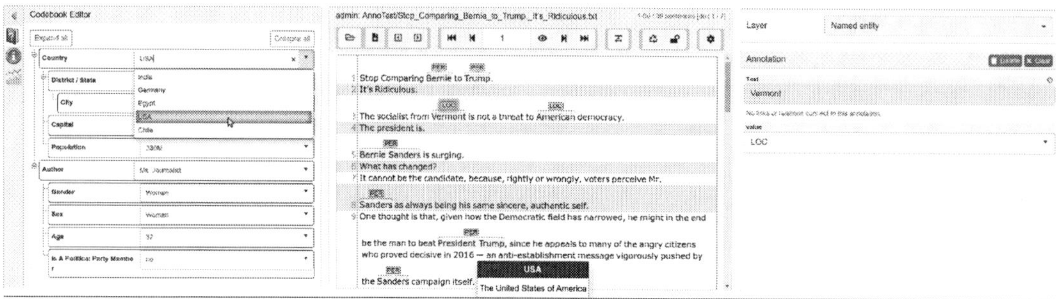

Figure 2: The CodaAnno annotation UI with the Codebook Editor for document-level annotations on the left, the document viewer in the middle, and the Layer Editor for span annotations on the right.

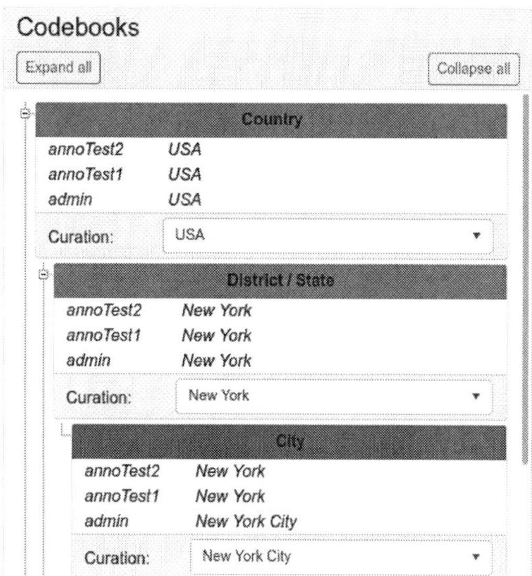

Figure 3: The CodaAnno Curation UI showing the Codebook annotations of different users. The curation user can select the "correct" Codebook from the dropdown menu at the bottom of each Codebook node.

to speed up the curation process.

With the Codebook Agreement feature, it is possible to calculate common inter-rater and intra-rater agreement measures per Codebook and project. For this purpose, the project manager first selects the respective project and Codebook. With a dropdown to select the measure, she can choose between Cohen's Kappa, Fleiss' Kappa, Krippendrof's Alpha, and Krippendorfs's Kappa. When the calculation has finished, the results are presented in a table like with layer annotation agreement in WebAnno.

3.3 Codebook Import and Export

CodeAnno features multiple new import and export functionalities. They are separated into import/export of the Codebook structure and the coded data belonging to each document. This separation allows reusing the Codebook structure by easily transferring it to a blank project without copying any document data. Since the Codebook is structured hierarchically, CodeBook uses the JSON format for import/export due to its convenient nesting of objects. As such, in the Codebook settings, it allows to import/export the whole CodeBook or only subtrees of it, thereby providing great flexibility to reuse only parts of CodeBook. The separated import/export in JSON of the Codebook (subtree) structure further has the advantage of being both human-readable and easy to manipulate in any text editor or even programmatically. Thus, changing many entries at once during construction of the Codebook, e.g. mass renaming, becomes very efficient. The import/export of Codebook data belonging to a document is possible in multiple ways. A document can be opened in CodeAnno and its Codebook annotations can be exported. In addition, the whole project can be exported, containing all documents and the Codebook structure. Importing documents previously exported is also possible through the Codebook settings. Thus, documents with Codebook annotations can be exported and later imported to move the documents to another project or make a backup.

4 CodeBook Automation (CBA)

Another major component of CodeAnno is the Codebook Automation (CBA) extension. As the name suggests, this functionality enables automatic annotation of Codebooks leveraging state-of-the-art machine learning technology to train and evaluate generic, user-specific classification models. The component consists of three parts: The CBA backend, the CBA WebApp, and the CBA integration in CodeAnno. An overview of the different parts is shown in Figure 4. The backend, which contains all logic and manages data and models, is accessible via a REST API. The CBA WebApp is a web-based user interface that consumes this API so

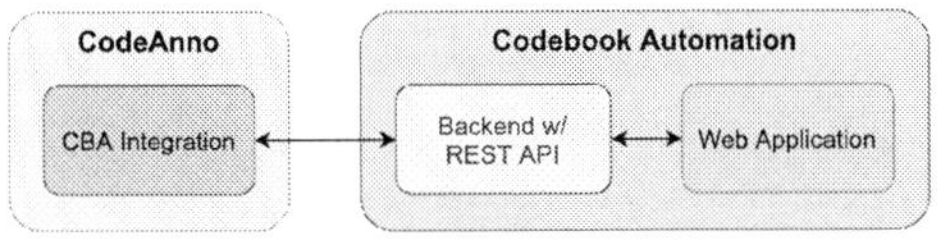

Figure 4: Overview of the Codebook Automation components. The communication between the components indicated by the arrows happens via HTTP.

that users can conveniently manage datasets, and create, train and test user-specific Codebook classifiers. Both parts are separated from CodeAnno and run independently. The third part is the CBA integration in CodeAnno to apply trained classifiers to annotate, i.e., predict documents with Codebooks automatically.

4.1 Backend Architecture of CBA

The CBA backend holds all logic to manage datasets and classifiers and exposes its functionality via a REST API. It is implemented using modern Python libraries and frameworks like FastAPI[3], pandas[4], Redis[5], and TensorFlow[6].

The process to train a classifier is schematically depicted in Figure 5. The dataset, uploaded by a

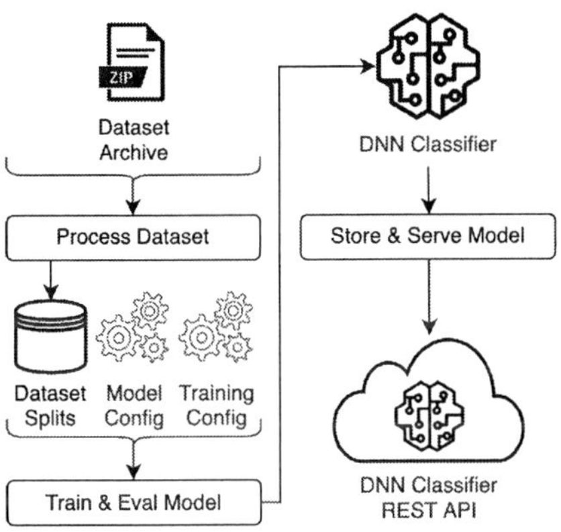

Figure 5: Schematic overview of the process to train a classifier in the Codebook Automation backend.

user, is a ZIP archive containing two CSV files for the training set and the evaluation set. Both files have to consist of two columns: The "text" column contains arbitrarily long text representing the document, and the "label" column contains the class or label for the sample. Further, the user must provide configurations defining the model architecture and training process. A model's architecture configuration contains the number of hidden layers and their respective hidden units, the activation function, the drop-out percentage, and the optimizer used for training. Further, the specification contains an URL pointing to a text-embedding model available on TensorFlow Hub[7]. A typical choice for this is, e.g., a Universal Sentence Encoder (Cer et al., 2018). The training process configuration specifies the batch size, the number of maximum training and evaluation steps, the optimizer, and if early stopping is activated or not. Once the model training is completed, it is persisted in the TensorFlow SavedModel format, supporting efficient model serving.

4.2 CBA WebApp and CodeAnno Integration

The CBA WebApp is the user interface for uploading or managing datasets and training or managing classifiers. The application consumes the REST API of the CBA backend and is implemented using NuxtJS[8].

Codebook Automation is also neatly integrated into CodeAnno so that human coders can leverage CBA classifiers to accelerate the Codebook annotation process. To use this functionality, a project administrator can start a bulk prediction process, in which all project documents are sent to the CBA backend and classified by the specified model. Another way is that annotators can send their currently processing document to the backend and let the default model set by an administrator classify the document.

The predictions are available in the Codebook Annotation UI when the process has been completed. Users can then easily accept or reject the suggestions from the CBA classifiers.

Details about the CBA WebApp and the CBA CodeAnno integration can be found on our GitHub[9][10] pages.

5 Case Studies

5.1 The NEPOCS Codebook

NEPOCS stands for Network of European Political Communication Scholars[11] established by a group of social science researchers who are working on political communication research. Each member is an expert on a particular European country, and the mission is to further internationally comparative political communication research. The work

[3] https://fastapi.tiangolo.com/
[4] https://pandas.pydata.org/
[5] https://redis.io
[6] https://www.tensorflow.org
[7] https://tfhub.dev
[8] https://nuxtjs.org/
[9] https://github.com/uhh-lt/codebook_automation
[10] https://github.com/uhh-lt/codeanno
[11] https://nepocs.eu/about-nepocs/

by Hopmann et al. (2017) discussed the methods and approaches they have used in coding around 7,500 news items gathered from 16 different European countries. The news items were collected considering different criteria such as consisting of comparable countries (established Western democracies) and media and political system level. As a source of the news item, televised news, newspapers, and online news outlets were considered. As part of the goal to the "2012 Journalism special issue", Hopmann et al. (2017) build a codebook as a contribution to *increasing standardization of how key concepts are conceptualized.* In collaboration with political communication science experts at Universität Hamburg, we have built standard codebook of NEPOCS, as shown in Figure 6 that can be released as part of CodeAnno for further use.

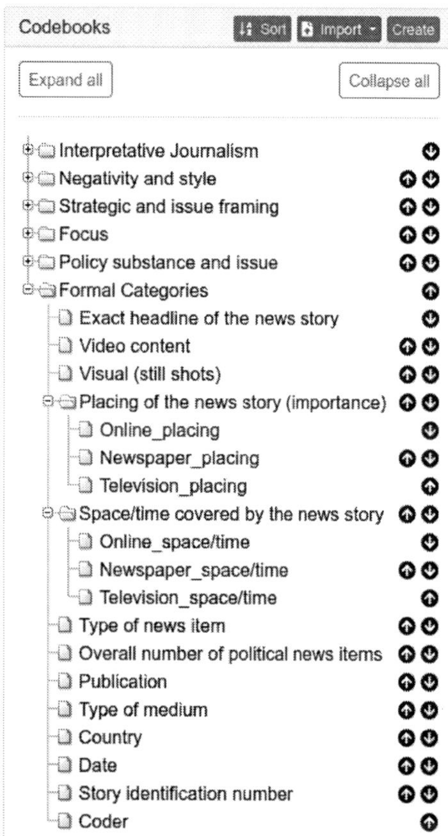

Figure 6: Parts of NEPOCS codebook designed with social science researchers.

5.2 CLICCS project

The Cluster of Excellence "Climate, Climatic Change, and Society" (CLICCS[12]) is following the overarching question: "Which climate futures are possible and which are plausible?" In the B1 sub-project researchers from journalism, media, and communication studies work on the question: "how do journalists frame climate futures?" For a quantitative study of climate future frames across countries, they have manually annotated hundreds of news articles in CodeAnno. Texts have been sampled from four countries (Germany, the United States, South Afrika and India) in German for Germany and English for the other three countries.

The researcher developed a sophisticated, hierarchical Codebook for the task based on a selected sample of documents. Coded are formal aspects like the type of text, author type and topic with a fixed number of categories. For the classification of future scenarios, they use hierarchically structured Codebooks for e.g. type of scenario, timeframe, geographic scope, plausibility, actors etc. In another sub-tree of the Codebook, the causes including attribution of blame and measures are structured into seven nested Codebooks.

In total, the whole Codebook comprises 26 aspects, each either coded as a Boolean or selection from multiple classes. To perform the annotation on the large sample, three coders have been trained on the developed Codebook. The CSV export of all coded documents has been used frequently to perform custom analysis on the annotations.

6 Conclusion

In this paper, we discussed main functionalities of CodeAnno, an extension of WebAnno that supports coding of social science documents using hierarchical Codebooks. Social science researchers usually employ traditional annotation tools, for example spreadsheet applications to code and analyze a text. This annotation process is cumbersome and hinders the development of predictive machine learning models. CodeAnno supports the creation of Codebooks, coding or annotating documents, and integration of custom machine learning models. Further, it eases the analysis of annotated documents and enables to import and export documents in different formats. Since CodeAnno intrinsically supports the annotation of entities and relations from WebAnno, we plan to integrate a functionality that provides automatic coding recommendations using the span-level entity and relation annotations. This facilitates the explainability of Codebook Annotations by linking back to the rationale in the document.

[12]https://www.cliccs.uni-hamburg.de/

Acknowledgement

This work is partly supported by the Cluster of Excellence CLICCS (EXC 2037), Universität Hamburg, funded by DFG, and the D-WISE project, funded by BMBF (grant ID 01UG2124).

References

Beto Boullosa, Richard Eckart de Castilho, Naveen Kumar, Jan-Christoph Klie, and Iryna Gurevych. 2018. Integrating Knowledge-Supported Search into the INCEpTION Annotation Platform. In *Proceedings of the 2018 Conference on Empirical Methods in Natural Language Processing: System Demonstrations*, pages 127–132, Brussels, Belgium.

Daniel Cer, Yinfei Yang, Sheng-yi Kong, Nan Hua, Nicole Limtiaco, Rhomni St John, Noah Constant, Mario Guajardo-Cespedes, Steve Yuan, Chris Tar, Brian Strope, and Ray Kurzweil. 2018. Universal Sentence Encoder for English. In *Proceedings of the 2018 Conference on Empirical Methods in Natural Language Processing: System Demonstrations*, pages 169–174, Brussels, Belgium.

Nan-Chen Chen, Margaret Drouhard, Rafal Kocielnik, Jina Suh, and Cecilia R. Aragon. 2018. Using Machine Learning to Support Qualitative Coding in Social Science: Shifting the Focus to Ambiguity. *ACM Trans. Interact. Intell. Syst.*, 8(2).

Richard Eckart de Castilho, Éva Mújdricza-Maydt, Seid Muhie Yimam, Silvana Hartmann, Iryna Gurevych, Anette Frank, and Chris Biemann. 2016. A Web-based Tool for the Integrated Annotation of Semantic and Syntactic Structures. In *Proceedings of the Workshop on Language Technology Resources and Tools for Digital Humanities (LT4DH)*, pages 76–84, Osaka, Japan.

David Nicolas Hopmann, Frank Esser, Claes de Vreese, Toril Aalberg, Peter Aelst, Rosa Berganza, Nicolas Hubé, Guido Legnante, Jörg Matthes, Stylianos Papathanassopoulos, Carsten Reinemann, Susana Salgado, Tamir Sheafer, James Stanyer, and Jesper Strömbäck. 2017. How We Did It: Approach and Methods. In *Comparing Political Journalism*, pages 10–21.

Hiroki Nakayama, Takahiro Kubo, Junya Kamura, Yasufumi Taniguchi, and Xu Liang. 2018. doccano: Text Annotation Tool for Human. Software available from https://github.com/doccano/doccano.

Mariana Neves and Jurica Ševa. 2019. An Extensive Review of Tools for Manual Annotation of Documents. *Briefings in Bioinformatics*, 22(1):146–163.

Tal Perry. 2021. LightTag: Text Annotation Platform. In *Proceedings of the 2021 Conference on Empirical Methods in Natural Language Processing: System Demonstrations*, pages 20–27, Online and Punta Cana, Dominican Republic.

Pontus Stenetorp, Sampo Pyysalo, Goran Topić, Tomoko Ohta, Sophia Ananiadou, and Jun'ichi Tsujii. 2012. brat: a Web-based Tool for NLP-Assisted Text Annotation. In *Proceedings of the Demonstrations at the 13th Conference of the European Chapter of the Association for Computational Linguistics*, pages 102–107, Avignon, France.

Max Wiechmann, Seid Muhie Yimam, and Chris Biemann. 2021. ActiveAnno: General-Purpose Document-Level Annotation Tool with Active Learning Integration. In *Proceedings of the 2021 Conference of the North American Chapter of the Association for Computational Linguistics: Human Language Technologies: Demonstrations*, pages 99–105, Online.

Seid Muhie Yimam, Chris Biemann, Richard Eckart de Castilho, and Iryna Gurevych. 2014. Automatic annotation suggestions and custom annotation layers in WebAnno. In *Proceedings of 52nd Annual Meeting of the Association for Computational Linguistics: System Demonstrations*, pages 91–96, Baltimore, Maryland.

Seid Muhie Yimam, Iryna Gurevych, Richard Eckart de Castilho, and Chris Biemann. 2013. Webanno: A flexible, web-based and visually supported system for distributed annotations. In *Proceedings of the 51st Annual Meeting of the Association for Computational Linguistics: System Demonstrations*, pages 1–6, Sofia, Bulgaria.

NLP Workbench: Efficient and Extensible Integration of State-of-the-art Text Mining Tools

Peiran Yao, Matej Kosmajac, Abeer Waheed,
Kostyantyn Guzhva, Natalie Hervieux, Denilson Barbosa
Department of Computing Science
University of Alberta
{peiran, denilson}@ualberta.ca

Abstract

NLP Workbench is a web-based platform for text mining that allows non-expert users to obtain semantic understanding of large-scale corpora using state-of-the-art text mining models. The platform is built upon latest pre-trained models and open source systems from academia that provide semantic analysis functionalities, including but not limited to entity linking, sentiment analysis, semantic parsing, and relation extraction. Its extensible design enables researchers and developers to smoothly replace an existing model or integrate a new one. To improve efficiency, we employ a microservice architecture that facilitates allocation of acceleration hardware and parallelization of computation. This paper presents the architecture of NLP Workbench and discusses the challenges we faced in designing it. We also discuss diverse use cases of NLP Workbench and the benefits of using it over other approaches. The platform is under active development, with its source code released under the MIT license[1]. A website[2] and a short video[3] demonstrating our platform are also available.

1 Introduction

Text mining, also known as *text analytics* or *text analysis*, is the process where a user interacts with machine-supported analysis tools that transform natural language text into structured data, to gain insights and new knowledge from the text (Feldman and Sanger, 2006a). For more than two decades, text mining systems have been built for applications in various domains, such as business intelligence, analytical sociology, and medical sciences (Hearst, 1999), demonstrating irreplaceable value. Analysis tools in text mining usually take the form of machine learning (ML) and natural language processing (NLP) models and span a large spectrum of ML and NLP subfields, such as entity linking, sentiment analysis, relation extraction, and text summarization.

Nearly every subfield of NLP involved in text mining has been rapidly evolving in recent years, with records on benchmarks being continuously broken[4]. A positive practice of releasing the code and models to the public has been adopted by a growing number of researchers[5] to address reproducibility and accessibility issues in the field[6]. Despite efforts to make new models more accessible, non-expert users such as digital humanists and business analysts still face entry barriers when trying to apply the latest models. Some salient issues include: (1) heterogenous software stacks required to run the models; (2) non-standardized, inconsistent input and output formats; (3) the lack of user-friendly interfaces to apply the models and visualize the results; and (4) the constraints on computation and networking resources. We build NLP Workbench with the goal of addressing these issues and further bridging the gap between state-of-the-art open NLP research and the use of these models and tools in text mining applications by non-experts.

NLP Workbench is designed with two fundamental principals in mind: for developers and NLP researchers, fast and easy adaptation of off-the-shelf models and tools; and for non-expert users such as sociologists, a user-friendly interface for both document-level and corpus-level analysis. Following these principles, NLP Workbench offers the following key features:

Platform NLP Workbench unifies corpus management, text mining tools, and visualization in a single platform. It provides a growing list of models and tools that are based on state-of-the-

[1] https://github.com/U-Alberta/NLPWorkbench/
[2] https://newskg.wdmuofa.ca
[3] https://vimeo.com/801006908

[4] http://nlpprogress.com
[5] https://paperswithcode.com
[6] https://aclrollingreview.org/responsibleNLPresearch/

Proceedings of the 17th Conference of the European Chapter of the Association for Computational Linguistics System Demonstrations, pages 18–26
May 2-4, 2023

art research, currently offering functionalities like named entity recognition, entity linking, relation extraction, semantic parsing, summarization, sentiment analysis, and social network analysis.

Interaction A web interface is included for user interactions with the ability to visualize the model results at document and corpus levels. Users could choose to interactively apply a model on a given document and have the results saved for future queries, or to apply models in batches on selected documents in a corpus.

Architecture For development, NLP Workbench adopts containerization, allowing new models to be added independent of the software stack of existing models. For deployment, its microservice architecture allows models to be deployed in a distributed way on machines that meet the computing and networking requirements of individual models, enabling horizontal scaling.

Interface Tools in NLP Workbench can be accessed in versatile ways. Besides the web interface, non-expert users could import new documents into the platform via a browser extension. For developers and researchers, NLP Workbench provides RESTful API and remote procedure call (RPC) interfaces for easy integration with other applications and pipelines.

2 Related Work

Hearst (1999) and Cunningham et al. (2002) identified three key aspects of an effective text mining system: management of text document collections (corpora), application of text processing algorithms on the collection, and visualization of results. LINDI (Hearst, 1999) is an early prototype of such a system used for gene function discovery. GATE (Cunningham et al., 2002), a framework that is still currently maintained, provides a unified architecture for all three aspects. Similarly, NLP Workbench tries to accommodate all three aspects in a single platform. Our platform uses containerized microservices instead of Java classes for each processing module, which avoids the restrictions of underlying programming frameworks for implementing NLP algorithms. Voyant Tools (Rockwell and Sinclair, 2016) is another web-based platform that provides tools for corpus analysis and the function to write user-defined scripts. Their built-in tools are mostly limited to count-based statistics and visualization, while we are integrating large deep learning models. UIMA (Ferrucci and Lally, 2004) attempts to define a standard protocol for managing corpora and NLP algorithms. It is more developer-oriented, unlike our application which provides a complete system that can be used for analysis directly by users.

A plethora of NLP toolkits focusing on building NLP pipelines have been developed in the past few decades, including Stanford CoreNLP (Manning et al., 2014), OpenNLP[7], NLTK (Bird et al., 2009), spaCy (Honnibal et al., 2020) and Transformers (Wolf et al., 2020). These toolkits could be used to address the text processing algorithm aspect of text mining systems, but they do not provide a full solution. The typical strategy to incorporate new models into these toolkits is to re-implement the model in the framework of the toolkit, while we try to re-use, as much as possible, the code and models released by researchers.

Some tools specialize in only the visualization aspect. To name a few, Blloshmi et al. (2021) and Cohen et al. (2021) built tools for visualizing the results of semantic parsers – a function that is also provided by our system.

Several libraries and tools are able to manage corpora or models from multiple sources. For example, Datasets library (Lhoest et al., 2021) provides an interface to access common NLP datasets, and DataLab (Xiao et al., 2022) is a platform to examine and analyze datasets. Transformers (Wolf et al., 2020) can access models and datasets from the Hugging Face Hub[8]. Beyond corpora and models, NLP Workbench also incorporates code from multiple sources.

3 Architecture

NLP Workbench is built on top of various open source software and incorporates the code and models from many research projects. We design our architecture to leverage off-the-shelf functionalities provided by these software and projects, and to minimize the effort of integrating new code from a research project.

3.1 Workflow

Figure 1 provides a high-level overview of how users interact with NLP Workbench and how the system handles the requests.

[7] https://opennlp.apache.org

[8] https://huggingface.co/docs/hub/index

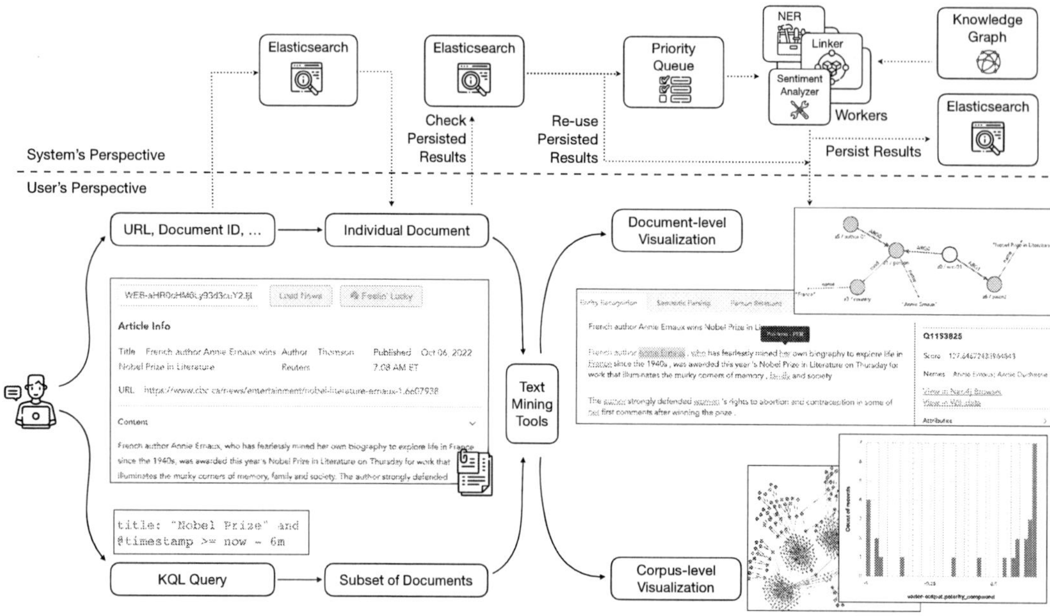

Figure 1: Workflow of NLP Workbench from the perspectives of the user and the system, as described in §3.1. For document-level visualization, we showcase the user interface for named entity recognition, coreference resolution, entity linking, and semantic parsing. For corpus-level visualization, this figure includes plots of a social network constructed from a tweet of the official Nobel Prize account, and the distribution of sentiment polarity scores of a sample of the built-in news corpus. Icons created by Freepik - Flaticon.

User Perspective From the perspective of a user, one could choose to apply text mining tools on a single document specified by its URL or ID, or apply them in batches on a set of documents specified by a query. Queries are written in the Kibana Query Language (KQL)[9], which is a simple and intuitive text-based query language. The outputs of the tools on a single document can be visualized in the web interface, with each tool having a separate panel. Using Kibana Lens[10], a user can visualize statistics calculated over the output of multiple documents, such as the distribution of sentiment polarity scores. The connected Neo4j Browser[11] provides an interactive web interface for exploring social networks constructed from a corpus.

System Perspective From the perspective of the system, both the corpus and the outputs of text mining tools are stored and indexed in Elasticsearch[12], a document indexing, search, and analytics engine. By storing and indexing tool outputs, we re-use previous results and avoid re-computation to improve efficiency. In addition to that, Elasticsearch provides convenient tools to filter documents based on the outputs of text mining tools and visualizing statistics, which are very useful for downstream analytics.

If running a tool is indeed necessary, the task is added to a priority queue. Ad hoc and interactive requests, issued when a user is examining a single document and applying tools on it, are prioritized over batched requests that run in the background. Each tool or model has workers processing the tasks in the queue. This ensures that users performing interactive analysis experience little latency even when the number of workers is limited, which is usually the case in practice as deep learning models are often resource-intensive and it is infeasible to have multiple instances running in parallel.

3.2 Pipelining and Scheduling

Text mining tools often rely on the outputs of other tools or NLP models and are built as pipelines. For example, both entity linking and relation extraction require named entity recognition and coreference resolution. To ensure efficiency, re-computing the outputs of tools that are already available should be avoided, and tools should be run in parallel if pos-

[9]https://www.elastic.co/guide/en/kibana/current/kuery-query.html

[10]https://www.elastic.co/kibana/kibana-lens

[11]https://neo4j.com/developer/neo4j-browser/

[12]https://www.elastic.co/what-is/elasticsearch

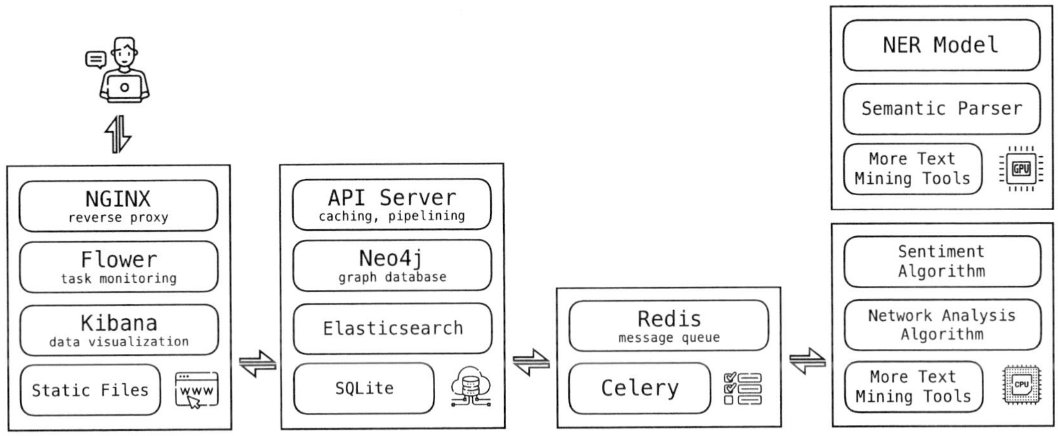

Figure 2: Microservice architecture of NLP Workbench. Each rectangle represents a physical machine, with its capability indicated by the icon at the bottom right corner. Each rounded rectangle represents a container, with the tool and function it provides indicated by the text inside. Container to physical machine allocation is for illustration purposes only and is adjusted to fit the need when the system is deployed in production.

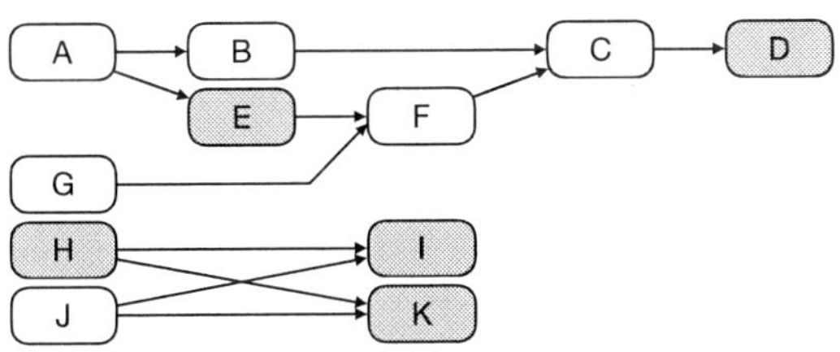

Figure 3: Example of a batched task with the directed acyclic graphs of dependencies. Shaded nodes represent tools that the user requests to run on the document, and unshaded nodes represent tools that are needed to provide the inputs to the shaded nodes.

sible. In addition to persisting and re-using outputs as discussed in Section 3.1, we design a pipelining and scheduling system that automatically detects the dependencies between tools and schedules the tasks in a way that eliminates re-computation and encourages parallelism.

The dependencies of a tool can naturally be represented as a directed acyclic graph (DAG), where inbound edges represent the dependencies. When multiple tools are requested to be run on a single document, we gather the direct and transitive dependencies of these tools in a single graph, as shown in Figure 3. The connected components of the graph are DAGs. Within each DAG, the tools are run in topological order; and disjoint DAGs are executed in parallel.

In the example illustrated in Figure 3, the user requests to run tool `E`, `D`, `H`, `I`, and `K` on a document. The scheduler will automatically find all dependencies (`A` to `K`) and run two chains in parallel: `A-B-E-G-F-C-D` and `H-J-I-K`[13].

3.3 Containerized Microservices

A major obstacle to integrating third party code is the *dependency hell* problem: it is an NP-complete problem to find a set of compatible versions of all software library dependencies (Burrows, 2005; Cox, 2016), and in reality a compatible set may not exist. This is especially true for deep learning models (Han et al., 2020; Huang et al., 2022), which often require specific versions of software libraries. In the case of popular deep learning frameworks, TensorFlow (Abadi et al., 2016) 2.0 introduces breaking API changes that are not back-compatible. Both TensorFlow and PyTorch (Paszke et al., 2019) are compiled with specific versions of CUDA (Nickolls et al., 2008) and cuDNN (Chetlur et al., 2014), and that makes different framework versions hard to coexist. Manually fixing the code to make it compatible with a specific version of a library is often tedious and error-prone (Han et al., 2020).

For deployment, a practical problem is that it is often difficult or costly to find a single physical machine that satisfies the computing and networking requirements of all the components: deep learning models require GPU for inference, database management systems consume large amounts of memory and disk space, and web servers need ac-

[13]There is more than one valid topological sorting for a DAG.

cess to the Internet. One solution to this problem is the ability to deploy components of NLP Workbench on multiple machines, which is achieved by our design.

We solve both problems discussed above at once by deploying both text mining tools and infrastructure components as *containerized microservices*. Each component is deployed as a Docker container (Merkel, 2014) that encapsulates the software and its dependencies. The containers communicate with each other via the RPC and message queue functions provided by Celery[14]. Figure 2 illustrates how the containerized microservices are deployed on separate machines with different capabilities. Such a microservice architecture allows us to overcome the problem of heterogeneous technologies and simplifies horizontal scaling when needed (Newman, 2015).

4 Components

NLP Workbench already includes a variety of tools and models for text mining. Most of the components come from state-of-the-art research in the respective subfields. Others are baseline implementations to demonstrate NLP Workbench's extensibility, showing that developers can straightforwardly incorporate new tools and build pipelines from existing ones. One benefit of the flexible and modular design as described in §3 is that all built-in tools and models can easily be replaced or upgraded. Existing tools and models in NLP Workbench include:

Named Entity Recognition The task, known as NER, is to identify mentions to entities such as people, organizations, and locations. We incorporated the NER model from PURE (Zhong and Chen, 2021), which achieved good performance by simply fine-tuning BERT (Devlin et al., 2019).

Coreference Resolution To determine which entity a pronoun refers to, we adopted the heuristic algorithm by Cunningham et al. (2002) that is based on recency and type agreement.

Entity Linking Mentions to entities in the text are disambiguated and linked to Wikidata (Vrandečić and Krötzsch, 2014) entities. Candidate entities are generated by a fuzzy match on name. In addition to name similarity, the ranking of candidates utilizes the cosine similarity between the sentence embeddings (Reimers and Gurevych, 2019) of the context and the descriptions of the candidate entity from Wikipedia and Wikidata.

Relation Extraction The user can extract structured facts in the form of knowledge triples like (*Annie Ernaux*, `Country`, *France*) from a text. The underlying model (Mesquita et al., 2019) combines syntax and semantic features as well as BERT embeddings to predict the relation between entities.

Semantic Parsing Semantic parsing provides a structured representation of the meaning of a sentence, allowing users to obtain information like who did what to whom, when, and where without caring about the form. NLP Workbench uses AMRBART (Bai et al., 2022), a sequence-to-sequence model based on BART (Lewis et al., 2020) and pretrained on a large graph corpus, to parse sentences into AMR graphs (Banarescu et al., 2013).

Summarization We build an application on top of semantic parsing to create natural language summaries of events related to people in the document, partly to demonstrate the simplicity of building pipelines in NLP Workbench. For each sentence in the document, we prune its AMR graph to only contain the nodes and edges of pattern *subject-predicate-object*, where the subject or object is a person. The pruned AMR graphs are then converted to natural language using AMRBART.

Sentiment Analysis The sentiment of a document is predicted by VADER (Hutto and Gilbert, 2014), a fast and accurate rule-based algorithm optimized for social media posts. A sentiment polarity score is produced and can be used to classify the sentiment as positive, neutral, or negative.

Social Network Analysis For corpora consisting of social media posts, NLP Workbench is equipped with a tool that builds graphs of social network interactions from posts. Powered by the graph database Neo4j[15], the tool can be used to visualize the network and perform analyses, such as running centrality algorithms like PageRank (Page et al., 1999) to identify influential users.

5 Use Cases

Text mining has been proven useful in a variety of domains, such as corporate finance, patent research, life sciences, and many others (Feldman

[14] `https://docs.celeryq.dev`

[15] `https://neo4j.com/`

and Sanger, 2006b). NLP Workbench, as a full-fledged text mining platform, has been or has the potential to be applied in many of these domains. Some of the use cases are described in this section.

Digital Humanities Accessible and reliable NLP tools are useful in digital humanities projects such as Linked Infrastructure for Networked Cultural Scholarship (LINCS)[16]. A major component of the LINCS project is to generate linked data from natural language cultural heritage texts. The key steps are NER, coreference resolution, entity linking, and relation extraction, all of which are made available in NLP Workbench. Through the simple user interface, digital humanists and their students can choose the available models that suit their data, and easily connect these steps into a custom workflow.

The Centre for Artificial Intelligence, Data, and Conflict (CAIDAC)[17] houses human right scholars interested in how armed groups and extremists use social media to promote their agendas. NLP Workbench offers such researchers convenient tools for collecting tweets[18] for analysis. Posts can be subjected to the NLP tools of interest, and the social network underlying the corpus can be visualized, explored, and analyzed. All of these tasks are done through an accessible interface, requiring no programming from the users, enabling them to perform more and larger studies in a fraction of the time otherwise required.

Business Analytics Business analysts ask questions like *"are recent news reports about Apple Inc. positive or negative?"*. These type of questions can easily be answered by NLP Workbench. After performing NER and entity linking on the news articles, the analyst can conduct a **semantic search** to find the articles that are related to *Apple Inc.* rather than apple the fruit. Then, the analyst can use the sentiment analysis tool and visualize the distribution of sentiment polarity scores with Kibana Lens, as shown in the bottom right screenshot in Figure 1.

NLP Research All NLP models in NLP Workbench can be accessed via RESTful API and RPC, or used directly as containers. For researchers who wish to perform inferences with the models on their own data, they could use the interfaces provided by NLP Workbench, without needing to set up the environment to run the models.

[16]`https://lincsproject.ca`

[17]`https://www.tracesofconflict.com/`

[18]Support for Telegram and other platforms is in progress.

6 Roadmap

NLP Workbench is still in its early stages of development, and we are actively working on improving the system. Besides usability, stability, and security updates, we plan to work on the following major features in the near future:

Human-in-the-loop NLP Adding annotation support to the web interface will allow users to provide feedback to the outputs of models. This will help researchers to collect domain-specific labelled data and improve the performance of the models in a human-in-the-loop fashion (Wang et al., 2021).

Improved Corpus Management Managing document collections is a crucial aspect of text mining (Hearst, 1999; Cunningham et al., 2002). Currently, corpora are manually imported into Elasticsearch or created by crawling social media. We hope to improve the way users access document collections. This can be done by connecting NLP Workbench to Datasets (Lhoest et al., 2021) and DataLab (Xiao et al., 2022) where popular text datasets are already available. In addition to crawling from social media, we also plan to support creating a new corpus by doing web search on a search engine.

More Text Mining Tools The extensible design of NLP Workbench allows us to keep existing tools and models up to date by replacing them when better models are released, and integrate emerging text mining tools to the system. For example, we hope to add claim extraction models to facilitate fact checking tasks (Hassan et al., 2017).

Multi-modal Analysis Social media posts often refer to or contain information in other modalities (images, video, audio) of interest. At the same time, there is growing interest in grounding NLP models and analysis on knowledge extracted from videos and other sources. While adding support for processing different media in NLP Workbench is as easy as adding more NLP tools, we are interested in integrating these models so that co-training or grounding can be automated to the extent possible.

7 Conclusion

We introduced NLP Workbench, a platform that caters to all three major aspects of text mining systems: corpus management, text mining tools, and user interface. We explained what design features make NLP Workbench efficient and extensible, and how it can be used in a variety of applications.

Limitations

We have already identified several important features that are not yet implemented in NLP Workbench, as discussed in §6: the platform needs an annotation feature for human-in-the-loop AI; it should have access to commonly used public corpora; and it should include text mining tools such as one for claim extraction. There are some intrinsic limitations that even the state-of-the-art models in NLP Workbench do not solve. For example, long tail entities may not be covered by the knowledge graph, and current entity linking models do not have a notion for out-of-knowledge-graph entities (Shen et al., 2023). This will result in long tail entities always being incorrectly linked. Beyond social network analysis, our current design does not have the user interface or models for other corpus-level analyses, such as topic modeling (Blei et al., 2003). And finally, all NLP models and algorithms in NLP Workbench are targeted at English text. Although we have been able to deal with corpora in other languages by translating them to English using Marian MT (Junczys-Dowmunt et al., 2018), it is not yet clear whether performance can be improved by directly using models trained on other languages.

Ethics Statement

By encapsulating the models, NLP Workbench lowers the entry barrier for non-experts to use state-of-the-art AI models. The microservice architecture, which allows models to be deployed on multiple servers with different capabilities rather than a single omnipotent server, also makes this text mining platform more accessible. Containerizing third-party models also helps with reproducibility and transparency. There have been attempts of using NLP Workbench to analyze datasets to help understand propaganda, misinformation, and disinformation related to war and terrorism. However, users must be warned that, as NLP Workbench uses third-party data and models without modification, outputs obtained from NLP Workbench are inevitably affected by the bias inherent in the datasets and models.

Acknowledgements

The work is supported in part by the Natural Sciences and Engineering Research Council of Canada (NSERC), the Canadian Foundation for Innovation (CFI), AI4Society[19] and a gift from Scotiabank. Certain computing resources are provided by the Digital Research Alliance of Canada.

References

Martín Abadi, Paul Barham, Jianmin Chen, Zhifeng Chen, Andy Davis, Jeffrey Dean, Matthieu Devin, Sanjay Ghemawat, Geoffrey Irving, Michael Isard, Manjunath Kudlur, Josh Levenberg, Rajat Monga, Sherry Moore, Derek Gordon Murray, Benoit Steiner, Paul A. Tucker, Vijay Vasudevan, Pete Warden, Martin Wicke, Yuan Yu, and Xiaoqiang Zheng. 2016. Tensorflow: A system for large-scale machine learning. In *12th USENIX Symposium on Operating Systems Design and Implementation, OSDI 2016, Savannah, GA, USA, November 2-4, 2016*, pages 265–283. USENIX Association.

Xuefeng Bai, Yulong Chen, and Yue Zhang. 2022. Graph pre-training for AMR parsing and generation. In *Proceedings of the 60th Annual Meeting of the Association for Computational Linguistics (Volume 1: Long Papers)*, pages 6001–6015, Dublin, Ireland. Association for Computational Linguistics.

Laura Banarescu, Claire Bonial, Shu Cai, Madalina Georgescu, Kira Griffitt, Ulf Hermjakob, Kevin Knight, Philipp Koehn, Martha Palmer, and Nathan Schneider. 2013. Abstract Meaning Representation for sembanking. In *Proceedings of the 7th Linguistic Annotation Workshop and Interoperability with Discourse*, pages 178–186, Sofia, Bulgaria. Association for Computational Linguistics.

Steven Bird, Edward Loper, and Ewan Klein. 2009. *Natural Language Processing with Python*. O'Reilly Media Inc.

David M. Blei, Andrew Y. Ng, and Michael I. Jordan. 2003. Latent dirichlet allocation. *J. Mach. Learn. Res.*, 3:993–1022.

Rexhina Blloshmi, Michele Bevilacqua, Edoardo Fabiano, Valentina Caruso, and Roberto Navigli. 2021. SPRING goes online: End-to-end AMR parsing and generation. In *Proceedings of the 2021 Conference on Empirical Methods in Natural Language Processing: System Demonstrations*, pages 134–142, Online and Punta Cana, Dominican Republic. Association for Computational Linguistics.

Daniel Burrows. 2005. Modelling and resolving software dependencies.

Sharan Chetlur, Cliff Woolley, Philippe Vandermersch, Jonathan Cohen, John Tran, Bryan Catanzaro, and Evan Shelhamer. 2014. cuDNN: Efficient primitives for deep learning. *CoRR*, abs/1410.0759.

Jaron Cohen, Roy Cohen, Edan Toledo, and Jan Buys. 2021. RepGraph: Visualising and analysing meaning

[19]https://ai4society.ca/

representation graphs. In *Proceedings of the 2021 Conference on Empirical Methods in Natural Language Processing: System Demonstrations*, pages 79–86, Online and Punta Cana, Dominican Republic. Association for Computational Linguistics.

Russ Cox. 2016. Version SAT. Retrieved November 29, 2022, from `https://research.swtch.com/version-sat`.

Hamish Cunningham, Diana Maynard, Kalina Bontcheva, and Valentin Tablan. 2002. GATE: an architecture for development of robust HLT applications. In *Proceedings of the 40th Annual Meeting of the Association for Computational Linguistics*, pages 168–175, Philadelphia, Pennsylvania, USA. Association for Computational Linguistics.

Jacob Devlin, Ming-Wei Chang, Kenton Lee, and Kristina Toutanova. 2019. BERT: pre-training of deep bidirectional transformers for language understanding. In *Proceedings of the 2019 Conference of the North American Chapter of the Association for Computational Linguistics: Human Language Technologies, NAACL-HLT 2019, Minneapolis, MN, USA, June 2-7, 2019, Volume 1 (Long and Short Papers)*, pages 4171–4186. Association for Computational Linguistics.

Ronen Feldman and James Sanger. 2006a. Introduction to text mining. In *The Text Mining Handbook: Advanced Approaches in Analyzing Unstructured Data*, page 1–18. Cambridge University Press.

Ronen Feldman and James Sanger. 2006b. Text mining applications. In *The Text Mining Handbook: Advanced Approaches in Analyzing Unstructured Data*, page 273–314. Cambridge University Press.

David Ferrucci and Adam Lally. 2004. UIMA: An Architectural Approach to Unstructured Information Processing in the Corporate Research Environment. *Natural Language Engineering*, 10(3-4):327–348.

Junxiao Han, Shuiguang Deng, David Lo, Chen Zhi, Jianwei Yin, and Xin Xia. 2020. An empirical study of the dependency networks of deep learning libraries. In *2020 IEEE International Conference on Software Maintenance and Evolution (ICSME)*, pages 868–878.

Naeemul Hassan, Gensheng Zhang, Fatma Arslan, Josue Caraballo, Damian Jimenez, Siddhant Gawsane, Shohedul Hasan, Minumol Joseph, Aaditya Kulkarni, Anil Kumar Nayak, Vikas Sable, Chengkai Li, and Mark Tremayne. 2017. Claimbuster: The first-ever end-to-end fact-checking system. *Proc. VLDB Endow.*, 10(12):1945–1948.

Marti A. Hearst. 1999. Untangling text data mining. In *Proceedings of the 37th Annual Meeting of the Association for Computational Linguistics*, pages 3–10, College Park, Maryland, USA. Association for Computational Linguistics.

Mattew Honnibal, Ines Montani, Sofie Van Landeghem, and Adriane Boyd. 2020. spaCy: Industrial-strength natural language processing in Python.

Kaifeng Huang, Bihuan Chen, Susheng Wu, Junmin Cao, Lei Ma, and Xin Peng. 2022. Demystifying dependency bugs in deep learning stack. *CoRR*, abs/2207.10347.

Clayton J. Hutto and Eric Gilbert. 2014. VADER: A parsimonious rule-based model for sentiment analysis of social media text. In *Proceedings of the Eighth International Conference on Weblogs and Social Media, ICWSM 2014, Ann Arbor, Michigan, USA, June 1-4, 2014*. The AAAI Press.

Marcin Junczys-Dowmunt, Roman Grundkiewicz, Tomasz Dwojak, Hieu Hoang, Kenneth Heafield, Tom Neckermann, Frank Seide, Ulrich Germann, Alham Fikri Aji, Nikolay Bogoychev, André F. T. Martins, and Alexandra Birch. 2018. Marian: Fast neural machine translation in C++. In *Proceedings of ACL 2018, System Demonstrations*, pages 116–121, Melbourne, Australia. Association for Computational Linguistics.

Mike Lewis, Yinhan Liu, Naman Goyal, Marjan Ghazvininejad, Abdelrahman Mohamed, Omer Levy, Veselin Stoyanov, and Luke Zettlemoyer. 2020. BART: denoising sequence-to-sequence pre-training for natural language generation, translation, and comprehension. In *Proceedings of the 58th Annual Meeting of the Association for Computational Linguistics, ACL 2020, Online, July 5-10, 2020*, pages 7871–7880. Association for Computational Linguistics.

Quentin Lhoest, Albert Villanova del Moral, Yacine Jernite, Abhishek Thakur, Patrick von Platen, Suraj Patil, Julien Chaumond, Mariama Drame, Julien Plu, Lewis Tunstall, Joe Davison, Mario Šaško, Gunjan Chhablani, Bhavitvya Malik, Simon Brandeis, Teven Le Scao, Victor Sanh, Canwen Xu, Nicolas Patry, Angelina McMillan-Major, Philipp Schmid, Sylvain Gugger, Clément Delangue, Théo Matussière, Lysandre Debut, Stas Bekman, Pierric Cistac, Thibault Goehringer, Victor Mustar, François Lagunas, Alexander Rush, and Thomas Wolf. 2021. Datasets: A community library for natural language processing. In *Proceedings of the 2021 Conference on Empirical Methods in Natural Language Processing: System Demonstrations*, pages 175–184, Online and Punta Cana, Dominican Republic. Association for Computational Linguistics.

Christopher Manning, Mihai Surdeanu, John Bauer, Jenny Finkel, Steven Bethard, and David McClosky. 2014. The Stanford CoreNLP natural language processing toolkit. In *Proceedings of 52nd Annual Meeting of the Association for Computational Linguistics: System Demonstrations*, pages 55–60, Baltimore, Maryland. Association for Computational Linguistics.

Dirk Merkel. 2014. Docker: Lightweight Linux containers for consistent development and deployment. *Linux J.*, 2014(239).

Filipe Mesquita, Matteo Cannaviccio, Jordan Schmidek, Paramita Mirza, and Denilson Barbosa. 2019. Knowledgenet: A benchmark dataset for knowledge base population. In *Proceedings of the 2019 Conference on Empirical Methods in Natural Language Processing and the 9th International Joint Conference on Natural Language Processing, EMNLP-IJCNLP 2019, Hong Kong, China, November 3-7, 2019*, pages 749–758. Association for Computational Linguistics.

Sam Newman. 2015. Microservices. In *Building Microservices*. O'Reilly Media, Inc.

John Nickolls, Ian Buck, Michael Garland, and Kevin Skadron. 2008. Scalable parallel programming with CUDA. *ACM Queue*, 6(2):40–53.

Lawrence Page, Sergey Brin, Rajeev Motwani, and Terry Winograd. 1999. The pagerank citation ranking: Bringing order to the web. Technical Report 1999-66, Stanford InfoLab. Previous number = SIDL-WP-1999-0120.

Adam Paszke, Sam Gross, Francisco Massa, Adam Lerer, James Bradbury, Gregory Chanan, Trevor Killeen, Zeming Lin, Natalia Gimelshein, Luca Antiga, Alban Desmaison, Andreas Köpf, Edward Z. Yang, Zachary DeVito, Martin Raison, Alykhan Tejani, Sasank Chilamkurthy, Benoit Steiner, Lu Fang, Junjie Bai, and Soumith Chintala. 2019. PyTorch: An imperative style, high-performance deep learning library. In *Advances in Neural Information Processing Systems 32: Annual Conference on Neural Information Processing Systems 2019, NeurIPS 2019, December 8-14, 2019, Vancouver, BC, Canada*, pages 8024–8035.

Nils Reimers and Iryna Gurevych. 2019. Sentence-BERT: Sentence embeddings using Siamese BERT-networks. In *Proceedings of the 2019 Conference on Empirical Methods in Natural Language Processing and the 9th International Joint Conference on Natural Language Processing (EMNLP-IJCNLP)*, pages 3982–3992, Hong Kong, China. Association for Computational Linguistics.

Geoffrey Rockwell and Stéfan Sinclair. 2016. *Hermeneutica: Computer-Assisted Interpretation in the Humanities*. The MIT Press.

Wei Shen, Yuhan Li, Yinan Liu, Jiawei Han, Jianyong Wang, and Xiaojie Yuan. 2023. Entity linking meets deep learning: Techniques and solutions. *IEEE Transactions on Knowledge and Data Engineering*, 35(3):2556–2578.

Denny Vrandečić and Markus Krötzsch. 2014. Wikidata: A free collaborative knowledgebase. *Commun. ACM*, 57(10):78–85.

Zijie J. Wang, Dongjin Choi, Shenyu Xu, and Diyi Yang. 2021. Putting humans in the natural language processing loop: A survey. In *Proceedings of the First Workshop on Bridging Human–Computer Interaction and Natural Language Processing*, pages 47–52, Online. Association for Computational Linguistics.

Thomas Wolf, Lysandre Debut, Victor Sanh, Julien Chaumond, Clement Delangue, Anthony Moi, Pierric Cistac, Tim Rault, Remi Louf, Morgan Funtowicz, Joe Davison, Sam Shleifer, Patrick von Platen, Clara Ma, Yacine Jernite, Julien Plu, Canwen Xu, Teven Le Scao, Sylvain Gugger, Mariama Drame, Quentin Lhoest, and Alexander Rush. 2020. Transformers: State-of-the-art natural language processing. In *Proceedings of the 2020 Conference on Empirical Methods in Natural Language Processing: System Demonstrations*, pages 38–45, Online. Association for Computational Linguistics.

Yang Xiao, Jinlan Fu, Weizhe Yuan, Vijay Viswanathan, Zhoumianze Liu, Yixin Liu, Graham Neubig, and Pengfei Liu. 2022. DataLab: A platform for data analysis and intervention. In *Proceedings of the 60th Annual Meeting of the Association for Computational Linguistics: System Demonstrations*, pages 182–195, Dublin, Ireland. Association for Computational Linguistics.

Zexuan Zhong and Danqi Chen. 2021. A frustratingly easy approach for entity and relation extraction. In *Proceedings of the 2021 Conference of the North American Chapter of the Association for Computational Linguistics: Human Language Technologies*, pages 50–61, Online. Association for Computational Linguistics.

jTLEX: a Java Library for TimeLine EXtraction

Mustafa Ocal, Akul Singh, Jared Hummer, Antonela Radas, & Mark Finlayson
Knight Foundation School of Computing and Information Sciences
Florida International University
CASE Building, Room 362, 11200 S.W. 8th Street, Miami, FL USA 33199
{mocal001,asing118,jhumm001,arada002,markaf}@fiu.edu

Abstract

jTLEX is a programming library that provides a Java implementation of the TimeLine EXtraction algorithm (TLEX; Finlayson et al., 2021), along with utilities for programmatic manipulation of TimeML graphs. Timelines are useful for a number of natural language understanding tasks, such as question answering, cross-document event coreference, and summarization & visualization. jTLEX provides functionality for (1) parsing TimeML annotations into Java objects, (2) construction of TimeML graphs from scratch, (3) partitioning of TimeML graphs into temporally connected subgraphs, (4) transforming temporally connected subgraphs into point algebra (PA) graphs, (5) extracting exact timeline of TimeML graphs, (6) detecting inconsistent subgraphs, and (7) calculating indeterminate sections of the timeline. The library has been tested on the entire TimeBank corpus, and comes with a suite of unit tests. We release the software as open source with a free license for non-commercial use.

1 Introduction

TimeML is a standardized temporal annotation scheme for annotating temporal information in texts (Pustejovsky et al., 2003a). TimeML annotations can be used to build temporal graphs, where nodes are events and temporal expressions (i.e., times), and edges are temporal relations. TimeML annotations can be generated using automatic analyzers (Chambers et al., 2014), manual annotation (Minard et al., 2016), or some combination of the two.

While temporal graphs derived from texts can be deeply informative, they usually only encode partial orderings of events and times. For many NLP tasks such as text summarization and visualization (Liu et al., 2012), question-answering (Saquete et al., 2004), and knowledge representation (Galton, 2009), a total order of all events and times (i.e., a timeline) is often more useful. Unfortunately, timelines are rarely explicit in texts and usually cannot be read off from texts directly. There have been a few prior attempts to extract timelines from temporal graphs, however, these works have certain limitations: they do not handle all TimeML relations, they do not separate "real-life" events and subordinated events, and they do not deal with multiple possible temporal orders.

These problems were addressed by an approach called TLEX (TimeLine EXtraction; Finlayson et al., 2021). TLEX presented a CSP-based solution that extracts *exact* timelines from a TimeML graph. TLEX also detects inconsistent TimeML subgraphs as well as temporal indeterminacy. TLEX is a formally correct method and the experimental evaluation on four different TimeML corpora showed that it has 100% accuracy for extracting timelines (Finlayson et al., 2021). TLEX has been used for several NLP tasks such as corpus validation, evaluating temporal dependency parsers, and narrative representation (Ocal et al., 2022a,b; Ocal and Finlayson, 2020). To enable better access to this approach for the community, we have implemented jTLEX, an open-source Java implementation of TLEX for other researchers in the field to use. We present jTLEX in this paper.

jTLEX provides several types of functionality. In its canonical usage, jTLEX takes a TimeML annotated file as input, then (1) parses the annotations into TimeML objects, (2) builds a TimeML graph, (3) partitions the TimeML graph into temporally connected graphs to separate real-life events and subordinated events, (4) transforms the temporally connected graphs into point algebra (PA) graphs, and (5) solves the PA graphs to extract a timeline. If a timeline cannot be extracted, meaning the graph is temporally inconsistent, (6) it detects the minimum inconsistent subgraph and returns it to the annotator to fix it. Finally, if the order of events and times are indeterminant (multiple possible order-

Proceedings of the 17th Conference of the European Chapter of the Association for Computational Linguistics System Demonstrations, pages 27–34
May 2-4, 2023 ©2023 Association for Computational Linguistics

ing), (7) it calculates the temporal indeterminacy. These steps correspond to steps of the TLEX algorithm as described in Finlayson et al. (2021).

We have tested jTLEX on the entire TimeBank corpus (Pustejovsky et al., 2003b) which is a reference corpus for TimeML that contains 183 TimeML annotated news articles. For each file, jTLEX took no longer than 1 second to extract all timelines on a currently available, standard consumer laptop (3.0 GHz Intel Core i7-1185G7 with 32GB of RAM) Our demonstration system as well as a screencast video demonstrating our system is available[1].

2 Library Overview

2.1 User Input

jTLEX processes and allows the manipulation of all the information available in a TimeML annotation. jTLEX can read in preexisting TimeML annotations from a `.tml` file, accept TimeML annotations directly via a JSON-style TimeML encoding, or accept the raw text of TimeML annotations as a Java String object. TimeML annotations can be generated via manual annotation by following the TimeML annotation guide (Sauri et al., 2006) or by using state-of-the-art TimeML annotators such as TARSQI (Verhagen et al., 2005), ClearTK (Bethard, 2013), CAEVO (Chambers et al., 2014), or CATENA (Mirza and Tonelli, 2016). Note that there are certain limitations when using automatic TimeML annotators such as information loss and temporal inconsistency (Ocal et al., 2022a). Fortunately, jTLEX can detect inconsistencies and help users to fix them as explained in Section 2.7.

2.2 TimeML Parser

TimeML is an SGML-based annotation scheme to annotate temporal information in texts. TimeML defines tags for events (<EVENT>), temporal expressions (<TIMEX>), temporal signals (<SIGNAL>), event instances (<MAKEINSTANCE>), and links between events and times, namely temporal link (<TLINK>), subordinated link (<SLINK>), and aspectual link (<ALINK>). Each tag has attributes that contain information about a TimeML object. For example, the "`polarity`" attribute of <MAKEINSTANCE> indicates whether an event is negated and it contains either `POS` or `NEG` values.

jTLEX provides a TimeML parser that can parse TimeML annotations into a set of TimeML Java objects, including events, times, and links. Additionally, it can strip the TimeML tags and return the raw text. The TimeML annotation guide identifies optional and non-optional attributes for each TimeML tag. If the input to jTLEX is missing a non-optional attribute, the parser returns an error message to the user about which attribute is missing for which object. Therefore, jTLEX's TimeML parser can be used to check compliance of annotations to the TimeML standard.

2.3 Graph Constructor

A TimeML graph is a graph where nodes are events and times, and edges are TimeML links (as shown in Figure 1). After jTLEX parses a TimeML annotations into the TimeML objects (events, times, links, etc.), it builds a TimeML graph. Any information about the graph can be then programmatically queried, such as the set of links, the set of nodes, a link by ID, a node by ID, a list of incoming or outgoing links, and much else.

jTLEX allows users to directly modify the TimeML graph if they wish. Users can add or remove links or nodes to the graph, and can also build their own custom graph by creating an empty graph and adding events, times, and links. The graph implementation has a method that returns a JSON output of the graph. This allows users to take advantage of existing graph visualization system such as React Flow (So, 2018) to inspect the TimeML annotations.

2.4 Partitioner

As mentioned in Section 2.2, there are three types of TimeML links. While <TLINK> and <ALINK> provide information about the temporal order of events and times, <SLINK> is used for contexts introducing possible (modal), counterfactual, or conditional relations between two events. An example is shown below.

(1) Amanda *forgot* to *buy* coffee.

The example indicates a counterfactual relationship between *forgot* and *buy*. The event of *buy* never happened in the world described in the text, i.e., the "real world", and therefore, it needs to be separated. As described in the TLEX paper, jTLEX implements this by partitioning a TimeML graph into temporally connected subgraphs. The partitioner has two steps: jTLEX walks the graph to partition the TimeML graph into connected subgraphs. Then

[1] https://cognac.cs.fiu.edu/jtlex/

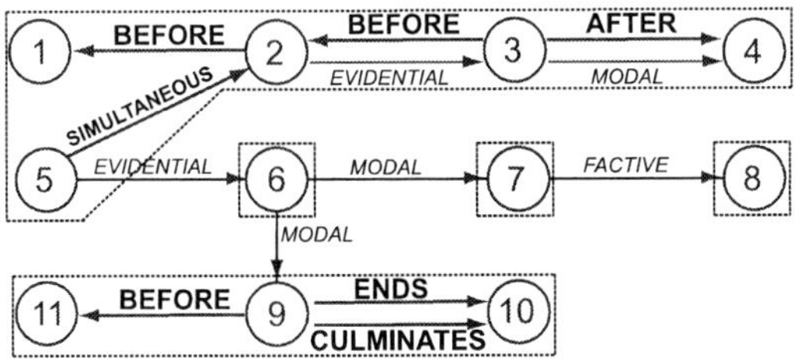

Figure 1: Visualization of partitioning the TimeML graph for wsj_0006.tml from the TimeBank corpus. TLINKs and ALINKs are given in bold, and SLINKs are in italic. jTLEX partitions the TimeML graph into five temporally and aspectually connected subgraphs, as shown by dashed lines.

it further partitions these connected subgraphs into subgraphs connected only with temporal and aspectual links. We name the subgraph(s) that contains "real world" events as *main* subgraph(s), and subgraphs that connect to main subgraphs via subordination links as *subordinated* subgraphs. A visual example of this process is shown in Figure 1.

2.5 Transformer

A point algebra (PA) graph is a graph where nodes are time points and edges are primitive temporal constraints such as {<, =}. As prescribed by the TLEX algorithm, jTLEX transforms each temporally connected subgraph into a PA graph. Each node and link in the subgraph can be expressed in time points and constraints. Assume we have two events (A and B) and A is *BEFORE* B. This can be represented in a PA graph as follows: $A^- < A^+ < B^- < B^+$, where $-$ and $+$ indicate the start and end time points of a node, respectively. An example of the transformation of the TimeML graph in Figure 1 into a PA graph is shown in Figure 2.

This transformation is necessary because the timeline is generated by solving the temporal constraint satisfaction problem (TCSP) represented by the PA graph, as discussed in Section 2.6.

2.6 Solver

After the transformer transforms each temporally connected subgraph into a PA graph, jTLEX assigns integers to each time point in the graph using Java Constraint Programming (JaCoP) library (Kuchcinski and Szymanek, 2013). The library then obtains a timeline after sorting the assigned integers. JaCoP is an open-source java library that offers a rich set of primitive, logical, conditional, and global constraints as well as configurable solution search methods. jTLEX by default produces the smallest solution, which starts at 1 and which represents each time point difference as a difference of 1. Users can also use jTLEX to produce a random solution.

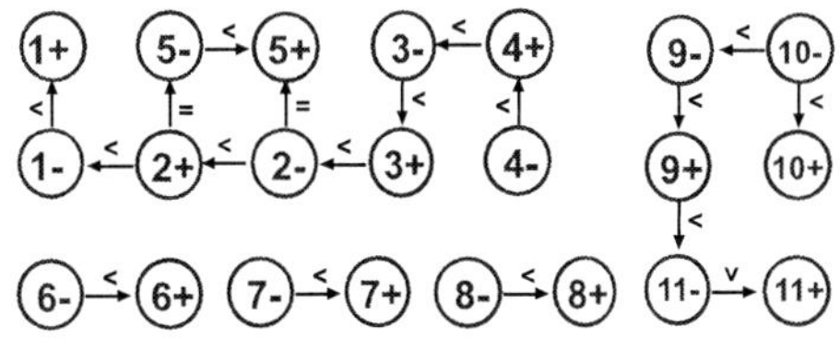

Figure 2: Visualization of the output of the transforming temporally connected subgraphs in Figure 1 into the PA graph.

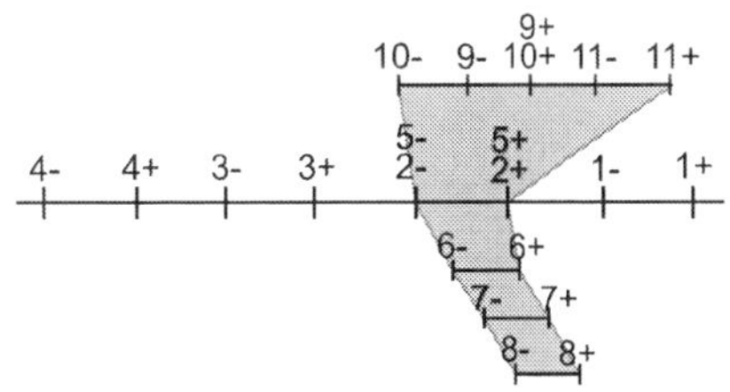

Figure 3: Visualization of the timeline of the TimeML graph in Figure 1. Grey regions indicate subordinating links between timelines.

When run over all the PA graphs, jTLEX produces an *exact* trunk-and-branch *timeline* where the trunk is the main timeline corresponding to the main subgraph and branches are subordinated timelines corresponding to the subordinated subgraphs as shown in Figure 3. Therefore, the main timeline consists the global order of "real world" events and times, while subordinated branches consist subordinated events. Users can retrieve the length of the timeline, the first and last time points, the main timeline, subordinated branches, the number of subordinated branches, the number of time points, and the list of attachment time points where subordinated branches are connected to the main timeline. Users can also retrieve the JSON output of the timeline, and therefore they can visualize the timeline using a third-party graph visualizer application.

2.7 Inconsistency Detector

As described in the TLEX work, the solver can only extract a timeline of the TimeML annotation if the annotation is temporally consistent. If the integer assignment is not possible, then it means the TimeML graph has temporal inconsistency (Barták

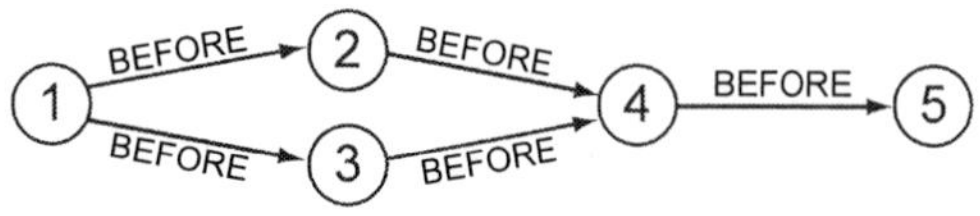

Figure 4: An example graph that has temporal indeterminacy.

et al., 2014). jTLEX provides an inconsistency detector to detect inconsistent cycles in the TimeML graph.

The inconsistency detection algorithm detects self-loops, where the start and end node of an edge is the same such as *A-AFTER->A*. This can be removed automatically as users request. For other non-self-loop cycles, it detects the minimum inconsistent subgraph in the TimeML graph. Further, in the case of two or more inconsistent subgraph overlaps (have a shared edge), it can distinguish the subgraphs and return each inconsistent cycle to the users. A jTLEX output of an inconsistent cycle is shown in Section 3.

Users can use jTLEX to check if their annotation is temporally consistent. If the annotation is not consistent, jTLEX returns the links that cause inconsistency, therefore, users can fix the inconsistent annotation. This could be used as a corpus validation after NLP researchers create a corpus.

2.8 Indeterminacy Calculator

In most cases, natural language texts lack enough information to specify a full ordering, meaning there could be multiple different global orderings of the same events and times. Figure 4 shows a TimeML graph with just such a temporal indeterminacy. The graph indicates a global order of $1^- < 1^+ < 2$ and $3 < 4^- < 4^+ < 5^- < 5^+$, but does not specify the relative order of 2 and 3.

jTLEX uses its own algorithm to measure temporal indeterminacy in a timeline. The algorithm extracts all possible timelines of the graph and compares the shortest timeline with all other possible timelines. More precisely, it checks whether every neighboring time point pair in the shortest timeline is a neighboring time point in other timelines. If they are not always adjacent, the order of that pair is indeterminate. With this result, we can actually represent indeterminate sections on the timeline as shown in Figure 5. This allows jTLEX to represent multiple different orderings in a single timeline.

Using jTLEX, users can retrieve the indeterminant sections of a timeline. jTLEX also provides a standard way of scoring the amount of indeterminacy present in particular timeline.

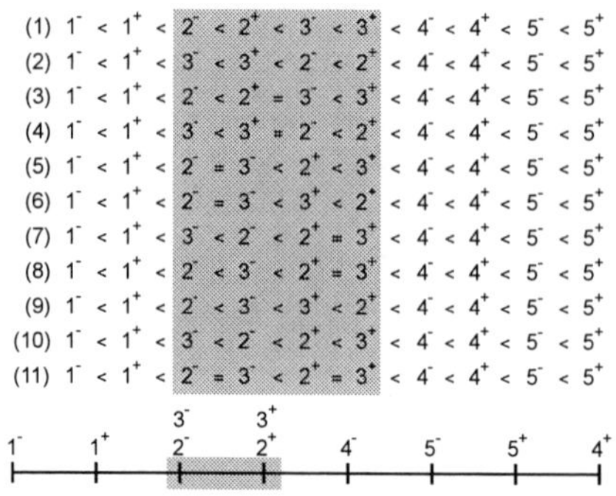

Figure 5: Illustration of the indeterminacy calculation process. The algorithm extracts all possible timelines. For the graph in Figure 4, between 2 and 3, there are 11 possible ordering. This temporal indeterminacy is shown in the grey area in the timeline. Therefore, multiple possible ordering can be represented in a single timeline.

3 Use Cases

A user guide and license information can be found on the jTLEX website[2]. Here we illustrate an approach for one of the TimeML annotations of the TimeBank corpus, called `wsj_0006.tml`. This file and the rest of the corpus can be obtained from LDC website[3]. The following text shown in Example (2), is a snippet of the TimeML-annotated text of `wsj_0006.tml`. The TimeML graph corresponding to the snippet text is shown in Figure 1, where we can see that the nodes of the graph are either events or times, and the edges are TimeML relations. Event instance IDs and timeIDs are given in square brackets (DCT = DOCUMENT CREATION TIME).

(2) [DCT:11/02/89$_{1[t9]}$]: Pacific First Financial Corp. **said**$_{2[ei73]}$ shareholders **approved**$_{3[ei74]}$ its **acquisition**$_{4[ei75]}$ by Royal Trustco Ltd. of Toronto for $27 a share, or $212 million. The thrift holding company **said**$_{5[ei76]}$ it **expects**$_{6[ei77]}$ to **obtain**$_{7[ei78]}$ regulatory **approval**$_{8[ei79]}$ and **complete[**$_{9[ei80]}$ the **transaction**$_{10[ei81]}$ by **year-end**$_{11[t10]}$.

Users can read the file and create the TimeML graph as follows:

[2]https://cognac.cs.fiu.edu/jtlex/

[3]https://catalog.ldc.upenn.edu/LDC2006T08

```
Link: {ID = 1, LinkTag = TLINK, Syntax
    = "", Temporal Relation = BEFORE,
    Origin = null
    Signal: {Id = sid12, String = "by"
        }
    Related to event - Timex: {tID =
        t10, Type = DATE, Value =
        1989-12-31 , Mod = null,
        Temporal Function = true,
        AnchorID = t9, Begin Point = t0
        , End Point = t0, Quantity =
        null, Frequency = null}
    Event Instance - Event Instance:
    {ID = eiid80, Tense = PRESENT,
        Aspect = NONE, Part of Speech =
        VERB, Polarity = POS, Modality
        = "null", Cardinality = "null"
        , Signal = null
        EVENT: eid = e7, class =
            ASPECTUAL, stem = complete}
    }
```

Listing 1: jTLEX parser output for printing the information about the first link of the graph.

```
Main Timeline: {
    eiid75- = 1
    eiid75+ = 2
    eiid74- = 3
    eiid74+ = 4
    eiid73- = 5
    eiid76- = 5
    eiid73+ = 6
    eiid76+ = 6
    t9- = 7
    t9+ = 8
}
Attachment Points: {eiid77->eiid78,
    eiid77->eiid80, eiid76->eiid77,
    eiid78->eiid79}
Subordinated Timelines: {
[eiid81- = 1, eiid80- = 2, eiid81+ =
    3, eiid80+ = 3, t10- = 4, t10+ =
    5],
[eiid79- = 1, eiid79+ = 2],
[eiid78- = 1, eiid78+ = 2],
[eiid77- = 1, eiid77+ = 2]}
```

Listing 2: jTLEX timeline output for the `wsj_0006.tml` file.

```
File tmlFile = new File(fName);
ITimeMLGraph graph = GraphReader.
    TimeMLGraph(tmlFile);
```

Here, `fName` is the path to the file. Users can retrieve any information about the graph such as links (all or one by ID), nodes (all or one by ID), incoming links, outgoing links, JSON output, number of nodes, number of links, number of link types, etc. Using the following code, users can retrieve the information of the first link:

```
System.out.print(graph.getLinkById(1));
```

The output will be as shown in Listing 1. As can be seen, jTLEX provides all the available information in the TimeML annotation about the link and its components using the TimeML parser.

After the TimeML graph is created, users can create a `TLEX` object to perform the timeline extraction including partitioning, transforming, solving, inconsistency detection (if the graph is inconsistent), and temporal indeterminacy. Creating the tlex object is as follows:

```
TLEX tlex = new TLEX(graph);
```

Users, can retrieve the *exact* trunk-and-branch timeline structure using:

```
tlex.getTimeline();
```

The output will be as shown in Listing 2. As can be seen, jTLEX returns the *main* timeline, subordinated timelines, and the attachment points for each subordinated timeline.

```
[Graph Type: Main Graph
Nodes Count = 2
Links count = 2
TLinkType: 2
ALinkType: 0
SLinkType: 0
Nodes:
eiid2048, t57
Links: (From -> To)
(t57 BEFORE eiid2048)
(eiid2048 BEFORE t57)
]
```

Listing 3: jTLEX inconsistent subgraph output for the `wsj_1011.tml` file.

Since the graph of `wsj_0006.tml` is consistent, jTLEX's inconsistency detection method returns an empty set. We illustrate the inconsistency detection algorithm using a temporally inconsistent file from the TimeBank corpus, called `wsj_1011.tml`.

After running the method for graph construction and creating the tlex object, users can simply call the method `tlex.getInconsistentSubGraphs()` and retrieve the inconsistent cycle. For this file, jTLEX returns the output show in Listing 3. As can be seen from the output, jTLEX returns the inconsistent subgraph along with the information about the subgraph.

4 Related Work

As we discussed in Section 1, TimeML is a standardized temporal markup language in the NLP community. Therefore, many tools have been developed for TimeML-related tasks. We can classify existing TimeML tools into two categories: producing TimeML annotations and analyzing TimeML annotations. NLP researchers have concentrated tools of the first type, in particular for both full automatic TimeML annotation—such as TARSQI (Verhagen et al., 2005), ClearTK (Bethard, 2013), and CAEVO (Chambers et al., 2014)—and tools of the automatic annotation of sub-parts of TimeML—such as Evita (Saurí et al., 2005) and NavyTime (Chambers, 2013) for event detection, GATE-Time (Derczynski et al., 2016) and SUTime (Chang and Manning, 2012) for temporal expression recognition, and CATENA (Mirza and Tonelli, 2016) and LCC-TE (Min et al., 2007) for temporal relation extraction.

There are only a small number of tools that evaluate TimeML annotations. Tango is a Java TimeML parser tool to parse the TimeML annotated documents and create a TimeML graph (Verhagen et al., 2006). Tango allows users to modify the graph and it checks the temporal consistency of the graph using temporal closure. Tango was used to evaluate the TimeBank corpus, however, Tango did not report any inconsistency on the TimeBank files. Using the <TIMEX> values, Tango displays the graph in a timeline form, where each section contains a <TIMEX> and the events connected to the <TIMEX>, however, it doesn't provide the global order of events. Similarly, TBOX (Verhagen, 2007) also generates a TimeML graph from a TimeML annotation, but it further removes the temporal closure links to display a simplified TimeML graph. TBOX displays each event in a box shape and places each box based on the temporal relation to present the timeline (e.g., if event A is before event B, then box-A would be on the left of box-B). However, this representation could be problematic considering temporal indeterminacy is already high in TimeML annotations.

TimeML-strict is a Java validation tool that parses TimeML annotations and validates them whether they follow strict TimeML annotation guide rules (Derczynski et al., 2013). It also fixes missing document creation time (DCT) and <TEXT> tags in the annotations. CAVaT is a Python tool that parses TimeML annotations and prints out the quantitative results such as distributions of the TimeML objects (Derczynski and Gaizauskas, 2012). Further, it detects self-loops as well as disconnectivity in the TimeML graphs. CAVaT detects the temporal inconsistency of the graph using inconsistent disclosure. If the graph is inconsistent, it returns the last added constraint to the inconsistent cycle. Determining the entire inconsistent cycle based on one edge is very difficult for the annotators considering the graph size. CAVaT detects 30 inconsistent files in the TimeBank corpus. However, CAVaT's inconsistency detection algorithm only deals with TLINKs and ignores ALINKs and SLINKs. Later, (Ocal et al., 2022b) showed that by taking ALINKs into consideration, the TimeBank corpus actually has 65 inconsistent files.

In addition to these TimeML tools, NLP researchers have also developed ML-based approaches to extract timelines from TimeML annotations (Mani et al., 2006; Do et al., 2012; Kolomiyets et al., 2012; Leeuwenberg and Moens, 2020). However, these approaches have certain limitations such as they do not deal with all temporal links (at most 6 out of 13), they do not distinguish the real-life events and subordinated events, and they do not handle temporal indeterminacy.

Unlike other tools and approaches, in this work we provide an open-source implementation of TLEX, a method for extracting *exact* timelines from a TimeML annotation. Like prior approaches, TLEX—and by extension, jTLEX—offers a TimeML parser and a graph constructor. However, it goes further by separating subordinated events from real-life events, presenting the global order of events and times in a novel trunk-and-branch timeline structure, detecting inconsistencies automatically and helping users to fix them, representing multiple different orders in a single timeline, and measuring the indeterminacy score.

5 Discussion

We perform an extensive evaluation of the TLEX algorithm using the jTLEX output in our forthcoming paper (Ocal and Finlayson, 2023). We perform sampling evaluation using Simple Random Sampling (Saunders et al., 2009, p. 222), which allows us to check the correctness of a specific feature of a set of n members randomly selected from a population with size N to obtain an estimate of the correctness of that feature over all the data. Sampling evaluation shows that jTLEX achieved 100% accuracy on time point ordering and indeterminacy identification with 95% confidence (Ocal and Finlayson, 2023).

Because jTLEX can detect temporal errors in the

annotations and measure temporal indeterminacy, it can be used to evaluate automatic TimeML tools and manual TimeML annotations. An example of using jTLEX to evaluate automatic TimeML annotators can be found in Ocal et al. (2022a), and for using it to evaluate gold-standard TimeML annotations, see Ocal et al. (2022b).

6 Conclusion

We presented jTLEX, an open-source Java library that, for the first time, allows the programmatic extraction of exact timelines from TimeML annotated texts using a standard Java API. jTLEX provides many useful methods for the TimeML community such as TimeML parsing, graph extraction, timeline extraction, inconsistency detection, and temporal indeterminacy calculation. jTLEX can for used on any TimeML annotations in any domain of natural language. We release jTLEX as an open source library that is free for non-commercial use[4].

References

R. Barták, R.A. Morris, and K.B. Venable. 2014. *An Introduction to Constraint-Based Temporal Reasoning*. Morgan & Claypool Publishers.

Steven Bethard. 2013. Cleartk-timeml: A minimalist approach to tempeval 2013. In *Second joint conference on lexical and computational semantics (* SEM), volume 2: proceedings of the seventh international workshop on semantic evaluation (SemEval 2013)*, pages 10–14.

Nathanael Chambers. 2013. Navytime: Event and time ordering from raw text. Technical report, NAVAL ACADEMY ANNAPOLIS MD.

Nathanael Chambers, Taylor Cassidy, Bill McDowell, and Steven Bethard. 2014. Dense event ordering with a multi-pass architecture. *Transactions of the Association for Computational Linguistics*, 2:273–284.

Angel X Chang and Christopher D Manning. 2012. Sutime: A library for recognizing and normalizing time expressions. In *Lrec*, volume 3735, page 3740.

Leon Derczynski and Robert Gaizauskas. 2012. Analysing temporally annotated corpora with cavat. *arXiv preprint arXiv:1203.5051*.

Leon Derczynski, Hector Llorens, and Naushad UzZaman. 2013. Timeml-strict: clarifying temporal annotation. *arXiv preprint arXiv:1304.7289*.

[4]`https://cognac.cs.fiu.edu/jtlex/`

Leon Derczynski, Jannik Strötgen, Diana Maynard, Mark A Greenwood, and Manuel Jung. 2016. Gatetime: Extraction of temporal expressions and event. In *10th Language Resources and Evaluation Conference*, pages 3702–3708. European Language Resources Association (ELRA).

Quang Xuan Do, Wei Lu, and Dan Roth. 2012. Joint inference for event timeline construction. In *Proceedings of the 2012 Joint Conference on Empirical Methods in Natural Language Processing and Computational Natural Language Learning (EMNLP-CoNLL'12)*, pages 677–687.

Mark A Finlayson, Andres Cremisini, and Mustafa Ocal. 2021. Extracting and aligning timelines. In *Computational Analysis of Storylines: Making Sense of Events*, page 87. Cambridge University Press.

Antony Galton. 2009. Spatial and temporal knowledge representation. *Earth Science Informatics*, 2(3):169–187.

Oleksandr Kolomiyets, Steven Bethard, and Marie-Francine Moens. 2012. Extracting narrative timelines as temporal dependency structures. In *Proceedings of the 50th Annual Meeting of the Association for Computational Linguistics (ACL'12)*, pages 88–97.

Krzysztof Kuchcinski and Radoslaw Szymanek. 2013. JaCoP: Java constraint programming solver. `http://jacop.cs.lth.se/`.

Artuur Leeuwenberg and Marie-Francine Moens. 2020. Towards extracting absolute event timelines from english clinical reports. *IEEE/ACM Transactions on Audio, Speech, and Language Processing*, 28:2710–2719.

Shixia Liu, Michelle X. Zhou, Shimei Pan, Yangqiu Song, Weihong Qian, Weijia Cai, and Xiaoxiao Lian. 2012. Tiara: Interactive, topic-based visual text summarization and analysis. *ACM Trans. Intell. Syst. Technol.*, 3(2):25:1–25:28.

Inderjeet Mani, Marc Verhagen, Ben Wellner, Chong Min Lee, and James Pustejovsky. 2006. Machine learning of temporal relations. In *Proceedings of the 21st International Conference on Computational Linguistics and the 44th Annual Meeting of the Association for Computational Linguistics (ICCL-ACL'06)*, pages 753–760. Sydney, Australia.

Congmin Min, Munirathnam Srikanth, and Abraham Fowler. 2007. Lcc-te: a hybrid approach to temporal relation identification in news text. In *Proceedings of the fourth international workshop on semantic evaluations (SemEval-2007)*, pages 219–222.

Anne-Lyse Minard, Manuela Speranza, Ruben Urizar, Begona Altuna, Marieke Van Erp, Anneleen Schoen, and Chantal Van Son. 2016. Meantime, the newsreader multilingual event and time corpus. In *Proceedings of the Tenth International Conference on Language Resources and Evaluation (LREC'16)*, pages 4417–4422.

Paramita Mirza and Sara Tonelli. 2016. Catena: Causal and temporal relation extraction from natural language texts. In *Proceedings of COLING 2016, the 26th International Conference on Computational Linguistics: Technical Papers*, pages 64–75.

Mustafa Ocal and Mark Finlayson. 2020. Evaluating information loss in temporal dependency trees. In *Proceedings of The 12th Language Resources and Evaluation Conference*, pages 2148–2156, Marseille, France. European Language Resources Association.

Mustafa Ocal and Mark A Finlayson. 2023. Tlex: A formally correct method for extracting exact timelines from timeml temporal graphs. *Journal of Artificial Intelligence Research (JAIR)*, Manuscript submitted for publication.

Mustafa Ocal, Adrian Perez, Antonela Radas, and Mark Finlayson. 2022a. Holistic evaluation of automatic timeml annotators. In *Proceedings of the Language Resources and Evaluation Conference*, pages 1444–1453, Marseille, France. European Language Resources Association.

Mustafa Ocal, Antonela Radas, Jared Hummer, Karine Megerdoomian, and Mark Finlayson. 2022b. A comprehensive evaluation and correction of the timebank corpus. In *Proceedings of the Language Resources and Evaluation Conference*, pages 2919–2927, Marseille, France. European Language Resources Association.

James Pustejovsky, José Castaño, Robert Ingria, Roser Saurí, Robert Gaizauskas, Andrea Setzer, and Graham Katz. 2003a. TimeML: robust specification of event and temporal expressions in text. In *Fifth International Workshop on Computational Semantics (IWCS-5)*, pages 1–11.

James Pustejovsky, Patrick Hanks, Roser Saurí, Andrew See, Rob Gaizauskas, Andrea Setzer, Dragomir Radev, Beth Sundheim, David Day, Lisa Ferro, and Marcia Lazo. 2003b. The TimeBank corpus. In *Proceedings of Corpus Linguistics Conference*, pages 647–656. Lancaster, UK.

E. Saquete, P. Martínez-Barco, R. Muñoz, and J. L. Vicedo. 2004. Splitting complex temporal questions for question answering systems. In *Proceedings of the 42Nd Annual Meeting on Association for Computational Linguistics*, ACL '04, Stroudsburg, PA, USA. Association for Computational Linguistics.

M.N.K. Saunders, Philip Lewis, and Adrian Thornhill. 2009. *Research Methods for Business Students, Fifth Edition*. Prentice Hall, New York.

Roser Saurí, Robert Knippen, Marc Verhagen, and James Pustejovsky. 2005. Evita: a robust event recognizer for qa systems. In *Proceedings of Human Language Technology Conference and Conference on Empirical Methods in Natural Language Processing*, pages 700–707.

Roser Sauri, Jessica Littman, Robert Gaizauskas, Andrea Setzer, and James Pustejovsky. 2006. TimeML annotation guidelines, version 1.2.1. `https://catalog.ldc.upenn.edu/docs/LDC2006T08/timeml_annguide_1.2.1.pdf`.

Preston So. 2018. React. In *Decoupled Drupal in Practice*, pages 313–334. Springer.

Marc Verhagen. 2007. Drawing timeml relations with tbox. In *Annotating, extracting and reasoning about time and events*, pages 7–28. Springer.

Marc Verhagen, Robert Knippen, Inderjeet Mani, and James Pustejovsky. 2006. Annotation of temporal relations with tango. In *LREC*, pages 2249–2252.

Marc Verhagen, Inderjeet Mani, Roser Saurí, Jessica Littman, Robert Knippen, Seok Bae Jang, Anna Rumshisky, John Phillips, and James Pustejovsky. 2005. Automating temporal annotation with tarsqi. In *ACL*, pages 81–84.

CovRelex-SE: Adding Semantic Information for Relation Search via Sequence Embedding

Dinh-Truong Do[1] **Chau Nguyen**[1] **Vu Tran**[2] **Ken Satoh**[3]
Yuji Matsumoto[4] **Minh Le Nguyen**[1]

[1]Japan Advanced Institute of Science and Technology
{truongdo,chau.nguyen,nguyenml}@jaist.ac.jp
[2]The Institute of Statistical Mathematics, Japan
vutran@ism.ac.jp
[3]National Institute of Informatics, Japan
ksatoh@nii.ac.jp
[4]RIKEN Center for Advanced Intelligence Project (AIP), Japan
yuji.matsumoto@riken.jp

Abstract

In recent years, COVID-19 has impacted all aspects of human life. As a result, numerous publications relating to this disease have been issued. Due to the massive volume of publications, some retrieval systems have been developed to provide researchers with useful information. In these systems, lexical searching methods are widely used, which raises many issues related to acronyms, synonyms, and rare keywords. In this paper, we present a hybrid relation retrieval system, CovRelex-SE, based on embeddings to provide high-quality search results. Our system can be accessed through the following URL: `https://www.jaist.ac.jp/is/labs/nguyen-lab/systems/covrelex-se/`.

Keywords: COVID-19, relation search, biomedical domain, relation extraction, entity recognition, semantic search.

1 Introduction

Scientific information related to the coronavirus disease has received a lot of attention in recent years. The number of COVID-19-relevant publications is increasing daily. In the record of CORD-19 dataset (Wang et al., 2020a), there are more than 900K papers introduced by March 31st, 2022. The huge number of documents demonstrates the importance of retrieval systems for providing researchers with informative knowledge.

A relation is an object that consists of three components ($arg1$, rel, $arg2$), where $arg1$, and $arg2$ are noun phrases that may contain biomedical entities and rel is an expression describing the relation between $arg1$ and $arg2$. A query is made up of partial information on a relation, which includes keywords regarding these components. Ideally, a relation retrieval system should return all relevant relations with the corresponding papers, which can be used to answer two different types of questions: single-hop and multi-hop. Regarding single-hop questions, such as *"COVID-19 disables which things?"*, we can input the query *("COVID-19", "disable", any-arg2)*, and then extract the answer by using the returned results of *arg2*. On the other hand, we can combine two queries: *("COVID-19", "cause", DISEASE)*, and *(CHEMICAL, "treat", DISEASE)* to answer the multi-hop question *"What are CHEMICAL that can treat some DISEASES caused by COVID-19?"*. By that, the answer can be extracted by using the returned results at the position of *CHEMICAL*.

In this paper, we propose CovRelex-SE, a hybrid retrieval system to search the relations that effectively tackles the issues raised by the lexical approach in the CovRelex system (Tran et al., 2021). Instead of searching relations using lexical methods, CovRelex-SE ranks their scores by utilizing the combination of lexical scores (based on the Elasticsearch[1] engine) and semantic scores (based on CORD19-BERT embeddings). In summary, our contributions in this paper are as follows: **(I)** A novel approach to ranking COVID-19-relevant relations, which combines the effectiveness of lexical approach and vector representation approach; **(II)** A new pre-trained language model,

[1]https://www.elastic.co/

Proceedings of the 17th Conference of the European Chapter of the Association for Computational Linguistics System Demonstrations, pages 35–42
May 2-4, 2023 ©2023 Association for Computational Linguistics

CORD19-BERT, which is pre-trained from scratch using the CORD-19 dataset; **(III)** A web-based relation search system, CovRelex-SE, which provides two search functions: Single-Relation Search and Graph Search; that aims to answer two type of questions: single-hop and multi-hop; **(IV)** An experimental evaluation, which shows the superior performance of CovRelex-SE system using the CORD-19 dataset by March 31st, 2022.

2 Related Work

Due to the COVID-19 outbreak, it is vital to collect crucial information from a huge number of COVID-19-related publications. Zhang et al. (2020) created Covidex, a search engine that allows users to query the COVID-19 Open Research Dataset and access inside information. Esteva et al. (2020) introduced Co-Search, a semantic search engine composed of a retriever and a ranker that was built to handle complex queries throughout the COVID-19 papers. Additionally, Wang et al. (2020b) created the EvidenceMiner web-based solution. Given a query as a natural language statement, EvidenceMiner retrieves textual evidence at the sentence level from the CORD-19 corpus for life sciences. More recently, Raza et al. (2022) present an Information Retrieval System that uses latent information to select relevant works related to specific concepts. Otegi et al. (2022) develop a Question Answering system that receives a set of questions asked by experts about the disease COVID-19 and SARS-CoV-2 virus, and provides a ranked list of expert-level answers to each question.

Conceptually, the most similar to our work, CovRelex (Tran et al., 2021), is a retrieval system for scientific publications that target entities and relations via relation extraction from COVID-19 scientific papers. However, there is still a lack of systems that automatically extract the diverse relations through papers and obtain the results using semantic information, especially given the rapid publication of COVID-19 papers. This issue motivates us to create the CovRelex-SE system.

3 Method

3.1 Overview

Figure 1 illustrates our proposed system, CovRelex-SE. From the raw text of document abstracts, we extract relations and recognize biomedical entities inside the extracted relations. For each relation, $arg1$, $arg2$, and rel are converted into vectors by using CORD19-BERT. Three Faiss (Johnson et al., 2019) indices are then trained using all of the embedding vectors. At the query time, the user input a query, which will be converted to embedding vectors. Following that, the Faiss indices will be looked up for the most similar relations according to the query and return semantic scores. The Elasticsearch engine will also look up the query and utilize the BM25 algorithm (Robertson et al., 1995) to calculate lexical scores. The system then combines the lexical scores and semantic scores as final scores for relations. Finally, CovRelex-SE returns the top-ranked triplets after filtering query entities using the Elasticsearch engine.

3.2 Relation Extraction & Entity Recognition

In this paper, to extract the relations in the documents as many as possible, we use a variety of relation extraction methods. As each method has its own characteristics, we can obtain more unique relations when combining all of them. The following are brief descriptions of the methods.

- **ReVerb** (Fader et al., 2011) tackles the issues of incoherent and uninformative relation extractions by introducing syntactic and lexical constraints on binary verb-based relations.
- **OLLIE** (Schmitz et al., 2012) overcomes the limitation of prior methods, which extract only relations mediated via verbs. OLLIE broadens the syntactic scope by identifying relations mediated by nouns, adjectives, etc.
- **ClausIE** (Del Corro and Gemulla, 2013) is a clause-based approach to open information extraction. It separates the detection of clauses and clause types from the actual generation of propositions.
- **Relink** (Tran and Nguyen, 2021) is a method inherited partly from ReVerb. It extracts relations from connected phrases, unlike ClauseIE which extracts clause types.
- **OpenIE** (Angeli et al., 2015) breaks a long sentence into short, coherent clauses, and then finds the maximally simple relations.

After extracting relations, we use the SpaCy[2] models provided by the SciSpacy (Neumann et al., 2019) library to recognize the biomedical entities.

[2]https://spacy.io/

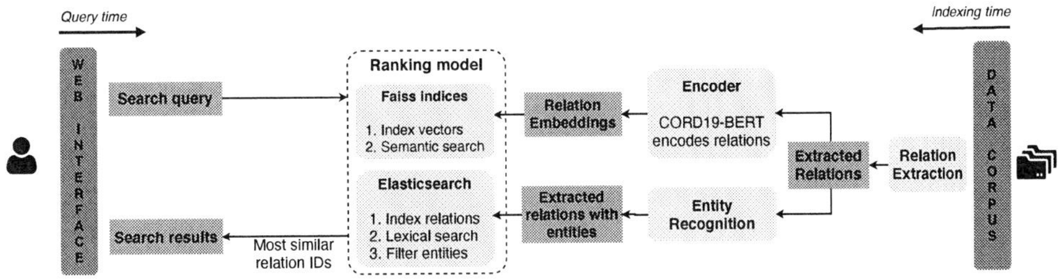

Figure 1: Overview of the CovRelex-SE system.

Since each model is trained on a different annotated corpus (Li et al., 2016; Bada et al., 2012; Kim et al., 2004; Pyysalo et al., 2015), it can recognize a different set of biomedical entities. Table 1 shows SciSpacy models that were utilized.

Table 1: SciSpacy models used in our system.

Models	Training corpus
en_ner_craft_md	CRAFT corpus (for cell types, chemicals, proteins, genes) (Bada et al., 2012)
en_ner_jnlpba_md	JNLPBA corpus (for cell lines, cell types, DNAs, RNAs, proteins) (Collier and Kim, 2004)
en_ner_bc5cdr_md	BC5CDR corpus (for chemicals and diseases) (Li et al., 2016)
en_ner_bionlp13cg_md	BioNLP13CG (for cancer genetics) (Pyysalo et al., 2015)

3.3 Embedding Extraction & Faiss Index

In recent years, domain-specific pre-trained models have led to effective results on many natural language processing tasks (Chalkidis et al., 2020; Lee et al., 2020). Generally, there are two common ways to pre-train a domain-specific language model: from scratch or continual over a general language model such as BERT (Devlin et al., 2018). However, Gu et al. (2020) show that if we have a large enough training data, pre-training from scratch would be better. The particular reasons for this circumstance are as follows: **(I)** The ability to develop a new vocabulary for the specific domain, **(II)** The fact that general documents basically differ from documents of this domain, increasing the likelihood of negative transfers that reduce the overall performance.

Based on the above points, we pre-train a new language model, CORD19-BERT, from scratch using the data of CORD-19 corpus. Figure 2 illustrates the relative coverages of the vocabularies of three models CORD19-BERT, PubMedBERT (Gu et al., 2020) and BERT-base (Devlin et al., 2018). There is a considerable variation in the three vocabularies. Especially, there are some common COVID-19 related words that do not exist in the vocabularies of BERT-base and PubMedBERT, such as *covid, unvaccinated, etc.* In this step, we use the masked language model task to pre-train CORD19-BERT. Following BERT, we mask 15% of tokens, and the model needs to predict the masked tokens in the sentence. We share our pre-trained CORD19-BERT model via Huggingface[3].

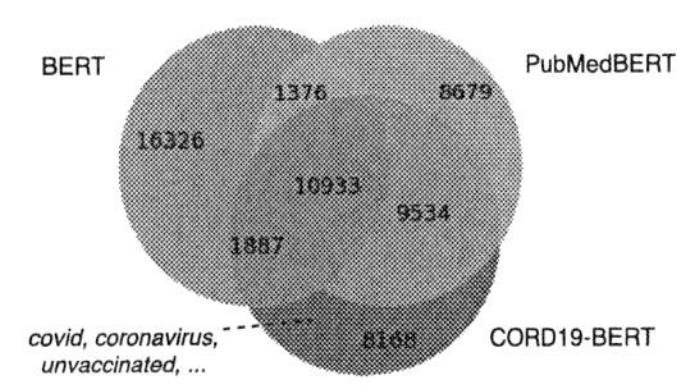

Figure 2: The relative coverages of three vocabularies of BERT, PubMedBERT, and CORD19-BERT. When the vocabulary size of each model is 30,522 tokens.

After pre-training the model, we use CORD19-BERT to extract the embeddings of relations. One issue with data processing is the excessive number of embedding vectors. Therefore, we used the Faiss index (Johnson et al., 2019) to resolve this problem. Faiss is a method for searching and grouping dense vectors in an efficient manner. More details about the Faiss settings used in this paper are shown in the experimental section.

3.4 Relation Scoring

The score of a relation ($arg1$, rel, $arg2$) is calculated based on semantic and lexical scores. The semantic score is determined using the embeddings from CORD19-BERT, whereas the lexical score is computed using the Elasticsearch engine. Specifically, let (*s_arg1*, *s_rel*, *s_arg2*) be the semantic

[3] https://huggingface.co/CovRelex-SE/CORD19-BERT

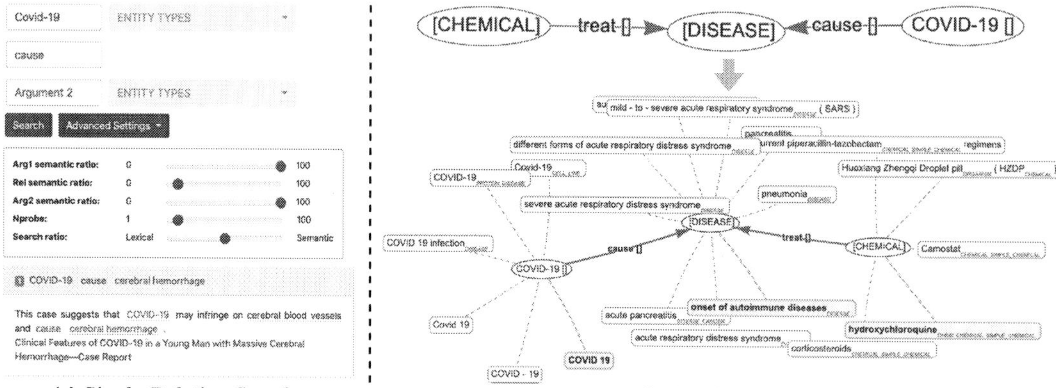

(a) Single-Relation Search

(b) Graph Search

Figure 3: Examples of Single-Relation Search and Graph Search.

scores of (*arl*, *rel*, *arg2*) calculated by Faiss indices based on squared Euclidean (L2) distance. Following that, the semantic score of a relation is calculated based on formula 1 with hyperparameters α, β, and γ. These parameters' values can be controlled by the users.

$$score_{se} = \alpha * s\_arg1 + \beta * s\_rel + \gamma * s\_arg2 \quad (1)$$

The Elasticsearch engine, which is based on the BM25 scoring algorithm, is used to compute the lexical score. After obtaining the semantic and lexical scores, the final score is calculated by combining these two scores using the formula 2. Additionally, there is a user-specified hyperparameter with θ, depending on whether the user wants to search exact match or by semantic similarity.

$$score_{final} = \theta * score_{se} + (1-\theta) * score_{lex} \quad (2)$$

3.5 Retrieval System

The retrieval system provides two different types of searching scenarios: **Single-Relation Search** and **Graph Search**. While **Single-Relation Search** provides a simple way to discover a specific relation, **Graph Search** aims to answer complex questions from users.

3.5.1 Single-Relation Search

In **Single-relation Search**, a query consists of partial information of a relation which can contain keywords about $arg1$, $arg2$, and rel, and the sliders which determine the values of the hyperparameters in formulas 1 and 2. The retrieved results are relevant relations along with their corresponding papers. An example of a single-relation query is illustrated in Fig. 3a. The query relation is *("Covid-19", "cause", "")*. The results are highest score relations, for instance, *("COVID-19", "cause", "cerebral hemorrhage")*.

3.5.2 Graph Search

In addition to single relation searching, we provide a multi-relation search tool called **Graph Search**. The input graph is a directed graph where each edge indicates a relation, and the label of the edge is determined by the value of *rel*. Each edge contains *arg1* and *arg2* as its source and target. The retrieved result is a graph that matches the query graph. The main purpose of **Graph Search** is to find out the answer for complex questions that are challenging to answer with single search searching. For example, the question *"What CHEMICAL can treat some DISEASE caused by COVID-19?"* can be represented as a graph with three nodes and two edges defining two relations *("COVID-19", "cause", DISEASE)*, and *(CHEMICAL, "treat", DISEASE)*. This allows us to perform the question on the system as a graph query, which will be answered by the retrieved results. Additionally, **Graph Search** is also a visualization of retrieved relations that makes users easier to understand the results. Figure 3b shows the outcome of the above query. One of the results is the graph with two relations *("COVID-19", "cause", "onset of autoimmune diseases")*, and *("hydroxychloroquine", "treat", "autoimmune diseases")*.

4 Experimental Results

4.1 Corpus

The CovRelex-SE system makes use of a snapshot of CORD-19 at March 31st, 2022. The dataset is a resource of over 900,000 scholarly articles about COVID-19 and related coronaviruses. Relation extraction and embedding extraction were performed on the abstracts of the papers.

4.2 Relation Extraction & Entity Recognition

As illustrated in Table 2, we extracted **107.4** million relations, **82.2** million of which were unique. On average, there are **160** unique relations extracted from a single document abstract. Among the methods, OpenIE generates the most results.

Table 2: Statistics of extracted relations.

Method	Non-uniq/corpus	Uniq/corpus	Uniq/abstract
ReVerb	5.5M	4.5M	8
OLLIE	11.0M	8.9M	17
ClausIE	20.9M	16.9M	32
Relink	12.7M	10.0M	20
OpenIE	57.3M	45.8M	90
Overall	107.4M	82.2M	160

As shown in Table 3, four entity recognition models have identified **15.1** million distinct entities from the corpus. An average of **24** recognized entities are present for each abstract of CORD-19. Among the models, **en_ner_jnlpba_md** generates the most results. The top 3 common recognized entities are AMINO_ACID, CANCER, and CELL.

Table 3: Statistics of recognized entities.

Model	/corpus	/abstract
en_ner_craft_md	3.1M	5
en_ner_jnlpba_md	6.6M	11
en_ner_bc5cdr_md	3.4M	5
en_ner_bionlp13cg_md	2.0M	3
Total	15.1M	24

4.3 Embedding Extraction & Faiss Index

To pre-train CORD19-BERT, we extract **52.8** million sentences from the CORD-19 corpus using both abstract and full-text of documents. We then pre-train the model following the BERT-base settings (110M parameters) (Devlin et al., 2018). In the initialization step, we use a peak learning rate **5e-05** and train for **4.7** million steps, Adam optimizer with epsilon **1e-08**, and batch size of **32** sequences with **512** tokens. Training took **99** hours on one NVIDIA A100 GPU. After that, we use the pre-trained model to perform embedding extractions. Each component of a relation is converted to a 768-dim vector using this model.

Using the Faiss package, we divide the searching space of embedding vectors into **100** clusters. When searching a query, the users can easily alter the value of parameter **nprobe**, which affects how many adjacent clusters are used to search. Table 4 shows the required time to search a query *("covid", "cause", DISEASE)* based on different values of **nprobe**. The increase of the **nprobe** implies longer search time. In general, there are three main factors that affected the search time of a query including the number of non-empty components in the query, the number of components with entity types, and the value of **nprobe**.

Table 4: Statistics of search time for different hyperparameter values of **nprobe**.

Hyperameter	Search time
Nprobe=1	5.92 s
Nprobe=10	6.86 s
Nprobe=50	19.46 s
Nprobe=100	23.19 s

4.4 Evaluation Settings and Results

To demonstrate the effectiveness of two search functions of our system, we conduct an evaluation task. The queries are created by using the content of sample articles in the corpus. There are 50 single-relation search queries and 30 graph search queries were created. Two evaluators work together to evaluate the returned results. Specifically, the evaluation process contains three phrases as follows:

- **Phase 1: How to use system.** Two evaluators carefully read the manual[4] of our system.
- **Phase 2: Evaluating.** Two evaluators separately determine whether the returned result of systems are correct or not. A correct result contains at least one relation that can be entailed from its corresponding paragraph and answer the query. After that, if any answers weren't identical, they adjudicated with each other.
- **Phase 3: Combining answers.** We collect the answers from two evaluators. Only answers that are accepted by both evaluators are counted as correct ones. In addition, we used Cohen's kappa coefficient (McHugh, 2012)

[4]https://www.jaist.ac.jp/is/labs/nguyen-lab/systems/covrelex-se/docs/

Table 5: Evaluation results on systems. **Correct I&II**: evaluated as correct results (can be entailed the expected answer from top-5 returned relations) by both the evaluators. **Kappa**: Cohen's kappa coefficient.

Function	Method	Correct I & II	Kappa
Single Relation Search	CovRelex	28 (56%)	0.78
	CovRelex with semantic	41 (82%)	0.85
	CovRelex-SE	**42 (84%)**	0.83
Graph Search	CovRelex	15 (50%)	0.72
	CovRelex-SE	**22 (73.3%)**	0.70

to estimate the agreement between the two evaluators.

As a baseline, we perform the queries on CovRelex using the system's default settings. Moreover, we add the semantic search component to the baseline and refer to this setting as CovRelex with semantic. For CovRelex with semantic and CovRelex-SE, we set the values of $(\alpha, \beta, \gamma, \theta)$ in section 3.4 to *(1.0, 0.1, 1.0, 0.5)*.

Table 5 shows the evaluation results. For single-relation search, we can see that using the semantic improves the system by 26% over using simply the lexical method. In addition, after employing the latest data corpus, the accuracy of our system enhances to 84%. For graph search, our system performs better than CovRelex by 23.3%. Moreover, Cohen's kappa coefficients of the methods are greater than or equal to 0.7, which is considered a good agreement (Fleiss et al., 2013).

4.5 Result Discussion

We observe that the proposed system is able to make more effective use of semantic information than the baseline CovRelex system. Specifically, instead of lexical matching only, the CovRelex-SE system also searches with the meaning of keywords. For example, there is a query *("", "shield", "lung")* that describes the question *"What thing shields the lungs?"*. Figure. 4 presents top-1 retrieved relations based on each system for this query. We can see that the CovRelex system can not return any results. On the other hand, the CovRelex-SE system knows the close meaning between *"shield"* and *"protect"* in this context and returns the relation *("ARBs", "protect", "lung")*.

There are some cases that the CovRelex-SE system with default settings fails to retrieve the correct relations in top-5 results, for example *("lung radiological image", "screen", "covid")*. In general,

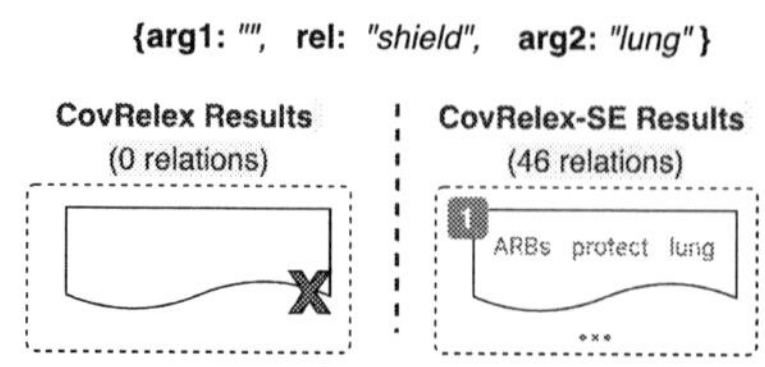

Figure 4: An example results of systems.

we can further improve the accuracy of the system by changing the values of hyperparameters such as **nprobe**. However, there is a trade-off between computation time and accuracy.

5 Threats to Validity

There are two main threats to validity in this study, which are described as follows.

5.1 Threat of Evaluation Settings

In this study, we evaluate the performance of the systems in Table 5 using the default settings. As a result, their configuration values might not be optimal for the systems. To reduce the threat, we run several queries through the systems, manually changing the value of each setting and selecting the one with the most relevant and consistent results. Also, we intend to use an evaluation task to determine the best settings for each system.

5.2 Threat of Extracting Relations

This threat mainly lies in the extracted relations that are used for ranking. The threat may come from the relation extraction methods that do not capture all available relations or extract the incorrect ones. To minimize the threat of extracting false positive relations, we carefully investigate the relation extraction methods. Also, we plan to use additional relation extraction methods to capture all possible relations in the documents.

6 Conclusions

In this paper, we present CovRelex-SE, a novel COVID-19 retrieval system for ranking relations in the CORD-19 corpus. The score of a relation is calculated based on semantic and lexical scores. The semantic score is determined using the embeddings from CORD19-BERT, whereas the lexical score is computed using the Elasticsearch engine. In order to evaluate the effectiveness of CovRelex-SE, we conducted an evaluation task. The experimental results show that our system outperforms the

CovRelex system in both single-relation search and graph search.

References

Gabor Angeli, Melvin Jose Johnson Premkumar, and Christopher D. Manning. 2015. Leveraging linguistic structure for open domain information extraction. In *Proceedings of the 53rd Annual Meeting of the Association for Computational Linguistics and the 7th International Joint Conference on Natural Language Processing (Volume 1: Long Papers)*, pages 344–354, Beijing, China. Association for Computational Linguistics.

Michael Bada, Miriam Eckert, Donald Evans, Kristin Garcia, Krista Shipley, Dmitry Sitnikov, William A Baumgartner, K Bretonnel Cohen, Karin Verspoor, Judith A Blake, et al. 2012. Concept annotation in the craft corpus. *BMC bioinformatics*, 13(1):1–20.

Ilias Chalkidis, Manos Fergadiotis, Prodromos Malakasiotis, Nikolaos Aletras, and Ion Androutsopoulos. 2020. Legal-bert: The muppets straight out of law school. *arXiv preprint arXiv:2010.02559*.

Nigel Collier and Jin-Dong Kim. 2004. Introduction to the bio-entity recognition task at jnlpba. In *Proceedings of the International Joint Workshop on Natural Language Processing in Biomedicine and its Applications (NLPBA/BioNLP)*, pages 73–78.

Luciano Del Corro and Rainer Gemulla. 2013. Clausie: clause-based open information extraction. In *Proceedings of the 22nd international conference on World Wide Web*, pages 355–366.

Jacob Devlin, Ming-Wei Chang, Kenton Lee, and Kristina Toutanova. 2018. Bert: Pre-training of deep bidirectional transformers for language understanding. *arXiv preprint arXiv:1810.04805*.

Andre Esteva, Anuprit Kale, Romain Paulus, Kazuma Hashimoto, Wenpeng Yin, Dragomir Radev, and Richard Socher. 2020. Co-search: Covid-19 information retrieval with semantic search, question answering, and abstractive summarization. *arXiv preprint arXiv:2006.09595*.

Anthony Fader, Stephen Soderland, and Oren Etzioni. 2011. Identifying relations for open information extraction. In *Proceedings of the 2011 conference on empirical methods in natural language processing*, pages 1535–1545.

Joseph L Fleiss, Bruce Levin, and Myunghee Cho Paik. 2013. *Statistical methods for rates and proportions*. john wiley & sons.

Yu Gu, Robert Tinn, Hao Cheng, Michael Lucas, Naoto Usuyama, Xiaodong Liu, Tristan Naumann, Jianfeng Gao, and Hoifung Poon. 2020. Domain-specific language model pretraining for biomedical natural language processing.

Jeff Johnson, Matthijs Douze, and Hervé Jégou. 2019. Billion-scale similarity search with GPUs. *IEEE Transactions on Big Data*, 7(3):535–547.

Jin-Dong Kim, Tomoko Ohta, Yoshimasa Tsuruoka, Yuka Tateisi, and Nigel Collier. 2004. Introduction to the bio-entity recognition task at jnlpba. In *Proceedings of the international joint workshop on natural language processing in biomedicine and its applications*, pages 70–75. Citeseer.

Jinhyuk Lee, Wonjin Yoon, Sungdong Kim, Donghyeon Kim, Sunkyu Kim, Chan Ho So, and Jaewoo Kang. 2020. Biobert: a pre-trained biomedical language representation model for biomedical text mining. *Bioinformatics*, 36(4):1234–1240.

Jiao Li, Yueping Sun, Robin J Johnson, Daniela Sciaky, Chih-Hsuan Wei, Robert Leaman, Allan Peter Davis, Carolyn J Mattingly, Thomas C Wiegers, and Zhiyong Lu. 2016. Biocreative v cdr task corpus: a resource for chemical disease relation extraction. *Database*, 2016.

Mary L McHugh. 2012. Interrater reliability: the kappa statistic. *Biochemia medica*, 22(3):276–282.

Mark Neumann, Daniel King, Iz Beltagy, and Waleed Ammar. 2019. Scispacy: fast and robust models for biomedical natural language processing. *arXiv preprint arXiv:1902.07669*.

Arantxa Otegi, Iñaki San Vicente, Xabier Saralegi, Anselmo Peñas, Borja Lozano, and Eneko Agirre. 2022. Information retrieval and question answering: A case study on covid-19 scientific literature. *Knowledge-Based Systems*, 240:108072.

Sampo Pyysalo, Tomoko Ohta, Rafal Rak, Andrew Rowley, Hong-Woo Chun, Sung-Jae Jung, Sung-Pil Choi, Jun'ichi Tsujii, and Sophia Ananiadou. 2015. Overview of the cancer genetics and pathway curation tasks of bionlp shared task 2013. *BMC bioinformatics*, 16(10):1–19.

Shaina Raza, Brian Schwartz, and Laura C Rosella. 2022. Coquad: a covid-19 question answering dataset system, facilitating research, benchmarking, and practice. *BMC bioinformatics*, 23(1):1–28.

Stephen E Robertson, Steve Walker, Susan Jones, Micheline M Hancock-Beaulieu, Mike Gatford, et al. 1995. Okapi at trec-3. *Nist Special Publication Sp*, 109:109.

Michael Schmitz, Stephen Soderland, Robert Bart, Oren Etzioni, et al. 2012. Open language learning for information extraction. In *Proceedings of the 2012 joint conference on empirical methods in natural language processing and computational natural language learning*, pages 523–534.

Vu Tran, Van-Hien Tran, Phuong Nguyen, Chau Nguyen, Ken Satoh, Yuji Matsumoto, and Minh Nguyen. 2021. Covrelex: A covid-19 retrieval system with relation extraction. In *Proceedings of the*

16th Conference of the European Chapter of the Association for Computational Linguistics: System Demonstrations, pages 24–31.

Xuan-Chien Tran and Le-Minh Nguyen. 2021. Relink: Open information extraction by linking phrases and its applications. In *International Conference on Distributed Computing and Internet Technology*, pages 44–62. Springer.

Lucy Lu Wang, Kyle Lo, Yoganand Chandrasekhar, Russell Reas, Jiangjiang Yang, Darrin Eide, Kathryn Funk, Rodney Kinney, Ziyang Liu, William Merrill, et al. 2020a. Cord-19: The covid-19 open research dataset. *ArXiv*.

Xuan Wang, Yingjun Guan, Weili Liu, Aabhas Chauhan, Enyi Jiang, Qi Li, David Liem, Dibakar Sigdel, John Caufield, Peipei Ping, et al. 2020b. Evidenceminer: Textual evidence discovery for life sciences. In *Proceedings of the 58th Annual Meeting of the Association for Computational Linguistics: System Demonstrations*, pages 56–62.

Edwin Zhang, Nikhil Gupta, Raphael Tang, Xiao Han, Ronak Pradeep, Kuang Lu, Yue Zhang, Rodrigo Nogueira, Kyunghyun Cho, Hui Fang, et al. 2020. Covidex: Neural ranking models and keyword search infrastructure for the covid-19 open research dataset. *arXiv preprint arXiv:2007.07846*.

A Appendix

A.1 Detailed settings of Faiss

One issue with data processing is the excessive number of embedding vectors; 82 million relations correspond to 246 million 758-dim vectors. Then calculating the query's embedding and iterating over all corpus relations' embeddings is impractical. Therefore, we used Faiss to resolve this issue. The detailed settings of Faiss[5] are shown in Table. 6.

Table 6: Detailed settings of Faiss.

Setting	Value
Version	1.7.2
Faiss Index	IndexIVFFlat
Faiss Quantizer	IndexFlatL2
Faiss **nlist**	100
Faiss **nprobe**	10 (default)

[5]See Faiss wiki page for the meaning of each setting: `https://github.com/facebookresearch/faiss/wiki/`

A.2 Examples appearing in CORD19-BERT Vocabulary

Table 7 shows some examples of subwords that exist in the CORD19-BERT vocabulary but not in BERT and PubMedBERT. From these examples, it can be seen that the embedding spaces of BERT and PubMedBERT are not capable of describing the important concepts of COVID-19-related documents directly. This can affect the model's performance on representing the semantic information of phrases. We provide subwords with explanations of them from Oxford Online Learner's Dictionary[6]. Most of these terms are related to the coronavirus.

Table 7: Examples appearing in CORD19-BERT vocabulary, not in BERT and PubMedBERT vocabularies.

Token	Explanation
covid	A disease caused by a coronavirus, especially Covid-19.
coronavirus	A type of virus that can cause pneumonia and other diseases in humans and animals.
respirator	A piece of equipment that makes it possible for somebody to breathe over a long period when they are unable to do so naturally.
quarantine	A period of time when an animal or a person that has or may have a disease is kept away from others in order to prevent the disease from spreading.
vaccinate	To give a person or an animal a vaccine, especially by injecting it, in order to protect them against a disease.
disinformation	False information that is given deliberately.
distancing	To become less involved or connected with somebody/something.
facemask	Something that you wear over part or all of your face, in order to protect it or to prevent the spread of disease.
lockdown	An official order to control the movement of people or vehicles because of a dangerous situation.
##infection	Wordpiece in words containing "infection" (e.g. reinfection, coinfection)

[6]`https://www.oxfordlearnersdictionaries.com/`

ITMT: Interactive Topic Model Trainer

L. Calvo-Bartolomé, J. A. Espinosa-Melchor, and J. Arenas-García
Universidad Carlos III de Madrid
Avda. Universidad, 30. 28911 Leganés, Madrid, Spain
lcalvo@pa.uc3m.es
joespino@pa.uc3m.es
jarenas@ing.uc3m.es

Abstract

Topic Modeling is a commonly used technique for analyzing unstructured data in various fields, but achieving accurate results and useful models can be challenging, especially for domain experts who lack the knowledge needed to optimize the parameters required by this natural language processing technique. From this perspective, we introduce an Interactive Topic Model Trainer (ITMT) developed within the EU-funded project IntelComp. ITMT is a user-in-the-loop topic modeling tool presented with a graphical user interface that allows the training and curation of different state-of-the-art topic extraction libraries, including some recent neural-based methods, oriented toward the usage by domain experts. This paper reviews ITMT's functionalities and key implementation aspects in this paper, including a comparison with other tools for topic modeling analysis.

1 Introduction

In the growing information age, today mostly dominated by an unprecedented interest in artificial intelligence (AI), as well as its deployment in a multitude of applications, topic modeling is still mostly preferred over other AI techniques for the automatic extraction of the main themes concurring in a collection of documents.

Nonetheless, the blind application of these topic extraction tools entails some difficulties, from which we can cite the presence of garbage topics (i.e., topics that describe the corpus under analysis as a whole, but not the relevant topics it consists of); the complicated adjustment of flat topic models when the corpus is characterized by topics with very different sizes, as they do not support hierarchical modeling; or challenges associated with finding a suitable tuning for each algorithm, which requires expertise and a good knowledge of their hyperparameters, just to mention some.

Moreover, when the knowledge of domain experts is available, it is worthwhile to offer tools that enable the incorporation of such understanding into the building of topic models, providing both appliances for visualization and guided adjustment of the model, specially designed for the usage of non-AI practitioners that are experts in their area. Nevertheless, it is essential that the models created for this purpose are easily interpretable by end users, i.e., avoid garbage or too broad topics, etc.

Hence, we present in this paper IntelComp's *Interactive Topic Model Trainer (ITMT)*, a tool developed within the *H2020 European project IntelComp*[1] for this purpose. IntelComp seeks the development of a platform that makes use of the latest generation of Artificial Intelligence and Natural Language Processing (NLP) tools to provide relevant information to assist public policies in Science, Technology, and Innovation (STI), geared toward aiding decision-making over the policy cycle. This requires a thorough analysis of documentary sources, which can entail up to hundreds of millions of documents (e.g., scientific articles, patents, etc.); therefore, here becomes fundamental the use of topic modeling to extract information with a level of detail greater than attainable through the inspection of these sources' metadata.

ITMT consists of a Python-based toolbox integrated within a PyQT6-based graphical user interface[2] for the training of topic models following an expert-in-the-loop approach that ultimately contributes to models that are more aligned with the prior experience and needs of IntelComp end users. The software package includes several state-of-the-art topic modeling solutions, seeking adequacy to the needs of each possible scenario, due to both the characteristics of the data sets and the scalability of the algorithms, but also the infrastructure available for training. Besides, the software contains a series of proprietary algorithmic improvements that allow

[1] http://intelcomp.eu

[2] The project will also make the tool accessible via a web service.

Proceedings of the 17th Conference of the European Chapter of the Association for Computational Linguistics
System Demonstrations, pages 43–49
May 2-4, 2023

Features	ITMT	Gensim	Mallet	StandfordTMT	STTM	Familia	TopicNet	ToModAPI	OCTIS	BigML
Pre-processing tools	✓	✓	✓	✓				✓	✓	✓
Bayesian based models	✓	✓	✓	✓	✓	✓	✓	✓	✓	✓
Neural topic models	✓							✓	✓	
Level-2 HTMs for granularity inspection	✓									
Topic visualization tools	✓						✓		✓	✓
Topic curation tools	✓									
Topic annotation tools	✓									
Hyper-parameters tuning		✓	✓	✓		✓			✓	
Global topic statistics	✓			✓						
Coherence metrics	✓	✓	✓		✓		✓	✓	✓	
Entropy metrics	✓									
Diversity metrics									✓	
Significance metrics									✓	
Classification metrics			✓		✓			✓	✓	
Domain-experts oriented	✓					✓	✓			

Table 1: Comparison of ITMT with other existing frameworks for topic modeling.

topic models to be evaluated and curated by experts.

Compared to other current topic modeling frameworks (McCallum, 2002; Rehurek and Sojka, 2010; Lisena et al., 2020; Silvia Terragni, et al., 2021), which typically focus on putting out topic modeling algorithms but ignore their interpretability and adequateness for the needs of end users, ITMT stands out as a tool for training topic models while including the knowledge of experts in the creation and curation of such models. A comparison summary between ITMT and other available frameworks is available in Table 1, while a detailed analysis is provided in Section 4.

The main contributions of our framework's current release are:

- Integration of several topic extraction libraries enabling users to easily train models under a common interface.
- Incorporation of a novel implementation of Hierarchical Topic Models (HTMs). In particular, we provide a level-2 HTM comprising tools that allow the user to pick which topics should be further split.
- Inclusion of topic evaluation, annotation, visualization, and curation tools aiming for the usage of domain experts, which are common and independent of the training algorithm.

ITMT has been published under a permissive MIT license in the GitHub Project `https://github.com/IntelCompH2020/topicmodeler`.

2 System overview

ITMT consists both of a PyQT6-based graphical user interface (GUI) as the front-end and a back-end service supporting all the operations that need to be carried out as a response to user interactions. The visualization itself and the actual training and optimization of the models are completely decoupled. The state management is performed on the back-end side, and it is sustained by the use of external folders given as input to the application, as described in Section 2.1. This provides the ITMT with both persistence and portability capabilities, as all structures (training datasets, models, etc.) created during the application's execution can be accessed and modified at a later time.

2.1 Input requirements

For the system to work, three input folders must be provided, namely 1) a *project folder* in which the application's output will be saved; 2) a *source folder* containing the datasets; 3) a *wordlists folder* to harbor the wordlists (i.e., lists created by the user outside the ITMT and the ones generated during the application's execution). For the time being, the datasets available in the source folder must be given in parquet format, and contain at least the raw version of the texts to be used for training, and, for some models, their contextualized embeddings.

Provided the three inputs, the project folder is set up with a fixed structure composed of 1) a configuration file with all the specifications and descriptions of variables implied in the ITMT; 2) a folder for the training datasets, and 3) a folder for the trained topic models.

2.2 The graphical user interface

So as to offer the distinct ITMT utilities in a user-friendly manner, the GUI is composed of four main subwindows, each of them relating to one of the functionalities offered by the application, leading the user through the different steps that must be followed for the creation of topic models; and one additional subwindow serving as a welcome page.

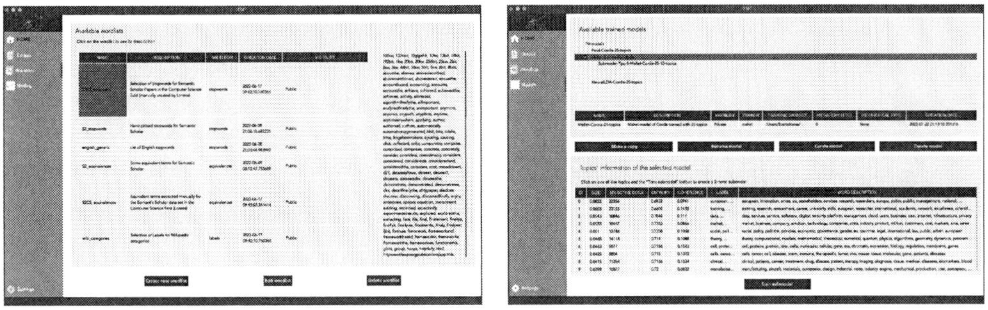

Figure 1: Wordlist management and Model management ITMT's subwindows. Left: Available wordlists and their information are listed, and the user can access their content by clicking on a wordlist's associated row; also, the user can access the menus for editing and creating a new wordlist, or delete any of them. Right: Available models (level-1 and level-2) are hierarchically listed; by clicking on any, the model's information, topical description, and metrics are displayed; windows for curation and training of submodels can be accessed from here.

In the following, we offer a summarized description of each of these subwindows, and for more details, the demo video available here[3] can be consulted.

Welcome page. It allows the selection of the project/source/wordlists folders through either the user's file system or a list of recently used folders and provides a shortcut and description to all functionalities.

Corpus management. It is composed of two views, each of them serving a different purpose: 1) visualizing and operating with the available local datasets (obtained from the source folder) and 2) visualizing and operating with the user-created training datasets. From 1) a training dataset can be created through a new window and from 2) the preprocessing + topic modeling training windows can be accessed.

Wordlist management. It supports the listing, creation, edition and deletion of *ad-hoc* word lists to incorporate information collected by domain experts (e.g., stopwords, equivalent terms or acronyms, etc.).

Model management. It assists the models' management functionalities (listing, copying, renaming, and deletion), as well as the visualization of the models' information and statistics. Also, a thematic analysis with different levels of resolution through the construction of second-level topic models can be pursued from here, and the curation, visualization and evaluation tools can be accessed.

Settings. It permits the user to configure all the settings available in the configuration file.

[3] https://youtu.be/e0YDsnnNHto

2.3 ITMT users' workflows

With the ITMT's subwindow division, we aim at guiding the user through the steps that are necessary for the procurement of high-quality models with interpretable topics, and as aligned as possible to the needs of the expert orchestrating the creation. To do so, we recommend following the succeeding five-stage process, summarized in Figure 2. Note that the tool itself does not impose the execution of this workflow, but it is the user who should be conscious of it.

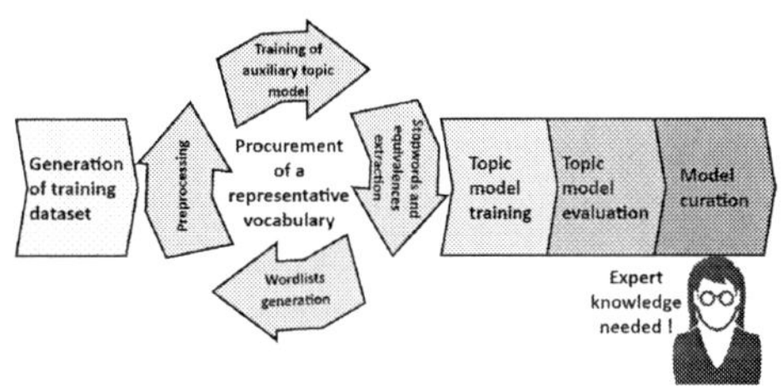

Figure 2: ITMT recommended workflow.

1. **Generation of a training dataset.** By utilizing the documents of one of the local datasets provided in the source folder, or the concatenation of several of them, the user can construct a training corpus through the Corpus management subwindow.

2. **Procurement of a representative vocabulary for the training corpus.** After the selection of the just created training dataset, its preprocessing and the creation of an initial auxiliary model with a moderate number of topics (e.g., 30-40 topics) through the preprocessing and training windows should be approached. Having the model constructed, the user benefits

from some topic evaluation and curation tools to clean the vocabulary as follows:

- Through the visual and manual inspection of the model, garbage topics can be identified. This allows the detection of uninformative terms for the corpus, which should be marked as stopwords.
- Terms that appear in several topics of varied nature should also be marked as stopwords.
- Equivalent terms coming from lemmatization errors, acronyms, and synonyms should be marked to be mapped to a common structure.

Based on the stopwords and equivalences detected, corresponding wordlists for filtering each of the latter can be created through the Wordlist management subwindow, which can be used for performing a new preprocessing of the training corpus. This process can be repeated any number of times until an adequate vocabulary for the dataset is obtained.

3. **Topic modeling training.** Having a representative vocabulary, the final training should be pursued. To obtain an easily interpretable model, slightly overestimating the number of training topics is a good practice.

4. **Topic modeling evaluation.** It could be advantageous for the user to train several models and then pick the one with the best performance metrics.

5. **Models curation.** Finally, the usage of curation tools is recommended for the final adjustment of the selected model. E.g., similar topics could be fused into a unique one or garbage topics removed; alternatively, the user can observe the presence of too broad topics, for which a level-2 exploration through the HTM techniques may be of use, etc.

3 Software components

As we have covered in the former section, the construction of a topic model is a procedure that requires the sequential execution of various tasks, each of them managed by a different component of the topic modeling service underlying the GUI. We present in this section each of these components.

3.1 Preprocessing pipeline

This section describes the tasks carried out by the ITMT's preprocessing pipeline. It is important to highlight it is not a complete NLP pipeline but only provides additional cleaning tasks usually recommended to obtain higher-quality topic models.

The transformations to which the documents inputted into the pipeline are subjected are based on a set of settings selected *ad-hoc* by the user, which includes the wordlists to be used for the vocabulary cleaning (i.e., steps 1 and 2 described below) and the parameters implied in steps 3 and 4 (e.g., vocabulary size, etc.).

1. **Removal of additional stopwords** which, while having meaning to a sentence, lack semantic interest for the dataset under analysis.

2. **Word replacements** by other equivalent ones so that they are treated as a single term during topic modeling.

3. **Filtering of short documents**, as they lack enough information for a robust estimation of their thematic composition.

4. **Vocabulary construction** by removing terms with a too high or too low probability of appearance in the corpus, and restricting the maximum vocabulary size.

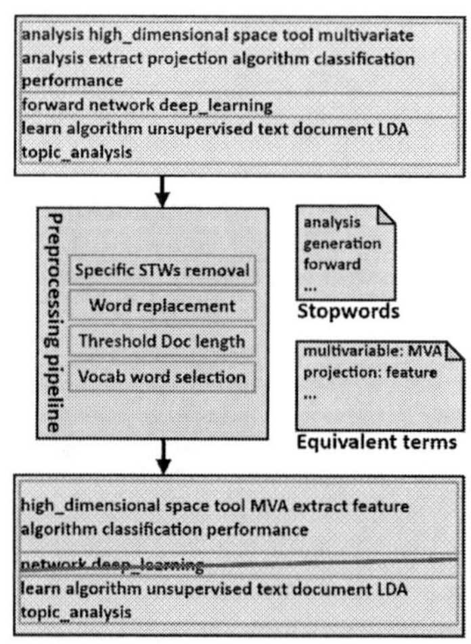

Figure 3: Illustration of the operation of the components in the ITMT preprocessing pipeline.

The output of the processing pipeline is therefore a subset of the input documents (those with sufficient length) in BoW format (besides its embeddings, in case the topic modeling algorithm in use requires them). The complete procedure has been illustrated in Figure 3 for a concrete example.

The tool includes two different implementations that allow high parallelization of the processes just described. The first one is based on Spark, so the execution can be easily distributed among the nodes of a Spark cluster if such a cluster is available. If the latter condition cannot be met, the parallelization is achieved through Dask.

3.2 Topic modeling technologies

This section describes the topic modeling technologies included in the toolbox so far. All the algorithms are provided with default parameters as presented in their original works, but can be customized by the user for each specific training.

Mallet (McCallum, 2002) is a popular Java library with a highly efficient parallelizable implementation of LDA (Blei et al., 2003) based on collapsed Gibbs sampling known for providing good performance in terms of topic coherence and scalability. It puts the available resources to good use leading to fast training due to its multi-threading capabilities.

Spark-LDA Spark incorporates a machine learning library, MLLIB (Xiangrui Meng, et al., 2016) with two LDA implementations, both of them integrated into the ITMT: a fast online method based on Variational Bayes and another based on an expectation-maximization algorithm. Spark-LDA is suitable for fast training using horizontal scaling, but requires the use of a Spark cluster.

Neural Topic Models Bayesian-based topic models (BTMs) have been useful for text analysis for almost two decades, but neural topic models (NTMs) have gained research interest in the last years for their performance and flexibility. ITMT evaluates three representative NTM techniques, Autoencoded Variational Inference for Topic Models *(AVITM)-based implementation of LDA* and *ProdLDA* (Product-of-Experts LDA), both proposed in Srivastava and Sutton (2017); and Contextualized Topic Models (Bianchi et al., 2021a,b), against classical approaches for performance comparison.

Second-level hierarchical topic models Flat topic models like the ones presented above do not permit a topical analysis with the degree of granularity sometimes required by domain experts. In this line, we have included in the ITMT two novel implementations of hierarchical topic models (HTMs) that lack complicated implementations like most state-of-the-art HTMs, thus making it straightforward to integrate the knowledge of domain experts in the model building. Concretely, the integrated models are *HTM with word selection (HTM-WS)* and *HTM with document selection (HTM-DS)*, which follow a three-step process: 1) level-1 topic modeling and expansion topic selection; 2) level-2 model's synthetic training corpus construction by either keeping the words each level-1 corpus's document assigned to the topic selected for expansion (HTM-WS) or those documents with a proportion of the expansion topic larger than a customized threshold (HTM-DS); 3) training of this corpus to generated the level-2 model.

3.3 User-oriented tools

We present in this section the topic modeling user-oriented tools integrated into the ITMT.

Evaluation tools. The tools currently available are a set of global topics statistics and metrics:

- Topics' relative size in the corpus.
- Topics' chemical description with a penalty for the most common terms, instead of the traditional way of presenting the words in descending order of appearance frequency.
- Number of active documents (i.e., number of documents in which each topic is present), which helps distinguish between "vertical" and "horizontal" topics, i.e., topics that are specific to a limited number of documents vs topics that are shared among most documents.
- Entropy of the model, which gives an idea of whether a topic is characterized by a reduced number of terms or by a broad set (each of them in a smaller proportion).
- Coherence metrics, to provide insight into the degree of cohesion of the high probability terms for a given topic. It can be used as an indicator to help the user decide which topics are good candidates to be further split.

Visualization and annotation tools. pyLDAvis graphs (Sievert and Shirley, 2014) are generated for each trained model and embedded into the ITMT to ease the interpretation of the topics. To improve identification, the ITMT also supports the automatic labeling of topics and their posterior modification through the user's manual labeling. For the automatic topic labeling system itself, i.e., the scheme that assigns to each collection of words characterizing one of the topics in the model a specific label from a customizable list of feasible terms, a zero-shot-classifier is used.

Curation tools. Aiming to improve the quality of the final model, the ITMT offers:

- Suggestions of similar topics, in the sense they co-occur with relative frequency, or the words characterizing them are the same.
- Fusion of topics (e.g., too similar topics) selected by the user, guaranteeing the probabilistic feasibility of the model.
- Sorting the topics of the model according to size, by placing the largest topics first.
- Topic deletion, which is useful to eliminate topics of little interest from the model.
- Topic model reset, allowing the user to discard all changes applied after training.

4 Existing frameworks

Probably the most widely used topic modeling frameworks are *Gensim* (Rehurek and Sojka, 2010) and Java-based package *Mallet* (McCallum, 2002), which include implementations of a handful of popular BTMs. They also provide pre-processing pipelines, hyper-parameters optimization, and the calculation of some coherence metrics. In the same direction, the *Stanford TMT* (Daniel Ramage, et al., 2009) is a set of topic modeling tools, including, inter alia, features such as the training of BTMs, the selection of parameters via a data-driven process, and the manipulation of texts from different spreadsheets.

Also released as a Java framework, *STTM* (Qiang et al., 2018) focuses on the integration of short text topic modeling algorithms, but it includes as well some long-text implementations and evaluation metrics. In Di Jiang, et al. (2021) the authors proposed a configurable framework named *Familia* that performs automatic parameter inference for a variety of topic models and supports the design of new topic models to best suit specific problems at hand. Aiming to bring additive regularization for topic modeling (ARTM) Vorontsov (2014); Kochedykov et al. (2017) accessible for the general public, Victor Bulatov, et al. (2020) proposed *TopicNet*, a Python module including a modular approach to topic model training and several visualization techniques, as well as semi-automated model selection and support for user-defined goal metrics.

Other state-of-the-art frameworks include *ToModAPI* (Lisena et al., 2020), a python-based API for the training, inference, and evaluation of different topic models; and *OCTIS* (Silvia Terragni, et al., 2021), also a Python-based framework + dashboard for the training of topic models, which additionally supports its analysis and comparison over several datasets and evaluation metrics, besides a bayesian-based hyperparameters optimization strategy. Lastly, BigML is a general tool for Machine Learning, that incorporates some Topic Modeling functionalities[4], including an optimized implementation of LDA for any text in seven languages, with preprocessing, training, inference, and visualization of models in a user-friendly dashboard, as well as the possibility of creating, configuring, and updating topic models programmatically via the BigML API and bindings.

Nonetheless, from the latter, only *ToModAPI* and *OCTIS* support the training of NTMs. Moreover, none of them allow the actual incorporation of knowledge expertise into the model building, nor allow for a thematic analysis with different levels of resolution. Hence, *ITMT* excels as an expert-in-the-loop oriented tool for the training at different resolution levels, curation, evaluation, and visualization of both BTMs and NTMs.

5 Conclusions

In this paper, we have presented IntelComp's Interactive Topic Model Trainer (ITMT), a Python-based tool that includes implementations of several state-of-the-art topic modeling algorithms orientated towards the usage of domain experts and a novelty implementation of second-level hierarchical topic models for granularity exploration. Moreover, the framework is provided with a set of tools for the evaluation, visualization, annotation, and curation of topic models, and a preprocessing pipeline.

For future work, we are active in offering each of the ITMT's components as a Docker container to transform the GUI into a web service.

Acknowledgements

This work has received funding from the European Union's Horizon 2020 research and innova-

[4]https://bigml.com/features/topic-model

tion program under grant agreement No 101004870, and from Grant TED2021-132366B-I00 funded by MCIN/AEI/10.13039/501100011033 and by the "European Union NextGenerationEU/PRTR".

References

Federico Bianchi, Silvia Terragni, and Dirk Hovy. 2021a. Pre-training is a hot topic: Contextualized document embeddings improve topic coherence. In *Proc. 59th Annual Meeting of the ACL and the 11th Intl. Joint Conf. on Natural Language Process. (Vol. 2: Short Papers)*, pages 759–766.

Federico Bianchi, Silvia Terragni, Dirk Hovy, Debora Nozza, and Elisabetta Fersini. 2021b. Cross-lingual contextualized topic models with zero-shot learning. In *Proc. 16th Conf. EACL*, pages 1676–1683.

David M Blei, Andrew Y Ng, and Michael I Jordan. 2003. Latent dirichlet allocation. *Journal of machine Learning research*, 3(Jan):993–1022.

Daniel Ramage, et al. 2009. Topic modeling for the social sciences. In *NIPS 2009 Workshop on applications for topic models: text and beyond*, volume 5, pages 1–4.

Di Jiang, et al. 2021. Familia: A configurable topic modeling framework for industrial text engineering. In *Proc. Intl. Conf. Database Systems for Advanced Applications*, pages 516–528. Springer.

Denis Kochedykov, Murat Apishev, Lev Golitsyn, and Konstantin Vorontsov. 2017. Fast and modular regularized topic modelling. In *2017 21st Conf. Open Innovations Association (FRUCT)*, pages 182–193. IEEE.

Pasquale Lisena, Ismail Harrando, Oussama Kandakji, and Raphaël Troncy. 2020. Tomodapi: a topic modeling api to train, use and compare topic models. In *Proc. NLP-OSS*, pages 132–140.

Andrew Kachites McCallum. 2002. Mallet: A machine learning for language toolkit. *http://mallet. cs. umass. edu*.

Jipeng Qiang, Yun Li, Yunhao Yuan, Wei Liu, and Xindong Wu. 2018. Sttm: A tool for short text topic modeling. *arXiv preprint arXiv:1808.02215*.

Radim Rehurek and Petr Sojka. 2010. Software framework for topic modelling with large corpora. In *Proc. LREC 2010 Workshop on new challenges for NLP frameworks*.

Carson Sievert and Kenneth Shirley. 2014. Ldavis: A method for visualizing and interpreting topics. In *Proc. Workshop on Interactive Language Learning, Visualization, and Interfaces*, pages 63–70.

Silvia Terragni, et al. 2021. OCTIS: comparing and optimizing topic models is simple! In *Proc. EACL: System Demonstrations*, pages 263–270.

Akash Srivastava and Charles Sutton. 2017. Autoencoding variational inference for topic models. *arXiv preprint arXiv:1703.01488*.

Victor Bulatov, et al. 2020. Topicnet: Making additive regularisation for topic modelling accessible. In *Proc. 12th LREC*, pages 6745–6752.

KV Vorontsov. 2014. Additive regularization for topic models of text collections. In *Doklady Mathematics*, volume 89, pages 301–304.

Xiangrui Meng, et al. 2016. Mllib: Machine learning in apache spark. *The Journal of Machine Learning Research*, 17(1):1235–1241.

FISH: A Financial Interactive System for Signal Highlighting

Ta-Wei Huang[1*], **Jia-Huei Ju**[1*], **Yu-Shiang Huang**[1], **Cheng-Wei Lin**[1], **Yi-Shyuan Chiang**[2], and **Chuan-Ju Wang**[1]

[1]Research Center of Information Technology Innovation, Academia Sinica
[2]Department of Computer Science, University of Illinois, Urbana-Champaign
a0917589225@gmail.com, {jhjoo, yushuang, lcw.1997}@citi.sinica.edu.tw,
ysc6@illinois.edu, cjwang@citi.sinica.edu.tw

Abstract

In this system demonstration, we seek to streamline the process of reviewing financial statements and provide insightful information for practitioners. We develop FISH, an interactive system that extracts and highlights crucial textual signals from financial statements efficiently and precisely. To achieve our goal, we integrate pre-trained BERT representations and a fine-tuned BERT highlighting model with a newly-proposed two-stage classify-then-highlight pipeline. We also conduct the human evaluation, showing FISH can provide accurate financial signals. FISH overcomes the limitations of existing research and more importantly benefits both academics and practitioners in finance as they can leverage state-of-the-art contextualized language models with their newly gained insights. The system is available online at `https://fish-web-fish.de.r.appspot.com/`, and a short video for introduction is at `https://youtu.be/ZbvZQ09i6aw`.

1 Introduction

Financial statements document the business activities and financial performance of a company. For example, the 10-K fillings required by SEC[1] are regulatory documents required of all public companies and are typically composed of several sections each. Considerable time and human resources are needed to digest such long and complicated texts. Accordingly, efficient analysis of complex and condensed documents is critical for financial practitioners. In this work, we introduce FISH—a **F**inancial **I**nteractive System for **S**ignal **H**ighlighting—as an effective and efficient system to review financial reports.

One common scenario in practice is when a company's report has just been released: financial professionals such as financial analysts and accountants must skim through the report and quickly prepare a preliminary summary. However, some parts of the report are minor or even trivial due to the established structure formulated by regulators or similar writing patterns from the same accounting firms. That is, there are often only a few sentences in the report that need to be carefully reviewed and analyzed. Although many studies leverage textual data in financial reports to provide soft evidence to support financial analysis (Liu et al., 2018; Du et al., 2019; Juan et al., 2021), most existing systems or studies still lack interactivity and do not directly provide off-the-shelf signals; such solutions are thereby considered impractical for many real-world usage scenarios.

2016 (Target)	*Our most critical accounting policies relate to revenue recognition, inventory, pension and other post-retirement benefit costs, goodwill, other intangible assets and long-lived assets and income taxes.*
2015 (Reference)	*Our most critical accounting policies relate to revenue recognition, inventory, pension and other post-retirement benefit costs, goodwill, other intangible assets and long-lived assets and income taxes.*

Table 1: A pair of highly similar segments from ITEM 7 in the financial 10-K reports of the Estée Lauder Companies Inc. in 2016.

We first recognize two challenges in the literature concerning textual information in long and complicated financial reports: (1) Many parts of a financial report are minor or even trivial; (2) It is difficult to utilize coarse information in empirical applications. To address these challenges, we propose a multi-stage financial analysis pipeline composed of two modules: a *segment classifier* and a *segment highlighter*.

To tackle the first one, we leverage the year-to-year structure of the annually released financial statements of a company. For example, as shown in Table 1, we observe that the target and reference segments appear identical, showing that these texts provide rather minor information and can be ignored for further analyses. For this part, we inte-

*These authors contributed equally to this work.
[1]Securities and Exchange Commission

Proceedings of the 17th Conference of the European Chapter of the Association for Computational Linguistics System Demonstrations, pages 50–56

grate a segment classifier that calculates the similarities for text pairs between years (i.e., the target year and the year previous to it). Given such a year-to-year similarity comparison, all segments in the report for a target year are classified as one of three types: (1) new segments, (2) highly similar segments, and (3) revised segments.

For the second challenge, the segment highlighter module provides straightforward and fine-grained signals in segments identified as the third type—revised segments—which are considered those revised from segments in the reports of the reference year. Specifically, this module highlights words in such segments by predicting the word importance based on the semantic context of the financial report and the differences between the two segments in a year-to-year pair. To accomplish this, we adopt contextualized representations from the pre-trained language model (Devlin et al., 2019) and further fine-tune the proposed module with a supervised token classification task.

In this demonstration, we showcase FISH, an interactive system to help financial professionals effectively and efficiently skim through financial reports in a straightforward manner. FISH is technically supported by the proposed two-module pipeline. In particular, we use financial 10-K reports collected by Loughran and McDonald (2011) to demonstrate our idea. FISH better visualizes the segment classifications in a target-year report and provides fine-grained information highlighting the essential information for the revised segments for financial professionals to review and analyze carefully.

2 Background and Related Work

Traditionally, research on financial statements focuses on quantitative data such as stock prices or other financial metrics. Textual information such as operation calls and forward-looking statements in reports are rarely carefully considered in conventional finance literature. Pioneering studies in both finance and computer science literature first adopted statistical or machine learning methods to identify crucial information in text data in financial reports. For example, Loughran and McDonald (2011) compile a large amount of 10-K reports and construct a finance-specific sentiment lexicon. Moreover, Jegadeesh and Wu (2013); Tsai and Wang (2017) leverage the sentiment signals in textual data to investigate relations between quantitative and textual information. More recently, distributed representation techniques have been introduced to analyze financial reports (Tsai et al., 2016; Rekabsaz et al., 2017; Lin et al., 2021).

Recent advancements in natural language processing (NLP) techniques have made it possible to develop useful information systems that can analyze textual information in financial reports. For example, Liu et al. (2018) leverage variants of pretrained word embedding models to identify financial risks and cues to support financial analysis. Du et al. (2019) integrate multiple representations of 10-K reports and further infuse financial sentiment aspects into word and sentence representations. HIVE (Juan et al., 2021) is an interactive system utilizing an attention mechanism to explore insights from financial reports. However, existing systems do not effectively address the two challenges mentioned earlier, nor do they utilize state-of-the-art and dominant deep contextualized language models such as BERT (Devlin et al., 2019) and its variants as their back-end engine.

3 Financial Data and Pre-processing

The Form 10-K Financial Statements. we used the Form 10-K filings collected from the Software Repository for Accounting and Finance,[2] where a Form 10-K is an annual report required by the U.S. SEC. Specifically, we used the 10-K filings ranging from 2011 to 2018, which comprise 63,336 filings from 12,960 public companies. To make the best use of the year-to-year information, we discarded companies for which the reports in some years are missing during the period; 3,849 companies (3,849 $\times$ 8 = 30,792 reports in total) remained after this filtering. Note that in this study, we randomly sample 200 companies from the 3,849 companies with their annual reports for demonstration purpose.

Coherent Text Segments. Every 10-K annual report contains 15 schedules (e.g., Items 1, 1A, 1B, 2, 3, ..., 7, 7A, ..., 15).[3] Each item section in a report is typically composed of multiple paragraphs, to which we first applied the SpaCy API[4] to divide each paragraph into sentences as our smallest unit of text. Moreover, as coherent text segments have been claimed to be beneficial to some downstream tasks such as information re-

[2] `https://sraf.nd.edu/sec-edgar-data/`
[3] `https://en.wikipedia.org/wiki/Form_10-K`
[4] Sentencizer: `https://spacy.io/api/sentencizer`

	#Segments/Report	#Tokens/Segment
Sentence	1,743	36
Segment*	677	94
Paragraph	474	134

Table 2: Statistics of pre-processed reports of 200 sampled companies. The two columns report the average numbers of segments in a report and the average numbers of tokens in a sentence/segment*/paragraph, respectively, where * indicates the documents are segmented by the cross-segment BERT.

trieval and other NLP applications (Koshorek et al., 2018; Shtekh et al., 2018), we further integrated the cross-segment BERT (Lukasik et al., 2020), a state-of-the-art text segmentation model, for the final pre-processing. Note that a segment may contain more than one sentence and usually reflects the proper length for the BERT-based models; thus, in our system, we take "segments" to be a basic unit as the input of the two proposed modules for classification and fine-grained highlighting. Table 2 is an overview of pre-processed segments with different levels of granularity and other data statistics.

4 The Multi-stage Pipeline

The proposed multi-stage pipeline is composed of the segment classifier and the segment highlighter modules, both of which leverage contextualized text representations from BERT-based models (Devlin et al., 2019; Reimers and Gurevych, 2019). With this pipeline we seek to examine year-to-year signals from the 10-K filings of each given company. Specifically, our interactive system targets each company's 10-K filings for a certain year; the company's report from the previous year is regarded as the reference document (see Table 1).

4.1 Segment Classifier

To leverage the year-to-year structure of a company's 10-K filing, we first denote the set of text segments from a company's year-t report as $\mathcal{S}_t = \{s_t^1, s_t^2, \ldots, s_t^n\}$, where n denotes the number of segments in the reports. As $\mathcal{S}_t$ is a target-year report, $\mathcal{S}_{t-1}$ is treated as a reference document. Accordingly, we perform year-to-year text ranking by treating segments in the target report $s_t^i \in \mathcal{S}_t$ as our queries and segments in the reference report $s_{t-1}^j \in \mathcal{S}_{t-1}$ as our references. In particular, the segment classifier calculates the similarity of each pair of target-reference text segments as

$$\phi(s_t^i, s_{t-1}^j),$$

where ϕ is a proximity function. In this study, we adopt two approaches for similarity calculation to account for both syntactic and semantic similarities. First, we use ROUGE-2 to measure the syntactic similarity, capturing bi-gram patterns in financial sentences (Lin, 2004). For semantic similarity, we utilize the fine-tuned SentenceBERT model (Reimers and Gurevych, 2019) to calculate the cosine similarity of each target-reference pair.

In this demonstration, each target text segment $s_t^i \in \mathcal{S}_t$ is classified into different groups by adopting the following heuristic rules with pre-defined thresholds τ and ϵ:[5]

$$s_t^i \text{ type} = \begin{cases} 1 & \text{if } \max(\{\phi_{\text{Rouge}}(s_t^i, s_{t-1}^j) | s_{t-1}^j \in \mathcal{S}_{t-1}\}) < \tau \\ 2 & \text{if } \max(\{\phi_{\text{Rouge}}(s_t^i, s_{t-1}^j) | s_{t-1}^j \in \mathcal{S}_{t-1}\}) \geq \tau \\ & \text{AND } \phi_{\text{BERT}}(s_t^i, s_{t-1}^{j^*}) \geq \epsilon, \\ 3 & \text{if } \max(\{\phi_{\text{Rouge}}(s_t^i, s_{t-1}^j) | s_{t-1}^j \in \mathcal{S}_{t-1}\}) \geq \tau \\ & \text{AND } \phi_{\text{BERT}}(s_t^i, s_{t-1}^{j^*}) < \epsilon, \end{cases} \quad (1)$$

where $j^* = \text{argmax}_j(\{\phi_{\text{Rouge}}(s_t^i, s_{t-1}^j) | s_{t-1}^j \in \mathcal{S}_{t-1}\})$ denotes the segment in the reference document with the maximum $\phi_{\text{Rouge}}(s_t^i, \cdot)$ similarity. Thus, a segment in the target report can be categorized according to the above three types:

1. **New segments** are new text segments which are syntactically distant from all of their corresponding relevant reference text segments (as shown in Table 3).

2. **Highly similar segments** are text segments possessing syntactic structures and semantic meanings that closely resemble those of the reference segments (as shown in Table 1).

3. **Revised segments** include segments that are syntactically similar to the reference segments but differ semantically in meaning. In practice, as financial professionals shall pay greater attention to these segments, we here adopt further fine-grained highlighting for these segments in our second-stage module (as shown in Table 3).

Note that we here use a simple yet intuitive procedure to classify segments in target reports for

[5] We set threshold τ as 0.1, resulting in approximately 10% of new segments in a report; the threshold ϵ is set to 0.99, resulting in discarding approximately 50% of highly similar segments in a report.

Figure 1: The main system interface of FISH. The left and right panels indicate the 10-K filings of a company in the target and reference years, respectively.

demonstration purposes; nevertheless, the classification can be much more complicated or involve professional adjustments of practitioners.

4.2 Segment Highlighter

The first-stage module narrows the considerations of what constitutes a (potentially) important segment. In the second module, we further focus on the third type of segments—the revised segments—and provide fine-grained information on these to enhance the readability of the documents. In particular, we seek to provide fine-grained (i.e., word-level) signals on such segments for practitioners, which in our demonstration of the interactive system is the basis for the highlighted words.

To build the highlighting model, we formulate the underlying word importance prediction problem as a token-level binary classification task by adding a classification linear layer on top of BERT. We further fine-tune the model using the e-SNLI dataset (Camburu et al., 2018), which was compiled for a natural language inference classification task that determines the entailment or contradiction relation for a given pair of sentences with human-annotated highlighted words. Fine-tuning takes around two hours on a V100 GPU, with less than 20GB of GPU memory usage.

At the inference stage, for each syntactically similar but semantically dissimilar pair $(s_t^{\tau}, s_{t-1}^{j^*})$, where s_t^{τ} is a revised segment, we construct the contextualized representation with BERT (Devlin et al., 2019) with the two special tokens (i.e., [CLS] and [SEP]) as:

$$h_{rj^*} = \mathrm{BERT}\big(\texttt{[CLS]}s_{t-1}^{j^*}\texttt{[SEP]}s_t^{\tau}\big). \quad (2)$$

Recall that in Eq. (2), $s_{t-1}^{j^*}$ denotes the most syntactically similar segment in the reference year against s_t^{τ}, but the cosine similarity between $s_{t-1}^{j^*}$ and s_t^{τ} is rather low (see Eq. (1)). In this demonstration, we consider that word-level signals for such *revised* segments (syntactically similar but semantic dissimilar to the reference segments) can help users examining these segments easily and deeply. The importance probability of each word w in each revised segment s_t^{τ} is then $P(w|s_t^{\tau}; s_{t-1}^{j^*}) = F(h_{rj^*}, w)$, where $F(\cdot,\cdot)$ denotes the fine-tuned model using the e-SNLI dataset; these probabilities are later used to indicate the word importance in our system using highlighting.

5 Demonstration

Figure 1 shows the main interactive interface of the proposed FISH, a web-based interactive analysis system for financial reports. For a better user experience, we lay out a concise system interface with user-friendly shortcuts to meet the needs of financial practitioners. In addition, we use both coarse-grained (segment-level) and fine-grained (word-level) signal highlighting features and interactive functions based on the proposed pipeline. FISH thereby facilitates more effective and efficient reviewing of financial reports.

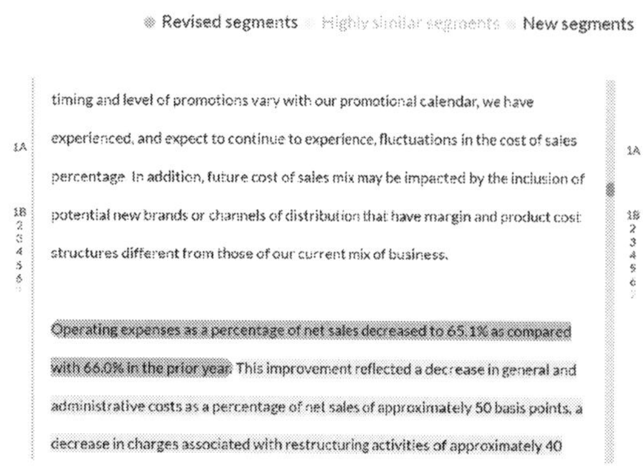

Figure 2: Highlighting has been disabled for highly similar segments; only new or revised segments remain highlighted.

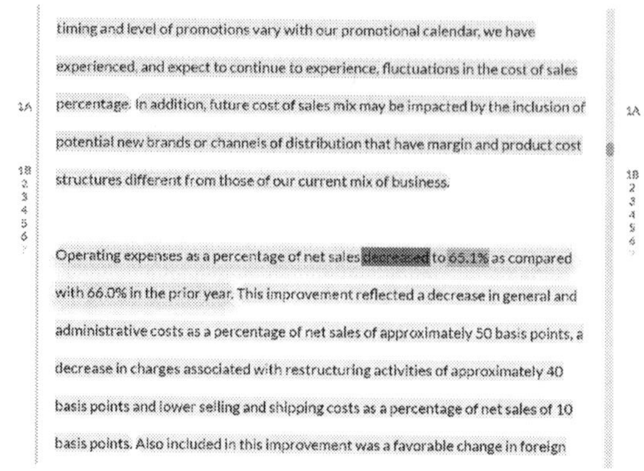

Figure 3: Segment- and word-level highlighting

5.1 User-friendly System Interface

The system includes the content of all available sections in the 10-K reports of the sampled 200 companies. As shown in (1) of Fig. 1, users can also scroll through drop-down menus at the top of the page to select the company and target year. Additionally, the ITEM navigation buttons on the left sidebar help users quickly locate the first line of the target ITEM, illustrated in (4) of the Fig. 1.

For year-to-year analysis, we adopt a two-panel interface (see (3) in Fig. 1) to make it easy for users to compare reports between consecutive years on the same screen. The left panel in the figure shows the contents of a financial report for the target year, and the right panel is regarded as the reference document and thus features a lower opacity. We also provide arrows on both sides of the screen by which to switch back and forth between target years, as shown in (6) of the Fig. 1.

5.2 Interactive Signal Highlighting

As described in Section 4, the proposed classify-then-highlight pipeline first classifies each segment in the target report as one of three types according to Eq. (1): new, highly similar, or revised. Each segment is highlighted in a color reflecting its type, as illustrated in the content panel of the figure. The three color indicator buttons on the right top of the page (shown in (2) of Fig. 1) allow users to enable/disable highlighting for each type of segment, as demonstrated in Fig. 2.

In addition to segment-level highlighting, we provide fine-grained information for revised segments. Recall that each *revised* segment s_t^{τ} in the report of interest (displayed in the left panel) is further passed to the segment highlighter along with the most syntactical similar segment $s_{t-1}^{j^*}$ in the reference document (see the condition of the third type in Eq. (1) and the description in Section 4.2). The embedding of the $(s_t^{\tau}, s_{t-1}^{j^*})$ segment pair in Eq. (2) is then fed to the fine-tuned model $F(\cdot, \cdot)$ to estimate the word importance of each word in s_t^{τ}. This importance is indicated with different color shades when users hover over the revised segments. As illustrated in Fig. 3, the words *decreased* and *65.1%* are darker than others, implying that these two words are judged to be more crucial than other words in the same segment.

Note that we additionally provide a segment alignment feature as shown in (5) of Fig. 1. This horizontally aligns the target segment s_t^i with the most syntactical similar segment $s_{t-1}^{j^*}$ from the reference report document for the highly similar and revised segments, where the right panel automatically redirects to the corresponding aligned segment in the reference document when the user clicks on such segments in the left panel.

6 Empirical Evaluation

In this section, we report real-world cases that FISH captured and evaluate FISH's highlighting results with human judgement.

Case studies We take the financial report of *Estée Lauder Companies Inc* in 2016 for example. Table 3 provides an example of *new segments* and *revised segments* along with their reference segments. Recall that the new segments capture content that is not syntactically similar to—or is less syntactically similar to—content from the previous year's document. As shown in the upper block in Table 3, the target segment (left) is identified

	Estee Lauder Cos. (2016) – target segment	*Estee Lauder Cos. (2015)* – reference segment
New	*On May 3, 2016, we announced a multi-year initiative (Leading Beauty Forward) to build on our strengths and better leverage our cost structure to free resources for investment to continue our growth momentum.*	*We also plan to continue to build upon and leverage our history of outstanding creativity, innovation and entrepreneurship in high quality products and services and engaging communications.*
Revised	*Based on this material weakness, the Company s management has concluded that, as of June 30, 2016, the Company s internal control over financial reporting was not effective...*	*Based on this assessment, the Company s management has concluded that, as of June 30, 2015, the Company s internal control over financial reporting was effective...*

Table 3: The cases of new and revised segment (left) with their corresponding reference segments s_{t-1}^{j*} (right).

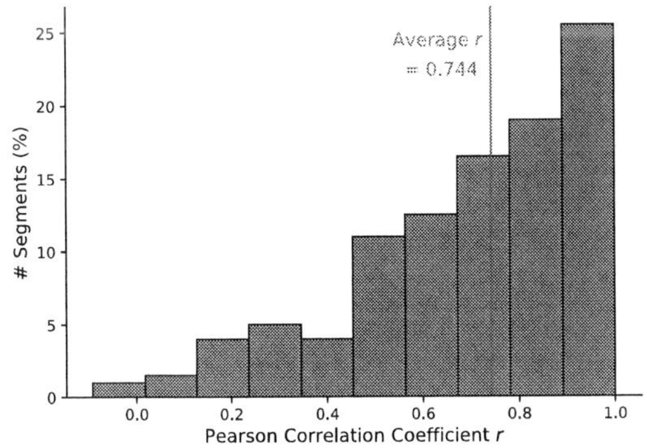

Figure 4: The histogram of the Pearson correlation coefficients r between human annotations and the outputs of our system. The red line is the average of all scores.

as a new segment by FISH as its corresponding most syntactically similar segment in the previous reference report is completely different. Indeed, with this example, we observe that the company is disclosing a new operational strategy in 2016, which is brand-new information compared to the previous year's report. As for the revised segments, which sometimes conceal important information such as changed income, expenses or management decisions such as new partnerships. In the lower block in Table 3, we observe what seems at first glance to be minor differences between reports in two consecutive years; however, the meanings behind these changes carry important financial signals (e.g. the highlighted words *weakness, was not effective*). With the highlighted words, we can then further attest the empirical effectiveness of these highlighted words.

Human Evaluation on Revised segments To verify the effectiveness of FISH's word-level highlighting on *revised* segments, we hire three assessors as potential users to select important words from the given segments. Specifically, the annotators should first identify the importance of each words-in-context of the revised segments and then label them as 1 or 0. As a result, for each sequence of words $[w_1, w_2, ...]$ in s_t^r, we calculate the Pearson correlation coefficient (denoted as Pearson's r, hereafter) between the human annotations[6] and the probabilities of word importance predicted by our system.

Our empirical evaluation data is composed of 200 *revised* segments randomly sampled from all revised segments classified by our system. As shown in Figure 4, most cases are with high values of Pearson's r, and only a few cases are with values lower than 0.5. Overall, FISH achieves a high average of 0.744 Pearson's r (the red vertical line in Figure 4).

7 Conclusion

We propose FISH, a financial statement signal-highlighting system integrated with a two-stage pipeline architecture, including a *segment classifier* and a *segment highlighter*. Both utilize BERT contextualized representations to strengthen the semantic comprehension of texts. Notably, our pipeline leverages the relationship of text segments between the target year and the previous year for automatic and interactive signal highlighting for financial professionals. The segment classifier first narrows the focus to new or revised segments instead of the entire report. As for the revised segments, we integrate a word-level highlighter to provide fine-grained financial signals via transfer learning on an external dataset. In addition, our human evaluation also suggests that FISH can provide effective highlighting results for empirical applications. To the best of our knowledge, FISH is the first interactive system not only made for practical financial applications but also leverages state-of-the-art contextualized language models, which shall greatly benefit both academics and finance practitioners to yield new insights.

[6] We take the average of three annotations as the final word importance (i.e., the ground truth) to avoid the personal subjective opinions.

References

Oana-Maria Camburu, Tim Rocktäschel, Thomas Lukasiewicz, and Phil Blunsom. 2018. e-snli: Natural language inference with natural language explanations. In *Proc. of NeurIPS*, pages 9539–9549.

Jacob Devlin, Ming-Wei Chang, Kenton Lee, and Kristina Toutanova. 2019. BERT: Pre-training of deep bidirectional Transformers for language understanding. In *Proc. of NAACL*, pages 4171–4186.

Chi-Han Du, Yi-Shyuan Chiang, Kun-Che Tsai, Liang-Chih Liu, Ming-Feng Tsai, and Chuan-Ju Wang. 2019. Fridays: A financial risk information detecting and analyzing system. In *Proc. of AAAI*, pages 9853–9854.

Narasimhan Jegadeesh and Di Wu. 2013. Word power: A new approach for content analysis. *J. Financ. Econ.*, 110(3):712–729.

Yi-Ning Juan, Yi-Shyuan Chiang, Shang-Chuan Liu, Ming-Feng Tsai, and Chuan-Ju Wang. 2021. HIVE: Hierarchical information visualization for explainability. In *Proc. of IJCAI*, pages 4988–4991.

Omri Koshorek, Adir Cohen, Noam Mor, Michael Rotman, and Jonathan Berant. 2018. Text segmentation as a supervised learning task. In *Proc. of NAACL*, pages 469–473.

Chin-Yew Lin. 2004. Rouge: a package for automatic evaluation of summaries. In *Proc. of ACL, Text Summarization Branches Out*, pages 74–81.

Ting-Wei Lin, Ruei-Yao Sun, Hsuan-Ling Chang, Chuan-Ju Wang, and Ming-Feng Tsai. 2021. XRR: Explainable risk ranking for financial reports. In *Proc. of ECML-PKDD*, pages 253–268.

Yu-Wen Liu, Liang-Chih Liu, Chuan-Ju Wang, and Ming-Feng Tsai. 2018. RiskFinder: A sentence-level risk detector for financial reports. In *Proc. of NAACL*, pages 81–85.

Tim Loughran and Bill McDonald. 2011. When is a liability not a liability? Textual analysis, dictionaries, and 10-Ks. *J. Finance*, 66(1):35–65.

Michal Lukasik, Boris Dadachev, Kishore Papineni, and Gonçalo Simões. 2020. Text segmentation by cross segment attention. In *Proc. of EMNLP*, pages 4707–4716.

Nils Reimers and Iryna Gurevych. 2019. Sentence-BERT: Sentence embeddings using Siamese BERT-networks. In *Proc. of EMNLP-IJCNLP*, pages 3982–3992.

Navid Rekabsaz, Mihai Lupu, Artem Baklanov, Alexander Dür, Linda Andersson, and Allan Hanbury. 2017. Volatility prediction using financial disclosures sentiments with word embedding-based IR models. In *Procs. of ACL*, pages 1712–1721.

Gennady Shtekh, Polina Kazakova, Nikita Nikitinsky, and Nikolay Skachkov. 2018. Applying topic segmentation to document-level information retrieval. In *Proc. of CEE-SECR*. Article no. 6.

Ming-Feng Tsai and Chuan-Ju Wang. 2017. On the risk prediction and analysis of soft information in finance reports. *Eur. J. Oper. Res.*, 257(1):243–250.

Ming-Feng Tsai, Chuan-Ju Wang, and Po-Chuan Chien. 2016. Discovering finance keywords via continuous-space language models. *ACM Trans. Manage. Inf. Syst.*, 7(7):1–17.

Yu Sheng: Human-in-Loop Classical Chinese Poetry Generation System

Jingkun Ma Runzhe Zhan Derek F. Wong*
NLP²CT Lab, Department of Computer and Information Science, University of Macau
nlp2ct.{jingkun, runzhe}@gmail.com, derekfw@um.edu.mo

Abstract

The development of poetry generation system mainly focuses on enhancing the capacity of generation model. However, the demands of customization and polishing are generally ignored, which highly reduces the scope of application. In this work, we present Yu Sheng, a web-based poetry generation system that is featured a human-in-loop generation framework, providing various customization options for users with different backgrounds to engage in the process of poetry composition. To this end, we propose two methods and train the models that can perform constrained generation and fine-grained polishing. The automatic and human evaluation results show that our system has a strong ability to generate and polish poetry compared to other vanilla models. Our system is publicly accessible at: https://yusheng.cis.um.edu.mo.[1]

1 Introduction

Classical Chinese poetry is written with specific rules such as historical period, phonology, etc., attracting researchers from different fields to study its writing mechanism. Apart from the in-depth analysis of poetry writing process, the automatic generation of classical Chinese poetry is an emerging research task of open-ended text generation.

Several research lines of poetry generation has been investigated in the past few years such as combinatory process (Queneau, 1961), template-based method (Gervás, 2001), machine learning (Levy, 2001), and deep learning (Yi et al., 2018). Recently, the pre-trained language model is utilized to capture poetry prior knowledge (Tian et al., 2021) and build the downstream generation models. Previous research focuses on building the generation model with an end-to-end pipeline, polishing (Yan, 2016) is an essential part of poetry generation that can be helpful to reduce linguistic errors and enhance the aesthetic. Although there are numerous online systems that can generate classical Chinese poetry based on the keywords,[2][3][4] few works integrate the polishing function into the generation system. Jiuge[5] allows the user to make the adjustment by providing candidate words but is limited to word-level replacements, which is not flexible in adjusting the poetry-level polishing. Moreover, the design of polishing services should be user-oriented. The current system (Zhipeng et al., 2019) allows users to select the candidate words, but it is not friendly for non-professional users due to their insufficient background in poetry composition, which is also limited for professional users to polish the results.

To alleviate the aforementioned problems, we design and implement a human-in-loop classical Chinese poetry generation system, Yu Sheng. Yu Sheng not only supports the poetry generation with diverse genres and constraints, but also provides fine-grained polishing functions where the unsatisfactory parts can be refined with automatic adjustment. In order to build models that are capable to handle the above functions, we propose two methods for constraint integration and poetry polishing. Specifically, the global attention mechanism is proposed to integrate different kinds of constraints. For building the polishing model, we utilize the multi-task learning approach to train the model with mask prediction and sentence reconstruction tasks. Moreover, the data augmentation techniques are also used to alleviate the scarcity of task-specific data. Both automatic and human evaluation results have shown the effectiveness of our proposed polishing-based generation model. By deploying the model trained with the above methods, Yu Sheng is characterized by customizable

*Corresponding author

[1]Our demonstration video is available at: https://vimeo.com/776525586.

[2]https://www.aichpoem.net/#/shisanbai/ctcouplet

[3]http://moonbrewer.com/poem/

[4]https://tssc.sinaapp.com/

[5]http://jiuge.thunlp.org

Proceedings of the 17th Conference of the European Chapter of the Association for Computational Linguistics System Demonstrations, pages 57–66
May 2-4, 2023

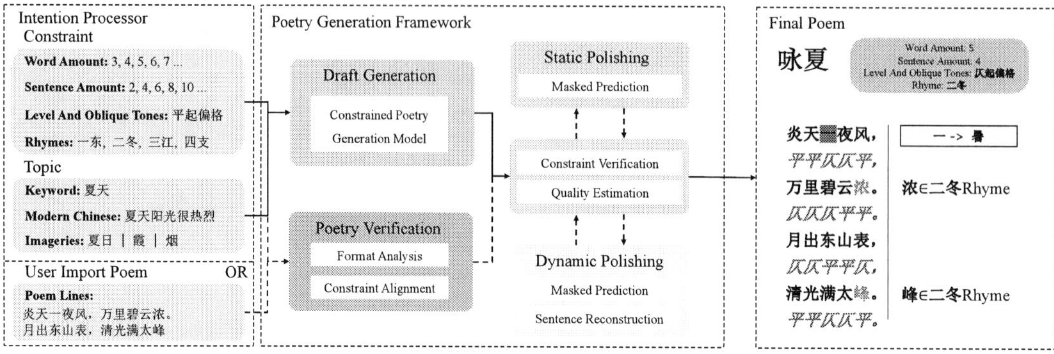

Figure 1: The overall architecture of system Yu Sheng. User input will be handled with an intention processor before sending into the essential poetry generation framework. Note that not all the modules in the generation framework are necessarily used before completing a composition.

generation and human-in-loop polishing, aiming to further improve the generation quality and flexibility of classical Chinese poetry.

2 Methodology

The generation pipeline of Yu Sheng includes two stages: poetry generation and poetry polishing. It not only supports automatic poetry generation from given information, but also accepts any existing poems as input for polishing. In this section, we first describe the proposed methods for building the generation and polishing models and introduce the data augmentation methods for compensating the data used in supervised training.

2.1 Constrained Poetry Generation

Global Attention As a typical literacy genre with predetermined features, poetry is designed, drafted, and polished under the subtle influence of different rigid features. These indispensable features not only affect the structures and multi-level morphology, but also the sentence semantics, and phonology beauty. Hence, the algorithm of extracting and integrating these features in different dimensions is crucial to the whole process of poetry generation. Global features of poetry include "Word Amount", "Sentence Amount", "Level and Oblique Tones", and "Rhyme". Apart from some features that can be directly measured, we specifically build a rule-based tool to extract other abstract features, such as "Level and Oblique Tones" and "Rhyme", by using an ancient rhyming dictionary called PingShuiYun (Branner, 2006). Specifically, we leverage the dictionary to annotate the tone of each word in poetry dataset and then automatically predict the rhyming condition determined by tone of end word in each poem sentence. In this section, we use Transformer-based architecture (Vaswani et al., 2017) to illustrate the proposed method for generation and polishing task. To introduce all the global features into the generation process as the constraints, they are formulated as text input $\mathbf{D}$ and encoded into the vectorized representation $\mathbf{S}$ with the model embedding. Finally, the self-attention mechanism is used to integrate these constraints, which can be formally expressed as:

$$\mathbf{S} = \mathbf{D}_y \oplus \mathbf{D}_j \oplus \mathbf{D}_p \oplus \mathbf{D}_r \oplus \mathbf{D}_i \tag{1}$$

$$\mathbf{G} = \text{EMBED}(\mathbf{S}) \tag{2}$$

$$\mathbf{C} = \text{SELF-ATT}\left(\mathbf{G}\mathbf{W}^Q, \mathbf{G}\mathbf{W}^K, \mathbf{G}\mathbf{W}^V\right) \tag{3}$$

where $\mathbf{D}_y, \mathbf{D}_j, \mathbf{D}_p, \mathbf{D}_r$, and $\mathbf{D}_i$ denote "Word Amount", "Sentence Amount", "Level and Oblique Tones", "Rhyme", and user input, respectively. The constraints are interacted with the inputs by self-attention calculation $\mathbf{C} = \text{SELF-ATT}(\cdot)$, acting as the global information to steer the generation of each time step t. The generation model is optimized by cross-entropy loss with constraints $\mathbf{C}$ as follows:

$$\mathcal{L}_{\text{gen}} = -\sum_{t=1}^{|\hat{\mathbf{y}}|} \log p\left(\hat{\mathbf{y}}_t \mid \mathbf{C}; \theta_{\text{gen}}\right) \tag{4}$$

where $\hat{\mathbf{y}}$ is the draft produced by the generation model θ_{gen}.

2.2 Poem Polishing

The polishing model θ_{pol} iteratively optimizes the generation draft $\mathbf{y}$ following the constraints $\mathbf{C}$.

Mask Prediction Strategy Previous works use the independent polishing model under practical scenarios. Deng et al. (2020) propose a BERT-based polishing scheme that highly relies on the mask-prediction pre-training task. However, this method generates the candidate words without considering original input and constraints. Li et al. (2020) successfully introduce the input into the polishing process through additional embedding modules. But it is not efficient to design an additional embedding module for newly introduced constraints due to computational cost, nor to ignore user input from the prior generation and only conduct masked prediction tasks. To this end, we design a polishing model that is capable to update the specific word and reconstruct the entire poetry. Within decoding process of polishing task, the model should provide word candidates predictions $\mathbf{w}$ for mask position $\mathbf{m}$ and generate polished sentence according to previous obtained poetry draft $\hat{\mathbf{y}}$ and feature constraints $\mathbf{C}$. For training the polishing model, a multi-task learning approach is applied to jointly optimize the loss of mask prediction and sentence reconstruction, which can be formulated as:

$$\mathcal{L}_{\text{mask}} = -\sum_{t=1}^{|\mathbf{m}|} \log p\left(\mathbf{w}_t \mid \mathbf{m}_t, \mathbf{C}; \theta_{\text{pol}}\right) \quad (5)$$

$$\mathcal{L}_{\text{rec}} = -\sum_{t=1}^{|\mathbf{y}|} \log p\left(\mathbf{y}_t \mid \hat{\mathbf{y}}_t, \mathbf{C}; \theta_{\text{pol}}\right) \quad (6)$$

where $\mathbf{y}$ is the ground truth. $\mathcal{L}_{\text{mask}}$ and $\mathcal{L}_{\text{rec}}$ are the cross-entropy loss of mask-prediction task and sentence reconstruction task, respectively. Finally, the model is optimized by two kinds of loss:

$$\mathcal{L} = \mathcal{L}_{\text{mask}} + \mathcal{L}_{\text{rec}} \quad (7)$$

2.3 Data Augmentation

Generation Augmentation For constrained generation task, combining poetry data with all the pre-determined constraints could limit the scope of application. In this case, hard constraints would restrict the diversity of model input, leading to limited customization choices in the deployment stage, let alone the generation case without constraint. Hence we propose a constraint-level masked-style data augmentation method. It masks the constraints with equal probabilities so that it can increase the diversity of data with different sets of pre-determined constraints. The model is forced to learn to generate diverse candidates based on augmented types of constraints, meanwhile, it also supports more flexible customization of poetry generation.

Polishing Augmentation Since there is no labeled data for training the polishing model, a pseudo dataset is built by masking the random tokens of ground truth text. To construct the masked sentences, we set up the mask ratio as 0.5, resulting in an equal probability for masked and unmasked tokens. Due to the randomness of the masking operation, the masked sentences will not cover all polishing scenarios. Hence, we further quadruple the polishing data for each poetry by masking the tokens that are different from the original pseudo data, covering a wider range of polishing requests.

2.4 Setup

We exploit GPT-2 (Radford et al., 2019) as our fundamental model and follow the pretrain-finetuning paradigm to build the downstream generation and polishing models. Our training corpus consists of 1,004,039 poems which are built based on open-source data[6][7]. The amount of training data reaches 4,016,159 instances after data augmentation techniques. For decoding settings, we employ Top-p sampling method with $p = 1$, and the temperature parameter $t = 1.0$ is applied to the softmax layer.

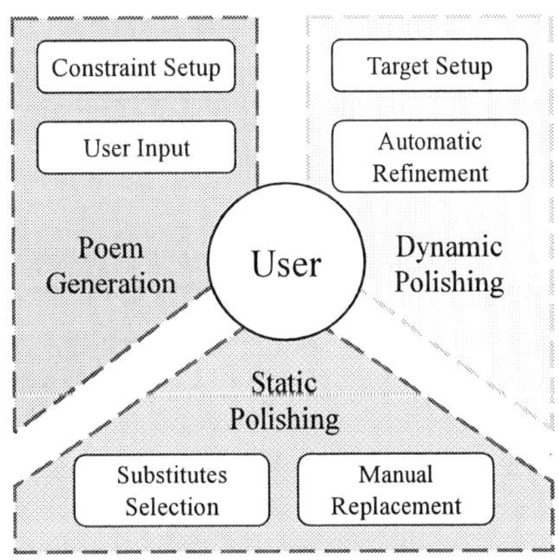

Figure 2: Overview of system functionality.

3 Functionality Design

As shown in Figure 2, we specially design three main functions for Yu Sheng system, meeting the

[6]https://github.com/Werneror/Poetry

[7]https://github.com/chinese-poetry/chinese-poetry

Model	Diversity (Distinct) ↑		F-Score ↑			
	Distinct-1	Distinct-2	Word Amount	Sentence Amount	Tones	Rhyme
Transformer	1.10	14.39	13.84	2.10	3.38	33.25
+ *Polish*	1.39	23.10	45.20	30.60	**99.96**	25.67
GPT-2	2.42	44.62	76.18	86.96	99.76	68.53
+ *Polish*	**2.45**	44.67	75.98	86.00	99.56	67.51
+ *Gen. Aug.*	2.42	44.97	**80.56**	87.24	99.72	**70.02**
+ *Polish Aug.*	2.44	44.61	74.51	**87.67**	99.72	69.11
+ *Both*	2.44	**45.02**	79.76	86.52	99.64	69.42

Table 1: Automatic evaluation results of generated poems with same input and constraints. Overall, the polishing model enhances the generation quality. "Gen." and "Aug." denote "generation" and "augmentation", respectively.

user's demand at different levels. As the fundamental function, the user can easily obtain poetry by indicating expected features. As for people who have advanced requirements of aesthetics, they can pay more effort into poetry generation by using two polishing modes for optimizing the generation draft. The dynamic polishing provides the functionality of poetry-level refinement. The user can simply select the unsatisfactory words or sentences as the target, and then the system will perform automatic polishing for updating the chosen parts. If the user wants to dive deeper and make subtle changes, static polishing can recommend substitutes for the unsatisfactory text, where the user can choose the proper candidate and manually replace the corresponding parts. Moreover, professional user can import their own poetry work and obtain inspiration from polishing candidates provided by Yu Sheng. To facilitate polishing process, the system will provide explanatory information of each feature to user for understanding the candidates. For improving the inference speed in a practical environment, we enable a inherit-based decoding trick for polishing task, which significantly reduces response time by preserving the unchanged tokens at each decoding step. The whole generation pipeline makes up of the aforementioned functions, and the specific use cases of each function are introduced in Appendix.

4 Evaluation

4.1 Automatic Evaluation

4.1.1 Data and Metrics

Data 2,522 constraint-poem pairs are filtered out from the original data as the test data, which is independent of the training corpus. This test set is passed to original vanilla Transformer and GPT-2 generation model to obtain initial poetry drafts and then used as the input of the polishing model. To simulate the users' operation, we randomly choose the polishing part of each poem.

Distinct is used to evaluate the diversity of generated poetry. It is calculated by dividing the number of words by the number of unique words in a sentence, which can be formulated as:

$$\text{Distinct}(n) = \frac{\text{Count(unique } N\text{-gram)}}{\text{Count(word)}} \tag{8}$$

F-score Since our system focuses on generating the poetry according to poetry-related constraints, F-score is utilized to evaluate the model accuracy and recall of constraint integration. We calculate micro-F1 score to evaluate the integration of different constraints due to large inter-class gap.

4.1.2 Results

The evaluation results are as shown in Table 1. In general, GPT-2 is a stronger generation model compared to vanilla Transformer. Hence, we choose GPT-2 as a testbed to further verify the effectiveness of different polishing strategies. Although all metrics show that basic polishing model improves the generation performance of vanilla Transformer, original GPT-2 model cannot benefit from the basic polishing model. The reason may be that the difficulty of polishing increases with the improvement of generation quality. Encouragingly, the polishing model trained with augmentation data improves the performance of most metrics, demonstrating the effectiveness of proposed augmentation methods.

Although the polishing model learns the diversified polishing cases from the augmentation data, both sentence reconstruction and mask prediction tasks cannot improve the generation diversity due to their objective functions. Hence, the scores of Distinct-1 and Distinct-2 are fluctuating for augmentation models. But the proposed methods gain stable improvement from the perspective of morphology, phonology, and lexical-related factors.

Overall, our proposed polishing model can further improve the quality of GPT-2 generation results by mending constraint errors with the aforementioned augmentation strategies, which demonstrates the effectiveness of proposed methodology. Therefore, we can realize that the system is capable to generate high-quality poetry together with flexible customization. To prove the competitiveness of our system, we also compare it with the existing system in Section 4.2.

4.2 Human Evaluation

4.2.1 Data and Metrics

The goal of poetry generation and polishing is conforming to human preference. To better understand the model's behavior from human points of view and evaluate the effectiveness of polishing, we conduct a human evaluation of the polished poetry. Besides model evaluation, we provide system comparison regarding generated poems based on poetry customization options that all systems support.

For each model and system, we randomly sample 60 poems from the generation results as evaluation data. Then we invite native Chinese speakers with poetry knowledge as evaluators to conduct evaluation using four metrics: Poeticness, Fluency, Meaning, and Coherency. Three evaluators are assigned to evaluate poems generated under different models and another four evaluators are assigned to conduct system comparison.

The rating criteria for each metric are listed below:

- **Poeticness** (Poe.): Score the current poem based on the sense of beauty: 0 (tedious), 1 (sense of beauty exists in partial sentence), 2 (all poem sentences contain a sense of beauty).
- **Fluency** (Flu.): Score the current poem based on the phonology and fluency: 0 (phonology crash), 1 (partial sentence is unreadable), 2 (all the sentences can be read fluently with smooth phonology).
- **Meaning** (Mea.): Score the current poem based on its relevance to the user intention: 0 (digress from the main subject), 1 (partial sentences are irrelevant), 2 (relevant to the subject).
- **Coherency** (Coh.): Score the current poem based on its coherency: 0 (all sentences are independent), 1 (partial sentence does not follow surrounding context), 2 (all the sentences are coherent with the other context).

Model	**Poe.**	**Flu.**	**Mea.**	**Coh.**
Transformer	0.88	0.87	0.43	0.63
+ *Polish*	0.62	0.52	0.55	0.50
GPT-2	1.27	0.82	0.55	0.50
+ *Polish*	1.12	0.82	1.13	0.77
+ *Gen. Aug.*	1.18	0.93	1.10	0.88
+ *Polish Aug.*	1.10	0.85	0.98	0.82
+ *Both*	**1.30**	**1.02**	**1.20**	**1.08**

Table 2: Human evaluation results of the poems generated by different models. By training the models with augmentation data, the poems generated/polished by our model are better than GPT-2 baseline. "Gen." and "Aug." denote "generation" and "augmentation", respectively.

System	**Poe.**	**Flu.**	**Mea.**	**Coh.**
Jiuge	1.40	1.25	1.15	1.17
Yu Sheng	**1.62**	**1.53**	**1.55**	**1.62**

Table 3: Human evaluation results of the poems generated by our system Yu Sheng and another system Jiuge. The poems were generated by each system based on poetry constraints that both systems are capable to customize. Overall quality of the poems generated by Yu Sheng is competitive with the other systems in terms of each metric.

4.2.2 Results

The human evaluation results are as shown in Table 2. It shows that polished poems achieve the highest score on poeticness, which supports the rationality of high F-score in the automatic evaluation. In our system, the model can generate poetry with accurate morphology by following the constraints given by the user, such as "Word Amount" and "Sentence Amount", and other high-level rhythmic options like "Rhyme" and "Level and Oblique Tones" could enhance the sense of beauty. Regarding fluency and coherency, the augmentation data highly improve their scores since the polishing model is trained by diversified constraints. System comparison in Table 3 shows high competitiveness of our

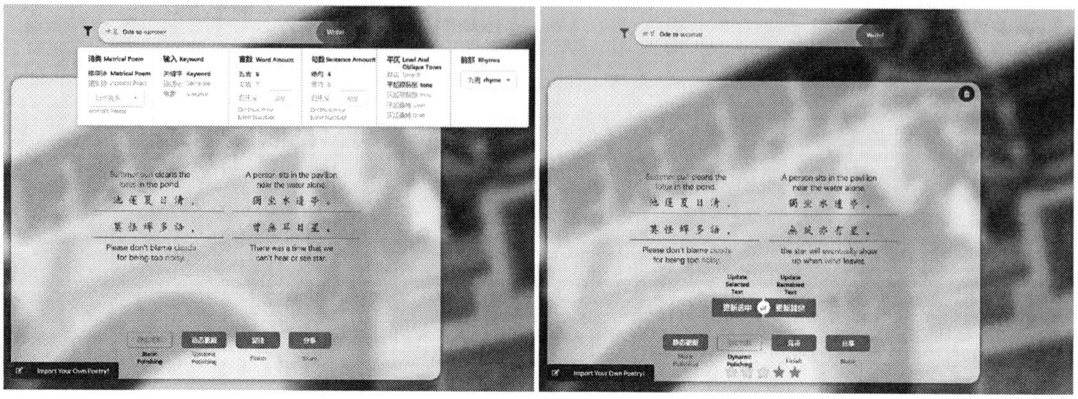

(a) Constrained generation.

(b) Poetry polishing.

Figure 3: Use cases of constrained poetry generation and polishing. Constraints customized in filter bar and topic words entered in input bar steer the constrained poetry generation. Refinement results are reflected on the demonstration panel, replacing the previous draft.

system regarding the same constraints supported by both systems.

5 Discussion

Figure 3 presents a case of using Yu Sheng to customize poetry generation with constraints.

Constrained Poem Generation As shown in Figure 3a, the user may first use the feature selector to customize all generation constraints. Then the user enters the topic words according to the type of keywords and click generate button, Yu Sheng will return the results in the demonstration panel.

Poem Polishing We also showcase the poetry polishing procedure on the automatic generation results or user-imported poem as illustrated in Figure 3b. The users can import their own poem into workspace by entering keywords and poem sentences into the import module. When the user switches to Dynamic Polishing mode and chooses "自", "有" as the unsatisfactory tokens, the system would perform polishing action and return the result with poetry-level adjustment. The user also can switch to static polishing mode, and then select specific word or sentence. The system would recommend different substitutes for words and sentences for replacement. Preliminary analysis of the poem would be automatically generated in the workspace for users to understand current features and structural information before performing next operation. At the end of poetry generation, Yu Sheng also allows users to evaluate the current composition and propose a beautiful share poster for sharing the poem work. More details can be founded in the Appendix due to page limitations.

More Backbone Models In this work, we focus on exploring the generation and polishing capability of general casual language model. Since other pre-trained models also inherit the Transformer architecture, we provide the results of vanilla Transformer to prove the generality of proposed method. The polishing model can greatly enhance the quality of model outputs in the first stage. However, the polishing model becomes less effective for high-quality poems. We are also passionate to explore in the future work.

6 Conclusion and Future Work

We propose Yu Sheng, a comprehensive, human-in-loop classical Chinese poetry generation system. Yu Sheng establishes a generation pipeline that covers multi-dimensional demands of generation and polishing, enabling amateurs to engage in the process of poetry generation, and provide inspirations for composition work of human poets. It provides the functionalities for users with different backgrounds to conduct poetry composition conveniently and flexibly. With the global attention mechanism and the human-in-loop poetry generation paradigm, Yu Sheng could be easily updated with diverse constraints and further extended to different languages. In the future, we will also collect the data and construct an annotated polishing corpus for training a more robust polishing model.

Limitations

The limitations of our system are three-folded. First, there is no public polishing dataset in the open-source community. To address this problem, we mask the tokens of human-written poetry to build the pseudo data. Since the polishing model aims to refine the machine-generated poetry, the pseudo data used to train our model is still far away from the realistic scenario compared to the annotated data. Secondly, polishing quality is hard to control due to knowledge background of users. Although poetry features can be easily checked and evaluated, aesthetics highly relies on the users' preferences. Non-professional users may hardly notice the subtle problem of the generated poetry and make the right decision on whether to polish it or not. Thirdly, polyphonic disambiguation is hard to solve due to the lack of phonology data, resulting mild corruption of sentence semantic.

Acknowledgements

This work was supported in part by the Science and Technology Development Fund, Macau SAR (Grant Nos. FDCT/0070/2022/AMJ, FDCT/060/2022/AFJ) and the Multi-year Research Grant from the University of Macau (Grant No. MYRG2020-00054-FST). This work was performed in part at SICC which is supported by SKL-IOTSC, and HPCC supported by ICTO of the University of Macau.

References

David Prager Branner. 2006. Introduction: What are rime tables and what do ti-ey mean? *The Chinese Rime Tables: Linguistic philosophy and historical-comparative phonology*, 271:1.

Liming Deng, Jie Wang, Hang-Ming Liang, Hui Chen, Zhiqiang Xie, Bojin Zhuang, Shaojun Wang, and Jing Xiao. 2020. An iterative polishing framework based on quality aware masked language model for chinese poetry generation. In *The Thirty-Fourth AAAI Conference on Artificial Intelligence, AAAI 2020, The Thirty-Second Innovative Applications of Artificial Intelligence Conference, IAAI 2020, The Tenth AAAI Symposium on Educational Advances in Artificial Intelligence, EAAI 2020, New York, NY, USA, February 7-12, 2020*, pages 7643–7650. AAAI Press.

Pablo Gervás. 2001. An expert system for the composition of formal spanish poetry. In *Applications and innovations in intelligent systems VIII*, pages 19–32. Springer.

Robert P Levy. 2001. A computational model of poetic creativity with neural network as measure of adaptive fitness. In *Proceedings of the ICCBR-01 Workshop on Creative Systems*. Citeseer.

Piji Li, Haisong Zhang, Xiaojiang Liu, and Shuming Shi. 2020. Rigid formats controlled text generation. In *Proceedings of the 58th Annual Meeting of the Association for Computational Linguistics*, pages 742–751, Online. Association for Computational Linguistics.

Raymond Queneau. 1961. 100.000. 000.000. 000 de poemes. *Gallimard Series. Schoenhof's Foreign Books, Incorporated.*

Alec Radford, Jeffrey Wu, Rewon Child, David Luan, Dario Amodei, Ilya Sutskever, et al. 2019. Language models are unsupervised multitask learners. *OpenAI blog*, 1(8):9.

Huishuang Tian, Kexin Yang, Dayiheng Liu, and Jiancheng Lv. 2021. Anchibert: a pre-trained model for ancient chinese language understanding and generation. In *2021 International Joint Conference on Neural Networks (IJCNN)*, pages 1–8. IEEE.

Ashish Vaswani, Noam Shazeer, Niki Parmar, Jakob Uszkoreit, Llion Jones, Aidan N. Gomez, Lukasz Kaiser, and Illia Polosukhin. 2017. Attention is all you need. In *Advances in Neural Information Processing Systems 30: Annual Conference on Neural Information Processing Systems 2017, December 4-9, 2017, Long Beach, CA, USA*, pages 5998–6008.

Rui Yan. 2016. i, poet: Automatic poetry composition through recurrent neural networks with iterative polishing schema. In *Proceedings of the Twenty-Fifth International Joint Conference on Artificial Intelligence, IJCAI 2016, New York, NY, USA, 9-15 July 2016*, pages 2238–2244. IJCAI/AAAI Press.

Xiaoyuan Yi, Maosong Sun, Ruoyu Li, and Wenhao Li. 2018. Automatic poetry generation with mutual reinforcement learning. In *Proceedings of the 2018 Conference on Empirical Methods in Natural Language Processing*, pages 3143–3153, Brussels, Belgium. Association for Computational Linguistics.

Guo Zhipeng, Xiaoyuan Yi, Maosong Sun, Wenhao Li, Cheng Yang, Jiannan Liang, Huimin Chen, Yuhui Zhang, and Ruoyu Li. 2019. Jiuge: A human-machine collaborative Chinese classical poetry generation system. In *Proceedings of the 57th Annual Meeting of the Association for Computational Linguistics: System Demonstrations*, pages 25–30, Florence, Italy. Association for Computational Linguistics.

A Appendix

A.1 Detailed Use Case

Constrained Generation Figure 1 presents a case study of using Yu Sheng to customize poetry generation task with constraints. As shown in Figure 1a, the user first uses the feature selector to customize all correlated features ("Poem Type" as "Metrical Poem", "Input Type" as "Keyword", "Word Amount" as 5, "Sentence Amount" as 4, "Level and Oblique Tones" as "平起黏格" and "Rhymes" as "九青"). Then the user enters the keyword "夏天"(Summer) as the topic word according to the chosen type of keywords and starts the generation by clicking the "Write" button on the right side of input bar.

Within a short time after receiving the generation request, Yu Sheng returns and presents the expected generated poem in the demonstration panel, which is shown in Figure 1b. The user can easily obtain diversified poems under the same constraints and topic setup by repeatedly clicking the "Write" button without limitation.

Poetry Polishing We also showcase the polishing functionalities as illustrated in Figure 2. With the upholding poem draft, a user stays in the static polishing mode and clicks on unsatisfactory word "無" and sentence "曾無耳目星". The system will provide different substitutes as shown in Figure 2a. The user can replace sentence "無風自有星" in the original draft with substitute "曾無耳目星" by clicking the preferred substitute block in the sentence recommendation panel. The updated poem is shown in 2b.

Then, the user switches to the dynamic polishing mode for automatic polishing. The words "自" and "有" are marked as targets as shown in Figure 2c. Then the user clicks "Update Selected Text" button to label the text with a low-quality tag. Yu Sheng will automatically polish these unsatisfactory words and returns the result with dynamic adjustment as shown in Figure 2d. Finally, the result meets the user's requirement after iterative polishing.

When the user decides to complete the current work, Yu Sheng allows the user to evaluate the presented composition by rating stars after clicking "Finish" button. The user can also click the "Share" button to generate a poster. The poster will pop up in the middle of the interface (Figure 2e, 2f) for downloading and sharing.

A.2 Examples

As shown in Table 1, we also present two examples obtained from our pipeline system.

B Revisions

To address the reviewers' concerns, we revised our paper as follows:

- We fixed the typos and added a link of system. Furthermore, a multilingual user interface has been added in Yu Sheng for serving the user comes from different language background.
- We offered more detailed explanations in terms of training loss and modelling approaches. Sentence reconstruction loss is formulated as the posterior probability of predicting words in the original poem sentence based on the draft and constraints.
- We described the rule-based method to extract tone and rhyme in Section 2.

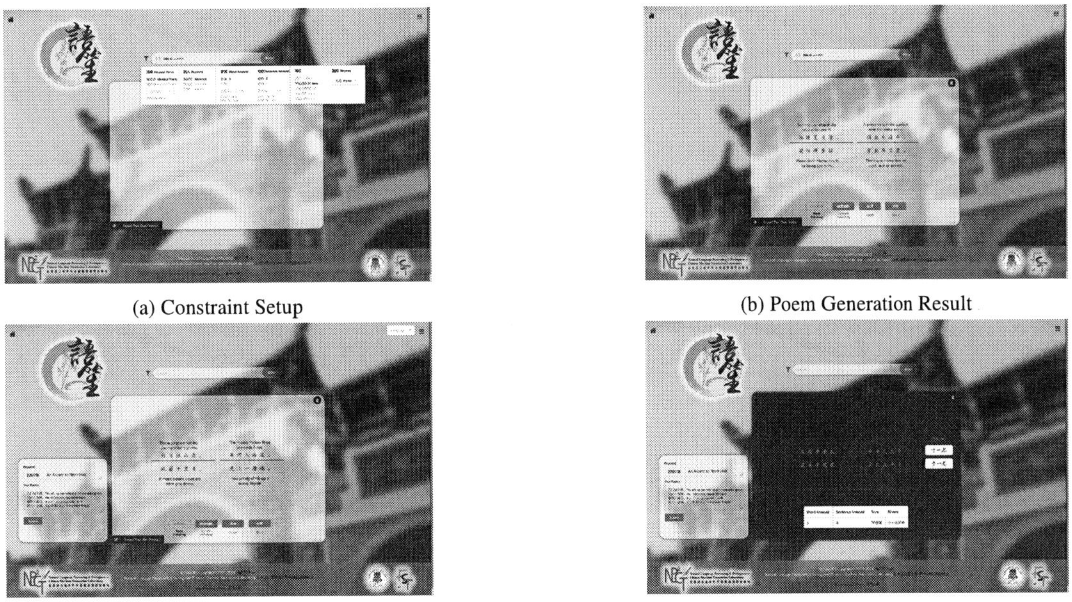

(a) Constraint Setup

(b) Poem Generation Result

(c) Import Poem

(d) Poem Analysis

Figure 1: Use Case: Constrained Poetry Generation

Constrained Generation	Setup	Topic Word: 夏天; Word Amount: 5; Sentence Amount 7; Rhyme: 九青; Tone: 平平仄仄平　仄仄仄平平　仄仄平平仄　平平仄仄平
	Result	池蓮夏日清，獨坐水邊亭。莫怪蟬多語，曾無耳目星。
Static Polishing	Result	池蓮夏日清，獨坐水邊亭。莫怪蟬多語，無風自有星。
Dynamic Polishing	Result	池蓮夏日清，獨坐水邊亭。莫怪蟬多語，無風亦有星。

Constrained Generation	Setup	Topic Word: 月下獨飲; Word Amount: 5; Sentence Amount 7; Rhyme: 十一尤; Tone: 仄仄仄平平　平平仄仄平　平平平仄仄　仄仄仄平平
	Result	月下弄鳴弦，秋聲滿樹頭。今來何處去，日夜憶南州。
Dynamic Polishing	Result	月下弄鳴弦，秋聲滿樹頭。今來何處去，此夜憶南州。
Static Polishing	Result	月下弄鳴弦，秋聲滿樹頭。何因逢老病，此夜憶南州。
Dynamic Polishing	Result	月下弄鳴弦，秋聲滿樹頭。何因驚老病，此夜憶南州。

Table 1: Examples of pipeline generation.

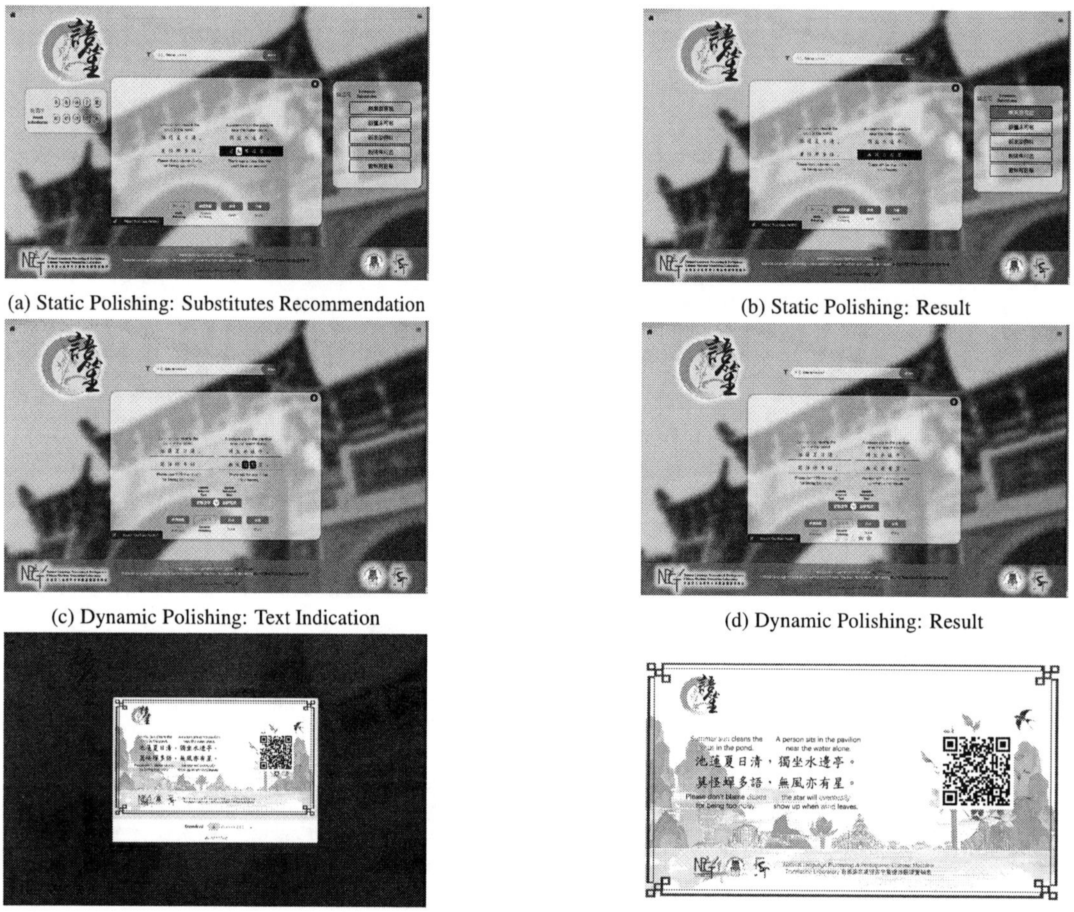

(a) Static Polishing: Substitutes Recommendation

(b) Static Polishing: Result

(c) Dynamic Polishing: Text Indication

(d) Dynamic Polishing: Result

(e) Share Page

(f) Poster

Figure 2: Use Case: Poem Polishing

PANACEA: An Automated Misinformation Detection System on COVID-19

Runcong Zhao[1,3], **Miguel Arana-Catania**[5], **Lixing Zhu**[1,3], **Elena Kochkina**[2,4], **Lin Gui**[3], **Arkaitz Zubiaga**[2], **Rob Procter**[1,4], **Maria Liakata**[1,2,4], **Yulan He**[1,3,4]
[1]University of Warwick, [2]Queen Mary University of London
[3]King's College London, [4]The Alan Turing Institute, [5]Cranfield University
{runcong.zhao, yulan.he}@kcl.ac.uk

Abstract

In this demo, we introduce a web-based misinformation detection system PANACEA on COVID-19 related claims, which has two modules, *fact-checking* and *rumour detection*. Our *fact-checking* module, which is supported by novel natural language inference methods with a self-attention network, outperforms state-of-the-art approaches. It is also able to give automated veracity assessment and ranked supporting evidence with the stance towards the claim to be checked. In addition, PANACEA adapts the bi-directional graph convolutional networks model, which is able to detect rumours based on comment networks of related tweets, instead of relying on the knowledge base. This *rumour detection* module assists by warning the users in the early stages when a knowledge base may not be available.

1 Introduction

The dangers of misinformation have become even more apparent to the general public during the COVID-19 pandemic. Following *false* treatment information has led to a high number of deaths and hospitalisations (Islam et al., 2020). Manual verification can not scale to the amount of misinformation being spread, therefore there is a need to develop automated tools to assist in this process.

In this work, we focus on automating misinformation detection using information from credible sources as well as social media. We produce a web-based tool that can be used by the general public to inspect relevant information about the claims that they want to check, see supporting or refuting evidence, and social media propagation patterns.

For *false* information, the commonly used and relatively reliable method for automated veracity assessment is to check the claim against a verified knowledge base, which we call *fact-checking*. Previous works such as EVIDENCEMINER (Wang et al., 2020b), PubMed[1] and COVID-19 fact-checking sites recommended by the NHS[2] are all designed to retrieve related documents/sentences from a reliable knowledge base. However, this approach leaves users to summarise a large amount of potentially conflicting evidence themselves. PANACEA, which is supported by novel natural language inference methods (Arana-Catania et al., 2022), is instead able to provide automated veracity assessment and supporting evidence for the input claim. In addition, previous works retrieve results using entities in the input claim, and thus often include results related to a keyword in the input claim instead of the whole query, while PANACEA considers the whole query for better result. The supporting pieces of evidence are also ranked by their relevance score and classified according to their stance towards the input claim.

In addition to *false* information, truthful information can also be misused to harm competitors or gain attention on social media (Pennycook et al., 2020; Tsfati et al., 2020). However, the latter is harder to be found by checking reliable knowledge bases as those are focused on *false* information. Regarding this issue, previous work has analysed the spread of misinformation using features such as stance (Zhu et al., 2021), sentiment, topics, geographical spread, the reliability of external links included in the tweet (Sharma et al., 2020), origin and propagation networks (Finn et al., 2014). However, it is still hard for users to identify rumours by directly looking at those features. Previous research shows that the propagation pattern is different between fake and real news, which would offer additional features for early detection of misinformation on social media (Zhao et al., 2020). PANACEA extends this by using tweets' propagation patterns to identify rumours. *Rumour detection* is not as reliable as *fact-checking*, but it generalises the system to various situations that *fact-checking*

[1]https://www.ncbi.nlm.nih.gov/pmc/

[2]https://library.hee.nhs.uk/covid-19/coronavirus-%28covid-19%29-misinformation

Proceedings of the 17th Conference of the European Chapter of the Association for Computational Linguistics System Demonstrations, pages 67–74
May 2-4, 2023 ©2023 Association for Computational Linguistics

cannot cover: First, *true* or *unverified* information with *intent to harm*; Second, scenarios where no verified knowledge database is available. *Rumour detection* cannot prove the truth of a claim but may alert the user about claims with a high risk of being misinformation.

Previous work have either retrieved tweets from a short fixed time period (Sharma et al., 2020) or search recent tweets (Finn et al., 2014), which is limited by Twitter to only the last 7 days. We instead maintain an updated database which is constituted of an annotated tweets dataset with popular claims and an unlabelled streaming of COVID-19 related tweets that are crawled and selected periodically to update the dataset. Besides building on the various analytic functionalities used in previous work, PANACEA improves the architecture of these elements and adds extra features to the updated dataset for more efficient results.

A screencast video introducing the system[3], illustrating its use in the checking of a COVID-19 claim, and the demo[4] are also available online. The system can be easily adapted to other claim topics.

PANACEA covers various types of misinformation detection related to COVID-19 with the following contributions:

- We built a new web-based system, PANACEA, which is able to perform both *fact-checking* and *rumour detection* with natural language claims submitted by users. The system includes visualisations of various statistical analyses of the results for a better user understanding.
- PANACEA performs automated veracity assessment and provides supporting evidence that can be ranked by various criteria, supported by novel natural language inference methods. The system is able to manage multiple user requests with low latency thanks to our development of a queuing system.
- PANACEA is able to perform automated rumour detection by exploiting state-of-the-art research on propagation patterns. The system uses an annotated dataset and streams of COVID-19 tweets are collected to maintain an updated database.

[3]https://www.youtube.com/watch?v=D1PN8_9oYso

[4]https://panacea2020.github.io/

2 Datasets

The following datasets are used in the project:

Knowledge Database This is used for fact-checking, and includes COVID-19 related documents from selected reliable sources [5]. The documents were cleaned and split into 300 token paragraphs to construct a reliable knowledge database, whose supporting documents are retrieved and visualised in our system.

PANACEA Dataset (Arana-Catania et al., 2022), constructed from COVID-19 related data sources[6] and using BM25 and MonoT5 (Nogueira et al., 2020) to remove duplicate claims. This dataset includes 5,143 labelled claims (1,810 *False* and 3,333 *True*), and their respective text, source and claim sub-type.

COVID-RV dataset In order to fine-tune our model, we constructed a new COVID-19 related propagation tree dataset for rumour detection. Similar previous datasets are Twitter15 and Twitter16 (Ma et al., 2018), which are widespread tweets' propagation trees with rumour labels, however, they are not COVID-19 related. Our dataset has been constructed by extending COVID-RV (Kochkina et al., 2023), including *the number of retweets, user id, post time, text, location* and *tweet reply ids* as metadata for each tweet. Each tree is annotated with a related claim chosen from our claim dataset and a stance label (chosen from *Support* or *Refute*) towards its related claim. Such a stance label for each tree is purely based on the content of the source tweet. In COVID-RV the conversations are annotated as either *True* or *False* based on the veracity of the claim and the stance of the source tweet towards it. Tweets supporting a false claim or challenging a true claim are annotated as *False*, tweets supporting true claims or challenging a false claim are annotated as *True*. Twitter15 and Twitter16 datasets also contain *Unverified* conversations, which are discussing claim that are neither confirmed or denied.

COVID Twitter Propagation Tree (Live) Besides the last dataset constructed for fine-tuning,

[5]*Centers for Disease Control and Prevention* (CDC), *European Centre for Disease Prevention and Control* (ECDC), *WebMD* and *World Health Organisation* (WHO)

[6]Corona VirusFacts Database, CoAID dataset (Cui and Lee, 2020), MM-COVID (Li et al., 2020), CovidLies (Hossain et al., 2020), TREC Health Misinformation track and TREC COVID challenge (Voorhees et al., 2021)

PANACEA also runs a crawler to collect a stream of COVID-19 tweets that are used to maintain an updated database. This live dataset is not annotated, instead, it is labelled by the pre-trained rumour detection model. As the Twitter's search API does not allow retrieval of tweets beyond a week window, we retrieve COVID-19 related historical tweets based on the widely used dataset of COVID-19-TweetIDs (Chen et al., 2020), which contains more than 1 billion tweet IDs. Considering the size of the dataset, and for the storage and retrieval efficiency, we filtered out the less popular tweets with limited impact. To date, more than 12k propagation trees have been collected, starting from January 2020. For each tweet, its pseudo rumour label is generated by the trained model.

3 Architecture of PANACEA

Figure 1 shows an overview of PANACEA, including two functions: *fact-checking* and *rumour detection* for COVID-19. For *fact-checking*, there are three modules: (1) resource allocation system; (2) veracity assessment; and (3) supporting evidence retrieval. PANACEA also supports a unique function, *rumour detection* by propagation patterns, which has the following modules: (1) tweet retrieval; (2) rumour detection; and (3) tweet meta-information analysis.

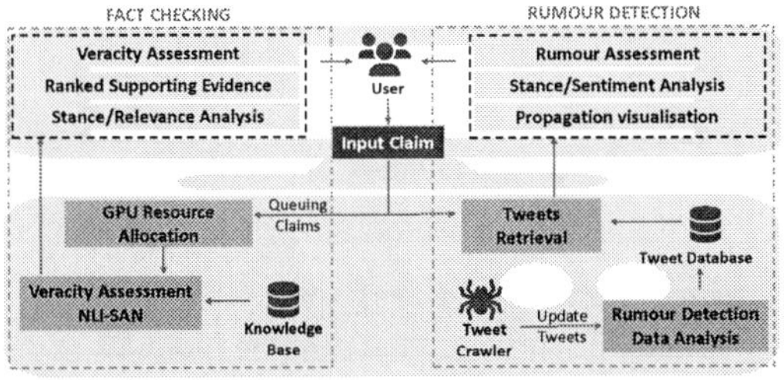

Figure 1: Architecture of PANACEA

3.1 Fact-Checking

Resource Allocation System Users can input natural language claims into our system, and PANACEA provides autocompleted input guesses based on the current input and the claims dataset. Claim autocompletion can help users to input the claim faster and the results included within the claims dataset can be pre-computed for faster retrieval. However, if the user cannot find what they would like to check through the claims dataset, the new claim would be passed to our model for real-time evaluation. Veracity assessment and evidence retrieval are based on our natural language inference model NLI-SAN (Arana-Catania et al., 2022), which needs GPU resources to run. Therefore we built a queuing system that manages the resources and queues the claims while the GPUs are being used. The results are sent to the user. To avoid duplicate searches, a temporary copy of this result is saved in our database based on the user's IP address until the user searches for a new claim or the saved period expires.

Veracity Assessment PANACEA is supported by NLI-SAN (Arana-Catania et al., 2022), which incorporates natural language inference results of claim-evidence pairs into a self-attention network. The input claim c is paired with each retrieved relevant evidence e_i to form claim-evidence pairs, where the relevant evidences are the retrieved sentences as described in the following paragraph. Each claim-evidence pair (c, e_i) is fed into both a RoBERTa-large[7] model to get a representation S_i and into a RoBERTa-large-MNLI[7] model to get a probability triplet I_i of stance (*contradiction*, *neutrality*, or *entailment*) between the pair. Next, S_i is mapped to a Key K and a Value V, while I_i is mapped onto a Query Q. $(Q, K, V)_i$ forms the input of the self-attention layer and the outputs O_i for all the claim-evidence pairs are concatenated together. The output is then passed to a MLP layer to get the veracity assessment result (*True* or *False*) as shown in Figure 2.

Supporting Evidence Retrieval This module includes three parts: document retrieval, sentence retrieval and corresponding meta-data generation. Multi-stage retrieval is applied, retrieving first the top 100 relevant documents with BM25, that then are re-ranked by MonoT5 (Nogueira et al., 2020) and the top 10 documents are selected. For each of those documents, the top 3 sentences are selected. Both documents and sentences are ranked by their relevance score, which is the cosine similarity between the documents/sentences and the input claim embeddings. Each of those texts are represented through embeddings obtained using Sentence-Transformers with the pre-trained model MiniLM-L12-v2 (Wang et al., 2020a). The corresponding metadata of the supporting documents, including type, source, relevance score, and stance towards the claim are also shown, together with the ranked documents/sentences. Users can also

[7] `https://huggingface.co/`

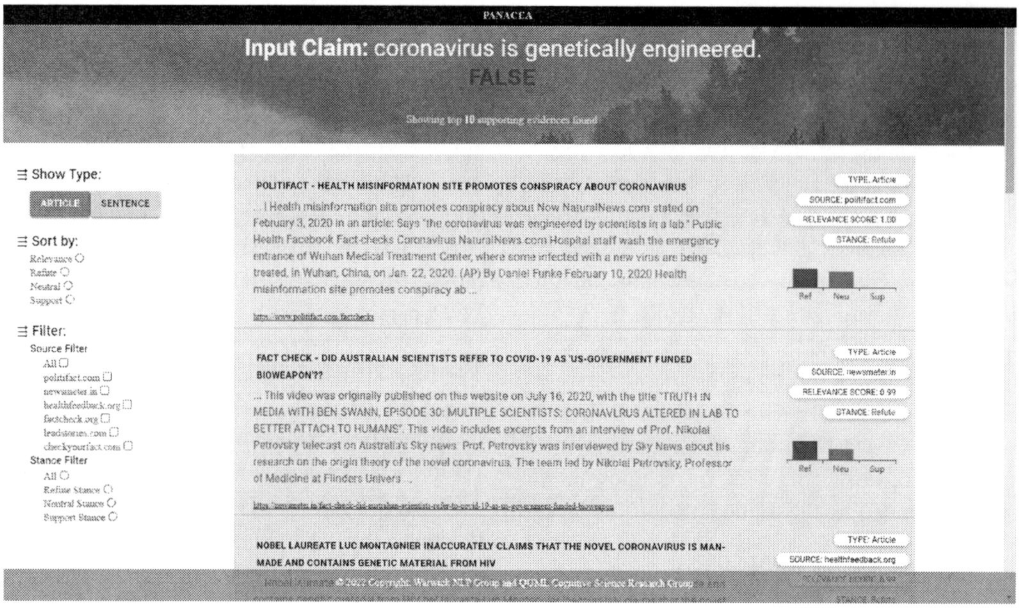

Figure 2: Fact checking result with input claim: *coronavirus is genetically engineered.*

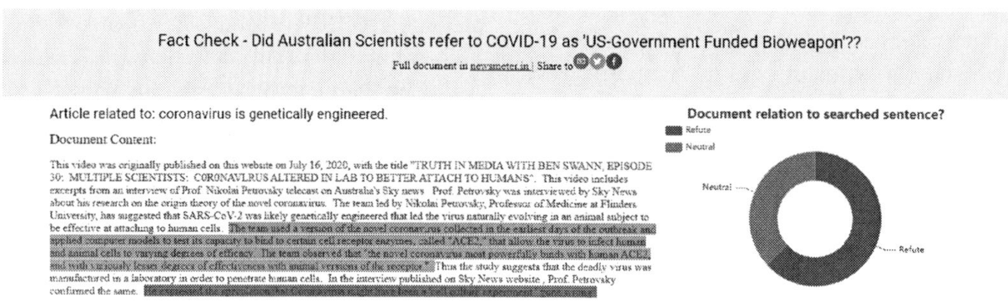

Figure 3: The detail page of user selected supporting document

filter or re-rank the result using the metadata. An example of documents retrieved is shown in Figure 2 and the corresponding detailed information visualisation is shown in Figure 3. On the details page, the whole document text is shown with the top 3 relevant sentences highlighted by their stance towards the input claim. The stance distribution, described in the veracity assessment module is also visualised.

3.2 Rumour Detection

Another approach to detecting rumours that has been found to be effective (Ma et al., 2018; Tian et al., 2022) is modelling user comments and propagation networks. Next we describe the relevant rumour detection modules of our system.

Claim-related tweets retrieval Similar to the fact-checking module, this module includes an autocomplete function for the user's natural language input claim that guesses the input from our claims dataset. The results for existing claims are also pre-computed to retrieve tweets faster. For a claim that is not in our claim dataset, we use BM25 to retrieve the related propagation trees from the large Twitter propagation tree database maintained by the active Twitter crawler.

Rumour Assessment and Data Analysis PANACEA adapts a bi-directional graph convolutional networks model (BiGCN) (Bian et al., 2020) to perform rumour detection, which is trained on Twitter16 and fine-tuned on our annotated propagation trees. The reason we chose BiGCN is that it behaves relatively better compared with

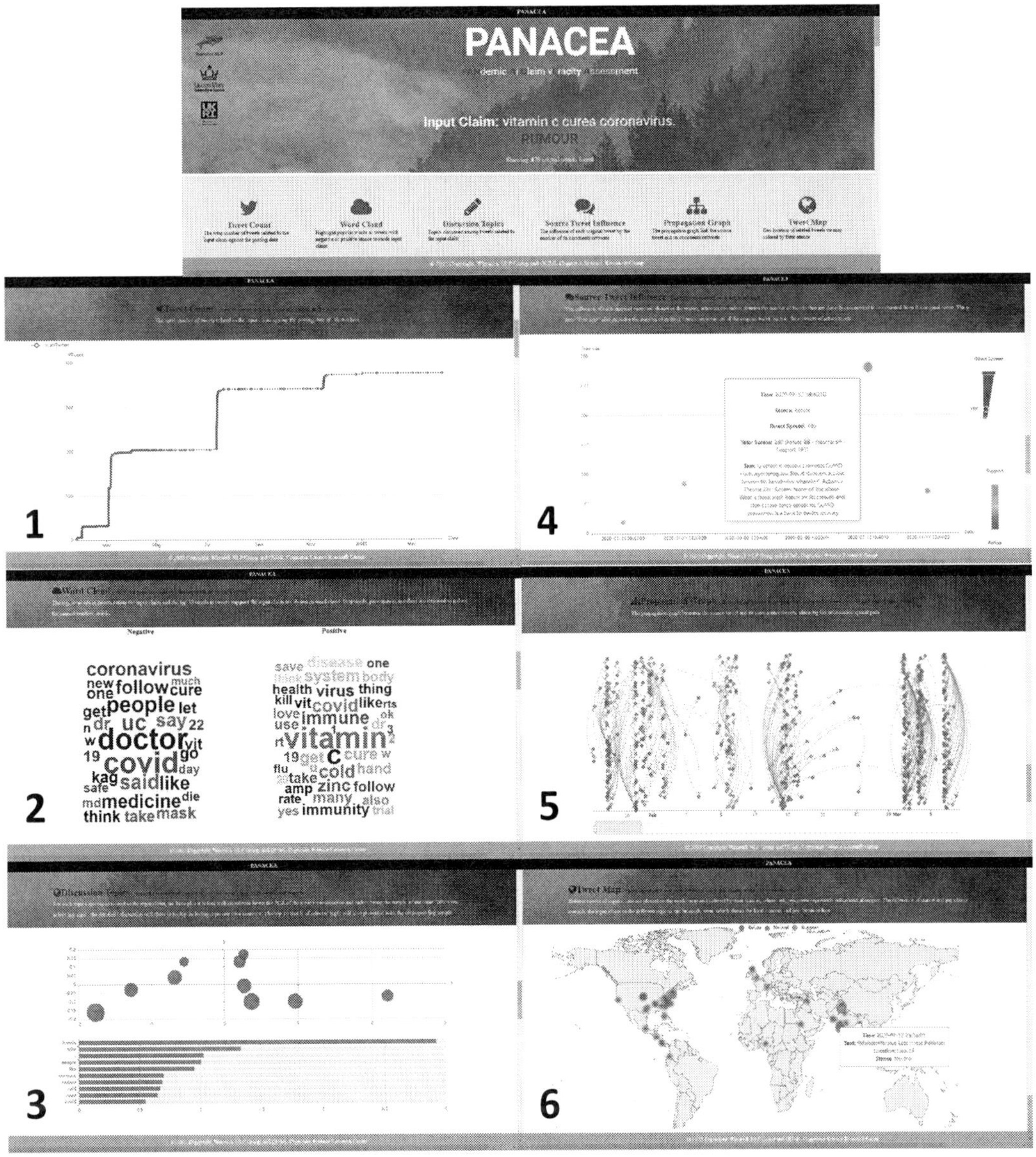

Figure 4: Rumour detection result with input claim: *vitamin c cures coronavirus.*

other models in cross-dataset evaluation (Kochkina et al., 2023). For an input claim, the system gives the rumour detection result generated by the weighted average of propagation trees' rumour assessment label, $\frac{\sum_{i \in T} n_i r_i}{\sum_{j \in T} n_j}$, where T is the set of retrieved propagation trees. We generate the sentiment labels of each tweet by VADER[8] and stance of tweet towards the input claims by natural language inference (Nie et al., 2020).

[8]https://www.nltk.org/api/nltk.sentiment.vader.html

Twitter propagation visualisation As shown in Figure 4, PANACEA has six modules, which use the metadata we crawled from the tweet and generated from data analysis to visualise the propagation pattern:

1. Tweet Count, showing the total number of tweets related to the input claim against the posting date, and aiming to reflect the total influence and scale of discussion of the claim.

2. Word Cloud, showing the top 30 words in tweets refuting the input claim and the top 30 words in tweets supporting the input claim.

Stopwords, punctuation, and numbers are removed to reduce non-informative words.

3. Discussion Topics, building on Latent Dirichlet Allocation (LDA), where each topic is encoded by COVID-Twitter-BERT [9] and the representative tweet is selected by its embedding similarity with respect to the topic. Principal component analysis (PCA) is applied to visualise each topic. Top 10 words and corresponding weights of the chosen topic are shown in a bar chart.
4. Tweet Spread, showing the influence of each original tweet in the scatter plot, where the radius denotes the number of tweets that are direct comments or retweets from the original tweet. The y-axis "Total Spread" also includes the number of indirect comments/retweets of the original tweet, such as the retweets of retweets, etc.
5. Propagation Graph, showing the propagation graph between the source tweet and its comments, showing the information spread path. 5 other claims are randomly chosen from popular claims for users to compare propagation patterns. This module aims to visualise propagation graphs in a straightforward way and help users see the difference between trees of different types.
6. Tweet Map. Related tweets to the input claim are plotted on the world map and coloured by their stances, where *red/yellow/blue* represents *refute/neutral/support*. The difference in stance and popularity towards the input claim in the different regions can be easily seen, which shows the local context and geolocation bias.

4 Evaluation Results

Fact-Checking We investigate the performance of our system in document retrieval and veracity assessment in (Arana-Catania et al., 2022). Table 1 shows that combining BM25 and MonoT5 is the most effective approach for document retrieval of the selected techniques. In addition, Figure 5 shows that NLI-SAN achieves similar performance with KGAT (Liu et al., 2020), while having a simpler architecture for the application, and outperforms GEAR (Zhou et al., 2019).

[9] https://huggingface.co/digitalepidemiologylab/covid-twitter-bert-v2

	AP@5	AP@10	AP@20	AP@100
BM25	0.54	0.56	0.58	0.62
BM25+MonoBERT	0.52	0.55	0.58	0.62
BM25+MonoBERT	**0.55**	**0.58**	**0.60**	**0.62**
BM25+RM3+MonoT5	0.51	0.53	0.55	0.57

Table 1: Document retrieval on the PANACEA dataset.

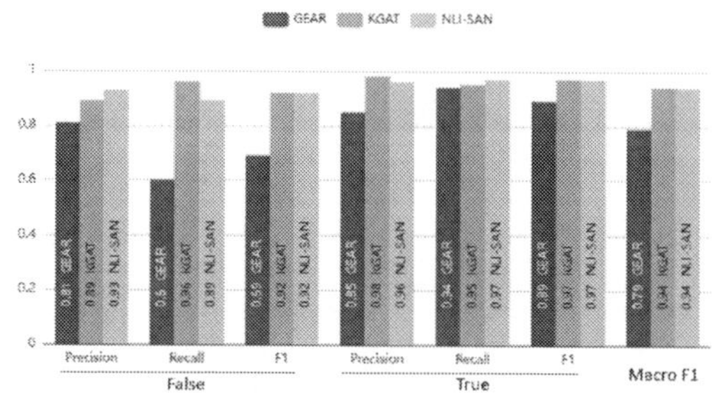

Figure 5: Veracity classification on the PANACEA dataset.

Rumour Detection As shown in Figure 6, our comparison (Kochkina et al., 2023) among various models, including branchLSTM (Kochkina and Liakata, 2020), TD-RvNN (Ma et al., 2018), BiGCN (Bian et al., 2020), SAVED (Dougrez-Lewis et al., 2021) and BERT (Devlin et al., 2019) for rumour detection evaluated on Twitter15, Twitter16 and PHEME (Kochkina et al., 2018), reveals there is no model that always performs the best. Although state-of-the-art models can achieve high accuracy on their training datasets, such performance drops quickly while evaluating on a different dataset (Kochkina et al., 2023). Due to the limitation of existing models in generalisation, users should interpret this result with caution as the system cannot guarantee output correctness.

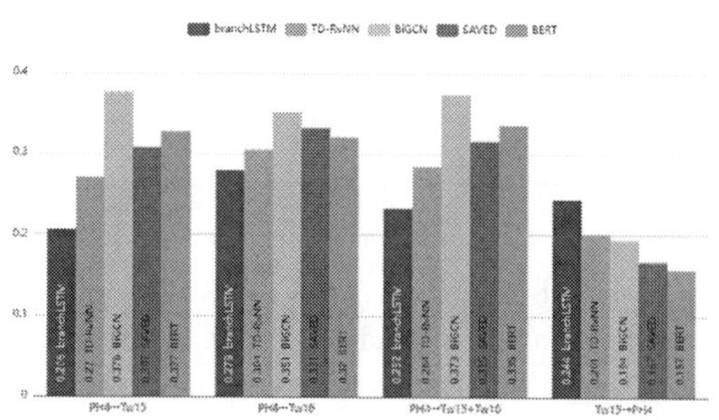

Figure 6: Cross-dataset evaluation of models train and test on different datasets, such as training on PHEME, testing on Twitter15/Twitter16 and vice versa.

5 Conclusion

This paper introduces a web-based system on *fact-checking* and *rumour detection* based on novel natural language processing models for COVID-19 misinformation detection. Going forward, we will keep updating the data and explore other methods for misinformation identification to improve the current system and introduce more functions to the system as part of our continuing efforts to support the general public to identify misinformation.

Acknowledgements

This work was supported by the UK Engineering and Physical Sciences Research Council (grant no. EP/V048597/1). YH and ML are each supported by a Turing AI Fellowship funded by the UK Research and Innovation (grant no. EP/V020579/1, EP/V030302/1).

References

Miguel Arana-Catania, Elena Kochkina, Arkaitz Zubiaga, Maria Liakata, Rob Procter, and Yulan He. 2022. Natural language inference with self-attention for veracity assessment of pandemic claims. In *Proceedings of the 2022 Annual Conference of the North American Chapter of the Association for Computational Linguistics*, pages 1496–1511.

Tian Bian, Xi Xiao, Tingyang Xu, Peilin Zhao, Wenbing Huang, Yu Rong, and Junzhou Huang. 2020. Rumor detection on social media with bi-directional graph convolutional networks. In *Proceedings of the 34th AAAI Conference on Artificial Intelligence*.

Emily Chen, Kristina Lerman, and Emilio Ferrara. 2020. Tracking social media discourse about the covid-19 pandemic: Development of a public coronavirus twitter data set. *JMIR Public Health Surveill*, 6(2).

Limeng Cui and Dongwon Lee. 2020. Coaid: Covid-19 healthcare misinformation dataset. *CoRR abs/2006.00885*.

Jacob Devlin, Ming-Wei Chang, Kenton Lee, and Kristina Toutanova. 2019. Bert: Pre-training of deep bidirectional transformers for language understanding. In *Proceedings of the 2019 conference of the North American chapter of the association for computational linguistics: human language technologies*, page 4171–4186.

John Dougrez-Lewis, Maria Liakata, Elena Kochkina, and Yulan He. 2021. Learning disentangled latent topics for twitter rumour veracity classification. In *Findings of the association for computational linguistics: ACL-IJCNLP 2021*, page 3902–3908.

Samantha Finn, Panagiotis Takis Metaxas, and Eni Mustafaraj. 2014. Investigating rumor propagation with twittertrails. *CoRR abs/1411.3550*.

Tamanna Hossain, Robert L. Logan IV, Arjuna Ugarte, Yoshitomo Matsubara, Sean Young, and Sameer Singh. 2020. Detecting covid-19 misinformation on social media. In *the 1st Workshop on NLP for COVID-19 (Part 2) at EMNLP 2020*.

Md Saiful Islam, Tonmoy Sarkar, Sazzad Hossain Khan, Abu-Hena Mostofa Kamal, SM Murshid Hasan, Alamgir Kabir, Dalia Yeasmin, Mohammad Ariful Islam, Kamal Ibne Amin Chowdhury, Kazi Selim Anwar, et al. 2020. Covid-19–related infodemic and its impact on public health: A global social media analysis. *The American journal of tropical medicine and hygiene*, 103(4):1621.

Elena Kochkina, Tamanna Hossainb, Robert L.Logan IV Miguel Arana-Catania, Rob Procter, Arkaitz Zubiaga, Sameer Singh, Yulan He, and Maria Liakata. 2023. Evaluating the generalisability of neural rumour verification models. *Information Processing & Management*, 60(1).

Elena Kochkina and Maria Liakata. 2020. Estimating predictive uncertainty for rumour verification models. In *Proceedings of the 58th Annual Meeting of the Association for Computational Linguistics*, page 6964–6981.

Elena Kochkina, Maria Liakata, and Arkaitz Zubiaga. 2018. All-in-one: Multi-task learning for rumour stance classification,detection and verification. In *Proceedings of the 27th International Conference on Computational Linguistics*, page 3402–3413.

Yichuan Li, Bohan Jiang, Kai Shu, and Huan Liu. 2020. Mm-covid: A multilingual and multimodal data repository for combating covid-19 disinformation. *CoRR abs/2011.04088*.

Zhenghao Liu, Chenyan Xiong, Maosong Sun, and Zhiyuan Liu. 2020. Fine-grained fact verification with kernel graph attention network. In *Proceedings of the 58th Annual Meeting of the Association for Computational Linguistics*, page 7342–7351.

Jing Ma, Wei Gao, and Kam-Fai Wong. 2018. Rumor detection on twitter with tree-structured recursive neural networks. In *Proceedings of the 56th Annual Meeting of the Association for Computational Linguistics*, page 1980–1989.

Yixin Nie, Adina Williams, Emily Dinan, Mohit Bansal, Jason Weston, and Douwe Kiela. 2020. Adversarial nli: A new benchmark for natural language understanding. In *Proceedings of the 58th Annual Meeting of the Association for Computational Linguistics*, page 4885–4901.

Rodrigo Nogueira, Zhiying Jiang, Ronak Pradeep, and Jimmy Lin. 2020. Document ranking with a pretrained sequence-to-sequence model. In *Proceedings of the 2020 Conference on Empirical Methods in Natural Language Processing: Findings*, page 708–718.

Gordon Pennycook, Ziv Epstein, Mohsen Mosleh, Antonio Arechar, Dean Eckles, and David Rand. 2020. Understanding and reducing the spread of misinformation online. *NA - Advances in Consumer Research*, 48:863–867.

Karishma Sharma, Sungyong Seo, Chuizheng Meng, Sirisha Rambhatla, and Yan Liu. 2020. Covid-19 on social media: Analyzing misinformation in twitter conversations. *CoRR abs/2003.12309*.

Lin Tian, Xiuzhen Zhang, and Jey Han Lau. 2022. Duck: Rumour detection on social media by modelling user and comment propagation networks. In *Proceedings of the North American Chapter of the Association for Computational Linguistics*, pages 4939 – 4949.

Yariv Tsfati, H. G. Boomgaarden, J. Strömbäck, R. Vliegenthart, A. Damstra, and E. Lindgren. 2020. Causes and consequences of mainstream media dissemination of fake news: literature review and synthesis. *Annals of the International Communication Association*, 44(2):157–173.

Ellen Voorhees, Tasmeer Alam, Steven Bedrick, Dina Demner-Fushman, William R Hersh, Kyle Lo, Kirk Roberts, Ian Soboroff, and Lucy Lu Wang. 2021. Trec-covid: constructing a pandemic information retrieval test collection. In *ACM SIGIR Forum*.

Wenhui Wang, Furu Wei, Li Dong, Hangbo Bao, Nan Yang, and Ming Zhou. 2020a. Minilm: Deep self-attention distillation for task-agnostic compression of pre-trained transformers. *CoRR abs/2002.10957*.

Xuan Wang, Yingjun Guan, Weili Liu, Aabhas Chauhan, Enyi Jiang, Qi Li, , David Liem, Dibakar Sigdel, J. Harry Caufield, Peipei Ping, and Jiawei Han. 2020b. Evidenceminer: Textual evidence discovery for life sciences. In *Proceedings of the 58th Annual Meeting of the Association for Computational Linguistics*, page 56–62.

Zilong Zhao, Jichang Zhao, Yukie Sano, Orr Levy, Hideki Takayasu, Misako Takayasu, Daqing Li, Junjie Wu, and Shlomo Havlin. 2020. Fake news propagates differently from real news even at early stages of spreading. *EPJ Data Science*, 9(7).

Jie Zhou, Xu Han, Cheng Yang, Zhiyuan Liu, Lifeng Wang, Changcheng Li, and Maosong Sun. 2019. Gear: Graph-based evidence aggregating and reasoning for fact verification. In *Proceedings of the 57th Annual Meeting of the Association for Computational Linguistics*, page 892–901.

Zhengyuan Zhu, Kevin Meng, Josue Caraballo, Israa Jaradat, Xiao Shi, Zeyu Zhang, Farahnaz Akrami, Fatma Arslan Haojin Liao, Damian Jimenez, Mohammed Samiul Saeef, Paras Pathak, and Chengkai Li. 2021. A dashboard for mitigating the covid-19 misinfodemic. In *Proceedings of the 16th Conference of the European Chapter of the Association for Computational Linguistics: System Demonstrations*, page 99–105.

NxPlain: A Web-based Tool for Discovery of Latent Concepts

Fahim Dalvi **Nadir Durrani** **Hassan Sajjad**[♣*]
Tamim Jaban **Mus'ab Husaini** **Ummar Abbas**
{faimaduddin,ndurrani}@hbku.edu.qa
Qatar Computing Research Institute, HBKU Research Complex, Doha, Qatar
[♣]Faculty of Computer Science, Dalhousie University, Halifax, Canada

Abstract

The proliferation of deep neural networks in various domains has seen an increased need for the interpretability of these models, especially in scenarios where fairness and trust are as important as model performance. A lot of independent work is being carried out to: i) analyze what linguistic and non-linguistic knowledge is learned within these models, and ii) highlight the salient parts of the input. We present **NxPlain**, a web application that provides an explanation of a model's prediction using latent concepts. NxPlain discovers latent concepts learned in a deep NLP model, provides an interpretation of the knowledge learned in the model, and explains its predictions based on the used concepts. The application allows users to browse through the latent concepts in an intuitive order, letting them efficiently scan through the most salient concepts with a global corpus-level view and a local sentence-level view. Our tool is useful for debugging, unraveling model bias, and for highlighting spurious correlations in a model. A hosted demo is available here: https://nxplain.qcri.org[1]

1 Introduction

Interpretation of deep neural networks (DNNs) has gained a lot of attention in recent years, especially in NLP, where state-of-the-art models are being widely deployed and used in practice. Work done in interpretation can be broadly classified into two branches: i) representation analysis and ii) attribution analysis. The former attempts to understand what knowledge is learned within the representation (Belinkov et al., 2017a; Tenney et al., 2019) and the latter is focused on how the model predicts the output (Linzen et al., 2016; Gulordava et al., 2018; Marvin and Linzen, 2018).[2]

A drawback of the methods in *representation analysis* is that it does not gauge whether the model uses what it has learned in making a prediction. On the other hand, the drawback of *attribution analysis* is that their explanations are limited to discrete units (e.g. words, some specific piece of the network), and the abstract nuances behind these discrete units are lost in the explanation, resulting in an inadequate or implausible explanation. Some efforts have been made in trying to connect representation and attribution analysis (Feder et al., 2021; Elazar et al., 2021).

In this work, we present **NxPlain**, a web-app that provides a holistic view by combining representation and attribution analysis. More specifically, we discover latent concepts in the model using the Latent Concept Analysis (Dalvi et al., 2022) and connect these concepts to specific predictions using Integrated Gradients (Sundararajan et al., 2017), a model and input saliency method.

NxPlain allows the users to:

- Discover latent concepts in *transformers* (Wolf et al., 2020) models via an interactive GUI
- Align the concepts using human-defined ontologies and task specific concepts
- Explain predictions using saliency-based attributions and extracted latent concepts

The analysis presented by **NxPlain** can enable a practitioner to understand a trained model better and be aware of the kinds of concepts a model is using to perform its tasks. For example, the word *immigrant* can appear as part of a neutral concept (if the model clusters it with other "roles" related to a person's status like "non-immigrant", "resident",

---

* This work was carried out while the author was at QCRI.

[1] A short video demo of the system is also available here: https://www.youtube.com/watch?v=C2Pi04fI5dk

[2] The following survey papers summarize the work done on *Representations Analysis* (Belinkov et al., 2020; Sajjad et al., 2021) and *Attribution Analysis* (Danilevsky et al., 2020)

Proceedings of the 17th Conference of the European Chapter of the Association for Computational Linguistics System Demonstrations, pages 75–83

(a) Terms used in hate-speech against immigration policies

(b) Syntactic concept of hyphenated words

(c) Concept made up of numbers

(d) Lexical concept (hyphenation) representing ages

(e) Morphological concept (*adjectives* with common suffix *est* signifying superlative adjectives

(f) Named entities in Germany

Figure 1: Examples of Latent Concepts.

etc), or it can appear as part of a negative concept (if the model clusters it with other hate-speech related terms like "alien", "illegal" etc.) as in Figure 1. Understanding which of these categorizations a model is learning and relying on can be a strong signal of the underlying biases of the model. A more benign example of debugging would also be able to see a purely lexical concept being used for prediction (say words ending in "y"), when the lexical property should not have any bearing on the task at hand. The target users for our system can be broadly divided into two categories: i) researchers/practitioners who want to understand their model better, and ii) other systems that want to use the concepts extracted by NxPlain to better explain predictions to their customers.

2 System Design

The overall system behind the **NxPlain** application is split into three distinct components. See Figure 2 for a pictorial representation.

- **`Backend`**: This part of the app integrates the `pipeline`, which handles i) extraction of latent concepts, ii) computation of various orderings, and iii) computation of the concepts relevant to particular sentences etc. A database is used to store all of the computed results so that the other two components can then use these results.
- **`Rest API`**: This piece displays the results from the `Backend` in an organized and machine-readable fashion. Users can use this to access the latent concepts and their relevant metadata for their applications.
- **`Frontend`**: This is the primary user-facing module of the app, and runs in a Web browser. The `frontend` provides an easy to use the graphical interface to add models to the computation queue and retrieve the extracted concepts once they are ready. Figure 4 shows the *Model Explanations* page, where one can browse all the extracted concepts, sort them according to various criteria and analyze the knowledge learned in the selected model.

Technical Details For extracting the concepts, we use the code provided by Dalvi et al. (2022). We then tag the input corpus with various human-defined tagsets such as Parts-of-Speech and Semantic tags, and align the latent concepts with these, as done by Sajjad et al. (2022). The results are then stored in a database, and retrieved later via a Python server implemented using Flask. The backend exposes a Rest API which can be used as-is by users in their own applications. We also provide an Angular frontend app that uses the Rest API to present the concepts in a GUI. For sentence-level explanations, we use the (Kokhlikyan et al.,

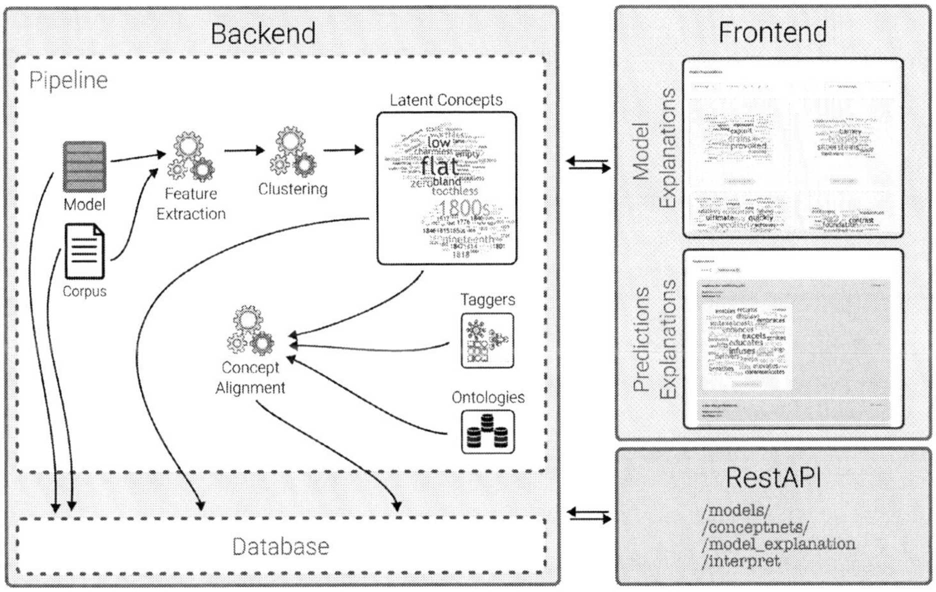

Figure 2: The architecture of NxPlain: The backend uses a pipeline to extract latent concepts and align them with various human ontologies and task-specific concepts. The frontend then uses the computed data to provide both global (model-level) and local (prediction-level) explanations. A RestAPI is also provided so a user can build upon the backend without having to use the provided frontend.

2020) tookit's Integrated Gradients implementation to perform attribution analysis.

3 Pipeline Components

The **NxPlain** application provides an easy interface to analyze the latent knowledge learned within a deep NLP model, as well as connect these latent concepts to specific predictions. In order to do this, the pipeline in the Backend relies on three key components proposed by recent literature: i) concept discovery, ii) concept alignment, and iii) attribution analysis.

3.1 Concept Discovery

The first component, responsible for extracting the latent concepts learned by a model is based on work done by Dalvi et al. (2022), called *Latent Concept Analysis*. At a high level, feature vectors (contextualized representations) are first generated by performing a forward pass on the model. These representations are then clustered using agglomerative hierarchical clustering (Gowda and Krishna, 1978) to discover the encoded concepts. The hypothesis is that contextualized word representations learned within pretrained language models capture *meaningful* groupings based on a coherent concept such as lexical, syntactic and semantic similarity, or any task or data specific pattern that groups the words together (Dalvi et al., 2022). Figure 1 shows example concepts discovered in the model space of a base and finetuned BERT model. The concepts discovered are a mix of linguistic, lexical and semantic concepts.

3.2 Concept Alignment

The second component uses an alignment framework proposed by Sajjad et al. (2022) to align each of the latent concepts to some pre-existing ontology like part-of-speech, semantic tags, WordNet etc. This enables richer explanations for the latent concepts, and also allows for the application to sort all of the concepts based on criteria relevant to the user. For instance, if the user is only interested in morphological latent concepts, the application can easily filter and sort all of the latent concepts based on this property after the alignment has been performed.

The alignment of a concept to a specific property (e.g. Noun) is done by checking if most of the words (above a certain threshold) in the concept are labeled with that property. For example, $C_{pos}(JJR) =$

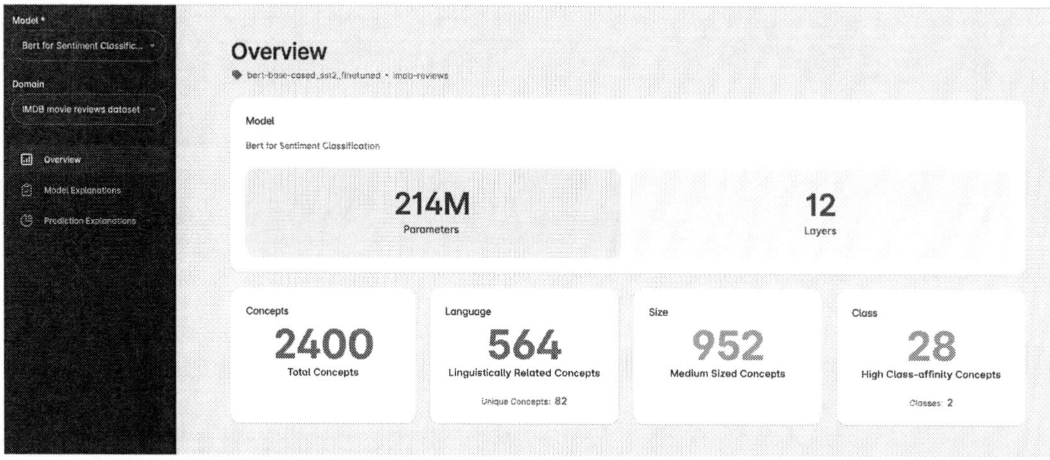

Figure 3: Sample overview page, providing high level statistics at a glance.

$\{greener, taller, happier, \ldots\}$ would be aligned to the property of "comparative adjectives" in the POS tagging task, $C_{sem}(MOY) = \{January, February, \ldots, December\}$ defines a concept containing months of the year in the semantic tagging task, and $C_{muslim}(names) = \{Ahmed, Muhammad, Karim, Hamdy, \ldots\}$ represents a concept of Muslim names. Explanations based on human-defined concepts are not always applicable or available as these models learn very fine-grained hierarchies of knowledge and concepts that are very task-specific, hence not every latent concept is aligned to some pre-existing tag/ontology.

3.3 Attribution Analysis

Our first two components are geared towards understanding what the model has learned, however, it does not necessarily imply that this knowledge is utilized during prediction and provides no insight into how these concepts are being used. To bridge this gap, our third component uses **Integrated Gradients** (IG) (Sundararajan et al., 2017), which is a powerful axiomatic attribution method for deep neural networks that computes the importance of input features and model components based on their contribution to model's prediction. More concretely, IG is used to extract the salient input features (words) used to make a certain prediction, and these salient features are then mapped to latent concepts to expand on the explanation. For example in Figure 5 highlights "captures" to be the most salient input feature used in predicting the sentiment of the sentence.

4 Frontend Views

The goal of **NxPlain** is to provide an easy method for users to extract and analyze latent knowledge learned within a deep NLP model and connect them to the prediction. The `Frontend` helps achieve this goal by providing a intuitive yet powerful GUI that can be used to interact with a model's latent concepts and predictions. The user can upload a model and a corpus that they want to analyze. The computational queue of the application discovers latent concepts and aligns them using the components mentioned in Section 3. The user can then use the `Frontend`, where they can switch between three major views:

Overall view: This view presents a high-level overview of the concepts learned by the model. Specifically, we can see i) the number of concepts learned, ii) statistics on the concepts aligned with the human-fined concepts, iii) a summary of the size distribution of these concepts, iv) and salient concepts in the data and model. Figure 3 shows a sample overview page for a Sentiment analysis model.

Model Explanations view: This view presents the latent concepts in a paginated view, along with controls to sort the concepts. Users can sort the concepts i) by size, ii) by their affinity to the linguistic phenomenon (using the alignments computed earlier), iii) by their relation to the various output classes (in classification models) and iv) by their overall relevance. Each concept is accompanied by a unique label to keep track of important concepts. See Figure 4 for a sample model explanation view.

Figure 4: The model-explanation page showing latent concepts for the selected model and domain. Sorting and pagination controls allow a user to effectively browse and analyze concepts learned by the model.

Prediction Explanations view: This view allows the user to look at concepts used in making a prediction and facilitates a deeper view of the behavior of the model on specific sentences. The *attribution analysis* component is used to get a salience map of the input tokens, as well as the matching concepts that contain these tokens in similar contexts. Figure 5 displays the prediction view, where the user can select the sentences that they want to analyze. Here NxPlain shows that "captures" was the most influential word used by the model to make the prediction. The model used a latent concept representing *positive verbs* to make the prediction.

5 Related Work

5.1 Toolkits

A number of toolkits have been made available to carry out analysis of neural network models. Google's What-If tool (Wexler et al., 2019) inspects machine learning models and provides users an insight into the trained model based on the predictions. Seq2Seq-Vis (Strobelt et al., 2018) enables the user to trace back the prediction decisions to the input in NMT models. Captum (Kokhlikyan et al., 2020) provides generic implementations of a number of gradient and perturbation-based attribution algorithms. NeuroX (Dalvi et al., 2019b) and Ecco (Alammar, 2021) use probing classifiers to examine the representations pre-trained language models. ConceptX (Alam et al., 2023) provides a framework for analyzing and annotating latent concepts in pre-trained language models. Tenney et al. (2020) facilitates debugging of pLMs through interactive visualizations. Our work is different from these toolkits. Our toolkit bridges the gap between representation analysis and causation by using attribution-based method. NxPlain provides enriched explanations using traditional linguistic knowledge and human-defined ontologies.

5.2 Research Works

A large number of studies primarily focus on understanding the knowledge learned within a trained model. Researchers have proposed numerous analysis frameworks such as diagnostic classifiers (Belinkov et al., 2017a; Hupkes et al., 2018), corpus analysis (Kádár et al., 2017; Poerner et al., 2018; Na et al., 2019), linguistic correlation analysis (Dalvi et al., 2019a; Lakretz et al., 2019). A plethora of work has been carried out using these analyses frameworks to analyze what concepts are learned within the representations through relevant extrinsic phenomenon varying from word morphology (Vylomova et al., 2017; Belinkov et al., 2017a; Dalvi et al., 2017) to high level concepts such as structure (Shi et al., 2016; Linzen et al., 2016) and semantics (Qian et al., 2016; Belinkov et al., 2017b) or more generic properties such as sentence length (Adi et al., 2016; Bau et al., 2019).

While the work done on representation analysis unwraps interesting insights about the knowledge learned within the network and how it is preserved,

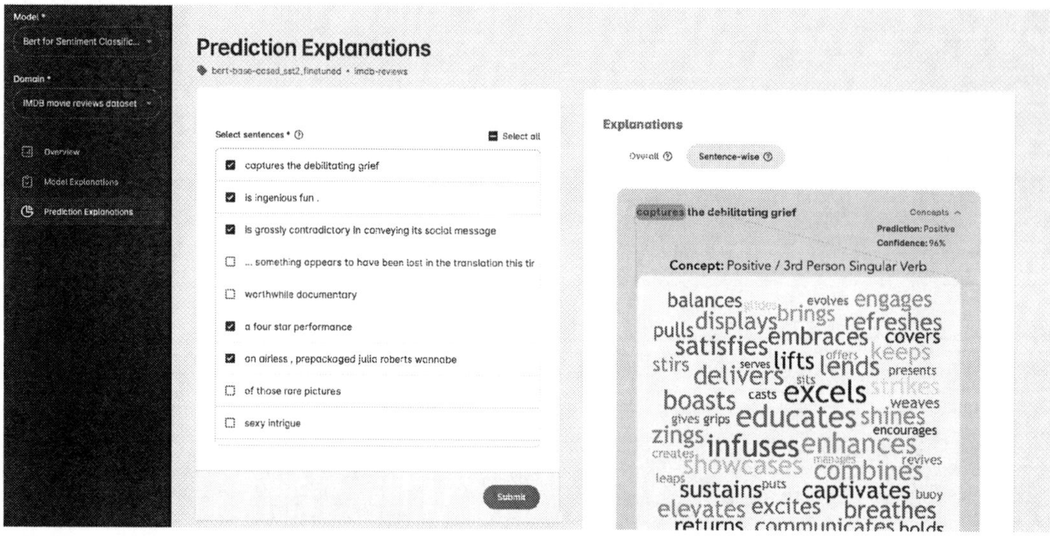

Figure 5: The prediction-explanation page showing latent concepts used during the prediction. The Integrated Gradients method highlights that capture is the most salient word used in the prediction. NxPlain connects it to the concept used along with its label. We observe here that the model used a concept representing positive verbs.

it's only limited to human-defined concepts. More recent work has discovered that these models capture novel ontologies (Michael et al., 2020; Dalvi et al., 2022; Fu and Lapata, 2022) learning linguistic concepts (Sajjad et al., 2022), as well as the task-specific concepts (Durrani et al., 2022) that emerge as the pre-trained language models are fine-tuned towards a task.

Another line of work in interpretability focuses on attribution analysis that characterizes the role of model components and input features towards a specific prediction (Linzen et al., 2016; Gulordava et al., 2018; Marvin and Linzen, 2018). The explanations are categorized based on two aspects: local or global (Guidotti et al., 2018). The former gives a view of explanation at a level of individual instance (Ribeiro et al., 2016; Alvarez-Melis and Jaakkola, 2017), whereas the latter explains the general behavior of the model at corpus level (Pryzant et al., 2018; Pröllochs et al., 2019).

6 Conclusion

We presented **NxPlain**, a web-app for connecting concept analysis with model prediction. The application bridges *representation analysis* and *attribution analysis* to better explain the models' predictions, and provides a intuitive, yet powerful graphical interface to explore the knowledge learned by a model, and also to pinpoint the knowledge used in specific predictions. In the future, we plan to enable human-in-the-loop to enhance concept alignment, as well as incorporate feedback into the explanation system. A hosted version of the application can be accessed at `https://nxplain.qcri.org`.

References

Yossi Adi, Einat Kermany, Yonatan Belinkov, Ofer Lavi, and Yoav Goldberg. 2016. Fine-grained Analysis of Sentence Embeddings Using Auxiliary Prediction Tasks. *arXiv preprint arXiv:1608.04207*.

Firoj Alam, Fahim Dalvi, Nadir Durrani, Hassan Sajjad, Abdul Rafae Khan, and Jia Xu. 2023. Conceptx: A framework for latent concept analysis. *Proceedings of the AAAI Conference on Artificial Intelligence*.

J Alammar. 2021. Ecco: an open source library for the explainability of transformer language models. In *Proceedings of the 59th Annual Meeting of the Association for Computational Linguistics and the 11th International Joint Conference on Natural Language Processing: System Demonstrations*, pages 249–257.

David Alvarez-Melis and Tommi Jaakkola. 2017. A causal framework for explaining the predictions of black-box sequence-to-sequence models. In *Proceedings of the 2017 Conference on Empirical Methods in Natural Language Processing*, pages 412–421, Copenhagen, Denmark. Association for Computational Linguistics.

Anthony Bau, Yonatan Belinkov, Hassan Sajjad, Nadir Durrani, Fahim Dalvi, and James Glass. 2019. Identifying and controlling important neurons in neural machine translation. In *Proceedings of the Seventh International Conference on Learning Representations*, ICLR '19, New Orleans, USA.

Yonatan Belinkov, Nadir Durrani, Fahim Dalvi, Hassan Sajjad, and James Glass. 2017a. What do neural machine translation models learn about morphology? In *Proceedings of the 55th Annual Meeting of the Association for Computational Linguistics*, ACL '17, pages 861–872, Vancouver, Canada. Association for Computational Linguistics.

Yonatan Belinkov, Nadir Durrani, Fahim Dalvi, Hassan Sajjad, and James Glass. 2020. On the linguistic representational power of neural machine translation models. *Computational Linguistics*, 45(1):1–57.

Yonatan Belinkov, Lluís Màrquez, Hassan Sajjad, Nadir Durrani, Fahim Dalvi, and James Glass. 2017b. Evaluating layers of representation in neural machine translation on part-of-speech and semantic tagging tasks. In *Proceedings of the Eighth International Joint Conference on Natural Language Processing*, IJCNLP '17, pages 1–10, Taipei, Taiwan. Asian Federation of Natural Language Processing.

Fahim Dalvi, Nadir Durrani, Hassan Sajjad, Yonatan Belinkov, D. Anthony Bau, and James Glass. 2019a. What is one grain of sand in the desert? analyzing individual neurons in deep nlp models. In *Proceedings of the Thirty-Third AAAI Conference on Artificial Intelligence*, AAAI '19, pages 6309–6317, Honolulu, Hawaii, USA. AAAI.

Fahim Dalvi, Nadir Durrani, Hassan Sajjad, Yonatan Belinkov, and Stephan Vogel. 2017. Understanding and Improving Morphological Learning in the Neural Machine Translation Decoder. In *Proceedings of the 8th International Joint Conference on Natural Language Processing (IJCNLP)*.

Fahim Dalvi, Abdul Rafae Khan, Firoj Alam, Nadir Durrani, Jia Xu, and Hassan Sajjad. 2022. Discovering latent concepts learned in BERT. In *Proceedings of the Tenth International Conference on Learning Representations*, ICLR '22, Online.

Fahim Dalvi, Avery Nortonsmith, D. Anthony Bau, Yonatan Belinkov, Hassan Sajjad, Nadir Durrani, and James Glass. 2019b. Neurox: A toolkit for analyzing individual neurons in neural networks. In *Proceedings of the AAAI Conference on Artificial Intelligence*, AAAI '19, pages 9851–9852, Honolulu, USA.

Marina Danilevsky, Kun Qian, Ranit Aharonov, Yannis Katsis, Ban Kawas, and Prithviraj Sen. 2020. A survey of the state of explainable AI for natural language processing. In *Proceedings of the 1st Conference of the Asia-Pacific Chapter of the Association for Computational Linguistics and the 10th International Joint Conference on Natural Language Processing*, pages 447–459, Suzhou, China. Association for Computational Linguistics.

Nadir Durrani, Hassan Sajjad, Fahim Dalvi, and Firoj Alam. 2022. On the transformation of latent space in fine-tuned nlp models. In *Proceedings of the 2022 Conference on Empirical Methods in Natural Language Processing*, EMNLP, Abu Dhabi, UAE. Association for Computational Linguistics.

Yanai Elazar, Shauli Ravfogel, Alon Jacovi, and Yoav Goldberg. 2021. Amnesic probing: Behavioral explanation with amnesic counterfactuals. *Transactions of the Association for Computational Linguistics*, 9:160–175.

Amir Feder, Nadav Oved, Uri Shalit, and Roi Reichart. 2021. CausaLM: Causal model explanation through counterfactual language models. *Computational Linguistics*, 47(2):333–386.

Yao Fu and Mirella Lapata. 2022. Latent topology induction for understanding contextualized representations.

K Chidananda Gowda and G Krishna. 1978. Agglomerative clustering using the concept of mutual nearest neighbourhood. *Pattern recognition*, 10(2):105–112.

Riccardo Guidotti, Anna Monreale, Franco Turini, Dino Pedreschi, and Fosca Giannotti. 2018. A survey of methods for explaining black box models. *CoRR*, abs/1802.01933.

Kristina Gulordava, Piotr Bojanowski, Edouard Grave, Tal Linzen, and Marco Baroni. 2018. Colorless green recurrent networks dream hierarchically. In *Proceedings of the 2018 Conference of the North American Chapter of the Association for Computational Linguistics: Human Language Technologies*, NAACL '18, pages 1195–1205, New Orleans, Louisiana, USA. Association for Computational Linguistics.

Dieuwke Hupkes, Sara Veldhoen, and Willem Zuidema. 2018. Visualisation and 'diagnostic classifiers' reveal how recurrent and recursive neural networks process hierarchical structure. *arXiv:1711.10203*.

Akos Kádár, Grzegorz Chrupała, and Afra Alishahi. 2017. Representation of linguistic form and function in recurrent neural networks. *Computational Linguistics*, 43(4):761–780.

Narine Kokhlikyan, Vivek Miglani, Miguel Martin, Edward Wang, Bilal Alsallakh, Jonathan Reynolds, Alexander Melnikov, Natalia Kliushkina, Carlos Araya, Siqi Yan, and Orion Reblitz-Richardson. 2020. Captum: A unified and generic model interpretability library for pytorch.

Yair Lakretz, German Kruszewski, Theo Desbordes, Dieuwke Hupkes, Stanislas Dehaene, and Marco Baroni. 2019. The emergence of number and syntax units in LSTM language models. In *Proceedings of the 2019 Conference of the North American Chapter of the Association for Computational Linguistics: Human Language Technologies, Volume 1 (Long and Short Papers)*, pages 11–20, Minneapolis, Minnesota. Association for Computational Linguistics.

Tal Linzen, Emmanuel Dupoux, and Yoav Goldberg. 2016. Assessing the ability of LSTMs to learn syntax-sensitive dependencies. *Transactions of the Association for Computational Linguistics*, 4:521– 535.

Rebecca Marvin and Tal Linzen. 2018. Targeted syntactic evaluation of language models. In *Proceedings of the 2018 Conference on Empirical Methods in Natural Language Processing*, pages 1192–1202, Brussels, Belgium. Association for Computational Linguistics.

Julian Michael, Jan A. Botha, and Ian Tenney. 2020. Asking without telling: Exploring latent ontologies in contextual representations. In *Proceedings of the 2020 Conference on Empirical Methods in Natural Language Processing*, EMNLP '20, pages 6792–6812, Online. Association for Computational Linguistics.

Seil Na, Yo Joong Choe, Dong-Hyun Lee, and Gunhee Kim. 2019. Discovery of natural language concepts in individual units of CNNs. *CoRR*, abs/1902.07249.

Nina Poerner, Benjamin Roth, and Hinrich Schütze. 2018. Interpretable textual neuron representations for NLP. In *Proceedings of the 2018 EMNLP Workshop BlackboxNLP: Analyzing and Interpreting Neural Networks for NLP*, pages 325–327, Brussels, Belgium. Association for Computational Linguistics.

Nicolas Pröllochs, Stefan Feuerriegel, and Dirk Neumann. 2019. Learning interpretable negation rules via weak supervision at document level: A reinforcement learning approach. In *Proceedings of the 2019 Conference of the North American Chapter of the Association for Computational Linguistics: Human Language Technologies, Volume 1 (Long and Short Papers)*, pages 407–413, Minneapolis, Minnesota. Association for Computational Linguistics.

Reid Pryzant, Sugato Basu, and Kazoo Sone. 2018. Interpretable neural architectures for attributing an ad's performance to its writing style. In *Proceedings of the 2018 EMNLP Workshop BlackboxNLP: Analyzing and Interpreting Neural Networks for NLP*, pages 125–135, Brussels, Belgium. Association for Computational Linguistics.

Peng Qian, Xipeng Qiu, and Xuanjing Huang. 2016. Investigating Language Universal and Specific Properties in Word Embeddings. In *Proceedings of the 54th Annual Meeting of the Association for Computational Linguistics*, ACL '16, pages 1478–1488, Berlin, Germany. Association for Computational Linguistics.

Marco Tulio Ribeiro, Sameer Singh, and Carlos Guestrin. 2016. "why should I trust you?": Explaining the predictions of any classifier. In *Proceedings of the 22nd ACM SIGKDD International Conference on Knowledge Discovery and Data Mining, San Francisco, CA, USA, August 13-17, 2016*, pages 1135–1144.

Hassan Sajjad, Nadir Durrani, and Fahim Dalvi. 2021. Neuron-level Interpretation of Deep NLP Models: A Survey. *CoRR*, abs/2108.13138.

Hassan Sajjad, Nadir Durrani, Fahim Dalvi, Firoj Alam, Abdul Khan, and Jia Xu. 2022. Analyzing encoded concepts in transformer language models. In *Proceedings of the 2022 Conference of the North American Chapter of the Association for Computational Linguistics: Human Language Technologies*, pages 3082–3101, Seattle, United States. Association for Computational Linguistics.

Xing Shi, Inkit Padhi, and Kevin Knight. 2016. Does string-based neural MT learn source syntax? In *Proceedings of the 2016 Conference on Empirical Methods in Natural Language Processing*, EMNLP '16, pages 1526–1534, Austin, TX, USA.

Hendrik Strobelt, Sebastian Gehrmann, Michael Behrisch, Adam Perer, Hanspeter Pfister, and Alexander Rush. 2018. Debugging sequence-to-sequence models with Seq2Seq-vis. In *Proceedings of the 2018 EMNLP Workshop BlackboxNLP: Analyzing and Interpreting Neural Networks for NLP*, pages 368–370, Brussels, Belgium. Association for Computational Linguistics.

Mukund Sundararajan, Ankur Taly, and Qiqi Yan. 2017. Axiomatic attribution for deep networks. *CoRR*, abs/1703.01365.

Ian Tenney, Dipanjan Das, and Ellie Pavlick. 2019. BERT rediscovers the classical NLP pipeline. In *Proceedings of the 57th Annual Meeting of the Association for Computational Linguistics*, pages 4593–4601, Florence, Italy. Association for Computational Linguistics.

Ian Tenney, James Wexler, Jasmijn Bastings, Tolga Bolukbasi, Andy Coenen, Sebastian Gehrmann, Ellen Jiang, Mahima Pushkarna, Carey Radebaugh, Emily Reif, and Ann Yuan. 2020. The language interpretability tool: Extensible, interactive visualizations and analysis for NLP models. In *Proceedings of the 2020 Conference on Empirical Methods in Natural Language Processing: System Demonstrations*, pages 107–118, Online. Association for Computational Linguistics.

Ekaterina Vylomova, Trevor Cohn, Xuanli He, and Gholamreza Haffari. 2017. Word representation models for morphologically rich languages in neural machine translation. In *Proceedings of the First Workshop on Subword and Character Level Models in NLP*, pages 103–108, Copenhagen, Denmark. Association for Computational Linguistics.

James Wexler, Mahima Pushkarna, Tolga Bolukbasi, Martin Wattenberg, Fernanda Viegas, and Jimbo Wilson. 2019. The what-if tool: Interactive probing of machine learning models. *IEEE Transactions on Visualization and Computer Graphics*, pages 1–1.

Thomas Wolf, Lysandre Debut, Victor Sanh, Julien Chaumond, Clement Delangue, Anthony Moi, Pierric Cistac, Tim Rault, Rémi Louf, Morgan Funtowicz, Joe Davison, Sam Shleifer, Patrick von Platen, Clara Ma, Yacine Jernite, Julien Plu, Canwen Xu, Teven Le

Scao, Sylvain Gugger, Mariama Drame, Quentin Lhoest, and Alexander M. Rush. 2020. Transformers: State-of-the-art natural language processing. In *Proceedings of the 2020 Conference on Empirical Methods in Natural Language Processing: System Demonstrations*, pages 38–45, Online. Association for Computational Linguistics.

Small-Text: Active Learning for Text Classification in Python

Christopher Schröder[1], **Lydia Müller**[1,2], **Andreas Niekler**[1], **Martin Potthast**[1,3]

[1]Leipzig University
[2]Institute for Applied Informatics (InfAI), Leipzig
[3]ScaDS.AI

Abstract

We introduce `small-text`, an easy-to-use active learning library, which offers pool-based active learning for single- and multi-label text classification in Python. It features numerous pre-implemented state-of-the-art query strategies, including some that leverage the GPU. Standardized interfaces allow the combination of a variety of classifiers, query strategies, and stopping criteria, facilitating a quick mix and match, and enabling a rapid and convenient development of both active learning experiments and applications. With the objective of making various classifiers and query strategies accessible for active learning, `small-text` integrates several well-known machine learning libraries, namely `scikit-learn`, `PyTorch`, and Hugging Face `transformers`. The latter integrations are optionally installable extensions, so GPUs can be used but are not required. Using this new library, we investigate the performance of the recently published SetFit training paradigm, which we compare to vanilla transformer fine-tuning, finding that it matches the latter in classification accuracy while outperforming it in area under the curve. The library is available under the MIT License at https://github.com/webis-de/small-text, in version 1.3.0 at the time of writing.

1 Introduction

Text classification, like most modern machine learning applications, requires large amounts of training data to achieve state-of-the-art effectiveness. However, in many real-world use cases, labeled data does not exist and is expensive to obtain, especially when domain expertise is required. *Active Learning* (Lewis and Gale, 1994) solves this problem by repeatedly selecting unlabeled data instances that are deemed informative according to a so-called *query strategy*, and then having them labeled by an expert (see Figure 1a). A new model is then trained on all previously labeled data, and this process is repeated until a specified stopping criterion is met.

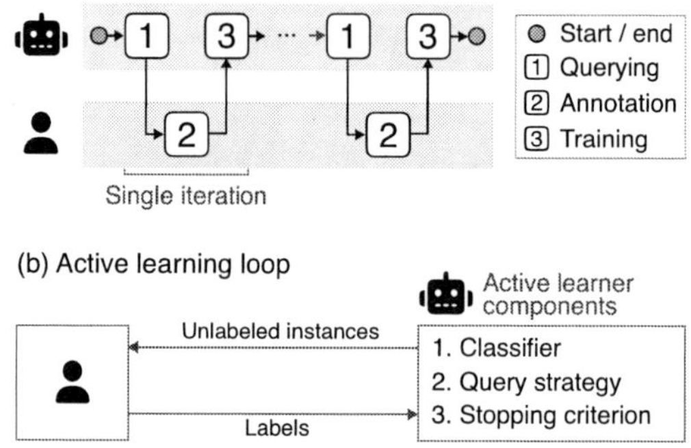

Figure 1: Illustrations of (a) the active learning process, and (b) the active learning setup with the components of the active learner.

Active learning aims to minimize the amount of labeled data required while maximizing the effectiveness (increase per iteration) of the model, e.g., in terms of classification accuracy.

An active learning setup, as shown in Figure 1b, generally consists of up to three components on the system side: a classifier, a query strategy, and an optional stopping criterion. Meanwhile, many approaches for each of these components have been proposed and studied. Determining appropriate combinations of these approaches is only possible experimentally, and efficient implementations are often nontrivial. In addition, the components often depend on each other, for example, when a query strategy relies on parts specific to certain model classes, such as gradients (Ash et al., 2020) or embeddings (Margatina et al., 2021). The more such non-trivial combinations are used together, the more the reproduction effort increases, making a modular library essential.

An obvious solution to the above problems is the use of open source libraries, which, among other benefits, accelerate research and facilitate technology transfer between researchers as well as into practice (Sonnenburg et al., 2007). While solu-

Proceedings of the 17th Conference of the European Chapter of the Association for Computational Linguistics System Demonstrations, pages 84–95
May 2-4, 2023

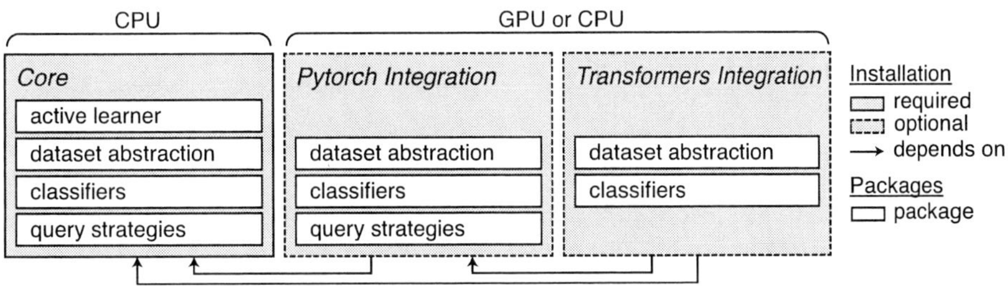

Figure 2: Module architecture of `small-text`. The core module can optionally be extended with a `PyTorch` and `transformers` integration, which enable to use GPU-based models and state-of-the-art transformer-based text classifiers of the Hugging Face `transformers` library, respectively. The dependencies between the module's packages have been omitted.

tions for active learning in general already exist, few address text classification, which requires features specific to natural language processing, such as word embeddings (Mikolov et al., 2013) or language models (Devlin et al., 2019). To fill this gap, we introduce `small-text`, an active learning library that provides tried and tested components for both experiments and applications.

2 Overview of Small-Text

The main goal of `small-text` is to offer state-of-the-art active learning for text classification in a convenient and robust way for both researchers and practitioners. For this purpose, we implemented a modular pool-based active learning mechanism, illustrated in Figure 2, which exposes interfaces for classifiers, query strategies, and stopping criteria. The core of `small-text` integrates `scikit-learn` (Pedregosa et al., 2011), enabling direct use of its classifiers. Overall, the library provides thirteen query strategies, including some that are only usable on text data, five stopping criteria, and two integrations of well-known machine learning libraries, namely `PyTorch` (Paszke et al., 2019) and `transformers` (Wolf et al., 2020). The integrations ease the use of CUDA-based GPU computing and transformer models, respectively. The modular architecture renders both integrations completely optional, resulting in a slim core that can also be used in a CPU-only scenario without unnecessary dependencies. Given the ability to combine a considerable variety of classifiers and query strategies, we can easily build a vast number of combinations of active learning setups.

The library provides relevant text classification baselines such as SVM (Joachims, 1998) and KimCNN (Kim, 2014), and many more can be used through `scikit-learn`. Recent transformer models such as BERT (Devlin et al., 2019) are available through the `transformers` integration. This integration also includes a wrapper that enables the use of the recently published SetFit training paradigm (Tunstall et al., 2022), which uses contrastive learning to fine-tune SBERT embeddings (Reimers and Gurevych, 2019) in a sample efficient manner.

As the query strategy, which selects the instances to be labeled, is the most salient component of an active learning setup, the range of alternative query strategies provided covers four paradigms at the time of writing: (i) confidence-based strategies: least confidence (Lewis and Gale, 1994; Culotta and McCallum, 2005), prediction entropy (Roy and McCallum, 2001), breaking ties (Luo et al., 2005), BALD (Houlsby et al., 2011), CVIRS (Reyes et al., 2018), and contrastive active learning (Margatina et al., 2021); (ii) embedding-based strategies: BADGE (Ash et al., 2020), BERT k-means (Yuan et al., 2020), discriminative active learning (Gissin and Shalev-Shwartz, 2019), and SEALS (Coleman et al., 2022); (iii) gradient-based strategies: expected gradient length (EGL; Settles et al., 2007), EGL-word (Zhang et al., 2017), and EGL-sm (Zhang et al., 2017); and (iv) coreset strategies: greedy coreset (Sener and Savarese, 2018) and lightweight coreset (Bachem et al., 2018). Since there is an abundance of query strategies, this list will likely never be exhaustive—also because strategies from other domains, such as computer vision, are not always applicable to the text domain, e.g., when using the geometry of images (Konyushkova et al., 2015), and thus will be disregarded here.

Furthermore, `small-text` includes a considerable amount of different stopping criteria: (i) stabilizing predictions (Bloodgood and Vijay-Shanker, 2009), (iv) overall-uncertainty (Zhu et al., 2008), (iii) classification-change (Zhu et al., 2008),

(ii) predicted change of F-measure (Altschuler and Bloodgood, 2019), and (v) a criterion that stops after a fixed number of iterations. Stopping criteria are often neglected in active learning although they exert a strong influence on labeling efficiency.

The library is available via the python packaging index and can be installed with just a single command: `pip install small-text`. Similarly, the integrations can be enabled using the extra requirements argument of Python's `setuptools`, e.g., the `transformers` integration is installed using `pip install small-text[transformers]`. The robustness of the implementation rests on extensive unit and integration tests. Detailed examples, an API documentation, and common usage patterns are available in the online documentation.[1]

3 Library versus Annotation Tool

We designed `small-text` for two types of settings: (i) experiments, which usually consist of either automated active learning evaluations or short-lived setups with one or more human annotators, and (ii) real-world applications, in which the final model is subsequently applied on unlabeled or unseen data. Both cases benefit from a library which offers a wide range of well-tested functionality.

To clarify on the distinction between a library and an annotation tool, `small-text` is a library, by which we mean a reusable set of functions and classes that can be used and combined within more complex programs. In contrast, annotation tools provide a graphical user interface and focus on the interaction between the user and the system. Obviously, `small-text` is still intended to be used by annotation tools but remains a standalone library. In this way it can be used (i) in combination with an annotation tool, (ii) within an experiment setting, or (iii) as part of a backend application, e.g. a web API. As a library it remains compatible to all of these use cases. This flexibility is supported by the library's modular architecture which is also in concordance with software engineering best practices, where high cohesion and low coupling (Myers, 1975) are known to contribute towards highly reusable software (Müller et al., 1993; Tonella, 2001). As a result, `small-text` should be compatible with most annotations tools that are extensible and support text classification.

[1] https://small-text.readthedocs.io

4 Code Example

In this section we show a code example to perform active learning with transformers models.

Dataset First, we create (for the sake of a simple example) a synthetic two-class spam dataset of 100 instances. The data is given by a list of texts and a list of integer labels. To define the tokenization strategy, we provide a `transformers` tokenizer. From these individual parts we construct a `TransformersDataset` object which is a dataset abstraction that can be used by the interfaces in `small-text`. This yields a binary text classification dataset containing 50 examples of the positive class (spam) and the negative class (ham) each:

```
import numpy as np
from small_text import TransformersDataset, \
    TransformerModelArguments
from transformers import AutoTokenizer

# Fake data example:
#    50 spam and 50 non-spam examples
text = np.array(['this is ham'] * 50 +
                ['this is spam'] * 50)
labels = np.array([0] * 50 + [1] * 50)

transformer_model = 'bert-base-uncased'
tokenizer = AutoTokenizer.from_pretrained(
    transformer_model)

train = TransformersDataset.from_arrays(
    text, labels, tokenizer,
    target_labels=np.array([0, 1]),
    max_length=10
)
```

Active Learning Configuration Next, we configure the classifier and query strategy. Although the active learner, query strategies, and stopping criteria components are dataset- and classifier-agnostic, classifier and dataset have to match (i.e. `TransformerBasedClassification` must be used with `TransformersDataset`) owing to the different underlying data structures:

```
from small_text import LeastConfidence, \
    TransformerBasedClassificationFactory \
    as TransformerFactory
num_classes = 2
model_args = TransformerModelArguments(
    transformer_model)

clf_factory = TransformerFactory(model_args,
    num_classes, kwargs={'device': 'cuda'})
query_strategy = LeastConfidence()
```

Since the active learner may need to instantiate a new classifier before the training step, a factory (Gamma et al., 1995) is responsible for creating new classifiers. Finally, we set the query strategy to least confidence (Culotta and McCallum, 2005).

Initialization There is a chicken-and-egg problem for active learning because most query strategies rely on the model, and a model in turn is trained on labeled instances which are selected by the query strategy. This problem can be solved by either providing an initial model (e.g. through manual labeling), or by using cold start approaches (Yuan et al., 2020). In this example we simulate a user-provided initialization by looking up the respective true labels and providing an initial model:

```
from small_text import \
    PoolBasedActiveLearner, \
    random_initialization_balanced as init

active_learner = PoolBasedActiveLearner(
    clf_factory, query_strategy, train)

# Provide initial data.
indices_initial = init(train.y, n_samples=10)

active_learner.initialize_data(
    indices_initial,
    train.y[indices_initial]
)
```

To provide an initial model in the experimental scenario (where true labels are accessible), `small-text` provides sampling methods, from which we use the balanced sampling to obtain a subset whose class distribution is balanced (or close thereto). In a real-world application, initialization would be accomplished through a starting set of labels supplied by the user. Alternatively, a cold start classifier or query strategy can be used instead.

Active Learning Loop After the previous code examples prepared the setting by loading a dataset, configuring the active learning setup, and providing an initial model, the following code block shows the actual active learning loop. In this example, we perform five queries during each of which ten instances are queried. During a query step the query strategy samples instances to be labeled. Subsequently, new labels for each instance are provided and passed to the `update` method, and then a new model is trained. In this example, it is a simulated response relying on true labels, but in a real-world application this part is the user's response.

```
from sklearn.metrics import accuracy_score

num_queries = 5
for i in range(num_queries):
    # Query 10 samples per iteration.
    indices_queried = active_learner.query(
        num_samples=10
    )

    # Simulate user interaction here.
    #   Replace this for real-world usage.
    y = train.y[indices_queried]

    # Provide labels for the queried indices.
    active_learner.update(y)

    # Evaluate accuracy on the train set
    print(f'Iteration {i+1}')
    y_pred = active_learner.classifier\
        .predict(train)
    print('Train accuracy: {:.2f}'.format(
        accuracy_score(y_pred, train.y)))
```

In summary, we built a full active learning setup in only very few lines of code. The actual active learning loop consists of just the previous code block and changing hyperparameters, e.g., using a different query strategy, is as easy as adapting the `query_strategy` variable.

5 Comparison to Previous Software

Unsurprisingly, after decades of research and development on active learning, numerous other libraries are available that focus on active learning as well. In the following we present a selection of the most relevant open-source projects for which either a related publication is available or a larger user base exists: `JCLAL` (Reyes et al., 2016) is a generic framework for active learning which is implemented in Java and can be used either through XML configurations or directly from the code. It offers an experimental setting which includes 18 query strategies. The aim of `libact` (Yang et al., 2017) is to provide active learning for real-world applications. Among 19 other strategies, it includes a well-known meta-learning strategy (Hsu and Lin, 2015). `BaaL` (Atighehchian et al., 2020) provides bayesian active learning including methods to obtain uncertainty estimates. The `modAL` library (Danka and Horvath, 2018) offers single- and multi-label active learning, provides 12 query strategies, also builds on `scikit-learn` by default, and offers instructions how to include GPU-based models using `Keras` and `PyTorch`. `ALiPy` (Tang et al., 2019) provides an active learning framework targeted at

Name	Active Learning			Code					
	QS	SC	Text Focus	GPU support	Unit Tests	Language	License	Last Update	Repository
JCLAL[1]	18	2	✖	✖	✖	Java	GPL	2017	
libact[2]	19	-	✖	✖	✔	Python	BSD-2-Clause	2021	
modAL[3]	12	-	✖	✔	✔	Python	MIT	2022	
ALiPy[4]	22	4	✖	✖	✔	Python	BSD-3-Clause	2022	
BaaL[5]	9	-	✖	✔	✔	Python	Apache 2.0	2023	
lrtc[6]	7	-	✔	✔	✖	Python	Apache 2.0	2021	
scikit-activeml[7]	29	-	✖	✔	✔	Python	BSD-3-Clause	2023	
ALToolbox[8]	19	-	✔	✔	✔	Python	MIT	2023	
small-text	14	5	✔	✔	✔	Python	MIT	2023	

Table 1: Comparison between `small-text` and relevant previous active learning libraries. We abbreviated the number of query strategies by "QS", the number of stopping criteria by "SC", and the `low-resource-text-classification` framework by `lrtc`. All information except "Publication Year" and "Code Repository" has been extracted from the linked GitHub repository of the respective library on February 24th, 2023. Random baselines were not counted towards the number of query strategies. Publications: [1]Reyes et al. (2016), [2]Yang et al. (2017), [3]Danka and Horvath (2018), [4]Tang et al. (2019), [5]Atighehchian et al. (2020), [6]Ein-Dor et al. (2020), [7]Kottke et al. (2021), [8]Tsvigun et al. (2022).

the experimental active learning setting. Apart from providing 22 query strategies, it supports alternative active learning settings, e.g., active learning with noisy annotators. The `low-resource-text-classification-framework` (`lrtc`; (Ein-Dor et al., 2020)) is an experimentation framework for the low resource scenario and supports which can be easily extended. It also focuses on text classification and has a number of built-in models, datasets, and query strategies to perform active learning experiments. Another recent library is `scikit-activeml` which offers general active learning built around `scikit-learn`. It comes with 29 query strategies but provides no stopping criteria. GPU-based functionality can be used via `skorch`,[2] a `PyTorch` wrapper, which is a ready-to-use adapter as opposed to our implemented classifier structures but is on the other hand restricted to the `scikit-learn` interfaces. `ALToolbox` (Tsvigun et al., 2022) is an active learning framework that provides an annotation interface and a benchmarking mechanism to develop new query strategies. While it has some overlap with `small-text`, it is not a library, but also focuses on text data, namely on text classification and sequence tagging.

In Table 1, we compare `small-text` to the previously mentioned libraries, and compare them based on several criteria related to active learning or to the respective code base: While all libraries provide a selection of query strategies, not all libraries offer stopping criteria, which are crucial to reducing the total annotation effort and thus directly influence the efficiency of the active learning process (Vlachos, 2008; Laws and Schütze, 2008; Olsson and Tomanek, 2009). We can also see a difference in the number of provided query strategies. While a higher number of query strategies is certainly not a disadvantage, it is more important to provide the most relevant strategies (either due to recency, domain-specificity, strong general performance, or because it is a baseline). Based on these criteria, `small-text` provides numerous recent strategies such as BADGE (Ash et al., 2020), BERT K-Means (Yuan et al., 2020), and contrastive active learning (Margatina et al., 2021), as well as the gradient-based strategies by Zhang et al. (2017), where the latter are unique to active learning for text classification. Selecting a subset of query strategies is especially important since active learning experiments are computationally expensive (Margatina et al., 2021; Schröder et al., 2022), and therefore not every strategy can be tested in the context of an experiment or application. Finally, only `small-text`, `lrtc`, and `ALToolbox` focus on text, and only about half of the libraries offer access to GPU-based deep learning, which has become indispensable for text classification due to the recent advances and ubiquity of transformer-based models (Vaswani et al., 2017; Devlin et al., 2019).

The distinguishing characteristic of `small-text` is the focus on text classification, paired with a multitude of interchangeable components. It of-

[2]We also evaluated the use of `skorch` but transformer models were not supported at that time.

Dataset Name (ID)	Type	Classes	Training	Test
AG's News[1] (AGN)	N	4	120,000	*7,600
Customer Reviews[2] (CR)	S	2	3,397	378
Movie Reviews[3] (MR)	S	2	9,596	1,066
Subjectivity[4] (SUBJ)	S	2	9,000	1,000
TREC-6[5] (TREC-6)	Q	6	5,500	*500

Table 2: Key characteristics about the examined datasets: [1]Zhang et al. (2015), [2]Hu and Liu (2004), [3]Pang and Lee (2005), [4]Pang and Lee (2004), [5]Li and Roth (2002). The dataset type was abbreviated by N (News), S (Sentiment), Q (Questions). ⋆: Predefined test sets were available and adopted.

fers the most comprehensive set of features (as shown in Table 1) and through the integrations these components can be mixed and matched to easily build numerous different active learning setups, with or without leveraging the GPU. Finally, it allows to use concepts from natural language processing (such as transformer models) and provides query strategies unique to text classification.

6 Experiment

We perform an active learning experiment comparing an SBERT model trained with the recent sentence transformers fine-tuning paradigm (SetFit; (Tunstall et al., 2022)) over a BERT model trained with standard fine-tuning. SetFit is a contrastive learning approach that trains on pairs of (dis)similar instances. Given a fixed amount of differently labeled instances, the number of possible pairs is considerably higher than the size of the original set, making this approach highly sample efficient (Chuang et al., 2020; Hénaff, 2020) and therefore interesting for active learning.

Setup We reproduce the setup of our previous work (Schröder et al., 2022) and evaluate on the datasets shown in Table 2 with an extended set of query strategies. Starting with a pool-based active learning setup with 25 initial samples, we perform 20 queries during each of which 25 instances are queried and labeled. Since SetFit has only been evaluated for single-label classification (Tunstall et al., 2022), we focus on single-label classification as well. The goal is to compare the following two models: (i) BERT (`bert-large-uncased`; (Devlin et al., 2019)) with 336M parameters and (ii) SBERT (`paraphrase-mpnet-base-v2`; (Reimers and Gurevych, 2019)) with 110M parameters. The first model is trained via vanilla fine-tuning and the second using SetFit. For the sake of brevity, we refer to the first as "BERT" and to the second as "SetFit". To compare their performance during active learning, we provide an extensive benchmark over multiple computationally inexpensive uncertainty-based query strategies, which were selected due to encouraging results in our previous work. Moreover, we include BALD, BADGE, and greedy coreset—all of which are computationally more expensive, but have been increasingly used in recent work (Ein-Dor et al., 2020; Yu et al., 2022).

Model	Strategy	Rank		Result	
		Acc.	AUC	Acc.	AUC
BERT	PE	2.20	2.80	0.917	0.858
	BT	**1.40**	**1.60**	**0.919**	**0.868**
	LC	3.80	3.20	0.916	0.863
	CA	4.20	5.00	0.915	0.857
	BA	3.00	5.20	0.917	0.855
	BD	6.20	4.60	0.909	0.862
	CS	6.60	7.60	0.910	0.843
	RS	7.80	5.40	0.901	0.856
SetFit	PE	2.80	3.20	0.927	0.906
	BT	2.80	**1.60**	0.926	**0.912**
	LC	**2.20**	2.60	**0.927**	0.908
	CA	4.80	3.80	0.924	0.907
	BA	5.20	6.20	0.923	0.902
	BD	6.60	5.60	0.915	0.904
	CS	2.80	4.40	0.927	0.909
	RS	6.60	6.80	0.907	0.899

Table 3: The "Rank" columns show the mean rank when ordered by mean accuracy (Acc.) and by area under curve (AUC). The "Result" columns show the mean accuracy and AUC. All values used in this table refer to state after the final iteration. Query strategies are abbreviated as follows: prediction entropy (PE), breaking ties (BT), least confidence (LC), contrastive active learning (CA), BALD (BA), BADGE (BD), greedy coreset (CS), and random sampling (RS).

Results In Table 3, the results show the summarized classification performance in terms of (i) final accuracy after the last iteration, and (ii) area under curve (AUC). We also compare strategies by ranking them from 1 (best) to 8 (worst) per model and dataset by accuracy and AUC. First, we can also confirm for SetFit the earlier finding that uncertainty-based strategies perform strong for BERT (Schröder et al., 2022). Second, SetFit configurations result in between 0.06 and 1.7 percentage points higher mean accuracy, and also in betwen 4.2 and 6.6 higher AUC when averaged over model and query strategy. Interestingly, the greedy coreset strategy (CS) is remarkably more successful for the SetFit runs compared to the BERT runs. Detailed results per configuration can be found

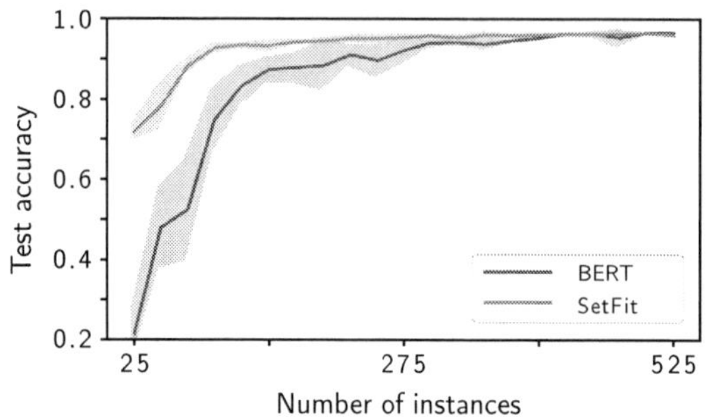

Figure 3: An exemplary learning curve showing the difference in test accuracy for breaking ties strategy on the TREC dataset, comparing BERT and SetFit. The tubes represent the standard deviation across five runs.

in the appendix, where it can be seen that SetFit reaches higher accuracy scores in most configurations, and better AUC scores in all configurations.

Discussion When trained with the new SetFit paradigm, models having only a third of the parameters compared to the large BERT model achieve results that are not only competitive, but slightly better regarding final accuracy and considerably better in terms of AUC. Since the final accuracy values are often within one percentage point or less to each other, it is obvious that the improvement in AUC stems from improvements in earlier queries, i.e. steeper learning curves. We suspect that this is at least partly owed to sample efficiency from SetFit's training that uses pairs of instances. Moreover, this has the additional benefit of reducing instability of transformer models (Mosbach et al., 2021) as can be exemplarily seen in Figure 3. This increasingly occurs when the training set is small (Mosbach et al., 2021), which is likely alleviated with the additional instance pairs. On the other hand, training cost increase linearly with the number of pairs per instance. In the low-data regime, however, this is a manageable additional cost that is worth the benefits.

7 Library Adoption

As recent publications have already adopted `small-text`, we present four examples which have already successfully utilized it for their experiments.

Abusive Language Detection Kirk et al. (2022) investigated the detection of abusive language using transformer-based active learning on six datasets of which two exhibited a balanced and four an imbalanced class distribution. They evaluated a pool-based binary active learning setup, and their main finding is that, when using active learning, a model for abusive language detection can be efficiently trained using only a fraction of the data.

Classification of Citizens' Contributions In order to support the automated classification of German texts from online citizen participation processes, Romberg and Escher (2022) used active learning to classify texts collected by three cities into eight different topics. They evaluated this real-world dataset both as a single- and multi-label active learning setup, finding that active learning can considerably reduce the annotation efforts.

Softmax Confidence Estimates Gonsior et al. (2022) examined several alternatives to the softmax function to obtain better confidence estimates for active learning. Their setup extended small-text to incorporate additional softmax alternatives and found that confidence-based methods mostly selected outliers. As a remedy to this they proposed and evaluated uncertainty clipping.

Revisiting Uncertainty-Based Strategies In a previous publication, we reevaluated traditional uncertainty-based query strategies with recent transformer models (Schröder et al., 2022). We found that uncertainty-based methods can still be highly effective and that the breaking ties strategy is a drop-in replacement for prediction entropy.

Not only have all of these works successfully applied small-text to a variety of different problems, but each work is also accompanied by a GitHub repository containing the experiment code, which is the outcome we had hoped for. We expect that `small-text` will continue to gain adoption within the active learning and text classification communities, so that future experiments will increasingly rely on it by both reusing existing components and by creating their own extensions, thereby supporting the field through open reproducible research.

8 Conclusion

We introduced `small-text`, a modular Python library, which offers state-of-the-art active learning for text classification. It integrates `scikit-learn`, `PyTorch`, and `transformers`, and provides robust components that can be mixed and matched to quickly apply active learning in both experiments and applications, thereby making active learning easily accessible to the Python ecosystem.

Limitations

Although a library can, among other things, lower the barrier of entry, save time, and speed up research, this can only be leveraged with basic knowledge of the Python programming language. All included algorithmic components are subject to their own limitations, e.g., the greedy coreset strategy quickly becomes computationally expensive as the amount labeled data increases. Moreover, some components have hyperparameters which require an understanding of the algorithm to achieve the best classification performance. In the end, we provide a powerful set of tools which still has to be properly used to achieve the best results.

As `small-text` covers numerous text classification models, query strategies, and stopping criteria, some limitations from natural language processing, text classification and active learning apply as well. For example, all included classification models rely on tokenization, which is inherently more difficult for languages which have no clear word boundaries such as Chinese, Japanese, Korean, or Thai.

Ethics Statement

In this paper, we presented `small-text`, a library which can—like any other software—be used for good or bad. It can be used to bootstrap classification models in scenarios where no labeled data is available. This could be used for good, e.g. for spam detection, hatespeech detection, or targeted news filtering, but also for bad, e.g., for creating models that detect certain topics that are to be censored in authoritarian regimes. While such systems already exist and are of sophisticated quality, `small-text` is unlikely to change anything at this point. On the contrary, being open-source software, these methods can now be used by a larger audience, which contributes towards the democratization of classification algorithms.

Acknowledgments

We thank the anonymous reviewers for their constructive advice and the early adopters of the library for their invaluable feedback.

This research was partially funded by the Development Bank of Saxony (SAB) under project numbers 100335729 and 100400221. Computations were done (in part) using resources of the Leipzig University Computing Centre.

References

Michael Altschuler and Michael Bloodgood. 2019. Stopping active learning based on predicted change of F measure for text classification. In *2019 IEEE 13th International Conference on Semantic Computing (ICSC)*, pages 47–54. IEEE.

Jordan T. Ash, Chicheng Zhang, Akshay Krishnamurthy, John Langford, and Alekh Agarwal. 2020. Deep batch active learning by diverse, uncertain gradient lower bounds. In *Proceedings of the 8th International Conference on Learning Representations (ICLR)*. OpenReview.net.

Parmida Atighehchian, Frédéric Branchaud-Charron, and Alexandre Lacoste. 2020. Bayesian active learning for production, a systematic study and a reusable library. *arXiv preprint arXiv:2006.09916*.

Olivier Bachem, Mario Lucic, and Andreas Krause. 2018. Scalable k-Means Clustering via Lightweight Coresets. In *Proceedings of the 24th ACM SIGKDD International Conference on Knowledge Discovery & Data Mining, (KDD)*, pages 1119–1127.

Michael Bloodgood and K. Vijay-Shanker. 2009. A method for stopping active learning based on stabilizing predictions and the need for user-adjustable stopping. In *Proceedings of the Thirteenth Conference on Computational Natural Language Learning (CoNLL-2009)*, pages 39–47, Boulder, Colorado. Association for Computational Linguistics.

Ching-Yao Chuang, Joshua Robinson, Yen-Chen Lin, Antonio Torralba, and Stefanie Jegelka. 2020. Debiased contrastive learning. In *Advances in Neural Information Processing Systems 33 (NeurIPS)*, volume 33, pages 8765–8775. Curran Associates, Inc.

Cody Coleman, Edward Chou, Julian Katz-Samuels, Sean Culatana, Peter Bailis, Alexander C. Berg, Robert Nowak, Roshan Sumbaly, Matei Zaharia, and I. Zeki Yalniz. 2022. Similarity search for efficient active learning and search of rare concepts. *Proceedings of the AAAI Conference on Artificial Intelligence (AAAI)*, 36(6):6402–6410.

Aron Culotta and Andrew McCallum. 2005. Reducing labeling effort for structured prediction tasks. In *Proceedings of the 20th National Conference on Artificial Intelligence (AAAI)*, volume 2, pages 746–751.

Tivadar Danka and Peter Horvath. 2018. modAL: A modular active learning framework for Python. *arXiv preprint arXiv:1805.00979*.

Jacob Devlin, Ming-Wei Chang, Kenton Lee, and Kristina Toutanova. 2019. BERT: Pre-training of deep bidirectional transformers for language understanding. In *Proceedings of the 2019 Conference of the North American Chapter of the Association for Computational Linguistics (NAACL)*, pages 4171–4186. Association for Computational Linguistics.

Liat Ein-Dor, Alon Halfon, Ariel Gera, Eyal Shnarch, Lena Dankin, Leshem Choshen, Marina Danilevsky, Ranit Aharonov, Yoav Katz, and Noam Slonim. 2020. Active Learning for BERT: An Empirical Study. In *Proceedings of the 2020 Conference on Empirical Methods in Natural Language Processing (EMNLP)*, pages 7949–7962, Online. Association for Computational Linguistics.

Erich Gamma, Richard Helm, Ralph Johnson, and John Vlissides. 1995. *Design Patterns: Elements of Reusable Object-Oriented Software*, 1 edition. Addison-Wesley Longman Publishing Co., Inc., USA. 37. Reprint.

Daniel Gissin and Shai Shalev-Shwartz. 2019. Discriminative active learning. *arXiv preprint arXiv:1907.06347*.

Julius Gonsior, Christian Falkenberg, Silvio Magino, Anja Reusch, Maik Thiele, and Wolfgang Lehner. 2022. To softmax, or not to softmax: that is the question when applying active learning for transformer models. *arXiv preprint arXiv:2210.03005*.

Olivier J. Hénaff. 2020. Data-efficient image recognition with contrastive predictive coding. In *Proceedings of the 37th International Conference on Machine Learning, ICML 2020, 13-18 July 2020, Virtual Event*, volume 119 of *Proceedings of Machine Learning Research*, pages 4182–4192. PMLR.

Neil Houlsby, Ferenc Huszar, Zoubin Ghahramani, and Máté Lengyel. 2011. Bayesian active learning for classification and preference learning. *arXiv preprint arXiv:1112.5745*.

Wei-Ning Hsu and Hsuan-Tien Lin. 2015. Active learning by learning. *Proceedings of the 29th AAAI Conference on Artificial Intelligence (AAAI)*, 29(1).

Minqing Hu and Bing Liu. 2004. Mining and summarizing customer reviews. In *Proceedings of the Tenth ACM SIGKDD International Conference on Knowledge Discovery and Data Mining*, KDD '04, pages 168–177, New York, NY, USA. Association for Computing Machinery.

Thorsten Joachims. 1998. Text categorization with support vector machines: Learning with many relevant features. In *Machine Learning: ECML-98, 10th European Conference on Machine Learning, Chemnitz, Germany, April 21-23, 1998, Proceedings*, volume 1398 of *Lecture Notes in Computer Science*, pages 137–142. Springer.

Yoon Kim. 2014. Convolutional neural networks for sentence classification. In *Proceedings of the 2014 Conference on Empirical Methods in Natural Language Processing (EMNLP)*, pages 1746–1751.

Hannah Kirk, Bertie Vidgen, and Scott Hale. 2022. Is More Data Better? Re-thinking the Importance of Efficiency in Abusive Language Detection with Transformers-Based Active Learning. In *Proceedings of the Third Workshop on Threat, Aggression and Cyberbullying (TRAC 2022)*, pages 52–61, Gyeongju, Republic of Korea. Association for Computational Linguistics.

Ksenia Konyushkova, Raphael Sznitman, and Pascal Fua. 2015. Introducing geometry in active learning for image segmentation. In *Proceedings of the IEEE International Conference on Computer Vision (ICCV)*, pages 2974–2982.

Daniel Kottke, Marek Herde, Tuan Pham Minh, Alexander Benz, Pascal Mergard, Atal Roghman, Christoph Sandrock, and Bernhard Sick. 2021. scikitactiveml: A Library and Toolbox for Active Learning Algorithms. *Preprints.org*.

Florian Laws and Hinrich Schütze. 2008. Stopping criteria for active learning of named entity recognition. In *Proceedings of the 22nd International Conference on Computational Linguistics (COLING)*, pages 465–472.

David D. Lewis and William A. Gale. 1994. A sequential algorithm for training text classifiers. In *Proceedings of the 17th Annual International ACM-SIGIR Conference on Research and Development in Information Retrieval*, pages 3–12.

Xin Li and Dan Roth. 2002. Learning question classifiers. In *Proceedings of the 19th International Conference on Computational Linguistics (COLING)*, volume 1 of *COLING '02*, pages 1–7, USA. Association for Computational Linguistics.

Tong Luo, Kurt Kramer, Dmitry B. Goldgof, Lawrence O. Hall, Scott Samson, Andrew Remsen, and Thomas Hopkins. 2005. Active Learning to Recognize Multiple Types of Plankton. *Journal of Machine Learning Research (JMLR)*, 6:589–613.

Katerina Margatina, Giorgos Vernikos, Loïc Barrault, and Nikolaos Aletras. 2021. Active learning by acquiring contrastive examples. In *Proceedings of the 2021 Conference on Empirical Methods in Natural Language Processing (EMNLP)*, pages 650–663.

Tomás Mikolov, Kai Chen, Greg Corrado, and Jeffrey Dean. 2013. Efficient estimation of word representations in vector space. In *Proceedings of the 1st International Conference on Learning Representations (ICLR)*.

Marius Mosbach, Maksym Andriushchenko, and Dietrich Klakow. 2021. On the stability of finetuning BERT: misconceptions, explanations, and strong baselines. In *Proceedings of the 9th International Conference on Learning Representations (ICLR 2021)*. OpenReview.net.

Hausi A. Müller, Mehmet A. Orgun, Scott R. Tilley, and James S. Uhl. 1993. A reverse-engineering approach to subsystem structure identification. *Journal of Software Maintenance: Research and Practice*, 5(4):181–204.

Glenford J. Myers. 1975. *Reliable Software through Composite Design*. Petrocelli/Charter.

Fredrik Olsson and Katrin Tomanek. 2009. An intrinsic stopping criterion for committee-based active learning. In *Proceedings of the Thirteenth Conference on Computational Natural Language Learning (CoNLL)*, pages 138–146.

Bo Pang and Lillian Lee. 2004. A sentimental education: Sentiment analysis using subjectivity summarization based on minimum cuts. In *Proceedings of the 42nd Annual Meeting of the Association for Computational Linguistics (ACL)*, pages 271–278, Barcelona, Spain.

Bo Pang and Lillian Lee. 2005. Seeing stars: Exploiting class relationships for sentiment categorization with respect to rating scales. In *Proceedings of the 43rd Annual Meeting of the Association for Computational Linguistics (ACL)*, pages 115–124, Ann Arbor, Michigan. Association for Computational Linguistics.

Adam Paszke, Sam Gross, Francisco Massa, Adam Lerer, James Bradbury, Gregory Chanan, Trevor Killeen, Zeming Lin, Natalia Gimelshein, Luca Antiga, Alban Desmaison, Andreas Kopf, Edward Yang, Zachary DeVito, Martin Raison, Alykhan Tejani, Sasank Chilamkurthy, Benoit Steiner, Lu Fang, Junjie Bai, and Soumith Chintala. 2019. Pytorch: An imperative style, high-performance deep learning library. In *Advances in Neural Information Processing Systems 32*, pages 8024–8035.

Fabian Pedregosa, Gaël Varoquaux, Alexandre Gramfort, Vincent Michel, Bertrand Thirion, Olivier Grisel, Mathieu Blondel, Peter Prettenhofer, Ron Weiss, Vincent Dubourg, Jake Vanderplas, Alexandre Passos, David Cournapeau, Matthieu Brucher, Matthieu Perrot, and Édouard Duchesnay. 2011. Scikit-learn: Machine learning in python. *Journal of Machine Learning Research (JMLR)*, 12(85):2825–2830.

Nils Reimers and Iryna Gurevych. 2019. Sentence-BERT: Sentence embeddings using Siamese BERT-networks. In *Proceedings of the 2019 Conference on Empirical Methods in Natural Language Processing and the 9th International Joint Conference on Natural Language Processing (EMNLP-IJCNLP)*, pages 3982–3992, Hong Kong, China. Association for Computational Linguistics.

Oscar Reyes, Carlos Morell, and Sebastián Ventura. 2018. Effective active learning strategy for multi-label learning. *Neurocomputing*, 273:494–508.

Oscar Reyes, Eduardo Pérez, María del Carmen Rodríguez-Hernández, Habib M. Fardoun, and Sebastián Ventura. 2016. JCLAL: A Java Framework for Active Learning. *Journal of Machine Learning Research (JMLR)*, 17(95):1–5.

Julia Romberg and Tobias Escher. 2022. Automated topic categorisation of citizens' contributions: Reducing manual labelling efforts through active learning. In *Electronic Government*, pages 369–385, Cham. Springer International Publishing.

Nicholas Roy and Andrew McCallum. 2001. Toward optimal active learning through sampling estimation of error reduction. In *Proceedings of the Eighteenth International Conference on Machine Learning (ICML)*, pages 441–448.

Christopher Schröder, Andreas Niekler, and Martin Potthast. 2022. Revisiting uncertainty-based query strategies for active learning with transformers. In *Findings of the Association for Computational Linguistics: ACL 2022 (Findings of ACL 2022)*, pages 2194–2203.

Ozan Sener and Silvio Savarese. 2018. Active learning for convolutional neural networks: A core-set approach. In *Proceedings of the 6th International Conference on Learning Representations (ICLR)*.

Burr Settles, Mark Craven, and Soumya Ray. 2007. Multiple-instance active learning. In *Proceedings of the 20th International Conference on Neural Information Processing Systems (NIPS)*, pages 1289–1296.

Sören Sonnenburg, Mikio L. Braun, Cheng Soon Ong, Samy Bengio, Leon Bottou, Geoffrey Holmes, Yann LeCun, Klaus-Robert Müller, Fernando Pereira, Carl Edward Rasmussen, Gunnar Rätsch, Bernhard Schölkopf, Alexander Smola, Pascal Vincent, Jason Weston, and Robert Williamson. 2007. The Need for Open Source Software in Machine Learning. *Journal of Machine Learning Research (JMLR)*, 8(81):2443–2466.

Ying-Peng Tang, Guo-Xiang Li, and Sheng-Jun Huang. 2019. ALiPy: Active learning in python. *arXiv preprint arXiv:1901.03802*.

Paolo Tonella. 2001. Concept analysis for module restructuring. *IEEE Trans. Software Eng.*, 27(4):351–363.

Akim Tsvigun, Leonid Sanochkin, Daniil Larionov, Gleb Kuzmin, Artem Vazhentsev, Ivan Lazichny, Nikita Khromov, Danil Kireev, Aleksandr Rubashevskii, and Olga Shahmatova. 2022. ALToolbox: A set of tools for active learning annotation of natural language texts. In *Proceedings of the The 2022 Conference on Empirical Methods in Natural Language Processing: System Demonstrations*, pages 406–434, Abu Dhabi, UAE. Association for Computational Linguistics.

Lewis Tunstall, Nils Reimers, Unso Eun Seo Jo, Luke Bates, Daniel Korat, Moshe Wasserblat, and Oren Pereg. 2022. Efficient few-shot learning without prompts. *arXiv preprint arXiv:2209.11055*.

Ashish Vaswani, Noam Shazeer, Niki Parmar, Jakob Uszkoreit, Llion Jones, Aidan N Gomez, Łukasz Kaiser, and Illia Polosukhin. 2017. Attention is all you need. In *Proceedings of the Advances in Neural Information Processing Systems 30 (NeurIPS)*, pages 5998–6008.

Andreas Vlachos. 2008. A stopping criterion for active learning. *Computer Speech & Language*, 22(3):295–312.

Thomas Wolf, Lysandre Debut, Victor Sanh, Julien Chaumond, Clement Delangue, Anthony Moi, Pierric Cistac, Tim Rault, Rémi Louf, Morgan Funtowicz, Joe Davison, Sam Shleifer, Patrick von Platen, Clara Ma, Yacine Jernite, Julien Plu, Canwen Xu, Teven Le Scao, Sylvain Gugger, Mariama Drame, Quentin Lhoest, and Alexander M. Rush. 2020. Transformers: State-of-the-art natural language processing. In *Proceedings of the 2020 Conference on Empirical Methods in Natural Language Processing: System Demonstrations (EMNLP)*, pages 38–45.

Yao-Yuan Yang, Shao-Chuan Lee, Yu-An Chung, Tung-En Wu, Si-An Chen, and Hsuan-Tien Lin. 2017. libact: Pool-based active learning in python. *arXiv preprint arXiv:1710.00379*.

Yue Yu, Lingkai Kong, Jieyu Zhang, Rongzhi Zhang, and Chao Zhang. 2022. AcTune: Uncertainty-based active self-training for active fine-tuning of pretrained language models. In *Proceedings of the 2022 Conference of the North American Chapter of the Association for Computational Linguistics: Human Language Technologies*, pages 1422–1436, Seattle, United States. Association for Computational Linguistics.

Michelle Yuan, Hsuan-Tien Lin, and Jordan Boyd-Graber. 2020. Cold-start active learning through self-supervised language modeling. In *Proceedings of the 2020 Conference on Empirical Methods in Natural Language Processing (EMNLP)*, pages 7935–7948. Association for Computational Linguistics.

Xiang Zhang, Junbo Zhao, and Yann LeCun. 2015. Character-level convolutional networks for text classification. In C. Cortes, N. D. Lawrence, D. D. Lee, M. Sugiyama, and R. Garnett, editors, *Proceedings of the Advances in Neural Information Processing Systems 28 (NIPS)*, pages 649–657. Curran Associates, Inc., Montreal, Quebec, Canada.

Ye Zhang, Matthew Lease, and Byron C. Wallace. 2017. Active discriminative text representation learning. In *Proceedings of the 31st AAAI Conference on Artificial Intelligence (AAAI)*, pages 3386–3392.

Jingbo Zhu, Huizhen Wang, and Eduard Hovy. 2008. Multi-criteria-based strategy to stop active learning for data annotation. In *Proceedings of the 22nd International Conference on Computational Linguistics (Coling 2008)*, pages 1129–1136, Manchester, UK. Coling 2008 Organizing Committee.

Supplementary Material

A Technical Environment

All experiments were conducted within a Python 3.8 environment. The system had CUDA 11.1 installed and was equipped with an NVIDIA GeForce RTX 2080 Ti (11GB VRAM).

B Experiments

Each experiment configuration represents a combination of model, dataset and query strategy, and has been run for five times.

B.1 Datasets

We used datasets that are well-known benchmarks in text classification and active learning. All datasets are accessible to the Python ecosystem via Python libraries that provide fast access to those datasets. We obtained CR and SUBJ using gluonnlp, and AGN, MR, and TREC using huggingface datasets.

B.2 Pre-Trained Models

In the experiments, we fine-tuned (i) a large BERT model (bert-large-uncased) and (ii) an SBERT paraphrase-mpnet-base model (sentence-transformers/paraphrase-mpnet-base-v2). Both are available via the huggingface model repository.

B.3 Hyperparameters

Maximum Sequence Length We set the maximum sequence length to the minimum multiple of ten, so that 95% of the given dataset's sentences contain at most that many tokens.

Transformer Models For BERT, we adopt the hyperparameters from Schröder et al. (2022). For SetFit, we use the same learning rate and optimizer parameters but we train for only one epoch.

C Evaluation

In Table 4 and Table 5 we report final accuracy and AUC scores including standard deviations, measured after the last iteration. Note that results obtained through PE, BT, and LC are equivalent for binary datasets.

C.1 Evaluation Metrics

Active learning was evaluated using standard metrics, namely accuracy und area under the learning curve. For both metrics, the respective scikit-learn implementation was used.

Dataset	Model	Query Strategy							
		PE	BT	LC	CA	BA	BD	CS	RS
AGN	BERT	0.898 0.003	0.901 0.004	0.900 0.001	0.889 0.010	0.889 0.008	0.894 0.003	0.881 0.006	0.886 0.004
	SetFit	0.900 0.002	0.902 0.004	**0.902 0.002**	0.892 0.006	0.887 0.010	0.896 0.003	0.896 0.003	0.877 0.005
CR	BERT	0.920 0.009	0.920 0.009	0.916 0.006	0.917 0.010	0.919 0.010	0.911 0.010	0.915 0.012	0.902 0.014
	SetFit	0.937 0.014	0.937 0.014	0.937 0.014	0.938 0.009	0.934 0.004	0.913 0.011	**0.939 0.011**	0.912 0.010
MR	BERT	0.850 0.005	0.850 0.005	0.846 0.008	0.844 0.008	0.859 0.003	0.835 0.017	0.843 0.006	0.831 0.020
	SetFit	0.871 0.009	0.871 0.009	0.871 0.009	0.869 0.004	0.867 0.005	0.864 0.008	0.870 0.008	**0.871 0.003**
SUBJ	BERT	0.959 0.005	0.959 0.005	0.958 0.003	0.958 0.008	0.959 0.003	0.948 0.006	0.957 0.004	0.937 0.006
	SetFit	0.962 0.004	0.962 0.004	0.962 0.004	0.960 0.002	**0.966 0.002**	0.942 0.002	0.963 0.003	0.932 0.005
TREC-6	BERT	0.960 0.002	0.966 0.003	0.960 0.008	0.965 0.006	0.958 0.007	0.958 0.009	0.952 0.015	0.947 0.009
	SetFit	0.966 0.005	0.961 0.005	0.966 0.005	0.963 0.008	0.961 0.005	0.958 0.005	**0.967 0.004**	0.946 0.009

Table 4: Final accuracy per dataset, model, and query strategy. We report the mean and standard deviation over five runs. The best result per dataset is printed in bold. Query strategies are abbreviated as follows: prediction entropy (PE), breaking ties (BT), least confidence (LC), contrastive active learning (CA), BALD (BA), BADGE (BD), greedy coreset (CS), and random sampling (RS). The best result per dataset is printed in bold.

Dataset	Model	Query Strategy							
		PE	BT	LC	CA	BA	BD	CS	RS
AGN	BERT	0.827 0.009	0.839 0.014	0.836 0.009	0.821 0.015	0.819 0.012	0.840 0.003	0.804 0.012	0.825 0.011
	SetFit	0.881 0.002	**0.889 0.003**	0.885 0.005	0.879 0.004	0.869 0.006	0.881 0.002	0.881 0.003	0.867 0.004
CR	BERT	0.885 0.007	0.885 0.007	0.881 0.007	0.881 0.011	0.882 0.006	0.876 0.005	0.874 0.011	0.877 0.011
	SetFit	0.925 0.001	0.925 0.001	0.925 0.001	0.927 0.003	0.924 0.005	0.910 0.005	**0.930 0.002**	0.908 0.008
MR	BERT	0.819 0.010	0.819 0.010	0.820 0.007	0.813 0.009	0.817 0.013	0.808 0.011	0.804 0.010	0.813 0.004
	SetFit	0.859 0.004	0.859 0.004	0.859 0.004	**0.859 0.003**	0.858 0.004	0.855 0.002	0.858 0.004	0.857 0.002
SUBJ	BERT	0.944 0.008	0.944 0.008	0.943 0.007	0.940 0.009	0.939 0.009	0.929 0.005	0.934 0.006	0.924 0.007
	SetFit	**0.953 0.002**	**0.953 0.002**	**0.953 0.002**	0.952 0.003	0.950 0.002	0.940 0.003	0.949 0.001	0.935 0.002
TREC-6	BERT	0.818 0.033	0.855 0.023	0.837 0.034	0.829 0.030	0.816 0.029	0.856 0.024	0.799 0.037	0.843 0.008
	SetFit	0.910 0.008	**0.934 0.005**	0.919 0.008	0.917 0.013	0.907 0.017	0.934 0.010	0.927 0.008	0.927 0.004

Table 5: Final area under curve (AUC) per dataset, model, and query strategy. We report the mean and standard deviation over five runs. The best result per dataset is printed in bold. Query strategies are abbreviated as follows: prediction entropy (PE), breaking ties (BT), least confidence (LC), contrastive active learning (CA), BALD (BA), BADGE (BD), greedy coreset (CS), and random sampling (RS). The best result per dataset is printed in bold.

D Library Adoption

As mentioned in Section 7, the experiment code of previous works documents how `small-text` was used and can be found at the following locations:

- Abusive Language Detection: https://github.com/HannahKirk/ActiveTransformers-for-AbusiveLanguage
- Classification of Citizens' Contributions: https://github.com/juliaromberg/egov-2022
- Softmax Confidence Estimates: https://github.com/jgonsior/btw-softmax-clipping
- Revisiting Uncertainty-Based Strategies: https://github.com/webis-de/ACL-22

kogito: A Commonsense Knowledge Inference Toolkit

Mete Ismayilzada
EPFL
mahammad.ismayilzada@epfl.ch

Antoine Bosselut
EPFL
antoine.bosselut@epfl.ch

Abstract

In this paper, we present kogito, an open-source tool for generating commonsense inferences about situations described in text. kogito provides an intuitive and extensible interface to interact with natural language generation models that can be used for hypothesizing commonsense knowledge inference from a textual input. In particular, kogito offers several features for targeted, multi-granularity knowledge generation. These include a standardized API for training and evaluating knowledge models, and generating and filtering inferences from them. We also include helper functions for converting natural language texts into a format ingestible by knowledge models — intermediate pipeline stages such as knowledge head extraction from text, heuristic and model-based knowledge head-relation matching, and an ability to define and use custom knowledge relations. We make the code for kogito available at https://github.com/epfl-nlp/kogito along with thorough documentation at https://kogito.readthedocs.io.

1 Introduction

In recent years, large-scale language models (Radford and Narasimhan, 2018; Devlin et al., 2019; Brown et al., 2020) trained on massive amounts of text have been conceptualized as implicit knowledge bases that encode knowledge about the world (Petroni et al., 2019; Roberts et al., 2020). As they are trained to receive natural language inputs, these models can be prompted to generate text that expresses a fact. Leveraging this property, *knowlege models* train on knowledge graph tuples (triplets of *head entity*, *relation*, *tail entity*) and learn to express knowledge encoded in the parameters of language models when provided with a *head entity* and *relation* (Bosselut et al., 2019; Hwang et al., 2021; Da et al., 2021; West et al., 2022).

The success of these *knowledge models* has inspired the field to deploy them in various downstream use-cases such as generating figurative language (Chakrabarty et al., 2020b), producing sarcastic responses (Chakrabarty et al., 2020a), designing plots for stories (Ammanabrolu et al., 2021) and text-based games (Dambekodi et al., 2020), and developing persona-grounded dialogue agents (Majumder et al., 2020). Given the prevalence of applications that benefit from augmenting NLP systems with commonsense inferences, we present a novel commonsense **K**n**O**wled**G**e **I**nference **TO**olkit, kogito, that standardizes commonsense inference generation from knowledge models. To the best of our knowledge, kogito is the first library that facilitates access to knowledge models through an easy-to-use, customizable interface. In particular, we make the following contributions:

1. A Python package[1] for knowledge inference with a customizable and extensible API.
2. A module to perform commonsense inference with a library of pretrained models, including GPT-2 (Radford et al., 2019), GPT-3 (Brown et al., 2020) and COMET (Hwang et al., 2021).
3. A standardized interface to train, evaluate and predict with knowledge models.
4. Modules to extract relevant candidates for commonsense inference (*i.e.*, head extraction) with support for customization and extension.
5. Modules to match relevant relations to extracted head entities (*i.e.*, relation matching) with support for customization and extension.
6. A module to filter commonsense inferences based on their contextual relevance using commonsense fact linkers (Gao et al., 2022)
7. Functionality to define novel knowledge relations on top of the built-in ATOMIC2020

[1] https://pypi.org/project/kogito/

Proceedings of the 17th Conference of the European Chapter of the Association for Computational Linguistics System Demonstrations, pages 96–104
May 2-4, 2023 ©2023 Association for Computational Linguistics

(Hwang et al., 2021) and ConceptNet (Speer and Havasi, 2013) relation sets.

8. Extensive documentation with User Guides and API Reference.[2]

The library is released under the Apache 2.0 License. We provide a demo video[3] for our library along with a live demo app.[4] Below, we outline the commonsense inference challenges addressed by this tool, its core design, and walk through its major components in more detail.

2 Challenges of Commonsense Inference

While many works use *knowledge models* as commonsense inference engines to augment natural language inputs, no work has formalized the pipeline for producing such inferences. Here, we outline the challenges of effectively setting up this pipeline.

Head Extraction Head extraction (*i.e.*, finding relevant concepts to produce commonsense inferences about) is a consistent challenge when using knowledge models. Typically, these inferences must be produced for more fine-grained textual units than full contexts (Bosselut et al., 2021). For instance, to understand figurative language, Chakrabarty et al. (2020b) extract concepts from similes such as *"Love is like a unicorn"*. Commonsense inferences are generated about entities such as *"unicorn"* (*e.g.*, unicorns are *rare*, *beautiful*, etc.), allowing them to produce literal interpretations of this figurative language: *"Love is rare"*. This use case motivates a need for fine-grained text extraction functionality in our tool. In Section 5, we outline our approach to address this challenge.

Relation Matching To generate commonsense inferences, knowledge models typically take as input a *(head, relation)* pair and produce a *tail* (*i.e.*, the commonsense inference about the *head* entity). Following this convention, once we have extracted candidate *heads* from a given text, they must be paired with relevant relations to produce valid commonsense inferences. For example, a head entity such as "go to mall" should not be paired with an `ObjectUse` relation as it is unlikely to produce a valid (and practical) commonsense inference. Consequently, a brute-force approach of matching all relations to presented head entities would be inadequate for most use cases. Current works often circumvent this challenge by manually selecting only a subset of available knowledge relations. As part of **kogito**, we implement various heuristic and model-based matching schemes to address this challenge, while also providing users with the ability to define their own matching mechanisms. We discuss these implementations in Section 6.

Inference Generation & Filtering Once a list of relevant *(head, relation)* pairs is produced, we run these examples through a knowledge model to generate tail entities about these examples. However, many of these generated inferences may not be relevant to the original context, particularly for extracted head entities that have been decontextualized. **kogito** leverages a model-based approach (Gao et al., 2022) to filter out irrelevant commonsense generations. While other works re-implement pipelines for performing these steps, **kogito** offers an all-in-one solution.

3 kogito: A Pipeline for Commonsense Inference

kogito is a pipeline for commonsense inference from text and supports various steps to specialize and customize inference behaviour. At full functionality, given a text input, **kogito** extracts relevant *knowledge heads* from textual inputs, and matches these heads to plausible *knowledge relations*, thereby constructing an incomplete *knowledge graph* of (*head*, *relation*) prompts. Then, this partial graph is input to a *knowledge model* to generate tails to complete the graph. Finally, these commonsense inferences (comprised of the *head*, *relation*, and *tail*) are filtered based on their relevance to the initial context. Below we provide a simple example of how this module can be used to generate commonsense inferences for the example *"PersonX becomes a great basketball player"*:

```
from kogito.models.bart.comet import COMETBART
from kogito.inference import CommonsenseInference

# Load pre-trained model from HuggingFace
model = COMETBART
        .from_pretrained("mismayil/comet-bart-ai2")

# Initialize inference module
csi = CommonsenseInference()

# Run inference
text = "PersonX becomes a great basketball player"
kgraph = csi.infer(text, model)

# Save output knowledge graph to JSON file
kgraph.to_jsonl("kgraph.json")
```

[2]https://kogito.readthedocs.io/

[3]https://www.youtube.com/watch?v=rFGzDrLCx00

[4]https://kogito.live

The resulting knowledge graph from the code above contains inferences such as *"PersonX needs to practice a lot"* and *"PersonX is athletic"*. Various parts of this pipeline can be customized and modified, allowing users to define their own modules. In the following sections, we discuss **kogito**'s core design, as well as the *head extraction*, *relation matching*, and *inference filtering* components of the pipeline. More details on these configuration options can be found in the kogito documentation.

4 Data Representation

To allow for standardization and ease of maintenance, **kogito** defines an interface to represent core concepts such as a *knowledge tuple*, a *commonsense knowledge graph*, and a *knowledge model*.

Commonsense Knowledge Tuple Commonsense knowledge graphs (Speer and Havasi, 2013; Hwang et al., 2021) and knowledge models (Bosselut et al., 2019) typically represent instances of knowledge as tuples of 3 elements: *(head, relation, tail)*. The *head* entity refers to the subject of a piece of knowledge (*e.g.*, objects such as *hammer*; events such as *"PersonX becomes a great basketball player"*). A *relation* provides an implicit question about the *head* (*e.g.*, `CapableOf` → *what is this head entity capable of?*; `xNeed` → *What does PersonX need before this event occurs?*). Finally, *tail* entities provide an answer option (among potentially many) to the relation with respect to the head (*e.g.*, *put nail in wood*; *to practice hard*). We often refer to the *tail* as the commonsense inference about the *head*.

Following this convention, we define a class with these elements and an additional two classes for knowledge *head* and *relation* representation. While knowledge *heads* and *tails* can be arbitrary text, we use predefined *relations* from the ATOMIC2020 (Hwang et al., 2021) and ConceptNet (Speer and Havasi, 2013) knowledge graphs.[5] Below is an example of defining a knowledge tuple in **kogito**:

```
from kogito.core.head import KnowledgeHead
from kogito.core.knowledge import Knowledge
from kogito.core.relation import X_NEED

head = KnowledgeHead("PersonX becomes a great
                      "basketball player")
kg = Knowledge(head=head, relation=X_NEED,
               tails=["practice hard"])
```

Knowledge Graph In addition to individual knowledge tuples, we also define a knowledge graph as a collection of knowledge tuples. In **kogito**, a knowledge graph serves as the standardized input object to (and output from) knowledge models, and has a simple API to manipulate knowledge instances collectively. In particular, a knowledge graph can be used to easily iterate over, read, and write a collection of knowledge instances to and from various files, and perform set-like operations on multiple knowledge graphs. These operations require a notion of equality, so we define two knowledge instances to be equal if they have the same head, relation and tail. Below is an example of defining and manipulating knowledge graphs:

```
from kogito.core.knowledge import KnowledgeGraph

# Read from csv
kgraph1 = KnowledgeGraph
          .from_csv("sample_graph1.csv",
                    sep="|", header=None)

# Read from jsonl (list of json objects)
kgraph2 = KnowledgeGraph
          .from_jsonl("sample_graph2.jsonl",
                      head_attr="source",
                      relation_attr="rel",
                      tails_attr="targets")

# Union
# kgraph1.union(kgraph2)
kgraph3 = kgraph1 + kgraph2

# Intersection
# kgraph1.intersection(kgraph2)
kgraph3 = kgraph1 & kgraph2

# Difference
# kgraph1.difference(kgraph2)
kgraph3 = kgraph1 - kgraph2

# Write to jsonl
kgraph3.to_jsonl("sample_graph3.jsonl")
```

Knowledge Model Knowledge models conceptually accept as input a *(head, relation)* pair and output an inferred knowledge tail. However, these models can sometimes expect a subtly different formats for these inputs and outputs. To increase the extensibility and interoperability of our tool, so that users can easily substitute one knowledge model for another, we define a model-agnostic abstraction over possible types of knowledge models. Consequently, knowledge models inherit from an abstract interface that defines core abstract methods, which users can implement to port new knowledge models into **kogito**. The *knowledge model* interface provides methods to train, generate from, evaluate these models, as well as save and load them. The input dataset for training, generating, or evaluating is given as a *knowledge graph* and the output dataset (in the case of generation) is returned as a *knowledge graph*.

kogito currently offers the following knowledge models: COMET-BART and COMET-GPT2

[5] **kogito** also supports defining new custom relations and using them to generate commonsense inferences (§8)

from Hwang et al. (2021), GPT2-zeroshot (Radford et al., 2019), and GPT3-zeroshot (Brown et al., 2020). Pre-trained COMET models can be loaded either from HuggingFace[6] by name or from local disk by model path. The GPT-3 model requires an API key. Each model method supports customization of various model-specific hyperparameters. `kogito` currently evaluates models using the following metrics: *BLEU* (Papineni et al., 2002), *ROUGE* (Lin, 2004), *METEOR* (Lavie and Agarwal, 2007), *CIDEr* (Vedantam et al., 2015) and *BERTScore* (Zhang et al., 2019).

Pipeline Design In the following sections, we discuss the *head extraction*, *relation matching*, and *inference filtering* components of this pipeline. We note that we provide a "dry-run" mode which allows for faster iteration on head extraction and relation matching by skipping the inference generation portion of `kogito`'s pipeline. More details on these configuration options can be found in the kogito docs.

5 Head Extraction

Head extraction refers to finding relevant chunks of a text in a sequence that can serve as knowledge heads (*i.e.*, the concepts commonsense inferences should be generated about). For example, given a text input *"PersonX becomes a great basketball player"*, we might be interested in generating inferences for the full sentence, but also about entities such as *"basketball player"*, *"basketball"*, or potentially *"become player"*. For different applications, different sets of head entities might be appropriate for generating inferences. Consequently, `kogito` allows the user to customize this behaviour and define arbitrary head extraction methods.[7]

At the same time, by default, `kogito` comes with a few standard head extraction methods. These built-in methods segment sentences, and then extract noun phrases (NP) and verb phrases (VP) using dependency parses produced from spaCy.[8] Extracted heads are deduplicated using string matching and passed onto the next stage of the pipeline, *relation matching*. We note that the *head extraction* stage itself is optional and the user can also provide a dedicated list of heads to `kogito`, which would replace the pre-processing of head entities.

[6] https://huggingface.co/models

[7] https://tinyurl.com/head-extraction

[8] https://spacy.io/

6 Relation Matching

Not all relations that a knowledge model is trained with will be relevant to each extracted head. For example, a head entity, *"hammer"*, would ideally be match to a relation such as `AtLocation`, while a relation such as `xWants` (*i.e.*, what does this head entity want) would not be matched. Similarly, *"PersonX becomes a basketball player"* might be matched to a relation such as `xIntent` (*i.e.*, what is the intent of the main persona in the head entity), while a relation such as `UsedFor` (*i.e.*, what is the head entity used for) would yield an incoherent inference. In this next stage, `kogito` matches relations to the given head input so that the resulting *(head, relation)* pair constitutes a sensible and plausible prompt for the knowledge model.

`kogito` supports relation matching as a preprocessing step before generating inferences. Suitable relation matches may be subjective depending on the use case, so `kogito` supports specifying subsets of relations and creation of custom relation matching modules developed by the user.[9]

In addition, `kogito` also provides native relation matching algorithms. These relation matchers follow the categorization of relations set out by Hwang et al. (2021), where relations were mapped into three categories: *Physical*, *Social* and *Event* types. Following this standard, we design relation matchers that identify a given head with whether it should be connected to the *Physical*, *Social* or *Event* categories, and match all relations in these categories to the head entity. Below, we describe three relation matching methods provided as part of `kogito`'s core library:

Base Matcher Every relation defined for a knowledge graph is matched to the head entities. This matcher is particularly useful if the user predefines a set of acceptable known relations or if they define new relations for their use case (§8).

Heuristic matcher The heuristic relation matcher matches extracted head entities that are noun phrases to ATOMIC2020 *Physical* relations and extracted head entities that are sentences or verb phrases to *Social* and *Event* relations. In our example, *"PersonX becomes a great basketball player"*, an extracted verb phrase such as *"become player"* would be matched to the *Social* and *Event* relations, while the extracted noun phrase

[9] https://tinyurl.com/relation-matching

Dataset	n_{train}	n_{test}	Overlap
Original	36,940	6,559	0.80 / 0.81
D_4	40,395	1,192	0.30 / 0.36
D_2	40,516	1,071	0.20 / 0.27
D_0	40,777	810	0.00 / 0.11

Table 1: Summary of Relation Matching datasets. The overlap column reports the degree of overlap with / without stopwords included.

Split	Head Entity	Labels
Train	PersonX acts funny	*event, social*
Train	accordion	*physical*
Train	big investment	*event*
Test	agenda	*physical*
Test	PersonX wreaks havoc	*event, social*
Test	PersonX motivates PersonY	*social*

Table 2: Samples from resplit train and test set D_0

"basketball player" would be matched to the *Physical* relations.

6.1 Model-based relation matching

The above matchers do not consider the semantic meaning of the head entities when matching them to relations. We also define model-based matchers that learn which heads and relations would be good matches. Relation matching is modeled as a classification problem. A head entity is given as input, and the model must determine the relation groups that match: *Physical, Social* and *Event.*

Dataset We use the ATOMIC2020 knowledge graph to train and evaluate the model-based relation matchers. First, we construct a dataset where the inputs are head entities and the label space corresponds to the three relation groups. If a head entity in the knowledge graph is connected to a relation from a particular group, we treat that relation group as a positive label for the head entity. As relations from multiple relation groups may be connected to a head entity, this labeling yields a multi-label prediction problem.

To evaluate the performance of our relation matchers (and test their generalization so they may be applicable to a broad scope of use cases), we split our dataset into both an in-distribution (ID) and an out-of-distribution (OOD) evaluation sample set. For the ID test set, we use the original ATOMIC2020 development set. For the OOD test set, we combine the train and test set of ATOMIC2020 and resplit this joint dataset while minimizing the word overlap between the train and test set. More specifically, we prepare 3 sets of (train, test) splits called D_0, D_2 and D_4 where n in D_n is defined as the maximum number of times a word in a particular test set example can occur in the training dataset (excluding stopwords). A bigger n indicates more overlap between these two sets. In D_0, the test set does not have any overlapping non-stopwords with the training set. Finally, we ensure that the resulting test set is balanced over each relation group. Table 1 provides the summary of the constructed datasets and Table 2 lists some examples from the D_0 dataset.

Models We report results for fine-tuned models using different pretrained embeddings: GloVe (Pennington et al., 2014), BERT (Devlin et al., 2019) and DistilBERT (Sanh et al., 2019). The GloVe model uses the technique of Shen et al. (2018) with average pooling over 100 dimensional GloVe embeddings and a projection layer on top. The BERT and DistilBERT models are finetuned on the task with a projection layer to predict the label.[10] These models are provided with `kogito`, and can be selected to match relations to head inputs.

In Table 3, we report the train, ID test and OOD test F1 scores for these models using different training datasets D_n, allowing users to understand their relative benefits and trade-offs.

7 Inference Filtering

By default, the commonsense inference module returns all generated tails without any filtering applied. However, many of these resulting inferences may be irrelevant to the initial context, particularly for extracted heads that have been decontextualized. Given most users may only be interested in relevant subsets of these commonsense inferences, `kogito` provides a separate module to determine the relevance of the given *knowledge tuples* with respect to the initial *context* from which it was extracted. In our running example, *"PersonX becomes a great basketball player"*, an extracted head entity *"player"* may yield contextually-irrelevant inferences such as *"player plays video games"* and *"player is at a soccer match"*, which

[10]All models are trained using binary cross-entropy loss and the Adam optimizer (Kingma and Ba, 2015) for 20 (for SWEM models) and 3 (for BERT and DistilBERT models) epochs with a batch size of 64.

Data	Model	Train F1	ID F1	OOD F1
D_4	Base	0.68	0.82	0.62
	Heuristic	0.84	0.80	0.69
	GloVe	0.90	0.91	0.82
	DistilBERT	**0.97**	0.91	0.85
	BERT	**0.97**	**0.91**	**0.86**
D_2	Base	0.68	0.82	0.61
	Heuristic	0.84	0.80	0.69
	GloVe	0.89	0.90	0.81
	DistilBERT	**0.97**	0.93	0.85
	BERT	**0.97**	**0.94**	**0.86**
D_0	Base	0.68	0.82	0.63
	Heuristic	0.84	0.80	0.73
	GloVe	0.89	0.90	0.76
	DistilBERT	**0.97**	**0.93**	0.84
	BERT	**0.97**	0.91	**0.85**

Table 3: Relation matcher performance on datasets D_n

would be filtered.

To filter inferences, `kogito` comes with the off-the-shelf DeBERTa-based commonsense fact linking model from Gao et al. (2022), which achieved a state-of-the-art average 72.5% F1 across multiple benchmarks. However, our setting is different from the one evaluated in Gao et al. (2022) as we evaluate generated commonsense inferences (rather than ones from an existing KB) for contextual relevance. To evaluate how well our method transfers to this new setting, we perform an expert study on the performance of the inference filtering model with respect to the knowledge generated from a knowledge model such as COMET. We randomly select 50 instances from the test split of ROC-ATOMIC dataset Gao et al. (2022) where each instance is composed of a *context* and a *fact* as a knowledge tuple *(head, relation, tail)*. We then run the default `kogito` inference pipeline (with full head extraction and heuristic relation matching) on the *heads* which produces several inferences per head instance. We select 100 results randomly from the output of the previous step and apply our inference filtering model. Finally, we ask a human expert to annotate each instance with the true relevance label of the fact and find that our model achieves a 75% F1 on the knowledge model generated inferences. We also offer a modular interface to define and plug in new filtering models in the future.

8 Defining New Relations

In previous knowledge modeling papers (Bosselut et al., 2019; Hwang et al., 2021), the set of relations that can be used in prompts is limited by the knowledge graph used to to train the knowledge model (*e.g.*, ATOMIC2020). However, a user may want to generate inferences for new dimensions of knowledge, define their own custom relations for them, and produce commonsense inferences based on these new properties. However, if there are no large KGs that use this schema, training a suitable knowledge model would pose a challenge.

`kogito` provides this functionality by implementing the approach of West et al. (2022), which allows a user to prompt large language models for knowledge using custom relations and has been shown to generate high-quality knowledge. Specifically, a user defines an instance of a *knowledge relation* class, a verbalizer function that describes how to convert the new relation into a natural language prompt (with a head and tail), and an instruction prompt to GPT-3. At inference time, the user provides a list of sample knowledge tuples that use the new relation. These tuples are verbalized using the verbalizer function and provided to the GPT-3 model along with the instruction prompt. Below, we illustrate this process with an example where a new relation, `xWishes`, which describes person's wishes, is defined using the sample code:

```
from kogito.core.relation import (KnowledgeRelation,
                                  register_relation)

def x_wishes_verbalizer(head, **kwargs):
    # index will be passed from the model
    # so that we can enumerate samples
    # which helps with inference
    index = kwargs.get("index")
    index_txt = f"{index}" if index is not None \
                                        else ""
    return f"Situation {index_txt}: {head}."
           "As a result, PersonX wishes"

X_WISHES = KnowledgeRelation("xWishes",
            verbalizer=x_wishes_verbalizer,
            prompt="How does this situation affect"
                   " each character's wishes?")
register_relation(X_WISHES)
```

Then, to use this new relation for inference, the user can provide a sample knowledge graph (*i.e.*, a prompt filled with example tuples using this relation), and a head such as *"PersonX makes a huge mistake"* to generate inferences about. Below, we show how such a sample knowledge graph could be verbalized into a prompt for GPT-3:

How does the situation affect the character's wishes?
Situation 1: John is at a party. As a result, John wishes to drink beer and dance
Situation 2: Terry bleeds a lot. As a result, Terry wishes to see a doctor
Situation 3: Eileen works as a cashier. As a result, Eileen wishes to be a store manager
Situation 4: James gets dirty. As a result, James wishes to clean up
Situation 5: Janice stays up all night studying. As a result, Janice wishes to sleep all day
Situation 6: Isaac makes a huge mistake. As a result, Isaac wishes...

The result of prompting GPT-3 with the above text is returned as the generated tail inference for the given head. Using this approach, users can instantiate a prompt defining a new relation, and use large language models to produce inferences for it.

9 Conclusion & Future Work

In this system description, we presented **kogito**, a toolkit for generating commonsense inferences for open-world text using knowledge models. **kogito** provides a foundational, customizable, and extensible interface for inference generation from knowledge models, and supports preprocessing and manipulation utilities such as head extraction, relation matching, and relation definition.

Future work may include improved head extraction, such as semantic head extraction (*e.g.*, paraphrased noun phrase extraction, etc.), new relation matching methods that more rigorously trade off performance and latency, support for new knowledge models trained on other knowledge graphs (*e.g.*, ANION; Jiang et al., 2021), and multimodal inputs such as images.

Acknowledgements

We thank Silin Gao, Deniz Bayazit, Beatriz Borges, Antoine Masanet, and other members of the EPFL NLP lab for their feedback on earlier iterations of this library. Significant portions of the model training and evaluation code for this tool have been adapted from the codebase[11] of Hwang et al. (2021). Antoine Bosselut gratefully acknowledges the support of Innosuisse under PFFS-21-29, the EPFL Science Seed Fund, the EPFL Center for Imaging, Sony Group Corporation, and the Allen Institute for AI.

[11]https://github.com/allenai/comet-atomic-2020

Ethical Considerations

kogito is a library that uses knowledge models such as COMET (Bosselut et al., 2019) to generate commonsense inferences from text. These knowledge models are seeded with pretrained language models and subsequently finetuned on knowledge graphs so that they may generate knowledge in the structure of the finetuning KG. Consequently, **kogito** could reflect harmful behaviors exhibited by language models and knowledge graphs that are used to train the knowledge models in its library. For example, language models have been shown to encode biases about race, gender, and many other demographic attributes (Sheng et al., 2020; Weidinger et al., 2021). They can also generate toxic outputs when prompted in overt (Wallace et al., 2019), but also seemingly innocuous (Gehman et al., 2020), ways. We encourage users of this library to consider the same precautions they would apply to other language models and methods that use noisy knowledge sources.

References

Prithviraj Ammanabrolu, Wesley Cheung, William Broniec, and Mark O. Riedl. 2021. Automated storytelling via causal, commonsense plot ordering. In *AAAI*.

Antoine Bosselut, Ronan Le Bras, and Yejin Choi. 2021. Dynamic neuro-symbolic knowledge graph construction for zero-shot commonsense question answering. In *Proceedings of the 35th AAAI Conference on Artificial Intelligence (AAAI)*.

Antoine Bosselut, Hannah Rashkin, Maarten Sap, Chaitanya Malaviya, Asli Celikyilmaz, and Yejin Choi. 2019. COMET: Commonsense transformers for automatic knowledge graph construction. In *Proceedings of the 57th Annual Meeting of the Association for Computational Linguistics*, pages 4762–4779, Florence, Italy. Association for Computational Linguistics.

Tom Brown, Benjamin Mann, Nick Ryder, Melanie Subbiah, Jared D Kaplan, Prafulla Dhariwal, Arvind Neelakantan, Pranav Shyam, Girish Sastry, Amanda Askell, Sandhini Agarwal, Ariel Herbert-Voss, Gretchen Krueger, Tom Henighan, Rewon Child, Aditya Ramesh, Daniel Ziegler, Jeffrey Wu, Clemens Winter, Chris Hesse, Mark Chen, Eric Sigler, Mateusz Litwin, Scott Gray, Benjamin Chess, Jack Clark, Christopher Berner, Sam McCandlish, Alec Radford, Ilya Sutskever, and Dario Amodei. 2020.

Language models are few-shot learners. In *Advances in Neural Information Processing Systems*, volume 33, pages 1877–1901. Curran Associates, Inc.

Tuhin Chakrabarty, Debanjan Ghosh, Smaranda Muresan, and Nanyun Peng. 2020a. R^3: Reverse, retrieve, and rank for sarcasm generation with commonsense knowledge. In *Proceedings of the 58th Annual Meeting of the Association for Computational Linguistics*, pages 7976–7986, Online. Association for Computational Linguistics.

Tuhin Chakrabarty, Smaranda Muresan, and Nanyun Peng. 2020b. Generating similes effortlessly like a pro: A style transfer approach for simile generation. In *Proceedings of the 2020 Conference on Empirical Methods in Natural Language Processing (EMNLP)*, pages 6455–6469, Online. Association for Computational Linguistics.

Jeff Da, Ronan Le Bras, Ximing Lu, Yejin Choi, and Antoine Bosselut. 2021. Analyzing commonsense emergence in few-shot knowledge models. In *Proceedings of the Conference on Automated Knowledge Base Construction (AKBC)*.

Sahith Dambekodi, Spencer Frazier, Prithviraj Ammanabrolu, and Mark Riedl. 2020. Playing text-based games with common sense.

Jacob Devlin, Ming-Wei Chang, Kenton Lee, and Kristina Toutanova. 2019. BERT: Pre-training of deep bidirectional transformers for language understanding. In *Proceedings of the 2019 Conference of the North American Chapter of the Association for Computational Linguistics: Human Language Technologies, Volume 1 (Long and Short Papers)*, pages 4171–4186, Minneapolis, Minnesota. Association for Computational Linguistics.

Silin Gao, Jena D. Hwang, Saya Kanno, Hiromi Wakaki, Yuki Mitsufuji, and Antoine Bosselut. 2022. Comfact: A benchmark for linking contextual commonsense knowledge. In *Findings of EMNLP*.

Samuel Gehman, Suchin Gururangan, Maarten Sap, Yejin Choi, and Noah A. Smith. 2020. Realtoxicityprompts: Evaluating neural toxic degeneration in language models. *ArXiv*, abs/2009.11462.

Jena D. Hwang, Chandra Bhagavatula, Ronan Le Bras, Jeff Da, Keisuke Sakaguchi, Antoine Bosselut, and Yejin Choi. 2021. Comet-atomic 2020: On symbolic and neural commonsense knowledge graphs. In *AAAI*.

Liwei Jiang, Antoine Bosselut, Chandra Bhagavatula, and Yejin Choi. 2021. "I'm not mad": Commonsense implications of negation and contradiction. In *Proceedings of the 2021 Conference of the North American Chapter of the Association for Computational Linguistics: Human Language Technologies*, pages 4380–4397, Online. Association for Computational Linguistics.

Diederik P. Kingma and Jimmy Ba. 2015. Adam: A method for stochastic optimization. In *ICLR (Poster)*.

Alon Lavie and Abhaya Agarwal. 2007. METEOR: An automatic metric for MT evaluation with high levels of correlation with human judgments. In *Proceedings of the Second Workshop on Statistical Machine Translation*, pages 228–231, Prague, Czech Republic. Association for Computational Linguistics.

Chin-Yew Lin. 2004. ROUGE: A package for automatic evaluation of summaries. In *Text Summarization Branches Out*, pages 74–81, Barcelona, Spain. Association for Computational Linguistics.

Bodhisattwa Prasad Majumder, Harsh Jhamtani, Taylor Berg-Kirkpatrick, and Julian McAuley. 2020. Like hiking? you probably enjoy nature: Persona-grounded dialog with commonsense expansions. In *Proceedings of the 2020 Conference on Empirical Methods in Natural Language Processing (EMNLP)*, pages 9194–9206, Online. Association for Computational Linguistics.

Kishore Papineni, Salim Roukos, Todd Ward, and Wei-Jing Zhu. 2002. Bleu: a method for automatic evaluation of machine translation. In *Proceedings of the 40th Annual Meeting of the Association for Computational Linguistics*, pages 311–318, Philadelphia, Pennsylvania, USA. Association for Computational Linguistics.

Jeffrey Pennington, Richard Socher, and Christopher Manning. 2014. GloVe: Global vectors for word representation. In *Proceedings of the 2014 Conference on Empirical Methods in Natural Language Processing (EMNLP)*, pages 1532–1543, Doha, Qatar. Association for Computational Linguistics.

Fabio Petroni, Tim Rocktäschel, Sebastian Riedel, Patrick Lewis, Anton Bakhtin, Yuxiang Wu, and Alexander Miller. 2019. Language models as knowledge bases? In *Proceedings of the 2019 Conference on Empirical Methods in Natural Language Processing and the 9th International Joint Conference on Natural Language Processing (EMNLP-IJCNLP)*, pages 2463–2473, Hong Kong, China. Association for Computational Linguistics.

Alec Radford and Karthik Narasimhan. 2018. Improving language understanding by generative pre-training.

Alec Radford, Jeff Wu, Rewon Child, David Luan, Dario Amodei, and Ilya Sutskever. 2019. Language models are unsupervised multitask learners.

Adam Roberts, Colin Raffel, and Noam Shazeer. 2020. How much knowledge can you pack into the parameters of a language model? In *Proceedings of the 2020 Conference on Empirical Methods in Natural Language Processing (EMNLP)*, pages 5418–5426, Online. Association for Computational Linguistics.

Victor Sanh, Lysandre Debut, Julien Chaumond, and Thomas Wolf. 2019. Distilbert, a distilled version of bert: smaller, faster, cheaper and lighter.

Dinghan Shen, Guoyin Wang, Wenlin Wang, Martin Renqiang Min, Qinliang Su, Yizhe Zhang, Chunyuan Li, Ricardo Henao, and Lawrence Carin. 2018. Baseline needs more love: On simple word-embedding-based models and associated pooling mechanisms. In *Proceedings of the 56th Annual Meeting of the Association for Computational Linguistics (Volume 1: Long Papers)*, pages 440–450, Melbourne, Australia. Association for Computational Linguistics.

Emily Sheng, Kai-Wei Chang, Prem Natarajan, and Nanyun Peng. 2020. Towards Controllable Biases in Language Generation. In *Findings of the Association for Computational Linguistics: EMNLP 2020*, pages 3239–3254, Online. Association for Computational Linguistics.

Robyn Speer and Catherine Havasi. 2013. Conceptnet 5: A large semantic network for relational knowledge. In *The People's Web Meets NLP*.

Ramakrishna Vedantam, C. Lawrence Zitnick, and Devi Parikh. 2015. Cider: Consensus-based image description evaluation. In *2015 IEEE Conference on Computer Vision and Pattern Recognition (CVPR)*, pages 4566–4575.

Eric Wallace, Shi Feng, Nikhil Kandpal, Matt Gardner, and Sameer Singh. 2019. Universal adversarial triggers for attacking and analyzing NLP. In *Proceedings of the 2019 Conference on Empirical Methods in Natural Language Processing and the 9th International Joint Conference on Natural Language Processing (EMNLP-IJCNLP)*, pages 2153–2162, Hong Kong, China. Association for Computational Linguistics.

Laura Weidinger, John Mellor, Maribeth Rauh, Conor Griffin, Jonathan Uesato, Po-Sen Huang, Myra Cheng, Mia Glaese, Borja Balle, Atoosa Kasirzadeh, Zac Kenton, Sasha Brown, Will Hawkins, Tom Stepleton, Courtney Biles, Abeba Birhane, Julia Haas, Laura Rimell, Lisa Anne Hendricks, William S. Isaac, Sean Legassick, Geoffrey Irving, and Iason Gabriel. 2021. Ethical and social risks of harm from language models. *CoRR*, abs/2112.04359.

Peter West, Chandrasekhar Bhagavatula, Jack Hessel, Jena D. Hwang, Liwei Jiang, Ronan Le Bras, Ximing Lu, Sean Welleck, and Yejin Choi. 2022. Symbolic knowledge distillation: from general language models to commonsense models. In *NAACL*.

Tianyi Zhang, Varsha Kishore, Felix Wu, Kilian Q. Weinberger, and Yoav Artzi. 2019. Bertscore: Evaluating text generation with bert.

Text-Blueprint: An Interactive Platform for Plan-based Conditional Generation

Fantine Huot, Joshua Maynez, Shashi Narayan,
Reinald Kim Amplayo, Kuzman Ganchev, Annie Louis,
Anders Sandholm, Dipanjan Das, Mirella Lapata
Google Research
fantinehuot@google.com, joshuahm@google.com, shashinarayan@google.com,
reinald@google.com, kuzman@google.com, annielouis@google.com,
sandholm@google.com, dipanjand@google.com, lapata@google.com

Abstract

While conditional generation models can now generate natural language well enough to create fluent text, it is still difficult to control the generation process, leading to irrelevant, repetitive, and hallucinated content. Recent work shows that planning can be a useful intermediate step to render conditional generation less opaque and more grounded. We present a web browser-based demonstration for query-focused summarization that uses a sequence of question-answer pairs, as a *blueprint* plan for guiding text generation (i.e., what to say and in what order). We illustrate how users may interact with the generated text and associated plan visualizations, e.g., by editing and modifying the blueprint in order to improve or control the generated output.

A short video demonstrating our system is available at https://goo.gle/text-blueprint-demo

1 Introduction

With the advent of encoder-decoder models (Bahdanau et al., 2014; Sutskever et al., 2014), Transformer-based architectures (Vaswani et al., 2017), and large-scale pretraining (Zhang et al., 2020; Lewis et al., 2020), deep learning models have achieved great performance on conditional generation tasks such as summarization (Rush et al., 2015; Nallapati et al., 2016; See et al., 2017; Liu and Lapata, 2019) or task-oriented dialogue modeling (Wen et al., 2018). However, it remains challenging to control the text generation, as these neural models tend to generate hallucinated (Song et al., 2018; Maynez et al., 2020; Kryscinski et al., 2020; Gabriel et al., 2021) or repetitive content (Suzuki and Nagata, 2017; Li et al., 2018), and struggle to identify which information is most relevant to include in the output text (Tan et al., 2017).

Recent work shows that planning can be a useful intermediate step to address some of these challenges (Puduppully et al., 2019; Moryossef et al., 2019; Narayan et al., 2021, 2022). In this work, we present Text-Blueprint, a demonstration for showcasing the approach described in Narayan et al. (2022), that uses a text plan, formulated as a sequence of question-answer pairs called the *blueprint*, to serve as an intermediate representation for content selection and organization of the generated text. It draws inspiration from the "Questions Under Discussion" theory of discourse which posits that the structure of a text can be derived by identifying the questions that are answered by each subsequent span of text (Carlson, 1983; Ginzburg, 1994; Van Kuppevelt, 1995; Larson, 2002; Roberts, 2012; Riester, 2019).

We implement this blueprint approach as an interactive web application for query-focused summarization. An example snapshot of our interface is shown in Figure 1. As can be seen, for a given generated summary, users can examine its corresponding blueprint, modify it to make it more faithful or relevant, and control its length by changing the number of question-answer pairs. Given a query and relevant documents, there can be multiple semantically-diverse summaries that meet the communicative goal of synthesizing the most important points. Traditional generation systems do well at *single-best* summaries, while our interactive demonstration allows users to explore *different* summaries for a given input, while directly observing the impact of changes to the plan on the generated text. The formulation of the blueprint plan as question-answer pairs makes it intuitive and user-friendly (e.g., users can inspect and ask questions without any instructions).

Our demonstration is an example of what can be achieved with human-in-the-loop conditional generation (Cheng et al., 2022). It allows users to revise the output text (i.e., by editing the blueprint) subject to their information needs. Additionally, it allows researchers to analyze what constitutes a good blueprint for various summarization tasks.

Proceedings of the 17th Conference of the European Chapter of the Association for Computational Linguistics System Demonstrations, pages 105–116
May 2-4, 2023 ©2023 Association for Computational Linguistics

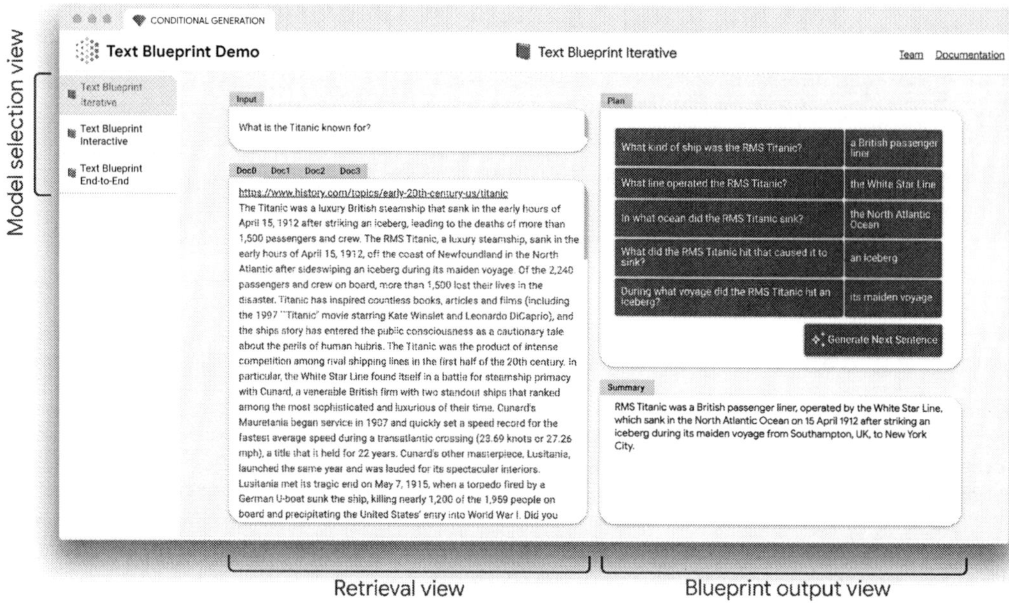

Figure 1: User interface of the web browser-based Text-Blueprint demonstration showcasing the iterative model.

2 Related Work

There are several libraries for broad NLP tasks, such as AllenNLP[1] or GluonNLP[2]. The Language Interpretability Tool (Tenney et al., 2020) is an interactive platform for examining model behavior, meant for rapid exploration and error analysis. A variety of toolkits have been developed recently that support generation tasks. For instance, Texar (Hu et al., 2019) is an open-source platform that unifies the development of diverse yet closely-related applications, such as machine translation, summarization, and dialog. TextBox (Li et al., 2021) is a modular framework that offers interfaces for various common functions in text generation models, allowing researchers and practitioners to reproduce baseline models and compare new models. The Giant Language Model Test Room, also known as GLTR (Gehrmann et al., 2019b), helps users differentiate automatically-generated text from human-written text.

For conditional generation, many demonstrations are summarization systems. For instance, Nyzam and Bossard (2019) present a modular tool for automatic summarization. Syed et al. (2021) showcase a visualization tool for summaries obtained by different summarization methods. The SummVis platform (Vig et al., 2021) serves a similar goal to the demonstration presented in this paper. It enables users to visually analyze the models, data, and evaluation metrics associated with abtractive summarization, e.g., by highlighting hallucinated entities in the generated text. While previous tools and frameworks are versatile and modular, their focus is not on empowering users with control over the generated text in an *interactive* environment.

In particular, studies on human-AI interaction for text summarization (Cheng et al., 2022; Lai et al., 2022) show that users' overall experience is better when they can control the generation process. Users preferred systems that allowed them to adjust and see the impact of their changes on the output directly, and the controllability improved their trust in the system when summarizing unfamiliar topics.

Systems more geared toward interactive text generation include chatbots such as Meena (Adiwardana et al., 2020) or other specialized dialogue systems such as ParlAI (Miller et al., 2017). Gehrmann et al. (2019a) present an approach called collaborative semantic inference that exposes latent variables to the user for interactive generation. Still, these tasks differ from conditional generation using planning for which our demonstration is designed.

3 Summarization Using Planning

This demonstration showcases query-focused summarization using planning as described in Narayan

[1] allennlp.org
[2] gluon-nlp.mxnet.io

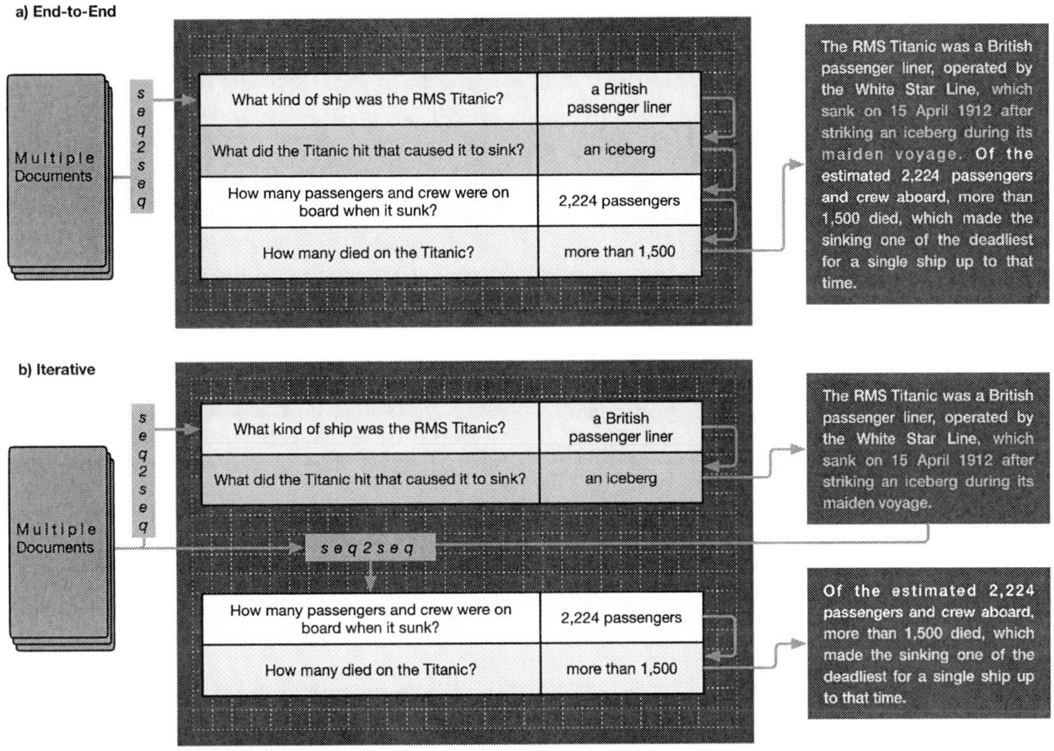

Figure 2: a) End-to-end and b) iterative Blueprint models. The end-to-end model generates the entire blueprint plan before generating the output text, while the iterative model plans and generates one proposition at a time, conditioning on the input and the sentences generated so far. Each portion of the output is color-coded with its corresponding question-answer pair.

et al. (2022).[3] In their approach, question-answer text plans, called blueprints, serve as intermediate representations for content selection and structuring of the generated text. We implement three Blueprint models in our demonstration, which we briefly describe below; they are all encoder-decoder variants instantiated from a Transformer (Vaswani et al., 2017) architecture.

Let d denote the input to our models, which is a user query concatenated with a document or a set of documents relevant to this query. From this input d, the model generates $b; s$, the blueprint b and its corresponding summary s. The blueprint itself is a sequence of question-answer pairs $\{(q_1, a_1), (q_2, a_2), \ldots, (q_m, a_m)\}$. Existing datasets do not contain such blueprints, they are typically designed as (d, s) pairs. Narayan et al. (2022) describe a suite of data enhancement methods for obtaining blueprint annotations (we refer the interested reader to their paper for details).

[3]Code and checkpoints to be released at `github.com/google-research`

End-to-End Model The end-to-end Blueprint model uses an encoder-decoder model to encode the input documents d and generate $b; s$, the concatenation of the blueprint and output text, *in one go* (Figure 2a). The decoder first predicts the blueprint b autoregressively and continues to generate the output s, conditioned on both b and d. In particular, it predicts b as $q_1; a_1; \ldots; q_m; a_m$, a concatenated sequence of question-answer pairs. In contrast to systems that use prompted encoders, such as CTRLSum (He et al., 2020), the Blueprint models use decoder prompting. As a consequence, the blueprint plan is entirely generated by the model, without human intervention or relying on external systems. After the generation, users can inspect the question-answer pairs and corresponding summary. If desired, they can then select question-answer pairs to remove from the plan. The system is fed the updated blueprint b' which prompts the decoder to generate the corresponding output s'.

Iterative Model It is generally challenging for encoder-decoder models to generate long output sequences (Ko and Li, 2020; Tan et al., 2021). The end-to-end model ultimately suffers from this problem as it aims to generate sequence $b; s$ instead of just s. The iterative Blueprint model mitigates this by adopting an incremental approach that interleaves planning with text generation rather than predicting a global plan before generating the output s (Figure 2b).

If we denote the output s as consisting of n sentences $\{s_1, s_2, \ldots, s_n\}$, then the corresponding blueprint b can be expressed as $\{b_1, b_2, \ldots, b_n\}$, where $b_i : \{(q_1^i, a_1^i), (q_2^i, a_2^i), \ldots, (q_k^i, a_k^i)\}$ consists of k question-answer pairs for sentence s_i. This model iteratively plans and generates one sentence at a time, conditioning on the input and the output sentences generated so far. In particular, it is trained such that the encoder first encodes the input d, while the decoder takes the output generated so far $\{s_1, \ldots, s_i\}$ as a forced prompt and generates the blueprint b_{i+1} for the following sentence s_{i+1}, followed by sentence s_{i+1} itself.

The iterative approach naturally addresses some of the issues the end-to-end model faces. In particular, it does not run into sequence length limitations as it predicts one sentence at a time.

Interactive Model The third model is an interactive Blueprint model that allows the user to modify the blueprint and directly change the generated output. It operates similarly to the end-to-end model previously described but in addition to letting the user select which elements of the plan to keep or remove, we design the system to allow the user to provide their own plan.

We do not expect users to be able to provide answers to all the questions they come up with when creating their own plans. Therefore, we modify the original paradigm set by Narayan et al. (2022) and develop a new model specifically for the interactive mode that uses a question-only blueprint instead of a question-answer blueprint. From the input documents d, we fine-tune this model to generate $b; s$, where b is a concatenated sequence of questions $q_1; q_2; \ldots; q_m$. For this new model, we use the same blueprint training data as the iterative and end-to-end models, but only use the question annotations during fine-tuning, ignoring the answers. In the interactive mode, the user can edit the plan by typing in questions they come up with. This process creates an updated blueprint b' which prompts the decoder to generate an updated summary s'.

Model Training The models made available in this demonstration are based on the LongT5 model (Guo et al., 2021), an extension of T5 (Raffel et al., 2020) designed to handle long inputs. Specifically, we fine-tune the XL 3B-parameter model[4] with maximum input and output sequence lengths of 4,096 and 512 tokens, respectively, on the AQuaMuSe dataset (Kulkarni et al., 2020). This is a query-focused multi-document summarization dataset which leverages the Google Natural Questions dataset (Kwiatkowski et al., 2019). The latter contains real user queries from Google search logs paired with crowd-sourced answer spans from Wikipedia, and matched with passages from web documents from Common Crawl. AQuaMuse uses the answer passages as summaries with the passages extracted from Common Crawl as the input documents. This dataset is query-focused, with long inputs and multi-sentence outputs, making it well-suited to a user-centric summarization system.

4 System Description

Our web browser-based demonstration is designed so that researchers and practitioners can inspect and interact with the different Blueprint models. We frame the summarization task around a user query, since in a real world scenario we would expect users to have a question or intent in mind. The system retrieves documents relevant to the query and displays their summary and its corresponding blueprint. Figure 1 provides a snapshot of the user interface (UI) and its components, namely the model selection, document retrieval, and Blueprint output views.

Model Selection View Using the left-side menu, the user selects which of the models to use: end-to-end, iterative, or interactive Blueprint. The UI then adapts to the selected model.

Retrieval View In the search bar at the top of the middle panel, the user can enter an information-seeking query. For instance, in the example from Figure 1: "What is the Titanic known for?". The system automatically retrieves documents relevant to the query and displays them underneath in different tabs, allowing the user to navigate between them and examine individual documents. The URL for each document is shown at the top. For longer documents, scrolling is also enabled.

[4]Using the checkpoints from `github.com/google-research/longt5`

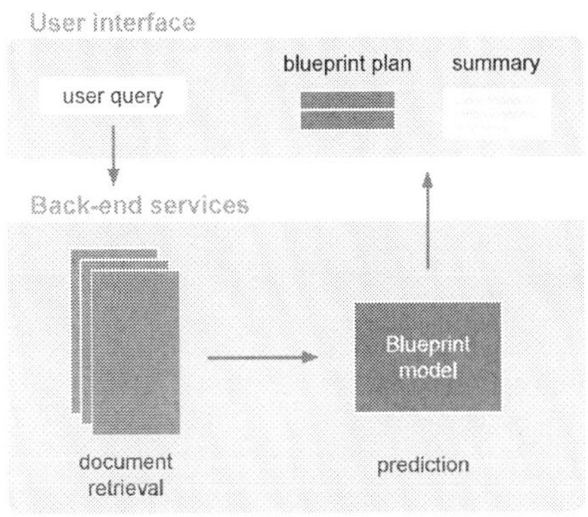

Figure 3: Schematic representation of the different components of the web browser-based demonstration.

The document retrieval component is query-focused in a similar style to the AQuaMuSe dataset (Kulkarni et al., 2020). It retrieves candidate URLs and ranks relevant passages for a query using an off-the-shelf retrieval system.[5] It extracts a text document from each of the best-ranking web pages, resulting in multi-document input for the Blueprint models. Documents are formatted similarly to AQuaMuse to closely match the data on which the models were trained.

Blueprint Output View The retrieved documents serve as inputs for the summarization. The outputs of the selected model are displayed on the right. The top-right box displays the blueprint b and the bottom-right box shows the corresponding generated output s. The question-answer blueprint (or question-only, in the case of the interactive model) highlights what the model deemed important, such as, in the example from Figure 1, "What kind of ship is the Titanic?" or "What did the Titanic hit that caused it to sink?". We see that the generated output closely follows the blueprint.

In the end-to-end and interactive models, the user can click on elements of the blueprint to include or exclude them from the plan to re-generate the summary. Furthermore, when using the interactive model, an additional text box allows the user to input and edit a custom question plan.

System Design Figure 3 shows the different components of the web application. The web interface is made interactive with LitElement[6] components and is implemented in HTML and TypeScript. The back-end services are implemented in Python and C++. Requests for document retrieval and blueprint model inference are sent to back-end services to be processed asynchronously. Outputs are then sent back to the front-end web interface.

5 Use Cases

In the following we explore some of the possibilities of human-in-the-loop summarization and illustrate different use cases for our demonstration.

Informative Blueprints While the inner workings of deep learning models might be opaque to a human user, the formulation of the blueprint as a sequence of questions makes the control of the system's output user-friendly. Users do not have to be machine learning experts to interact with the system through questions and answers. Moreover, the ability to change the blueprint and observe the result on the summary, provides the user with immediate feedback.

The planning step also brings some insight into the often black-box nature of conditional generation. This property is especially valuable when the user summarizes complex or difficult information, since it breaks down the generation process into a sequence of questions. The blueprint plan offers context for the information in the generated output, which has been shown to be a desirable property in human-AI interaction for text summarization (Cheng et al., 2022). Plan agnostic models do not provide details as to why certain pieces of information were included. In contrast, as seen in Figure 4, the blueprint plan anchors conditional generation, providing the user with a question-answer explanation for each proposition.

Improved Faithfulness Narayan et al. (2021) evaluate the Blueprint models across several datasets and show improvements in faithfulness over models that do not use planning. Moreover, they also evaluate the impact of automated blueprint edits on the output summary. For each generated blueprint, they automatically remove question-answer pairs for which the answer is not contained in the input, thus eliminating questions that cannot be answered based on the input documents. They then prompt the decoder with the modified blueprint to generate the summary, following a similar setting as in our system demonstration. Their results confirm that this automatic filtering of the generated blueprint further improves

[5] `github.com/google-research/t5x_retrieval`

[6] See `lit.dev` for details.

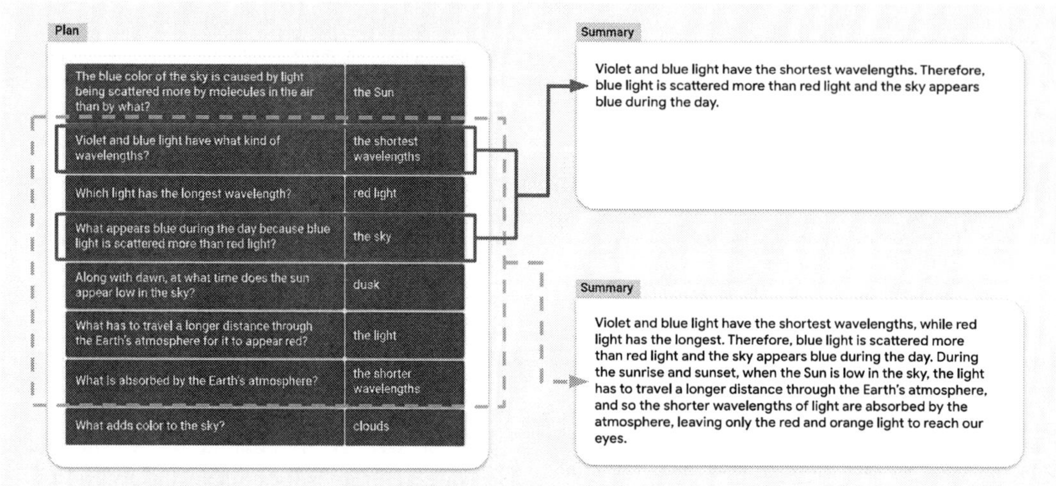

Figure 4: Example snapshot of the results obtained with the end-to-end Blueprint model for the user query "Why is the sky blue?". Depending on which question-answer pairs the user selects, different summaries can be generated.

faithfulness. Their experiment further underscores the importance of letting users interactively modify the plan, since we expect manual editing of the blueprint to have greater potential than automated filtering alone. In addition to unanswerable questions, users can remove questions with incorrect answers and irrelevant questions. A quantitative evaluation of the full scope of various human edits (e.g., remove an element of the blueprint, reorder the blueprint, add human-written questions) is left for future work.

Controllable Blueprints In the example in Figure 4, we examine the blueprint results obtained with the end-to-end model for the user query "Why is the sky blue?". The first question-answer pair of the blueprint is actually incorrect, but likely would not have been caught by simple heuristics since it seems fluent and its answer is present in the input documents. The user selects the subset of question-answers that are deemed most relevant, leading to higher-quality output than would have been generated without the blueprint control step. In particular, we see that the output does not contain the inaccuracies from the first question-answer pair.

This example also shows how the user can control the length of the generated summary by including more or less question-answer pairs in the blueprint. For instance, the user can restrict the summary to contain only the explanation for blue skies as shown at the top in Figure 4, or decide to include information about orange skies at sunset, as shown at the bottom. For a given query and source documents, the system can lead to diverse summaries by selecting different blueprints. Moreover, while it would be difficult for a user to come up with a plan from scratch if they are unfamiliar with the topic of their query, the provided blueprint can serve as a starting point from which the user can select what they would like to keep. As we discuss next, the user could also elaborate on their initial query by adding questions in the blueprint.

Personalized Generation Going beyond selecting and removing questions, in Figure 5, we illustrate results obtained with the interactive model and a user-provided blueprint. The user can edit the blueprint with their own follow-on questions, leading to an updated summary with information it did not contain originally. When summarizing unfamiliar topics, it might be difficult for the user to come up with many new questions, and such cases might be better served by the end-to-end model. In Appendix A, we provide additional examples of manually-edited blueprints and their corresponding summary. We observe that editing the plan allows the user to guide the generation to include certain elements in the output summary.

6 Conclusions

This demonstration showcases a novel approach to query-focused summarization that uses a blueprint to plan the generated text. By implementing it within an interactive framework, we transform it into an example of human-in-the-loop conditional generation. Our demonstration is designed in a

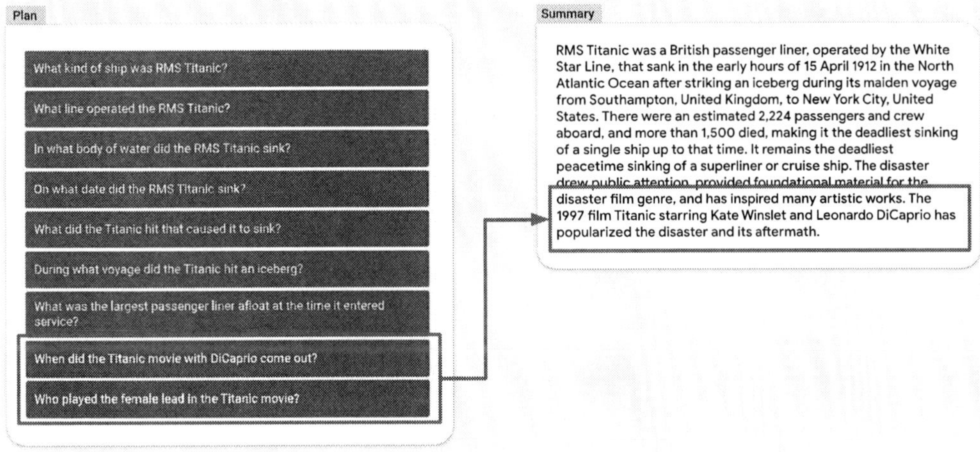

Figure 5: Snapshot of the results obtained with the interactive Blueprint model for the query "What is the Titanic known for?". Questions highlighted in red were manually added by the user, leading to a different output.

query-focused summarization setting; it retrieves multiple documents for a given query and uses them as input for the summarization. The system offers three different model variations, namely an end-to-end, iterative, and interactive Blueprint approach. The interactive model, in particular, allows users to examine and edit the blueprint plans, offering a more personalized experience. Since the blueprint is formulated as a sequence of questions, it provides a natural way for the user to interact with the generated output, e.g., by selecting relevant question-answer pairs, which in turn helps reduce inaccuracies and hallucinations.

We hope this demonstration will spur further exploration into controllable and interpretable conditional generation systems and how human interaction can be an integral component in generating personalized outputs. We further expect interactive tools like the one presented here to assist in summary creation and editing, e.g., for data augmentation in low-resource settings or for more robust system evaluation by generating multiple outputs for a given document.

7 Ethics statement

An ethical consideration with generative language models is the problem of misinformation. While the work we present here makes a step towards improving the faithfulness and factual consistency of text generation systems, it is important to note that current systems are still far from being perfect in this respect, and thus should be used with caution. While we did not observe harmful speech with typical queries, such a system can still be abused and additional controls and filters on both the queries and the system's output could help mitigate this.

Acknowledgements

We thank Sebastian Gehrmann, Ankur Parikh, and William Cohen for their feedback on earlier versions of this work.

References

Daniel Adiwardana, Minh-Thang Luong, David R So, Jamie Hall, Noah Fiedel, Romal Thoppilan, Zi Yang, Apoorv Kulshreshtha, Gaurav Nemade, Yifeng Lu, et al. 2020. Towards a human-like open-domain chatbot. *arXiv preprint arXiv:2001.09977*.

Dzmitry Bahdanau, Kyunghyun Cho, and Yoshua Bengio. 2014. Neural machine translation by jointly learning to align and translate. *arXiv preprint arXiv:1409.0473*.

L Carlson. 1983. *Dialogue Games: An Approach to Discourse Analysis*. Riedel, Dordrecht.

Ruijia Cheng, Alison Smith-Renner, Ke Zhang, Joel Tetreault, and Alejandro Jaimes-Larrarte. 2022. Mapping the design space of human-AI interaction in text summarization. In *Proceedings of the 2022 Conference of the North American Chapter of the Association for Computational Linguistics: Human Language Technologies*, pages 431–455, Seattle, United States. Association for Computational Linguistics.

Saadia Gabriel, Asli Celikyilmaz, Rahul Jha, Yejin Choi, and Jianfeng Gao. 2021. GO FIGURE: A meta evaluation of factuality in summarization. In *Findings of the Association for Computational Linguistics: ACL-IJCNLP 2021*, pages 478–487, Online. Association for Computational Linguistics.

Sebastian Gehrmann, Hendrik Strobelt, Robert Krüger, Hanspeter Pfister, and Alexander M Rush. 2019a. Visual interaction with deep learning models through collaborative semantic inference. *IEEE transactions on visualization and computer graphics*, 26(1):884–894.

Sebastian Gehrmann, Hendrik Strobelt, and Alexander Rush. 2019b. GLTR: Statistical detection and visualization of generated text. In *Proceedings of the 57th Annual Meeting of the Association for Computational Linguistics: System Demonstrations*, pages 111–116, Florence, Italy. Association for Computational Linguistics.

Jonathan Ginzburg. 1994. An update semantics for dialogue. In *In Proceedings of the 1st Tilburg International Workshop on Computational Semantics*, Tilburg, The Netherlands.

Mandy Guo, Joshua Ainslie, David C. Uthus, Santiago Ontañón, Jianmo Ni, Yun-Hsuan Sung, and Yinfei Yang. 2021. LongT5: Efficient text-to-text transformer for long sequences. *CoRR*, abs/2112.07916.

Junxian He, Wojciech Kryściński, Bryan McCann, Nazneen Rajani, and Caiming Xiong. 2020. Ctrlsum: Towards generic controllable text summarization. *arXiv preprint arXiv:2012.04281*.

Zhiting Hu, Haoran Shi, Bowen Tan, Wentao Wang, Zichao Yang, Tiancheng Zhao, Junxian He, Lianhui Qin, Di Wang, Xuezhe Ma, Zhengzhong Liu, Xiaodan Liang, Wanrong Zhu, Devendra Sachan, and Eric Xing. 2019. Texar: A modularized, versatile, and extensible toolkit for text generation. In *Proceedings of the 57th Annual Meeting of the Association for Computational Linguistics: System Demonstrations*, pages 159–164, Florence, Italy. Association for Computational Linguistics.

Wei-Jen Ko and Junyi Jessy Li. 2020. Assessing discourse relations in language generation from GPT-2. In *Proceedings of the 13th International Conference on Natural Language Generation*, pages 52–59, Dublin, Ireland. Association for Computational Linguistics.

Wojciech Kryscinski, Bryan McCann, Caiming Xiong, and Richard Socher. 2020. Evaluating the factual consistency of abstractive text summarization. In *Proceedings of the 2020 Conference on Empirical Methods in Natural Language Processing (EMNLP)*, pages 9332–9346, Online. Association for Computational Linguistics.

Sayali Kulkarni, Sheide Chammas, Wan Zhu, Fei Sha, and Eugene Ie. 2020. Aquamuse: Automatically generating datasets for query-based multi-document summarization. *arXiv preprint arXiv:2010.12694*.

Tom Kwiatkowski, Jennimaria Palomaki, Olivia Redfield, Michael Collins, Ankur Parikh, Chris Alberti, Danielle Epstein, Illia Polosukhin, Jacob Devlin, Kenton Lee, Kristina Toutanova, Llion Jones, Matthew Kelcey, Ming-Wei Chang, Andrew M. Dai, Jakob Uszkoreit, Quoc Le, and Slav Petrov. 2019. Natural questions: A benchmark for question answering research. *Transactions of the Association for Computational Linguistics*, 7:452–466.

Vivian Lai, Alison Smith-Renner, Ke Zhang, Ruijia Cheng, Wenjuan Zhang, Joel Tetreault, and Alejandro Jaimes-Larrarte. 2022. An exploration of post-editing effectiveness in text summarization. In *Proceedings of the 2022 Conference of the North American Chapter of the Association for Computational Linguistics: Human Language Technologies*, pages 475–493, Seattle, United States. Association for Computational Linguistics.

Staffan Larson. 2002. *Issue-based Dialogue Management*. Ph.D. thesis, Göteborg University, Sweden.

Mike Lewis, Yinhan Liu, Naman Goyal, Marjan Ghazvininejad, Abdelrahman Mohamed, Omer Levy, Veselin Stoyanov, and Luke Zettlemoyer. 2020. BART: Denoising sequence-to-sequence pretraining for natural language generation, translation, and comprehension. In *Proceedings of the 58th Annual Meeting of the Association for Computational Linguistics*, pages 7871–7880, Online. Association for Computational Linguistics.

Junyi Li, Tianyi Tang, Gaole He, Jinhao Jiang, Xiaoxuan Hu, Puzhao Xie, Zhipeng Chen, Zhuohao Yu, Wayne Xin Zhao, and Ji-Rong Wen. 2021. TextBox: A unified, modularized, and extensible framework for text generation. In *Proceedings of the 59th Annual Meeting of the Association for Computational Linguistics and the 11th International Joint Conference on Natural Language Processing: System Demonstrations*, pages 30–39, Online. Association for Computational Linguistics.

Wei Li, Xinyan Xiao, Yajuan Lyu, and Yuanzhuo Wang. 2018. Improving neural abstractive document summarization with explicit information selection modeling. In *Proceedings of the 2018 Conference on Empirical Methods in Natural Language Processing*, pages 1787–1796, Brussels, Belgium. Association for Computational Linguistics.

Yang Liu and Mirella Lapata. 2019. Text summarization with pretrained encoders. In *Proceedings of the 2019 Conference on Empirical Methods in Natural Language Processing and the 9th International Joint Conference on Natural Language Processing (EMNLP-IJCNLP)*, pages 3730–3740, Hong Kong, China. Association for Computational Linguistics.

Joshua Maynez, Shashi Narayan, Bernd Bohnet, and Ryan McDonald. 2020. On faithfulness and factuality in abstractive summarization. In *Proceedings of the 58th Annual Meeting of the Association for Computational Linguistics*, pages 1906–1919, Online. Association for Computational Linguistics.

Alexander H Miller, Will Feng, Adam Fisch, Jiasen Lu, Dhruv Batra, Antoine Bordes, Devi Parikh, and Jason Weston. 2017. Parlai: A dialog research software platform. *arXiv preprint arXiv:1705.06476*.

Amit Moryossef, Yoav Goldberg, and Ido Dagan. 2019. Step-by-step: Separating planning from realization in neural data-to-text generation. In *Proceedings of the 2019 Conference of the North American Chapter of the Association for Computational Linguistics: Human Language Technologies, Volume 1 (Long and Short Papers)*, pages 2267–2277, Minneapolis, Minnesota. Association for Computational Linguistics.

Ramesh Nallapati, Bowen Zhou, Cicero dos Santos, Çağlar Gulçehre, and Bing Xiang. 2016. Abstractive text summarization using sequence-to-sequence RNNs and beyond. In *Proceedings of The 20th SIGNLL Conference on Computational Natural Language Learning*, pages 280–290, Berlin, Germany. Association for Computational Linguistics.

Shashi Narayan, Joshua Maynez, Reinald Kim Amplayo, Kuzman Ganchev, Annie Louis, Fantine Huot, Dipanjan Das, and Mirella Lapata. 2022. Conditional generation with a question-answering blueprint. *arXiv preprint arXiv:2207.00397*.

Shashi Narayan, Yao Zhao, Joshua Maynez, Gonçalo Simões, Vitaly Nikolaev, and Ryan McDonald. 2021. Planning with learned entity prompts for abstractive summarization. *Transactions of the Association for Computational Linguistics*, 9:1475–1492.

Valentin Nyzam and Aurélien Bossard. 2019. A modular tool for automatic summarization. In *Proceedings of the 57th Annual Meeting of the Association for Computational Linguistics: System Demonstrations*, pages 189–194, Florence, Italy. Association for Computational Linguistics.

Ratish Puduppully, Li Dong, and Mirella Lapata. 2019. Data-to-text generation with content selection and planning. In *Proceedings of the 33rd AAAI Conference on Artificial Intelligence*, Honolulu, Hawaii.

Colin Raffel, Noam Shazeer, Adam Roberts, Katherine Lee, Sharan Narang, Michael Matena, Yanqi Zhou, Wei Li, and Peter J. Liu. 2020. Exploring the limits of transfer learning with a unified text-to-text transformer. *Journal of Machine Learning Research*, 21(140):1–67.

Arndt Riester. 2019. Constructing qud trees. In *Questions in Discourse*, volume 2: Pragmatics, pages 164–193. Brill.

Craige Roberts. 2012. Information structure in discourse: Towards an integrated formal theory of pragmatics. *Semantics and Pragmatics*, 5(6):1–69.

Alexander M. Rush, Sumit Chopra, and Jason Weston. 2015. A neural attention model for abstractive sentence summarization. In *Proceedings of the 2015 Conference on Empirical Methods in Natural Language Processing*, pages 379–389, Lisbon, Portugal. Association for Computational Linguistics.

Abigail See, Peter J. Liu, and Christopher D. Manning. 2017. Get to the point: Summarization with pointer-generator networks. In *Proceedings of the 55th Annual Meeting of the Association for Computational Linguistics (Volume 1: Long Papers)*, pages 1073–1083, Vancouver, Canada. Association for Computational Linguistics.

Kaiqiang Song, Lin Zhao, and Fei Liu. 2018. Structure-infused copy mechanisms for abstractive summarization. In *Proceedings of the 27th International Conference on Computational Linguistics*, pages 1717–1729, Santa Fe, New Mexico, USA. Association for Computational Linguistics.

Ilya Sutskever, Oriol Vinyals, and Quoc V Le. 2014. Sequence to sequence learning with neural networks. In Z. Ghahramani, M. Welling, C. Cortes, N. D. Lawrence, and K. Q. Weinberger, editors, *Advances in Neural Information Processing Systems 27*, pages 3104–3112. Curran Associates, Inc.

Jun Suzuki and Masaaki Nagata. 2017. Cutting-off redundant repeating generations for neural abstractive summarization. In *Proceedings of the 15th Conference of the European Chapter of the Association for Computational Linguistics: Volume 2, Short Papers*, pages 291–297, Valencia, Spain. Association for Computational Linguistics.

Shahbaz Syed, Tariq Yousef, Khalid Al Khatib, Stefan Jänicke, and Martin Potthast. 2021. Summary explorer: Visualizing the state of the art in text summarization. In *Proceedings of the 2021 Conference on Empirical Methods in Natural Language Processing: System Demonstrations*, pages 185–194, Online and Punta Cana, Dominican Republic. Association for Computational Linguistics.

Bowen Tan, Zichao Yang, Maruan Al-Shedivat, Eric Xing, and Zhiting Hu. 2021. Progressive generation of long text with pretrained language models. In *Proceedings of the 2021 Conference of the North American Chapter of the Association for Computational Linguistics: Human Language Technologies*, pages 4313–4324, Online. Association for Computational Linguistics.

Jiwei Tan, Xiaojun Wan, and Jianguo Xiao. 2017. Abstractive document summarization with a graph-based attentional neural model. In *Proceedings of the 55th Annual Meeting of the Association for Computational Linguistics (Volume 1: Long Papers)*, pages 1171–1181, Vancouver, Canada. Association for Computational Linguistics.

Ian Tenney, James Wexler, Jasmijn Bastings, Tolga Bolukbasi, Andy Coenen, Sebastian Gehrmann, Ellen Jiang, Mahima Pushkarna, Carey Radebaugh,

Emily Reif, et al. 2020. The language interpretability tool: Extensible, interactive visualizations and analysis for nlp models. *arXiv preprint arXiv:2008.05122*.

Jan Van Kuppevelt. 1995. Discourse structure, topicality and questioning. *Journal of linguistics*, 31(1):109–147.

Ashish Vaswani, Noam Shazeer, Niki Parmar, Jakob Uszkoreit, Llion Jones, Aidan N Gomez, Ł ukasz Kaiser, and Illia Polosukhin. 2017. Attention is all you need. In I. Guyon, U. V. Luxburg, S. Bengio, H. Wallach, R. Fergus, S. Vishwanathan, and R. Garnett, editors, *Advances in Neural Information Processing Systems 30*, pages 5998–6008. Curran Associates, Inc.

Jesse Vig, Wojciech Kryscinski, Karan Goel, and Nazneen Rajani. 2021. SummVis: Interactive visual analysis of models, data, and evaluation for text summarization. In *Proceedings of the 59th Annual Meeting of the Association for Computational Linguistics and the 11th International Joint Conference on Natural Language Processing: System Demonstrations*, pages 150–158, Online. Association for Computational Linguistics.

Haoyang Wen, Yijia Liu, Wanxiang Che, Libo Qin, and Ting Liu. 2018. Sequence-to-sequence learning for task-oriented dialogue with dialogue state representation. In *Proceedings of the 27th International Conference on Computational Linguistics*, pages 3781–3792, Santa Fe, New Mexico, USA. Association for Computational Linguistics.

Jingqing Zhang, Yao Zhao, Mohammad Saleh, and Peter Liu. 2020. PEGASUS: Pre-training with extracted gap-sentences for abstractive summarization. In *Proceedings of the 37th International Conference on Machine Learning*, volume 119 of *Proceedings of Machine Learning Research*, pages 11328–11339. PMLR.

A Appendix

Tables 1 and 2 on the following pages show examples of manually-edited plans and their corresponding summaries.

	Plan	Summary
Why did France give the US the Statue of Liberty?		
MACHINE-GENERATED PLAN	Q_1: Who proposed that a statue be built as a gift from France to the United States to commemorate the friendship between France and the United States? Q_2: In what year was the Statue of Liberty designed? Q_3: Who designed the Statue of Liberty? Q_4: Along with freedom and democracy, what did Laboulaye want the Statue of Liberty to represent? Q_5: To whom was the Statue of Liberty presented? Q_6: In what city was the Statue of Liberty presented to the U.S. ambassador? Q_7: Gustave Eiffel helped build what for the Statue of Liberty?	In 1865, French political thinker and abolitionist Édouard de Laboulaye proposed that a statue be built as a gift from France to the United States to commemorate the friendship between France and the United States and to commemorate the 100th anniversary of U.S. independence. Designed by sculptor Auguste Bartholdi, the statue was meant to symbolize the American welcome of immigrants and refugee seekers. It was presented to the U.S. ambassador Levi Morton in Paris on July 4, 1881, by French Marshal Nicolas Luckner as a commemoration of the friendship between France and the United States. Gustave Eiffel helped build the pedestal for the Statue of Liberty.
MANUALLY-EDITED PLAN	Q_1: Who proposed that a statue be built as a gift from France to the United States to commemorate the friendship between France and the United States? Q_2: In what year was the Statue of Liberty designed? Q_3: Who designed the Statue of Liberty? Q_4: Along with freedom and democracy, what did Laboulaye want the Statue of Liberty to represent? Q_5: To whom was the Statue of Liberty presented? Q_6: In what city was the Statue of Liberty presented to the U.S. ambassador? **Q_7: How was the Statue of Liberty transported to New York City?**	In 1865, French political thinker and abolitionist Édouard de Laboulaye proposed that a statue be built as a gift from France to the United States to commemorate the friendship between France and the United States and to commemorate the 100th anniversary of the United States' independence. Designed by sculptor Auguste Bartholdi, the statue was meant to symbolize the American welcome of immigrants and refugee seekers. It was presented to the U.S. ambassador Levi Morton in Paris on July 4, 1881, **and later transported to New York City where it was reconstructed.**
Who plays Queen Lannister in Game of Thrones?		
MACHINE-GENERATED PLAN	Q_1: Who is the actress who played Cersei Lannister? Q_2: What is Cersei Lannister's role in Game of Thrones? Q_3: What is the name of the book series in which Cersei Lannister appears? Q_4: Who wrote 'A Song of Ice and Fire'? Q_5: What is Game of Thrones based on? Q_6: When did Game of Thrones first air? Q_7: What is one of the wealthiest and most powerful families in Westeros? Q_8: In what year did Cersei Lannister first appear in the books?	Cersei Lannister is a fictional character in the A Song of Ice and Fire series of epic fantasy novels by American author George R.R. Martin, and its television adaptation Game of Thrones, where she is portrayed by Bermudian-English actress Lena Headey. Introduced in 1996's A Game of Thrones, Cersei is a member of House Lannister, one of the wealthiest and most powerful families on the continent of Westeros. She subsequently appears in A Clash of Kings (1998) and A Storm of Swords (2000), and becomes a prominent point of view character beginning with A Feast for Crows (2005).
MANUALLY-EDITED PLAN	Q_1: Who is the actress who played Cersei Lannister? Q_2: What is Cersei Lannister's role in Game of Thrones? **Q_3: Has the actress received any awards?** **Q_4: Is the actress famous?**	Cersei Lannister is a fictional character in the A Song of Ice and Fire series of epic fantasy novels by American author George R.R. Martin, and its television adaptation Game of Thrones, where she is portrayed by Bermudian-English actress Lena Headey. **Headey has received widespread critical acclaim for her portrayal of the character, making her one of the most popular and longest-running actors on television.**
Who said my enemy's enemy is my friend?		
MACHINE-GENERATED PLAN	Q_1: What did the Latin phrase "Amicus meus, inimicus inimici mei" mean? Q_2: During what time period did the Latin phrase "Amicus meus, inimicus inimici mei" become common? Q_3: When did the English version of the phrase "the enemy of my enemy is my friend" first appear? Q_4: Who was the first person to use the modern English version of the phrase "the enemy of my enemy is my friend"? Q_5: When did the English version of the phrase "the enemy of my enemy is my friend" first appear?	The exact meaning of the modern phrase was first expressed in the Latin phrase "Amicus meus, inimicus inimici mei" ("my friend, the enemy of my enemy"), which had become common throughout Europe by the early 1700s, while the first recorded use of the current English version came in 1884. The first recorded instance for this phrasing comes from Gabriel Manigault, who in his 1884 Political Creed described the sense that "the enemy of my enemy is my friend" as a "natural feeling".
MANUALLY-EDITED PLAN	**Q_1: Who was the first person to use the modern English version of the phrase "the enemy of my enemy is my friend"?** **Q_2: What did Gabriel Manigault describe as a natural feeling?**	**The first recorded instance for this phrasing comes from Gabriel Manigault, who in his 1884 Political Creed described the sense that "the enemy of my enemy is my friend" as a "natural feeling".**

Table 1: Examples of machine-generated and manually-edited plans and their corresponding summaries. We highlight in bold changes made by the user and the resulting changes to the summary.

	Plan	Summary
Is it illegal to have a bald eagle?		
MACHINE-GENERATED PLAN	Q_1: What is the section number of the Bald and Golden Eagle Protection Act in the United States Code? Q_2: What is the Bald and Golden Eagle Protection Act? Q_3: What does the Bald and Golden Eagle Protection Act prohibit the taking of? Q_4: Along with golden eagles, what bald eagle is protected by the Bald and Golden Eagle Protection Act? Q_5: The Bald and Golden Eagle Protection Act prohibits the taking of bald eagles, their parts, nests, and what else? Q_6: Who is required to obtain a permit from the Secretary of the Interior to take bald eagles? Q_7: What can result in a fine of up to \$100,000? Q_8: How much is the fine for a first offense of taking a bald eagle?	The Bald and Golden Eagle Protection Act (16 U.S.C. 668-668d), enacted in 1940, and amended several times since, prohibits anyone, without a permit issued by the Secretary of the Interior, from "taking" bald or golden eagles, including their parts (including feathers), nests, or eggs. The Act provides criminal penalties for persons who take, possess, sell, purchase, barter, offer to sell, purchase or barter, transport, export or import, at any time or any manner, any bald eagle (or any golden eagle), alive or dead, or any part (including feathers), nest, or egg thereof. A violation of the Act can result in a fine of up to \$100,000 (\$200,000 for organizations), imprisonment for one year, or both, for a first offense.
MANUALLY-EDITED PLAN	Q_1: What is the Bald and Golden Eagle Protection Act? **Q_2: Can Native Americans ask for an eagle permit?**	The Bald and Golden Eagle Protection Act (16 U.S.C. 668-668d), enacted in 1940, and amended several times since, prohibits anyone, without a permit issued by the Secretary of the Interior, from "taking" bald or golden eagles, including their parts (including feathers), nests, or eggs. **Native Americans may ask for an eagle permit.**
Is software engineer a good job?		
MACHINE-GENERATED PLAN	Q_1: What is projected to grow 22% from 2020 to 2030? Q_2: What is the average salary for a software engineer? Q_3: What is the average salary for a software engineer? Q_4: Along with management, in what area do software engineers earn more than most other workers?	Employment of software developers is projected to grow 22% from 2020 to 2030, which is much higher than the national average for other occupations. The average salary for a software engineer is \$99,400 with an average yearly growth rate of 7%. In addition, software engineers earn more than most other workers in the more traditional business aspects such as management and sales.
MANUALLY-EDITED PLAN	Q_1: What is the average salary for a software engineer? **Q_2: What degree should you get to become a software engineer?**	The average salary for a software engineer is \$99,400 according to the BLS. **Having a bachelor's degree in computer science or software engineering is recommended, though a master's degree may be more beneficial.**

Table 2: Examples of machine-generated and manually-edited plans and their corresponding summaries (Continued). We highlight in bold changes made by the user and the resulting changes to the summary.

ALAMBIC : Active Learning Automation with Methods to Battle Inefficient Curation

Charlotte Nachtegael
Machine Learning Group, ULB
IBsquare, ULB-VUB
charlotte.nachtegael@ulb.be

Jacopo De Stefani
TPM-ESS-ICT, TUDelft
Machine Learning Group, ULB
J.deStefani@tudelft.nl

Tom Lenaerts
Machine Learning Group, ULB
IBsquare, ULB-VUB
AI Lab, VUB
Tom.Lenaerts@ulb.be

Abstract

In this paper, we present ALAMBIC, an open-source dockerized web-based platform for annotating text data through active learning for classification tasks. Active learning is known to reduce the need of labelling, a time-consuming task, by selecting the most informative instances among the unlabelled instances, reaching an optimal accuracy faster than by just randomly labelling data. ALAMBIC integrates all the steps from data import to customization of the (active) learning process and annotation of the data, with indications of the progress of the trained model that can be downloaded and used in downstream tasks. Its architecture also allows the easy integration of other types of models, features and active learning strategies. The code is available on https://trusted-ai-labs.github/ALAMBIC/ and a video demonstration is available on https://youtu.be/4oh8UADfEmY.

1 Introduction

Data annotation is crucial for any machine learning task. Datasets of high-quality are obtained through manual labelling which requires both considerable time and sometimes also expertise. Active learning aims to reduce the need for labelled data by starting from a partially labelled dataset and gradually selecting the most informative instances among the unlabelled instances (Settles, 2009; Baldridge and Palmer, 2009). This incremental training of a machine learning model can thus actively select the instances it finds to be the most informative, asking the person involved to provide a true label for the selected data. Several strategies exist to define informativeness, such as those based on uncertainty of the predictions obtained for unlabelled instances (Settles, 2009) or based on the difference of their features with respect to the training set (Sener and Savarese, 2018). The model is then trained with the newly obtained labelled set and can again select instances to be labeled. This process is repeated up until a specific criterion is reached, such as a desired accuracy or a maximum number of instances labelled.

We present in this work **ALAMBIC** (**A**ctive **L**earning **A**utomation with **M**ethods to **B**attle **I**nefficient **C**uration), an open-source dockerized web-based platform for active-learning-based text classification, allowing for a full customisation of the active learning process, from the choice of the model, its features and parameters, and the active learning strategy[1]. It allows the study of the usefulness of active learning on a given labelled dataset and model, as well as the annotation of text instances with active learning.

2 Related works

Several active learning libraries have been developed, such as ALiPy (Tang et al., 2019), modAL (Danka and Horvath), scikit-activeml (Kottke et al., 2021), for traditional machine learning methods and DISTIL (Beck et al., 2021), SmallText (Schröder et al., 2021), the low-resource Text classification framework (Ein-Dor et al., 2020) or the ALToolbox (Tsvigun et al., 2022) which also contains active learning methods for deep learning. However, these libraries do not provide user interface or if they do, they require the user to be reasonably skilled in coding. Tools such as Prodigy [2], APLenty (Nghiem and Ananiadou, 2018), AlpacaTag (Lin et al., 2019), Paladin (Nghiem et al.,

[1] Code source available on https://github.com/Trusted-AI-Labs/ALAMBIC

[2] https://prodi.gy/

Proceedings of the 17th Conference of the European Chapter of the Association for Computational Linguistics System Demonstrations, pages 117–127
May 2-4, 2023 ©2023 Association for Computational Linguistics

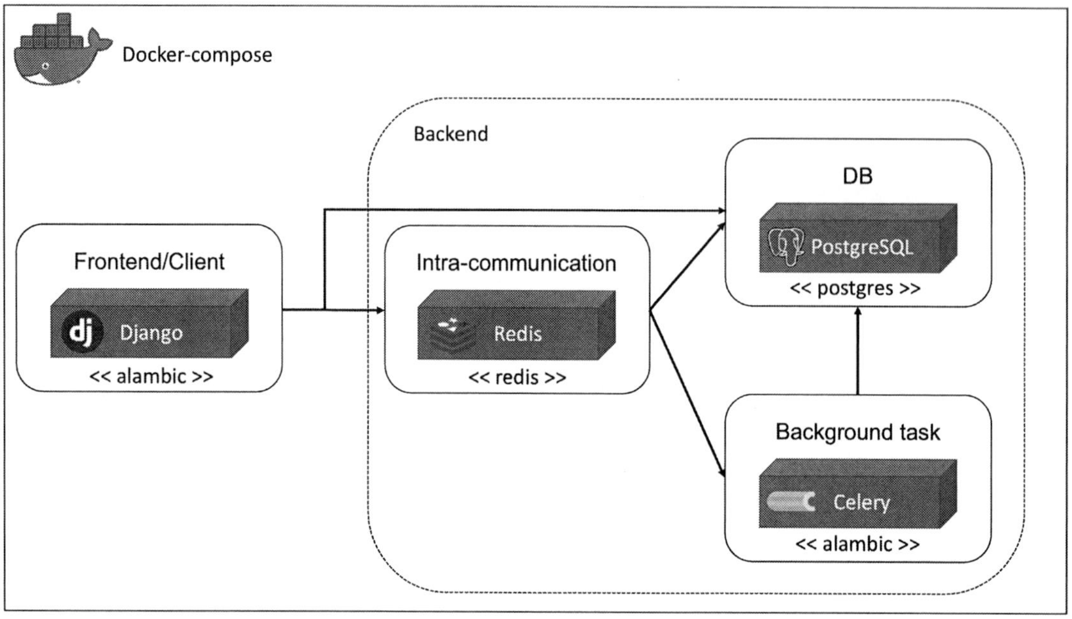

Figure 1: Diagram of the orchestrated deployment for ALAMBIC. Each box with a full line corresponds to a container. The blue box inside the container is the main service of the container. The name of the docker image for each container is indicated below the blue box.

2021), or Label Sleuth (Shnarch et al., 2022) tried to fill the gap by offering a user interface for the annotation process combined with an active learning setting. While these tools offer a friendly user-interface to annotate text classification or sequence labelling tasks, they either require a high-to-expert knowledge in programming languages, are not open source or are limited in the choice of the parameters in the active learning process, such as the model or the selection strategy.

At the time of writing, and to the best of our knowledge, **ALAMBIC** is the first free annotation tool for text classification with a user-friendly interface allowing a complete control of the user on the parameters of the features, model and active learning strategy, with no coding skills needed. Moreover, in addition to support the annotation task, it also allows the study of different active learning strategies with chosen features and models to evaluate the best strategy within that specific context. Its dockerized form also allows for an easy deployment and usage on diverse platforms.

3 Design and implementation

ALAMBIC is a web-based platform built in Python using Django framework [3], combined with Celery [4], Redis [5] and PostgreSQL [6] in a Docker Compose setting (Fig. 1). The installation requires only few command lines and is quite easy, even for people not familiar with Docker or GitHub (see Appendix A). The framework is divided in five main interfaces : (i) the import data interface, (ii) the setup and customisation of the (active) learning process, (iii) the progress of the active learning process, (iv) annotation interface and (v) the result interface. Each of these interfaces will be described below in detail[7].

3.1 Data import and task choice

ALAMBIC supports the import of the data in raw text with a reference file containing the path of the files and their labels if already available. The supported format is a TSV file with the path of the text files and their optional labels.

The user can also choose the annotation task. At the moment only multi-class classification is implemented.

Future developments will include annotation for relation extraction, as well as additional formats, such as JSON and XML, for import.

[3]https://www.djangoproject.com/

[4]https://github.com/celery/celery

[5]https://redis.io/

[6]https://www.postgresql.org/

[7]Full documentation is available at https://trusted-ai-labs.github.io/ALAMBIC/

If several files are provided, the user can choose among them through the dedicated user interface. Once imported, the data is accessible through the Django admin interface.

3.2 Setup of the learning process

Once the data has been added to the database, the user can setup each part of the learning process, from the model, its parameters and the features used as inputs.

The user can then choose to either analyse the impact of different active learning strategies in order to evaluate which one would be the most suitable with their data and choice of learning process, or use a specific active learning strategy to annotate the unlabeled part of the dataset. In the first case, the user is invited to choose the number of cross-validation folds, number of repetitions and size of the initial training seed, as well as which strategies they want to evaluate, ensuring a robust analysis of the process. In the second case, the user can choose the portion of the dataset to use as test set to evaluate the performance of the model at each iteration of the active learning process, the size of the training seed, the active learning strategy and the stop criterion, which will stop the active process once a specific criteria is met, such as a minimum accuracy, or a number of annotations done.

Model and feature implementations are based on scikit-learn (Pedregosa et al., 2011). While only a fraction of these are currently implemented, the architecture allows for an easy extension to functionalities already implemented in scikit-learn or having a similar programming interface. Our documentation offers a dedicated section for people more at ease in coding with Python to guide them through the integration of new models or features.

Active learning strategies are implemented from the ALiPy library (Tang et al., 2019). We choose to use only the strategies using the trained model in a pool-based scenario, i.e. all the unlabelled instances are considered for labelling at each iteration step.

3.3 Analysis and annotation interface

Once either type of processes, i.e. study of different active learning strategies or annotation, is launched, the process can be followed on an interface, displaying a plot of the performance of the model up until the current iteration.

All the plots are interactive, meaning that the user can zoom to observe a specific range of data, highlight and make disappear specific observations as to not crowd the graphic.

3.3.1 Study of different active learning strategies

In this case, the interface shows the performance in terms of accuracy of each of the strategies while the model goes through the different cross-validation folds and repetitions. The entire process is automated and can be followed in real-time.

Once the process is finished, the user can download the performances of the model generated during the whole analysis. Performances measures currently include accuracy, precision, recall, F-score and Matthews correlation coefficient.

3.3.2 Annotation using active learning

During the training of the model and the selection of the instances to label, the user can also observe in real time the accuracy of the model with the currently labelled data used as a training set.

Once instances have been selected to be labelled, the user is brought to a page where the text to label is displayed (Fig 2). They can either select an existing label or create a new one in the below drop-down menu. Above the text, a interactive plot with all the performance measures across the iterations is shown. This should have a positive impact on the motivation of the annotator by showing the effect of their work directly during the learning process.

3.4 Results interface

Once the process finished, the user can download for both types of processes the performances visualized in the plots. If ALAMBIC is used for annotating a dataset, the annotated dataset and the trained model during the last iteration can also be downloaded.

The performances are available in a CSV format with the different performance measures for each iteration, and optionally the repetitions, of the active learning process.

The annotated dataset format is a CSV file with the path of the text file, the ground-truth label if available, the manual label given during the anntation process, the label predicted by the model trained with ALAMBIC, as well as if the instance was part of the training set, the test set or none of them.

The model is exported in a compressed joblib format, compatible with most of the machine learning libraries for downstream import and usage.

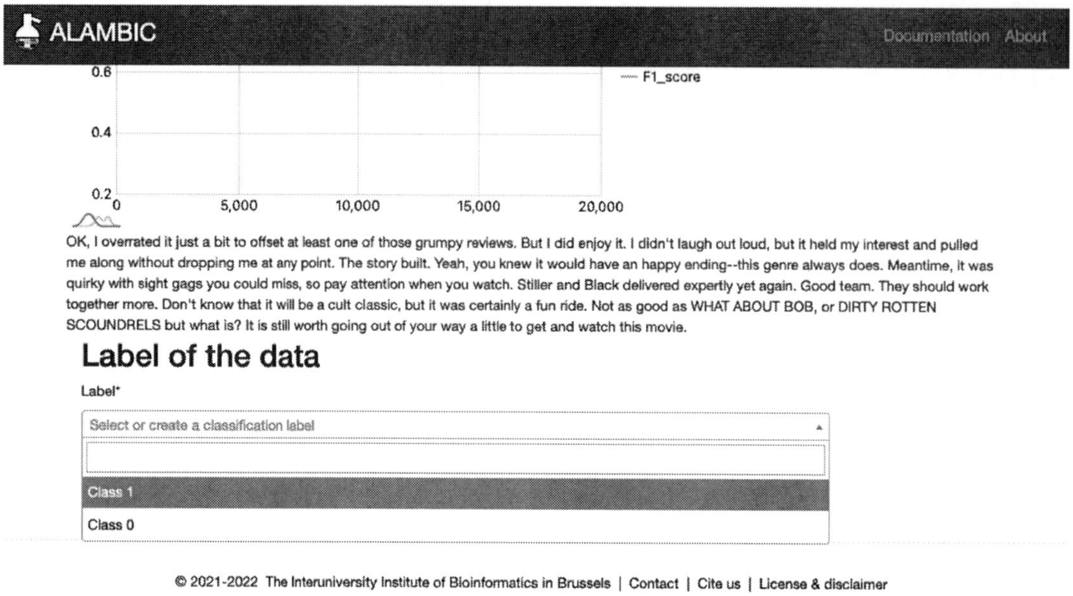

Figure 2: Annotation interface for text classification in ALAMBIC. The text to label is displayed below an interactive plot showing the performances of the model trained on the labelled data across the active learning iterations. The dropdown menu below the text to annotate allows the selection of an existing label or the creation of a new one by typing the new label in the text box.

4 Use Cases

The platform supposes that the user has a partially labelled dataset, a preferred model and features to use, and wants to label a portion of the remaining unlabelled dataset in a way that this portion will be the most informative to obtain a high-performance model. ALAMBIC can be used for two main use cases :

- **Comparison of active learning strategies:** ALAMBIC can be used to compare the performance of different active learning strategies, to determine which strategy to choose under given parameters/conditions.
- **Annotation of datasets:** ALAMBIC allows to choose one of the implemented active learning strategies and proceed with the annotation. The resulting annotations, performances measures and trained model can be exported and used for downstream analysis or automatic annotation.

5 Experiments and Results

We used the training set of the *Large Movie Review Dataset* (Maas et al., 2011), consisting in 25,000 highly polarized movie reviews, 12,500 positive and 12,500 negative.

For the analysis, we selected randomly 500 instances from each class.

Using ALAMBIC, we tested several active learning methods, including an uncertainty-based strategy (Settles, 2009), i.e. strategy based on different measures of uncertainty computed with the prediction output of the model; Core-set (Sener and Savarese, 2018), a selection method which tries to select the most different from the current training set and representative subset of unlabelled instances; and of course the random sampling as a baseline.

Each active learning method was tested for five folds of cross-validation, with three repetitions of the active learning process for the same test set with different initial training seeds (of a size of 10% of the remaining dataset). This means that 15 experiments were conducted for each strategy. Resulting performances are averaged for each iteration step. For each step, 50 instances are selected to be added.

The experiment was conducted with a Support Vector Machine (SVM) and a Random Forest (RF), with the default parameters proposed in their im-

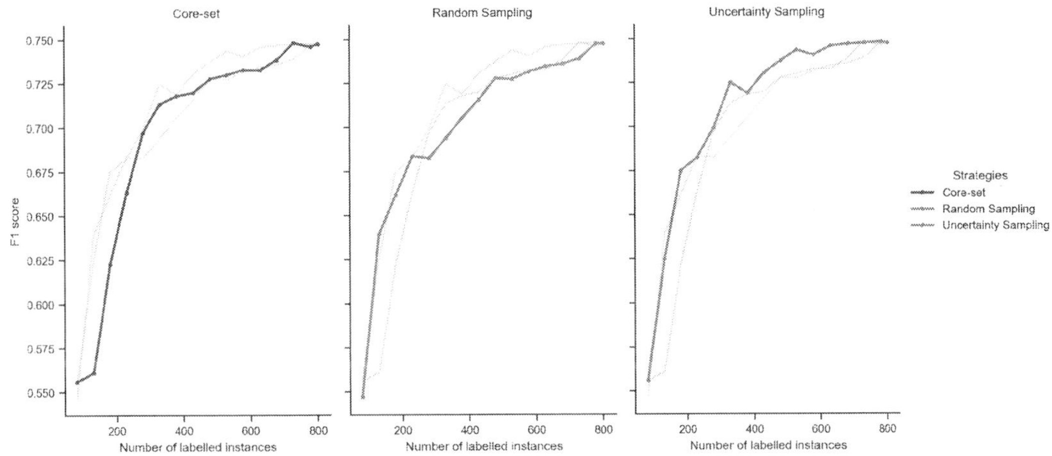

Figure 3: F-score obtained during the analysis of several active learning strategies with the SVM for a subset of 1000 samples of the Large Movie Reviews Dataset. Each panel highlights the results obtained for one specific strategy, with the other strategies greyed out.

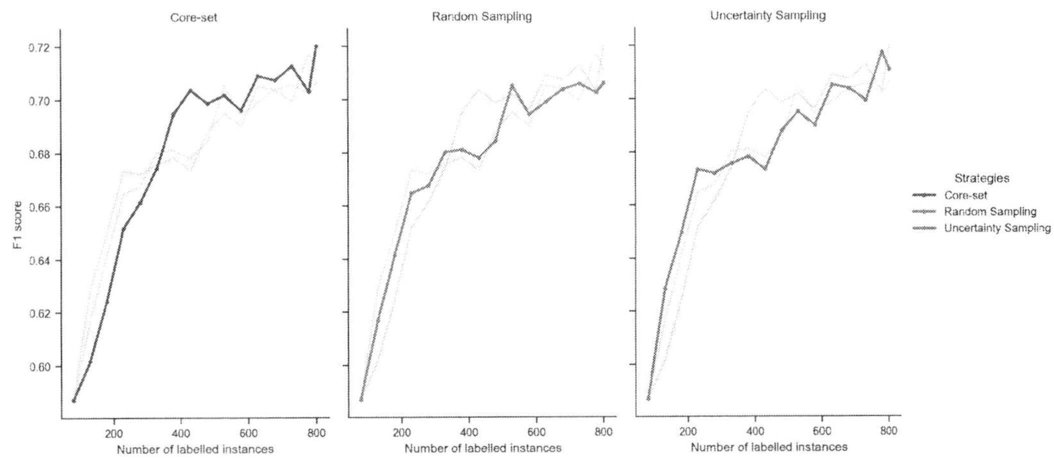

Figure 4: F-score obtained during the analysis of several active learning strategies with the RF for a subset of 1000 samples of the Large Movie Reviews Dataset. Each panel highlights the results obtained for one specific strategy, with the other strategies greyed out.

plementation in scikit-learn. The text was first pre-processed by ignoring the stop words, then the Term Frequency -Inverse Document Frequency (TF-IDF) was computed for each term, with a minimum document frequency of 0.1 and a maximum of 0.9. Only the top 3000 features were kept to build the vocabulary, ordered by term frequency across the corpus.

Figure 3 and 4 display the F-scores obtained for the subset of 1000 samples. We could observe that it would be preferable to use the uncertainty sampling method coupled with the SVM, as we see that while it performs less efficiently in the first few iterations, it clearly performs better and reached an optimal performance earlier than the random sampling or core-set method. However, if one wanted to use a RF, then it would be better to use the core-set method, as while it does not perform well in the first iterations, it outperforms the outer two selection methods. Moreover, for the RF, the uncertainty method has a similar performance as the random sampling.

Those observations highlight the importance of such analysis before using active learning in a real setting in order to choose the most optimal strategy. More advanced cases will be explored outside this paper.

6 Conclusion and Future Work

We presented ALAMBIC, an open-source web-based platform for the study and use of active learning in text classification. It can help people with low-to-no coding skills to use in the most efficient way active learning methods to build high-quality NLP datasets at a faster pace. First, they can compare with their choice of parameters and models different active learning strategies and then annotate their data with the strategy obtaining the best performance.

Further developments of the tools include the addition of other NLP annotation tasks, the integration of deep learning models and their related active learning methods. While the later development would reduce the ease of deployment for non-experts in coding, this would offer more state-of-the-art models for further automatic annotation.

Limitations

At the moment, only traditional machine learning methods can be used with our framework. The expansion to deep learning methods would bring models with better accuracy and make disappear the need to study also different features.

Using active learning in practice is also subject to several limitations. First, finding the right initial pool for an active learning setting will have an important impact on the overall performance of the active learning process. Moreover, the choice of the evaluation set is difficult as 1) it has to be representative of a dataset whom distribution could be unknown and 2) large enough to evaluate the performances of the model (such as recall, notably sensitive to class distribution). The latter aspect in particular would be in conflict with the spirit of active learning which tries to limit the annotation as much as possible. Finally, one has to keep in mind that the oracle/annotator is not always right and could in consequence introduce noise in the active learning process. While some strategies could be implemented to fight those practical issues (Yang and Loog, 2022; Paul et al., 2020), they were not implemented or taken into account in our work.

While it only supports few models and features at the moment, it can be easily extended to any models and features developed by scikit-learn.

ALAMBIC has only been tested and implemented for the English language. Spacy (Honnibal et al., 2020), which is used for some pre-processing steps, can be however adapted for many other languages.

The platform has also not been developed for a multi-annotators or crowd annotator contexts, which means that only one annotator can work at a time on the annotation task.

Acknowledgements

Basic architecture and design was largely inspired by the work done by Alexandre Renaux for ORVAL[8] (Renaux et al., 2019). This work was supported by Service Public de Wallonie Recherche under grant n° 2010235 - ARIAC by DIGITALWALLONIA4.AI. We would also like to thank the anonymous reviewers for their helpful comments.

References

Jason Baldridge and Alexis Palmer. 2009. How well does active learning *actually* work? Time-based evaluation of cost-reduction strategies for language documentation. In *Proceedings of the 2009 Conference on Empirical Methods in Natural Language Processing*, pages 296–305, Singapore. Association for Computational Linguistics.

Nathan Beck, Durga Sivasubramanian, Apurva Dani, Ganesh Ramakrishnan, and Rishabh Iyer. 2021. Effective evaluation of deep active learning on image classification tasks.

Tivadar Danka and Peter Horvath. modAL: A modular active learning framework for Python. Available on arXiv at `https://arxiv.org/abs/1805.00979`.

Liat Ein-Dor, Alon Halfon, Ariel Gera, Eyal Shnarch, Lena Dankin, Leshem Choshen, Marina Danilevsky, Ranit Aharonov, Yoav Katz, and Noam Slonim. 2020. Active learning for BERT: An empirical study. In *Proceedings of the 2020 Conference on Empirical Methods in Natural Language Processing (EMNLP)*, pages 7949–7962, Online. Association for Computational Linguistics.

Matthew Honnibal, Ines Montani, Sofie Van Landeghem, and Adriane Boyd. 2020. spaCy: Industrial-strength Natural Language Processing in Python.

Daniel Kottke, Marek Herde, Tuan Pham Minh, Alexander Benz, Pascal Mergard, Atal Roghman, Christoph Sandrock, and Bernhard Sick. 2021. scikitactiveml: A library and toolbox for active learning algorithms. *Preprints*.

Bill Yuchen Lin, Dong-Ho Lee, Frank F. Xu, Ouyu Lan, and Xiang Ren. 2019. AlpacaTag: An active learning-based crowd annotation framework for sequence tagging. In *Proceedings of the 57th Annual Meeting of*

[8] `https://orval.ibsquare.be`

the Association for Computational Linguistics: System Demonstrations, pages 58–63, Florence, Italy. Association for Computational Linguistics.

Andrew L. Maas, Raymond E. Daly, Peter T. Pham, Dan Huang, Andrew Y. Ng, and Christopher Potts. 2011. Learning word vectors for sentiment analysis. In *Proceedings of the 49th Annual Meeting of the Association for Computational Linguistics: Human Language Technologies*, pages 142–150, Portland, Oregon, USA. Association for Computational Linguistics.

Minh-Quoc Nghiem and Sophia Ananiadou. 2018. APLenty: annotation tool for creating high-quality datasets using active and proactive learning. In *Proceedings of the 2018 Conference on Empirical Methods in Natural Language Processing: System Demonstrations*, pages 108–113, Brussels, Belgium. Association for Computational Linguistics.

Minh-Quoc Nghiem, Paul Baylis, and Sophia Ananiadou. 2021. Paladin: an annotation tool based on active and proactive learning. In *Proceedings of the 16th Conference of the European Chapter of the Association for Computational Linguistics: System Demonstrations*, pages 238–243, Online. Association for Computational Linguistics.

Sudipta Paul, Shivkumar Chandrasekaran, B. S. Manjunath, and Amit K. Roy-Chowdhury. 2020. Exploiting context for robustness to label noise in active learning. *ArXiv*, abs/2010.09066.

F. Pedregosa, G. Varoquaux, A. Gramfort, V. Michel, B. Thirion, O. Grisel, M. Blondel, P. Prettenhofer, R. Weiss, V. Dubourg, J. Vanderplas, A. Passos, D. Cournapeau, M. Brucher, M. Perrot, and E. Duchesnay. 2011. Scikit-learn: Machine learning in Python. *Journal of Machine Learning Research*, 12:2825–2830.

Alexandre Renaux, Sofia Papadimitriou, Nassim Versbraegen, Charlotte Nachtegael, Simon Boutry, Ann Nowé, Guillaume Smits, and Tom Lenaerts. 2019. ORVAL: a novel platform for the prediction and exploration of disease-causing oligogenic variant combinations. *Nucleic Acids Research*, 47(W1):W93–W98.

Christopher Schröder, Lydia Müller, Andreas Niekler, and Martin Potthast. 2021. Small-text: Active learning for text classification in python.

Ozan Sener and Silvio Savarese. 2018. Active learning for convolutional neural networks: A core-set approach. In *International Conference on Learning Representations*.

Burr Settles. 2009. Active learning literature survey. Technical report, University of Wisconsin–Madison.

Eyal Shnarch, Alon Halfon, Ariel Gera, Marina Danilevsky, Yannis Katsis, Leshem Choshen, Martin Santillan Cooper, Dina Epelboim, Zheng Zhang, Dakuo Wang, Lucy Yip, Liat Ein-Dor, Lena Dankin, Ilya Shnayderman, Ranit Aharonov, Yunyao Li, Naftali Liberman, Philip Levin Slesarev, Gwilym Newton, Shila Ofek-Koifman, Noam Slonim, and Yoav Katz. 2022. Label Sleuth: From unlabeled text to a classifier in a few hours. In *Proceedings of the 2022 Conference on Empirical Methods in Natural Language Processing: System Demonstrations*. Association for Computational Linguistics.

Ying-Peng Tang, Guo-Xiang Li, and Sheng-Jun Huang. 2019. ALiPy: Active learning in python. Technical report, Nanjing University of Aeronautics and Astronautics. Available as arXiv preprint `https://arxiv.org/abs/1901.03802`.

Akim Tsvigun, Leonid Sanochkin, Daniil Larionov, Gleb Kuzmin, Artem Vazhentsev, Ivan Lazichny, Nikita Khromov, Danil Kireev, Aleksandr Rubashevskii, Alexander Panchenko, Olga Shahmatova, Dmitry Dylov, Igor Galitskiy, and Artem Shelmanov. 2022. ALToolbox: A set of tools for active learning annotation of natural language texts. In *Proceedings of the The 2022 Conference on Empirical Methods in Natural Language Processing: System Demonstrations*, pages 406–434, Abu Dhabi, UAE. Association for Computational Linguistics.

Yazhou Yang and Marco Loog. 2022. To actively initialize active learning. *Pattern Recognition*, 131:108836.

Ethics Statement

We have considered eventual ethical impacts of our developed tool and evaluated the following questions :

- **Does the paper describe how the technology would be deployed in actual use cases?** Yes, our tool is dockerized, thusly easily deployable. We give further details on the deployment in our documentation[9]. Our aim is to offer a tool which is easy to use for non-coding experts.
- **Does the task carried out by the computer match how it would be deployed?** Yes, it is exactly as described in the paper, as we created a tool directly destined for users for annotation purposes.
- **Does the paper address possible harms when the technology is being used as intended and functioning correctly?** The tool can only be used in a local setting for an optimised, faster annotation. No harm can be directly induced by the tool itself. However, the users could use the tool to annotate in an harmful way data and maliciously spread the dataset, with biases and false information.

[9] `https://trusted-ai-labs.github.io/ALAMBIC/`

- **Does the paper address possible harms when the technology is being used as intended but giving incorrect results?** As the task concerns annotation, the only harm brought by the tool would come from the inefficient selection of instances to be labelled, which would only impact the performance of the labelling, but not bring harm directly to the human user.
- **Does the paper address possible harms following from potential misuse of the technology?** It highly depends on which type of data the user wants to annotate. The misuse would come from the data content and what will do the user with this data, such as spreading wrongly annotated datasets.
- **If the system learns from user input once deployed, does the paper describe checks and limitations to the learning?** The trained model learns from the labelled dataset, which is expanded by the user during the annotation process. However, the learning process is limited to the annotation process or the analysis process.

A Installation commands

Docker, Docker compose and git needs to be installed. The commands to install the tool and launch everything can be resumed in :

- Clone the repository
- Build the docker

Listing 1: Commands to install ALAMBIC

```
git clone https://github.com/Trusted-AI-Labs/ALAMBIC.git
cd ALAMBIC/
docker-compose up
```

B Interfaces examples

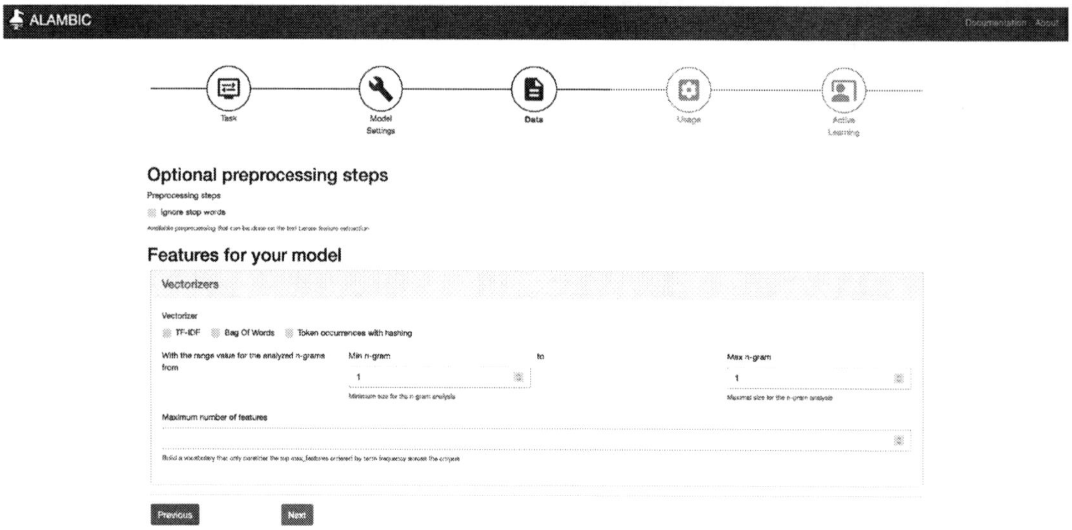

Figure 5: Choice of the model inputs/features.

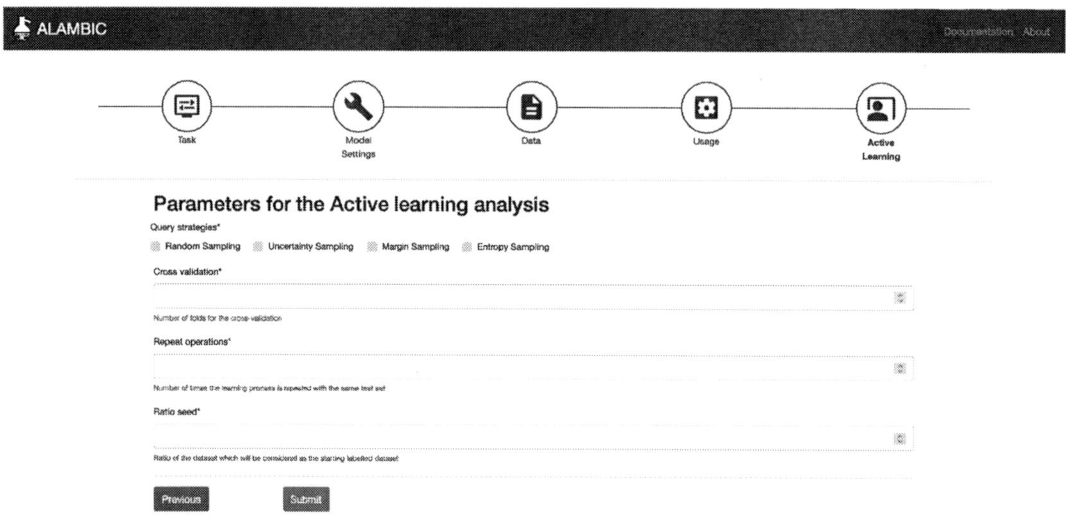

Figure 6: Parameters choice for an analysis of the use of different active learning strategies. Specific parameters include which strategies to evaluated, the number of cross-validations, number of repeats with different training seed and the ratio of the labelled set to be used as training seed.

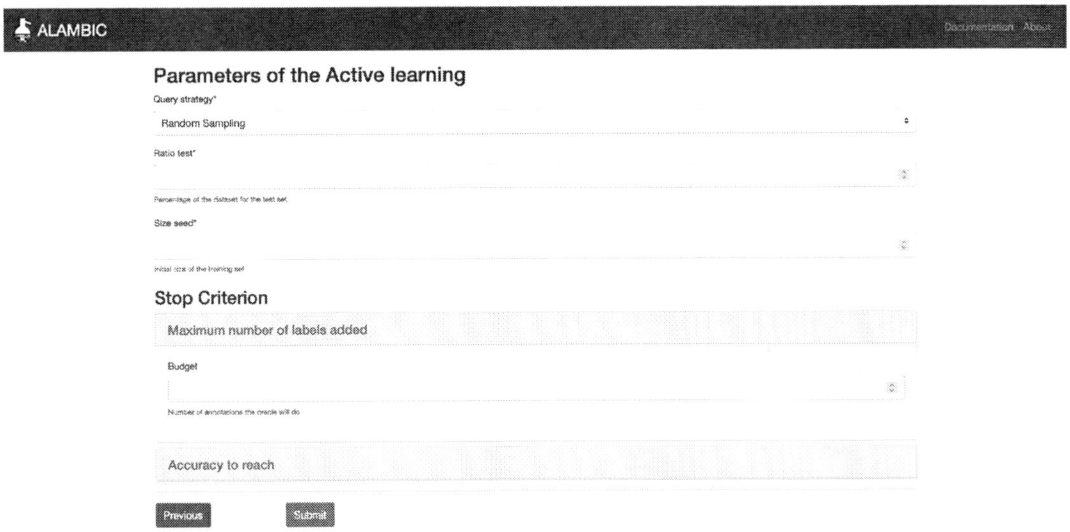

Figure 7: Parameters choice for the annotation using active learning. Specific parameters include the strategy to use, the ratio of the dataset to use as a test set, the size of the training seed and the stop criterion of the active learning process.

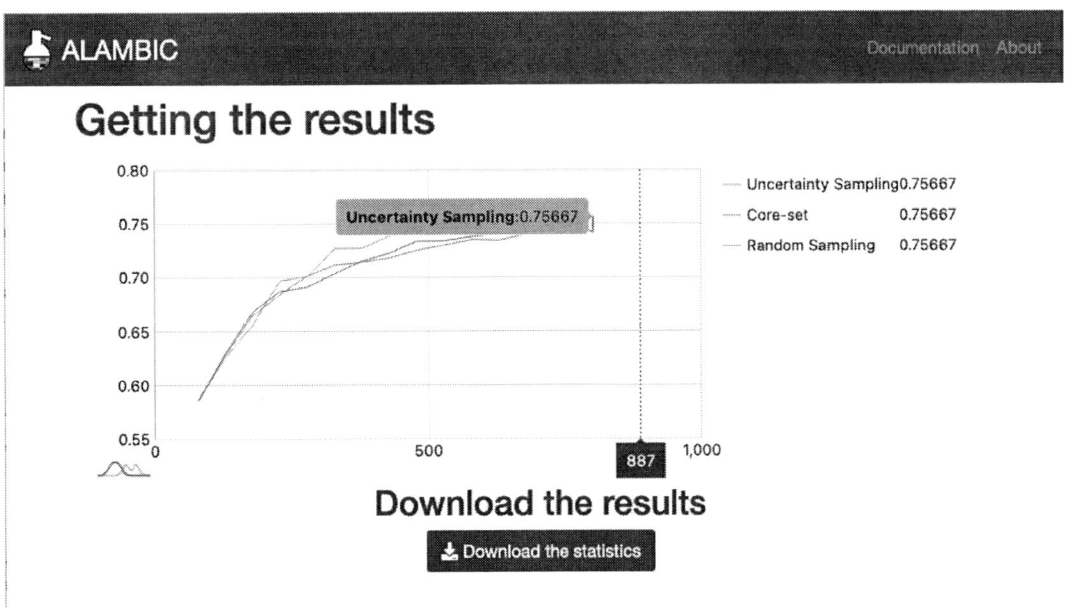

Figure 8: Example of result for the analysis of different active learning strategies.

SPINDLE: Spinning Raw Text into Lambda Terms with Graph Attention

Konstantinos Kogkalidis[◇] and **Michael Moortgat**[◇] and **Richard Moot**[□]
◇ Institute for Language Sciences, Utrecht University
□ LIRMM, Université de Montpellier, CNRS
{k.kogkalidis,m.j.moortgat}@uu.nl, richard.moot@lirmm.fr

Abstract

This paper describes SPINDLE[1] – an open source Python module implementing an efficient and accurate parser for written Dutch that transforms raw text input to programs for meaning composition, expressed as λ terms. The parser integrates a number of breakthrough advances made in recent years. Its output consists of hi-res derivations of a multimodal type-logical grammar, capturing two orthogonal axes of syntax, namely deep function-argument structures and dependency relations. These are produced by three interdependent systems: a static type-checker asserting the well-formedness of grammatical analyses, a state-of-the-art, structurally-aware supertagger based on heterogeneous graph convolutions, and a massively parallel proof search component based on Sinkhorn iterations. Packed in the software are also handy utilities and extras for proof visualization and inference, intended to facilitate end-user utilization.

1 Introduction

The transparency and formal well-behavedness of lambda calculi make them the ideal format for expressing compositional structures, a fact that has been duly emphasized by parsers and tools with a predominant focus on semantics. Lambda calculi form a key ingredient of type-logical grammars, where they find use as the computational counterpart of a so-called *grammar logic*, a substructural logic of the intuitionistic linear variety that is designed to capture (aspects of) natural language syntax and semantics (Moortgat, 1997). For type-logical grammars, the Curry-Howard isomorphism guarantees a straightforward passage between logical rules, type constructors and term-forming operators; put simply, Parse ≡ Proof ≡ Program, and Category ≡ Proposition ≡ Type. The modus operandi is straightforward: a lexicon associates words with logical formulas, and the logic's rules of inference decide how formulas may interact with one another.

By extension, words may only combine in a strict, well-typed manner, forming larger phrases in the process. Parsing becomes a process of logical deduction, at the end of which the result (a proof) gives rise to a recipe for meaning assembly (a program). This program is turned into executable code as soon as one plugs in appropriate interpretations for the lexical constants (words) and for the term operations (composition instructions). The set-up is general-purpose in that it readily accommodates different choices for these interpretations; valid targets can for instance be found in (truth-conditional) formal semantics, distributional-compositional models (Sadrzadeh and Muskens, 2018), or tableau-based theorem provers (Abzianidze, 2017).

In this work, we are interested in what happens prior to semantic execution; that is, we abstract away from lexical semantics and seek to reveal the compositional recipe underlying a natural language utterance. To that end, we employ a type grammar aimed at capturing two different *syntactic* axes, only rarely observed together in the wild: function-argument structures and dependency relations. To procure a derivation from an input phrase, we design and implement a system combining three distinct but communicating components. Component number one is the implementation of the grammar's type system — it comes packed with a number of useful facilities, most important being a static type checker that verifies the syntactic well-formedness of the analyses construed. Component number two is a supertagger responsible for assigning a type to each input word — the tagger is formulated on the basis of a hyper-efficient heterogeneous graph convolution kernel that boasts state-of-the-art accuracy among categorial grammar datasets. The third and last component is a neural permutation module that

[1] Stylized spind[2]λe and standing for **s**pindle **p**arses **in**to **d**ependency-**d**ecorated λ **e**xpressions. Source code and user instructions can be found at `https://github.com/konstantinosKokos/spindle`.

Proceedings of the 17th Conference of the European Chapter of the Association for Computational Linguistics System Demonstrations, pages 128–135
May 2-4, 2023 ©2023 Association for Computational Linguistics

exploits the linearity constraint of the target logic to simplify proof search as optimal transport learning (Peyré et al., 2019) — this reformulation allows for a massively parallel and easily optimizable implementation. The three components alternate roles through the processing pipeline, switching between phases of low level linear algebra routines and high level logical reasoning (GPU and CPU intensive, respectively). Their integration yields a lightspeed-fast and highly accurate neurosymbolic parser, neatly packaged and made publicly available.

2 System Decomposition

2.1 Type Grammar

The system's theoretical backbone is its type logic – a uniquely flavoured, semantics-first type-logical grammar that strays from the categorial norm in two major ways. First, it focuses on deep syntactic structure (or tectogrammar, in Curry's terms) rather than surface form; its functional types are therefore oblivious to directional or positional constraints, abiding only to the linearity condition: every occurrence of an atomic proposition must be used once and exactly once. Second, it dresses functional types up, so as to have them encode grammatical functions, making a three-way distinction between complements, heads and adjuncts.

A full exposition of the grammar is beyond the scope of this paper, but a superficial and simplified rundown should help shed light on what is to follow. Its first aspect, **function-argument structures**, is modeled using linear logic's implication arrow, $\multimap$, which gives us access to resource-conscious versions of function application and variable abstraction (Girard, 1987; Abramsky, 1993). In their linguistic usecase, functional types of the form $\mathrm{A}\multimap\mathrm{B}$ denote predicates that *consume* a single occurrence of some object of type A, the result being a composite phrase of type B. Reasoning about gaps, ellipses and the like is accomplished with the aid of higher-order types, i.e. instances of the previous scheme where A is itself a function — these higher-order types launch a process of **hypothetical reasoning**, whereby we may temporarily assume the existence of a resource to produce a derivation locally, only to later withdraw the hypothesis, creating a new function in the process. The second aspect, **dependency relations**, are modeled using a labeled assortment of residuated pairs of unary operators lent from temporal logic. Atomic types without any

$$\frac{}{\mathsf{x}:\mathrm{A}\vdash\mathsf{x}:\mathrm{A}}\ \mathrm{id} \qquad \frac{(\mathsf{c}\mapsto\mathrm{A})\in\mathcal{L}}{\mathsf{c}:\mathrm{A}\vdash\mathsf{c}:\mathrm{A}}\ \mathrm{lex}$$

$$\frac{\Gamma\vdash\mathsf{s}:\mathrm{A}\multimap\mathrm{B}\quad\Delta\vdash\mathsf{t}:\mathrm{A}}{\Gamma,\Delta\vdash\mathsf{s}\,\mathsf{t}:\mathrm{B}}\ {\multimap}E \qquad \frac{\Gamma,\mathsf{x}:\mathrm{A}\vdash\mathsf{s}:\mathrm{B}}{\Gamma\vdash\lambda\mathsf{x}.\mathsf{s}:\mathrm{A}\multimap\mathrm{B}}\ {\multimap}I$$

$$\frac{\Gamma\vdash\mathsf{s}:\Box_\delta\mathrm{A}}{\langle\Gamma\rangle^\delta\vdash\blacktriangledown_\delta\mathsf{s}:\mathrm{A}}\ \Box_\delta E \qquad \frac{\Gamma\vdash\mathsf{s}:\mathrm{A}}{\langle\Gamma\rangle^\delta\vdash\vartriangle_\delta\mathsf{s}:\Diamond_\delta\mathrm{A}}\ \Diamond_\delta I$$

Figure 1: Logical rules of inference used by the type grammar (subset). The id rule instantiates a fresh variable of arbitrary type A. The lex rule provides declares a constant c as being of type A, given type assignment $\mathsf{c}\mapsto\mathrm{A}$ pulled from the lexicon $\mathcal{L}$ (or, in the post-neural era, the supertagger). Introduction rules are complex types constructors, elimination rules are destructors. The ${\multimap}E$ rule says a term s of type $\mathrm{A}\multimap\mathrm{B}$ derived from premises Γ can apply to a term t of type A derived from premises Δ, producing a complex term $\mathsf{s}\,\mathsf{t}$ of type B derived from the merger of Γ and Δ. The ${\multimap}I$ rule says that if the premises of some term s of type B include a variable x of type A, we can abstract over the latter, producing a term $\lambda\mathsf{x}.\mathsf{s}$ of type $\mathrm{A}\multimap\mathrm{B}$. The $\Box_\delta E$ rule removes the box from a term s of type $\Box_\delta\mathrm{A}$, producing term $\blacktriangledown_\delta\mathsf{s}$ of type A and enclosing the premises under brackets $\langle\_\rangle^\delta$. Dually, the $\Diamond_\delta I$ rule puts a term s of type A under the scope of a diamond, producing term $\vartriangle_\delta\mathsf{s}$ of type $\Diamond_\delta\mathrm{A}$ and again enclosing the premises under brackets $\langle\_\rangle^\delta$.

dependency decorations are assigned to linguistically autonomous units and phrases, e.g. NP for a noun phrase. Functional types denoting heads impose a diamond $\Diamond_\mathsf{c}$ on the complements they select for, label c being the dependency slot the complement is to occupy, e.g. $\Diamond_{\mathsf{su}}\mathrm{NP}\multimap\mathrm{S}_{\mathsf{main}}$ for an intransitive verb looking for a subject-marked noun phrase to produce a matrix clause. Dually, functional types denoting adjuncts are themselves decorated with a box $\Box_\mathsf{a}$, label a now being the dependency role projected by the adjunct prior to application, e.g. $\Box_{\mathsf{mod}}(\mathrm{NP}\multimap\mathrm{NP})$ for an adjective, promising to provide a function over noun phrases if one is to remove its box. Introducing a diamond or eliminating a box leaves a *structural* imprint that encloses complete phrases under brackets, and a *computational* imprint that calls for a special treatment of the wrapped term – both labeled by the grammatical function of the diamond (resp. box) that was introduced (resp. eliminated). The key logical rules of the type grammar and their isomorphic term operations are presented in Figure 1.

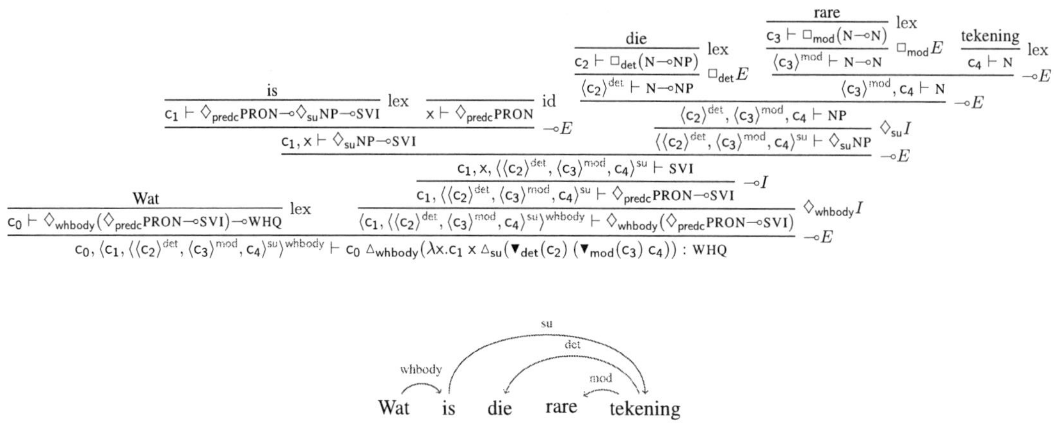

Figure 2: Natural deduction proof for the sentence *Wat is die rare tekening?* 'What is that strange drawing?'. For space economy, compositional λ term is only explicitly written in the endsequent (bottom of the proof). From the antecedent structure of the endsequent, we may also recover a dependency tree. Color coding serves to informally differentiate between complement (red) vs. adjunct (green) structural brackets/dependency arcs.

2.1.1 Proof Representation

Proofs in the type logic are traditionally served in the tree-like **natural deduction** format. Proofs in natural deduction benefit from an easy translation to (i) λ expressions, by following the rules of Figure 1, and (ii) dependency trees, by simply casting structural brackets to dependency arcs, going from the head of each phrase to (the heads of) its dependents. Figure 2 presents a visual example. An alternative representation is in the far less verbose format of a **proof net**, a geometric construction that abstracts away from the bureaucratic book-keeping of hypothetical reasoning and tree-structured rule ordering. Figure 3 presents the proof net equivalent of the running example. Proof nets are easier to reason about in a neural setup by allowing us to treat parsing as the vastly simplified problem of matching each occurrence of an atomic proposition in *negative* position, i.e. a prerequisite of a conditional implication, with an occurrence in *positive* position, i.e. a (conditionally) proven statement. The parallel nature of proof nets allows the matching to occur simultaneously across the entire proof; that is, all decisions are done in a single instant, without the bottleneck of having to wait for conditionals to be satisfied in a bottom-up fashion. On the other hand, proof nets are slightly underspecified compared to natural deduction proofs, being explicit only with respect to function-argument structures – translating from one format to another requires establishing some conventions on what constitutes a canonical proof.

2.1.2 Implementation

The syntax of the type system is implemented as a tiny DSL written in Python.[2] It is used as the representation format of Æthel (Kogkalidis et al., 2020a), a dataset of some 70 000 analyses of written Dutch, which also constitutes the system's training data. The implementation was originally designed to assert the type-safety of the dataset, to facilitate the conversion between natural deduction trees, λ terms and proof nets, and to ease third-party corpus analysis by providing niceties such as search and pretty printing utilities, cross compilation to LaTeX for visualization purposes, interfaces for proof transformations, etc. All these functionalities are imported unchanged. The conversion routines allow us to conduct neural proof search in the favorable regime of proof nets, and convert the result to natural deduction format only at the very end, just for the sake of presentation and/or sanity testing. Importantly, the type-checker is repurposed as a tool for verifying the correctness of analyses constructed – an analysis that does not amount to a valid proof will fail to pass the checker, throwing a type error and alerting us to the fact. In other words, we can blindly trust anything the parser gives us as correct, at least in the sense of (proof-theoretic) syntactic validity.

[2] Source code can be found at `https://github.com/konstantinosKokos/aethel`.

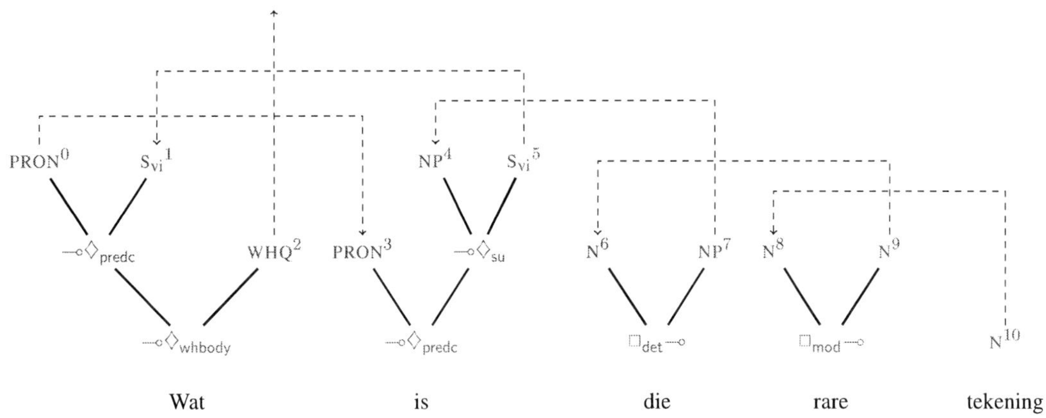

Figure 3: Proof net equivalent of the proof of Figure 2, with unary diamonds (resp. boxes) fused with the implication dominating (resp. dominated by) them for depth compression. Atomic propositions are indexed by enumeration for identification purposes. Color coding here serves to differentiate between resources we have (green) and resources we need (red) – the rule is start green from the bottom, change (resp. keep) color for the left (resp. right) daughter of an implication. Bold edges denote the tree structure underlying type assignments. Dashed edges denote the correct matching between resources of opposite polarity.

2.2 Supertagging Module

Lexical type ambiguity and lexical type sparsity are common and pervasive problems for any categorial grammar. The de facto approach rests on a supertagger, a neural module replacing the fixed lexicon, traditionally formulated as a sequence classifier and trained to produce the most plausible type assignments for each word in the context of an input sentence. Here, these problems are exacerbated by the highly elaborated type system. Some 80% of Æthel's approx. 6 000 types are rare (i.e. have less than 10 occurrences in the corpus), and some 10% of the total sentences contain at least 1 such rare type. This necessitates a more ambitious treatment than the standard "set-and-forget" approach of completely discarding rare type assignments as inconsequential. The solution comes in the form of a **constructive supertagger**, an auto-regressive neural decoder that is trained to construct types on the fly according to their algebraic decomposition, rather than treat them as singular, opaque blocks (Kogkalidis et al., 2019). This configuration enables the construction of valid types regardless of whether they have been seen before or not, extending coverage beyond the training data. The supertagger employed here follows a geometrically informed, task-specific decoding order, whereby types are represented as the structural unfolding of binary trees. Following Prange et al. (2021), trees are decoded in parallel across the entire batch of input sequences, establishing an upper temporal bound on decoding that scales with the maximal tree depth – in practice, a constant. To circumvent the locality of a standard tree decoder, the target output being not a batch of trees but a batch of **sequences of trees** (see Figure 3), the supertagger is formulated as a a graph neural network, utilizing message-passing connections to transfer feedback from tree nodes to their lexical roots and from lexical roots to their neighbours, ensuring that decisions made at each decoding step are influenced by prior decisions across the entire output (Kogkalidis and Moortgat, 2022). As a result, it strikes the perfect balance between the speed and memory efficiency of a tree-shaped architecture, allowing for more training iterations and faster inference, and the stronger autoregressive properties of a seq2seq model, improving performance. Further, being inherently constrained to trees, its output is structurally correct-by-construction – under no circumstance can any of the types produced be ill-formed. Used in isolation, the architecture currently sits at the top of the accuracy leaderboard for categorial grammar supertagging across different formalisms and languages – the performance is marginally inferior in the multi-task training setup adopted here.

2.3 Permutation Module

Conducting search over proof nets is typically ill-advised. The problem traditionally involves examining all possible bijections between positive and negative atomic propositions. The number of such bijections scales factorial to the number of atomic propositions, quickly becoming prohibitive. To navigate this combinatorially explosive landscape, **neural proof nets** relax proof search into a continuous, differentiable problem, where finding the correct bijection is translated to a transportation problem (Kogkalidis et al., 2020b) learned by yet another graph neural network. Concretely, the representations of all occurrences of atomic propositions are extracted from the decoder and binned according to their sentential index, sign and polarity (e.g. a single bin would be all occurrences of a positive NP in sentence #13 of the input batch). Each bin is contrasted with its inverse polarity counterpart using some similarity metric (here a weighted inner product). The result is a collection of square matrices, each matrix containing attention weights (or similarity scores) in the cartesian product of positive and negative items of the same sign and sentence. These matrices are grouped by their cardinality, and the Sinkhorn operator (Sinkhorn and Knopp, 1967) is used to push them towards binarity and bistochacity, yielding approximations of permutation matrices representing the goal bijections (Mena et al., 2018).

To make things concrete using the running example of Figure 3, each of the atomic types S_{vi}, NP and PRON has a single negative and a single positive occurrence, therefore their bijections are trivial (a testament to supertagging being almost parsing). The single positive occurrence of WHQ stands for the goal type of the phrase, and remains unmatched. Only N requires a decision, having two possible bijections. The correct candidate is encoded by the permutation table below, where rows enumerate positive and columns negative items:

$$\Pi_{N} := \begin{array}{c|c|c|} & 6 & 8 \\ \hline 9 & \checkmark & \\ \hline 10 & & \checkmark \\ \hline \end{array}$$

This reformulation entails a tremendous speedup: the painstakingly slow problem of symbolic proof search is cast into simple, well-optimized and batchable matrix operations. The current parser builds on the insight that the permutation module is invariant to the source of atomic symbol representations, and in fact greatly benefits from the faster and more accurate task-adapted supertagger.

2.4 Integration

Neurosymbolic integration yields an end-to-end pipeline that consists of the following phases. First, the user inputs a list of sentences to be parsed. Contextualized token representations are obtained from a fine-tuned $\text{BERT}_{\text{BASE}}$ model, which are then aggregated according to the input's word boundaries. The resulting word representations act as initial seeds for decoding to begin on an empty canvas. During decoding, types are progressively constructed, while seeds are updated by exchanging messages with one another on the basis of their sequential proximity. After a small number of decoding steps, the process terminates, yielding a sequence of type assignments for each input sentence. A rudimentary invariance check is then performed, controlling whether each sequence counts an equal number of atomic propositions of each polarity. Sentences failing the invariance check are not eligible for proof search, and their analysis stops early. Passing sentences are symbolically processed to obtain a collection of sparse indexing tensors, used to gather the decoder's representations into the bins described earlier. Bins are batched and contrasted, and a small number of Sinkhorn iterations is employed as a 2-dimensional softmax analogue. The soft Sinkhorn distances are discretized using the Hungarian algorithm in order to enforce bijectivity (Jonker and Volgenant, 1987). Bijections are reassociated with their origin symbols and sentences, using the reverse of the previous indexing operation. Control is then passed to the symbolic component, which attempts to traverse the candidate proof nets, verifying the correctness criteria of acyclicity and connectedness in the process (Danos and Regnier, 1989). The traversal coincides with a translation to a natural deduction format, the construction of which corresponds to static type checking of the output (Lamarche, 2008). Assuming no type mismatches are caught, the output is a proof proper, which by Curry-Howard isomorphism is rewritten as a dependency-decorated λ term. The user is finally presented with an analysis for each input sentence – ideally, a λ term, but occasionally a rejected intermediate result together with an error description.

3 Evaluation

3.1 Performance

The system has been evaluated on the test set of Æthel. Without any pre-filtering or post-processing training wheels (i.e. no constraints on sentence length, type rarity/depth or cardinality of bijections), the parser produces a proof that satisfies strict syntactic equality with the ground truth in 3 191 of the 5 770 test set samples. This amounts to a significant 55.30% of the test sentences being analyzed without a single error with respect to type assignments, phrasal chunking, function-argument structures and dependency annotations produced[3] In total, 4 901 sentences are assigned a passing analysis, which sets the coverage to a more modest 84.94%. The discrepancy between the high accuracy and low coverage is due to the rigidness of the type system: only 5 010 of the sentences satisfy the invariance check, being thus amenable to any proof. This signals that the performance bottleneck lies on the supertagger rather than the permutation module; a parse is assigned to 97.82% of parsable sentences, and it's also the perfect parse 75.30% of the time. These findings are summarized in Table 1.

parsability (some proof obtainable)	**coverage** (some proof obtained)
86.83	84.94
types correct (correct proof obtainable)	**accuracy** (correct proof obtained)
56.88	55.30

Table 1: Sentential-level evaluation of the parser.

To obtain a more refined perspective on performance, we employ an adaptation of the parsing community's favorite F_1-score. Concretely, we gather all samples for which a proof was produced, and decompose both prediction and ground truth into their respective sets of subproofs. We measure tp as the two sets' intersection, fp as the difference between predicted and correct subproofs and fn as the difference between correct and predicted subproofs, from which we may obtain precision as $p = {}^{tp}/_{(tp+fp)}$, recall as $r = {}^{tp}/_{(tp+fn)}$ and their harmonic mean as $F_1 = {}^{2pr}/_{(p+r)}$. On top of the vanilla versions of these metrics, we can also examine relaxations by incorporating a combination of two modulo factors. Relaxation one targets the functional core of the logic, applying a forgetful transformation that strips proofs of their modalities in order to examine typed function-argument structures in isolation. Relaxation two targets the modal enhancement of the logic, collapsing the set of atomic types into a single point (thus treating all functional types of the same *shape* as equal) in order to examine dependency structures in isolation. Relaxing on both axes at once is essentially replacing type constants by type variables, where all we care about are the type- and dependency-agnostic linear function-argument structures – this is the metric most comparable to external theories.[4] Note that relaxations are performed only *after* inference – the point being that a strict proof must have been produced for its relaxations to be considered (i.e. lax accuracy is still bottlenecked by strict coverage). The results are averaged over covered samples[5] and presented in Table 2.

modulo	**local metrics** p	r	F_1
–	89.52	89.68	89.39
modalities	90.93	91.13	90.85
functional types	91.09	91.26	90.97
both	92.31	92.52	92.24

Table 2: Decomposition metrics and relaxations.

3.2 Efficiency

Regarding efficiency, the architecture contains a non-negligible total of 117M parameters, 94% of which are inherited from the underlying BERT model. The memory footprint of the network's forward pass does not exceed 3.5GB on the test set with a batch size of 64, making it reasonably lightweight for use at home. Using a middle range laptop GPU, the network takes about 15 seconds to tag the full test set (i.e. 370 sents/sec or 6 000 tokens/sec), and 80 seconds to tag and parse it (i.e. 70 sents/sec), including tokenization and post-processing. Note, however, that sentence-level batching is not yet implemented for inference mode proof search, i.e. sentences are tagged in parallel but proven sequentially. Cross-sentential padding and batching of Sinkhorn inputs is in the works – benchmarking shows that the asymptotic behavior of a forward pass over batches of 64 matrices only starts becoming apparent when they exceed

[3]This is comparable to the state-of-the-art for the similar (in fact simpler) problem of CCG parsing; see Clark (2021) for an up-to-date overview.

[4]Proofs are in β and η normal, so no free points from abstractions. Variables are only equal if they match in both name and type, so no free points from variable instantiations either.

[5]Averaging over the full test set would artificially inflate p and deflate r scores, since no partial proofs are returned from failing samples.

```
>>> from inference import InferenceWrapper as IW
>>> from aethel.utils.tex import compile_tex, sample_to_tex
>>> parser = IW(weight_path='./data/model_weights.pt')
>>> analysis = parser.analyze(['Wat is die rare tekening?'])[0]
>>> analysis
Analysis(
    lexical_phrases=(
        LexicalPhrase(string=Wat, type=(◇whbody(◇predc(VNW)⟶SV1))⟶WHQ, len=1),
        LexicalPhrase(string=is, type=◇predc(VNW)⟶◇su(NP)⟶SV1, len=1),
        LexicalPhrase(string=die, type=□det(N⟶NP), len=1),
        LexicalPhrase(string=rare, type=□mod(N⟶N), len=1),
        LexicalPhrase(string=tekening, type=N, len=1),
        LexicalPhrase(string=?, type=PUNCT, len=1)),
    proof=c0, ⟨c1, ⟨⟨c2⟩det, ⟨c3⟩mod, c4⟩su⟩whbody ⊢ c0 ▵whbody((λx0.c1 x0 ▵su(▾det(c2) (▾mod(c3) c4)))) : WHQ)
>>> tex_proof = compile_tex(sample_to_tex(analysis))  # see Figure 2 for output :)
```

Figure 4: User interaction example in python console.

the order of 2^7, being locked at an insubstantial 1ms prior to that.[6]

4 User Interface

The user interface is bare-bones, but simple and easy to use. The parser is currently packaged as a code repository, which, once downloaded, can be used as a python module. A front-end class wraps around the scary inner workings of the parser and provides easy access to an inference routine. Structure checking is handled internally and error handling is graceful: the user is guaranteed an output even in the case of a partial failure. The output implements the same protocols as samples of the Æthel corpus, and is thus compatible with all of the latter's bells and whistles. Proofs can be pretty-printed, interactively processed and transformed (e.g. for semantic applications), or visualized using LaTeX as a middlewoman. For the more ambitious, training and evaluation utilities are also available.

5 Conclusion & Future Work

Thus concludes the demonstration tour of spind$^2\lambda$e: a unique neurosymbolic parser that can accurately and efficiently convert raw text into λ expressions. Unlike cheaper alternatives, these λ expressions are not structureless ad-hoc imitations produced from arbitrary decoding, but executable, type-safe and 100% **guaranteed correct** programs. The software focuses on Dutch, but the universality of the intuitionistic linear core allows easy cross-lingual adaptation that essentially boils down to retraining with a new type lexicon; a French implementation is currently in the works (De Pourtales et al., 2023).

As to what the future holds, the intention is to keep the module synchronized and up-to-date with Æthel: any upcoming major release of the latter will be reflected in an update of the former (be it soft patching or retraining). Compatibility aside, planned features include deploying the module as a web service, compiling it as a stand-alone package and documenting the annotations (so as to be more inclusive towards the type-uninitiated). Any performance, stability or efficiency improvements stemming from related research or moments of engineering inspiration are also likely to find their way to the user-facing front. Contributions and feedback are always welcome.

Limitations

The implementation described capitalizes on a disentanglement between neural and symbolic operations to improve efficiency. But doing so comes at the heavy price of a unidirectional data flow that lacks feedback. The symbolic component has the singular role of testing and verifying the neural output, but emits back no messages of its own. Failures may be caught, but they are nonetheless irrecoverable – a partial output that fails some structural constraint signifies an abrupt and non-negotiable end to the processing pipeline, significantly reducing coverage. A better operationalization would be to use the symbolic core to continuously ask for neural output as long as the structural constraints are not met (or the user is not satisfied with the parse provided). However, this would only be feasible if the neural components were to be extended with some notion of backtracking. In that sense, the parallel nature of both the supertagger and the parser becomes now a double-edged sword, hindering the potential applicability of standard heuristic algorithms like beam search.

More generally, the software carries the standard

[6]To comprehend how extremely unrealistic 2^7 is, consider that this would amount to finding the correct bijection out of $2^7! = 3.9 \times 10^{215}$ possibilities across 64 pairs of sets in parallel.

risks of any NLP architecture reliant on machine learning, namely linguistic biases inherited from the unsupervised pretraining of the incorporated language model and annotation biases derived from the supervised training over human-labeled data.

Acknowledgements

This software described was developed with funds from the Dutch Research Council (NWO, grant nr. 360-89-070).

References

Samson Abramsky. 1993. Computational interpretations of linear logic. *Theoretical computer science*, 111(1-2):3–57.

Lasha Abzianidze. 2017. LangPro: Natural language theorem prover. In *Proceedings of the 2017 Conference on Empirical Methods in Natural Language Processing: System Demonstrations*, pages 115–120, Copenhagen, Denmark. Association for Computational Linguistics.

Stephen Clark. 2021. Something old, something new: Grammar-based CCG parsing with transformer models. *CoRR*, abs/2109.10044.

Haskell B Curry. 1961. Some logical aspects of grammatical structure. *Structure of language and its mathematical aspects*, 12:56–68.

Vincent Danos and Laurent Regnier. 1989. The structure of multiplicatives. *Archive for Mathematical logic*, 28(3):181–203.

Caroline De Pourtales, Julien Rabault, Konstantinos Kogkalidis, and Richard Moot. 2023. DeepGrail: Neural proof nets for French. Technical report, LIRMM. Forthcoming.

Matthias Fey and Jan Eric Lenssen. 2019. Fast graph representation learning with pytorch geometric. *arXiv preprint arXiv:1903.02428*.

Jean-Yves Girard. 1987. Linear logic. *Theoretical computer science*, 50(1):1–101.

Roy Jonker and Anton Volgenant. 1987. A shortest augmenting path algorithm for dense and sparse linear assignment problems. *Computing*, 38(4):325–340.

Konstantinos Kogkalidis and Michael Moortgat. 2022. Geometry-aware supertagging with heterogeneous dynamic convolutions.

Konstantinos Kogkalidis, Michael Moortgat, and Tejaswini Deoskar. 2019. Constructive type-logical supertagging with self-attention networks. In *Proceedings of the 4th Workshop on Representation Learning for NLP (RepL4NLP-2019)*, pages 113–123, Florence, Italy. Association for Computational Linguistics.

Konstantinos Kogkalidis, Michael Moortgat, and Richard Moot. 2020a. ÆTHEL: Automatically extracted typelogical derivations for Dutch. In *Proceedings of the 12th Language Resources and Evaluation Conference*, pages 5257–5266, Marseille, France. European Language Resources Association.

Konstantinos Kogkalidis, Michael Moortgat, and Richard Moot. 2020b. Neural proof nets. In *Proceedings of the 24th Conference on Computational Natural Language Learning*, pages 26–40, Online. Association for Computational Linguistics.

François Lamarche. 2008. Proof nets for intuitionistic linear logic: Essential nets.

Gonzalo Mena, David Belanger, Scott Linderman, and Jasper Snoek. 2018. Learning latent permutations with gumbel-sinkhorn networks. In *International Conference on Learning Representations*.

Michael Moortgat. 1997. Categorial type logics. In *Handbook of logic and language*, pages 93–177. Elsevier.

Gabriel Peyré, Marco Cuturi, et al. 2019. Computational optimal transport: With applications to data science. *Foundations and Trends® in Machine Learning*, 11(5-6):355–607.

Jakob Prange, Nathan Schneider, and Vivek Srikumar. 2021. Supertagging the long tail with tree-structured decoding of complex categories. *Transactions of the Association for Computational Linguistics*, 9:243–260.

Mehrnoosh Sadrzadeh and Reinhard Muskens. 2018. Static and dynamic vector semantics for lambda calculus models of natural language. *J. Lang. Model.*, 6(2):319–351.

Richard Sinkhorn and Paul Knopp. 1967. Concerning nonnegative matrices and doubly stochastic matrices. *Pacific Journal of Mathematics*, 21(2):343–348.

Linguistic Constructs Represent the Domain Model in Intelligent Language Tutoring

Anisia Katinskaia[1,2], Jue Hou[1,2], Anh-Duc Vu[1,2], Roman Yangarber[2]
[1] Department of Computer Science, University of Helsinki
[2] Department of Digital Humanities, University of Helsinki
first.last@helsinki.fi

Abstract

This paper presents the development of the AI-based language-learning platform, Revita. It is an intelligent online tutor, developed to support learners of multiple languages, from lower-intermediate toward advanced levels. It has been in pilot use with hundreds of students at several universities, whose feedback and needs shape the development. One of the main emerging features of Revita is the system of *linguistic constructs* to represent the domain knowledge. The system of constructs is developed in collaboration with experts in language pedagogy. Constructs define the types of exercises, the content of the feedback, and enable detailed modeling and evaluation of learner progress.

1 Introduction

The focus of this paper is the novel Domain Model in Revita,[1] an Intelligent Tutoring System (ITS) for language learning (Katinskaia et al., 2018, 2017). Revita follows the classic design of ITS—with a Domain model, Student model, and Instruction model. The *Domain Model* describes what must be mastered by the learner: concepts, rules, etc.—known as *skills* in ITS literature—and *relationships* among them (Wenger, 2014; Polson et al., 1988). We represent the Domain Model as a system of *linguistic constructs*—a wide range of linguistic phenomena, including inflexion of various paradigms, government relations, collocations, complex syntactic constructions, etc. The system of constructs is developed in collaboration with experts in language teaching. It impacts all apcects and components of Revita—the variety of exercises that it generates automatically, the intelligent feedback given to the learner, modeling of learner knowledge, and evaluation of learner progress.

The *Student model* represents the learner's proficiency. It is based on the history of answers given by the learner to many exercises, and tries to build a detailed picture of what the user knows vs. does not know. The *Instruction model* embodies the pedagogical principles that lie behind the decisions: which exercises the learner is best prepared for next, and which feedback should be provided to guide the learner toward the right answer. These models are interconnected in ITS.

Revita is currently undergoing pilot studies with real-world learners and teachers at several universities (Stoyanova et al., 2021). Revita's main target group are learners who have passed beyond the beginner level — above A2 on the CEFR scale.[2] Revita is developed as a tool for learners and teachers of several languages: Finnish and Russian are currently the most developed languages. Several "beta" languages, including Italian, German, Swedish, and others, are in earlier stages of development. The user interface also works in several languages (English, Finnish, Russian, Chinese, Italian). Revita is not meant to replace the teacher. For students, it provides 24/7 access to an unlimited amount of personalized exercises for practice matching the learner's current level, with immediate feedback and progress estimation. For teachers, it provides time-saving benefits by allowing them to delegate the mundane work of creating hundreds of exercises for each topic for students at different levels. Revita allows the teachers to share learning materials, create their own exercises, work with groups, and monitor progress and evaluation.

The paper is organized as follows: Section 2 briefly reviews work on intelligent computer-assisted language learning (ICALL). The principles and ideas behind Revita are described in Section 3. It also describes its main components: linguistic constructs, automatic generation of exercises and feedback, and modeling of learner knowledge. Section 4 describes tools for learners and teachers. Section presents the conclusions and future work.

[1]revita.cs.helsinki.fi — Link to a short demo here.

[2]The Common European Framework of Reference for Languages: Learning, Teaching, Assessment

Proceedings of the 17th Conference of the European Chapter of the Association for Computational Linguistics System Demonstrations, pages 136–144
May 2-4, 2023 ©2023 Association for Computational Linguistics

2 Prior Work

Interest in computer-assisted language learning (CALL) is growing with the rapid development of language technology. CALL is seen as the "study of applications of the computer in language teaching and learning" (Levy, 1997). Applying ITS to language learning and supporting CALL by intelligent and/or adaptive methodologies, such as expert systems (ES), natural language processing (NLP), automatic speech recognition (ASR), etc.—is the domain of intelligent CALL, or ICALL. The goal of ICALL is building advanced applications for language learning using NLP and linguistic resources—corpora, lexicons, etc. (Volodina et al., 2014).

The number of academic and commercial tools for language learning is growing drastically, e.g., popular commercial systems like Duolingo, Rosetta Stone, Babbel, Busuu, iTalki, etc. Some CALL systems aim to give learners access to *authentic* materials (White and Reinders, 2010), the opportunity to interact with teachers and native speakers (e.g., the app *Lingoda* is a platform for live video classes), and provide text or sound feedback based on learner needs and knowledge (Bodnar et al., 2017). Modern CALL systems are also mobile, which increases their accessibility (Derakhshan and Khodabakhshzadeh, 2011; Rosell-Aguilar, 2018; Kacetl and Klímová, 2019).

In developing CALL, pedagogical goals—rather than technological means—should be the primary focus (Gray, 2008). It has been shown that using ICALL systems for education improves learner motivation and attitudes, increases options for self-study (Golonka et al., 2014), improves retention of various learning concepts, communication between students and teachers, academic self-efficacy (Bandura, 1977; Rachels and Rockinson-Szapkiw, 2018), and overall language skills (Yeh and Lai, 2019; Zhang and Zou, 2022).

Despite having existed for decades, ICALL still has a number of serious limitations to overcome. Apart from platforms where teachers directly interact with students in video classes, most existing ICALL systems are based on the so-called "canned" approach—the available sets of exercises are pre-made, and therefore limited. This limits the level of personalization: pre-made exercises can be arranged into different individual programs, but no personalized exercises can be provided.

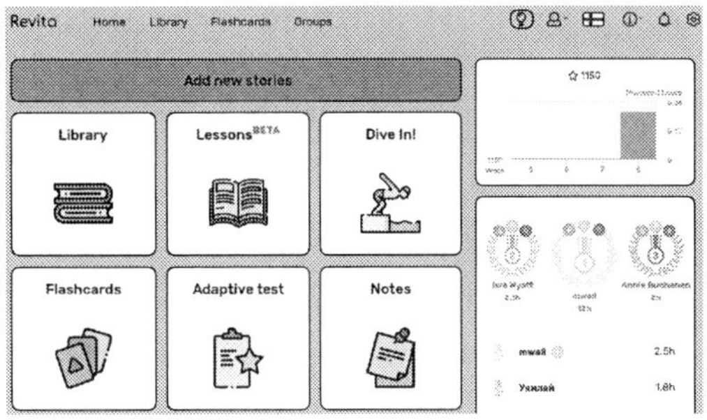

Figure 1: Revita's home page, with the main activities.

3 Core Components of Revita

3.1 Main Principles

Revita's approach is founded on the following primary principles:

1. *Practice should be based on authentic content.* By authentic we mean a text which is not artificial and written for learning purposes. The learner (or teacher) can upload any text from the Internet using a URL, upload any file, etc., to use it directly as learning content.
2. *Exercises are automatically generated* based on any authentic text chosen by the user, including any texts uploaded to the system.
3. *Exercises are personalized* to match the learner's current skill levels, so that each new exercise is selected to be a challenge that the learner is able to meet.
4. *Immediate feedback*: rather than saying only "right/wrong", the tutor *gradually guides* the learner toward finding the correct answer by providing *hints*, which begin as general hints about the context and then give more and more specific information about the answer.
5. *Continual assessment* of skills allows Revita to select exercises optimally personalized for each learner based on past performance.

The first principle is the bedrock of Revita's philosophy—in the story-based approach, all learning activities are based on authentic texts, which should be *inherently interesting* for the learner to read, which motivates her to practice longer. A few sample texts are available in the system's "public" library for each language; also, several new stories are recommended daily as "Stories of the day"—crawled daily from several selected websites. But the main idea is that texts be chosen and uploaded by the learners themselves (or teachers). The button "Add new stories" on the home page (see Figure 1)

Constructs	Examples
Finnish	
(1) Necessive construction: Present passive participle, with *-ttava* ending	*Energiakriisin lähestyessä kaikki keinot on **otettava** käyntiin.* (With the energy crisis approaching, all means must **be taken** into action.)
(2) Transitive vs. intransitive verbs	*Voisitko **sammuttaa** valon?* (Could you **turn off** the light?)
(3) Verb government: translative case	*Kaupungit eivät ole muuttuneet **energiatehokkaammiksi**.* (Cities have not become **more energy efficient**.)
(4) Substitute clause: participle substitutes for "that"-relative clause	*Maija kertoi **vanhempien asuvan** kaupungissa.* (Maija said that **her parents live** in the city.)
Russian	
(5) Verb: II conjugation	*Мы скоро **увидим** восход.* (We **will see** the sunrise soon.)
(6) Complex pronoun:	*Нам нужно **кое о чем** поговорить.* (We need to talk **about something**)
(7) Perfective vs. imperfective aspect	*Страны **согласовали** проект о будущих отношениях.* (The countries **agreed on** a draft on future relations.)
(8) Dative subject & impersonal verb	***Мне** необходимо поговорить с врачом.* (**I** need to talk to a doctor.)
German	
(9) Past perfect tense	*Ich **wäre** mit ihm **gekommen**, aber er wurde krank.* (I **would have come** with him, but he got sick.)
(10) Weak masculine nouns	*Ich möchte **den Jungen** kennenlernen.* (I want to meet **the boy**.)
(11) Prepositions governing dative case	*Wir sind **aus dem** Haus gelaufen.* (We ran **out of the** house.)

Table 1: Examples of *grammatical constructs* found in sentences (underlined). ***Candidates*** are words that will be chosen for exercises about the constructs (marked in bold).

allows the user to upload new text material into her private library.

3.2 Linguistic Constructs

At the core of Revita's approach is the system of linguistic constructs that are represented in the Domain model. *Constructs* are linguistic phenomena or rules, that vary in specificity: e.g., a construct (in Finnish) may be *verb government*: the verb *tutustua* ("to become acquainted") requires its argument to be in the illative case (*"into something"*), while *tykätä* ("to like") requires its argument in the elative case (*"from something"*), etc. Constructs also include all *constructions*, as conceived in Construction Grammar (CG). CG treats many phenomena—grammatical constructs, multi-word expressions, collocations, idioms, etc.—within a unified formalism. Examples of constructs for several languages are shown in Table 1.

When customizing the system for a new language, we engage experts in language teaching in creating the inventory of constructs, which need to be mastered by the learners. Currently, Finnish and Russian have the most developed system of constructs, each with over 200 constructs. Potentially, the number of constructs can be much larger. The Russian constructs evolved from the extensive grammatical inventory covered in tests for second language (L2) learners developed at the University of Helsinki (Kopotev, 2012). The Finnish constructs are based on inventories of grammatical topics developed by experts in teaching Finnish as L2.

As shown in the examples in Table 1, each construct needs to be identified in the text, when the text is uploaded to Revita. For this purpose, we use finite-state morphological analyzers (e.g., HFST[3]), neural dependency parsers,[4] and rule-based pattern detection. Each morphological analyzer is wrapped into a "Revita" analyzer which modifies the output analyses into a uniform standard set of features used in the system. Considering that none of these tools can provide perfect performance alone, we rely on the agreement between morphological analyzers, parsers, and rules.

In Example (1), for construct "Present passive participle with *-ttava* ending," the rule matches the participle *"otettava"* by morphological features: participle, present tense, passive voice. This form is then recognized as the head of the "necessive" construction *"on otettava"* ("must be taken"), detected by a rule that matches: the singular 3rd person present form of modal verb *"olla"* ("to be") and the present passive participle, in the nominative case. The matching rule has to agree with the output of a dependency parser. In Example (2), the construct "Transitive vs. intransitive verbs" is detected

[3]GiellaLT

[4]Turku NLP, DeepPavlov

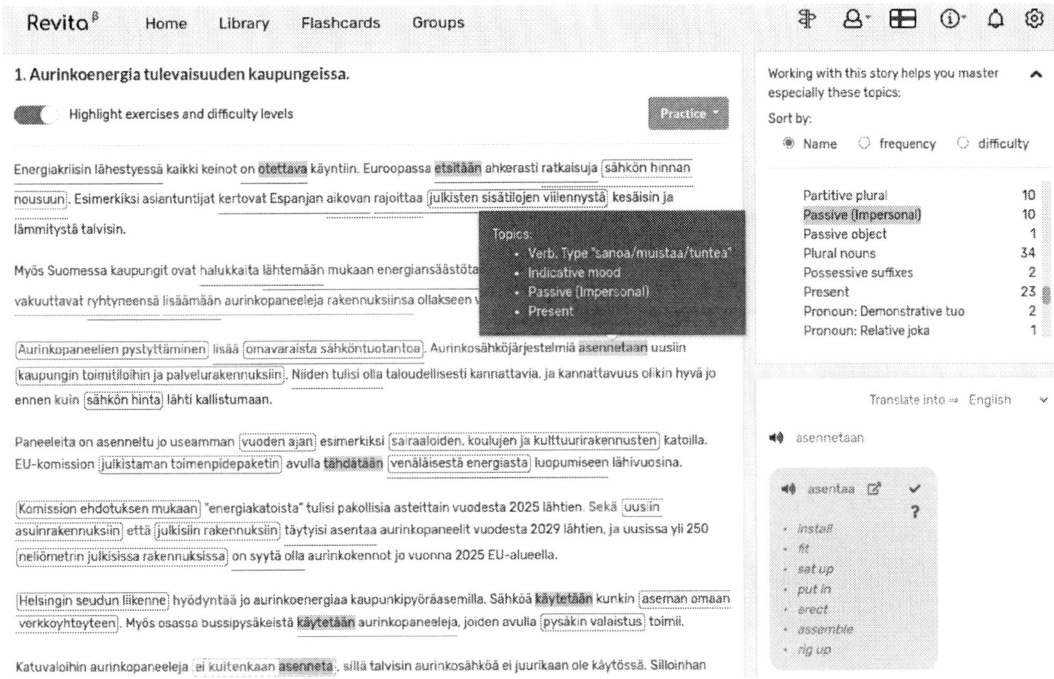

Figure 2: Preview mode for a story (before practice). All purple words can appear in an exercise. Noun phrases and prepositional phrases are circled in red. Government relations and constructions are underlined. Top-right corner—the list of constructs found in the story. Bottom-right corner—translation of the clicked word: "asennetaan", into English (target language can be selected). The green box over the clicked word lists all constructs related to it.

by using dictionaries of verb lemmas or by rules that detect regular transitive/intransitive ending patterns in verb lemmas (e.g., *sammut**taa*** vs. *sammu**a***, "turn something off" vs. "turn itself off"). Dictionaries contain hundreds of the most frequent Finnish lemmas and are continually updated.

Verb government is detected by several components: large sets of government patterns (2000-3000 per language); pattern matching for noun phrases, prepositional phrases, and analytic verb forms; dependency relations detected by parsers. Each rule for government pattern tests the dependency roles of the arguments as conditions. In Example (3), a government pattern for the intransitive verb *"muuttua"* ("to change") requires an argument in the translative case—here, the comparative adjective *energiatehokkaammiksi* ("more energy-efficient"). The government detector will find an argument of *"muuttua"* regardless of its position in the sentence, and for any form of the verb, including complex analytic forms, e.g., the negative perfect tense *"eivät ole muuttuneet."*

Detecting longer and more complex syntactic constructions relies on all of the components mentioned above. In (4), to match the complex construction *"kertoi vanhempien asuvan"*, we use a rule states that the verb *"kertoi"* ("said") must govern a subordinate clause starting with *"että"* ("that"); the *substitute* clause contains a noun phrase in the genitive case, which acts as the subject (*"vanhempien"*) and a genitive active participle (*"asuvan"*).

The user can preview all constructs identified in a story in the Preview Mode prior to practice, see Figure 2. All noun and preposition phrases are circled, government relations and syntactic constructions are underlined. A list of all constructs found in the story is in the top-right window: clicking on a construct highlights all instances of the construct in the story. Figure 2 shows all impersonal passive forms highlighted in blue. Clicking on any word in the story will also show all constructs linked to it (green box above the clicked word, the see word *"asennetaan"*). The translation of the clicked word into the learner's chosen language (English here) is in the bottom-right. This lets the learner (or teacher) see what can be exercised in the given text.

3.3 Exercise Generation Based on Constructs

Revita offers several practice modes; the main activity for the learner is the Grammar Practice Mode

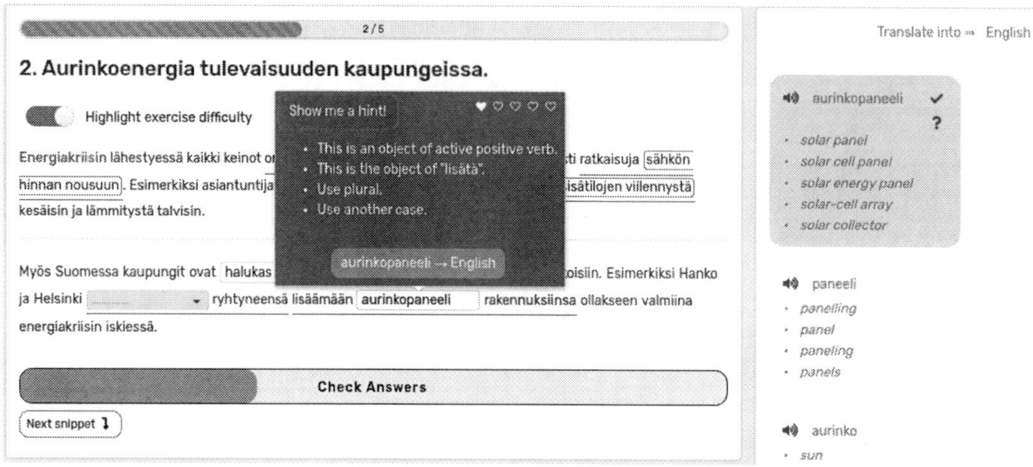

Figure 3: Practice mode with a story. Figure shows the second paragraph of a story with three exercises: two clozes ("halukas" and "aurinkopaneeli") and one MC. Previous answers are marked green and blue—correct and incorrect. The green box shows the hints requested so far for the cloze exercise.

based on a story from the public or private library, see Figure 3. Practice mode offers "cloze" (fill-in-the-blank) and multiple-choice (MC) exercises. A cloze exercise is shown as a text box, with the lemma of the expected answer given as a hint to the learner. In Figure 3, the lemma in the box is *aurinkopaneeli* ("sun panel"). The learner is expected to insert the correct form of this word that suits the context; here, it is the plural partitive case (*"aurinkopaneeleja"*)—the expected answer is the original word form from the story, which was replaced with the exercise. Each word picked to be exercised must be disambiguated—we must know the correct lemma to show to the learner. Disambiguation is performed by agreement rules and by dependency parsers. For *analytic* verb forms, such as *"on otettava"* ("should be taken"), the cloze box will show the lemma of the *head* verb: *ottaa* ("to take").

All *candidates*—potential exercises in practice mode—are based on the constructs detected in the story. In Example (3) for Finnish in Table 1, an exercise on the construct "Verb government" is in bold: the learner will see the lemma *energiatehokas* ("energy-efficient"). To insert the correct form in the translative case, the learner needs to know which case is required by the governing verb. MC exercises are more targeted: the options to choose from—known as "distractors"—are generated based on the exercised construct. Therefore, the same word or construction may have more than one set of distractors, since more than one construct may be linked to the candidate.

Distractors are created by rules and morphological generators. In Example (6), for the construct "Complex pronoun", tests the knowledge of joint vs. hyphenated spelling—a rule generates distractors like: *"кое о чем"*, *"кое-о-чем"*, *"о кое-чем"* ("about something"). For transitive vs. intransitive verbs, we use dictionaries of lemma pairs. However, the distractors must be *inflected* forms that fit the context, not lemmas. We use morphological generators to produce the required inflected forms.

MC distractors are often an effective way of learning a particular construct, and choosing good distractors is a task that requires pedagogical expertise. In Example (4), e.g., the construction requires the subject to be in genitive case. It is useful to offer the lemma *"vanhemmat"* ("parents") in other cases which can mark the subject in other constructions, e.g., nominative, partitive, etc. These forms, which differ only by case, are produced by the morphological generator.

In addition to the mentioned exercise types, Revita generates MC exercises for stress in Russian.[5] Distractors are generated using the finite-state morphological analyser UDAR[6] (Reynolds, 2016). Another kind of exercises is based on Text-to-Speech technology[7]—the learner needs to to listen to a spoken fragment and insert the missing forms. These exercises are not generated based on constructs, and are therefore outside the scope of the paper.

[5] Stress is a very complex topic in learning Russian.
[6] https://github.com/reynoldsnlp/udar
[7] Text-to-Speech

3.4 Feedback

Feedback is a second essential feature of Revita. The learner gets *multiple attempts* for every exercise. Feedback is designed to gradually guide the learner toward the correct answer by providing a sequence of hints that (a) depend on the context, (b) on the constructs linked to the exercise, and (c) on the answer that was given by the learner. Feedback hints are ordered so they become more specific on subsequent attempts: starting from referring to syntactic construction or word paradigms and then to grammatical features required in the answer. For example, for an object of a verb governs the partitive case, the feedback sequence may be: *"The is the object of the verb 'xyz'."* →*"Use another case."* →*"Use partitive case."* The learner can also request hints *before* giving an answer: as seen in the green box in Figure 3, four of the available hints are already "used up" (one heart remaining). Requesting hints indicates that the learner has *not* mastered the construct, and affects the learner's scores.

Feedback that depends on the context gives information on whether a word in question is part of some construction or relies on a governing word (verb, noun, or adjective), etc. Hints also appear as *underlining* of syntactically related elements in the context. These hints are generated based on detected syntactic constructions.

Some feedback hints are generated in the stage when the construct is linked to the text. For example, a hint *"Use past perfect tense"* will be attached to *"wäre gekommen"* (see example (9) in Table 1). A more complicated example is for an exercise with the participle *"asuvan"* in *substitute that-clause* construction (see example (4) in Table 1). We generate the feedback for it: *This is equivalent to "...kertoi että vanhemmat asuvat..."* ("...said that parents live...")—by generating the actual clause which is substituted by the participle. To produce this feedback message, Revita uses information about the syntactic roles of each word in the original construction *"kentoi vanhempien asuvan"*, and the required grammatical features of the forms in the feedback—to produce these forms, we use the morphological generator.

When the learner inserts an answer which does not match the expected one (i.e, the one in the original story), Revita analyzes the answer and checks which grammatical features are incorrect. To give feedback on these features in the order of increased specificity, Revita uses a language-specific hierarchy of features. For example, in Russian, the hierarchy specifies that the hint about an incorrect gender of an adjective is shown before hints about an incorrect number or case.

All mechanisms which define the order and the content of feedback hints and algorithms of sampling exercises for students are part of the Instruction Model of Revita.

3.5 Learner Modeling and Exercise Sampling

All learner answers and all requested hints to each exercise are recorded. A learner may attempt to answer each exercise multiple times. For each attempt, Revita analyzes the answers and the requested hints to calculate *credits and penalties* for the corresponding language constructs. Partial correctness of answers is taken into account, e.g., if the answer used the correct tense but wrong number, only number will be penalized, and tense will receive credit.

The collected information on performance with constructs is used to model learner skills and the difficulty of the constructs. To model learner skills and exercise difficulty, we use Item Response Theory (IRT) (Embretson and Reise, 2013; van der Linden and Hambleton, 2013). IRT comes from psychometrics and is widely used in education (Klinkenberg et al., 2011). The *Item* in IRT is a task that the learner should solve. Most IRT applications have a clear definition of an *item*, and a clear credit standard. The classic example of an item is a test question in mathematics: it is unambiguous and there is a clear judgment of the answer—correct or wrong. Our major challenge is that language constructs are not directly judged, as test items in other learning domains. It is challenging to determine the credit and penalty for each construct based on the student's answer, because the link from exercise to constructs is *one-to-many*.

We leave the details of modeling difficulty with IRT outside the scope of this paper. To date, we have collected 570K answers for Russian exercises. Experiments with this data show a strong correlation between students' proficiency estimated by IRT vs. by their teachers. This suggests that with IRT we are able to reliably model learner proficiency. Interestingly, the estimates of exercise difficulty do not correlate with teachers' judgments, which agrees with the findings of other researchers (Abbakumov and Lebedeva, 2016).

At present, we assume that the difficulty of an exercise depends on the *hardest* construct linked to it.

Thus, exercises are sampled for practice based on the difficulty of the hardest construct linked to each exercise. The difficulty of constructs is modeled by IRT. We aim to provide exercises that are best suited to each student's proficiency level. For each possible exercise, IRT first estimates the probability that the student will answer the exercise correctly—then the probability of picking this exercise for practice is sampled from a normal distribution around the mean of a 50% chance that the learner would answer correctly. Thus, on average, the exercises are not too difficult and not too easy.

For languages with insufficient learner data for training IRT, we ask teachers to assign manually CEFR difficulty levels to constructs. Earlier experiments using specialized Elo ratings[8] for assessing learner skills and evaluating the difficulty of linguistic constructs based on the learner data collected by Revita are presented in Hou et al. (2019).

4 Tools for Students and Teachers

At any time, the student can set her CEFR proficiency level manually or take an *adaptive* placement test to estimate proficiency (see the button "Adaptive Test" on Figure 1). The test draws on a bank of questions prepared by teachers; the sampling of questions is driven by an IRT model trained on learner data. After that, the estimate of the learner's proficiency levels is adjusted according to the correctness of answers to exercises.

The learner can upload a story from any website or a local file. To each uploaded text, Revita applies classification by semantic topic—culture, science, sport, politics—and difficulty classifiers. In case the learner does not want to choose a text for practice, there is a "Dive-in" option to practice with a randomly sampled story from a selected category (private vs. public or story tagged by a semantic topic). Another option is to choose a "story of the day" suggested by Revita.

The *Preview mode* (see Figure 2) allows the user to read a story, edit it (in case it was extracted from a web page inaccurately), and review the grammatical topics that can be learnt through practice with this story. Clicking on each word provides its translation into a number of languages. The learner can mark whether she knows a word or not. All unfamiliar words are added to the learner's personal set of flashcards, which are used for Vocabulary Practice.

[8]The Elo rating system is a method for calculating the relative skill levels of players in zero-sum games such as chess.

The *Practice mode* presents the grammar and listening exercises—the learner can hear a segment of text in context and is expected to type the missing words correctly in the empty box. The user can also practice with a story in the Competition Mode, against a bot: the difference from normal practice is that the learner needs to do the exercises faster than the bot—whose skill levels approximately match those of the learner. Another option is to practice with a Crossword built on the authentic text—the translations of words are used as hints. Practice mode also allows the user to create notes during practice, which can be attached to words in the story. All learner's notes are collected together (see button "Notes" in Figure 1) for easy review; each note has a reference to words in the story it was attached to.

Revita offers various statistics and info-graphics to track progress on grammar constructs and vocabulary. These analytics are available to the learner and to the teacher. Revita allows teachers to build groups of students, share texts with them, and create tailored exercises that can be shared with the group. Revita allows teachers to track how their students practice and how well they perform on various tasks.

5 Conclusions and Future Work

This paper presents an in-depth discussion of the novel core component of the Revita language learning system—the Domain model embodied in a system of linguistic constructs. This system of constructs underlies and supports all aspects of the learning experience in Revita, it supports the generation of the quality exercises and feedback. It also supports the modeling of learner skills more accurately to provide informative progress analytics, and to offer exercises most appropriate for the learner's current level.

We have results from pilot studies with Finnish and Russian L2 learners using the new Domain Model, but the discussion of the results is beyond the scope of this paper. In the future, we plan to improve the Domain Model by adding more information about the *interactions* and dependencies among the constructs—which will enable the creation of more intelligent learning paths. We also plan to add new types of activities, e.g., speech exercises.

Limitations

Revita works with many languages, however, at present, only Finnish and Russian have a sufficiently developed inventory of constructs that can be actually used by students in real-world scenarios. Most other languages have a limited set of constructs, which affects the quality and variety of the exercises, as well as limited feedback. Developing a substantial inventory of constructs is a complex task, that requires expertise in computational linguistics, as well as in language pedagogy. As mentioned above, Finnish and Russian have the order of 200 constructs. Meanwhile, "the Great Finnish Grammar" has over 1500 articles (Vilkuna et al., 2004), each of which introduces at least one construct, which, in principle, constitutes an aspect of the linguistic competency of a native speaker. A fascinating research challenge is determining the "essential" core inventory of constructs, which can support effective learning. Our experience so far with the rather modest inventories suggests that they already bring enormous value to learners and teachers (Stoyanova et al., 2021).

Revita's approach relies on arbitrary authentic texts being uploaded from the web; sometimes these texts cannot be extracted from the website without some inaccuracies. Also, the original texts may contain typos, mistakes, etc. These problems should be fixed manually by editing the text. Of course, learners with a low proficiency level cannot do that independently. To avoid having these mistakes negatively affect learning, the stories can be checked by a human teacher/tutor. We also plan to employ strong language models for grammatical error detection to identify such potential problems and highlight them to alert the user that additional checking may be needed.

Revita relies on the text when checking the learner's answers. Currently, only one correct answer is allowed—the one that is present in the story. Sometimes the word form entered by the learner may also be valid in the given story context—"alternative correct" answers. In such cases, Revita may still tell the learner that the answer is not correct. This is one of the important problems that we are researching at present, using neural models for the detection of grammatical errors (Katinskaia et al., 2019; Katinskaia and Yangarber, 2021).

Revita also has certain limitations related to the use of external tools and services: dependency parsers, morphological analyzers, and external dictionaries—all may contain inaccuracies and errors. All of these factors can be a source of mistakes in the intelligent tutor: wrong analyses, incorrectly disambiguated lemmas, missing translations, etc. The system tries to collect *multiple sources of evidence* for its predictions to raise the confidence in—and precision of—the predictions. When the confidence is low—e.g., in the presence of conflicting evidence—the exercise, feedback, etc., is *not* offered to the learner.

Ethics Statement

Revita is designed to carefully guard the privacy of its users—learners and teachers. It does not share any personal information collected during the learner's practice with any third parties. The teacher can track the learner's performance only if the learner has explicitly accepted the invitation to join the teacher's group.

Any authentic text material uploaded into the system is visible only in the user's personal *private* library. If the teacher shares a story with a group of students, it is visible only inside the group library, never to anyone outside the group. Texts pre-loaded into Revita's public library come either from sources that have given us explicit permission to use their content or from the public domain.

Acknowledgements

References

Dmitry Abbakumov and Maria Lebedeva. 2016. The RFL grammar and vocabulary placement test: design, pilot test and psychometric analysis. *Russian Language Abroad*, (5).

Albert Bandura. 1977. Self-efficacy: toward a unifying theory of behavioral change. *Psychological review*, 84(2):191.

Stephen Bodnar, Catia Cucchiarini, Bart Penning de Vries, Helmer Strik, and Roeland van Hout. 2017. Learner affect in computerised l2 oral grammar prac tice with corrective feedback. *Computer Assisted Language Learning*, 30(3-4):223–246.

Ali Derakhshan and Hossein Khodabakhshzadeh. 2011. Why call why not mall: An in-depth review of text-message vocabulary learning. *Theory and Practice in Language Studies*, 1(9):1150–1159.

Susan E Embretson and Steven P Reise. 2013. *Item response theory*. Psychology Press.

Ewa M Golonka, Anita R Bowles, Victor M Frank, Dorna L Richardson, and Suzanne Freynik. 2014. Technologies for foreign language learning: A review of technology types and their effectiveness. *Computer assisted language learning*, 27(1):70–105.

Lisa Gray. 2008. Effective practice with e-portfolios. *Higher Education Funding Council for England, JISC, Bristol.*

Jue Hou, Koppatz Maximilian, José María Hoya Quecedo, Nataliya Stoyanova, and Roman Yangarber. 2019. Modeling language learning using specialized elo rating. In *Proceedings of the Fourteenth Workshop on Innovative Use of NLP for Building Educational Applications*, pages 494–506, Florence, Italy. Association for Computational Linguistics.

Jaroslav Kacetl and Blanka Klímová. 2019. Use of smartphone applications in English language learning—a challenge for foreign language education. *Education Sciences*, 9(3):179.

Anisia Katinskaia, Sardana Ivanova, and Roman Yangarber. 2019. Multiple admissibility in language learning: judging grammaticality using unlabeled data. In *Proceedings of BSNLP: the 7th Workshop on Balto-Slavic Natural Language Processing, ACL: 56th Annual Meeting of the Association for Computational Linguistics.*

Anisia Katinskaia, Javad Nouri, and Roman Yangarber. 2017. Revita: a system for language learning and supporting endangered languages. In *6th Workshop on NLP for CALL and 2nd Workshop on NLP for Research on Language Acquisition, at NoDaLiDa*, Gothenburg, Sweden.

Anisia Katinskaia, Javad Nouri, and Roman Yangarber. 2018. Revita: a language-learning platform at the intersection of ITS and CALL. In *Proceedings of the Eleventh International Conference on Language Resources and Evaluation (LREC 2018)*, Miyazaki, Japan. European Language Resources Association (ELRA).

Anisia Katinskaia and Roman Yangarber. 2021. Assessing grammatical correctness in language learning. In *Proceedings of the 16th Workshop on Innovative Use of NLP for Building Educational Applications*. The Association for Computational Linguistics.

Sharon Klinkenberg, Marthe Straatemeier, and Han LJ van der Maas. 2011. Computer adaptive practice of maths ability using a new item response model for on-the-fly ability and difficulty estimation. *Computers & Education*, 57(2):1813–1824.

Mikhail Kopotev. 2012. Karttu: результаты языкового тестирования в школе и вузе (Karttu: results of language testing in schools and universities). *Формирование и оценка коммуникативной компетенции билингвов в процессе двуязычного образования (Formation and assessment of communicative competency of bilinguals in bilingual education)*, pages 312–339.

Michael Levy. 1997. *Computer-assisted language learning: Context and conceptualization*. Oxford University Press.

Martha C. Polson, J. Jeffrey Richardson, and Elliot Soloway. 1988. *Foundations of intelligent tutoring systems*. Hillsdale, N.J.: L. Erlbaum Associates.

Jason R Rachels and Amanda J Rockinson-Szapkiw. 2018. The effects of a mobile gamification app on elementary students' spanish achievement and self-efficacy. *Computer Assisted Language Learning*, 31(1-2):72–89.

Robert Reynolds. 2016. Russian natural language processing for computer-assisted language learning: capturing the benefits of deep morphological analysis in real-life applications.

Fernando Rosell-Aguilar. 2018. Autonomous language learning through a mobile application: a user evaluation of the busuu app. *Computer Assisted Language Learning*, 31(8):854–881.

Nataliya Stoyanova, Jue Hou, Mikhail Kopotev, and Roman Yangarber. 2021. Integration of computer-aided language learning into formal university-level l2 instruction. *L'analisi linguistica e letteraria*.

Wim J van der Linden and Ronald K Hambleton. 2013. Handbook of modern item response theory. Springer Science & Business Media.

Maria Vilkuna, Riitta Korhonen, V Kovisto, Tarja Riitta Heinonen, and Irja Alho. 2004. *Iso suomen kielioppi (The Great Finnish grammar)*. Suomalaisen Kirjallisuuden Seura.

Elena Volodina, Ildikó Pilán, Lars Borin, and Therese Lindström Tiedemann. 2014. A flexible language learning platform based on language resources and web services. In *Proceedings of LREC: the Ninth International Conference on Language Resources and Evaluation*, pages 3973–3978.

Etienne Wenger. 2014. *Artificial intelligence and tutoring systems: computational and cognitive approaches to the communication of knowledge*. Morgan Kaufmann.

Cynthia White and Hayo Reinders. 2010. The theory and practice of technology in materials development and task design. Cambridge University Press.

Hui-Chin Yeh and Wei-Yun Lai. 2019. Speaking progress and meaning negotiation processes in synchronous online tutoring. *System*, 81:179–191.

Ruofei Zhang and Di Zou. 2022. Types, purposes, and effectiveness of state-of-the-art technologies for second and foreign language learning. *Computer Assisted Language Learning*, 35(4):696–742.

GATE Teamware 2: An open-source tool for collaborative document classification annotation

David Wilby and **Twin Karmakharm**
Research Software Engineering Team

Ian Roberts, Xingyi Song and **Kalina Bontcheva**
Natural Language Processing Research Group
Department of Computer Science
The University of Sheffield

Abstract

We present GATE Teamware 2: an open-source web-based platform for managing teams of annotators working on document classification tasks. GATE Teamware 2 is an entirely re-engineered successor to GATE Teamware, using contemporary web frameworks. The software allows the management of teams of multiple annotators, project managers and administrators - including the management of annotators - across multiple projects. Projects can be configured to control and monitor the annotation statistics and have a highly flexible JSON-configurable annotation display which can include arbitrary HTML. Optionally, documents can be uploaded with pre-existing annotations and documents are served to annotators in a random order by default to reduce bias. Crucially, annotators can be trained on applying the annotation guidelines correctly and then screened for quality assurance purposes, prior to being cleared for independent annotation. GATE Teamware 2 can be self-deployed, including in container orchestration environments, or provided as private, hosted cloud instances. GATE Teamware 2 is an open-source software and can be downloaded from Github.[1] A demonstration video of the system has also been made available.[2]

1 Introduction

Machine learning models are an important element of modern natural language processing (Cunningham et al., 2013; Otter et al., 2021). These models need to be trained and evaluated on gold-standard human-annotated datasets. Depending on the purpose of the model, there are two types of annotations: *classification* and *chunking*. Chunking tasks (e.g. named entity recognition) require the annotators to identify the subset (or span) of the given text, while classification tasks (such as sentiment and stance classification) require annotators to assign labels to the given text. GATE Teamware 2 focuses on classification annotation tasks specifically.

Depending on text length or specific machine learning tasks, the classification annotation could vary from word level to document level, or single-label to multi-label annotation. In addition, other information (e.g. confidence score for the annotations) may also be needed. This requires annotation tools to be configurable and flexible to adapt to different classification annotation tasks.

Furthermore, machine learning model performance is highly dependent on annotation quality and as such, large annotation tasks often hire multiple annotators to collaborate to remedy this. Personal biases may be unknowingly introduced into annotations, so being able to collaborate with numerous annotators is a way to reduce the effect of this (Hovy and Prabhumoye, 2021).

Here we introduce GATE Teamware 2 (Karmakharm et al., 2022), a free open-source software tool for the management of teams of human annotators engaged in annotating datasets for document level classification, referred to here simply as document classification tasks. GATE Teamware 2 provides a highly flexible annotation configuration mechanism. Annotators can participate in more than one project. In order to ensure high quality human annotations, GATE Teamware 2 also provides functionality for training and testing annotators on a subset of example documents, prior to qualifying them to perform the given annotation task independently. GATE Teamware 2 is the spiritual successor to the popular GATE Teamware (Bontcheva et al., 2013), but has been entirely re-implemented in modern web frameworks with a containerised deployment architecture, as well as extended with new functionalities.

Teamware 2 has a number of unique features for an application specifically targeted at creating datasets for document classification tasks, includ-

[1] https://github.com/GATENLP/gate-teamware
[2] https://youtu.be/KoXkuhc4fmM

Proceedings of the 17th Conference of the European Chapter of the Association for Computational Linguistics
System Demonstrations, pages 145–151
May 2-4, 2023

ing:

- defined user roles and permissions,
- providing automatically 'pre-annotated' data, which the human annotators correct, rather than annotate from scratch, and
- optional training and testing qualification stages for annotators.

As a demonstration of its utility, Teamware 2 has already been used successfully for the annotation of several datasets consisting of tens of thousands of documents by numerous annotators per project on research topics such as COVID vaccine hesitancy on Twitter, stance detection in tweets (Figure 1) and emotion recognition.

2 Related Work

There is an abundance of software tools facilitating document annotation serving a variety of concerns in this area. Neves and Ševa (2020) collated a searchable directory of over 90 such tools and their features. In this section, the focus will be on the review of tools which can perform document classification while also offering collaborative features that allow multiple users to annotate the same set of documents.

According to Neves and Ševa (2020) and additional web searches, four annotation tools are available, which can:

- facilitate collaborative corpus annotation in document classification NLP tasks;
- permit management of multiple users;
- are actively maintained;
- and are available for general use.

These tools are doccano (Nakayama et al., 2018), tagtog (Cejuela et al., 2014), Universal Data Tool (Ibarluzea et al., 2022), and Label Studio (Tkachenko et al., 2020-2022).

These four tools all allow self-hosting of the software, enable multiple annotators to annotate documents through a web interface on a single hosted instance, and support a wide variety of annotation tasks out of the box in addition to document classification. However, they vary widely in availability of collaborative features and handling of document classification tasks.

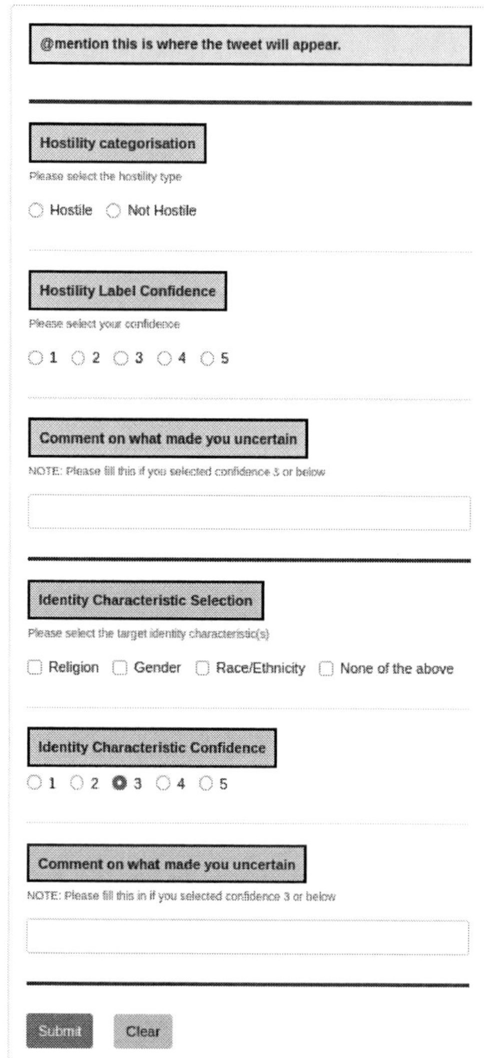

Figure 1: An example of Teamware 2's annotation interface, customised for the task of hostile tweet response classification. Actual tweet is not shown due to its sensitive nature. The application is able to capture multiple groups of labels in a single annotation using standard HTML form components (radio buttons, checkboxes, drop-down selectors and text boxes). Documents can be fully styled through HTML and CSS to suit various tasks.

In terms of suitability for document classification, while tagtog (Cejuela et al., 2014) can perform document classification as it allows document-wide labels to be captured, its focus is on sequence labelling tasks, and this is reflected in the user interface where these document-wide labels are only located in the sidebar, making it unsuitable for use especially when document classification is the only annotation task. Both Universal Data Tool (Ibarluzea et al., 2022) and doccano (Nakayama et al., 2018) have recipes for performing document classification, but both are only able to capture a single category; expect a fixed document layout; and have no options to customise the presentation of the text to be annotated by the user.

Label Studio (Tkachenko et al., 2020-2022) is perhaps the most similar tool to GATE Teamware 2 in that it provides a fine-grained way to customise the number of labels, their layout, and how the text to be annotated can be formatted and presented to the annotator.

In terms of collaborative features, Universal Data Tool (Ibarluzea et al., 2022), unlike the other tools, does not have user accounts and collaborators can join an annotation project through a generated link which would make the tool more suitable for smaller and shorter annotation projects. The free version of Label Studio (Tkachenko et al., 2020-2022) does not allow multiple users with clearly-defined user roles – all users are able to add and modify documents and annotations freely, though this may be different under a paid subscription. Finally, tagtog (Cejuela et al., 2014) and doccano (Nakayama et al., 2018) are the only two applications that have clear definition of user roles and limit annotators to performing annotation tasks, preventing them from modifying annotation project settings.

With these four tools, the expectation is for annotators to annotate every document in the project. With larger annotation projects that can contain thousands of documents, in order to limit the number of documents that have to be annotated by each individual annotator, it becomes necessary to split the corpus into multiple projects, recruiting different sets of annotators to each one. GATE Teamware 2 solves this problem by allowing limits to be placed on the number of annotations a document requires and the maximum proportion of the corpus a single annotator can annotate. This means annotation tasks can instead be automatically distributed to annotators within the project whilst avoiding the problem of annotators having too many annotation tasks.

Relation to GATE Teamware

As stated above, GATE Teamware 2 is intended as a successor to GATE Teamware version 1 (Bontcheva et al., 2013). Many of the design concepts in GATE Teamware 2 originate in the original GATE Teamware, for example the management of teams of human annotators, their assignment to annotation projects, monitoring of the average time-per-document for each annotator, and the option for the project manager to provide "pre-annotations" for the annotators to correct, rather than having them annotate every document from scratch. However, the original GATE Teamware was designed around the annotation of *spans* of characters within text and is poorly suited to more general document classification tasks of the sort required for modern ML models. In GATE Teamware, annotation schemas can be provided to control the sets of labels and features that annotators may assign, but every label must be tied to a specific span within a longer document, which increases the cognitive load on annotators.

There are other desirable features missing from GATE Teamware, notably:

- Annotator training and validation – GATE Teamware included tools to facilitate resolution of disagreements among annotators or between a single annotator and a gold standard annotation set, but there is no real-time feedback to the annotators on how well they are following the annotation guidelines and no way to automatically check that annotators have reached a certain quality threshold before starting on a real project.

- Limiting the number of documents each annotator can consume – GATE Teamware ensured that each document is annotated by a set number of *annotators*, but cannot ensure that each annotator sees the same number of *documents*. An annotator will continue to be assigned documents until either all documents have been fully annotated, or they have been presented with every available document. In many cases, it is desirable to better balance the documents across annotators.

In addition, GATE Teamware was built as a Java

web application using a complex stack of software libraries, while the annotator interface was derived from the annotation editor of GATE Developer, a desktop Java Swing application. The interface was delivered to annotators as a Java Web Start application[3], but this technology ceased to be supported by Oracle with the release of Java 11 in 2018, and is very difficult to operate in modern browsers. One of the key motivations for starting from scratch when implementing GATE Teamware 2 was to be able to use a more modern and performant development framework and purely browser-based user interface, vastly simplifying both server-side deployment and annotator on-boarding.

3 GATE Teamware 2 Overview

GATE Teamware 2 provides a database-backed web application for managing groups of annotators and providing document classification annotations. It is written in the modern web frameworks Django and Vue.js with a PostgreSQL database.

A Teamware 2 instance is set up by an administrator for a set group of users who can act as project managers and/or annotators. Project managers can create projects, which represent annotation tasks and are configured for the annotation of a single corpus of documents. Annotators can then be added to a project to create annotations according to the guidelines and configuration for that project.

4 User Roles

There are 3 user roles in Teamware 2:

Annotator: Can only annotate via the annotation view, when assigned to a project with annotation tasks available to them. Once a task is complete, they must contact a manager to be added to any new projects. This is the default role assigned to newly registered users. See section 6.

Manager: Can annotate as the annotator above. Also has the ability to create new projects and edit all existing projects on the instance. See section 5.

Admin: As roles above; also has total responsibility over an entire Teamware 2 instance, including the ability to promote annotator users to manager, and manage all users.

5 Annotation Projects

Annotation in GATE Teamware 2 is organised into 'Projects', each of which has a manager, who owns the project.

Managers create projects simply through a web interface which populates the configuration form with default options. Alternatively, an existing project can be 'cloned' to create a new project with no documents or annotators, but an identical configuration.

Projects are configured to include a description and annotator guidelines, both of which can contain text formatted as markdown or HTML and can be previewed by the project manager. Annotation parameters are set at this stage to include: the total number of annotations required per document; the maximum proportion of documents in the corpus that any one user can annotate; and how long an annotator assigned a document has to annotate it before it is returned to the pool of documents. In the interface, each of these options has concise inline help text to remove ambiguity and streamline the project setup process.

5.1 Configuring annotation display and collected labels

Configuring how annotations will be presented and the details of collected labels is performed with a highly flexible JSON format in which elements are defined as JSON objects (see Figure 2a). Detailed documentation and examples are provided. Annotations can include HTML, fields or columns from the document data (see subsection 5.2), widgets such as radio buttons, free text fields, checkboxes, and drop-down menus. The result of the configuration JSON is previewed alongside its input in the form (e.g. Figure 2c), allowing managers to experiment with the best display for their project.

5.2 Documents

Under the 'Documents & Annotations' tab of the project management page, a corpus can be uploaded for annotation via single or multiple file upload, or by dragging and dropping files. Documents can be provided as JSON or CSV, and users can set a global preference for how they view documents for either one of these formats. Once documents are uploaded to the project, they are shown in a searchable list along with annotation statistics including how many annotations for each document are complete, aborted, rejected, timed out, and pending.

[3] https://docs.oracle.com/javase/8/docs/technotes/guides/javaws/

```
[
  {
    "name": "htmldisplay",
    "text": "{{{text}}}",
    "type": "html"
  },
  {
    "name": "sentiment",
    "type": "radio",
    "title": "Sentiment",
    "options": {
      "neutral": "Neutral",
      "negative": "Negative",
      "positive": "Positive"
    },
    "description": "Please select a
       ↪ sentiment of the text above."
  }
]
```

(a) Example project configuration JSON.

```
{
  "text": "<p>Document text can be
      ↪ <strong>arbitrarily
      ↪ styled</strong> using
      ↪ HTML.</p><p>Second
      ↪ paragraph.</p>"
}
```

(b) Example document JSON containing styling HTML.

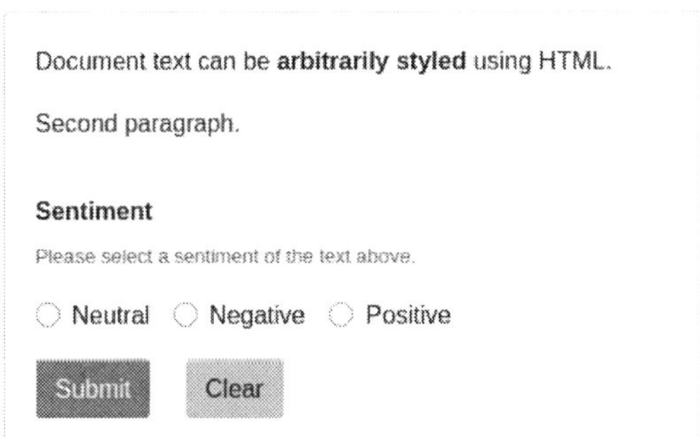

(c) Example annotation display produced by configuration in Figure 2a and document text field in Figure 2b.

Figure 2: Example simple project configuration and document text with the resulting annotation view.

5.3 Pre-Annotation

A project can be configured to look for a field in the document that contains pre-annotation information. At the annotation stage, the annotation display will be pre-filled if the configured pre-annotation field exists in the document and contains data in the same layout as the expected annotation output. An example annotation output can be obtained by filling out the annotation display preview in the project configuration page.

5.4 Managing a Project

Currently available annotators can be added from a pool of those available, using a list of annotators which is searchable by email and username. Once added to the project, user status can be monitored with respect to completion of training and testing stages (optional) and annotations. Annotators can then be marked as complete or rejected from a project, as well as made active again in a project, provided that they have not met their quota of annotations. These user management actions can also be performed in batch mode to save time.

The status of documents and their annotations can be monitored throughout the project, including icons showing the number of annotations and their status. Annotations can also be edited by project managers. Similarly, annotator status is shown in the 'Annotators' tab.

5.5 Training & Testing Annotators

Training and testing stages can be enabled for any project to ensure quality in annotations. Training mode allows project managers to supply interactive examples for annotators to complete, prior to participating in a project. Similarly, a testing stage can be enforced with a threshold of correct answers that an annotator must achieve before being allowed to annotate. For both options, a lightweight JSON format, similar to the main project documents, is used, with an additional field indicating the correct answers.

Depending on choice at the project configuration stage, annotators can be automatically advanced to the annotation stage once they have successfully scored over the pass threshold or, from the project management screen, be approved by a project manager or admin.

5.6 Collected Annotations

Annotations can be exported as CSV, JSON or JSONL format, of which the latter two can be either formatted in the same style as uploaded JSON documents or in the format used by GATE[4]. The project configuration (section 5 & Figure 2a) also defines how the annotations are exported.

By default, each exported annotation contains a unique numerical key associated to an annotator instead of the annotator's username. This is to ensure anonymisation when sharing the dataset, while at the same time allowing cross-referencing of annotators between exported datasets from the same Teamware 2 instance. An option is available to export with usernames instead if required.

6 Annotating with GATE Teamware 2

Once logged in, annotators are only able to view the annotation view, which presents them with the next annotation task assigned to them. Depending on the project configuration, there are several options made available; such as rejecting an annotation, or adding a training or test stage to the project. Once there are no more documents available, they are instructed to contact the project manager to be assigned to a new project (if applicable).

During an annotation task, annotators are able to go back to the previous annotation to make a correction. Annotations can also be changed at any stage by visiting the 'My Annotations' view which displays all of an annotator's annotations. A complete history of all annotations and changes made is kept for posterity.

7 Using GATE Teamware 2

GATE Teamware 2 is available under an open source AGPL license and as such is free to use and deploy. However, subject to arrangements, private hosted instances can be provided for NLP projects[5] as a low-overhead way to set up an instance of the software. For hosting your own instance, GATE Teamware 2 has been designed so users can deploy via a container orchestration tool such as Kubernetes or Docker Compose, for instance on a cloud service. Deployment options can be chosen by editing a single text file and without changing the source code, enabling easy annotation task management.

8 Software Quality Assurance

Quality and consistency of GATE Teamware 2's source code is ensured via extensive software testing using `pytest` for the back end unit tests, `jest` for the front end unit tests and `Cypress` for integration testing. Testing currently covers 85% of the codebase. The software is under active development and uses a continuous integration approach using GitHub Actions to run tests on all changes to the source code, therefore reducing breaking changes to functionality.

9 Conclusions & Future work

GATE Teamware 2 is a fast and simple to use platform for facilitating collaborative document annotation, and includes a number of important features such as pre-annotation upload, flexible annotation configuration and multiple user management.

The software is under active development and a number of valuable features will be coming to the software soon. For instance, in addition to document classification, sequence labelling is planned to be integrated in the future, allowing it to be used in an even greater range of NLP annotation tasks. Other planned future features include: calculation of inter-annotator agreement metrics, ability to define hierarchical/dependent annotations, exposing an annotation management API for integration with active learning algorithms, control over project visibility and ownership, and availability of the platform as a cloud service.

Limitations

The major current limitations of GATE Teamware 2 align closely with the future work above and so many of its limitations will be resolved in the short to medium term. Primarily, Teamware 2 is designed for document classification tasks and so at present cannot be used for chunk annotation. There is no facility yet for calculation of inter-annotator agreements within the application, though these can be simply calculated from the exported annotation data. Similarly, Teamware 2 does not yet have web-based annotation adjudication capabilities and annotation quality can only be evaluated based on exported data. Hierarchical annotations, *i.e.* nested options which depend on the initial annotation, are not yet available. As Teamware 2 is designed so

[4] `https://gate.ac.uk/userguide/sec:creole:gatejson`

[5] Please contact the team at https://gate.ac.uk/g8/contact to arrange.

far, all projects are visible and editable by all other managers and admins on the instance, however this is something that may become an option to change in the future. In the mean time if such separation is required (e.g. to protect data from one project being seen by managers of another), a workaround is possible by having the different annotation projects run on separate GATE Teamware 2 deployments.

Ethics Statement

The development of GATE Teamware 2 as an annotation tool was in line with the ethical clearances of the respective research projects that provided the funding. Ethical approvals for each annotated dataset and the respective volunteer annotators recruited for that project may need to be sought in addition, in line with the ethical guidelines of the user's institution and any data protection and privacy laws that apply to the managing organisation and to the annotators if they are located in a different jurisdiction. For example, for the authors' own annotation projects, individual ethical approvals have been obtained via the standard University of Sheffield research ethics process, and it is envisaged that similar processes would be followed by users at other institutions.

A limited amount of personally identifiable information, namely an email address and username, is collected from each annotator who registers an account with a given installation of GATE Teamware 2. This is made clear to users in a privacy policy prior to registration, and provision is made to remove all personal identifiers from the user's account if they choose to withdraw from participating in annotation projects on that installation. The annotations they have performed so far are not necessarily deleted[6], and will remain linked to the dormant account, so that it is still possible to determine whether disparate sets of annotations were created by the same individual, but the username and email address on their account profile are replaced by anonymous placeholders so the account is no longer linked to an identifiable person.

Acknowledgements

This work has been partially supported by a European Union – Horizon 2020 Program, grant no. 824091 (RISIS 2), the European Union Horizon 2020 Program under the scheme "INFRAIA-01-2018-2019 – Integrating Activities for Advanced Communities", Grant Agreement n.871042("SoBigData++: European Integrated Infrastructure for Social Mining and Big Data Analytics"(http://www.sobigdata.eu)) and a UKRI grant no. EP/W011212/1.

[6] Whether a user's pre-existing annotations must be deleted is a matter for the ethical approval of the particular project or projects they are working on, not something enforced at the platform level.

References

Kalina Bontcheva, Hamish Cunningham, Ian Roberts, Angus Roberts, Valentin Tablan, Niraj Aswani, and Genevieve Gorrell. 2013. GATE teamware: a web-based, collaborative text annotation framework. *Language Resources and Evaluation*, 47(4):1007–1029.

Juan Miguel Cejuela, Peter McQuilton, Laura Ponting, Steven J. Marygold, Raymund Stefancsik, Gillian H. Millburn, Burkhard Rost, and the FlyBase Consortium. 2014. tagtog: interactive and text-mining-assisted annotation of gene mentions in PLOS full-text articles. *Database*, 2014. Bau033.

Hamish Cunningham, Valentin Tablan, Angus Roberts, and Kalina Bontcheva. 2013. Getting More Out of Biomedical Documents with GATE's Full Lifecycle Open Source Text Analytics. *PLOS Computational Biology*, 9(2):e1002854. Publisher: Public Library of Science.

Dirk Hovy and Shrimai Prabhumoye. 2021. Five sources of bias in natural language processing. *Language and Linguistics Compass*, 15(8):e12432.

Severin Ibarluzea et al. 2022. Universal data tool. `https://github.com/UniversalDataTool/universal-data-tool`.

Twin Karmakharm, David Wilby, Ian Roberts, and Kalina Bontcheva. 2022. GATE Teamware. Open source software available from `https://github.com/GATENLP/gate-teamware`.

Hiroki Nakayama, Takahiro Kubo, Junya Kamura, Yasufumi Taniguchi, and Xu Liang. 2018. doccano: Text annotation tool for human. Software available from `https://github.com/doccano/doccano`.

Mariana Neves and Jurica Ševa. 2020. Annotationsaurus: A searchable directory of annotation tools.

Daniel W. Otter, Julian R. Medina, and Jugal K. Kalita. 2021. A Survey of the Usages of Deep Learning for Natural Language Processing. *IEEE Transactions on Neural Networks and Learning Systems*, 32(2):604–624. Conference Name: IEEE Transactions on Neural Networks and Learning Systems.

Maxim Tkachenko, Mikhail Malyuk, Andrey Holmanyuk, and Nikolai Liubimov. 2020-2022. Label Studio: Data labeling software. Open source software available from `https://github.com/heartexlabs/label-studio`.

GameQA: Gamified Mobile App Platform for Building Multiple-Domain Question-Answering Datasets

Njáll Skarphéðinsson[1,2], **Breki Guðmundsson**[2], **Steinar Þ. Smári**[1], **Marta K. Lárusdóttir**[1], **Hafsteinn Einarsson**[3], **Abuzar Khan**[2], **Eric Nyberg**[2], **Hrafn Loftsson**[1]

[1] Department of Computer Science, Reykjavik University, Reykjavik, Iceland
[2] Language Technologies Institute, Carnegie Mellon University, PA, USA
[3] Department of Computer Science, University of Iceland, Reykjavik, Iceland
{nskarphe, abuzark, en09}@andrew.cmu.edu, hafsteinne@hi.is
{brekig18, steinars21, marta, hrafn}@ru.is

Abstract

The methods used to create many of the well-known Question-Answering (QA) datasets are hard to replicate for low-resource languages. A commonality amongst these methods is hiring annotators to source answers from the internet by querying a single answer source, such as Wikipedia. Applying these methods for low-resource languages can be problematic since there is no single large answer source for these languages. Consequently, this can result in a high ratio of unanswered questions, since the amount of information in any single source is limited. To address this problem, we developed a novel crowd-sourcing platform to gather multiple-domain QA data for low-resource languages. Our platform, which consists of a mobile app and a web API, gamifies the data collection process. We successfully released the app for Icelandic (a low-resource language with about 350,000 native speakers) to build a dataset which rivals large QA datasets for high-resource languages both in terms of size and ratio of answered questions. We have made the platform open source with instructions on how to localize and deploy it to gather data for other low-resource languages.

1 Introduction

Replicating well known Question-Answering (QA) data collection methods, such as those used to create the SQuAD (Rajpurkar et al., 2016) and TyDi (Clark et al., 2020) datasets, for low-resource languages poses a few problems. First, many large-scale QA datasets are gathered using a single source for answers, e.g. Wikipedia. This is problematic since low-resource languages do not have access to any single, large knowledge base from which information can be extracted to create such a dataset. Second, QA datasets gathered in an information-seeking manner (where the question is asked prior to finding the answer), will have questions that cannot be answered by the answer source(s). As we will show, the ratio of answerable questions is positively correlated with the amount of content in an answer source. Third, many of these methods rely on paid workers to perform the laborious task of annotating data and the necessary funds may not be available in regions of low-resource languages.

In this paper, we introduce GameQA, a crowd-sourcing platform to build QA datasets. GameQA consists of a mobile trivia app (for iOS and Android) and a web API. GameQA, which is open source, is specifically designed to gather QA data for low-resource languages. It can be trivially localized and published for specific geographical regions. The main contributions of GameQA are as follows:

- **Gamification:** It incorporates numerous aspects of gamification to increase the number of annotations provided per user. This includes rewarding points, level-ups, streaks, avatar upgrades, and prestige tokens to users as they contribute to the data collection.
- **Social features:** The users are made aware of their contributions relative to other users. This includes a leaderboard and notifying users once another user has answered their question.
- **Cultural relevance:** Our results show that GameQA gathers questions which are relevant to the culture, history, and geography of the region in which it is employed.
- **Multiple Answer Sources:** The platform's API integrates Google's Programmable Search Engine[1] to allow users to find answers

[1] https://developers.google.com/custom-search/v1/introduction

Proceedings of the 17th Conference of the European Chapter of the Association for Computational Linguistics System Demonstrations, pages 152–160
May 2-4, 2023

on multiple websites, thus seamlessly constructing a multiple-domain QA dataset.

To spur QA research for low-resource languages, we have made the GameQA platform open source with instructions on how to localize it and subsequently release it for any geographical area[2].

2 Related Work

In recent years, the literature has seen an explosion in the number and diversity of QA datasets (Cambazoglu et al., 2021). The most prevalent type of QA datasets are sentence classification and span-prediction datasets. These include documents, questions, and demarcated answer spans that a machine learning model must learn to predict for a given question. Rajpurkar et al. (2016) introduced SQuAD, one of the first large span-prediction datasets. They crowd-sourced the creation of the dataset by showing crowd-workers an excerpt from Wikipedia and tasking them with writing a question whose answer is contained within the excerpt. This results in QA data with a high lexical overlap between questions and answer paragraphs (Ribeiro et al., 2019; Gan and Ng, 2019) which can lead to biased data (Shinoda et al., 2021). In this paper, we will refer to span-prediction datasets constructed in this manner as being *squad-like*. CoQa (Reddy et al., 2019), NarrativeQA (Kočiský et al., 2018), and NewsQA (Trischler et al., 2016) are other examples of datasets falling into this category.

To address the problems associated with squad-like datasets, researchers have developed ways that encourage information-seeking behavior during question elicitation. The aim is to emulate human curiosity by having annotators ask questions about something they do not know the answer to. WikiQA (Yang et al., 2015), which poses the problem as a sentence classification problem instead of span prediction, is orders of magnitude smaller than SQuAD (3,047 vs. 100,000 questions, respectively). However, WikiQA brings forth interesting ideas, such as collecting QA data in an information-seeking manner and using web-search queries as a means to capture the curiosity of information-seeking users. This web-search query-based approach was later adopted by larger information-seeking QA datasets, such as MS-Marco (Bajaj et al., 2016), SearchQA (Dunn et al., 2017), and Natural Questions (Kwiatkowski et al., 2019). TyDi is an example of an information-seeking dataset constructed using answer paragraphs from the encyclopedic domain (Clark et al., 2020). Clark et al. showed crowd-workers a paragraph from Wikipedia, but instructed them to ask a question that was not answerable by the paragraph.

Just as QA datasets can differ in terms of how they source their questions (e.g., squad-like or information-seeking), they can also be categorized in terms of where their answer paragraphs are sourced, i.e. the domain that contains the answers. A very common practice is to constrain a dataset to a single domain – this is the case for the majority of over 80 QA datasets reviewed by Rogers et al. (2020). SQuAD, WikiQA, TyDi, and Natural Questions are examples of such single-source datasets, i.e. they all source answer paragraphs from Wikipedia only. Examples of datasets sourcing answers from another notable domain, the news domain, are NewsQA and CNN/Daily Mail (Hermann et al., 2015). However, low-resource languages are unlikely to have access to a single source that contains enough information to construct a large QA dataset.

Multiple-domain QA datasets have also been created. MS-Marco, which utilized Bing[3] search queries, used a proprietary state-of-the-art passage retrieval system at Bing to match queries with answer paragraphs on the internet. Since MS-Marco relies on such an algorithm, replicating their methods (i.e. for other languages) is impossible. MMQA, a multiple-domain, squad-like dataset in English and Hindi, was created by web-crawling and subsequently having annotators write questions about the crawled articles (Gupta et al., 2018). However, it is likely that it suffers from the same problems as other squad-like datasets. To the best of our knowledge, there exists no easily reproducible method in the literature to gather a multi-domain dataset where the questions reflect information-seeking intent.

2.1 QA for Icelandic

In the last few years, Icelandic has been growing considerably with regard to language resources (Nikulásdóttir et al., 2022). However, for many natural language processing tasks it still lacks the necessary resources. For reading comprehension and open QA tasks, there only exists one dataset

[2]https://github.com/cadia-lvl/GameQA

[3]https://www.bing.com

for Icelandic (Snæbjarnarson and Einarsson, 2022). It was created using the same information-seeking process as was introduced with TyDi. Furthermore, the authors specifically mentioned that they exhausted the Icelandic Wikipedia[4] when creating questions for the dataset, thereby highlighting the need to include more domains both for question elicitation and answer annotation.

3 The GameQA Platform

Our crowd-sourcing platform consists of a mobile app and web API. The mobile app was written in React Native, the web server in Node.js, and the underlying database is MongoDB.

We recruited users by sending an email to all students at Reykjavik University and by advertising the app on social media platforms. The app was distributed through Apple App Store (iOS version) and Google Play Store (Android version), and, in both cases, only made accessible in Iceland.

The users form a community where they help each other finding answers to user generated questions. For example, the app might ask a user to write a question. Later on, another user would be tasked with reviewing it. Once it passes peer review, a third user would be tasked with finding a specific paragraph on a web page containing the answer, using an integrated web-search interface. Lastly, another user would verify the answer. These tasks are served randomly and users are not able to review their own content.

3.1 User centered development

In the design and development of GameQA, we applied user-centred design methodology through iterative development and three prototypes. In the first iteration, a web-based interface was evaluated. As a result, in the second iteration, the interface was simplified and gamification was added. When evaluating the second version, users pointed out the need for a mobile phone interface. In the final iteration, the mobile app was thus developed and evaluated. Involving users in the design and the development of the application improved the final result and the user experience. By qualitatively analysing the user interface prior to launch, we were able to understand which gamification features could increase adoption and usage of the app.

[4]At the time, the Icelandic Wikipedia had only 3,730 pages with more than 250 characters.

4 Gamification and Social Features

Gathering and annotating QA data is a laborious and repetitive task. Since the crowd-workers of GameQA are not financially compensated for their contributions, and thus have little incentive to participate, GameQA leverages gamification to incentivize the users and to give them positive feedback when they contribute to the data collection.

4.1 User levels and avatars

Every user collects points by completing tasks. For each completed task, the user is rewarded with 1 point. Upon completing a certain number of tasks, the user is awarded with a "level-up". We used an ad-hoc formula (see Equation 1) to calculate the number of tasks T in order to complete a specific level L:

$$T_L = \lfloor 2.5 \times L^{1.1} \rfloor \quad (1)$$

Here $T_L \in \mathbb{N}, \forall L \in \mathbb{N}$. For example, a user would have to complete $\lfloor 2.5 \times 1^{1.1} \rfloor = 2$ tasks for the first "level-up", and $\sum_{l=1}^{20} T_l = 667$ tasks to complete all 20 levels.

Users are also given avatars which change as the users level up. Since users can see each other's avatars, they are a signal from a user to the community about their status.

4.2 Prestige tokens

Once we rolled out the data collection, we were doubtful that any user would finish the 667 tasks required to complete all 20 levels. After the first day, however, we realized that a few completed 667 tasks within 24 hours and, subsequently, stopped playing. We hypothesized that this was because users had little motivation to continue annotating once they had reached the maximum level. As a result, taking inspiration from gaming franchises like `Call of Duty`[5], we added *Prestige Tokens*. The prestige tokens work as follows: Users are prompted when they finish level 20 to restart the game at level 1, but with a token that appears next to their avatar which signals to other users that they have finished the game once over. The prestige tokens then change color, every time the user reaches level 20.

4.3 Leaderboard

We implemented a live leaderboard within GameQA which allows users to see how they are

[5]`https://www.activision.com/`

performing relative to other users. We observed significant competitiveness amongst some users after adding this feature. For example, some users spent several hours per day annotating data, in order to achieve the highest rank. The avatar of the highest ranking user was given a crown to further incentive users to compete for the highest rank.

It is worth mentioning that even though users competed to achieve high ranks they were informed that the data collection was a collaborative effort, for the purpose of compiling a training corpus for Icelandic QA models.

4.4 User notifications

Once a question has been answered by the community, a notification is sent to the author of the question telling them that they can see the answer (and who answered it) in the app. This serves as an important way for users to see that their contribution is impacting the data collection.

5 Data Collection Steps

In total, the data collection consists of five different stages that each QA pair has to pass: 1) question elicitation, 2) question review, 3) web search and answer paragraph selection, 4) answer span marking, and 5) answer review[6]. Tasks are randomly served to users – subsequent tasks are thus independent of one another.

For our Icelandic QA dataset, which we call *RUQuAD* (Reykjavik University Question Answering Dataset)[7], we sourced answers from five sources in four separate domains: The Icelandic Wikipedia[8], "Vísindavefurinn" (The Icelandic Web of Science)[9], the news websites `mbl.is` and `visir.is`, and "Stjórnarráðið" (The Icelandic Government Information website)[10].

5.1 Question elicitation

Users are shown an image and asked to write a question that comes to mind. However, users are not constrained to ask a question about the image itself. Instead, the image serves as a stimulus for curiosity. To gather the set of images, we first constructed a list of 78 broad topics. From there, we found one image related to each topic.

[6]Demonstrated in a YouTube video: https://www.youtube.com/watch?v=PmCR7v_KDhQ

[7]https://github.com/cadia-lvl/RUQuAD

[8]https://is.wikipedia.org/wiki/

[9]https://www.visindavefur.is/

[10]https://www.stjornarradid.is/

5.2 Question review

Since we seek to gather questions based on the users' curiosity with minimal guidance and influence, we purposefully place little restrictions on the nature of the questions. Users are asked to rate questions given the following criteria:

Clarity If it is clear what the author of the question is asking for.

Consistency If the answer is unlikely to change depending on whom or when you ask.

Answer length If it seems like this question could be answered in three sentences or less.

We chose to include the *Answer Length* criteria in order to simplify other annotation tasks such as answer reviews. Each question has to pass all of these criteria in two separate reviews performed by two separate users. Researchers seeking to localize GameQA can modify these criteria if needed.

5.3 Web search and paragraph selection

A distinguishing feature of our data collection is the users' ability to find answers in various different sources and domains instead of only linking a question to a Wikipedia article. When searching for an article online containing an answer to a given question, the users form a search string that they believe will lead to success, i.e. for which an answer will be found (see Figure 1). This is carried out in very much the same way as a user of a search engine performs a web search.

Once the users find a website that contains the information necessary to answer the question, they select the exact paragraph that contains the answer. If annotators are not able to find an answer, they can mark it as *unanswerable*.

5.4 Answer span marking

Once a question has been linked to an answer paragraph, the question and the attached paragraph is shown to users. First, they are asked whether or not they think that the answer is contained within the paragraph. If the user responds in the affirmative, they are then tasked with selecting the first and last word (the span) of the answer (see Figure 2). However, if the question is a YES or NO question, then the user will mark it as such with the right answer.

Figure 1: A screenshot from the mobile app demonstrating the interface for the *Web search and paragraph selection* task. The question (in Icelandic) presented to the user is "Hver drap Frankenstein" (Who killed Frankenstein). The user has formed the search string "Frankenstein", and a list of search results from the five sources appears below. At the top, the users can see their avatar, level, position on the leaderboard, and their progress towards their next level.

Figure 2: A screenshot from the mobile app demonstrating the interface for the *Answer span marking* task. The question (in Icelandic) presented to the user is "Í hvaða heimsálfu er Perú" (In which continent is Peru). The user has marked "Suður-Ameríku" (South America) as the answer.

5.5 Answer review

The last step in this pipeline is the answer review step. Similar to the question review step, each answer has to pass two separate reviews from two separate users. The review step consists of a single question, asking users if they believe an answer shown to them to be correct or not. The users are not required to know the precise answer to the question, instead they use their reading comprehension skills and judgement to determine if the answer seems correct.

6 Results and Data Analysis

Throughout our QA collection process for Icelandic using GameQA, 1,524 users created an account. Roughly $\frac{2}{3}$ of those (1,024 users) contributed content to the creation of the RUQuAD dataset. By the end, they had generated 23,036 questions, 20,730 (90%) of which passed the double peer review. 12,772 answers were annotated and reviewed, resulting in an unanswerable ratio of 38.4%. A preliminary analysis suggests that approximately 30% of the questions that either failed the peer review or were marked as unanswerable might have been mislabeled as such. As a result, the unanswerable rate might become considerably lower with additional labeling after crowd-sourcing the data.

There is a remarkable diversity in the number of answer articles. 7,835 articles were gathered in total for the 12,722 answers, i.e. 1.64 answers per article. This ratio is roughly 2.05 and 200 for TyDi and SQuAD, respectively. We expect that more diverse answer paragraphs will help a machine learning model, trained on the data, to generalize better. The distribution of articles over the sources is as follows: 68.3% came from the Icelandic Wikipedia, 18.4% from The Icelandic Web of Science, 13.1% from the two news websites, and 0.2% from the Government Information website.

6.1 Understanding user contributions

Since the crowd-workers weren't paid, but rather users playing a game in their own free time, the strength of each users contribution was mostly impacted by the time they were willing to spend on the app. In total, the users performed 137,972 annotation tasks (elicit questions, review questions, find answers, label answers, review answers). As Figure 3 shows, the amount of work performed per user follows a pareto distribution.

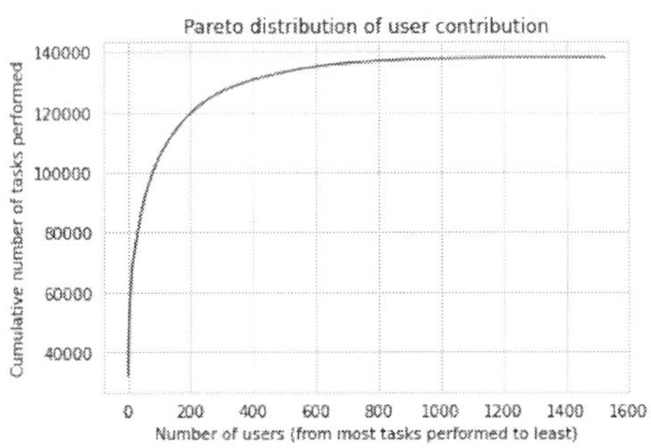

Figure 3: Tasks completed per user follow a pareto distribution where a minority of the 1,524 users contributed a majority of the content.

6.2 Unanswerable Questions

As mentioned in Section 2, a particular problem with information-seeking methods for low-resource languages is the high ratio of unanswerable questions – this can be observed in Table 1.

Icelandic has fewer Wikipedia articles (54,121) than all languages in TyDi. Yet, by leveraging multiple answer sources with GameQA, we achieved an unanswerable rate of 38% which is lower than all languages in TyDi, except Arabic.

6.3 Span length distribution

Out of the five annotation steps, marking answer spans is the step that requires the highest degree of standardization of annotation. Without such standards (or precise guidelines) and a way of enforcing them, the annotators will not mark answer spans in a consistent manner.

Language	Number of Wikipedia articles	Ratio of questions with an answer span
Russian	1,816,916	51%
Japanese	1,324,304	32%
Arabic	1,165,575	69%
Indonesian	620,863	34%
Korean	587,573	22%
Finnish	530,420	41%
Thai	147,378	43%
Bengali	122,041	35%
Telugu	76,259	27%
Kiswahili	71,570	22%

Table 1: A comparison of the ratio of questions, which had an answer span, with the number of Wikipedia articles, for each of the 10 non-English languages in the TyDi dataset. The Pearson correlation coefficient is $p = 0.54$.

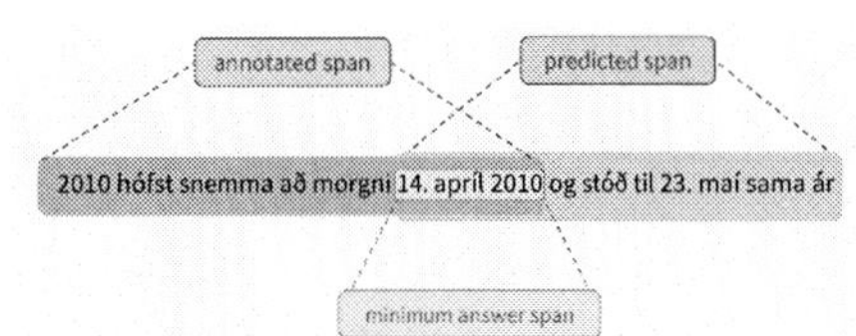

Figure 4: A comparison of the minimum answer span with the annotated and predicted spans. The underlying subsentence is: "hófst snemma að morgni 4. apríl 2010 og stóð til 23. maí sama ár" (started early in the morning on April 4, 2010 and lasted until May 23 of the same year).

Figure 4 shows a comparison of the minimum answer span (needed to answer a question) with the span annotated by a user and the span predicted by the IceBERT model (Snæbjarnarson et al., 2022), fine-tuned on our dataset. We expect this discrepancy between ground truth labels and the prediction to be a result of lack of alignment amongst annotators when marking answer spans. We propose that researchers that localize GameQA standardize and shorten the answer spans where needed, once the crowd-sourcing has concluded.

Table 2 shows summary statistics for the answer span lengths for three different datasets. Higher variance in answer span lengths in RUQuAD is to be expected since enforcing annotation standards across thousands of crowd-workers is non-trivial.

Dataset	Span Length	Standard Deviation
SQuAD	19.75	20.73
TyDi	25.77	46.12
RUQuAD	75.64	91.52

Table 2: Summary statistics of answer span lengths (character count)

6.4 Cost-effective data collection

A clear advantage of localizing GameQA for data collection for other languages is the possibility of gathering QA data in a cost-effective manner. By gamifying the data collection, we were able to create a large-scale QA data set, gathered by thousands of crowd-workers without the need of hiring, training, and managing annotators. The majority of the cost we incurred with GameQA was the cost of developing the platform. By making the code open source, we hope to enable researchers around the world to gather cost-effective large-scale multiple-domain QA data for low-resource languages.

6.5 Cultural relevance

As a result of having thousands of annotators, we observe a considerable diversity in terms of the range of topics users asked about. Furthermore, we notice that our proposed method is able to gather questions which are representative of the local history and culture. In order to build QA systems, researchers for low-resource languages might be tempted to translate large English datasets. However, translation of English datasets will not produce questions relevant to local culture, history, geography, etc. Out of 100 questions from our dataset, sampled uniformly at random, 33 were directly asking about local (Icelandic) culture, history, or geography. This emphasis on culture-related questions can possibly be attributed to some extent to the images used in the prompting step, but it also highlights how the right combination of annotators and prompts can lead to greater culture focus in the resulting data.

7 Conclusion

In this paper, we have presented GameQA – a novel mobile trivia game platform for collecting QA data for low-resource languages. We successfully gamified the experience to increase the number of annotations tasks performed per user and conducted different iterations of user experience testing. The QA data gathered by GameQA's users is culturally relevant for the language and/or geographical region in question. We have made GameQA open source, with instructions on how to localize and subsequently release it for particular geographical areas.

We believe that our platform can help to reduce the cost and time associated with collecting QA data for low-resource languages. Our method opens up new areas of research e.g. comparing different prompting methods, such as image vs. text prompts, as well as possible advancements for QA research in languages where traditional methods might fail to gather a large-scale QA dataset.

Given the success of the gamification for collecting QA data, we propose that gamified crowdsourcing can be leveraged to gather data for other NLP tasks as well. For an app such as GameQA, there is a target user base that is interested in triva and knowledge and thus willing to annotate data in this manner. Similarly, for other NLP tasks, such as machine translation, there exists a potential user base of multilingual persons that are greatly interested in languages and translation. We see great potential in applying the knowledge learned through implementing GameQA for such tasks.

Limitations

The question elicitation part of GameQA is different from prior work. An image is shown to the user instead of a textual prompt to inspire questions. It is unclear what effect that decision has on the chances of the question being answerable since users could make more or less challenging questions when prompted with images instead of text. Furthermore, the source from which the images are taken could further influence answerability. Future work will need to reveal the difference between prompting with text or images.

In GameQA, the user is responsible for finding the article that could contain an answer to a given question. This step was automated in prior work by selecting top search engine results. This approach gives the user more freedom when looking for the answer. Still, it could also limit their ability to find answers since they are responsible for performing Google search queries themselves. Although an answer might exist, their queries might not suffice to identify relevant candidate pages.

Furthermore, it is likely that some of the questions asked are ambiguous, i.e. that for a given question more than one correct answer is possible. In such cases, a rewrite of the question, for the purpose of clarifying its interpretation, might be beneficial (Min et al., 2020). In GameQA, this would require an additional task in the question review step (see Section 5.2).

Ethics Statement

The data collection process in GameQA consists of collecting paragraphs, from a set of sources/domains (see Section 5), in which answers can be found to given questions. Before starting our RUQuAD corpus collection process, we obtained formal permissions from The Icelandic Web of Science, the news cites `mbl.is` and `visir.is`, and the Icelandic Government Information website, to freely include paragraphs from their sources in our corpus. For the last domain, the Icelandic Wikipedia, formal permission was not needed because its material is already freely licensed.

As a part of the data collection, we did not collect any information about the users aside from their email address which was necessary to verify an account after registration. The data collection was GDPR compliant and we offered to remove any annotations or datapoints belonging to a users should they request that. However, no user made such a request.

As discussed in Section 4, GameQA is a game open to any user in a particular geographic area and does not compensate crowd-workers financially.

Acknowledgements

We thank The Icelandic Web of Science, `mbl.is`, `visir.is`, and the Government Information website for allowing us to include paragraphs, from articles on their websites, in our RuQuAD corpus.

References

Payal Bajaj, Daniel Campos, Nick Craswell, Li Deng, Jianfeng Gao, Xiaodong Liu, Rangan Majumder, Andrew McNamara, Bhaskar Mitra, Tri Nguyen, Mir Rosenberg, Xia Song, Alina Stoica, Saurabh Tiwary, and Tong Wang. 2016. MS MARCO: A Human Generated MAchine Reading COmprehension Dataset. *arXiv:1611.09268*.

B. Barla Cambazoglu, Mark Sanderson, Falk Scholer, and Bruce Croft. 2021. A Review of Public Datasets in Question Answering Research. *SIGIR Forum*, 54(2).

Jonathan H. Clark, Eunsol Choi, Michael Collins, Dan Garrette, Tom Kwiatkowski, Vitaly Nikolaev, and Jennimaria Palomaki. 2020. TyDi QA: A benchmark for information-seeking question answering in typologically diverse languages. *Transactions of the Association for Computational Linguistics*, 8:454–470.

Matthew Dunn, Levent Sagun, Mike Higgins, V. Ugur Guney, Volkan Cirik, and Kyunghyun Cho. 2017. SearchQA: A New Q&A Dataset Augmented with Context from a Search Engine. *arXiv:1704.05179*.

Wee Chung Gan and Hwee Tou Ng. 2019. Improving the robustness of question answering systems to question paraphrasing. In *Proceedings of the 57th Annual Meeting of the Association for Computational Linguistics*, pages 6065–6075, Florence, Italy. Association for Computational Linguistics.

Deepak Gupta, Surabhi Kumari, Asif Ekbal, and Pushpak Bhattacharyya. 2018. MMQA: A multi-domain multi-lingual question-answering framework for English and Hindi. In *Proceedings of the Eleventh International Conference on Language Resources and Evaluation (LREC 2018)*, Miyazaki, Japan. European Language Resources Association (ELRA).

Karl Moritz Hermann, Tomáš Kočiský, Edward Grefenstette, Lasse Espeholt, Will Kay, Mustafa Suleyman, and Phil Blunsom. 2015. Teaching machines to read and comprehend. In *Proceedings of the 28th International Conference on Neural Information Processing Systems - Volume 1*, NIPS'15, page 1693–1701, Cambridge, MA, USA. MIT Press.

Tomáš Kočiský, Jonathan Schwarz, Phil Blunsom, Chris Dyer, Karl Moritz Hermann, Gábor Melis, and Edward Grefenstette. 2018. The NarrativeQA reading comprehension challenge. *Transactions of the Association for Computational Linguistics*, 6:317–328.

Tom Kwiatkowski, Jennimaria Palomaki, Olivia Redfield, Michael Collins, Ankur Parikh, Chris Alberti, Danielle Epstein, Illia Polosukhin, Jacob Devlin, Kenton Lee, Kristina Toutanova, Llion Jones, Matthew Kelcey, Ming-Wei Chang, Andrew M. Dai, Jakob Uszkoreit, Quoc Le, and Slav Petrov. 2019. Natural questions: A benchmark for question answering research. *Transactions of the Association for Computational Linguistics*, 7:452–466.

Sewon Min, Julian Michael, Hannaneh Hajishirzi, and Luke Zettlemoyer. 2020. AmbigQA: Answering ambiguous open-domain questions. In *Proceedings of the 2020 Conference on Empirical Methods in Natural Language Processing (EMNLP)*, pages 5783–5797, Online. Association for Computational Linguistics.

Anna Björk Nikulásdóttir, Þórunn Arnardóttir, Starkaður Barkarson, Jón Guðnason, Þorsteinn Daði Gunnarsson, Anton Karl Ingason, Haukur Páll Jónsson, Hrafn Loftsson, Hulda Óladóttir, Eiríkur Rögnvaldsson, Einar Freyr Sigurðssona, Atli Þór Sigurgeirsson, Vésteinn Snæbjarnarson, Steinþór

Steingrímsson, and Gunnar Thor Örnólfsson. 2022. Help Yourself from the Buffet: National Language Technology Infrastructure Initiative on CLARIN-IS. In *Selected Papers from the CLARIN Annual Conference 2021, Linköping Electronic Conference Proceedings 189.*

Pranav Rajpurkar, Jian Zhang, Konstantin Lopyrev, and Percy Liang. 2016. SQuAD: 100,000+ questions for machine comprehension of text. In *Proceedings of the 2016 Conference on Empirical Methods in Natural Language Processing*, pages 2383–2392, Austin, Texas. Association for Computational Linguistics.

Siva Reddy, Danqi Chen, and Christopher D. Manning. 2019. CoQA: A conversational question answering challenge. *Transactions of the Association for Computational Linguistics*, 7:249–266.

Marco Tulio Ribeiro, Carlos Guestrin, and Sameer Singh. 2019. Are red roses red? evaluating consistency of question-answering models. In *Proceedings of the 57th Annual Meeting of the Association for Computational Linguistics*, pages 6174–6184, Florence, Italy. Association for Computational Linguistics.

Anna Rogers, Olga Kovaleva, Matthew Downey, and Anna Rumshisky. 2020. Getting Closer to AI Complete Question Answering: A Set of Prerequisite Real Tasks. *Proceedings of the AAAI Conference on Artificial Intelligence*, 34(05):8722–8731.

Kazutoshi Shinoda, Saku Sugawara, and Akiko Aizawa. 2021. Can question generation debias question answering models? a case study on question–context lexical overlap. In *Proceedings of the 3rd Workshop on Machine Reading for Question Answering*, pages 63–72, Punta Cana, Dominican Republic. Association for Computational Linguistics.

Vésteinn Snæbjarnarson and Hafsteinn Einarsson. 2022. Natural Questions in Icelandic. In *Proceedings of the Thirteenth Language Resources and Evaluation Conference*, pages 4488–4496, Marseille, France. European Language Resources Association.

Vésteinn Snæbjarnarson, Haukur Barri Símonarson, Pétur Orri Ragnarsson, Svanhvít Lilja Ingólfsdóttir, Haukur Jónsson, Vilhjalmur Thorsteinsson, and Hafsteinn Einarsson. 2022. A Warm Start and a Clean Crawled Corpus - A Recipe for Good Language Models. In *Proceedings of the Thirteenth Language Resources and Evaluation Conference*, pages 4356–4366, Marseille, France. European Language Resources Association.

Adam Trischler, Tong Wang, Xingdi Yuan, Justin Harris, Alessandro Sordoni, Philip Bachman, and Kaheer Suleman. 2016. NewsQA: A Machine Comprehension Dataset. *arXiv:1611.09830.*

Yi Yang, Wen-tau Yih, and Christopher Meek. 2015. WikiQA: A challenge dataset for open-domain question answering. In *Proceedings of the 2015 Conference on Empirical Methods in Natural Language Processing*, pages 2013–2018, Lisbon, Portugal. Association for Computational Linguistics.

Towards Speech to Speech Machine Translation focusing on Indian Languages

Vandan Mujadia[1], S. Umesh[2], Hema A. Murthy[2], Rajeev Sangal[1], Dipti Misra Sharma[1]
[1]IIIT Hyderabad, India; [2]IIT Madras, India
vandan.mu@research.iiit.ac.in,umeshs@ee.iitm.ac.in
hema@cse.iitm.ac.in, sangal@iiit.ac.in, dipti@iiit.ac.in

Abstract

We introduce an SSMT (Speech to Speech Machine Translation, aka Speech to Speech Video Translation) Pipeline[1], as a web application for translating videos from one language to another by cascading multiple language modules. Our speech translation system combines highly accurate speech to text (ASR) for Indian English, pre-possessing modules to bridge ASR-MT gaps such as spoken disfluency and punctuation, robust machine translation (MT) systems for multiple language pairs, SRT module for translated text, text to speech (TTS) module and a module to render translated synthesized audio on the original video. It is user-friendly, flexible, and easily accessible system. We aim to provide a complete configurable speech translation experience to users and researchers with this system. It also supports human intervention where users can edit outputs of different modules and the edited output can then be used for subsequent processing to improve overall output quality. By adopting a human-in-the-loop approach, the aim is to configure technology in such a way where it can assist humans and help to reduce the involved human efforts in speech translation involving English and Indian languages. As per our understanding, this is the first fully integrated system for English to Indian languages (Hindi, Telugu, Gujarati, Marathi, and Punjabi) video translation. Our evaluation shows that one can get 3.5+ MOS score using the developed pipeline with human intervention for English to Hindi. A short video demonstrating our system is available at https://youtu.be/MVftzoeRg48.

1 Introduction

India writes in many languages and speaks in many more tongues [2]. It is a geographically vast multilingual society with 22 recognized languages. The languages constitute 1.17+ billion speakers across 28 states and 7 union territories. According to the 2011 Census, while 129 million (10.6%) Indians speak English, only 259,678 (0.02%) Indians speak it as their first language. And only 8% Indians read newspapers in English while others prefer news in their local languages. As stated in a report from karnataka (gfgc.kar.nic.in, 2014), about 40% of all enrolled students from non-metropolitan regions fail to achieve their educational goals because they are unable to cope with English and very few study materials are available in native Indian languages [3]. Same is true for medical and health awareness related content. There is a huge void of content in Indian languages that necessitates urgent action. One solution for this problem is to use translation. Such translations can help different language speakers to seamlessly communicate with each other. With this work, we aim to ease this language barrier through speech to speech machine translation (SSMT) by providing a baseline system for video translation.

Generally, there are two ways to implement speech-to-speech translation (SSMT): the first approach is to cascade systems of Automatic Speech Recognition (ASR), Machine Translation (MT), and Text-to-Speech (TTS); second, direct end to end speech translation. Cascaded SSMT systems have been successfully demonstrated for English and European languages, but one finds minimal work done for Indian languages. Recent work in direct end to end speech translation (Translatotron) (Jia et al., 2019, 2022) attempts to directly translate speech from one language into speech in another language with the source speaker's voice in the translated speech. It achieves high translation quality on two Spanish to English datasets, although the reported performance is poorer than a baseline cascade of speech translation and TTS models (Jia et al., 2019, 2022). We are not aware of any cascaded or direct speech-to-speech translation work involving Indian languages.

[1]https://ssmt.iiit.ac.in/ssmtiiith
[2]shorturl.at/dnSV8
[3]shorturl.at/crCJ7

Proceedings of the 17th Conference of the European Chapter of the Association for Computational Linguistics System Demonstrations, pages 161–168

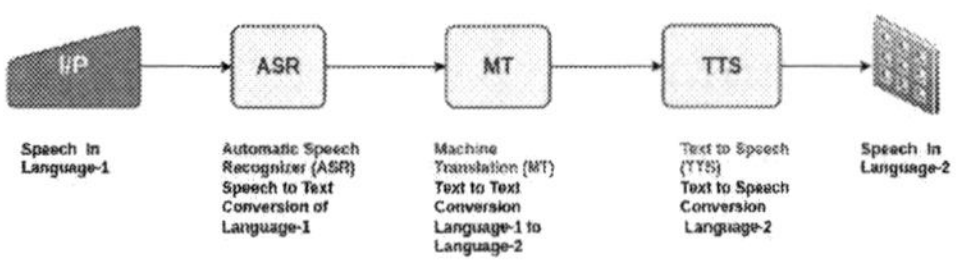

Figure 1: Speech to Speech Machine Translation: Cascading Approach

For the purpose of our work, we decided to implement a cascaded SSMT system. We also analyse gaps between the automatic modules and address them with pre-processing and post-processing tools. These gaps are :speech disfluencies, domain processing, and target language subtitling. Our system takes an English video as an input and outputs the same video in the chosen Indian language. Our proposed video translation pipeline is user-friendly, flexible, and easily accessible with following key modules:

1. highly accurate speech to text (ASR) for Indian English, 2. pre-possessing modules to bridge ASR-MT gaps such as spoken disfluency and punctuation, 3. robust machine translation (MT) systems for multiple language pairs, 4. SRT module for translated text, 5. text to speech (TTS) module, and 6. a module to render translated synthesized audio on the original video.

2 Approaches

The canonical approach as shown in Figure-1 includes automatic speech recognition (ASR) to transcribe source language speech to text and then, machine translation (MT) to translate transcribed text into target language, and at the end, text to speech synthesis (TTS) to generate speech in target language from the translated text (Sperber and Paulik, 2020; Wahlster, 2000; Lavie et al., 1997).

In this work, we aim to develop a system which can translate speech or video in English to selected Indian languages. While following a cascaded approach, one can not directly chain modules such as ASR, MT, and TTS as it is a well known fact that spoken language has various idiosyncrasies. These include lack of well-formed sentences and disfluencies (Rao et al., 2007). Traditional machine translation systems are trained on well formed, written, and grammatical pairs of sentences. Therefore, it is crucial to address these aspects before directly translating transcribed text using machine translation. Similarly, to sync original video with the translated text, time-stamping translated text is an essential step before text to speech synthesis. Also, video content syncing (speaker lip, video content) with the generated speech is another important factor in making system complete.

In recent times, technological advancements have enabled ASR, MT, and TTS to make quantum leaps. Today, computers are capable of doing these with greater accuracy and efficiency than ever before. But they cannot be expected to be 100% accurate. Human effort is still required to correct or edit these outputs. Therefore, in our pipeline, we also include steps where a human can intervene after each automatic module which eventually reduces the overall human effort for the task. For the translation of technical lectures, domain processing is one of the important steps before translating transcribed text into the target language. Domain processing is included as a pre-processing step, where identification of domain and domain terms are carried out before machine translation.

In this pipeline, we also aim to develop an interface for state-of-the-art video to video machine translation between English to 5 Indian languages (Hindi, Telugu, Gujarati, Marathi, and Punjabi) along with pre-processing of ASR output to make it translatable as well as post-processing of machine translation output to make it suitable for dubbing and video syncing. The subsequent section explains the SSMT pipeline, the interface, and the process in it. In section 4, we discuss the pipeline performance and conclude in section 5.

3 Process

Here, our task is to combine technologies to make video to video translation possible for English to Indian languages as shown in Figure-2. As discussed earlier, there are gaps between the components that need special processing. In order to fill these gaps, we link the major components with pre/post processing support tools with the provision of human interventions. These are before and after each major language component. Therefore, as visible in different colors in Figure-2, we categorize the overall process into 4 major parts: **Input/Output**, **Core technology**, **Pre/Post Processing Support Tools**, and **Pre/Post Editing** as Human Intervention.

3.1 Input/Output

In this, we deal with the input and output process, tools, and the user interface of the pipeline. This includes uploading a video, processing the video,

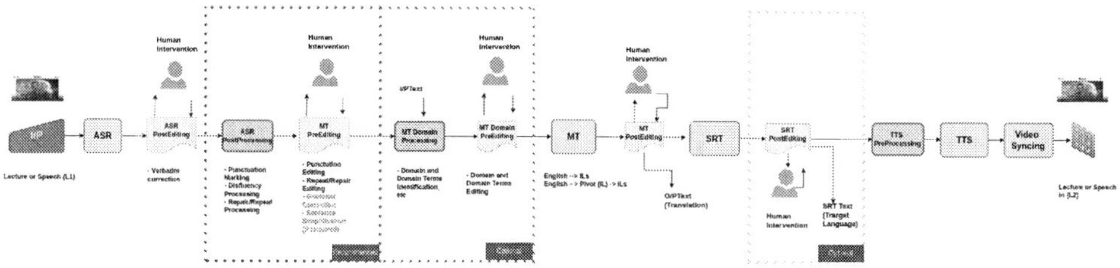

Figure 2: Worked out Speech to Speech Video Translation Process

displaying the translated video and subtitling in the target language. These are shown in dark blue color in Figure-2 at start and end. Figure-3 shows the application page where users can upload video, select one of the target languages, gender for target video voice, and start the process by clicking *START* button. Figure-4 shows the screenshot of the interface after it completes the entire process (visible as Speech to Text, English to Indian Language MT, and Text to Speech). Users can play the source language video and choose the subtitled language either as English or the opted one. Users can play the same video in the opted language by clicking the language button as shown in blue color Figure-4.

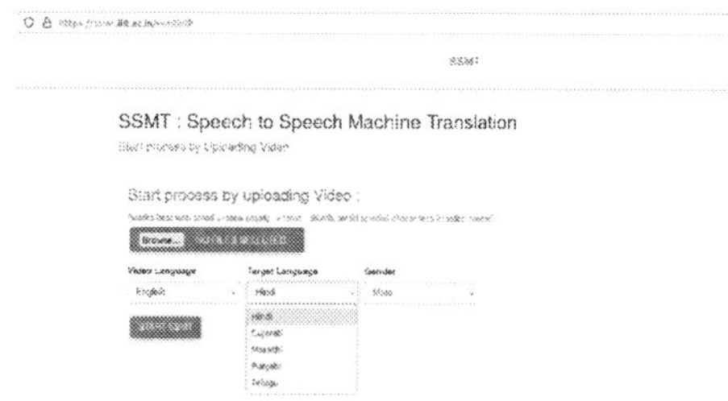

Figure 3: Speech to Speech Video Translation: Input Screen

3.2 Core Technology

This category includes core components such as ASR, MT, SRT, TTS, and Video Syncing. They are in sky blue color boxes in Figure-2. We describe each of these core components in detail and also point out where human intervention is required.

3.2.1 ASR for Transcription

Transcription is the process of translating an audio (of a video lecture) into text. This is usually carried out using automatic speech recognition (ASR) technology, human transcriptionists, or a combination of the two. ASR refers to the technologies developed to process human speech automatically and convert it into text (Juang and Rabiner, 2005). For this work, we have integrated the ASR developed by IIT-Madras (Shetty et al., 2020; Arunkumar and Umesh, 2022). Along with the verbatim output, ASR is also tuned to provide timestamp for each token which is directly used to create subtitle for the video/audio. The ASR system achieves 6 and 13 WER (Favre et al., 2013)[4] on the general and technical domain, respectively. The different categories of errors in the automatically transcribed text constitute missed words, wrongly transcribed words, spelling errors etc (Zafar et al., 2004). An editing functionality will be helpful to correct these errors for further processing.

3.2.2 MT for Translation

Translation is the process through which text content is transferred from a source language into a target language. The translation task can be carried out using machine translation systems or by human translators (Somers, 2011). For this task, we have integrated an MT system deployed by LTRC-IIIT-Hyderabad using methods presented in (Mujadia and Sharma, 2022, 2021a,b). The MT systems [5] achieved 36.33, 21.61, 18.73, 18.36, 15.89 BLEU scores (Post, 2018) on Flores Benchmarks (Goyal et al., 2022) for English-Hindi, English-Telugu, English-Gujarati, English-Punjabi, and English-Marathi language pairs, respectively. The state-of-the-art MT technology has not yet reached a level where it can directly provide publishable, usable, and accurate output in the target language. To address this, providing multiple translation options could be one possible solution. Our interface supports multiple translation options by leveraging multiple MT models for the involved language pairs. In this process, a user can choose one translation output from the available choices that can then

[4]https://github.com/Speech-Lab-IITM/English_ASR_Challenge

[5]http://ssmt.iiit.ac.in/translate

Figure 4: Speech to Speech Video Translation: Output Screen

be used for all the subsequent processing. The machine translation task becomes even more challenging when it encounters technical text. To support technical domain translation, we integrated fine-tuned machine translation systems which learn to retain already marked domain terms in the source script (Bak et al., 2021) along with domain adaptation (Ala et al., 2021; Ala and Sharma, 2020).

On top of this, human intervention in the form of post-editing is necessary to achieve fluency, adequacy, and faithfulness for the translated text. We have added the functionality for post-editing machine translation outputs that can later be used for further processing.

3.2.3 SRT - Subtitling Translated Text

Subtitling is the process of displaying spoken utterance as a text on the video screen. It is an audiovisual translation with a set of rules and guidelines [6]. The subtitle for a video is derived using the utterance speech and word alignment from ASR. We have developed an in-house mapping module which places translated text into timestamps based subtitles using source text mapping. It plays a vital role in speech to speech video translation as it helps to keep the translated text in sync with the video frame.

3.2.4 TTS for Text to Speech & Video Syncing

We integrated a Text to Speech (TTS) and video syncing system from IIT-Madras [7] (M et al., 2021; Mukherjeee et al., 2021). It uses target language subtitles and source speaker pauses to synthesize speech in the target language. To match and align the source video and synthesized audio duration, a video syncing module interpolates several frames in the middle of two adjacent frames of the original video. The integrated TTS and video syncing system has average Mean Opinion Score (MOS) (1-5) of 4 and 3.5, respectively.

3.3 Pre/Post Processing Support Tools

As discussed, to fill the gaps between core components, we have introduced pre and post processing tools. They are shown in pink color boxes in Figure-2. To bridge the gap between ASR and MT, we are using ASR post-processing tools such as punctuation marker/corrector, speech disfluency removal, repair and repeat identifier and processing. Similarly, for technical lectures, identification of domain and domain terms play an important role in translation. Therefore, we added these as a pre-processing utility to the machine translation system. Below subsections discuss each of these support tools in detail.

3.3.1 ASR Post-Processing

To prepare the raw ASR text for MT, we included 3 supporting tools as shown in Figure-2. We call these as ASR post-processing steps. First comes the **Punctuation Marker**. It is a standalone tool where it corrects, deletes, adds existing punctuation from ASR. We have integrated it for English (Mujadia et al., 2021). The second step involves **Disfluency Processing** where it removes filled pause (ahh, uhh, ah, etc) and Pet Phrases (okay, ok, so, right, etc) which are very frequent in speech. The final pre-processing step is **Repair/Repeat Processing** (Heeman, 1997), where it identifies repeated occurrences for a given ASR transcript and remove duplicate word sequences.

3.3.2 MT Domain Pre-Processing

After the ASR Post-Processing, we have integrated text based domain identification (a classification task) and text based domain term identifier as shown in Figure-2. Here, once the domain of a text is identified using the domain classifier (Sharma et al., 2020a), a domain term identifier (Sharma et al., 2020b) is used which is based on domain specific dictionaries and TextRank (Mihalcea and Tarau, 2004). These are later fed into the machine translation system which handles these identified domain terms differently in target language translation. For the purpose of this work, we integrated

[6] https://www.ted.com/participate/translate/subtitling-tips

[7] https://www.iitm.ac.in/donlab/tts/

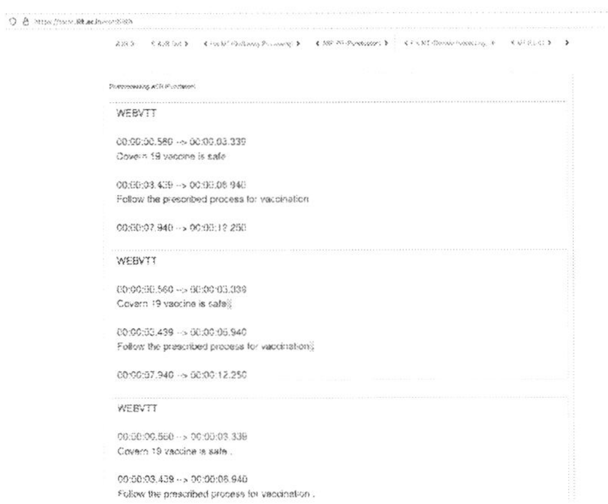

Figure 5: SSMT: ASR Post-processing for Punctuation

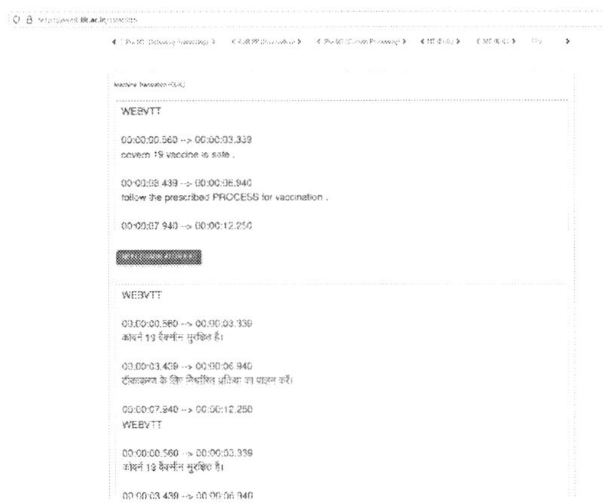

Figure 6: SSMT: MT Post-editing for Machine Translation

a domain classifier and domain dictionaries for law, computer science, biochemistry, general health awareness, and communication skill domains.

3.3.3 TTS Pre-Processing

Translated subtitled text or SRT text is a sequence of words along with a timestamp following certain language subtitling rules[8]. A valid SRT block may or may not represent a valid sentence. It can have multiple sentences or a part of a sentence as a SRT block. TTS requires valid sentences as an input to maintain target language speech flow. Therefore, the TTS pre-processing tool adjusts the subtitle timeline and keeps a valid sentence in one timeline. This tool is positioned after the SRT module in the SSMT pipeline as shown in Figure-2.

3.4 Pre/Post Editing as Human Intervention

Automatic tools are not 100% accurate. This warrants human intervention in the process. It is also required to control error propagation from one component to another. For this, we introduce a human intervention step after every automatic process Figure-2 shows them in yellow color boxes. In our interface, one just needs to press"Edit"button to enable the editing mode after it completes processing as can be seen in Figure-4.

Figure-5 shows the editing page for punctuation marking post ASR tool. Here, it has 3 different text boxes, where 1st shows the input text to the tool (here punctuation marker), 2nd shows the output of the module where the differences can be viewed in green color. A user can edit in the 3rd text box to make any further corrections. After this, the user needs to press the "Next" button to rerun the pipeline with the updates. Similar visual structures have been provided for editing throughout the interface. The user can navigate between different steps in the whole pipeline by clicking on the "Next" and "Previous" buttons.

Figure-6 shows the edit page for machine translation. Here, the 1st text box shows the input for the MT which is received after the domain preprocessing step. Here, automatic domain terms are being shown in upper case. 2nd, 3rd and 4th text boxes show translation outputs generated by different translation models. A user can pick one of them by clicking it or post-editing it. This edited/selected text box will be used for further processing in the pipeline. At each stage, the interface also gives flexibility to skip the human intervention and run the pipeline directly. As mentioned in Figure-1, we recommend that the post editing for ASR and MT output is quintessential; MT pre editing is done if required while other editing can be optional.

Core components and pre/post processing tools have been plugged based on their performance and availability. If better efficient systems are made available in future, then the pipeline has modularity to easily integrate them.

4 Performance

We evaluate the performance of the developed pipeline with two different metrics. They are: time taken to execute the pipeline and performance of major modules on their known evaluation metrics. One can access and execute presented SSMT pipeline using internet without installing specialized tools. The execution time for pipeline depends

[8]https://www.ted.com/participate/translate/subtitling-tips

V 1 CS	Options	Duration	ASR Verbatim (WER)	ASRtoMT (WER)	Eng-Hin MT (BLEU)	Eng-Hin MT + Domain (BLEU)	MOS (1-5)
1	Direct + No Punct	0:00:59	14.29%	21.74%	5.81	5.81	-
2	+ Fix len Punct	0:00:59	14.29%	23.23%	15.79	15.89	2.0
3	+ Punct by ASR	0:00:59	14.29%	22.28%	21.29	25.56	3.0
4	+ ASR PostPro	0:00:59	14.29%	18.48%	25.41	28.06	3.45
5	+ MT PreEdit	0:00:59	Gold	Gold	33.45	39.34	3.65
6	+ MT PostEdit	0:00:59	Gold	Gold	Gold	Gold	4.0
V 2 CS 1	Direct + No Punct	0:01:00	9.57%	18.48%	3.4	3.4	-
2	+ Fix len Punct	0:01:00	9.57%	19.47%	20.26	20.26	2.0
3	+ Punct by ASR	0:01:00	9.57%	16.11%	22.32	25.46	3.0
4	+ ASR PostPro	0:01:00	9.57%	12.32%	23.3	25.57	3.2
5	+ MT PreEdit	0:01:00	Gold	Gold	35.26	37.92	3.5
6	+ MT PostEdit	0:01:00	Gold	Gold	Gold	Gold	4.1

Table 1: Speech to Speech Video Translation Pipeline Evaluation at each stage; WER for ASR and ASERtoMT, BLEU for MT, Mean Opinion Score (MOS) score is for generated video in target language. Gold indicates human editing was carried out at that stage.

on the video length. On an average, it takes 1/3 of the video time for execution on a single GPU (NVIDIA-3080Ti) system. Due to resource constraints, for now we have set the input video length limit to 1 min in the interface, but this can be increased based on availability of compute infrastructure.

We created an evaluation dataset of 2 small English technical videos of **computer science domain for English-Hindi translation direction**. We hired experienced language professionals to carry out manual transcription and Hindi translation for these videos. We used WER (Favre et al., 2013) to evaluate **ASR verbatim (WER)** and **ASRtoMT Gaps (WER)** (that is verbatim + correct punctuation and without spoken disfluency). We used BLEU (Post, 2018) to evaluate English to Hindi machine translation **Eng-Hin MT (BLEU)** performance without and with domain pre-processing **Eng-Hin MT + Domain (BLEU)** to the MT. Mean Opinion Score (MOS) is used to evaluate generated Hindi speech and synced video. Table-1 shows the evaluation results for SSMT pipeline for 2 videos. 1st rows "Direct + No Punct" of video 1 and video 2 show the results when ASR verbatim (without punctuation), MT, TTS, and video syncing modules are used. The 2nd rows "+ Fix len Punct" of video 1 & 2 show the results when a punctuation symbol is placed after every 20 tokens on the direct ASR verbatim. The 3rd rows "+ Punct by ASR" of video 1 & 2 show the results when punctuations are given by ASR along with ASR verbatim. The 4th rows "+ Punct by ASR" of video 1 & 2 show the results when punctuation and disfluency processing are given by ASR post processing tools. Here, we can notice that rows from 1 to 4 for both the videos denote results for a fully automatic pipeline. For both the videos, ASR post processing tools along with domain processing for machine translation give best 18.48% and 12.32% WER scores for ASRtoMT respectively. Similarly, highest BLEU scores of 28.06 and 25.57 were achieved for machine translation with domain processing. Here, we got 3.45 and 3.2 MOS scores respectively for the Hindi audio synced video.

We have also measured the performance of the pipeline when there is human involvement in editing at major steps of the pipeline. Rows 5 of video 1 and 2 show the results after performing pre-editing for machine translation. Here, we clearly see a 12 BLEU score and 0.25 MOS score improvement in the machine translation and TTS quality, respectively when corrected texts are given to it. Rows 6 of both videos show results when post-edited machine translation output was passed to TTS and video syncing module. On the post-edited translation, we see an improvement of 0.5 MOS score. This indicates that speech to speech translation technology needs human intervention to get the best possible translated video. As speech-to-speech translation involving Indian languages is relatively a new area of research, it is difficult to compare our work with any end-to-end speech translation models.

5 Conclusion and Future Work

In this paper, we introduce an SSMT pipeline, an intelligent Speech to Speech Video Translation interface for English to Hindi, Telugu, Gujarati, Marathi, and Punjabi. This work demonstrates that speech to speech (video to video) translation is possible with a cascaded pipeline and support tools. We believe that large scale deployment of this can help lower the language barrier. The results also point out that human intervention is necessary to get high quality video translation output. In the near future, we aim to come up with benchmark corpora for speech to speech machine translation and evaluation involving English and multiple Indian Languages. We also plan to further improve the developed pipeline and its components to reduce involved human effort over a period of time. We will also plan to add multiple language directions to the pipeline in future.

Acknowledgement

We thank the reviewers for their insightful comments. We thank Pruthwik Mishra and Arafat Ahsan for their input at various stages of this work. This work is supported[9][10] by the Ministry of Electronics and Information Technology, Government of India.

References

Hema Ala, Vandan Mujadia, and Dipti Sharma. 2021. Domain adaptation for Hindi-Telugu machine translation using domain specific back translation. In *Proceedings of the International Conference on Recent Advances in Natural Language Processing (RANLP 2021)*, pages 26–34, Held Online. INCOMA Ltd.

Hema Ala and Dipti Sharma. 2020. AdapNMT : Neural machine translation with technical domain adaptation for indic languages. In *Proceedings of the 17th International Conference on Natural Language Processing (ICON): Adap-MT 2020 Shared Task*, pages 6–10, Patna, India. NLP Association of India (NLPAI).

A Arunkumar and Srinivasan Umesh. 2022. Joint encoder-decoder self-supervised pre-training for asr. *Proc. Interspeech 2022*, pages 3418–3422.

Yunju Bak, Jimin Sun, Jay Kim, Sungwon Lyu, and Changmin Lee. 2021. Kakao enterprise's WMT21 machine translation using terminologies task submission. In *Proceedings of the Sixth Conference on Machine Translation*, pages 804–812, Online. Association for Computational Linguistics.

Benoit Favre, Kyla Cheung, Siavash Kazemian, Adam Lee, Yang Liu, Cosmin Munteanu, Ani Nenkova, Dennis Ochei, Gerald Penn, Stephen Tratz, et al. 2013. Automatic human utility evaluation of asr systems: Does wer really predict performance? In *INTERSPEECH*, pages 3463–3467.

gfgc.kar.nic.in. 2014. Barriers of rural students in learning english in karnataka. `https://gfgc.kar.nic.in/krpuram/FileHandler/9-4fa6882f-fb7e-4f38-b81c-cd344d1a73d9`. (Accessed on 12/02/2022).

Naman Goyal, Cynthia Gao, Vishrav Chaudhary, Peng-Jen Chen, Guillaume Wenzek, Da Ju, Sanjana Krishnan, Marc'Aurelio Ranzato, Francisco Guzman, and Angela Fan. 2022. The flores-101 evaluation benchmark for low-resource and multilingual machine translation. *Transactions of the Association for Computational Linguistics*, 10:522–538.

Peter Anthony Heeman. 1997. *Speech repairs, intonational boundaries and discourse markers: Modeling speakers' utterances in spoken dialog*. University of Rochester.

Ye Jia, Michelle Tadmor Ramanovich, Tal Remez, and Roi Pomerantz. 2022. Translatotron 2: High-quality direct speech-to-speech translation with voice preservation. In *International Conference on Machine Learning*, pages 10120–10134. PMLR.

Ye Jia, Ron J Weiss, Fadi Biadsy, Wolfgang Macherey, Melvin Johnson, Zhifeng Chen, and Yonghui Wu. 2019. Direct speech-to-speech translation with a sequence-to-sequence model. *arXiv preprint arXiv:1904.06037*.

Biing-Hwang Juang and Lawrence R Rabiner. 2005. Automatic speech recognition–a brief history of the technology development. *Georgia Institute of Technology. Atlanta Rutgers University and the University of California. Santa Barbara*, 1:67.

Alon Lavie, Alex Waibel, Lori Levin, Michael Finke, Donna Gates, Marsal Gavalda, Torsten Zeppenfeld, and Puming Zhan. 1997. Janus-iii: Speech-to-speech translation in multiple languages. In *1997 IEEE International Conference on Acoustics, Speech, and Signal Processing*, volume 1, pages 99–102. IEEE.

[9]Sanction Order: 11(1)/2022-HCC(TDIL)-Part(2)/A/B/C

[10]Administrative Approval: 11(1)/2022-HCC(TDIL)-Part(2)

Mano Ranjith Kumar M, Jom Kuriakose, Karthik Pandia D S, and Hema A Murthy. 2021. Lipsyncing efforts for transcreating lecture videos in Indian languages. In *Proc. 11th ISCA Speech Synthesis Workshop (SSW 11)*, pages 216–221.

Rada Mihalcea and Paul Tarau. 2004. Textrank: Bringing order into text. In *Proceedings of the 2004 conference on empirical methods in natural language processing*, pages 404–411.

Vandan Mujadia, Pruthwik Mishra, and Dipti Misra Sharma. 2021. Deep contextual punctuator for NLG text (short paper). In *Proceedings of the Swiss Text Analytics Conference 2021, Winterthur, Switzerland, June 14-16, 2021 (held online due to COVID19 pandemic)*, volume 2957 of *CEUR Workshop Proceedings*. CEUR-WS.org.

Vandan Mujadia and Dipti Sharma. 2021a. Low resource similar language neural machine translation for Tamil-Telugu. In *Proceedings of the Sixth Conference on Machine Translation*, pages 288–291, Online. Association for Computational Linguistics.

Vandan Mujadia and Dipti Misra Sharma. 2021b. English-Marathi neural machine translation for LoResMT 2021. In *Proceedings of the 4th Workshop on Technologies for MT of Low Resource Languages (LoResMT2021)*, pages 151–157, Virtual. Association for Machine Translation in the Americas.

Vandan Mujadia and Dipti Misra Sharma. 2022. The ltrc hindi-telugu parallel corpus. In *Proceedings of the Thirteenth Language Resources and Evaluation Conference*, pages 3417–3424.

Bhagyashree Mukherjeee, Anusha Prakash, and Hema A. Murthy. 2021. Analysis of conversational speech with application to voice adaptation. In *2021 IEEE Automatic Speech Recognition and Understanding Workshop (ASRU)*, pages 765–772.

Matt Post. 2018. A call for clarity in reporting bleu scores. *arXiv preprint arXiv:1804.08771*.

Sharath Rao, Ian Lane, and Tanja Schultz. 2007. Improving spoken language translation by automatic disfluency removal: Evidence from conversational speech transcripts. In *Proceedings of Machine Translation Summit XI: Papers*.

Dipti Misra Sharma, Asif Ekbal, Karunesh Arora, Sudip Kumar Naskar, Dipankar Ganguly, Sobha L, Radhika Mamidi, Sunita Arora, Pruthwik Mishra, and Vandan Mujadia, editors. 2020a. *Proceedings of the 17th International Conference on Natural Language Processing (ICON): TechDOfication 2020 Shared Task*. NLP Association of India (NLPAI), Patna, India.

Dipti Misra Sharma, Asif Ekbal, Karunesh Arora, Sudip Kumar Naskar, Dipankar Ganguly, Sobha L, Radhika Mamidi, Sunita Arora, Pruthwik Mishra, and Vandan Mujadia, editors. 2020b. *Proceedings of the 17th International Conference on Natural Language Processing (ICON): TermTraction 2020 Shared Task*. NLP Association of India (NLPAI), Patna, India.

Vishwas M Shetty, S Umesh, et al. 2020. Investigation of speaker-adaptation methods in transformer based asr. *arXiv preprint arXiv:2008.03247*.

Harold Somers. 2011. Machine translation: History, development, and limitations.

Matthias Sperber and Matthias Paulik. 2020. Speech translation and the end-to-end promise: Taking stock of where we are. *arXiv preprint arXiv:2004.06358*.

Wolfgang Wahlster. 2000. Mobile speech-to-speech translation of spontaneous dialogs: An overview of the final verbmobil system. *Verbmobil: Foundations of speech-to-speech translation*, pages 3–21.

Atif Zafar, Burke Mamlin, Susan Perkins, Anne M Belsito, J Marc Overhage, and Clement J McDonald. 2004. A simple error classification system for understanding sources of error in automatic speech recognition and human transcription. *International Journal of Medical Informatics*, 73(9-10):719–730.

TEXTWORLDEXPRESS: Simulating Text Games at One Million Steps Per Second

Peter Jansen
University of Arizona, Tucson, USA
pajansen@arizona.edu

Marc-Alexandre Côté
Microsoft Research Montréal
macote@microsoft.com

Abstract

Text-based games offer a challenging test bed to evaluate virtual agents at language understanding, multi-step problem-solving, and common-sense reasoning. However, speed is a major limitation of current text-based games, capping at 300 steps per second, mainly due to the use of legacy tooling. In this work we present TEXTWORLDEXPRESS, a high-performance simulator that includes implementations of three common text game benchmarks that increases simulation throughput by approximately **three orders of magnitude**, reaching over one million steps per second on common desktop hardware. This significantly reduces experiment runtime, enabling billion-step-scale experiments in about one day.[1] [2] [3]

1 Introduction

One of the long standing goals of artificial intelligence is to create agents that can work and reason in embodied environments. Toward this goal, a variety of virtual environments have been created that allow simulated robots the opportunity to learn to a variety of tasks, in settings from household environments (Kolve et al., 2017; Shridhar et al., 2020a) to Minecraft (Guss et al., 2019). Because high-fidelity 3D virtual environments are challenging and resource intensive to develop, simpler 2D environments have also been proposed (e.g. Chevalier-Boisvert et al., 2019; Küttler et al., 2020) that allow agents to focus on learning skills such as search or navigation in graphically simpler environments.

Recently, text games – or environments rendered entirely in natural language – have emerged as an alternate research methodology for embodied agent research, centrally due to their low barrier to entry compared to 3D games, coupled with their ability to easily model complex tasks at a high-level (see Jansen, 2022, for review). For example, a cooking game might require an agent to read a recipe, find ingredients, then prepare those ingredients to create a meal. Text games model an agent as they navigate an environment, rendering their observations in text (e.g. *"You are in the kitchen. You see..."*). Similarly, agents interact with the environment through abstracted high-level natural language commands (e.g. *"move south"*, or *"pick up carrot"*), rather than lower-level actions common in 3D environments (e.g. *rotate agent 2 degrees clockwise*).

Text games require a variety of common-sense knowledge to complete successfully (Ryu et al., 2022; Murugesan et al., 2021b), including understanding common procedures (such as how to read and follow instructions), as well as affordances about the world – for example, that buildings have rooms, containers must be opened before their con-

Environment Simulator	SPS
2D/3D Simulators[4]	
AI2THOR (Kolve et al., 2017)	30†
MINERL (Guss et al., 2019)	180†
BABYAI (Chevalier-Boisvert et al., 2019)	3k
NETHACK (Küttler et al., 2020)	14k
MEGAVERSE (Petrenko et al., 2021)	327k†
Text Game Simulators[5]	
TEXTWORLD (Côté et al., 2018)	300
JERICHO (Hausknecht et al., 2020)	1
SCIENCEWORLD (Wang et al., 2022)	20
TEXTWORLDEXPRESS *(online,* PYTHON*)*	32k
TEXTWORLDEXPRESS *(precrawled,* PYTHON*)*	316k
TEXTWORLDEXPRESS *(online,* JAVA*)*	212k
TEXTWORLDEXPRESS *(precrawled,* JAVA*)*	4M

Table 1: Single-thread simulation speed of common 2D, 3D, and text-game environment simulators. Speed is measured in terms of Steps Per Second (SPS). † symbolizes that simulation is carried out on GPUs. TEXTWORLDEXPRESS outperforms other text game simulators by approximately three orders of magnitude.

[1] Code: github.com/cognitiveailab/TextWorldExpress
[2] Video: youtu.be/HLFAnRKuTlE
[3] Demo: marccote-textworldexpress.hf.space

[4] Performance reported from (Zholus et al., 2022).
[5] Benchmark scripts provided in the code repository.

Proceedings of the 17th Conference of the European Chapter of the Association for Computational Linguistics System Demonstrations, pages 169–177

tents can be observed or removed, and so forth. As such, text games are still extremely challenging for agents, with current state-of-the-art performance at only 12% for classic interactive fiction games such as *Zork* (Yao et al., 2021; Ammanabrolu et al., 2021). Similarly, interactivity and explicit step-by-step reasoning appears challenging for agents. For example, there appears to be a large dissociation between a model's ability to answer questions about topics (e.g., science exam questions) and its ability to perform very similar experiments in interactive text environments, even with substantial training (Wang et al., 2022). This suggests that explicit interactive multi-step reasoning is still very challenging for contemporary methods like language models, and that accurate procedural knowledge is currently difficult to generate. Together, these highlight the importance of using text games as a vehicle for explicit, embodied, step-by-step reasoning about the world.

To help support these efforts, a number of simulators have recently been developed for text game research, shown in Table 1. Current tooling for text games is built on legacy code bases, providing strong limitations in rendering speed – at present, most simulators are limited to running at between 1 and 300 steps per second. This generally limits agents from using modeling paradigms with fast iteration cycles and high sample requirements (such as reinforcement learning, or evolutionary learning), and restricts users to modeling techniques with large train and inference cycles (such as language models) where the simulator no longer becomes the bottleneck in experiment runtimes.

In this work, we develop a high-speed framework for text-based games in natural language processing research. Our contributions are:

1. TEXTWORLDEXPRESS, a highly optimized simulator that includes reimplementations of three text game benchmarks focusing on instruction following, commonsense reasoning, and object identification, as well as other newer benchmarks for evaluating arithmetic, navigation, and neurosymbolic reasoning.

2. We empirically demonstrate that this simulator runs up to *three orders of magnitude* faster than current tooling, reaching 300k steps per second (SPS) on a single thread, and exceeding 1M SPS on modest multi-core desktop hardware. This substantially reduces experiment times (from weeks to hours) for sample-heavy machine learning agents.

2 Related Work

Research Paradigm: Text games are a rapidly expanding research paradigm for learning and evaluating situated natural language processing agents on a variety of tasks, with over 100 papers written using this paradigm in the last few years (see Jansen, 2022, for review). This may be in part due to language providing useful abstractions for more efficient exploration and planning (Karch et al., 2020; Colas et al., 2020; Mu et al., 2022; Tam et al., 2022), making task modeling at the level of language more easily approached than with lower-level 3D simulations.

Agent Modeling: Agent modeling has explored a variety of modeling paradigms, including reinforcement learning approaches (Osborne et al., 2021; Xu et al., 2021), combined with reading comprehension techniques (Narasimhan et al., 2015; Tamari et al., 2019; Guo et al., 2020; Yao et al., 2020, 2021), commonsense reasoning (Ryu et al., 2022; Murugesan et al., 2021b), graph-based networks (Ammanabrolu and Riedl, 2019), and neurosymbolic logic (Kimura et al., 2021b; Chaudhury et al., 2021; Kimura et al., 2021a). Most recent agents make use of large pretrained language models (e.g. Devlin et al., 2019), though these can pose challenges both in inference speed, as well as generalization to interactive environments. For example, a model that can correctly answer 90% of multiple choice elementary science exam questions fails to solve text games that test that same knowledge but in a step-by-step procedural setting, even with significant training (Wang et al., 2022).

Simulation Speed: A variety of simulators currently exist for text games, typically focusing on providing domain-general tooling for creating small procedurally generated research environments (e.g. Côté et al., 2018), or interfacing to the existing body of large interactive fiction games such as Zork (Lebling et al., 1979) from the 1980s and 1990s by providing tooling and APIs (Hausknecht et al., 2020). Nearly all frameworks ultimately generate and run games as *Z-machine* code (e.g. Nelson, 2014), an almost 40-year-old domain specific language designed for portability rather than simulation speed. One of the central challenges in building fast research tooling is *valid* *action generation*. Because games implement different sets of actions, and at different levels of granularity, nearly all contemporary agents require the simulator to supply a list of possible valid actions (such as *put coat in closet*) that could be undertaken by the agent at a given time step. Action spaces can be large – hundreds of thousands of action-object combinations are frequently possible at a given step in most games – and existing frameworks (e.g. Hausknecht et al., 2020) built on legacy tooling perform valid action generation by enumerating then running all possible action-object combinations at each game step then recording which ones are valid. This is extremely costly, substantially reducing simulation performance (as shown in Table 1). In this work, TEXTWORLDEXPRESS has been built from the ground-up using heavily optimized and profiled code to quickly render environments while simultaneously generating an exhaustive list of possible next valid actions for agents, greatly speeding simulation time.

3 Environments

TEXTWORLDEXPRESS offers high-speed versions of three popular benchmark environments frequently used in text game research, as well as a number of newer environments for evaluating specific reasoning competencies:

CookingWorld: The CookingWorld environment (Côté et al., 2018) tasks agents with preparing meals by following the instructions in a recipe that is provided in the environment.[6] Agents must first collect required food ingredients (e.g. milk, bell pepper, flour, salt) that can be found in the environment in canonical locations (e.g. kitchen, pantry, supermarket, garden) and containers (e.g. fridge, cupboard). Randomly generated recipes require agents to first use a knife to prepare food by *slicing, dicing,* or *chopping* a subset of ingredients, then additionally using an appropriate heating appliance to *fry, roast,* or *barbeque* the ingredients. If all ingredients are prepared according to the recipe, the agent can use an action to *prepare the meal*, and finally *eat the meal* to complete the task successfully. Task complexity can be controlled by varying the number of locations in the environment, the number of ingredients required for the recipe, and the number of distractor ingredients randomly placed in the environment that are not required for the recipe. The recipes and environments are parametrically generated, with subsets of ingredients and specific preparations held out between training, development, and test sets to prevent overfitting. An example CookingWorld task is shown in Table 2.

CookingWorld Game
North of House You are in the kitchen. In one part of the room you see a fridge that is closed. There is also a dining chair, that has nothing on it. You also see a dishwasher that is closed. In another part of the room you see a trash can that is closed. In one part of the room you see an oven. There is also a cutlery drawer that is closed. You also see a stove. In another part of the room you see a counter that has a **cookbook**, a <u>green apple</u>, and a <u>red hot pepper</u> on it. In one part of the room you see a kitchen cupboard that is closed. To the South you see the backyard. To the West you see the pantry. > *read **cookbook***
Gather all following ingredients and follow the directions to prepare this tasty meal. Ingredients: **purple potato, yellow bell pepper**. Directions: dice the **purple potato**, fry the **purple potato**, roast the **yellow bell pepper**, prepare meal. > *open cutlery drawer*
You open the cutlery drawer. The cutlery drawer contains a **knife**. > *take **knife***
You take the knife. > *move south*
You are in the backyard. In one part of the room you see a barbeque. There is also a patio chair, that has nothing on it. You also see a clothes line, that has nothing on it. In another part of the room you see a garden that has a raw **purple potato**, and a **yellow bell pepper** on it. In one part of the room you see a workbench, that has nothing on it. There is also a patio table, that has nothing on it. To the North you see the kitchen. > *take **purple potato***
You take the **purple potato**. > *take **yellow bell pepper***
You take the **yellow bell pepper**. > *move north*
You are in the kitchen. > *dice **purple potato***
You dice the **purple potato**. > *cook **purple potato** in stove*
You fry the **purple potato** with the stove. > *cook **yellow bell pepper** with the oven*
You roast the **yellow bell pepper** with the oven. > *prepare meal*
The meal has been added to your inventory. > *eat meal*
Game completed.

Table 2: An example CookingWorld text game, requiring the agent to read a recipe, collect ingredients, and follow preparation instructions. User or agent-entered *actions* for the 12-step solution are italicized. Relevant **task objects** are bolded, while <u>distractor objects</u> are underlined. Here, an easy-level parametric game was generated consisting of 3 locations *(kitchen, backyard, pantry)*, 2 required ingredients *(potato, bell pepper)*, and 2 distractor ingredients *(apple, hot pepper)*.

TextWorld Commonsense (TWC): Text game agents frequently learn the dynamics of environment – such as the need to open a door before one can move through it – from interacting with the environment itself, rather than using a pre-

[6]This task was used as part of the First TextWorld Problems competition (`https://aka.ms/ftwp`) and named by (Madotto et al., 2020).

existing knowledge base of common sense facts or object affordances that would speed task learning. TextWorld Commonsense (Murugesan et al., 2021a) aims to evaluate agents on common sense knowledge that can not be directly learned from the environment by providing agents a clean-up task where the agent must place common household objects (e.g. *a dirty dish*) in their canonical locations (e.g. *the dishwasher*) that can be found in knowledge bases such as ConceptNet (Liu and Singh, 2004; Speer et al., 2017). Separate lists of objects are used in the training, development, and test sets, meaning the agent can not learn object locations from the training set alone, and must rely on an external common sense knowledge base to perform well on the development and test sets. Murugesan et al. (2021a) specify three task difficulty levels, with the easiest including a single location and object to put away, while the hard setting includes two location and up to 7 objects.

Coin Collector: Agents frequently find tasks such as object search, environment navigation, or pick-and-place tasks challenging (Shridhar et al., 2020b). The Coin Collector game (Yuan et al., 2018) distills these into a single benchmark where an agent must explore a series of rooms to locate and pick up a single coin. In the original implementation, the game map typically takes the form of a connected loop or chain, such that continually moving to new locations means the agent will eventually discover the coin – while including medium and hard modes that add in one or more "dead-end" paths. To control for environment difficulty across games, the TEXTWORLDEXPRESS reimplementation uses the same map generator across environments, and generates arbitrary home environments rather than connected loops. The user maintains control of other measures of difficulty, including the total number of rooms, and the number of distractor objects placed in the environment.

Adding new games: New games can be added to TEXTWORLDEXPRESS, and 4 additional games that benchmark arithmetic, navigation, and neurosymbolic reasoning have been added since its initial release[7]. Adding new games takes about a day of coding, which can be more effortful than using the domain-specific implementation languages of existing game engines (e.g. Côté et al., 2018).

[7]See full list at https://github.com/cognitiveailab/TextWorldExpress#environments.

Action	Description
Generic actions	
look around	*describe current location*
inventory	*list agent inventory*
examine **OBJ**	*examine an object*
move **DIR**	*move north, east, south, or west*
open **OBJ**	*open a door or container*
close **OBJ**	*close a door or container*
take **OBJ**	*pick up an object*
put **OBJ** in **OBJ**	*put an object in a container*
Extended actions (CookingWorld)	
read **OBJ**	*read a recipe book*
cook **OBJ** in **OBJ**	*cook an ingredient*
chop **OBJ**	*chop an ingredient*
slice **OBJ**	*slice an ingredient*
dice **OBJ**	*dice an ingredient*
eat **OBJ**	*eat an ingredient*
prepare meal	*prepare the meal*

Table 3: The action space of the environments, as well as descriptions of each action. Actions can take zero, one, or two object (OBJ) or direction (DIR) arguments.

3.1 Action Space and Valid Action Generation

The three benchmark games each have up to 15 different types of actions available to agents, described in Table 3. These include common text-game actions such as *taking objects*, *moving locations*, and *opening doors*, as well as domain-specific actions such as *slicing* or *cooking ingredients* for the cooking-domain game. Actions may take zero (e.g. *look around*), one (e.g. *take shirt*), or two (e.g. *put shirt in closet*) objects as arguments.

Most contemporary high-performance game agents (e.g. Ammanabrolu and Hausknecht, 2020; Murugesan et al., 2021a) make use of a "valid-action handicap" – that is, at each step, they require a list of possible valid actions that can be taken in the environment, from which they select a single action to undertake. For example, a kitchen agent might wish to *dice the carrot*, but such an action would only be available to the agent if it currently possessed both a carrot and a knife in its inventory. This valid-action detection is typically implemented overtop of existing interactive fiction games (such as *Zork*) by an interface framework (e.g., Jericho; Hausknecht et al., 2020) at significant loss to the simulation framerate. In contrast, TEXTWORLDEXPRESS was designed from the ground-up to provide fast valid action generation to maintain high framerates.

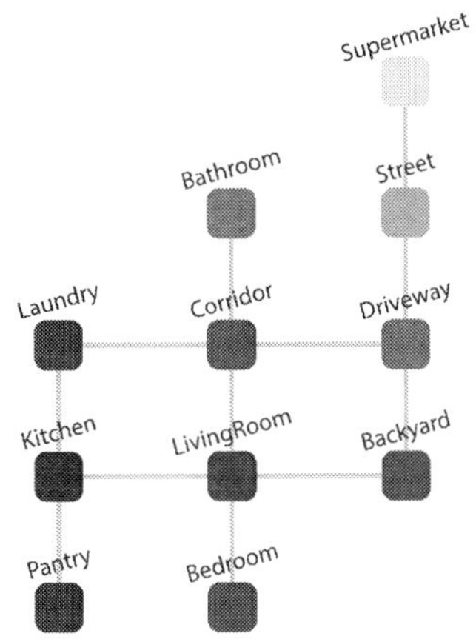

Figure 1: An example of the random map generation process, containing 11 separate locations. Locations are iteratively placed on a 7x7 grid, then interconnected (edges) on the four cardinal directions *(north, east, south, west)* based on connection preferences. For example, the *Pantry* prefers to connect to the *Kitchen*, and will never connect to the *Bedroom*.

3.2 Map Generation

Navigation tasks – such as exploring an environment, or navigating to a specific location – are typically challenging for contemporary text game agents. Because of this, games typically reduce the burden of navigation by providing simplified maps. At one end of the extreme, the original *TextWorld Commonsense* uses small maps containing only one or two locations, while at the other extreme *CookingWorld* creates maps with over a dozen locations interconnected in common ways (i.e. a *kitchen* is usually connected to a *pantry*, *backyard*, and/or *corridor*, but is never directly connected to a *supermarket*). To control for the difficulty of the navigation task across environments, TEXTWORLDEXPRESS uses the same map generator across all three benchmark games, while allowing the user to specify parameters such as the number of map locations to control the difficulty of the navigation task.

Environments can consist of up to 11 locations, consisting of locations common to both the *TWC* and *CookingWorld* games. Maps are randomly generated at the start of each game, and allow navigation on four cardinal directions (north, south, east, west). Optionally, rooms may be connected with doors that an agent is required to open before allowing passage, increasing task complexity. Figure 1 shows an example map produced by the generator.

3.3 Object Library

Task objects, room objects, and distractor objects are populated from the object libraries provided by the TextWorld Commonsense and CookingWorld games. This results in approximately 500 possible objects that can populate environments, including containers (e.g. *fridge*, *shelf*, *countertop*), and movable objects (e.g. *red onion, dirty shirt*).

3.4 Parametric Variation

To reduce overfitting, generated tasks and environments vary in their requirements and presentation. Tasks typically vary in task-critical objects, such as the specific objects that need to be cleaned up in *TextWorld Commonsense*, or the recipe, ingredients, and their locations in *CookingWorld*. Environments parametrically vary, centrally in the environment map (how the rooms are interconnected), while also allowing different numbers of distractor objects to be generated in different randomized locations in the environment. Critically, games are deterministic and the generation is repeatable and controlled by a single random seed, such that the same game can be regenerated during agent training and evaluation. To create independent train, development, and test sets, in addition to each game having specific task objects that are unique across training and evaluation sets, we also assign blocks of random seeds to the train, development, and sets. This allows generating thousands of possible parametric variations for each set, while ensuring that the tasks and environments remain unique.

3.5 Scoring

At each time step, the simulator provides the agent a score that signifies the agent's progress in solving a given task. Games typically assign rewards for critical task steps, such as picking up correct ingredients, or preparing ingredients correctly. Because the total score required to complete a game can vary both across games and across task complexity, scores are provided both as raw counts, as well as normalized to between zero (no task progress) and one (task completion). Each game has specific success and failure criterion, which are automatically detected by the simulator, and provided to the agent by the API. For example, if a recipe requires a *carrot* to be *chopped*, but the agent instead *slices* it, this will cause a task failure, and can be used as a reward signal for the agent model to use in adjusting its action policy.

4 Speed Comparison

4.1 Online and Precrawled Generation

To enable extremely fast simulations, TEXTWORLDEXPRESS supports two game generation modes: normal (online) generation, and precrawled generation. In *online generation*, games are parametrically generated and played at runtime, allowing a large number of parametric game variations to be generated, and games to be played up to any number of steps. Conversely, where speed is of critical importance, the simulator supports *precrawling* all possible paths an agent might take in a given environment, and pre-caching these to disk as a JSON file. This allows extremely fast game playing – at essentially the speed of updating a pointer to a particular node in the precrawled state tree – at the expense of generating and loading large files, that pragmatically limit the total number of steps that can be crawled and precached in the environment.[8] Precrawling is a unique feature offered by TEXTWORLDEXPRESS, as games taking minutes to crawl in this framework can take days or weeks to crawl in TEXTWORLD.

4.2 Evaluating Simulation Speed

We empirically compare the simulation speed of TEXTWORLDEXPRESS with three frameworks.

TextWorld (Côté et al., 2018) is a framework for generating parametric text games for natural language processing research. Games are specified using predicate logic (to define action rules) and a context-free grammar (to generate text), which TextWorld reformulates into Inform7 code (Nelson, 2006), that is then ultimately compiled to a Z-Machine game (Nelson, 2014). The three benchmark games reimplemented in TEXTWORLDEXPRESS were originally implemented in TextWorld.

Jericho (Hausknecht et al., 2020) provides a research interface to the existing body of interactive fiction games, such as Zork (Lebling et al., 1979), that were originally written for the Z-Machine interpreter. Critically, Jericho provides facilities for action template extraction and valid-action generation, to reduce the difficulty of interfacing classic interactive fiction games with language agents.

ScienceWorld (Wang et al., 2022) is a science-domain text game simulator that provides the ability to train and evaluate agents on scientific tasks normally learned by elementary science students, such as changes of states of matter (melting, boiling, freezing), life cycles of plants and animals, and basic chemistry. Supporting this is a series of complex simulation engines (e.g., thermodynamics, electrical conductivity, genetics) which increase simulation fidelity at the cost of speed. Similar to TextWorld and Jericho, ScienceWorld supports generating valid actions at each time step.

The results of this evaluation, using random agents to traverse the environments, are shown in Table 1. The highly optimized TEXTWORLDEXPRESS is able to simulate games in *online* generation mode at an average of *212k* frames per second per thread, or nearly three orders of magnitude faster than other frameworks.[9] This varies between *256k* steps per second for the fastest environment with the least complex action space *(Coin Collector)*, to *155k* steps per second for the most complex action space *(CookingWorld)*. On an 8-core workstation, this enables million-step experiments to be simulated per second, with billion-step experiments possible in approximately one hour.[10] In contrast, one billion steps would take approximately 38 days using the original TextWorld implementations. In *precrawled* mode, where game states are precached, single-thread speeds of up to 4 million steps per second are possible. Our fastest multi-threaded benchmark on desktop hardware (an AMD 3950X 16-core, 32-thread CPU) reaches 34M steps per second, enabling billion-step-scale simulations in approximately 30 seconds.

5 Conclusion

We present TEXTWORLDEXPRESS, a fast simulator for text-game research that reimplements three benchmark environments while running three orders of magnitude faster than their original implementations. New games can be added using existing games as templates, and four new games benchmarking specific reasoning competencies like arithmetic and navigation have been added since its initial release. The simulator supports common features (such as valid action detection), while providing new enabling features, such as quickly precrawling entire game state trees. This work is released as open source.

[8] As an example, a 1GB file can typically store precrawled game trees for a single game variation up to between 8 and 12 steps, depending on the complexity of the action space.

[9] PYTHON performance is 10X slower than JAVA/SCALA performance due to the speed of PYTHON-JVM binders.

[10] Using pre-crawled paths, we managed to run *billion-game* experiment on a 32-core server in about a day.

6 Broader Impacts

Embodied agents require a variety of commonsense reasoning skills and competencies about the world in order to successfully perform tasks. Text games distill task learning to a high level of abstraction, allowing conceptual-level procedural knowledge to be acquired without simultaneously learning challenging low-level perceptual or motor tasks as in 3D simulators (e.g. Shridhar et al., 2020a; Petrenko et al., 2021), while reducing the computational requirements to run experiments from expensive GPU servers to common desktop hardware. Futher, Shirdhar et al. (2020b) have empirically demonstrated that agents can be inexpensively pretrained on tasks in a text world environment, then transfer much of their performance to more realistic 3D environments, speeding training. TEXTWORLDEXPRESS, which increases the speed of text game experiments by three orders of magnitude, enables running experiments faster, at greater scale, or using alternate sample-heavy machine learning frameworks than currently available simulators.

7 Limitations

TEXTWORLDEXPRESS has two main limitations compared to existing simulators. TEXTWORLDEXPRESS gains much of its speed by developing a highly-profiled simulator with hard-coded implementations of text games. Unlike the original TEXTWORLD simulator, which is designed to allow new environments to be implemented with a domain-specific language, adding new environments to TEXTWORLDEXPRESS is more effortful and requires coding in SCALA, a derivative of JAVA. Similarly, for speed, the TEXTWORLDEXPRESS user input parser is simplified, and it only recognizes valid actions as it presents them to the agent, without facilities for alternate surface forms, misspellings, or other variations. While it is common for agents to select actions from a valid action list, the lack of a diverse input parser limits utility for human participants who might choose to play these games.

Acknowledgements

This work supported in part by National Science Foundation (NSF) award #1815948 to PJ, and gift from the Allen Institute for Artificial Intelligence (AI2).

References

Prithviraj Ammanabrolu and Matthew Hausknecht. 2020. Graph constrained reinforcement learning for natural language action spaces. In *International Conference on Learning Representations*.

Prithviraj Ammanabrolu and Mark Riedl. 2019. Playing text-adventure games with graph-based deep reinforcement learning. In *Proceedings of the 2019 Conference of the North American Chapter of the Association for Computational Linguistics: Human Language Technologies, Volume 1 (Long and Short Papers)*, pages 3557–3565, Minneapolis, Minnesota. Association for Computational Linguistics.

Prithviraj Ammanabrolu, Jack Urbanek, Margaret Li, Arthur Szlam, Tim Rocktäschel, and Jason Weston. 2021. How to motivate your dragon: Teaching goal-driven agents to speak and act in fantasy worlds. In *Proceedings of the 2021 Conference of the North American Chapter of the Association for Computational Linguistics: Human Language Technologies*, pages 807–833.

Subhajit Chaudhury, Prithviraj Sen, Masaki Ono, Daiki Kimura, Michiaki Tatsubori, and Asim Munawar. 2021. Neuro-symbolic approaches for text-based policy learning. In *Proceedings of the 2021 Conference on Empirical Methods in Natural Language Processing*, pages 3073–3078, Online and Punta Cana, Dominican Republic. Association for Computational Linguistics.

Maxime Chevalier-Boisvert, Dzmitry Bahdanau, Salem Lahlou, Lucas Willems, Chitwan Saharia, Thien Huu Nguyen, and Yoshua Bengio. 2019. Babyai: First steps towards grounded language learning with a human in the loop. In *International Conference on Learning Representations*, volume 105.

Cédric Colas, Tristan Karch, Nicolas Lair, Jean-Michel Dussoux, Clément Moulin-Frier, Peter Ford Dominey, and Pierre-Yves Oudeyer. 2020. Language as a cognitive tool to imagine goals in curiosity-driven exploration. *ArXiv*, abs/2002.09253.

Marc-Alexandre Côté, Ákos Kádár, Xingdi Yuan, Ben A. Kybartas, Tavian Barnes, Emery Fine, James Moore, Matthew J. Hausknecht, Layla El Asri, Mahmoud Adada, Wendy Tay, and Adam Trischler. 2018. Textworld: A learning environment for text-based games. In *CGW@IJCAI*.

Jacob Devlin, Ming-Wei Chang, Kenton Lee, and Kristina Toutanova. 2019. BERT: Pre-training of deep bidirectional transformers for language understanding. In *Proceedings of the 2019 Conference of the North American Chapter of the Association for Computational Linguistics: Human Language Technologies, Volume 1 (Long and Short Papers)*, pages 4171–4186, Minneapolis, Minnesota. Association for Computational Linguistics.

Xiaoxiao Guo, Mo Yu, Yupeng Gao, Chuang Gan, Murray Campbell, and Shiyu Chang. 2020. Interactive fiction game playing as multi-paragraph reading comprehension with reinforcement learning. In *Proceedings of the 2020 Conference on Empirical Methods in Natural Language Processing (EMNLP)*, pages 7755–7765, Online. Association for Computational Linguistics.

William H Guss, Brandon Houghton, Nicholay Topin, Phillip Wang, Cayden Codel, Manuela Veloso, and Ruslan Salakhutdinov. 2019. Minerl: a large-scale dataset of minecraft demonstrations. In *Proceedings of the 28th International Joint Conference on Artificial Intelligence*, pages 2442–2448.

Matthew J. Hausknecht, Prithviraj Ammanabrolu, Marc-Alexandre Côté, and Xingdi Yuan. 2020. Interactive fiction games: A colossal adventure. In *AAAI*.

Peter A Jansen. 2022. A systematic survey of text worlds as embodied natural language environments. In *WordPlay Workshop: When Language Meets Games*.

Tristan Karch, Nicolas Lair, Cédric Colas, Jean-Michel Dussoux, Clément Moulin-Frier, Peter Ford Dominey, and Pierre-Yves Oudeyer. 2020. Language-goal imagination to foster creative exploration in deep rl.

Daiki Kimura, Subhajit Chaudhury, Masaki Ono, Michiaki Tatsubori, Don Joven Agravante, Asim Munawar, Akifumi Wachi, Ryosuke Kohita, and Alexander Gray. 2021a. LOA: Logical optimal actions for text-based interaction games. In *Proceedings of the 59th Annual Meeting of the Association for Computational Linguistics and the 11th International Joint Conference on Natural Language Processing: System Demonstrations*, pages 227–231, Online. Association for Computational Linguistics.

Daiki Kimura, Masaki Ono, Subhajit Chaudhury, Ryosuke Kohita, Akifumi Wachi, Don Joven Agravante, Michiaki Tatsubori, Asim Munawar, and Alexander G. Gray. 2021b. Neuro-symbolic reinforcement learning with first-order logic. In *EMNLP*.

Eric Kolve, Roozbeh Mottaghi, Winson Han, Eli VanderBilt, Luca Weihs, Alvaro Herrasti, Daniel Gordon, Yuke Zhu, Abhinav Gupta, and Ali Farhadi. 2017. Ai2-thor: An interactive 3d environment for visual ai. *arXiv preprint arXiv:1712.05474*.

Heinrich Küttler, Nantas Nardelli, Alexander Miller, Roberta Raileanu, Marco Selvatici, Edward Grefenstette, and Tim Rocktäschel. 2020. The nethack learning environment. *Advances in Neural Information Processing Systems*, 33:7671–7684.

P David Lebling, Marc S Blank, and Timothy A Anderson. 1979. Zork: a computerized fantasy simulation game. *Computer*, 12(04):51–59.

Hugo Liu and Push Singh. 2004. Conceptnet—a practical commonsense reasoning tool-kit. *BT technology journal*, 22(4):211–226.

Andrea Madotto, Mahdi Namazifar, Joost Huizinga, Piero Molino, Adrien Ecoffet, Huaixiu Zheng, Alexandros Papangelis, Dian Yu, Chandra Khatri, and Gokhan Tur. 2020. Exploration based language learning for text-based games. In *Proceedings of the Twenty-Ninth International Joint Conference on Artificial Intelligence, IJCAI-20*, pages 1488–1494. International Joint Conferences on Artificial Intelligence Organization. Main track.

Jesse Mu, Victor Zhong, Roberta Raileanu, Minqi Jiang, Noah D. Goodman, Tim Rocktaschel, and Edward Grefenstette. 2022. Improving intrinsic exploration with language abstractions. *ArXiv*, abs/2202.08938.

Keerthiram Murugesan, Mattia Atzeni, Pavan Kapanipathi, Pushkar Shukla, Sadhana Kumaravel, Gerald Tesauro, Kartik Talamadupula, Mrinmaya Sachan, and Murray Campbell. 2021a. Text-based rl agents with commonsense knowledge: New challenges, environments and baselines. In *AAAI*.

Keerthiram Murugesan, Mattia Atzeni, Pavan Kapanipathi, Kartik Talamadupula, Mrinmaya Sachan, and Murray Campbell. 2021b. Efficient text-based reinforcement learning by jointly leveraging state and commonsense graph representations. In *Proceedings of the 59th Annual Meeting of the Association for Computational Linguistics and the 11th International Joint Conference on Natural Language Processing (Volume 2: Short Papers)*, pages 719–725, Online. Association for Computational Linguistics.

Karthik Narasimhan, Tejas Kulkarni, and Regina Barzilay. 2015. Language understanding for text-based games using deep reinforcement learning. In *Proceedings of the 2015 Conference on Empirical Methods in Natural Language Processing*, pages 1–11, Lisbon, Portugal. Association for Computational Linguistics.

Graham Nelson. 2006. Natural language, semantic analysis, and interactive fiction. *IF Theory Reader*, 141:99–104.

Graham Nelson. 2014. The z-machine standards document version 1.1.

Philip Osborne, Heido Nomm, and André Freitas. 2021. A survey of text games for reinforcement learning informed by natural language. *ArXiv*, abs/2109.09478.

Aleksei Petrenko, Erik Wijmans, Brennan Shacklett, and Vladlen Koltun. 2021. Megaverse: Simulating embodied agents at one million experiences per second. In *International Conference on Machine Learning*, pages 8556–8566. PMLR.

Dongwon Ryu, Ehsan Shareghi, Meng Fang, Yunqiu Xu, Shirui Pan, and Reza Haf. 2022. Fire burns, sword cuts: Commonsense inductive bias for exploration in text-based games. In *Proceedings of the 60th Annual Meeting of the Association for Computational Linguistics (Volume 2: Short Papers)*, pages 515–522, Dublin, Ireland. Association for Computational Linguistics.

Mohit Shridhar, Jesse Thomason, Daniel Gordon, Yonatan Bisk, Winson Han, Roozbeh Mottaghi, Luke Zettlemoyer, and Dieter Fox. 2020a. ALFRED: A Benchmark for Interpreting Grounded Instructions for Everyday Tasks. In *The IEEE Conference on Computer Vision and Pattern Recognition (CVPR)*.

Mohit Shridhar, Xingdi Yuan, Marc-Alexandre Cote, Yonatan Bisk, Adam Trischler, and Matthew Hausknecht. 2020b. Alfworld: Aligning text and embodied environments for interactive learning. In *International Conference on Learning Representations*.

Robyn Speer, Joshua Chin, and Catherine Havasi. 2017. Conceptnet 5.5: An open multilingual graph of general knowledge. In *Thirty-first AAAI conference on artificial intelligence*.

Allison C. Tam, Neil C. Rabinowitz, Andrew Kyle Lampinen, Nicholas A. Roy, Stephanie C. Y. Chan, DJ Strouse, Jane X. Wang, Andrea Banino, and Felix Hill. 2022. Semantic exploration from language abstractions and pretrained representations. *ArXiv*, abs/2204.05080.

Ronen Tamari, Hiroyuki Shindo, Dafna Shahaf, and Yuji Matsumoto. 2019. Playing by the book: An interactive game approach for action graph extraction from text. In *Proceedings of the Workshop on Extracting Structured Knowledge from Scientific Publications*, pages 62–71, Minneapolis, Minnesota. Association for Computational Linguistics.

Ruoyao Wang, Peter Alexander Jansen, Marc-Alexandre Côté, and Prithviraj Ammanabrolu. 2022. Scienceworld: Is your agent smarter than a 5th grader? *ArXiv*, abs/2203.07540.

Yunqiu Xu, Meng Fang, Ling Chen, Yali Du, and Chengqi Zhang. 2021. Generalization in text-based games via hierarchical reinforcement learning. In *Findings of the Association for Computational Linguistics: EMNLP 2021*, pages 1343–1353, Punta Cana, Dominican Republic. Association for Computational Linguistics.

Shunyu Yao, Karthik Narasimhan, and Matthew Hausknecht. 2021. Reading and acting while blindfolded: The need for semantics in text game agents. In *Proceedings of the 2021 Conference of the North American Chapter of the Association for Computational Linguistics: Human Language Technologies*, pages 3097–3102, Online. Association for Computational Linguistics.

Shunyu Yao, Rohan Rao, Matthew Hausknecht, and Karthik Narasimhan. 2020. Keep CALM and explore: Language models for action generation in text-based games. In *Proceedings of the 2020 Conference on Empirical Methods in Natural Language Processing (EMNLP)*, pages 8736–8754, Online. Association for Computational Linguistics.

Xingdi Yuan, Marc-Alexandre Côté, Alessandro Sordoni, Romain Laroche, Rémi Tachet des Combes, Matthew J. Hausknecht, and Adam Trischler. 2018. Counting to explore and generalize in text-based games. *ArXiv*, abs/1806.11525.

Artem Zholus, Alexey Skrynnik, Shrestha Mohanty, Zoya Volovikova, Julia Kiseleva, Arthur Szlam, Marc-Alexandre Côté, and Aleksandr I. Panov. 2022. IGLU gridworld: Simple and fast environment for embodied dialog agents. *CoRR*, abs/2206.00142.

TermoUD — a language-independent terminology extraction tool

Małgorzata Marciniak and **Piotr Rychlik** and **Agnieszka Mykowiecka**
Institute of Computer Science, Polish Academy of Sciences
Jana Kazimierza 5, 01-248 Warsaw, Poland

Abstract

The paper addresses TermoUD — a language-independent terminology extraction tool. Its previous version, i.e. TermoPL (Marciniak et al., 2016; Rychlik et al., 2022), uses language dependent shallow grammar which selects candidate terms. The goal behind the development of TermoUD is to make the procedure as universal as possible, while taking care of the linguistic correctness of selected phrases. The tool is suitable for languages for which the Universal Dependencies (UD) parser exists. We describe a method of candidate term extraction based on UD POS tags and UD relations. The candidate ranking is performed by the C-value metric (contexts counting is adapted to the UD formalism), which doesn't need any additional language resources. The performance of the tool has been tested on texts in English, French, Dutch, and Slovenian. The results are evaluated on the manually annotated datasets: ACTER, RD-TEC 2.0, GENIA and RSDO5, and compared to those obtained by other tools.

1 Introduction

The purpose of automatic term extraction (ATE) is to identify recurring phrases that are relevant to the domain of a given text. Such phrases can then be interpreted as candidates for key phrases, index terms or potential domain lexicon entries.

The first among many approaches to this problem is selecting term candidates based on one of the following methods: n-grams (Rose et al., 2010); a set of patterns defining sequences of part-of-speech (POS) tags allowed within phrases (Hulth, 2003); phrases identified by a syntactical parser or an NP-chunker (Cram and Daille, 2016). All the generated candidate terms are then ranked with an ordering procedure based, among other things, on tf/idf (Salton, 1988), the C-value (Frantzi et al., 2000), or the mutual information value. The top elements of the obtained list are treated as domain terminology. Methods based solely on n-grams are language independent but achieve worse results (especially for inflectional languages) than those based on shallow-parsers which are language dependent. One of the important objectives of developers of ATE tools is to make them language independent. The JATE system (Zhang et al., 2016) selects candidate terms on the basis of syntactic analysis. However, it is designed to make it easy to adapt to different domains and/or languages — a flexible mechanism to determine how candidate phrases are constructed has been defined.

The second approach to ATE involves combining solely statistical features extracted from the processed text used in heuristics selecting terminology. An example of this approach is YAKE! (Campos et al., 2020), which supports 9 languages. The score assignment in YAKE! combines features such as letter case, a position within the text, word frequency and the number of different sentences in which a given term appears and, finally, the number of different contexts in which a term appears. Scores for 1-grams are combined to give the ranking of n-grams. The method gives good results for keyphrase extraction from short texts. The method doesn't work so well for inflection-rich languages, as the statistics are counted on forms, moreover; the processing of texts longer than a few pages is time-consuming.

The newest approach solves the problem of terminology extraction as a sequential tagging task and applies machine learning methods similar to the Named Entities Recognition. This approach was first used in the Termeval 2020 shared task (Rigouts Terryn et al., 2020), whose organisers published English, French and Dutch data collected in the Annotated Corpora for Term Extraction Research (ACTER) (Terryn et al., 2020).

All of the above approaches have various limitations. Although the latter approach has proven quite effective on the ACTER corpus, its use is limited to cases where we have annotated data, which

Proceedings of the 17th Conference of the European Chapter of the Association for Computational Linguistics
System Demonstrations, pages 178–186

are quite rare. Using only statistical heuristics to identify phrases has proven ineffective, especially for highly inflected languages, and defining POS patterns or grammatical rules requires knowledge of the language in question. Here we propose a method that, while not completely universal, can be used without additional modifications or resources for a great many languages.

Our tool for terminology extraction performs selection of candidate terms by using dependency parsing. The presented method is language independent and time-efficient. Nowadays, dependency parsers are very popular and are available for many languages (e.g. SpaCy works for 20, and Stanza for 70 languages) and are robust enough to be used in NLP applications. They are quite naturally used a lot in relation extraction, e.g. (Fundel et al., 2006) or (Geng et al., 2020), but there is still little interest in using dependency parsing in terminology extraction. The only two known approaches are (Gamallo, 2017) and (Liu et al., 2018). Gamallo used dependency parsers for bilingual term alignment. In the second paper, the authors used dependency parses for candidate selection for Chinese and achieved better results (both in terms of recall and precision) than using only POS based rules. In (Marciniak et al., 2020), the authors proposed the post-processing of selected phrase-candidates by checking the consistency of dependency parses of already selected phrases.

2 Extraction Process

To make our program as universal as possible, we had to define a set of rules to identify, without any changes, noun phrases in dependency trees constructed by parsers processing sentences in different languages.

2.1 Identification of Candidate Phrases

The UD project assumes a consistent structure of annotation schemes for many languages. In the terminology candidate identification algorithm described below, we use this consistency to define rules for selecting nominal phrases that are based on four sets of information. Two sets consist of UD POSs. The first – `head-pos` – contains UD POSs of nodes that can be heads of the term phrases, i.e. `NOUN`, `PROPN` and `VERB` (if the considered node is classified as a gerund). The second – `non-head-pos` – contains UD POSs of nodes that can be part of the term phrases but not their

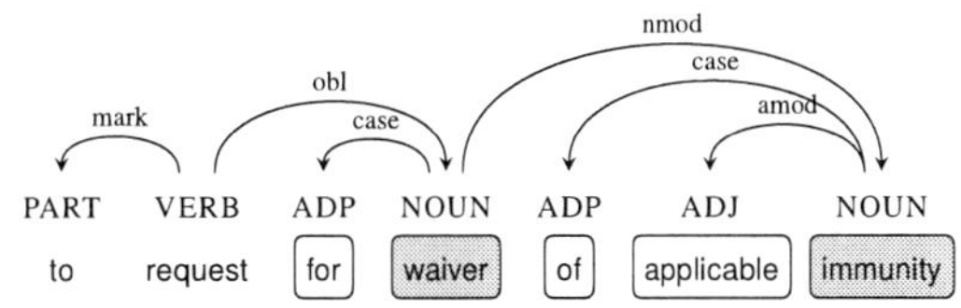

Figure 1: Dependency graph corresponding to phrase: *to request for waiver of applicable immunity*. All framed words are terminology nodes, heads are gray; obligatory relations: `case`, facultative relation: `amod`, `nmod`, `obl`.

heads, i.e. `ADJ`, `ADP`, `ADV`, `DET` and `NUM`. The next two sets consist of relations: `obligatory-rel` and `facultative-rel`. The first set groups relations between words that should appear together in terminology phrases, while the second set contains relations between words that may or may not appear in a sentence. The appropriate relations are listed below:

`obligatory-rel:` `amod:flat`, `case`, `case:poss`, `ccomp`, `compound`, `compound:prt`, `expl:pv`, `fixed`, `flat`, `iobj`, `nmod:arg`, `nmod:flat`, `nsubj:ger`,`obj`, `obl:agent`,`obl:arg`, `xcomp`.

`facultative-rel:` `acl`, `advmod`, `advmod:emph`,`amod`, `appos`, `nmod`, `nmod:poss`, `nummod`, `nummod:gov`, `obl`

Note that even if we add the relations that are only typical for a certain language to the lists, it will not destroy the generality of the solution. These relations will not affect the results obtained for other languages.

To create UD structures from plain text, we use the Stanza (Qi et al., 2020) dependency parser. The structure obtained in this way consists of sentence nodes with relations pointing to their dependent nodes, see Fig. 1. We select all nodes which may be included in terminology phrases creating the list of potential terminology nodes. This list includes all nodes whose UD POS belong to one of the above-mentioned sets: `head-pos` or `non-head-pos`. For hyphenated compound words, which are allowed in many languages, all nodes of the UD structures representing them are placed in the list of potential terminology nodes. All nodes from structures representing hyphenated compound words, except those that are heads of these structures, are also placed in the list of hyphenated nodes. Each of the nodes in the list of hyphenated nodes will be selected for creating phrases if and only if its head is also selected.

In the structure, we leave only relations between the terminology nodes and check if, for each node, all obligatory-relations are in the current structure. Doing so, we avoid some truncated phrases, as we do not want to create phrases with nodes that have unrealized requirements.

We repeat the process of making phrases in the loop for all nodes from the list of potential terminology nodes. For each node we take into account all combinations of dependent nodes, where nodes connected by obligatory-relations and those from the list of hyphenated nodes must be included in the phrase, while nodes connected by facultative-relations may be omitted. As the candidate term phrase, we accept only those for which the head element is included in the head-pos set. The list of established phrases for the considered node is passed to the upper node (if relevant), and the considered node is removed from the list of potential terminology nodes. The whole procedure is repeated until the list of potential terminology nodes is empty. Pseudocode for the algorithm is given in the Appendix A.

Many forms of a given term can occur in the processed texts, especially in the case of inflectional languages. Therefore, the program identifies terms by their lemmatized forms. To present terms in a more readable way, we choose their most frequently occurring forms, preferably from those in nominative case (if applicable) and/or in the singular.

The method described above allows the extraction of discontinuous phrases. Figure 1 gives a phrase from the ACTER part of the corpus on corruption. Our method extracts 5 term candidates for this structure, i.e., *waiver, applicable immunity, immunity, waiver of applicable immunity* and the phrase with a gap: *waiver of immunity*. All phrases, except the second one, are terms according to the manual annotation.

While our goal is to build a tool that can process texts in many languages, we are aware that omitting all language-dependent features may degrade the results. One such feature is the use of determiners, which for some languages are obligatory while in others they are used sporadically. Some pronouns, (indicative, possesive), which are usually excluded from terminological phrases, can also play role of determiners, so we focused not on syntactic classes but on the det relation. In Table 1, we have included the ratio (multiplied by 100) of the number of det relations to the number of nouns (both common and proper) for 20 languages from the PUD set used for CoNLL 2017 shared task (Zeman et al., 2017). Its value varies from above 60 for French to 2.4 for Japanese. We have chosen an arbitrary threshold equal to 20 below which we assume that terminology phrases do not include determiners. For languages with this coefficient larger than 20 we allow for determiners within terminological phases. In this case we include determiners to the set non-head-pos and make det relation obligatory.

name	tokens	N	PN	det-rel	%
French	24,131	4,672	1,272	3,857	64.9
Portuguese	21,917	4,600	1,393	3,726	62.2
Italian	22,182	4,392	1,756	3,751	61.0
Spanish	22,822	4,818	1,250	3,514	57.9
German	21,000	4,249	1,219	2,771	50.7
English	21,176	4,036	1,741	2,047	35.4
Swedish	19,076	4,035	1,216	1,017	19.4
Hindi	23,829	5,597	1,358	791	11.4
Indonesian	19,034	4,687	2,113	718	10.6
Turkish	16,536	5,829	1,525	686	9.3
Russian	19,355	4,897	1,209	476	7.8
Czech	18,565	4,482	1,091	423	7.6
Icelandic	18,831	4,101	1,464	318	5.7
Thai	22,322	6,052	1,491	413	5.5
Chinese	21,415	5,410	1,361	338	5.0
Korean	16,584	8,052	1,677	457	4.7
Finnish	15,807	4,223	1,504	245	4.3
Arabic	20,747	5,578	1,728	285	3.9
Polish	18,338	4,504	1,326	196	3.4
Japanese	28,788	7,424	1,363	210	2.4

Table 1: Frequency of using det relations in the corpora used for training dependency parsers. The columns include number of nouns, proper nouns, det dependency relations and the ratio (multiplied by 100) by the latter to the sum of all nouns.

2.2 Ranking of Phrases

The method of identifying term candidates described above leads a large number of phrases including their subphrases. For ranking candidates we use C-value coefficient which depends on the frequency of an evaluated phrase (the higher the frequency of the phrase in the text under study, the higher the C-value), its length (longer terms are preferred) and the number of different contexts in which it occurs (the C-value increases with the number of different contexts). We adapted this method to rank term candidates extracted using dependency relations. In particular, since the obtained phrases can be discontinuous, the definition of phrase contexts had to be reformulated.

When determining the context of a given phrase, we take into account its UD structure and the maximum structure that contains it. For example, for the phrase *waiver of immunity* from Figure 1, the maximum structure will be the structure corresponding to the maximum phrase *waiver of applicable immunity*. From the maximum structure, we select those nodes that do not belong to the structure of the examined phrase and are directly adjacent to some of its nodes. We then concatenate the lemmas of the tokens corresponding to the nodes found in the order in which these tokens appear in the sentence. We treat the resulting string of characters as the context of the examined phrase. For the phrase *waiver of immunity*, its context is *applicable*.

3 Evaluation

To compare the results with other approaches, we evaluate our tool on the following corpora annotated with terminology: ACTER, GENIA, ACL RD-TEC, and RDSO5. So, we tested the method on four languages: English, French, Dutch and Slovenian. For comparison, the D-Terminer (Rigouts Terryn, 2021; Rigouts Terryn et al., 2022a) and Sketch Engine (Jakubíček et al., 2014) were also used to process the same datasets. In the case of TermoUD, we tested the plain tool without additional existing filters developed for TermoPL, e.g., removing stopwords from candidate terms.

The result of TermoUD is a sorted list of all detected phrases, with no indication of where a split between terms and non-terms is suggested. Since the ranking method used in the tool assigns the same values to many terms, the evaluation cannot be carried out at any point in the ranking list, but only in those places where the value changes. Therefore, it is not possible to compare our method with others for the lists of terms of the same length.

3.1 ACL RD-TEC

The ACL Reference Dataset for Terminology Extraction and Classification, version 2.0 (ACL RD-TEC 2.0) (QasemiZadeh and Schumann, 2016) has been developed with the aim of providing a benchmark for the evaluation of term and entity recognition tasks based on specialised text from the computational linguistics domain. It consists of 300 abstracts from articles published between 1978 and 2006 in which both single and multi-word lexical units with a specialised meaning are manually annotated. 6,818 occurrences of terms are identified in total and 1918 of them are different strings.

To compare the results of TermoUD with the best tool for English, i.e. D-terminer, we use both to extract terms and compare the results. To make the comparison more reliable, we unify upper and lower case letters, so *natural language processing* and *Natural Language Processing* are treated as the same phrase. If phrases have different character sets, we consider that they are different, e.g., *word-sense disambiguation algorithms* and *word sense disambiguation algorithms*. The results of the comparison are given in Table 3. For the comparison, we select the number of elements returned by TermoUD, which is similar to the length of the manually annotated list of terms. A specific problem with the manually annotated ACL RD-TEC data is the high number of phrases containing acronyms surrounded by parentheses (128 cases), e.g., *Question Answering (QA) systems*. Neither of the two tools recognised these phrases, in effect lowering results equally. The D-terminer doesn't indicate any phrase with an acronym inside, while TermoUD indicates them without parentheses.

	selected terms	prec.	recall	F1
D-terminer	613	0.51	0.16	0.25
TermoUD(1)	171	0.60	0.05	0.10
TermoUD(2)	1276	0.26	0.17	0.21
TermoUD(3)	2610	0.28	0.38	0.33

Table 2: Results for D-terminer and TermoUD applied to the ACL RD-TEC corpus. Three lists of TermoUD differ in the numbers of selected terms and are given for three consecutive C-values.

3.2 Genia

The GENIA corpus (Kim et al., 2003) consists of 2000 MEDLINE abstracts containing about 400K words. Included in the collection are articles containing such MeSH terms as human, blood cell and transcription factor. The annotation for biological terms refers to concepts defined within the GENIA ontology, which contains 47 biologically relevant nominal categories. From a linguistic point of view, the selected terms were nominal phrases in which the noun was followed by an optional sequence of adjectives and noun modifiers. There are about 80K annotated phrases in the corpus. The data is challenging because the structure of biological terms varies widely, and the vast majority of terms (76% of 36230) occur only once.

As with the previous data set, we used the D-terminer to identify terms in the Genia corpus. It performed very well, achieving an F1 value of 0.45 and finding almost 40% (13,487) of all annotated terms. As expected for such data (many singular occurrences), our program performed worse in terms of precision at the top of the returned list (Table 3). We tested phrases with lengths up to 4 and 6 elements. The method recognized 116,499 phrases with length up to 4 tokens. The list contains 71% of manually annotated terms. While the list of phrases with length up to 6 tokens is longer and consists of 153,122 elements, but it contains only slightly more of manually annotated phrases – 73%. The top of the lists (the first 8,986 elements) is the same for both tested lengths of phrases and the precision is 0.52. Significant differences appear in the terms that were placed in positions above 33,000.

	terms selected	good	prec.	recall	F1
D-terminer	23,813	13,487	0.57	0.37	0.45
TermoUD					
4&6 top(1)	1173	740	0.63	0.02	0.04
4&6 top(2)	8,986	4,665	0.52	0.13	0.21
4 (1)	32,688	9,856	0.30	0.27	0.28
4 (2)	43,939	14,412	0.33	0.40	0.36
6 (1)	33,066	9,905	0.30	0.27	0.28
6 (2)	57,664	14,940	0.26	0.41	0.32

Table 3: Results for D-terminer and TermoUD applied to GENIA. The following results are reported for TermoUD: a) two results for the top parts of the lists (common for longer and shorter phrases) b) two results (consecutive C-values) for phrases of lenghts up to 4 and 6 which have the number of selected terms below and above the number of manually selected terms.

3.3 ACTER

The Annotated Corpora for Term Extraction Research (ACTER) dataset (Rigouts Terryn et al., 2022b) includes domain-specific corpora in three languages (English, French, and Dutch) and four domains (corruption, dressage (equitation), heart failure, and wind energy). Manual annotations are available for terms and Named Entities for each corpus, with almost 20k unique annotations in total. The corpus was used by those participating in the shared task at the Computerm workshop (Rigouts Terryn et al., 2020). The best result was achieved by a BERT based architecture used for sequential token classification, TALN-LS2N (Hazem et al., 2020). As the corpus contains a relatively short texts, our ranking methods are not too efficient, so the results for the top part of the candidate terms lists, shown in Table 4, are significantly worse (similar to the results of the standard methods taking part in the shared task). The worst result were obtained for Dutch texts. The TALN-LS2N results demonstrate some differences in the data across languages. For English, recall is much higher than precision, while for French they are similar. In our experiment, for English data, precision was higher than recall. The D-terminer application was trained on ACTER data, so we cannot use it as a comparison.

	all	terms selected	good	prec.	recall	F1
TermoUD, English						
corp	1087	1008	245	0.24	0.23	0.23
equi	1427	661	255	0.39	0.18	0.24
htfl	2459	3466	494	0.14	0.20	0.17
wind	1434	1028	282	0.27	0.20	0.23
TermoUD, French						
corp	1103	1230	245	0.20	0.22	0.21
equi	1079	619	192	0.31	0.18	0.23
htfl	2202	3305	453	0.14	0.21	0.16
wind	870	840	152	0.18	0.17	0.18
TermoUD, Dutch						
corp	1215	845	161	0.19	0.13	0.16
equi	1457	1673	182	0.11	0.12	0.12
htfl	2137	2586	193	0.07	0.09	0.08
wind	1159	735	96	0.13	0.08	0.10
TALN-LS2N, English						
htfl	2479	-	-	0.35	0.71	0.47
TALN-LS2N, French						
htfl	2220	-	-	0.46	0.52	0.48

Table 4: Results for ACTER data. The 'all' column represents the number of different terms annotated within the data. htfl data was used as test data for TALN-LS2N while the other sets were used as train data. In the TALN-LS2N approach there was no initially selected list of terms – all tokens were tested.

3.4 RSDO5

The Slovenian corpus RDSO5 (Jemec Tomazin et al., 2021) was created to train tools for automatic term identification. It consists of around 250,000 tokens and gathers texts from four domains: biomechanics, linguistics, chemistry, and veterinary. 38,000 phrases were manually marked as terms in the data, among them 6165 different strings. Slovenian is an inflectional language, which means that each term may occur in many forms, e.g. *virusni sev* 'virus strain' has the following inflected forms in the data: *virusnih sevov, virusni sevi, virusnimi sevi, virusnim sevom, virusni sev, virusnega seva, virusnih sevih, virusnemu sevu, virusna seva*. TermoUD gives a list of unique terms as its output, so we join various manually selected term forms with the help of the lemmas provided by the Stanza parser. As a result, we obtain a list of 4200 items.

Table 5 contains the results of applying the TermoUD tool to four subcorpora of the RSDO5 corpus. The third column of Table 5 gives the number of various terms (not term forms) which are identified in the data. For the evaluation we took lists of terms that have a length equal to the list of manually selected phrases. For this reason, the values of the precision, recall and F1 measure are equal. In the table, we give only the first value.

	tokens	diff. terms	prec. (nb)
bim	61,375	797	0.21 (169)
jez	109,421	1000	0.25 (249)
kem	65,620	773	0.24 (186)
vet	76,138	1630	0.21 (349)

Table 5: Results for TermoUD applied to RSDO5

We are not aware of other experiments performed on the RSDO5 corpus, so we have no data to evaluate the quality of TermoUD's performance. We decide to compare the obtained results with the free trial Skech Engine (Jakubíček et al., 2014) which gives the first 100 one-word terms and the first 100 multi-word terms, and almost all of them are unique terms. We select the same number of terms in the same proportion from our lists. The results of selected terms are given in Table 6. A comparison of the results shows that TermoUD is better at providing the first 100 one- and multi-words terms. Only the results for multi-word terms of biomechanic texts are at a similar level.

	Sketch Engine		TermoUD	
	one	multi	one	multi
bim	0.13	0.17	0.45	0.19
jez	0.26	0.31	0.42	0.47
kem	0.23	0.17	0.45	0.38
vet	0.14	0.24	0.53	0.46

Table 6: Precision of 100 extracted terms by Sketch Engine and TermoUD.

4 Conclusion and Future Work

TermoUD's method of selecting traditional candidate terms restricted to nominal phrases allows multiple languages to be processed with the same tool. As linguistic knowledge is already contained in the UD parsers, no language adjustments are needed. For example, it is irrelevant whether adjectives can come before or after a noun in a given language. An additional, unique feature of UD-based candidate term selection is its ability to extract discontinuous phrases, see Figure 1.

The best current methods of terminology extraction use machine learning and sequential tagging. The results obtained by these methods are much better than TermoUD's, especially measured by precision. These methods also facilitate the expansion of term types, e.g. to include those which are adjectives and verbs. However, the methods require the preparation of training data, that exists for only a few languages, text types and domains.

The quality of the results obtained by TermoUD depends on the quality of the parser for the language in question, especially how good the lemmatisation is. This feature is particularly important for languages with rich morphology, as we need to recognise and join various inflected forms of candidate terms.

The important feature that differentiates the two approaches is the list of results. For the classification-based methods, we get a list of terms, whereas TermoUD generates a sorted list of all term candidates. The disadvantage of the TermoUD tool is the need to establish where the list is divided into terms and non-terms, but the advantage is we can choose how many of the candidates we would like to choose. Machine learning methods only provide a list of accepted terms, which is fragmentary knowledge as we do not know the phrases that were rejected and should have been classified as terms. As the ranking coefficient used in TermoUD is highly dependent on term frequencies, our method gives much better results for larger data. Terms used in text only once are always located very low on the final list.

In the near future, we plan to deal with the analysis of coordinated phrases, which are quite a challenge for all terminology extraction tools and the UD mechanism seems to enable their correct handling. Moreover we should test the tool on languages from other families, and improve the term ordering method. as our lists contain on average about 80% of terms, changes in ordering method may significantly improve the results.

TermoUD[1] is available from `http://zil.ipipan.waw.pl/TermoPL`, the same page as TermoPL, the previous version of the tool described in the paper. TermoPL is also a part of Korpusomat (Kieraś and Kobyliński, 2021), a simple tool for creating linguistic corpora in Polish `https://korpusomat.pl/`. TermoUD will be available from the multilingual version of the Korpusomat tool currently under development.

[1] A system demonstration and the results of the tool are available from the same page.

5 Limitations

ThermoUD requires the existence of a UD parser. It does not consider candidate terms like adjectives, verbs, coordinated phrases and phrases containing coordinated phrases. We only evaluated the tool on Indo-European languages as we are not aware of any terminology-annotated datasets for other languages. We used our extraction method to extract terminology from Finish texts. Used texts and obtained results are available on the project page given above.

References

Ricardo Campos, Vítor Mangaravite, Arian Pasquali, Alípio Jorge, Célia Nunes, and Adam Jatowt. 2020. Yake! keyword extraction from single documents using multiple local features. *Information Sciences*, 509:257 - 289.

Damien Cram and Beatrice Daille. 2016. TermSuite: Terminology extraction with term variant detection. In *Proceedings of the 54th Annual Meeting of the Association for Computational Linguistics—System Demonstrations*, pages 13–18. Association for Computational Linguistics.

Katerina Frantzi, Sophia Ananiadou, and Hideki Mima. 2000. Automatic recognition of multi-word terms: the C-value/NC-value method. *Int. Journal on Digital Libraries*, 3:115–130.

Katrin Fundel, Robert Küffner, and Ralf Zimmer. 2006. RelEx—Relation extraction using dependency parse trees. *Bioinformatics*, 23(3):365–371.

Pablo Gamallo. 2017. Citius at SemEval-2017 task 2: Cross-lingual similarity from comparable corpora and dependency-based contexts. In *Proceedings of the 11th International Workshop on Semantic Evaluation*, pages 226–229. Association for Computational Linguistics.

ZhiQiang Geng, GuoFei Chen, YongMing Han, Gang Lu, and Fang Li. 2020. Semantic relation extraction using sequential and tree-structured LSTM with attention. *Information Sciences*, 509:183 - 192.

Amir Hazem, Mérieme Bouhandi, Florian Boudin, and Beatrice Daille. 2020. TermEval 2020: TALN-LS2N system for automatic term extraction. In *Proceedings of the 6th International Workshop on Computational Terminology*, pages 95–100, Marseille, France. European Language Resources Association.

Anette Hulth. 2003. Improved automatic keyword extraction given more linguistic knowledge. In *Proceedings of the 2003 Conference on Empirical Methods in Natural Language Processing*.

Miloš Jakubíček, Adam Kilgarriff, Vojtěch Kovář, Pavel Rychlý, and Vít Suchomel. 2014. Finding terms in corpora for many languages with the Sketch Engine. In *Proceedings of the Demonstrations at the 14th Conference of the European Chapter of the Association for Computational Linguistics*, pages 53–56, Gothenburg, Sweden. Association for Computational Linguistics.

Mateja Jemec Tomazin, Mitja Trojar, Simon Atelšek, Tanja Fajfar, Tomaž Erjavec, and Mojca Žagar Karer. 2021. Corpus of term-annotated texts RSDO5 1.1. Slovenian language resource repository CLARIN.SI.

Witold Kieraś and Łukasz Kobyliński. 2021. Korpusomat – stan obecny i przyszłość projektu. *Język Polski*, (2):49–58.

J.-D. Kim, T. Ohta, Y. Tateisi, and J. Tsujii. 2003. GENIA corpus—a semantically annotated corpus for bio-textmining. *Bioinformatics*, 19(suppl_1):i180–i182.

Ying Liu, Tianlin Zhang, Pei Quan, Yueran Wen, Kaichao Wu, and Hongbo He. 2018. A novel parsing-based automatic domain terminology extraction method. In Shi Y. et al., editor, *Computational Science – ICCS 2018. Lecture Notes in Computer Science, vol 10862*, pages 796–802. Springer, Cham.

Małgorzata Marciniak, Agnieszka Mykowiecka, and Piotr Rychlik. 2016. TermoPL — a flexible tool for terminology extraction. In *Proceedings of the Tenth International Conference on Language Resources and Evaluation, LREC 2016*, pages 2278–2284, Portorož, Slovenia. ELRA, European Language Resources Association (ELRA).

Małgorzata Marciniak, Piotr Rychlik, and Agnieszka Mykowiecka. 2020. Supporting terminology extraction with dependency parses. In *Proceedings of the 6th International Workshop on Computational Terminology*, pages 72–79, Marseille, France. European Language Resources Association.

Behrang QasemiZadeh and Anne-Kathrin Schumann. 2016. The ACL RD-TEC 2.0: A language resource for evaluating term extraction and entity recognition methods. In *Proceedings of the Tenth International Conference on Language Resources and Evaluation (LREC'16)*, pages 1862–1868, Portorož, Slovenia. European Language Resources Association (ELRA).

Peng Qi, Yuhao Zhang, Yuhui Zhang, Jason Bolton, and Christopher D. Manning. 2020. Stanza: A Python natural language processing toolkit for many human languages. In *Proceedings of the 58th Annual Meeting of the Association for Computational Linguistics: System Demonstrations*.

Ayla Rigouts Terryn. 2021. *D-TERMINE : data-driven term extraction methodologies investigated*. Ph.D. thesis.

Ayla Rigouts Terryn, Veronique Hoste, Patrick Drouin, and Els Lefever. 2020. TermEval 2020: Shared task on automatic term extraction using the annotated corpora for term extraction research (ACTER) dataset. In *Proceedings of the 6th International Workshop on Computational Terminology*, pages 85–94, Marseille, France. European Language Resources Association.

Ayla Rigouts Terryn, Veronique Hoste, and Els Lefever. 2022a. D-terminer: Online demo for monolingual and bilingual automatic term extraction. In *Proceedings of the Workshop on Terminology in the 21st century: many faces, many places*, pages 33–40, Marseille, France. European Language Resources Association.

Ayla Rigouts Terryn, Véronique Hoste, and Els Lefever. 2022b. Acter 1.5: Annotated corpora for term extraction research.

Stuart Rose, Dave Engel, Nick Cramer, and Wendy Cowley. 2010. Automatic keyword extraction from individual documents. *Text Mining: Applications and Theory*, pages 1 – 20.

Piotr Rychlik, Małgorzata Marciniak, and Agnieszka Mykowiecka. 2022. Termopl: A tool for extracting and clustering domain related terms. In *Proceedings of the 22nd ACM/IEEE Joint Conference on Digital Libraries*, JCDL '22, New York, NY, USA. Association for Computing Machinery.

Gerard Salton. 1988. Syntactic approaches to automatic book indexing. In *Proceedings of the 26th Annual Meeting on Association for Computational Linguistics*, ACL '88, pages 204–210, Stroudsburg, PA, USA. Association for Computational Linguistics.

Ayla Rigouts Terryn, Véronique Hoste, and Els Lefever. 2020. In no uncertain terms: a dataset for monolingual and multilingual automatic term extraction from comparable corpora. *Language Resources and Evaluation*.

Daniel Zeman, Martin Popel, Milan Straka, Jan Hajic, Joakim Nivre, Filip Ginter, Juhani Luotolahti, Sampo Pyysalo, Slav Petrov, Martin Potthast, Francis Tyers, Elena Badmaeva, Memduh Gokirmak, Anna Nedoluzhko, Silvie Cinkova, Jan Hajic jr., Jaroslava Hlavacova, Václava Kettnerová, Zdenka Uresova, Jenna Kanerva, Stina Ojala, Anna Missilä, Christopher D. Manning, Sebastian Schuster, Siva Reddy, Dima Taji, Nizar Habash, Herman Leung, Marie-Catherine de Marneffe, Manuela Sanguinetti, Maria Simi, Hiroshi Kanayama, Valeria dePaiva, Kira Droganova, Héctor Martínez Alonso, Çağrı Çöltekin, Umut Sulubacak, Hans Uszkoreit, Vivien Macketanz, Aljoscha Burchardt, Kim Harris, Katrin Marheinecke, Georg Rehm, Tolga Kayadelen, Mohammed Attia, Ali Elkahky, Zhuoran Yu, Emily Pitler, Saran Lertpradit, Michael Mandl, Jesse Kirchner, Hector Fernandez Alcalde, Jana Strnadová, Esha Banerjee, Ruli Manurung, Antonio Stella, Atsuko Shimada, Sookyoung Kwak, Gustavo Mendonca, Tatiana Lando, Rattima Nitisaroj, and Josie Li. 2017. Conll 2017 shared task: Multilingual parsing from raw text to universal dependencies. In *Proceedings of the CoNLL 2017 Shared Task: Multilingual Parsing from Raw Text to Universal Dependencies*, pages 1–19, Vancouver, Canada. Association for Computational Linguistics.

Ziqi Zhang, Jie Gao, and Fabio Ciravegna. 2016. JATE 2.0: Java automatic term extraction with Apache Solr. In *Proceedings of the Tenth International Conference on Language Resources and Evaluation (LREC'16)*, pages 2262–2269, Portorož, Slovenia. European Language Resources Association (ELRA).

A Candidate phrase extraction from UD structures (pseudocode for the algorithm)

1. Define sets:

`head-pos`, `non-head-pos`, `obligatory-rel`, `facultative-rel`.

2. Create the structure `ud`: for every token `j` in a sentence create a node n_j and define `ud[`n_j`]` as a set of pairs (`n`$_i$, `r`$_i$), where `n`$_i$ is the dependant (in the sense of the dependency relation `r`$_i$) of `n`$_j$ and corresponds to the token `i`.

3. Create the list `T-nodes` consisting of all nodes that might be included in term phrases. `T-nodes` will contain all nodes from `ud` with POS in `head-pos` or `non-head-pos`.

4. Identify the structures corresponding to hyphenated compound words. Add all nodes from this structures to `T-nodes`. Select all nodes from the identified structures that are not their heads and put them in the list `H-nodes`.

5. Remove nodes from the structure `ud` that are not in the list `T-nodes`.

6. Check if obligatory relations lead to the nodes that may create terms:

for each element `e` of `T-nodes`:
  for each pair `(n,r)` ∈ `ud[e]`:
    if `r` ∈ `obligatory-rel`:
      if `n` ∉ `T-nodes`:
        delete `e` from `T-nodes`;
    else: # `r` *is facultative*
      if *n* ∉ `T-nodes`:
        delete pair `(n,r)` from `ud[e]`;

7. For each node `n` in `T-nodes`, create an empty set `P[n]`. This set will contain lists of all possible phrases `p[d]` for which `d` is the head element, for all dependants `d` of `n`. These phrases will be represented by sets of nodes. After determining the

set P[n], the list p[n] can be created. Each phrase from p[n] must contain:

(a) node n,
(b) all nodes from one phrase in p[d],
    if (d,r) ∈ ud[h] and
    r ∈ obligatory-rel,
(c) none or all nodes from one phrase in p[d],
    if (d,r) ∈ ud[h] and
    r ∈ facultative-rel,
(d) all nodes x ∈ H-nodes, if (x,r) ∈ ud[n].

8. Select candidates for terminology phrases:

```
create empty list terms;
while T-nodes is not empty:
  for each n ∈ T-nodes:
    if ud[n] is empty:
      # phrases are established for all
      # dependent nodes of n
      remove n from T-nodes;
      create p[n];
      find the head node h of n;
      if h∈T-nodes:
        add p[n] to P[h];
        remove all pairs (n,r) from ud[h];
      if POS(n) ∈ head-pos:
        add all phrases from p[n] to terms;
```

9. Clean up:

(a) sort each element of terms according to the position of the nodes in the sentence,
(b) remove the node from the begining of a phrase, if it is a preposition referring to the head of the sentence, or if it is a determiner.

INCOGNITUS: A Toolbox for Automated Clinical Notes Anonymization

Bruno Ribeiro
Fraunhofer Portugal AICOS
R. Alfredo Allen 455,
4200-135 Porto

Vitor Rolla
Fraunhofer Portugal AICOS
R. Alfredo Allen 455,
4200-135 Porto

Ricardo Santos
Fraunhofer Portugal AICOS
& LIBPhys, Physics Department
FCT/NOVA, 2829-516 Caparica

Abstract

Automated text anonymization is a classical problem in Natural Language Processing (NLP). The topic has evolved immensely throughout the years, with the first list-search and rule-based solutions evolving to statistical modeling approaches and later to advanced systems that rely on powerful state-of-the-art language models. Even so, these solutions fail to be widely implemented in the most privacy-demanding areas of activity, such as healthcare; none of them is perfect, and most can not guarantee rigorous anonymization. This paper presents INCOGNITUS, a flexible platform for the automated anonymization of clinical notes that offers the possibility of applying different techniques. The available tools include an underexplored yet promising method that guarantees 100% recall by replacing each word with a semantically identical one. In addition, the presented framework incorporates a performance evaluation module to compute a novel metric for information loss assessment in real-time.

1 Introduction

The digitization of medical textual data has allowed for a whole new range of possibilities, such as the development of tools for the summarization of clinical notes or the automated identification of the International Classification of Diseases (ICD) codes in clinical text. However, clinical data contains sensitive information regarding both patients and health professionals. These entities are protected by the General Data Protection Regulation (GDPR), which grants equal data protection rights to all European Union (EU) citizens (GDPR, 2018). Therefore, information systems must be compliant to maintain such information private. This poses a challenge when considering the publication of clinical data for secondary usage.

The GDPR (GDPR, 2018) defines anonymization as the process through which "personal data (is) rendered anonymous in such a manner that the data subject is not or no longer identifiable" (Recital 26). However, achieving true anonymization is not a simple task, especially when considering unstructured data such as clinical notes. In fact, despite the fact that many literature works propose strategies for the automated anonymization of clinical text, their implementation in real contexts is still scarce. Consequently, the problematic access to clinical text data for secondary usage remains a barrier to scientific research.

This demonstration paper presents the INCOGNITUS platform for automated clinical notes anonymization. The beta version is available online at `https://tospe-incognitusfhp.streamlit.app/`. An overview video can be watched at `https://www.youtube.com/watch?v=4lePn19ZwJE`. Besides offering a wide range of methods to perform anonymization tasks, INCOGNITUS was designed to address two common flaws of similar systems: (i) the inability to provide truly anonymized outputs (100% sensitive information removal) (Abdalla et al., 2020) and (ii) the lack of an assessment on the quantity of relevant information that gets lost in the anonymization process (Mozes and Kleinberg, 2021).

The remainder of the manuscript is organized as follows. The next section contextualizes text anonymization literature, mainly focusing on the clinical domain. Then, the platform proposed is described, along with its composing methods and models. The experimental setup followed to develop each component is detailed in Section 4. The results associated with these experiments are then discussed in Section 5. In the last section, the main conclusions of this work are presented.

2 Background

The list of literature publications focused on clinical text anonymization is extensive. This section presents a chronological overview of the developments achieved in this area of research, culminating

Proceedings of the 17th Conference of the European Chapter of the Association for Computational Linguistics
System Demonstrations, pages 187–194
May 2-4, 2023 ©2023 Association for Computational Linguistics

in a final discussion on the main findings regarding the strengths and flaws of current techniques and future research tendencies.

2.1 First Approaches

The first works on clinical text de-identification involved the development of simple systems relying on handcrafted sets of rules, dictionary and medical thesaurus lookups, and pattern matching algorithms (Sweeney, 1996; Ruch et al., 2000; Thomas et al., 2002; Gupta et al., 2004; Douglass et al., 2004). These methods established the potential of applying Natural Language Processing (NLP) techniques to the anonymization problem, reporting performances between 94% and 99% in terms of recall. Even so, since they were usually highly adapted to the characteristics shared by the very notes that they were tested upon, their generalization ability was poor.

2.2 Conditional Random Fields

Following these early developments, two events boosted the scientific knowledge around clinical text data de-identification: the 2006 and 2014 Informatics for Integrating Biology to the Bedside (i2b2) challenges (Uzuner et al., 2007; Stubbs et al., 2015). These competitions encouraged researchers to produce innovative solutions to approach unstructured data anonymization. At this point, solutions based in Conditional Random Fields (CRF) took over as the best-performing methods (Aramaki et al., 2006; Wellner et al., 2007; Gardner and Xiong, 2008; Dehghan et al., 2015; Liu et al., 2015; Yang and Garibaldi, 2015). These systems leveraged features such as Part-of-Speech (POS) tags, surrounding words, position within the document, word form, and capitalization to identify sensitive information within the text. Some of them also included regular expression matching and list search modules along with the main CRF model (Wellner et al., 2007; Dehghan et al., 2015; Liu et al., 2015; Yang and Garibaldi, 2015). In 2006, all the proposed methodologies achieved f1-scores higher than 95%, while the best-performing method in 2014 reported a value of 93.6%.

2.3 Deep Learning

As the scientific community's focus shifted towards Deep Learning (DL) strategies, many studies were published where these models were trained on the anonymization task. Most of these studies implement long short-term memory (LSTM) recurrent neural networks (RNN), which are known to be effective in Named Entity Recognition (NER) tasks (Dernoncourt et al., 2016; Liu et al., 2017; Stubbs et al., 2017; Yang et al., 2019). Some of these consisted of hybrid approaches, complementing the DL models with CRF-based and even simpler modules.

Friedrich et al. (Friedrich et al., 2019) proposed an adversarial learning approach based on an LSTM-CRF architecture. Their solution prevents two procedures that can be used to re-construct Personal Health Identifiers (PHIs): (i) the development of a model which can learn the reverse transformation mechanism; and (ii) a look-up table with all the inputs and their respective representations. An adversarial representation is trained to perform two tasks directly following these two procedures. The goal is to achieve a secure solution where the best adversarial/negative representation cannot re-construct the PHIs.

Recently, Abdalla et al. (Abdalla et al., 2020) presented an innovative approach that leverages proximity measures between word embeddings. They argue that solutions based on NER techniques are insufficient to guarantee that no sensitive information gets overlooked, as search algorithms are never perfect. To counter this possibility, they propose the substitution of each token with a semantically proximate from the embedding space. This obfuscation strategy ensures that all sensitive information gets removed at the cost of a low readability. Even so, the authors report that little influence is observed on clinical machine learning tasks by taking the anonymized data as input (up to a 5% decrease in f1-score) since the contextualized token substitution allows for the preservation of data patterns that are useful in those tasks.

2.4 Discussion

While most of the discussed methods present extremely high performance considering the traditional metrics (f1-score and recall), their success remains mostly scientific, and thus the problem of automated text anonymization remains unsolved. This might be due to problems such as low generalization to external data and high production of false positives, which constitute huge barriers to real-world deployment and application. The Track 1A of the CEGS de-identification challenges (Stubbs et al., 2017) exposed these limitations by using test data collected from a different source than the train data. Although this is a fundamental measure to attain a reliable performance assessment, it is not usually adopted in most literary works around this topic (Yang et al., 2019). The state-of-the-art methods could not maintain their success rates in the mentioned task. The higher-performing solution presented an f1-score of approximately 80%, way below the above-90% scores reported in most literary works.

A recent paper by Mozes and Kleinberg (Mozes and Kleinberg, 2021) alerted for the necessity of reliable performance assessment strategies, putting forward an innovative method based on three criteria: i) technical evaluation through the commonly used evaluation metrics, ii) information loss estimation, and iii) de-anonymization tests. In addition, Pilán et al. (Pilán et al., 2022) also proposed a new set of metrics focused on privacy protection and utility preservation to evaluate text-anonymization solutions.

3 INCOGNITUS Framework

INCOGNITUS is a flexible and intuitive toolbox aimed at transparent and accountable automated text anonymization. This framework offers the possibility to employ different techniques while providing performance measures relating to the anonymization task itself and the resultant loss of information. All this content is displayed and accessible through an interactive, user-friendly interface, which can be seen in Figure 1. With these insights, the user can consciously select the adequate approach to anonymization, considering the specifications of each application context.

The flow of information circulating through INCOGNITUS is represented in the diagram of Figure 2. First, the user uploads or writes the content of a clinical note. The anonymization may then be performed through any of the available techniques. As the anonymization is completed, an ICD-10 classification model runs in the background, and its outputs are leveraged to estimate the ratio of information that got lost in the anonymization process. By the end of the calculation, this measure is displayed in the user interface, as well as the values of the standard performance metrics (recall, precision, and f1-score) associated with the technique selected. The user can then choose to (i) download the anonymized content or (ii) select another technique and repeat the process.

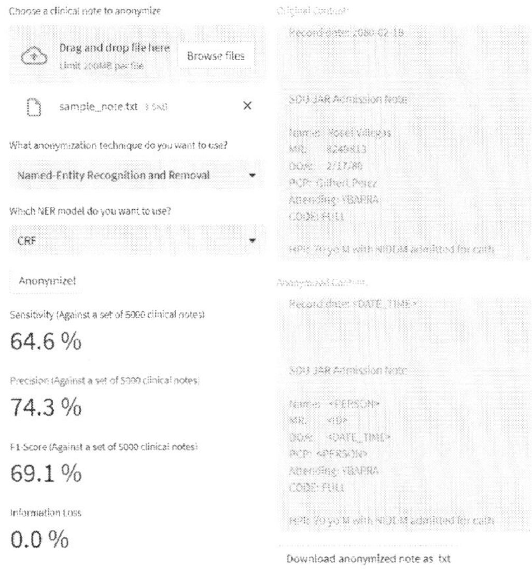

Figure 1: INCOGNITUS interface's outlook. In the depicted scenario, the user selected a NER approach based on a CRF model. On the right side of the page, the user can consult the contents of the original (top) and anonymized (bottom) versions of the uploaded sample note. A performance report is presented on the bottom left corner of the page, regarding the estimated values of recall, f1-score, precision, and Information Loss for the selected approach.

3.1 Components

Currently, INCOGNITUS comprises four NLP models that fulfill different purposes. First, there are two NER models for de-identification: a CRF classifier (Lafferty et al., 2001) and a pre-trained Spacy model (Montani et al., 2020). A Word2Vec embeddings model (Mikolov et al., 2013) is used to fuel the K-Nearest Embeddings Obfuscation technique (KNEO) based on the work of Abdalla et al. (Abdalla et al., 2020). And finally, a pre-trained BioBERT-based model (Lee et al., 2020) fine-tuned on the MIMIC III dataset (Johnson et al., 2016) is employed to infer the information loss over an ICD-10 classification problem.

3.1.1 Named Entity Recognition and Removal

CRF classifiers are standard in NLP and considered reliable benchmarks in de-identification tasks. On the other hand, Microsoft Presidio (Mendels and Balter) is a powerful tool designed to ensure that sensitive data, such as credit card numbers, names, locations, and financial data, is appropriately identified and anonymized in text. It comprises two modules: an analyzer based on NER techniques to

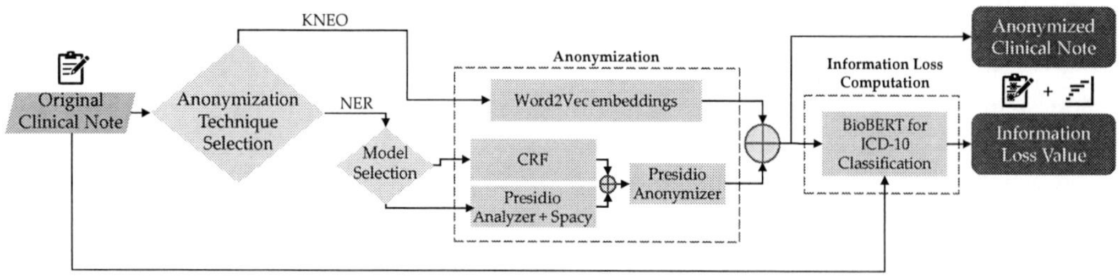

Figure 2: INCOGNITUS pipeline flowchart. After the clinical text content is uploaded to the platform, the user selects the technique and model desired to perform the anonymization task. The anonymization is performed, by employing the methodologies selected. Both the output of the anonymization phase and the original content is then fed into an ICD-10 classification model, which provides lists of the top ICD-10 code categories associated with each input. These results are leveraged to estimate the loss of information associated with the anonymization process. Finally, the user interface presents the anonymized content and the information loss estimate, along with other traditional metrics measured a priori. At the end of this process, the user may choose to download the anonymized version of the uploaded content or repeat the whole process using a different anonymization technique.

determine the sensitive entities and an anonymizer that takes the locations of those entities and removes or replaces them.

INCOGNITUS offers two possibilities for the recognition of sensitive entities: a CRF model trained upon the joint content of the training datasets of the i2b2 challenges (Uzuner et al., 2007; Stubbs et al., 2015), and an implementation of Presidio's analyzer module, receiving a Spacy model as input. Spacy is a Python package that provides accurate and up-to-date language models.

Once the identification of entities is performed through either of these NER-based techniques, the outputs are provided to the Presidio anonymizer, which returns a version of the original note where categorized tags replaced the identified entities.

3.1.2 K-Nearest Embeddings Obfuscation

A fundamental component of INCOGNITUS is its obfuscation module, which integrates a version of the algorithm proposed by Abdalla et al. (Abdalla et al., 2020). This approach is referred to as K-Nearest Embeddings Obfuscation (KNEO) in this work. It consists of randomly replacing each token composing a given text with one of the K semantically nearest ones within a space of embeddings. This methodology guarantees 100% recall in the anonymization task since no token is left unaltered.

3.1.3 Performance and Information Loss

Another innovative feature of this toolbox is the provision of a case-specific estimation of the information lost during the anonymization process, apart from the general performance metrics associated with each solution provided.

Before and after the anonymization of a clinical record, a pre-trained model (BioBERT fine-tuned on MIMIC III data (Lee et al., 2020; Johnson et al., 2016)) is used to identify the top N most frequent ICD-10 code categories (out of 157 possible) of both the original and anonymized versions of the same document. The value of Information Loss (IL) is inferred by dividing the number of classes simultaneously present in both prediction lists by the number N of top categories considered. Equation 1 presents the formalization of the proposed metric, where y_{orig} and y_{anon} represent the list of top N codes predicted in the original and anonymized versions of the same document, respectively. In INCOGNITUS, $N = 10$.

$$IL = (1 - \frac{\sum_{i=1}^{N}(y_{anon_i} \in y_{orig})}{N}) \times 100 \quad (1)$$

4 Experimental Setup

4.1 Datasets

Three distinct datasets were used to develop and evaluate the different anonymization strategies available at the INCOGNITUS platform.

MIMIC-III (Johnson et al., 2016) is an extensive, freely-available database comprising health-related data of over 40,000 patients who stayed in critical care units of the Beth Israel Deaconess Medical Center between 2001 and 2012. This dataset contains 1.2 million notes, including radiology reports, nursing notes, and discharge summaries.

The i2b2 project organized two challenges on automatically removing PHIs from medical records

(Uzuner et al., 2007; Stubbs et al., 2015). Both datasets released for the competitions are utilized in this research. The 2006 dataset contains 669 notes for training and 220 for testing, while the one used in 2014 counts 790 training samples and 514 testing samples.

4.2 Preprocessing

The original splits of both i2b2 datasets were maintained. As for the MIMIC III data, only discharge summaries were considered for this study, totaling 59,652 clinical notes, of which 5,000 were selected to test the different anonymization approaches. The remaining 54,652 were used to train the Word2Vec embeddings model employed in the KNEO approach.

Both i2b2 datasets contain fake PHI to simulate real, non-anonymized clinical records. The same is not valid for the MIMIC III notes, where all the sensitive information appears replaced by categorized entity tags. In order to re-establish a realistic clinical note structure, the Faker library for Python (Faraglia) was used to create fake entities according to each tag category.

4.3 NER Models

The first method developed was the CRF model. For this purpose, the following features were considered regarding each token and their immediate neighbors: POS tag, the last 2 and 3 constituting characters, whether it starts with a capital letter, whether it is a title, and whether it is a digit. This model was trained upon the train datasets of both i2b2 challenges, adding up to 1389 clinical notes.

For the second NER approach, Presidio Analyzer was used together with a language model from spacy, pre-trained on the OntoNotes 5 dataset (Ralph Weischedel, 2013), and reporting F1-score and recall values of 90% on the NER task. This solution was used as an off-the-shelf method; therefore, the language models were not re-trained upon any of the working train sets.

4.4 Word Embeddings

The training of embedding models is a complex task that requires extensive data. As such, the INCOGNITUS embeddings model was trained upon the subset of 54,652 discharge summaries retrieved exclusively from MIMIC III, following a Word2Vec strategy (Mikolov et al., 2013).

5 Results

To estimate the performance of the offered strategies in the anonymization task, they were tested against the working test sets. For each experiment, the f1-score regarding the binary task of classifying sensitive information was calculated. The mean IL associated with anonymizing each clinical note was also measured, based on Equation 1. The results of this experiment are displayed in Table 1.

		f1-score	**IL**
$i2b2_{2006}$	CRF	94.8	15.8 ± 11.4
	Presidio	73.0	21.6 ± 13.0
	KNEO	-	$59,9 \pm 21.3$
$i2b2_{2014}$	CRF	87.8	15.7 ± 12.4
	Presidio	64.6	21.3 ± 14.0
	KNEO	-	58.4 ± 21.1
$MIMIC$	CRF	69.1	21.3 ± 13.8
	Presidio	66.6	24.9 ± 14.6
	KNEO	-	63.4 ± 18.4

Table 1: Values of f1-score and mean $\pm$ standard deviation of the IL, attained by each of the anonymization methods offered by INCOGNITUS, in each test set.

By looking at the f1-score values in Table 1, it is clear that achieving high performance through fairly simple NER techniques is possible, as is evident by the results attained by the CRF model. These are in line with most reported values in the literature for similar tasks, when the data used for the test follows the same structure as the training data. Suppose one considers the results attained through the Presidio Analyzer instead, which uses a model trained upon the OntoNotes dataset. In that case, one can observe a clear drop in performance compared to that achieved with CRF. This might seem strange initially, considering that the configuration used by Presidio incorporates much more complex methods than those involved in training the CRF model. The fact that the NER models used by Presidio were not re-trained in any of the available clinical datasets might be the reason behind this. In fact, when the CRF model was tested against an external dataset (MIMIC III discharge notes subset), it presented a drop in performance of almost 20%, much closer to the values attained by presidio. These results are concerning because expecting access to notes for training in real application contexts is somewhat unrealistic. To have that, one would need access to content anonymized in a non-automated way or not anonymized at all, which defeats the purpose of these tools.

Furthermore, while f1-scores of 95% are high, these values can never comply with the GDPR definition of anonymization. Even if these rose to 100%, the underlying risk of existing particular identifiers not being considered during training is still a threat. In this regard, the traditional methods of automated anonymization (NER-based) cannot compete with the KNEO strategy, since the latter replaces every single token from the original text, guaranteeing no such occurrences. Since every original token is exchanged, the f1-score calculation becomes inappropriate for the KNEO methodology. On the one hand, by replacing every token, it is guaranteed that none of the original content gets overlooked, ensuring 100% recall. On the other hand, since the replacement of every original word is the fundamental ideology behind this method, the concept of false positives makes little sense. One could argue that every non-sensitive token replaced might be regarded as a false positive. Still, such an interpretation ignores the role of neighbor word embeddings in preserving the information encoded.

Even so, although KNEO outperforms both NER-based strategies in preventing sensitive information leaks, the quantity of relevant information lost in the process is undeniably higher than what is observed for the other methods. Looking at the information loss values, this tendency is clear: around 60% of the original content is lost when applying the KNEO strategy. This means that, on average, the obfuscator hides the information related to six of the ten codes identified in the original notes. This becomes even more concerning if we consider that the classification task used to compute the IL metric simplifies a much more complex one: identifying individual ICD10 codes. Therefore, applying this strategy before performing advanced text processing tasks, such as clinical note summarization, could be problematic. The rates of information lost for the NER-based strategies are much lower, although it is visible that some information also gets hidden (around 20%).

In sum, since no technique is flawless, it is fundamental to understand (i) the context of application and (ii) the pros and cons of applying each technique. INCOGNITUS answers to the second necessity by providing various solutions and estimating performance during anonymization. In this way, it allows the users to switch between strategies according to their needs and the characteristics of each method.

6 Conclusions

This paper introduced INCOGNITUS, a user-friendly platform to prompt conscious automated anonymization of clinical text. It provides two distinct NER-based methods and a recently proposed alternative that guarantees proper anonymization (100% recall) at the cost of information loss and low readability. Employing a pre-trained classifier of ICD-10 code categories, INCOGNITUS brings a new way of estimating the information lost during anonymization. This framework moves the research around clinical text anonymization forward, towards accountable strategies and fair performance assessments.

Acknowledgements

This article is a result of work conducted under two projects: "ConnectedHealth" (n.°46858), supported by the Competitiveness and Internationalisation Operational Programme, Portugal (POCI) and Lisbon Regional Operational Programme (LISBOA 2020), under the PORTUGAL 2020 Partnership Agreement, through the European Regional Development Fund (ERDF); and "CardioFollow.AI: An intelligent system to improve patients' safety and remote surveillance in follow-up for cardiothoracic surgery", and supported by national funds through 'FCT – Portuguese Foundation for Science and Technology, I.P.', with reference DSAIPA/AI/0094/2020.

References

Mohamed Abdalla, Moustafa Abdalla, Frank Rudzicz, and Graeme Hirst. 2020. Using word embeddings to improve the privacy of clinical notes. *Journal of the American Medical Informatics Association*, 27(6):901–907.

Eiji Aramaki, Takeshi Imai, Kengo Miyo, and Kazuhiko Ohe. 2006. Automatic deidentification by using sentence features and label consistency. In *i2b2 Workshop on Challenges in Natural Language Processing for Clinical Data*.

Azad Dehghan, Aleksandar Kovacevic, George Karystianis, John A. Keane, and Goran Nenadic. 2015. Combining knowledge- and data-driven methods for de-identification of clinical narratives. *Journal of Biomedical Informatics*, 58:S53–S59. Supplement: Proceedings of the 2014 i2b2/UTHealth

Shared-Tasks and Workshop on Challenges in Natural Language Processing for Clinical Data.

Franck Dernoncourt, Ji Young Lee, Ozlem Uzuner, and Peter Szolovits. 2016. De-identification of patient notes with recurrent neural networks. *Journal of the American Medical Informatics Association*, 24(3):596–606.

M. Douglass, Gari D. Clifford, A. Reisner, George B. Moody, and Mark Rg. 2004. Computer-assisted de-identification of free text in the mimic ii database. *Computers in Cardiology, 2004*, pages 341–344.

Daniele Faraglia. Faker. `https://github.com/joke2k/faker`.

Max Friedrich, Arne Köhn, Gregor Wiedemann, and Chris Biemann. 2019. Adversarial learning of privacy-preserving text representations for de-identification of medical records. In *Proceedings of the 57th Annual Meeting of the Association for Computational Linguistics*, pages 5829–5839, Florence, Italy. Association for Computational Linguistics.

James Gardner and Li Xiong. 2008. Hide: An integrated system for health information de-identification. In *2008 21st IEEE International Symposium on Computer-Based Medical Systems*, pages 254–259.

GDPR. 2018. General data protection regulation. Official website of the European Union.

Dilipkumar Gupta, Melissa I. Saul, and John R. Gilbertson. 2004. Evaluation of a deidentification (de-id) software engine to share pathology reports and clinical documents for research. *American journal of clinical pathology*, 121(2):176–86.

Alistair E. W. Johnson, Tom J. Pollard, Lu Shen, Li wei H. Lehman, Mengling Feng, Mohammad Mahdi Ghassemi, Benjamin Moody, Peter Szolovits, Leo Anthony Celi, and Roger G. Mark. 2016. Mimic-iii, a freely accessible critical care database. *Scientific Data*, 3.

John Lafferty, Andrew McCallum, and Fernando CN Pereira. 2001. Conditional random fields: Probabilistic models for segmenting and labeling sequence data.

Jinhyuk Lee, Wonjin Yoon, Sungdong Kim, Donghyeon Kim, Sunkyu Kim, Chan Ho So, and Jaewoo Kang. 2020. Biobert: a pre-trained biomedical language representation model for biomedical text mining. *Bioinformatics*, 36(4):1234 – 1240.

Zengjian Liu, Yangxin Chen, Buzhou Tang, Xiaolong Wang, Qingcai Chen, Haodi Li, Jingfeng Wang, Qiwen Deng, and Suisong Zhu. 2015. Automatic de-identification of electronic medical records using token-level and character-level conditional random fields. *Journal of Biomedical Informatics*, 58:S47–S52. Supplement: Proceedings of the 2014 i2b2/UTHealth Shared-Tasks and Workshop on Challenges in Natural Language Processing for Clinical Data.

Zengjian Liu, Buzhou Tang, Xiaolong Wang, and Qingcai Chen. 2017. De-identification of clinical notes via recurrent neural network and conditional random field. *Journal of Biomedical Informatics*, 75:S34–S42. Supplement: A Natural Language Processing Challenge for Clinical Records: Research Domains Criteria (RDoC) for Psychiatry.

Omri Mendels and Avishay Balter. Presidio: Context aware, pluggable and customizable data protection and de-identification sdk for text and images.

Tomas Mikolov, Kai Chen, Gregory S. Corrado, and Jeffrey Dean. 2013. Efficient estimation of word representations in vector space. In *International Conference on Learning Representations*.

Ines Montani, Matthew Honnibal, Matthew Honnibal, Sofie Van Landeghem, Adriane Boyd, Henning Peters, Maxim Samsonov, Jim Geovedi, Jim Regan, György Orosz, Paul O'Leary McCann, Søren Lind Kristiansen, Duygu Altinok, Roman, Leander Fiedler, Grégory Howard, Wannaphong Phatthiyaphaibun, Explosion Bot, Sam Bozek, Mark Amery, Yohei Tamura, Björn Böing, Pradeep Kumar Tippa, Leif Uwe Vogelsang, Ramanan Balakrishnan, Vadim Mazaev, GregDubbin, jeannefukumaru, Jens Dahl Møllerhøj, and Avadh Patel. 2020. explosion/spaCy: v3.0.0rc: Transformer-based pipelines, new training system, project templates, custom models, improved component API, type hints & lots more.

Maximilian Mozes and Bennett Kleinberg. 2021. No intruder, no validity: Evaluation criteria for privacy-preserving text anonymization.

Ildikó Pilán, Pierre Lison, Lilja Øvrelid, Anthi Papadopoulou, David Sánchez, and Montserrat Batet. 2022. The text anonymization benchmark (tab): A dedicated corpus and evaluation framework for text anonymization.

Mitchell Marcus Eduard Hovy Sameer Pradhan Lance Ramshaw Nianwen Xue Ann Taylor Jeff Kaufman Michelle Franchini Mohammed El-Bachouti Robert Belvin Ann Houston Ralph Weischedel, Martha Palmer. 2013. Ontonotes release 5. Philadelphia: Linguistic Data Consortium.

Patrick Ruch, Robert H. Baud, Anne-Marie Rassinoux, Pierrette Bouillon, and Gilbert Robert. 2000. Medical document anonymization with a semantic lexicon. *Proceedings. AMIA Symposium*, pages 729–33.

Amber Stubbs, Michele Filannino, and Özlem Uzuner. 2017. De-identification of psychiatric intake records: Overview of 2016 cegs n-grid shared tasks track 1. *Journal of Biomedical Informatics*, 75:S4–S18. Supplement: A Natural Language Processing Challenge for Clinical Records: Research Domains Criteria (RDoC) for Psychiatry.

Amber Stubbs, Christopher Kotfila, and Özlem Uzuner. 2015. Automated systems for the de-identification of longitudinal clinical narratives: Overview of 2014 i2b2/uthealth shared task track 1. *Journal of Biomedical Informatics*, 58:S11–S19. Supplement: Proceedings of the 2014 i2b2/UTHealth Shared-Tasks and Workshop on Challenges in Natural Language Processing for Clinical Data.

Latanya Sweeney. 1996. Replacing personally-identifying information in medical records, the scrub system. *Proceedings : a conference of the American Medical Informatics Association. AMIA Fall Symposium*, pages 333–7.

Sean M. Thomas, Burke W. Mamlin, Gunther Schadow, and Clement J. McDonald. 2002. A successful technique for removing names in pathology reports using an augmented search and replace method. *Proceedings. AMIA Symposium*, pages 777–81.

Özlem Uzuner, Yuan Luo, and Peter Szolovits. 2007. Evaluating the State-of-the-Art in Automatic De-identification. *Journal of the American Medical Informatics Association*, 14(5):550–563.

Ben Wellner, Matt Huyck, Scott Mardis, John Aberdeen, Alex Morgan, Leonid Peshkin, Alex Yeh, Janet Hitzeman, and Lynette Hirschman. 2007. Rapidly Retargetable Approaches to De-identification in Medical Records. *Journal of the American Medical Informatics Association*, 14(5):564–573.

Hui Yang and Jonathan M. Garibaldi. 2015. Automatic detection of protected health information from clinic narratives. *Journal of Biomedical Informatics*, 58:S30–S38. Supplement: Proceedings of the 2014 i2b2/UTHealth Shared-Tasks and Workshop on Challenges in Natural Language Processing for Clinical Data.

Xi Yang, Tianchen Lyu, Qian Li, Chih-Yin Lee, Jiang Bian, William R Hogan, and Yonghui Wu. 2019. A study of deep learning methods for de-identification of clinical notes in cross-institute settings. *BMC medical informatics and decision making*, 19(5):232.

CoTEVer: Chain of Thought Prompting Annotation Toolkit for Explanation Verification

Seungone Kim[1,2] **Sejune Joo**[1,2] **Yul Jang**[2] **Hyungjoo Chae**[2] **Jinyoung Yeo**[2]

KAIST AI[1] Yonsei University[2]
louisdebroglie@kaist.ac.kr
{sr7418,blaze,mapoout,jinyeo}@yonsei.ac.kr

Abstract

Chain-of-thought (CoT) prompting enables large language models (LLMs) to solve complex reasoning tasks by generating an explanation before the final prediction. Despite it's promising ability, a critical downside of CoT prompting is that the performance is greatly affected by the factuality of the generated explanation. To improve the correctness of the explanations, fine-tuning language models with explanation data is needed. However, there exists only a few datasets that can be used for such approaches, and no data collection tool for building them. Thus, we introduce **CoTEVer**, a tool-kit for annotating the factual correctness of generated explanations and collecting revision data of wrong explanations. Furthermore, we suggest several use cases where the data collected with **CoTEVer** can be utilized for enhancing the faithfulness of explanations. Our toolkit is publicly available at https://github.com/SeungoneKim/CoTEVer.

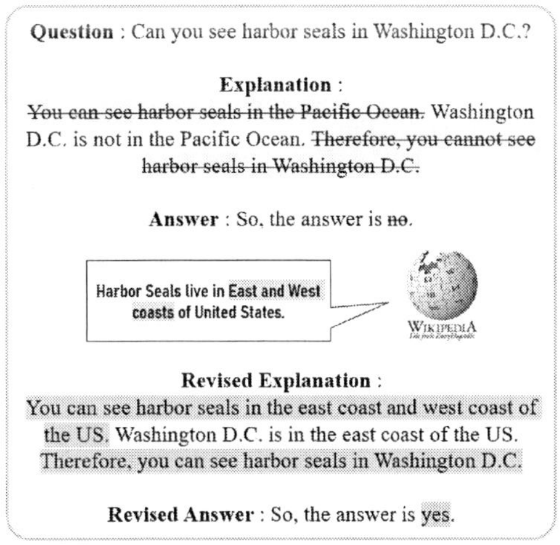

Figure 1: Example of Explanation Verification and Answer Verification of GPT-3's output. Explanation Verification requires additional knowledge which makes it hard for annotators to intuitively write a revised explanation and answer.

1 Introduction

Chain-of-thought prompting (Wei et al., 2022b) generates an explanation before the answer to elicit the reasoning capabilities of large language models. An intuitive way to interpret chain-of-thought prompting is that the process of '*generating an explanation*' is analogous to '*decomposing multiple step problems into smaller sub-problems*', which enables to solve complex reasoning tasks. Therefore, generating a plausible explanation is crucial to derive the correct answer (Wang et al., 2022).

To generate a plausible explanation, previous works have attempted to generate multiple explanations and use a task-specific verifier that would access the quality of the explanations and choose one of them (Cobbe et al., 2021; Shen et al., 2021; Thoppilan et al., 2022; Li et al., 2022). A more fundamental solution to this problem is fine-tuning the underlying language model with high-quality annotated explanations (Ling et al., 2017; Cobbe et al., 2021; Zelikman et al., 2022; Huang et al., 2022; Chung et al., 2022). However, fine-tuning would require to gather large amounts of annotated explanation data, which is impractical.

Collecting large amounts of annotated explanation data is difficult for several reasons. First, while existing works gather explanation data by asking annotators to manually write explanations using existing datasets (Wiegreffe and Marasovic, 2021), gathering human authored labels is often expensive in terms of time and cost (West et al., 2021). Second, writing a good quality explanation from scratch is difficult because it requires sufficient background knowledge (Geva et al., 2021a).

In this paper, we address the question: can we gather explanation data in a more *efficient* manner? Inspired by human-in-the-loop methods, we ask annotators to verify a machine generated explanation instead of manually writing them (Wallace et al., 2019; Weber et al., 2021; Du et al., 2022). In other

Proceedings of the 17th Conference of the European Chapter of the Association for Computational Linguistics System Demonstrations, pages 195–208

words, annotators get to check whether the underlying language model *hallucinate* (i.e., generate explanations that are factually incorrect) (Shuster et al., 2021; Lin et al., 2022a). To do this, we provide a set of supporting evidence documents retrieved from the web. Annotators access the quality of the given explanation, and provide a feedback score along with a better alternative.

As shown in Figure 1, let's consider gathering an explanation and answer for the question, 'Can you see harbor seals in Washington D.C.?'[1]. In this example, GPT-3 generates an explanation '1) You can see harbor seals in the Pacific Ocean. 2) Washington D.C. is not in the Pacific Ocean. 3) Therefore you cannot see harbor seals in Washington D.C.' and predicts 'No' as the answer. In this case, the first sentence of the explanation missed the point that harbor seals not only live in the west coast, but also in the east coast of the US. By providing the background knowledge 'Harbor Seals live in east and west coasts of United States', annotators could successfully revise the explanation.

To this end, we propose **CoTEVer** (Chain of Thought Prompting Annotation Toolkit for Explanation Verification), which is designed to *efficiently* gather explanation data, by 1) alleviating the role of annotators to verify instead of writing from scratch and 2) supplementing the required background knowledge via evidence documents. With the gathered explanation data, researchers could use them for CoT fine-tuning (Chung et al., 2022) or transform them into other knowledge intensive datasets.

2 Related Works

2.1 Tool-kits for Data Annotation

There exists a number of interactive tool-kits for annotating and verifying labels (Götze et al., 2022; Lin et al., 2022b; Friedrich et al., 2021; Bach et al., 2022; Thrush et al., 2022). For instance, Promptsource (Bach et al., 2022), is a framework designed to try out diverse set of prompts that can be used in in-context learning (Liu et al., 2021), or instruction tuning (Sanh et al., 2021; Wei et al., 2021; Min et al., 2021; Ye et al., 2022; Jang et al., 2023). Other human-in-the-loop annotation toolkits (Wallace et al., 2019; Weber et al., 2021; Du et al., 2022) provides functionality for annotators to verify the neural model's prediction instead of manually creating them. Compared to these toolkits, **CoTEver** provides additional features specifically designed for gathering explanation data such as retrieving evidence documents and supporting different Chain of Thought prompts.

2.2 Explanation Data

Chain of Thought Prompting is an in-context learning based methodology that generates an explanation before the answer. Instead of directly answering to the question, Wei et al. (2022b) conjectures that generating an explanation on-the-fly (explain-and-generate) enhances the reasoning capabilities of large language models. Wei et al. (2022a) argues that the ability to solve complex reasoning only appears when using large-scale language models, and defines this phenomenon as '*Emergent Abilities*'. **CoTEver** uses Chain of Thought Prompting to generate an explanation that could serve as a starting point for annotators to verify.

Recently, Chung et al. (2022) has shown that fine-tuning with explanation data unlocks the emergent abilities in large language models and achieves good performance not only at seen tasks (Ling et al., 2017; Cobbe et al., 2021; Zelikman et al., 2022), but also unseen tasks. The explanation data collected by **CoTEVer** could be used for CoT Fine-tuning since we collect a revised explanation.

2.3 Hallucination in Language Models

Hallucination is a phenomenon where a model generates a falsehood output that may contradict with the factual knowledge. Lin et al. (2022a) reported that as the model size increases, the less truthful they tend to be. Lewis et al. (2020) explains that models that rely only on parametric memory (e.g., GPT-3) are more likely to suffer from hallucination. When collecting explanation data from annotators, hallucination is a critical issue because the model may generate an unfaithful but very fluent output that is not easily distinguishable (Gao et al., 2022). To collect factually correct explanations from annotators, we provide supporting evidence documents using a search engine.

3 System Design and Workflow

In Figure 2, we present an illustration of the overall explanation verification process of **CoTEver** with 3 steps and show how the annotated explanations could be obtained effectively. We assume a scenario where a researcher requests a group of annotators to query a large language model and

[1]Example from StrategyQA (Geva et al., 2021b)

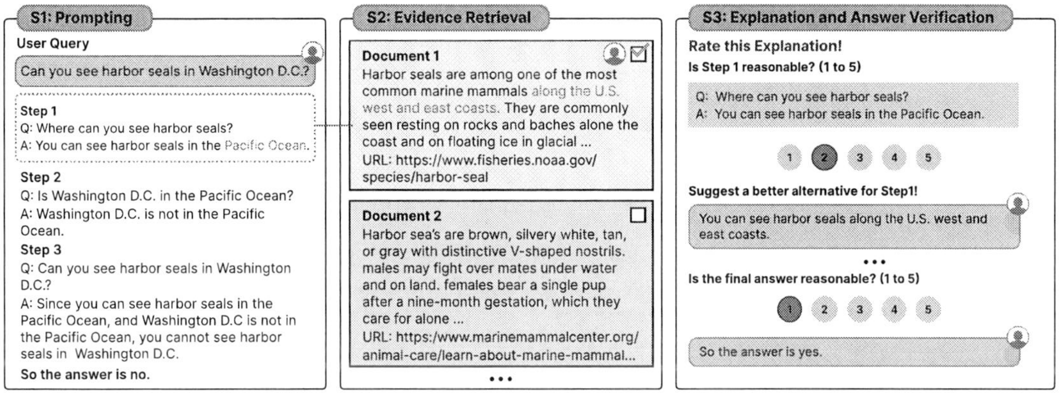

Figure 2: The overall illustration of **CoTEver**. An annotator asks a question to **CoTEver** and receives an explanation, supporting evidence documents, and a prediction. Then, the annotator's rating of the explanation (5 for most relevant), suggestions for a better explanation is stored in the Database which can be used for research purposes.

verify the explanations and predictions to collect explanation data. Although **CoTEVer** could support gathering free-form questions from annotators, it would either require 1) the researcher to make predefined few-shot demonstrations and retrieving them on-the-fly or 2) generating the explanation in a zero-shot setting (Kojima et al., 2022), which is both challenging to gather good quality explanations. Therefore, we define a scenario where a researcher assign users to query specific type of questions, such as 'Ask a question that could be answered with yes/no'(Answer Format) or 'Ask a question that is related to economics'(Domain). In this case, we could assume that the researcher prepared few-shot demonstrations beforehand.

3.1 S1: Prompting

Prompting Composition. We use GPT-3 (Brown et al., 2020) which is one of the standard large language models for CoT prompting (Wei et al., 2022b; Kojima et al., 2022). CoT prompting has limitations in that the generated explanations does not have a unified format, which makes verification harder. So, we adopt Self Ask (Press et al., 2022) as our prompting method to generate explanations composed of sub-questions and sub-answers. We provide more details of our prompt in Table 4.

Explanation Generation. As a first step, annotators are asked to explore our framework by querying a variety of different questions under the designated requirements. The user question is concatenated to the demonstrations as an input for the model. We then send a request via OpenAI API and get a response which contains the output of GPT-3. Upon obtaining the responses, we decompose the output into reasoning steps consist of a sub-question and sub-answer.

3.2 S2: Evidence Retrieval

Document Retrieval. To help the annotators' judgement, we provide documents that can be used as evidence to the generated explanation. For that, we retrieve documents using the sub-question directly as a query for document retrieval. Note that while Press et al. (2022) use the sub-questions to retrieve and answer to the question, we instead use them to retrieve and help annotators verify the explanations. In order to retrieve documents that are not outdated from the Web database, we use Google Search API [2]. We use the top-10 documents as candidates for reranking.

Document Reranking. We first split the retrieved documents into smaller chunks of maximum 512 tokens, the maximum number of input tokens acceptable in our reranking module. To provide reliable evidence documents to the annotators, we rerank the documents candidates and choose the order to be displayed on the user interface. We obtain the embeddings of the query and the supporting document candidates using Sentence-T5 (Ni et al., 2021), a state-of-the-art sentence embedding model trained to capture the semantic textual similarity between two input sequences. We then rank the retrieved documents with a cosine similarity score between the document and query embedding.

[2] https://pypi.org/project/google-api-python-client/

Error Type	Example	
	Do all crustaceans live in the ocean?	
Insufficient Knowledge 18%	Q#1: What are crustaceans? A#1: Crustaceans are a group of animals that include crabs, lobsters, and shrimp. Q#2: Where do crabs live? A#2: Crabs live in the ocean. Q#3: Where do lobsters live? A#3: Lobsters live in the ocean. Q#4: Where do shrimp live? A#4: Shrimp live in the ocean. Q#5: Do all crustaceans live in the ocean? A#5: Since crabs, lobsters, and shrimp live in the ocean, all crustaceans live in the ocean.	Crabs can be found in all oceans and in freshwater. Some crabs live on land, sometimes several miles from water. Species such as the fiddler crab live in burrows in the sand or mud, where they stay during winter and high tides. Shrimp occur in all oceans—in shallow and deep water—and in freshwater lakes and streams.
	Could a single bitcoin ever cover cost of a Volkswagen Jetta?	
Out of Date 22%	Q#1: How much is a single bitcoin? A#1: A single bitcoin is about $6,000. Q#2: How much is a Volkswagen Jetta? A#2: A Volkswagen Jetta is about $18,645. Q#3: Could a single bitcoin ever cover cost of a Volkswagen Jetta? A#3: Since a single bitcoin is about $ 6,000, and a Volkswagen Jetta is about $ 18,645, and $ 6,000 is smaller than $ 18,645, single bitcoin could not cover the cost of a Volkswagen Jetta.	Bitcoin's price today is $ 21,282.48, with a 24-hour trading volume of $ 37.84 B.
	Can a lifeboat rescue people in the Hooke Sea?	
Wrong Fact 43%	Q#1: What is the Hooke Sea? A#1: The Hooke Sea is a sea in Antarctica. Q#2: Is the Hooke Sea a dangerous place? A#2: The Hooke Sea is a dangerous place because it is a sea in Antarctica. Q#3: What is a lifeboat? A#3: A lifeboat is a boat designed for rescuing people in danger. Q#4: Can a lifeboat rescue people in the Hooke Sea? A#4: Since the Hooke Sea is a dangerous place in Antarctica, and a lifeboat is a boat designed for rescuing people in danger, lifeboat can rescue people in the Hooke Sea.	Hooke Crater is an impact crater in the Argyre quadrangle on Mars at 45.2°S and 44.4°W and is 139.0 km in diameter. It was named after British physicist-astronomer Robert Hooke.[1]

Table 1: Examples of frequent error types within explanations. The left side is the original explanation generated by a language model, and the right side is the retrieved evidence document. The evidence documents could provide the required knowledge when revising the original explanation.

3.3 S3: Explanation and Answer Verification

Explanation verification. In light of the provided evidence documents, annotators could easily check the correctness of the given explanation and give a 1-5 star Likert scale rating for each step in the explanation. In cases where the explanation needs to be revised, annotators can submit a better alternative. Our main intuition is that compared to writing a new explanation from scratch, revising an explanation with the evidence documents is much more easier for the annotators. Also, it is more likely that the revised explanation would be factually correct because the evidence documents would ground the required knowledge during annotation. The rating data is further used to determine the quality of a given explanation, which we further explain in Section 5

During the verification process, the annotators also label which evidence document is used as an evidence. For example, in Step 2 of Figure 2, the annotator put a check mark on the document that contains the information about the habitat of harbor seals which contradicts to the sub-answer in the first step, "*You can see harbor seals in the Pacific Ocean.*". We further explain how this data could be utilized in Section 5.

Answer verification. Lastly, annotators are asked to verify the correctness of the model's final prediction. Since large language models tend to output incorrect conclusions when the explanation is factually mistaken (Wang et al., 2022), it is very likely that the answer would be wrong when the original explanation got a low score in S3.

4 Analysis of Explanation Data

In this section, we analyze what error cases are abundant within an explanation and show how they can be revised using evidence documents retrieved by **CoTEVer**. As mentioned in Section 3.1, we adopt a Self-Ask style prompt and use TEXT-DAVINCI-002 (Ouyang et al., 2022) to generate a corresponding explanation and answer for the train set of StrategyQA (Geva et al., 2021b). Then, we sample 300 instances where the prediction is incorrect, ask annotators to classify the error type and revise the explanation using **CoTEVer**.

While we analyze the error types of explanations using human evaluation, automatic evaluation metrics proposed to measure the quality of a given explanation (Golovneva et al., 2022; Chen et al., 2022) is another promising direction, and we leave for future work. Also, we provide more detail of the human evaluation experiment process in Appendix B. Table 1 shows three frequently observed errors types, **Insufficient Knowledge**, **Out of Date** and **Wrong Fact** along with the corresponding percentage among the error cases (18%, 22%, 43% respectively).

Insufficient Knowledge. It is well known that language models mainly learn from high-frequency patterns and largely fail when tested on low resource tasks such as few-shot learning (Tänzer et al., 2021). Such behavior can be seen in the first example of Table 1. In general, it may be correct that crabs, lobsters and shrimp live in the oceans. However, the important point of the question is whether *all* crustaceans live in the ocean, making the generated explanation *insufficient*. The knowledge needed in such situation is included in the evidence documents, where it indicates that crabs and shrimp also live in freshwater.

Out of Date. The static nature of the text data that large language models are trained on makes it difficult to cope with rapidly changing real world situations (Jang et al., 2021). For instance, in the second example of Table 1, bitcoin is a highly volatile asset that has gone up significantly in the past few years. According to the retrieved evidence document, it is no longer \$6000 but actually more than \$20k which exceeds the price of a Volkswagen Jetta. These types of updates need to be done frequently through retrieval of up-to-date documents.

Wrong Fact. As shown in the third example of Table 1, large language models also generate false facts within the explanation. In this case, the first step within the explanation quoting, "The Hooke Sea is a sea in Antarctica." is not true. Because the Hooke Sea is not in Antarctica but on Mars, it isn't actually a sea, eliminating the lifeboat scenario. This fact can also be found in the retrieved document.

5 How to Utilize Explanation Data gathered with CoTEVer

In this section, we suggest three promising directions on how the explanation data collected with **CoTEVer** can be utilized. We define $\mathcal{E}$ and $\mathcal{A}$ to be the original explanation and answer generated by a language model, respectively. Similarly, the revised explanation and answer from the annotator can be defined as $\mathcal{E}^*$ and $\mathcal{A}^*$. Explanations consist of pairs of sub-questions sq_i and sub-answers sa_i which brings the following definition:

- Explanation $\mathcal{E}$ with N pairs of $e_i = (sq_i, sa_i)$ is $\mathcal{E} = \{e_i\}_{i=1}^{N}$
- A revised explanation $\mathcal{E}^*$ with N^* pairs of $e^* = (sq^*{}_i, sa^*{}_i)$ is $\mathcal{E}^* = \{e_i^*\}_{i=1}^{N^*}$

Now for an explanation, sets of documents $\mathcal{D}_i$ are retrieved for each pair e_i, based on sq_i. Within $\mathcal{D}_i$, we define the top-k^{th} document aligned by the re-ranking module as $\mathcal{D}_i^k$. Finally, $\tilde{\mathcal{D}}_i$ is defined as the evidence document chosen by the annotator upon the set $\mathcal{D}_i$.

5.1 Chain of Thought Fine-tuning

Chung et al. (2022) indicated that fine-tuning language models to generate an explanation is effective to improve reasoning abilities of language models. We suggest training a model using the revised explanation collected by **CoTEVer** instead of using manually collected explanations. The objective could be formalized such as:

$$\mathcal{L}_{e^*} = -\sum_{i=1}^{|\mathcal{E}^*|}\sum_{j=1}^{|e_i^*|} \log P(e_{i,j}^*|e_{<i}^*, e_{i,<j}^*) \quad (1)$$

$$\mathcal{L}_{a^*} = -\sum_{i=1}^{|\mathcal{A}^*|} \log P(a_i^*|a_{<i}, \mathcal{E}^*) \quad (2)$$

where the ith explanation e^* consists of $|e_i^*|$ tokens. Note that in CoT Fine-tuning, the explanation is first generated by conditioning on the question, and then the answer is generated by conditioning on the question and explanation (explain-and-generate).

Unlikelihood Training In addition to using the revised explanation to teach language models to generate an explanation coupled with the final prediction, we also suggest using the incorrect explanations for knowledge unlearning via unlikelihood training (Welleck et al., 2019). Prior work proposed that simply negating the original cross entropy loss is effective in knowledge unlearning (Jang et al., 2022). In the case of explanation data, models can forget incorrect explanations and learn the correct explanations instead. Using the rating score provided by the annotators, we could define how much room of improvement there was between the original explanation and the revised explanation. We could use 'original explanations with relatively low scores' among the collected explanations as hard negatives. Then, the objective could be formalized such as:

$$\mathcal{L}_{e} = -\sum_{i=1}^{|\mathcal{E}|}\sum_{j=1}^{|e_i|} \log(1 - P(e_{i,j}|e_{<i}, e_{i,<j})) \quad (3)$$

Future work could consider analyzing whether forgetting the incorrect explanation before learning the correct explanation is more effective, or vice versa. Also, a more sophisticated definition of how to determine 'incorrect explanations' and 'correct explanations' using the user's feedback score could be explored.

5.2 Knowledge-Intensive Tasks

As we show in Table 1, large language models tend to generate unfaithful explanations, which is especially problematic when solving knowledge-intensive tasks (Lewis et al., 2020). We suggest two approaches that could resolve this issue by building datasets for fact verification and information retrieval from the revised explanations and the evidence documents.

Fact Verification. Following the task definition of FEVER (Thorne et al., 2018), we define labels for each pair of sub-answer sa_i and a evidence document from $\mathcal{D}_i$ as either SUPPORTED, REFUTED, and NOTENOUGHINFO.

Since the annotators use $\tilde{\mathcal{D}}_i$ as evidence when finding contradictions, sa_i rated as 1 and $\tilde{\mathcal{D}}_i$ can be labeled as REFUTED. Similarly, the pair of sa_i^*[3] and document $\tilde{\mathcal{D}}_i$ can be labeled as SUPPORTED. As low-ranked documents $\mathcal{D}_i^{10}$ from our re-ranking module are less likely to contain information that supports nor refutes the explanations, we use them as examples for NOTENOUGHINFO. The fact verification data obtained with **CoTEVer** could be used to to train a factual error correction model (Thorne and Vlachos, 2021).

Information Retrieval. Karpukhin et al. (2020) explains that using negative examples helps substantially, whilst they mitigated the difficulty in obtaining them via setting in-batch negatives. **CoTEVer** is effective to acquire hard negative as well as positive pairs using the sub-questions sq_i and a evidence document from $\mathcal{D}_i$.

Since the annotators find $\tilde{\mathcal{D}}_i$ to contain the most helpful information when revising sa_i rated as 1 to sa_i^*, $\tilde{\mathcal{D}}_i$ would form a positive relation with sq_i. Meanwhile, $\mathcal{D}_i^{10}$, which was ranked low by our re-ranking module would serve as a hard negative for sq_i. The information retrieval data obtained with **CoTEVer** could be used to train a enhanced dense embedding model (Gao et al., 2021; Chuang et al., 2022).

6 Conclusion

In this work, we introduce **CoTEver**, an interactive annotation framework designed to verify unfaithful outputs and gather truthful explanation data from annotators. To reduce the cost of manually

[3] sa_i^* where the original sa_i was rated as 1, which is the lowest score.

searching for evidence while verifying an explanation, we provide supporting evidence documents via a search engine. Next, we analyze some of the abundant reasons where large language models generated incorrect explanations. Also, we suggest three directions on how explanation data gathered with **CoTEVer** can be utilized. We hope **CoTEVer** will contribute to gather high quality explanation data used for future research.

Acknowledgements

We thank Minkyeong Moon for helping make the demonstration video; Sangwon Park, Sehwan Jeon, Imsung Yu, and Donghwan Park for helping implement the frontend and backend of CoTEVer; Seonghyeon Ye, Hoyeon Chang, Joel Jang, Yongho Song, and anonymous reviewers for helpful feedback. This work was partly supported by Institute of Information & communications Technology Planning & Evaluation (IITP) grant funded by the Korea government(MSIT) (No. 2020-0-01361, Artificial Intelligence Graduate School Program (Yonsei University)), (No.2021-0-02068, Artificial Intelligence Innovation Hub), and (No. 2022-0-00077, AI Technology Development for Commonsense Extraction, Reasoning, and Inference from Heterogeneous Data). Jinyoung Yeo is the corresponding author.

References

Stephen H Bach, Victor Sanh, Zheng-Xin Yong, Albert Webson, Colin Raffel, Nihal V Nayak, Abheesht Sharma, Taewoon Kim, M Saiful Bari, Thibault Fevry, et al. 2022. Promptsource: An integrated development environment and repository for natural language prompts. *arXiv preprint arXiv:2202.01279*.

Tom Brown, Benjamin Mann, Nick Ryder, Melanie Subbiah, Jared D Kaplan, Prafulla Dhariwal, Arvind Neelakantan, Pranav Shyam, Girish Sastry, Amanda Askell, et al. 2020. Language models are few-shot learners. *Advances in neural information processing systems*, 33:1877–1901.

Hanjie Chen, Faeze Brahman, Xiang Ren, Yangfeng Ji, Yejin Choi, and Swabha Swayamdipta. 2022. Rev: Information-theoretic evaluation of free-text rationales. *arXiv preprint arXiv:2210.04982*.

Yung-Sung Chuang, Rumen Dangovski, Hongyin Luo, Yang Zhang, Shiyu Chang, Marin Soljačić, Shang-Wen Li, Wen-tau Yih, Yoon Kim, and James Glass. 2022. Diffcse: Difference-based contrastive learning for sentence embeddings. *arXiv preprint arXiv:2204.10298*.

Hyung Won Chung, Le Hou, Shayne Longpre, Barret Zoph, Yi Tay, William Fedus, Eric Li, Xuezhi Wang, Mostafa Dehghani, Siddhartha Brahma, et al. 2022. Scaling instruction-finetuned language models. *arXiv preprint arXiv:2210.11416*.

Karl Cobbe, Vineet Kosaraju, Mohammad Bavarian, Jacob Hilton, Reiichiro Nakano, Christopher Hesse, and John Schulman. 2021. Training verifiers to solve math word problems. *arXiv preprint arXiv:2110.14168*.

Wanyu Du, Zae Myung Kim, Vipul Raheja, Dhruv Kumar, and Dongyeop Kang. 2022. Read, revise, repeat: A system demonstration for human-in-the-loop iterative text revision. In *Proceedings of the First Workshop on Intelligent and Interactive Writing Assistants (In2Writing 2022)*, pages 96–108.

Niklas Friedrich, Kiril Gashteovski, Mingying Yu, Bhushan Kotnis, Carolin Lawrence, Mathias Niepert, and Goran Glavaš. 2021. Annie: An annotation platform for constructing complete open information extraction benchmark. *arXiv preprint arXiv:2109.07464*.

Luyu Gao, Zhuyun Dai, Panupong Pasupat, Anthony Chen, Arun Tejasvi Chaganty, Yicheng Fan, Vincent Y Zhao, Ni Lao, Hongrae Lee, Da-Cheng Juan, et al. 2022. Attributed text generation via post-hoc research and revision. *arXiv preprint arXiv:2210.08726*.

Tianyu Gao, Xingcheng Yao, and Danqi Chen. 2021. Simcse: Simple contrastive learning of sentence embeddings. In *Proceedings of the 2021 Conference on Empirical Methods in Natural Language Processing*, pages 6894–6910.

Mor Geva, Daniel Khashabi, Elad Segal, Tushar Khot, Dan Roth, and Jonathan Berant. 2021a. Did aristotle use a laptop? a question answering benchmark with implicit reasoning strategies. *Transactions of the Association for Computational Linguistics*, 9:346–361.

Mor Geva, Daniel Khashabi, Elad Segal, Tushar Khot, Dan Roth, and Jonathan Berant. 2021b. Did aristotle use a laptop? a question answering benchmark with implicit reasoning strategies. *Transactions of the Association for Computational Linguistics*, 9:346–361.

Olga Golovneva, Moya Chen, Spencer Poff, Martin Corredor, Luke Zettlemoyer, Maryam Fazel-Zarandi, and Asli Celikyilmaz. 2022. Roscoe: A suite of metrics for scoring step-by-step reasoning. *arXiv preprint arXiv:2212.07919*.

Jana Götze, Maike Paetzel-Prüsmann, Wencke Liermann, Tim Diekmann, and David Schlangen. 2022. The slurk interaction server framework: Better data for better dialog models. *arXiv preprint arXiv:2202.01155*.

Jiaxin Huang, Shixiang Shane Gu, Le Hou, Yuexin Wu, Xuezhi Wang, Hongkun Yu, and Jiawei Han. 2022. Large language models can self-improve. *arXiv preprint arXiv:2210.11610*.

Joel Jang, Seungone Kim, Seonghyeon Ye, Doyoung Kim, Lajanugen Logeswaran, Moontae Lee, Kyungjae Lee, and Minjoon Seo. 2023. Exploring the benefits of training expert language models over instruction tuning. *arXiv preprint arXiv:2302.03202*.

Joel Jang, Seonghyeon Ye, Sohee Yang, Joongbo Shin, Janghoon Han, Gyeonghun Kim, Stanley Jungkyu Choi, and Minjoon Seo. 2021. Towards continual knowledge learning of language models. *arXiv preprint arXiv:2110.03215*.

Joel Jang, Dongkeun Yoon, Sohee Yang, Sungmin Cha, Moontae Lee, Lajanugen Logeswaran, and Minjoon Seo. 2022. Knowledge unlearning for mitigating privacy risks in language models. *arXiv preprint arXiv:2210.01504*.

Vladimir Karpukhin, Barlas Oguz, Sewon Min, Patrick Lewis, Ledell Wu, Sergey Edunov, Danqi Chen, and Wen-tau Yih. 2020. Dense passage retrieval for open-domain question answering. In *Proceedings of the 2020 Conference on Empirical Methods in Natural Language Processing (EMNLP)*, pages 6769–6781.

Takeshi Kojima, Shixiang Shane Gu, Machel Reid, Yutaka Matsuo, and Yusuke Iwasawa. 2022. Large language models are zero-shot reasoners. *arXiv preprint arXiv:2205.11916*.

Patrick Lewis, Ethan Perez, Aleksandra Piktus, Fabio Petroni, Vladimir Karpukhin, Naman Goyal, Heinrich Küttler, Mike Lewis, Wen-tau Yih, Tim Rocktäschel, et al. 2020. Retrieval-augmented generation for knowledge-intensive nlp tasks. *Advances in Neural Information Processing Systems*, 33:9459–9474.

Yifei Li, Zeqi Lin, Shizhuo Zhang, Qiang Fu, Bei Chen, Jian-Guang Lou, and Weizhu Chen. 2022. On the advance of making language models better reasoners. *arXiv preprint arXiv:2206.02336*.

Stephanie Lin, Jacob Hilton, and Owain Evans. 2022a. Truthfulqa: Measuring how models mimic human falsehoods. In *Proceedings of the 60th Annual Meeting of the Association for Computational Linguistics (Volume 1: Long Papers)*, pages 3214–3252.

Yupian Lin, Tong Ruan, Ming Liang, Tingting Cai, Wen Du, and Yi Wang. 2022b. Dotat: A domain-oriented text annotation tool. In *Proceedings of the 60th Annual Meeting of the Association for Computational Linguistics: System Demonstrations*, pages 1–8.

Wang Ling, Dani Yogatama, Chris Dyer, and Phil Blunsom. 2017. Program induction by rationale generation: Learning to solve and explain algebraic word problems. In *Proceedings of the 55th Annual Meeting of the Association for Computational Linguistics (Volume 1: Long Papers)*, pages 158–167.

Jiachang Liu, Dinghan Shen, Yizhe Zhang, Bill Dolan, Lawrence Carin, and Weizhu Chen. 2021. What makes good in-context examples for gpt-3? *arXiv preprint arXiv:2101.06804*.

Sewon Min, Mike Lewis, Luke Zettlemoyer, and Hannaneh Hajishirzi. 2021. Metaicl: Learning to learn in context. *arXiv preprint arXiv:2110.15943*.

Jianmo Ni, Gustavo Hernández Ábrego, Noah Constant, Ji Ma, Keith B Hall, Daniel Cer, and Yinfei Yang. 2021. Sentence-t5: Scalable sentence encoders from pre-trained text-to-text models. *arXiv preprint arXiv:2108.08877*.

Long Ouyang, Jeff Wu, Xu Jiang, Diogo Almeida, Carroll L Wainwright, Pamela Mishkin, Chong Zhang, Sandhini Agarwal, Katarina Slama, Alex Ray, et al. 2022. Training language models to follow instructions with human feedback. *arXiv preprint arXiv:2203.02155*.

Ofir Press, Muru Zhang, Sewon Min, Ludwig Schmidt, Noah A Smith, and Mike Lewis. 2022. Measuring and narrowing the compositionality gap in language models. *arXiv preprint arXiv:2210.03350*.

Victor Sanh, Albert Webson, Colin Raffel, Stephen H Bach, Lintang Sutawika, Zaid Alyafeai, Antoine Chaffin, Arnaud Stiegler, Teven Le Scao, Arun Raja, et al. 2021. Multitask prompted training enables zero-shot task generalization. *arXiv preprint arXiv:2110.08207*.

Jianhao Shen, Yichun Yin, Lin Li, Lifeng Shang, Xin Jiang, Ming Zhang, and Qun Liu. 2021. Generate & rank: A multi-task framework for math word problems. *arXiv preprint arXiv:2109.03034*.

Kurt Shuster, Spencer Poff, Moya Chen, Douwe Kiela, and Jason Weston. 2021. Retrieval augmentation reduces hallucination in conversation. In *Findings of the Association for Computational Linguistics: EMNLP 2021*, pages 3784–3803.

Aarohi Srivastava, Abhinav Rastogi, Abhishek Rao, Abu Awal Md Shoeb, Abubakar Abid, Adam Fisch, Adam R Brown, Adam Santoro, Aditya Gupta, Adrià Garriga-Alonso, et al. 2022. Beyond the imitation game: Quantifying and extrapolating the capabilities of language models. *arXiv preprint arXiv:2206.04615*.

Michael Tänzer, Sebastian Ruder, and Marek Rei. 2021. Bert memorisation and pitfalls in low-resource scenarios. *arXiv preprint arXiv:2105.00828*.

Romal Thoppilan, Daniel De Freitas, Jamie Hall, Noam Shazeer, Apoorv Kulshreshtha, Heng-Tze Cheng, Alicia Jin, Taylor Bos, Leslie Baker, Yu Du, et al. 2022. Lamda: Language models for dialog applications. *arXiv preprint arXiv:2201.08239*.

James Thorne and Andreas Vlachos. 2021. Evidence-based factual error correction. In *Proceedings of the*

59th Annual Meeting of the Association for Computational Linguistics and the 11th International Joint Conference on Natural Language Processing (Volume 1: Long Papers)*, pages 3298–3309.

James Thorne, Andreas Vlachos, Christos Christodoulopoulos, and Arpit Mittal. 2018. Fever: a large-scale dataset for fact extraction and verification. In *Proceedings of the 2018 Conference of the North American Chapter of the Association for Computational Linguistics: Human Language Technologies, Volume 1 (Long Papers)*, pages 809–819.

Tristan Thrush, Kushal Tirumala, Anmol Gupta, Max Bartolo, Pedro Rodriguez, Tariq Kane, William Gaviria Rojas, Peter Mattson, Adina Williams, and Douwe Kiela. 2022. Dynatask: A framework for creating dynamic ai benchmark tasks. *arXiv preprint arXiv:2204.01906*.

Eric Wallace, Pedro Rodriguez, Shi Feng, Ikuya Yamada, and Jordan Boyd-Graber. 2019. Trick me if you can: Human-in-the-loop generation of adversarial examples for question answering. *Transactions of the Association for Computational Linguistics*, 7:387–401.

Xuezhi Wang, Jason Wei, Dale Schuurmans, Quoc Le, Ed Chi, and Denny Zhou. 2022. Self-consistency improves chain of thought reasoning in language models. *arXiv preprint arXiv:2203.11171*.

Verena Weber, Enrico Piovano, and Melanie Bradford. 2021. It is better to verify: Semi-supervised learning with a human in the loop for large-scale nlu models. In *Proceedings of the Second Workshop on Data Science with Human in the Loop: Language Advances*, pages 8–15.

Jason Wei, Maarten Bosma, Vincent Y Zhao, Kelvin Guu, Adams Wei Yu, Brian Lester, Nan Du, Andrew M Dai, and Quoc V Le. 2021. Finetuned language models are zero-shot learners. *arXiv preprint arXiv:2109.01652*.

Jason Wei, Yi Tay, Rishi Bommasani, Colin Raffel, Barret Zoph, Sebastian Borgeaud, Dani Yogatama, Maarten Bosma, Denny Zhou, Donald Metzler, et al. 2022a. Emergent abilities of large language models. *arXiv preprint arXiv:2206.07682*.

Jason Wei, Xuezhi Wang, Dale Schuurmans, Maarten Bosma, Ed Chi, Quoc Le, and Denny Zhou. 2022b. Chain of thought prompting elicits reasoning in large language models. *arXiv preprint arXiv:2201.11903*.

Sean Welleck, Ilia Kulikov, Stephen Roller, Emily Dinan, Kyunghyun Cho, and Jason Weston. 2019. Neural text generation with unlikelihood training. *arXiv preprint arXiv:1908.04319*.

Peter West, Chandra Bhagavatula, Jack Hessel, Jena D Hwang, Liwei Jiang, Ronan Le Bras, Ximing Lu, Sean Welleck, and Yejin Choi. 2021. Symbolic knowledge distillation: from general language models to commonsense models. *arXiv preprint arXiv:2110.07178*.

Sarah Wiegreffe and Ana Marasovic. 2021. Teach me to explain: A review of datasets for explainable natural language processing. In *Thirty-fifth Conference on Neural Information Processing Systems Datasets and Benchmarks Track (Round 1)*.

Seonghyeon Ye, Doyoung Kim, Joel Jang, Joongbo Shin, and Minjoon Seo. 2022. Guess the instruction! making language models stronger zero-shot learners. *arXiv preprint arXiv:2210.02969*.

Eric Zelikman, Yuhuai Wu, and Noah D Goodman. 2022. Star: Bootstrapping reasoning with reasoning. *arXiv preprint arXiv:2203.14465*.

A Link to Video & Code

The link to our video and code is as follows:

1. **Demonstration Video**: Link
2. **Official Code**: Link

B Experiment Details for Human Evaluation

Following Wei et al. (2022b), we use the open-domain setting (question-only set) of StrategyQA (Geva et al., 2021a) from Srivastava et al. (2022). We use TEXT-DAVINCI-002 to generate explanations. We set the temperature as 0.

The 6-shot prompt we used are shown in Table 4. Our prompt are divided into sub-questions and sub-answers where the sub-questions are used as a query for retrieving the evidence documents.

strategyQA	
CoT (Wei et al., 2022b)	CoTEVer (Ours)
65.4	70.52

Table 2: Few-shot Prompting accuracy on StrategyQA(question-only set). Our prompt consists of sub-questions and sub-answers.

Table 2 shows the performance when using our designed prompt. Although our purpose of consisting prompts with sub-questions was for evidence retrieval, Self-Ask (Press et al., 2022) style prompts achieves better performance compared to the prompts used in Wei et al. (2022b). Also, these results support the fact that the incorrect explanations(29.18%) were not generated due to the quality of our prompt.

To analyze the error types, we sample 300 incorrect instances since the explanation is likely to be wrong when the prediction is incorrect (Wang et al., 2022). We ask 20 annotators with background in deep learning and proficient English skills to 1)classify the error type and 2)revise the explanation using **CoTEVer**. While the error types introduced in Table 1 (total 83%) could be revised based on the supporting evidence documents, 17% were error types were GPT-3 didn't generate a final prediction by keep repeating itself, or error types where the knowledge was all correct, but the reasoning was incorrect. In this case, retrieving evidence documents does not help during explanation verification.

C Limitations

The following are the limitations of **CoTEVer**.

Dependency on Prompt Design. While we experimented with prompts from StrategyQA, where only yes/no questions are given, annotators could type in any form of questions such as multiple choice questions or 'why' style questions. In this case, the prompts used to query a large language model should be changed. Therefore, we provide functionality where the researcher using **CoTEVer** could change the prompt. To prevent unexpected behavior of large language models, it is recommended to instruct annotators what types of questions they should ask. Also beside output format, large language models are also sensitive to the domain of the question. For example, when annotators ask questions requiring financial of legal domain knowledge, the prompts we provided might not perform well. In this case, researchers should change the prompts to their needs.

Prevention on Usage for Unethical Use Cases. Large language models often tend to generate toxic outputs. This is a critical issue when annotators use our framework. Our annotation toolkit is built on top of the Open AI API, where there has been various attempts to mitigate the toxic behavior of GPT-3. For instance, their TEXT-DAVINCI-002 version uses reinforcement learning to align towards non-toxic language.

Cases when Explanation is wrong due to Incorrect Reasoning. While **CoTEVer** could supplement insufficient knowledge for annotators, it couldn't tell which step within the explanation contains incorrect reasoning.

<table>
<tr><th>Error Type</th><th colspan="2">Example</th></tr>
<tr><td rowspan="2">Incomplete Answer</td><td colspan="2">Is Black Lives Matter connected with capsaicin?</td></tr>
<tr><td>#Q1 : What is capsaicin?
#A1 : Capsaicin is a chemical compound
that can be found in chili peppers.
#Q1 : What is Black Lives Matter?
#A1 : Black Lives Matter is a movement that fights against
racism and violence towards black people.
#Q2 : Is Black Lives Matter connected with capsaicin?
#A2 : Since Black Lives Matter is a movement that fights
against racism and violence towards black people,
and capsaicin is a chemical compound that can be found
in chili peppers, Black Lives Matter is not connected
with capsaicin.
So the answer is no.</td><td>Capsaicin (8-methyl-N-vanillyl-6-none
namide) is an active component of
chili peppers, which are plants
belonging to the genus Capsicum.
It is a chemical irritant for mammals,
including humans, and produces a
sensation of burning in any tissue
with which it comes into contact.</td></tr>
<tr><td rowspan="2">Wrong Fact</td><td colspan="2">Does Soylent use Pea for their source of protein?</td></tr>
<tr><td>#Q1 : What is Soylent?
#A1 : Soylent is a meal replacement drink.
#Q2 : What is the source of protein for Soylent?
#A2 : Soylent uses pea protein.
#Q3 : Does Soylent use Pea for their source
#A3 : Since Soylent uses pea protein, Soylent uses pea for
their source of protein.
So the answer is yes.</td><td>Soy protein isolate is the ingredient
we use in Soylent as our source
of protein.</td></tr>
<tr><td rowspan="3">Update Required</td><td colspan="2">Has Kelly Clarkson outsold season 4 American Idol winner?</td></tr>
<tr><td rowspan="2">#Q1 : Who won season 4 of American Idol?
#A1 : Carrie Underwood won season 4 of American Idol.
#Q2 : How many albums did Carrie Underwood sell?
#A2 : Carrie Underwood sold over 15 million albums.
#Q2 : How many albums did Kelly Clarkson sell?
#A2 : Kelly Clarkson sold over 25 million albums.
#Q3 : Has Kelly Clarkson outsold season 4 American Idol
winner?
#A3 : Since Kelly Clarkson sold over 25 million albums, and
Carrie Underwood sold over 15 million albums, Kelly
Clarkson sold more albums than Carrie Underwood.
So the answer is yes.</td><td>To date, Clarkson has sold over
28 million albums and 54 million
singles worldwide.</td></tr>
<tr><td>Throughout her career, Underwood has
sold 66 million albums worldwide. In
the United States, she remains the best
-selling album artist from American
Idol franchise with a total of 16.3
million albums sold</td></tr>
</table>

Table 3: Additional Examples of frequent error types within explanations. The left side is the original explanation generated by a language model, and the right side is the retrieved evidence document. The evidence documents could provide the required knowledge when revising the original explanation.

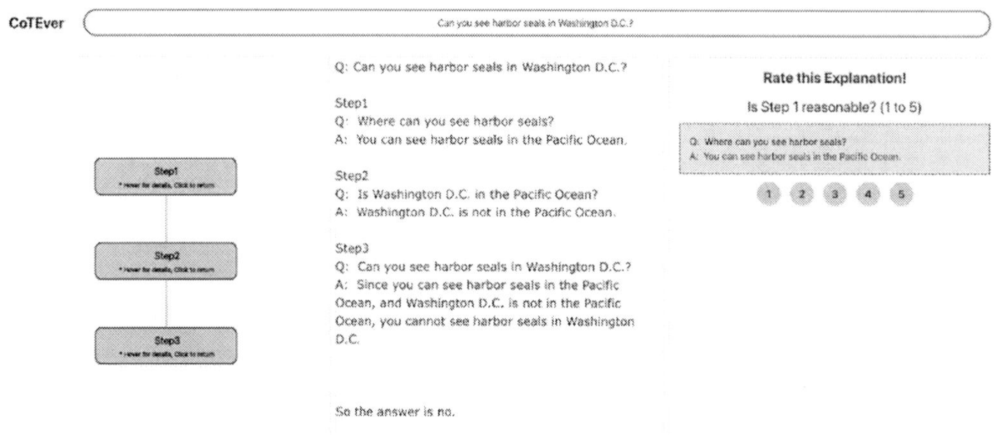

Figure 3: Snapshot of **CoTEVer**. Annotator gets to type in a question, and receive the output of a large language model(e.g., GPT-3).

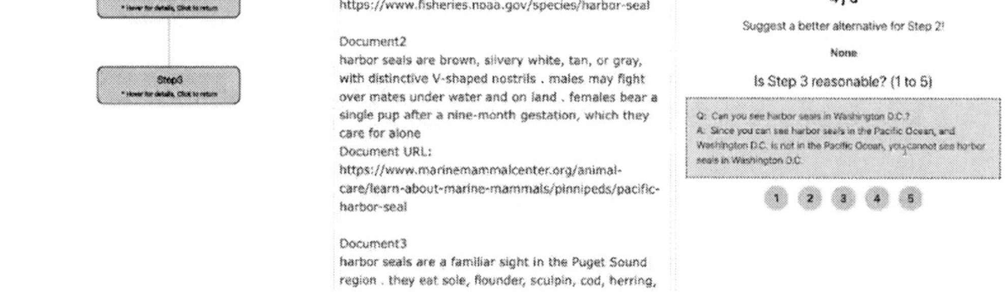

Figure 4: Snapshot of **CoTEVer**. Annotator could check the retrieved evidence documents in order to verify each step within the explanation.

Prompt
[Example 1] Question: Do hamsters provide food for any animals? Output: Sub Question #0 : What type of animals are hamsters? Sub Answer #0 : Hamsters are prey animals. Sub Question #1 : Can prey animals be food for other animals? Sub Answer #1 : Prey are food for predators. Sub Question #2 : Do hamsters provide food for any animals? Sub Answer #2 : Since hamsters are prey animals, and prey are food for predetors, hamsters provide food for some animals. Final Answer : So the answer is yes. [Example 2] Question: Could Brooke Shields succeed at University of Pennsylvania? Output: Sub question #0 : What university did Brooke Shields went to? Sub answer #0 : Brooke Shields went to Princeton University. Sub question #1 : Did Brooke Shields succeed at Princeton University? Sub answer #1 : At Princeton University, she got all As and Bs while pursing her bachelor's degree in French literature, meaning she had a successful school life. Sub question #2 : How rigorous is Princeton University compared to University of Pennsylvania? Sub answer #2 : Princeton University is about as academically rigorous as the University of Pennsylvania because they have a similar ranking according to U.S. News Rankings. Sub question #3 : Could Brooke Shields succeed at University of Pennsylvania? Sub answer #3 : Since University of Pennsylvania and University of Princeton are in similar circumstances, Brooke Shields has been successful in University of Princeton, Brooke Shields could also succeed at the University of Pennsylvania. So the answer is yes. [Example 3] Question: Hydrogen\u2019s atomic number squared exceeds number of Spice Girls? Output: Sub question #0 : What is the atomic number of Hydrogen? Sub answer #0 : Hydrogen has an atomic number of 1. Sub question #1 : What is 1 squared? Sub answer #1 : 1 squared is 1. Sub question #2 : How much Spice Girls are there? Sub answer #2 : There are 5 Spice Girls. Sub question #3 : Hydrogen\u2019s atomic number squared exceeds number of Spice Girls? Sub answer #3 : Since Hydrogen's atomic number squared is 1, the number of Spice Girls are 5, and 1 is smaller than 5, Hydrogen\u2019s atomic number squared is less than the number of Spice Girls. So the answer is no.

[Example 4]
Question: Is it common to see frost during some college commencements?
Output:
Sub question #0 : When does College commencement ceremonies usually happen?
Sub answer #0 : College commencement ceremonies can happen in December, May, and June.
Sub question #1 : Does it usually frost in December?
Sub answer #1 : December is in the winter, so there can be frost.
Sub question #2 : Is it common to see frost during some college commencements?
Sub answer #2 : Since there can be frost in December and a college commencement are held in December, there could be frost at some commencements.
So the answer is yes.

[Example 5]
Question: Could a llama birth twice during War in Vietnam (1945-46)?
Output:
Sub question #0 : How long was the Vietnam war?
Sub answer #0 : The War in Vietnam was 6 months.
Sub question #1 : How long is the gestation period?
Sub answer #1 : The gestation period for a llama is 11 months.
Sub question #2 : How long does it take for a llama to birth twice?
Sub answer #2 : Since the gestation period for a llama is 11 months, and 11 times 2 is 22, it will take 22 months.
Sub question #3 : Could a llama birth twice during War in Vietnam (1945-46)?
Sub answer #3 : Since it takes 22 months for a llama to birth twice, War in Vietnam was 6 months, and 22 is bigger than 6, llama could not give birth twice during the War in Vietnam.
So the answer is no.

[Example 6]
Question: Would a pear sink in water?
Output:
Sub question #0 : What is the density of a pear?
Sub answer #0 : The density of a pear is about 0.6g/cm3.
Sub question #1 : What is the density of water?
Sub answer #1 : The density of water is 1g/cm3.
Sub question #2 : Is the density of pear smaller than water?
Sub answer #2 : Since 0.6 is smaller than 1, the density of pear is smaller than water.
Sub question #3 : If the density of an object is less than water, what happens?
Sub answer #3 : Objects less dense than water float.
Sub question #4 : Would a pear sink in water?
Sub answer #4 : Since a pear has a smaller density than water, a pear would float.
So the answer is no.

[Example 7]

Table 4: Prompt used to gather explanations for human evaluation experiments.

OLEA: Tool and Infrastructure for Offensive Language Error Analysis in English

Marie Grace*, **Xajavion "Jay" Seabrum***, **Dananjay Srinivas***, **Alexis Palmer**
University of Colorado Boulder
first.last@colorado.edu; olea.ask@gmail.com†

Abstract

State-of-the-art models for identifying offensive language often fail to generalize over more nuanced or implicit cases of offensive and hateful language. Understanding model performance on complex cases is key for building robust models that are effective in real-world settings. To help researchers efficiently evaluate their models, we introduce OLEA, a diagnostic, open-source, extensible Python library that provides easy-to-use tools for error analysis in the context of detecting offensive language in English. OLEA packages analyses and datasets proposed by prior scholarship, empowering researchers to build effective, explainable and generalizable offensive language classifiers.

1 Introduction

Offensive language[1] detection models are integral to online platforms' moderation systems. Such systems excel at detecting and filtering out messages with explicit keywords and mentions, however these systems are known (1) to perform poorly on messages that are implicitly offensive or have negation (Röttger et al., 2020; Palmer et al., 2020); (2) to be subject to annotator biases (Sap et al., 2021); (3) not to be robust to diachronic language (Florio et al., 2020); and (4) to be insensitive to and to overdetect AAE as offensive language (Sap et al., 2021; Blodgett et al., 2016). Failing to address these issues and gaps can cause marginalized groups to be further dehumanized or attacked (Mathew et al., 2021; Kennedy et al., 2020).

Models have been shown to be ineffective at generalizing across these complexities (Yin and Zubiaga, 2021), tending to aggregate different types of hate speech under broad labels, causing large within-class variances (Waseem et al., 2017a). In response, prior research has curated diagnostic datasets such as HateCheck (Röttger et al., 2020) and COLD (Palmer et al., 2020), to evaluate existing models on specific types of hate speech. Such evaluation datasets allow us to view model performance as a continuum, and move away from monolithic F1 scores that can obscure a model's limitations and explainability (Kennedy et al., 2020).

We introduce OLEA,[2,3] an extensible, open-source Offensive Language Error Analysis tool and infrastructure designed to a) evaluate offensive language classifiers on different types of problematic language use, and b) provide detailed feedback about model performance. The library makes it convenient for researchers to analyze their models by providing an extensive set of error-analysis methods, callable with minimal coding, to measure case-specific model performances. In addition, the library provides a common interface for comparing different offensive language classifiers on granular linguistic categories. OLEA provides:

- nuanced error analysis methods focused on understanding model performance on specific linguistic occurrences;
- interfaces to two evaluation datasets that compile a broad typology of offensive language phenomena; and
- scaffolding to support easy distribution of new datasets and associated analysis methods.

OLEA formats evaluation datasets to be easily interpreted, and uses popular Python packages such as Pandas (Wes McKinney, 2010) and Matplotlib (Hunter, 2007) to encapsulate the data and error analysis methods.

2 Background and Related Work

Offensive language is complex, and systems for detecting it automatically need to be able to handle both explicit *and* implicit cases (Schmidt and

* The first three authors contributed equally.

† Please direct inquiries about the library to this email.

[1] We use the term "offensive language" to encompass offensive language and hate speech. This paper contains censored offensive language examples.

[2] https://pypi.org/project/olea/

[3] https://www.youtube.com/watch?v=e8VVhP6kNlY

Proceedings of the 17th Conference of the European Chapter of the Association for Computational Linguistics System Demonstrations, pages 209–218
May 2-4, 2023

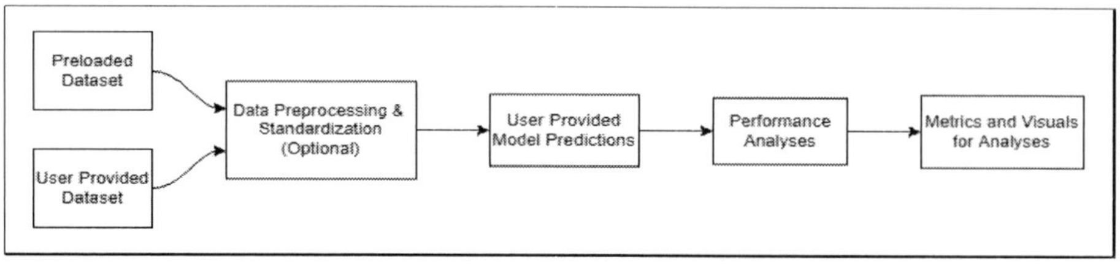

Figure 1: Diagram of the OLEA Library pipeline.

Wiegand, 2017; Waseem et al., 2017b). Detecting explicit offensive language often relies on keyword detection (Wiegand et al., 2019), but keyword-driven systems can lead to messages being falsely flagged, causing unchecked or unnoticed racial biases to propagate in the system's decisions (Sap et al., 2021; Blodgett et al., 2016). Implicit offensive language is generally more difficult to detect than its explicit counterpart (ElSherief et al., 2021; Caselli et al., 2020). It is also more likely to change over time, as the world changes, and as users coin new phrases and terms to implicitly refer to minority groups (Florio et al., 2020).

Datasets for this task address different (often overlapping) concerns, making direct comparison difficult. HateXplain (Mathew et al., 2021) and CAD (Vidgen et al., 2021) both provide rationales indicating where annotators see offensive content. OLID (Zampieri et al., 2019a) identifies offensive text and the specific targeted minority group in a three-tiered labeling structure. HateCheck (Röttger et al., 2020) and COLD (Palmer et al., 2020) are described more in Section 3.1.

Linguistic explainability of the prediction *failures* of NLP models has lagged behind performance gains according to benchmark datasets (Hovy, 2022). McMillan-Major et al. (2022) provide an interactive system mostly for end users of offensive language detection systems. Their system helps users explore datasets and understand how different models score and classify individual text inputs.OLEA has complementary functionality, focusing on fine-grained analysis of model performance (especially misclassifications) across existing evaluation datasets. **We focus instead on model developers, providing streamlined error analysis and interpretation of system outputs relative to linguistically-grounded categorizations.**

3 Library Tour and Design

Figure 1 shows an overview of OLEA's core functionalities. Users submit their model's predictions (3.2) on OLEA's preloaded datasets (3.1) and then call error analysis and evaluation functions (3.3). Users may also extend OLEA with new datasets and may write new analysis functions, adding to the library's capabilities (3.4). Most of OLEA's modules expect a Pandas[4] dataframe with the text of the instance to be classified, one or more labels indicating offensiveness, and a predicted label for the instance. Dataframes may include columns with additional information related to the instance and/or its annotation.

3.1 Preloaded diagnostic datasets

The primary function of OLEA is to make it easy for users to evaluate the capabilities of their models in a fine-grained way. We provide interfaces (via HuggingFace's datasets library[5] and the HuggingFace Hub) to two offensive language datasets, both designed specifically for diagnostic evaluation of detection systems. Both datasets include fine-grained annotations and binary offensiveness labels and were curated to compare model performance with linguistic phenomena. Tables 1 and 2 list the features available for analysis.

The **HateCheck** (Röttger et al., 2020) test suite includes labels reflecting specific linguistic constructions often seen in online hate speech, such as use of spelling changes to obscure hateful language and presence of threatening language. HateCheck also includes annotations of specific identities targeted in each instance of hate speech.

COLD (Palmer et al., 2020) provides fine-grained labels of some linguistic phenomena relevant for implicit/complex offensive language. Two examples are presence/absence of slur terms and presence/absence of adjectival nominalizations.

3.2 Submitting predictions

Before using the analysis functions described below, the user needs to submit their model's predic-

[4]https://pandas.pydata.org/docs/

[5]https://huggingface.co/docs/datasets/index

Feature	Description
functionality	The shorthand for the functionality tested by the test case.
case_id	The unique ID of the test case (assigned to each of the 3,901 cases initially generated)
test_case	The text of the test case.
label_gold	The gold standard label (hateful/non-hateful) of the test case. All test cases within a given functionality have the same gold standard label.
target_ident	Where applicable, the protected group targeted or referenced by the test case. We cover seven protected groups in the test suite: women, trans people, gay people, black people, disabled people, Muslims and immigrants.
direction	For hateful cases, the binary secondary label indicating whether they are directed at an individual as part of a protected group or aimed at the group in general.
focus_words	Where applicable, the key word or phrase in a given test case (e.g. "cut their throats").
focus_lemma	Where applicable, the corresponding lemma (e.g. "cut sb. throat").
ref_case_id	For hateful cases, where applicable, the ID of the simpler hateful case which was perturbed to generate them. For non-hateful cases, where applicable, the ID of the hateful case which is contrasted.
ref_templ_id	The equivalent, but for template IDs.
templ_id	The unique ID of the template from which the test case was generated (assigned to each of the 866 cases and templates from which we generated the 3,901 initial cases).

Table 1: Features available via the HateCheck dataset. Names and descriptions from Röttger et al. (2020).

Feature	Description
ID	The unique ID for the text
Text	The text containing social media messages (some containing offensive language)
Cat	The gold label category of the text
Off	Offensive or not? (Y / N) Majority Vote
Off1, Off2, Off3	Individual annotator labels for Off (Y / N)
Slur	Contains a slur? (Y / N) Majority Vote
Slur1, Slur2, Slur3	Individual annotator labels for Slur (Y / N)
Nom	Contains adjectival nominalization? (Y / N) Majority Vote
Nom1, Nom2, Nom3	Individual annotator labels for Slur (Y / N)
Dist	Contains linguistic distancing? (Y / N) Majority Vote
Dist1, Dist2, Dist3	Individual annotator labels for Dist (Y / N)

Table 2: Features available as part of the COLD dataset. Names and descriptions from Palmer et al. (2020).

tions on the selected dataset, as well as a mapping between the model's predicted labels (e.g. 1, 0) and the labels in the selected dataset (e.g. `hateful`, `non-hateful`).[6] The code snippet below illustrates the process and assumes that the user's data has been stored as a Pandas dataframe named `user_data`. In this example, the model predictions are found in a column called `predictions`. The user has selected three features for potential analysis: `Text`, `is_slur` and `text_length`.

```
from olea.data import Dataset
setup = Dataset(
          data = user_data,
          features = ["Text","is_slur",
                      "text_length"],
          gold_column = "gold_labels",
          text_column = "Text")
predictions = user_data["predictions"]
mapping = {"hateful": 1,
           "non-hateful": 0}
data_submit = setup.submit(
            batch = user_data,
            predictions = predictions,
            map = mapping)
```

The `submit` method passes the relevant parameters to the analysis module.

3.3 Error analysis functions

The heart of our library is a collection of functions for detailed evaluation and error analysis. **Throughout, we evaluate the model's coarse-grained classification performance (e.g. offensive vs. not offensive) for subsets of instances grouped according to a particular feature. The features generally correspond to dataframe columns. For example, we may compare performance for instances containing a slur term to performance for instances with no slur term.** Plots are produced using Matplotlib (Hunter, 2007), and we include the option to save plots to files. Section 4 shows concrete examples of the analysis outputs, and code examples appear in Appendix A.

`analyze_on`. In its most general version, this function evaluates model performance for a categorical column specified by the user. OLEA includes versions of `analyze_on` customized to the two preloaded datasets. The COLD-specific version evaluates performance for features constructed from combinations of four binary features: offensiveness, presence of slur term, presence of adjectival nominalization, and presence of linguistic distancing. The HateCheck-specific version includes linguistic features (e.g. negation, derogation, or profanity) and features related to the identity of the targeted individual or class (e.g. trans people, Muslims, or disabled people).

`check_anno_agreement`. This function is intended for datasets which include labels from multiple annotators, such as COLD. The function compares performance on instances with full annotator

[6] Note that this process applies both for preloaded datasets and for datasets read in from the user's own system.

agreement for the label of offensiveness to performance on instances with partial agreement. Full annotator agreement is taken as a proxy for instances that are "easy" to classify, and partial agreement indicates more complex cases.

`aave`. This function evaluates performance for instances (likely) written using African American English. The scores are calculated using the TwitterAAE model (Blodgett et al., 2016). These scores represent an inference of the proportion of words in the instance that come from a demographically-associated language/dialect.

`check_substring`. Given a user-specified text string, this function compares performance on instances with the substring to instances without.

`str_len_analysis`. This function outputs a histogram showing model performance on instances of different lengths (character or word count).

3.4 Adding datasets and analyses

Extensibility is a key principle guiding the design of OLEA, with the goal of providing an easy-to-use, uniform platform for error analysis in the context of offensive language detection. In addition to the two preloaded datasets, users can submit their own datasets using the process described in 4.2. To add a dataset, users need only define an interface (using the Dataset class) indicating where to find both target labels and features relevant for analysis.

OLEA has a helper function for preprocessing English text to remove user names and URLs and convert emoji to their textual descriptions.[7]

```
from olea.utils.preprocess_text import
    PreprocessText as pt
processed_text = pt.execute(user_data["
    raw_text"])
user_data["preprocessed_text"] =
    preprocessed_text
```

For example, the preprocessor converts "@username_1 Have you seen the video that @another_user made? 👀 🔥 https://fakelink.io" to "USER have you seen the video that USER made? eyes fire HTML".

Finally, users can write and share their own analysis functions, focusing on user-specified dimensions, as in 4.2.2. OLEA's code is modularized such that adding a new analysis requires enough Python knowledge to write the function, but not a detailed understanding of the entire codebase.

[7]Preprocessing scheme is described in Palmer et al. (2020).

4 Use Case Demonstrations

OLEA aids model development by providing an easy and comparable platform to test and build robust offensive language classifiers. We demonstrate three use cases: a) analysis on preloaded datasets (4.1), including model comparison (4.1.4), b) analysis on custom data (4.2), and c) sharing datasets and analysis functions (4.2).

4.1 User model performance evaluation using preloaded datasets

This section demonstrates how to use OLEA for detailed analysis of the strengths and weaknesses of existing offensive language detection models. For this demo, we use roBERTa-offensive (Barbieri et al., 2020), a pre-trained generic language model, fine-tuned on the SemEval2019 OffensEval dataset (Zampieri et al., 2019b). We use this model to make top-level predictions (offensive or not) for both COLD and HateCheck. Although they use different labels (offensive vs hateful), COLD and HateCheck align in their definitions by taking into account non-offensive uses of slurs and classifying derogatory text as offensive. Users explicitly run individual error analyses and specify whether a plot of the results should automatically be generated. These individual analysis functions show the model's performance with respect to a particular feature (i.e. an existing dataframe column, or a new one added by the function).

Each function returns two dataframes. The `metrics` dataframe contains a classification report for the analysis.[8] This dataframe uses OLEA's built in `Metrics` function, which is built upon and uses Scikit-learn's (Pedregosa et al., 2011) metrics library. The `plot_info` dataframe contains details of the analysis for the selected dimension, plus computed accuracy and the option to show textual examples. If `show_examples = True`, the function returns one randomly-selected incorrectly-classified instance for each value of the dimension being analyzed.[9] If the plot option is selected, the plots are built from the `plot_info` dataframe.

4.1.1 Generic analysis functions

Table 3 shows the classification report for roBERTa-offensive on COLD. Here, the classification report

[8]Appendix A provides more code examples for loading in data and starting generic analyses.

[9]The variable `show_examples` defaults to false to avoid accidental viewing of hateful or offensive language.

	N	Y	macro avg	weighted avg
precision	0.743	0.587	0.665	0.670
recall	0.502	0.803	0.652	0.643
f1-score	0.599	0.678	0.639	0.636
support	1072	944	2016	2016

Table 3: `Metrics` classification report for roBERTa-offensive on COLD, using `analyze_on` on the dimension of offensiveness. N=not offensive, Y=offensive.

Annotator Agreement	Full	Partial
Total	1431	585
Total Correct	1004	292
Accuracy	0.702	0.499
Incorrect Classification Example	an illegal is not an immigrant and illegals do take american jobs considering they are not americans.	USER yooo i was thinking bout that the other day lol.. you only really speaking of one person my n*ggah
Example's Predicted Label	N	Y
Example's Gold Label	Y	N

Table 4: `plot_info` report for roBERTa-offensive on COLD, using `check_anno_agreement` (full vs. partial), with randomly-selected examples.

provides F1, precision, and recall for the two categories of offensive and non-offensive, as well as the macros and weighted averages. This model performs better overall on offensive instances, with high recall, but shows much better precision for non-offensive instances. These reports can be easily modified to analyze subsets of the data.

Table 4 shows `plot_info` for roBERTa-offensive on COLD, using `check_anno_agreement`. The table shows accuracy for each category (full vs. partial) and one example incorrect prediction. Accuracy is much higher for instances with full agreement than for those with some disagreement. Offensiveness can be subjective, so it is useful to examine model performance on these different cases. Showing examples allows users to review difficult cases and may provide insights for model improvement.

4.1.2 COLD analysis

The next analysis (Fig. 2) is on the fine-grained COLD categories. roBERTa performs well on offensive tweets containing slurs and poorly on the reclaimed category (non-offensive tweets containing slurs). The model also performs poorly on offensive tweets containing adjectival nominalization. These insights suggest that the model relies too much on slurs for identifying offensive language.

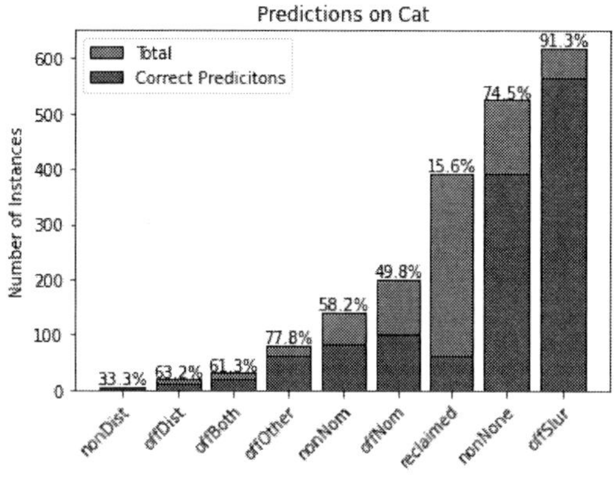

Figure 2: Results for roBERTa-offensive on COLD, focusing on fine-grained categories. Percent value above a bar shows percent accuracy for that category.

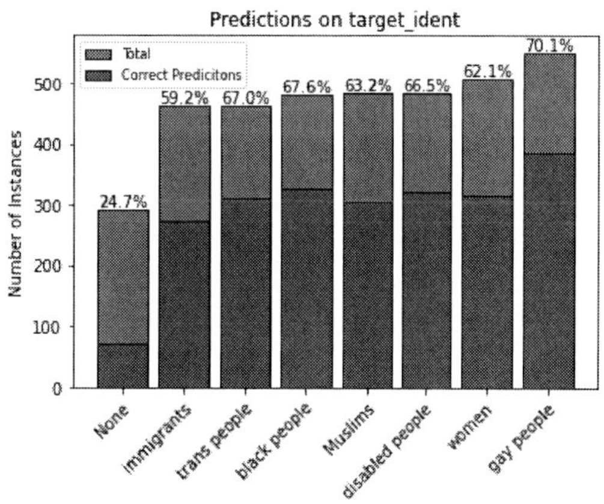

Figure 3: Results for roBERTa-offensive on HateCheck, focusing on identity of the target.

4.1.3 HateCheck analysis

HateCheck includes a column identifying the targeted group of the offensive language. This analysis can help identify which groups a model is more or less sensitive to. Figure 3 shows that the model does a better job of recognizing hateful speech when an identity is targeted than when one is not.

Figure 4a analyzes the performance of roBERTa-offensive on the fine-grained HateCheck categories; complete table is in Appendix B. Most instances of counter-speech (when hate speech is quoted or is referred to with a non-hateful effect) are incorrectly classified. An example of counter-speech is "I lost all respect for you when you said women are pathetic". Instances belonging to the categories of derogation, identity, threats, pronoun references, and phrasing are mostly correctly classified.

Figure 4: Comparison of HateXplain and roBERTa models on the fine-grained HateCheck categories. The category labels are followed by either (h) to denote that it is comprised of only hateful instances, (nh) for only non-hateful instances, or nothing to denote a mix of hateful and non-hateful instances

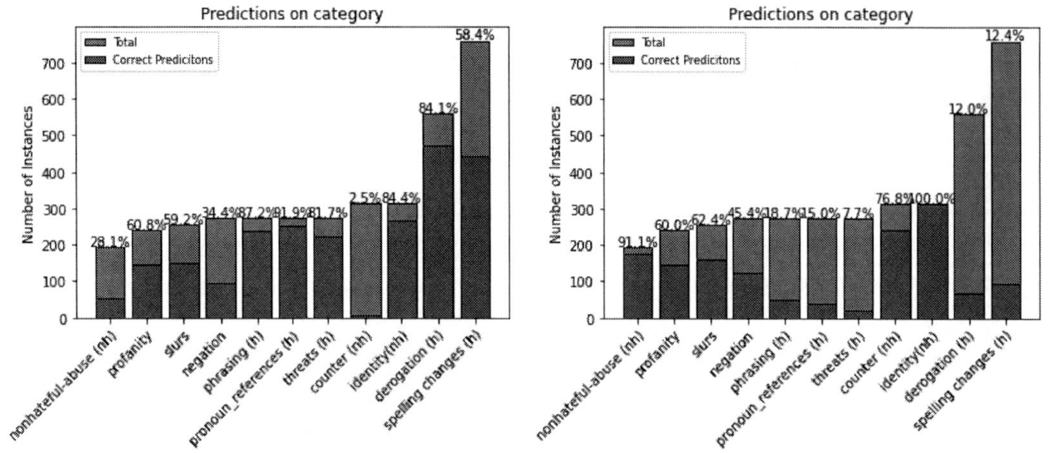

(a) Results for roBERTa-offensive on HateCheck, focusing on fine-grained categories.

(b) Results for HateXplain on HateCheck, focusing on fine-grained categories.

4.1.4 Model comparison

So far we have compared one model's performance on two different datasets. Next, we compare two different models on the same dataset. The second model is HateXplain (Mathew et al., 2021). Both models of course suffer when classifying data sourced from outside their training domain.[10,11] But we get a much truer sense of the models' out-of-domain capabilities when we look at the side-by-side analysis of the two models for the fine-grained HateCheck categories (Figures 4a and 4b). While roBERTa-offensive does not perform well on counter-speech, HateXplain correctly classifies most counter-speech instances. And while HateXplain struggles to recognize hateful expressions with spelling changes, roBERTa does much better.

4.2 OLEA as infrastructure: Extending functionality

OLEA is open-source[12] and has been designed to be extensible with new datasets and new analyses.

4.2.1 Analysis on custom data

The analysis methods described above can be easily applied to new corpora. The code below shows the process of loading the OLID dataset (Zampieri et al., 2019a) as a pandas dataframe. The user only needs to specify a path to the data and the relevant column headings. The `Dataset` class acts as a wrapper for the data loaded from disk and allows the user to access class utilities such as `generator()`, which in turn is helpful for accessing data in batches.

```
olid = pd.read_csv('data/olid/
    olid_levela.csv')
olid_dataset = Dataset(data = olid,
                features = 'Text',
                gold_column = 'label',
                text_column = 'Text')
data_gen = olid_dataset.generator(
    batch_size=64)
data = next(data_gen)
```

We can now submit model predictions, returning a `DatasetSubmissionObject` which can be used to conduct the generic analyses previously described; code in Appendix A.

4.2.2 Sharing datasets and analysis patterns

With just a bit of coding, interfaces new datasets can be added to the OLEA library more permanently, and for the benefit of all users.[13] We demonstrate again using OLID,[14] establishing the new `OLIDDataset` class which inherits from `Dataset`.

```
class OLIDDataset(Dataset) :
    text_column = 'Text'
```

[10] roBERTa-offensive reports an F1 of 0.78 on OLID but drops to 0.62 on HateCheck. HateXplain reports F1 of 0.69 on the HateXplain dataset, and drops to 0.37 on HateCheck.

[11] We map HateXplain's "offensive" and "hate speech" labels both to HateCheck's "hateful".

[12] `https://github.com/alexispalmer/olea`, Licensed under MIT License

[13] OLEA is not currently hosting datasets. The preloaded datasets are hosted via HuggingFace's datasets library.

[14] Note that we only consider OLID's "level-A" annotations.

```
    gold_column = 'label'
    features = ['Text','label_id']
def __init__(self, olid_csv_path:str) :
    self.olid_csv_path = olid_csv_path
    self._data = self._load_data()
def _load_data(self) -> pd.DataFrame:
    return pd.read_csv(self.
    olid_csv_path)
```

To accommodate the properties of the new dataset, we need to override some attributes of the `Dataset` class and to modify the method for loading data.

OLEA's scaffolding minimizes the amount of new code needed to add a new dataset, as well as automatically handling helper utilities such as mapping model predictions to the custom `Dataset` object. The library also runs sanity checks on submitted predictions before returning a `DatasetSubmissionObject`.

The advantage of using a native `DatasetSubmissionObject` is that users may run `Generic` analyses on it. However, if authors have a unique analysis that they wish to couple with their dataset, they may specify a special `Analysis` class that can operate on submissions. The class methods can be modified to accommodate patterns or properties specific to the dataset.

```
class OLIDAnalysis(object) :
    @classmethod
    def analyze_on(cls, submission:
    DatasetSubmissionObject, on:str) :
        '''
        Unique OLID analysis goes here!
        '''
        return get_metrics(submission,
    on)
```

5 Conclusion and Future Directions

This paper introduces OLEA, a tool for easy, in-depth error analysis and an infrastructure for sharing new datasets and analysis methods. OLEA helps researchers understand the strengths and weaknesses of their offensive language detection models. In the near term, we will continue to add new analysis methods and datasets, including methods for corpus exploration, and providing automatic trends and insights of model performance without users needing to run explicit analyses. Mid term, we plan to extend OLEA to additional languages, and eventually we would like to expand OLEA into a general error analysis library for a range of language classification tasks. Because OLEA is a convenient way for authors to share datasets and analyses, it is our hope that a community will develop around the library, and that models ultimately will improve as we learn more about what they can and cannot do.

Ethical Considerations. We acknowledge the ethical implications of releasing a tool that encourages accessing hate speech datasets where tweet author anonymity may not be ensured. This tool is to help researchers identify how their offensive language model can improve, with the intended benefit of more accurate identification of language that negatively affects vulnerable populations, and should not be used for any task that promotes or spreads the usage of hate speech or unnecessarily exposes people to hate speech. Even when used as intended and functioning correctly, users may react negatively to seeing offensive language, so we take steps to minimize exposure by defaulting `show_examples` to `False` during analysis, though researchers belonging to vulnerable populations might be more negatively affected. If the tool gives incorrect results, researchers might overestimate their model performance, which could directly hurt vulnerable populations depending on the deployments of the model. This tool relies on datasets that often categorize people based on their identity, and it supports analyses based on these categories. We believe that these categorizations are necessary for a granular understanding and examination of offensive language classification.

Limitations. OLEA is restricted in the languages that it can be applied to. Currently, for the substring analyses, it assumes that the language is delimited by spaces. Additionally, the library is primarily focused on providing error analyses for offensive language applications. Its use outside of this domain is not known or well-defined. Though we focus on error analysis for offensive language identification, the system makes no binding assumptions as to the proper definitions of offensive language and hate speech, nor does it assert (or assume) any difference between these two categories which can complicate cross-model comparison. Furthermore, this tool is just an analysis tool; it does not address concerns regarding language drift and other sociolinguistic biases that may be present within a user's dataset, nor does it address any annotator biases present in original datasets.

Acknowledgments. Thanks to the anonymous reviewers for useful feedback. Thanks also to Cutter Dalton for testing, and to members of the 2021-2023 CLASIC cohort for helpful discussions!

References

Francesco Barbieri, José Camacho-Collados, Leonardo Neves, and Luis Espinosa Anke. 2020. Tweeteval: Unified benchmark and comparative evaluation for tweet classification. *CoRR*, abs/2010.12421.

Su Lin Blodgett, Lisa Green, and Brendan O'Connor. 2016. Demographic dialectal variation in social media: A case study of African-American English. In *Proceedings of the 2016 Conference on Empirical Methods in Natural Language Processing*, pages 1119–1130, Austin, Texas. Association for Computational Linguistics.

Tommaso Caselli, Valerio Basile, Jelena Mitrović, Inga Kartoziya, and Michael Granitzer. 2020. I feel offended, don't be abusive! implicit/explicit messages in offensive and abusive language. In *Proceedings of the 12th Language Resources and Evaluation Conference*, pages 6193–6202, Marseille, France. European Language Resources Association.

Mai ElSherief, Caleb Ziems, David Muchlinski, Vaishnavi Anupindi, Jordyn Seybolt, Munmun De Choudhury, and Diyi Yang. 2021. Latent hatred: A benchmark for understanding implicit hate speech. In *Proceedings of the 2021 Conference on Empirical Methods in Natural Language Processing*, pages 345–363, Online and Punta Cana, Dominican Republic. Association for Computational Linguistics.

Komal Florio, Valerio Basile, Marco Polignano, Pierpaolo Basile, and Viviana Patti. 2020. Time of your hate: The challenge of time in hate speech detection on social media. *Applied Sciences*, 10(12):4180.

Eduard Hovy. 2022. Rediscovering the need for representation and knowledge. ACL 2022 - 60th Annual Meeting of the Association for Computational Linguistics.

J. D. Hunter. 2007. Matplotlib: A 2d graphics environment. *Computing in Science & Engineering*, 9(3):90–95.

Chris J Kennedy, Geoff Bacon, Alexander Sahn, and Claudia von Vacano. 2020. Constructing interval variables via faceted rasch measurement and multitask deep learning: a hate speech application. *arXiv preprint arXiv:2009.10277*.

Binny Mathew, Punyajoy Saha, Seid Muhie Yimam, Chris Biemann, Pawan Goyal, and Animesh Mukherjee. 2021. Hatexplain: A benchmark dataset for explainable hate speech detection. In *Proceedings of the AAAI Conference on Artificial Intelligence*, volume 35, pages 14867–14875.

Angelina McMillan-Major, Amandalynne Paullada, and Yacine Jernite. 2022. An interactive exploratory tool for the task of hate speech detection. In *Proceedings of the Second Workshop on Bridging Human–Computer Interaction and Natural Language Processing*, pages 11–20, Seattle, Washington. Association for Computational Linguistics.

Alexis Palmer, Christine Carr, Melissa Robinson, and Jordan Sanders. 2020. COLD: Annotation scheme and evaluation data set for complex offensive language in English. *Journal for Language Technology and Computational Linguistics*, 34(1):1–28.

F. Pedregosa, G. Varoquaux, A. Gramfort, V. Michel, B. Thirion, O. Grisel, M. Blondel, P. Prettenhofer, R. Weiss, V. Dubourg, J. Vanderplas, A. Passos, D. Cournapeau, M. Brucher, M. Perrot, and E. Duchesnay. 2011. Scikit-learn: Machine learning in Python. *Journal of Machine Learning Research*, 12:2825–2830.

Paul Röttger, Bertram Vidgen, Dong Nguyen, Zeerak Waseem, Helen Margetts, and Janet B Pierrehumbert. 2020. Hatecheck: Functional tests for hate speech detection models. *arXiv preprint arXiv:2012.15606*.

Maarten Sap, Swabha Swayamdipta, Laura Vianna, Xuhui Zhou, Yejin Choi, and Noah A Smith. 2021. Annotators with attitudes: How annotator beliefs and identities bias toxic language detection. *arXiv preprint arXiv:2111.07997*.

Anna Schmidt and Michael Wiegand. 2017. A survey on hate speech detection using natural language processing. In *Proceedings of the Fifth International Workshop on Natural Language Processing for Social Media*, pages 1–10, Valencia, Spain. Association for Computational Linguistics.

Bertie Vidgen, Dong Nguyen, Helen Margetts, Patricia Rossini, and Rebekah Tromble. 2021. Introducing CAD: the contextual abuse dataset. In *Proceedings of the 2021 Conference of the North American Chapter of the Association for Computational Linguistics: Human Language Technologies*, pages 2289–2303, Online. Association for Computational Linguistics.

Zeerak Waseem, Thomas Davidson, Dana Warmsley, and Ingmar Weber. 2017a. Understanding abuse: A typology of abusive language detection subtasks. *arXiv preprint arXiv:1705.09899*.

Zeerak Waseem, Thomas Davidson, Dana Warmsley, and Ingmar Weber. 2017b. Understanding abuse: A typology of abusive language detection subtasks. In *Proceedings of the First Workshop on Abusive Language Online*, pages 78–84, Vancouver, BC, Canada. Association for Computational Linguistics.

Wes McKinney. 2010. Data Structures for Statistical Computing in Python. In *Proceedings of the 9th Python in Science Conference*, pages 56 – 61.

Michael Wiegand, Josef Ruppenhofer, and Thomas Kleinbauer. 2019. Detection of Abusive Language: the Problem of Biased Datasets. In *Proceedings of the 2019 Conference of the North American Chapter of the Association for Computational Linguistics: Human Language Technologies, Volume 1 (Long and Short Papers)*, pages 602–608, Minneapolis, Minnesota. Association for Computational Linguistics.

Wenjie Yin and Arkaitz Zubiaga. 2021. Towards generalisable hate speech detection: a review on obstacles and solutions. *PeerJ Computer Science*, 7:e598.

Marcos Zampieri, Shervin Malmasi, Preslav Nakov, Sara Rosenthal, Noura Farra, and Ritesh Kumar. 2019a. Predicting the Type and Target of Offensive Posts in Social Media. In *Proceedings of NAACL*.

Marcos Zampieri, Shervin Malmasi, Preslav Nakov, Sara Rosenthal, Noura Farra, and Ritesh Kumar. 2019b. SemEval-2019 task 6: Identifying and categorizing offensive language in social media (OffensEval). In *Proceedings of the 13th International Workshop on Semantic Evaluation*, pages 75–86, Minneapolis, Minnesota, USA. Association for Computational Linguistics.

A Code Examples

In this appendix, we provide code snippets corresponding to Section 4.

A.1 Preliminaries

Installation

```
pip install olea
```

Import Statements

```
import pandas as pd
from olea.data.cold import COLD,
    COLDSubmissionObject
from olea.data.hatecheck import
    HateCheck
from olea.analysis.cold import
    COLDAnalysis
from olea.analysis.generic import
    Generic
from olea.analysis.hatecheck import
    HateCheckAnalysis
from olea.utils import preprocess_text
```

A.2 Code examples for Section 4.1

Download and Preprocess COLD text:

```
cold = COLD()
pt = preprocess_text.PreprocessText()
processed_text = pt.execute(cold.data()[
    "Text"])
cold.data()["Text"] =processed_text
```

Create predictions using roBERTa-offensive

```
from transformers import AutoTokenizer,
    AutoModelForSequenceClassification
from transformers import
    TextClassificationPipeline

 link = "cardiffnlp/twitter-roberta-base
    -offensive"
 tokenizer = AutoTokenizer.
    from_pretrained(link)
        model =
    AutoModelForSequenceClassification.
    from_pretrained(link)
        #Create Pipeline for Predicting
        pipe =
    TextClassificationPipeline(model=
    model, tokenizer=tokenizer)
        preds = pd.DataFrame(pipe(list(
    cold.data()["Text"])))["label"]
```

Create Submission Objects:

```
cold_so = cold.submit(
    batch = cold.data(),
    predictions = preds,
    map = {"LABEL_0": 'N', 'LABEL_1': "Y
    "})

hc_so = hc.submit(
    batch = hc.data(),
    predictions = preds,
    map = {"LABEL_0": 'non-hateful', '
    LABEL_1': "hateful"})
```

Generate Table 3:

```
plot_info, metrics = Generic.analyze_on(
    cold_so,
    'Cat',
    show_examples = False,
    plot = False)
```

Generate Table 3 and Save plot to file:

```
plot_info, metrics = Generic.analyze_on(
    cold_so,
    'Cat',
    show_examples = False,
    plot = False,
    savePlotToFile= "cold_cats.png")
```

Generate Table 4:

```
plot_info, metrics = Generic.
    check_anno_agreement(cold_so, ["Off1
    ","Off2","Off3"],show_examples =
    True, plot = False)
```

Generate Figure 2:

```
plot_info, metrics =COLDAnalysis.
    analyze_on(
    cold_so,
    'Cat',
    show_examples = False,
    plot = True)
```

Generate Figure 3:

```
plot_info, metrics = Generic.analyze_on(
    hc_so,
    'target_ident')
```

Generate Figure 4a, Figure 4b, and Table 5:

```
plot_info, metrics = HateCheckAnalysis.
    analyze_on(
    hc_so,
    'category')
```

A.3 Code examples for Section 4.2

Run analysis functions on local custom data:

```
predictions = model.predict(data)
submission = olid_dataset.submit(
            batch = data,
            predictions = predictions,
            map = {1:'OFF', 0:'NOT'})
# performance on AAVE
Generic.aave(submission)
# performance on texts containing
   substring 'female'
Generic.check_substring(submission, "
   female")
```

Submit predictions for newly-established dataset class `OLIDDataset`:

```
olid = OLIDDataset('data/olid.csv')
datagen = olid.generator(64)
data = next(datagen)
preds = model.predict(data)
map = {'OFF' : 1.0 , 'NOT' : 0.0}
submission = olid.submit(batch = data,
            predictions = preds,
            map = map)
```

B Full Results Table for Figure 4a

category	Metrics	precision	recall	f1-score	support
counter (nh)	hateful	0.000	0.000	0.000	0
counter (nh)	non-hateful	1.000	0.038	0.074	314
counter (nh)	macro avg	0.500	0.019	0.037	314
counter (nh)	weighted avg	1.000	0.038	0.074	314
derogation (h)	hateful	1.000	0.805	0.892	560
derogation (h)	non-hateful	0.000	0.000	0.000	0
derogation (h)	macro avg	0.500	0.403	0.446	560
derogation (h)	weighted avg	1.000	0.805	0.892	560
identity(nh)	hateful	0.000	0.000	0.000	0
identity(nh)	non-hateful	1.000	0.892	0.943	315
identity(nh)	macro avg	0.500	0.446	0.471	315
identity(nh)	weighted avg	1.000	0.892	0.943	315
negation	hateful	0.295	0.236	0.262	140
negation	non-hateful	0.335	0.406	0.367	133
negation	macro avg	0.315	0.321	0.315	273
negation	weighted avg	0.315	0.319	0.313	273
nonhateful-abuse (nh)	hateful	0.000	0.000	0.000	0
nonhateful-abuse (nh)	non-hateful	1.000	0.339	0.506	192
nonhateful-abuse (nh)	macro avg	0.500	0.169	0.253	192
nonhateful-abuse (nh)	weighted avg	1.000	0.339	0.506	192
phrasing (h)	hateful	1.000	0.868	0.929	273
phrasing (h)	non-hateful	0.000	0.000	0.000	0
phrasing (h)	macro avg	0.500	0.434	0.465	273
phrasing (h)	weighted avg	1.000	0.868	0.929	273
profanity	hateful	0.601	1.000	0.751	140
profanity	non-hateful	1.000	0.070	0.131	100
profanity	macro avg	0.800	0.535	0.441	240
profanity	weighted avg	0.767	0.613	0.492	240
pronoun-references (h)	hateful	1.000	0.908	0.952	273
pronoun-references (h)	non-hateful	0.000	0.000	0.000	0
pronoun-references (h)	macro avg	0.500	0.454	0.476	273
pronoun-references (h)	weighted avg	1.000	0.908	0.952	273
slurs	hateful	0.593	0.778	0.673	144
slurs	non-hateful	0.515	0.306	0.384	111
slurs	macro avg	0.554	0.542	0.528	255
slurs	weighted avg	0.559	0.573	0.547	255
spelling changes (h)	hateful	1.000	0.549	0.709	760
spelling changes (h)	non-hateful	0.000	0.000	0.000	0
spelling changes (h)	macro avg	0.500	0.274	0.354	760
spelling changes (h)	weighted avg	1.000	0.549	0.709	760
threats (h)	hateful	1.000	0.810	0.895	273
threats (h)	non-hateful	0.000	0.000	0.000	0
threats (h)	macro avg	0.500	0.405	0.447	273
threats (h)	weighted avg	1.000	0.810	0.895	273

Table 5: The `Metrics` classification report for roBERTa-offensive on HateCheck

TULAP - An Accessible and Sustainable Platform for Turkish Natural Language Processing Resources

Susan Üsküdarlı
suzan.uskudarli@boun.edu.tr

Muhammet Şen
muhammet.sen@boun.edu.tr

Furkan Akkurt
furkan.akkurt@boun.edu.tr

Merve Gürbüz
merve.gurbuz@boun.edu.tr

Onur Güngör
onurgu@boun.edu.tr

Arzucan Özgür
arzucan.ozgur@boun.edu.tr

Tunga Güngör
gungort@boun.edu.tr

Abstract

Access to natural language processing resources is essential for their continuous improvement. This can be especially challenging in educational institutions where the software development effort required to package and release research outcomes may be overwhelming and under-recognized. Access to well-prepared and reliable research outcomes is important both for their developers as well as the greater research community. This paper presents an approach to address this concern with two main goals: (1) to create an open-source easily deployable platform where resources can be easily shared and explored, and (2) to use this platform to publish open-source Turkish NLP resources (datasets and tools) created by a research lab. The Turkish Natural Language Processing (TULAP) was designed and developed as an easy-to-use platform to share dataset and tool resources which supports interactive tool demos. Numerous open access Turkish NLP resources have been shared on TULAP. All tools are containerized to support portability for custom use. This paper describes the design, implementation, and deployment of TULAP with use cases (available at `https://tulap.cmpe.boun.edu.tr/`). A short video demonstrating our system is available at `https://figshare.com/articles/media/TULAP_Demo/22179047`.

1 Introduction and Motivation

There is a growing interest in the field of natural language processing (NLP) due to the recent advances in deep learning-based approaches, such as transformer architectures and pretrained language models. This interest shows itself in the demand both for applications solving NLP tasks and for high-quality corpora that can be used in machine learning models. Although there are plenty of such resources for well-studied languages such as English, there is a scarcity of these resources in most of the other languages. In addition to developing such resources, there is a need for building software environments that collect these resources within a platform and offer them to the NLP community with easy-to-use interfaces.

This paper introduces TULAP (Turkish Language Processing Platform) that aims to provide a variety of Turkish NLP resources (datasets and tools). TULAP provides a user-friendly user interface (UI) where users can easily discover and examine NLP resources. Tools can be explored without the hassle of having to build and install them. All tools are containerized APIs (Application Programming Interface) to facilitate easy installation and use. The tools served on TULAP are provided as open-source to facilitate further research and development. This is particularly important in educational institutions where students tend not to package their code appropriately, leading to to loss of time and effort for those who wish to use their work.

The main motivation of TULAP is to develop a platform that supports the continuous contribution of NLP resources generated by our research lab, TABILab[1]. For the initial deployment, we gathered previously developed resources, created APIs, and containerized them. Hereafter, the resource developers will be able to make their contributions with an easy-to-use interface. The aim is to provide an up-to-date NLP platform with resources that are easy to discover and explore as well as to contribute new resources produced by researchers.

The main contributions of this work are summarized as follows:

- The creation of an NLP platform (TULAP)[2] that supports access to Turkish NLP datasets and tools, provides interactive demos, enables easy end-user contribution of datasets and tools, and open access to all resources;

[1] Text Analytics and BioInformatics Lab (TABILab) is a research lab of the Computer Engineering Department of Boğaziçi University. `https://tabilab.cmpe.boun.edu.tr/`

[2] `https://tulap.cmpe.boun.edu.tr/`

Proceedings of the 17th Conference of the European Chapter of the Association for Computational Linguistics System Demonstrations, pages 219–227
May 2-4, 2023 ©2023 Association for Computational Linguistics

- Systematic documentation of the Turkish NLP datasets and tools with access information [3];
- Creation of APIs and containerized versions of the tools to facilitate accessibility;
- Introduction of a general archival process to support continuous contributions by developing a research output platform[4];
- A monitoring system to identify problems and track how the platform is being used, and
- A deployment that aggregates Turkish NLP resources developed at Boğaziçi University.

The remainder of this paper is organized as follows: Section 2 provides an overview of NLP platforms; Section 3 describes the platform requirements, design, and implementation; Section 4 describes the resources on TULAP with use-cases in Section 5. Finally, Section 6 discusses the current state and future work with concluding remarks.

2 Related Work

The goal of collecting NLP resources under a unified framework and thus making implementing various types of applications easier has led to the development of NLP platforms in several languages. In this section, we briefly review a few of the widely-used NLP platforms with different functionalities including those specific to the Turkish language.

NLTK (Bird, 2006) is one of the earliest NLP libraries consisting of tools as a hierarchy of modules. It supports a wide range of tasks as well as corpora that can be used in various NLP tasks. AllenNLP (Gardner et al., 2018) is a library for deep learning-based NLP research. The users can build their own models using common deep learning operations. Stanford CoreNLP toolkit (Manning et al., 2014) provides a pipeline of preprocessing operations and downstream NLP tasks in various languages. It is one of the most widely used NLP platforms partly due to its simple design. Users can also integrate new NLP tasks to the pipeline.

The Hugging Face platform (Hugging Face, Inc., 2023) is one of the most popular platforms that is actively used in current NLP research. It includes a wide range of libraries that consist of different types of software such as machine learning models, datasets, demos, and evaluation tools. The `transformers` library (Wolf et al., 2020) includes open-source implementations of state-of-the-art transformer-based models. The users can easily share the resources they have developed in the platform via the Hugging Face Hub.

Among the platforms specific to Turkish, İTÜ Turkish NLP Web Service (Eryiğit, 2014) offers a variety of tools that can be used in Turkish NLP studies. The tools in the platform can be used either as a pipeline or as stand-alone components. Since the platform has been designed for Turkish, it includes tools that are specific to Turkish such as diacritic restorer. A recently-developed platform is Mukayese (Safaya et al., 2022), which is a benchmarking platform that provides a set of datasets and benchmarks for seven different types of Turkish NLP tasks. The Mukayese platform is also a part of the Turkish Data Depository (TDD) project[5] for building a repository of Turkish NLP resources.

The platform that we introduce in this work, TULAP, bears commonalities with these earlier works as well as different functionalities. Unlike most other platforms, we offer both NLP datasets and software tools. The tools can be used as ready-to-use stand-alone applications, while the datasets can be utilized for training machine learning models or for other purposes. With respect to the tool set, TULAP is similar to the Stanford CoreNLP framework in the sense that both preprocessing and downstream operations are supported, and the platform is extendable with new tools. There are several differences of TULAP from the currently available Turkish platforms. While these platforms mostly provide preprocessing operations, TULAP also supports a wide range of more complex tasks like text summarization and question answering. Furthermore, all the resources are made accessible with open-source or Creative Commons licenses and all tools are containerized for portability purposes. Finally, the platform is extensible with support for end-user contribution of new tools and datasets.

3 Platform Design & Implementation

3.1 Requirements

The main goals of the platform are to: (1) provide information and access to NLP resources (datasets and tools); (2) demonstrate the use of tools; (3) facilitate acquisition and use of resources; and (4) contribute new resources. There are three types of users: end users, resource providers, and system administrators. The main requirements are:

[3] https://github.com/BOUN-TABILab-TULAP

[4] https://github.com/BOUN-TABILab-TULAP/tabi-rop

[5] https://tdd.ai/?language=en

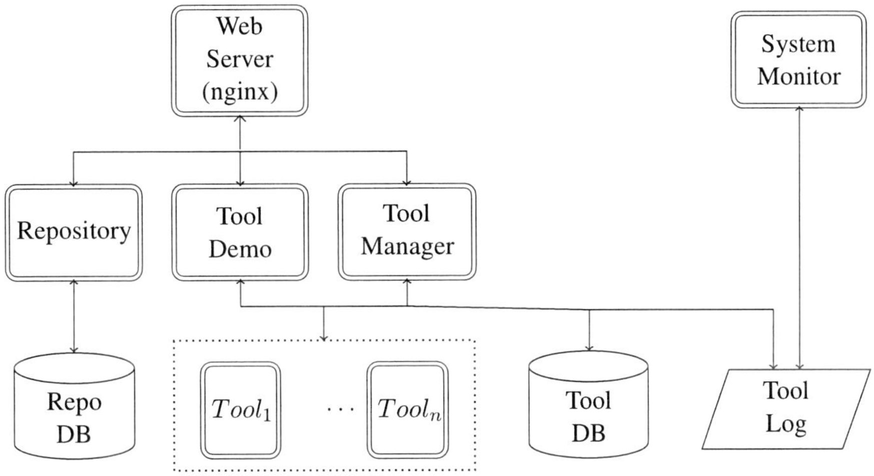

Figure 1: An overview of TULAP. The containers (docker) are indicated with double borders.

- A user should be able to browse and search the resources by keywords, tags, and authors.
- Resource providers should be able to specify or modify information (authors, language, etc.) related to the resources they contribute.
- The system should provide a demo interface that processes the input and returns the results.
- The system should provide installation and tool usage instructions.
- Containerization should be used to support portability, executability and scalability.
- All resources should be easy to obtain and use to support accessibility and extensibility.
- System administrators should be able to control and monitor the use of the tools.

3.2 Design and Implementation

The design of TULAP addresses the description, discovery and access to NLP-related dataset and tool resources. To support the portability and ease of building we chose to implement the platform with containerized components using Docker (Boettiger, 2015). Furthermore, all tools that are hosted on the platform must also be containerized. Thus, the platform as well as the tools it hosts are easily reusable.

The TULAP platform consists of several containers (Figure 1): An Nginx (NGINX, 2022) container serves as a reverse proxy for TULAP services and static files. There are two main functions that TULAP serves: (1) the specification and the access to information regarding NLP-related resources, and (2) demonstration of how tools function. The first part is addressed with the *Repository*, based on CLARIN-DSPACE (UFAL, 2022) (Common Language Resources and Technology Infrastructure) which is widely used for repositories. Users may browse and search about structured information related to datasets and tools, including references to corresponding academic articles. A PostgreSQL (PostgreSQL, 2022) container is used to persist data related to these resources.

Tool-related functionality is handled with the *Tool Manager* and *Tool Demo* containers. The *Tool Manager* supports the addition of new tool demos which involves specifying project source code (dockerized), information about the input & output types, and a user guide (see Section 5). *Tool Demo* enables the interactive exploration of tool demos using predefined or user-provided input. Figure 2 shows a sequence diagram of how a user interacts with a specific tool demo. First, the tool specification is fetched to generate a user interface (form). The input provided by the user is used to generate an API request which is sent to the tool. The response is processed according to the output specification and presented to the user.

Tools must be open-source, dockerized, and provide an application programming interface (API). Tool specifications are used to generate user interfaces to support interaction with demos. The front-end of tool demos is handled with a Node container[6] and the back-end (API calls) is handled with a Python container[7]. A MongoDB container[8] stores tool specifications and their usage information. The aim to provide ease of access and use to

[6]https://hub.docker.com/_/node
[7]https://hub.docker.com/_/python
[8]https://hub.docker.com/_/mongo

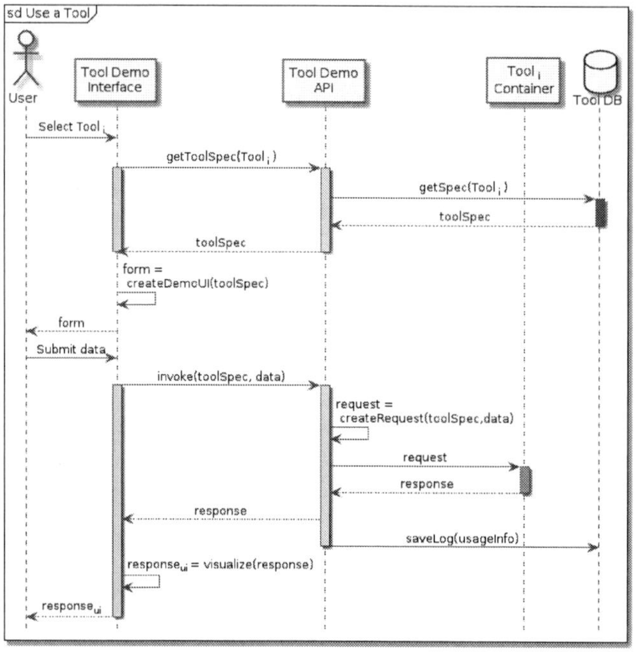

Figure 2: The sequence diagram for using a specific tool.

tools is the reason for imposing these criteria. As tools are dockerized, they can be fetched, built, and used for custom purposes.

Finally, the *System Monitor* allows the system administrators to gain insight into which, when, and how tools have been accessed. The system health is tracked to ensure that tools are up and running and to mitigate any problems.

3.3 Adding New Tools to the Demo Platform

Tool developers and system administrators are authorized to add new tools to the platform. Tools can be contributed by specifying four kinds of information: (1) *general* information which includes name & description (in Turkish and English), Git repository link, contact email, and API endpoint; (2) *input* specification which includes a name and type for each field type, at least one sample input, and the corresponding parameter name used by the tool; (3) *output* specification which includes the name and type of fields in the response provided by the tool; and (4) *user guide* which describes the input and output expected by the tool demo. This tool specification is posted to the *Tool Demo* which clones the Git repository and builds a Docker image. Then it creates a container from the image and stores the container details for future invocations. Once the container starts, it can handle requests.

4 TULAP Deployment

At the time of the writing of this article, TULAP includes 12 datasets and 16 tools which are shown in Table 1 and Table 2, respectively.

NLP Datasets
BOUN Dependency Treebank **v2.8** (Türk et al., 2019; Türk et al., 2021); **v2.11** (Marşan et al., 2022; Marşan, 2022)
Question Answering Corpus (Derici et al., 2018b,a)
Scientific Abstracts Corpus (Öztürk et al., 2014b,a)
Sentiment Analysis Corpus (Köksal and Özgür, 2021c,b)
Sign Language Corpus (Buz and Güngör, 2019a,b)
Türkiye Büyük Millet Meclisi (Grand National Assembly of Turkey) Corpus (Güngör et al., 2018a,b)
Turkish-English Parallel Corpus (Taşçı et al., 2006a,b)
Turkish Multi-document Summarization Corpus (Nuzumlalı and Özgür, 2014a,b)
Turkish Question Answering Dataset (SQuAD-TR) (Budur et al., 2020)
Web Corpus (Sak et al., 2011, 2010)
Word Embeddings (Güngör and Yıldız, 2017a,b)

Table 1: The datasets provided on TULAP

The tools on the platform are dynamically updated with new contributions. The platform itself is open-source and accessible at: `https://github.com/BOUN-TABILab-TULAP/tabi-rop`.

5 Using TULAP

This section describes how TULAP can be used through use cases. The landing page of TULAP

NLP Tools
Tokenizer (Ak and Güngör, 2022c)
Sentence Splitter (Ak and Güngör, 2022b)
Deasciifier (Ak and Güngör, 2022a)
Lemmatizer (Köksal, 2018)
Morphological Analyzer (Sak et al., 2007a,b)
Morphological Disambiguator (Sak et al., 2007a,c)
Dependency Parser (Özateş et al., 2018, 2020)
Verbal Multiword Expression Identifier (Yirmibeşoğlu and Güngör, 2020a,b)
Named Entity Recognizer (Güngör et al., 2018c,d)
Question Answerer (Derici et al., 2018b,c)
Relation Extractor (Köksal and Özgür, 2020, 2021a)
Sentiment Analyzer. i) Binary (Aydın and Güngör, 2020; Aydın et al., 2021); ii) Ternary (Köksal and Özgür, 2021c,b)
Text Summarizer (Baykara and Güngör, 2022b,a)
Grammar Annotation Tool. i) Standalone (Türk et al., 2022; Berk and Köksal, 2021); ii) Web (Akkurt et al., 2022; Akkurt and Uskudarli, 2022)

Table 2: The tools provided on TULAP

allows users to browse and search for datasets and tools. Dataset resources can be easily searched, inspected, and downloaded. Due to space limitations, in this section we focus on describing tool handling as it is significantly more complicated. The following use cases demonstrate how users: (1) discover and inspect tools; (2) contribute new resources; (3) fetch, build, and use tools independently; and (4) monitor the use of TULAP:

(1) Tool Discovery and Demo Figure 3a shows the repository where users can browse and search for resources. The user has searched for "named entity" for which resources that include either keyword are shown. Figure 3b shows the details pages when the "Named Entity Recognition" tool is selected. Figure 3c [9] shows the use of the demo with the Turkish sentence *İstanbul Barosu'ndaki Yapay Zekâ, Robotlar ve Hukuk Konferansı'nda pirimiz Alan Turing'i anmadan olmazdı*[10]. The tool returns the entity tags for tokens, for which the demo provides two alternative presentations (BRAT (Stenetorp et al., 2012) and JSON).

(2) Adding new tools Adding a new tool to the repository consists of providing information about the source-code (Git) and executable demo (URL) of the tool as well as academic information such as related papers, authors, and funding.

(3) Executing tools TULAP provides all the resources related to the tools along with an interface to demonstrate their functionality. All the tools provided in TULAP are open-source and are also independently available at TULAP repository[11]. For those who wish to utilize a tool beyond the demo interface (e.g. to recognize named entities in a large dataset using the NER tool), we have dockerized their APIs for easy deployment. TULAP itself utilizes the dockerized tools along with an interface we generate to demonstrate their functionality. Anyone can easily build the dockerized tools in their environment to use the APIs to their specific purposes. Listing 1 shows how easily the *Named Entity Recognition* tool can be built and used. Note that the API call is the one for the example shown in Figure 3c.

(4) Monitoring Tool Demos System administrators use the *System Monitor* to observe metrics like the number of requests and response times for the tools. These metrics are collected and visualized using Grafana (Grafana, 2022).

6 Discussion and Conclusions

This work's primary focus was to create an accessible and sustainable platform for Turkish NLP resources produced at Boğaziçi University. For this, we developed a *research output platform* (*tabi-rop*) where open access to datasets and tools that result from research activities related to NLP or other fields can be shared. TULAP was developed using *tabi-rop* and hosts numerous resources produced by our research lab. One of the most challenging tasks was the collection and packaging of previously developed resources. This fact validated the need for such a platform – a sentiment also expressed by the research lab alumni when reviewing TULAP. We continuously monitor TULAP as well as maintain *tabi-rop*[12]. Currently, we are upgrading the *Repository* component to benefit from DSpace v7 (Lyrasis, 2022) improvements.

Moving forward, we plan to include preprocessing tasks, new tasks, and improved versions of present tools. We are pleased that new resources have been contributed subsequently to the initial release. Other future work includes platform maintenance and improvements to the presentation of and interaction with resources.

While many platforms have been emerging to

[9]For higher resolution of the images see `https://figshare.com/articles/figure/TULAP_NER/21629549`

[10]Translation: *It is impossible not to remember our sage Alan Turing during the Artificial Intelligence, Robots, and Law Conference held at the Bar Association of Istanbul.*

[11]URL: `https://github.com/BOUN-TABILab-TULAP`

[12]`https://github.com/BOUN-TABILab-TULAP/tabi-rop`

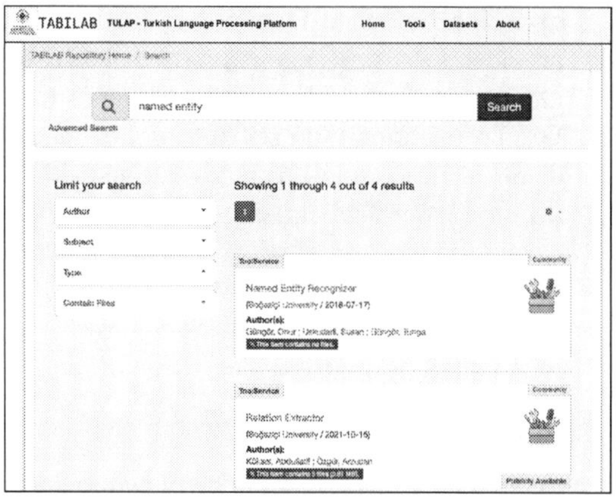

(a) Search for resources including the keywords *named entity*

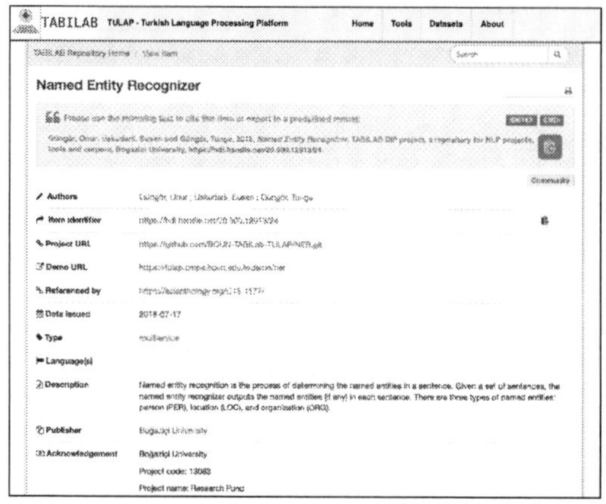

(b) Details for the Named Entity Recognizer.

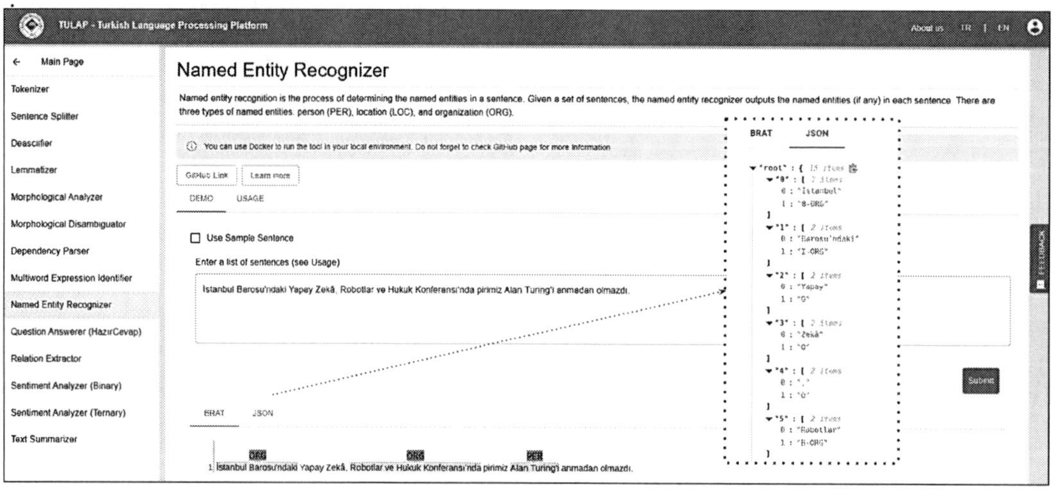

(c) NER for sentence: *İstanbul Barosu'ndaki Yapay Zekâ, Robotlar ve Hukuk Konferansı'nda pirimiz Alan Turing'i anmadan olmazdı*. Response is in BRAT format. The JSON serialization is shown in the dotted frame.

Figure 3: Searching (a), inspecting (b), and using a tool (c) in TULAP.

```
$ git clone https://github.com/BOUN-TABILab-TULAP/NER.git
$ docker build -t ner .
// docker console feedback omitted
$ docker run -d -p 8080:8080 ner
$ curl -X POST http://localhost:8080/ner/predict/ -H 'Content-Type: application/json' -d '{"text":"İstanbul
    Barosu'ndaki Yapay Zekâ, Robotlar ve Hukuk Konferansı'nda pirimiz Alan Turing'i anmadan olmazdı."}'

{'tagger_output': {'0': ['İstanbul', 'B-ORG'], '1': ["Barosu'ndaki", 'I-ORG'], '2': ['Yapay', 'O'], '3':
    ['Zekâ', 'O'],...}
```

Listing 1: The commands to acquire, build, run the NER tool and an API request. The output of the *docker build* and API response are truncated due to space limitation.

submit various resources, we expect that research teams will strongly benefit from a repository where reference versions of their work are collected in a single platform. The systematic publication of research outcomes supports the sustainability and continuity of research. Having control over the body of work makes it easier to track and include resources valued by the team that may not meet the criteria of external repositories. Similarly, it reduced the risks of relying solely on other repositories. This is not to imply that we do not support contributing our work on all relevant platforms. We expect that consistent effort in preparing reference material will result in following good practices that enhance the preparation of resources that can also be shared on all relevant platforms.

We approached the development of this platform as a software project starting from requirements elicitation, design, implementation, deployment, and maintenance. The project was managed with weekly meetings, version management, and issue-tracking tools. We believe that this approach was instrumental to achieving our goals. We note that the research output platform (*tabi-rop*) which we designed and developed for TULAP supports sharing computational research outputs in general and stands as a valuable contribution in its own right. It is not restricted to the deployment of TULAP and it can serve as an underlying platform in other domains and languages.

Our hope is that TULAP facilitates research and development efforts in Turkish NLP with information, demos, open-source resources, and easily accessible/usable reference versions of data and tools that we have provided.

Acknowledgements

This work was supported by Boğaziçi University Research Fund Grant Number 16909. We are grateful to all resource providers and the TABILab alumni who provided valuable feedback.

References

Buse Ak and Tunga Güngör. 2022a. Deasciifier. [Online; https://hdl.handle.net/20.500.12913/28; last accessed 19 July 2022].

Buse Ak and Tunga Güngör. 2022b. Sentence Splitter. [Online; https://hdl.handle.net/20.500.12913/26; last accessed 19 July 2022].

Buse Ak and Tunga Güngör. 2022c. Tokenizer. [Online; https://hdl.handle.net/20.500.12913/25; last accessed 19 July 2022].

Salih Furkan Akkurt, Büşra Marşan, and Susan Uskudarli. 2022. Boat v2 – a web-based dependency annotation tool with focus on agglutinative languages. This paper was presented at The International Conference and Workshop On Agglutinative Language Technologies as a Challenge of Natural Language Processing (ALTNLP) 2022.

Salih Furkan Akkurt and Susan Uskudarli. 2022. Bogazici Annotation Tool (BoAT) v2 - Web based Grammar Annotation tool for Morphologically Rich Languages. [Online; https://hdl.handle.net/20.500.12913/31; last accessed 19 July 2022].

Cem Rıfkı Aydın and Tunga Güngör. 2020. Combination of recursive and recurrent neural networks for aspect-based sentiment analysis using inter-aspect relations. *IEEE Access*, 8:77820–77832.

Cem Rıfkı Aydın, Tunga Güngör, and Ali Erkan. 2021. Sentiment Analyzer. [Online; https://hdl.handle.net/20.500.12913/9; last accessed 19 July 2022].

Batuhan Baykara and Tunga Güngör. 2022a. Text Summarizer. [Online; https://hdl.handle.net/20.500.12913/30; last accessed 19 July 2022].

Batuhan Baykara and Tunga Güngör. 2022b. Turkish abstractive text summarization using pretrained sequence-to-sequence models. *Natural Language Engineering*, page 1–30.

Gözde Berk and Abdüllatif Köksal. 2021. Bogazici Annotation Tool (BoAT) v1. [Online; https://hdl.handle.net/99999/38; last accessed 19 July 2022].

Steven Bird. 2006. NLTK: the natural language toolkit. In *Proceedings of the COLING/ACL 2006 Interactive Presentation Sessions*, pages 69–72.

Carl Boettiger. 2015. An introduction to Docker for reproducible research. *ACM SIGOPS Operating Systems Review*, 49(1):71–79.

Emrah Budur, Rıza Özçelik, Tunga Gungor, and Christopher Potts. 2020. Data and Representation for Turkish Natural Language Inference. In *Proceedings of the 2020 Conference on Empirical Methods in Natural Language Processing (EMNLP)*, pages 8253–8267, Online. Association for Computational Linguistics.

Buse Buz and Tunga Güngör. 2019a. Developing a statistical Turkish Sign Language translation system for primary school students. In *2019 IEEE International Symposium on INnovations in Intelligent SysTems and Applications (INISTA)*, pages 1–6.

Buse Buz and Tunga Güngör. 2019b. Sign Language Corpus. [Online; https://hdl.handle.net/20.500.12913/23; last accessed 19 July 2022].

Caner Derici, Yiğit Aydın, Çiğdem Yenialaca, and Nihal Yağmur Aydın. 2018a. Question Answering Corpus. [Online; https://hdl.handle.net/20.500.12913/22; last accessed 19 July 2022].

Caner Derici, Yiğit Aydın, Çiğdem Yenialaca, Nihal Yağmur Aydın, Günizi Kartal, Arzucan Özgür, and Tunga Güngör. 2018b. A closed-domain question answering framework using reliable resources to assist students. *Natural Language Engineering*, 24(5):725–762.

Caner Derici, Yiğit Aydın, Çiğdem Yenialaca, Nihal Yağmur Aydın, Günizi Kartal, Arzucan Özgür, and Tunga Güngör. 2018c. Question Answerer. [Online; https://hdl.handle.net/20.500.12913/29; last accessed 19 July 2022].

Gülşen Eryiğit. 2014. ITU Turkish NLP web service. In *Proceedings of the Demonstrations at the 14th Conference of the European Chapter of the Association for Computational Linguistics*, pages 1–4.

Matt Gardner, Joel Grus, Mark Neumann, Oyvind Tafjord, Pradeep Dasigi, Nelson F Liu, Matthew Peters, Michael Schmitz, and Luke Zettlemoyer. 2018. AllenNLP: A Deep Semantic Natural Language Processing Platform.

Grafana. 2022. Grafana. [Online; https://grafana.com/; last accessed 30 July 2022].

Onur Güngör, Mert Tiftikçi, and Çağıl Sönmez. 2018a. A corpus of Grand National Assembly of Turkish Parliament's transcripts. In *Proceedings of the Eleventh International Conference on Language Resources and Evaluation (LREC 2018)*, Paris, France. European Language Resources Association (ELRA).

Onur Güngör, Mert Tiftikçi, and Çağıl Sönmez. 2018b. TBMM Corpus. [Online; https://hdl.handle.net/20.500.12913/20; last accessed 19 July 2022].

Onur Güngör and Eray Yıldız. 2017a. Linguistic features in Turkish word representations. In *2017 25th Signal Processing and Communications Applications Conference (SIU)*, pages 1–4.

Onur Güngör and Eray Yıldız. 2017b. Word Embeddings. [Online; https://hdl.handle.net/20.500.12913/18; last accessed 19 July 2022].

Onur Güngör, Suzan Üsküdarlı, and Tunga Güngör. 2018c. Improving named entity recognition by jointly learning to disambiguate morphological tags. In *Proceedings of the 27th International Conference on Computational Linguistics (COLING)*, pages 2082–2092, Santa Fe, New Mexico, USA. Association for Computational Linguistics.

Onur Güngör, Suzan Üsküdarlı, and Tunga Güngör. 2018d. Named Entity Recognizer. [Online; https://hdl.handle.net/20.500.12913/24; last accessed 19 July 2022].

Hugging Face, Inc. 2023. Hugging Face. [Online; https://huggingface.co; last accessed 22 February 2023].

Abdullatif Köksal. 2018. Lemmatizer. [Online; https://hdl.handle.net/20.500.12913/27; last accessed 19 July 2022].

Abdullatif Köksal and Arzucan Özgür. 2020. The RELX dataset and matching the multilingual blanks for cross-lingual relation classification. In *Findings of the Association for Computational Linguistics: EMNLP 2020*, pages 340–350, Online. Association for Computational Linguistics.

Abdullatif Köksal and Arzucan Özgür. 2021a. Relation Extractor. [Online; https://hdl.handle.net/20.500.12913/5; last accessed 19 July 2022].

Abdullatif Köksal and Arzucan Özgür. 2021b. Sentiment Analyzer. [Online; https://hdl.handle.net/20.500.12913/7; last accessed 19 July 2022].

Abdullatif Köksal and Arzucan Özgür. 2021c. Twitter dataset and evaluation of transformers for Turkish sentiment analysis. In *2021 29th Signal Processing and Communications Applications Conference (SIU)*, pages 1–4.

Lyrasis. 2022. DSpace 7.x Documentation . [Online; https://wiki.lyrasis.org/display/DSDOC7x; last accessed 1 December 2022].

Christopher D Manning, Mihai Surdeanu, John Bauer, Jenny Rose Finkel, Steven Bethard, and David McClosky. 2014. The Stanford CoreNLP natural language processing toolkit. In *Proceedings of 52nd annual meeting of the association for computational linguistics: system demonstrations*, pages 55–60.

Büşra Marşan. 2022. BOUN Treebank v2. [Online; https://hdl.handle.net/99999/39; last accessed 28 July 2022].

Büşra Marşan, Salih Furkan Akkurt, Muhammet Şen, Merve Gürbüz, Onur Güngör, Şaziye Betül Özateş, Suzan Üsküdarlı, Arzucan Özgür, Tunga Güngör, and Balkız Öztürk. 2022. Enhancements to the BOUN Treebank Reflecting the Agglutinative Nature of Turkish. This paper was presented at The International Conference and Workshop On Agglutinative Language Technologies as a Challenge of Natural Language Processing (ALTNLP) 2022.

NGINX. 2022. NGINX. [Online; https://www.nginx.com; last accessed 1 Aug 2022].

Muhammed Yavuz Nuzumlalı and Arzucan Özgür. 2014a. Analyzing stemming approaches for Turkish multi-document summarization. In *Proceedings of the 2014 Conference on Empirical Methods in Natural Language Processing (EMNLP)*, pages 702–706, Doha, Qatar. Association for Computational Linguistics.

Muhammed Yavuz Nuzumlalı and Arzucan Özgür. 2014b. Turkish MDS Data Set. [Online; https://hdl.handle.net/20.500.12913/17; last accessed 19 July 2022].

PostgreSQL. 2022. PostgreSQL. [Online; https://www.postgresql.org/; last accessed 1 Aug 2022].

Ali Safaya, Emirhan Kurtuluş, Arda Goktogan, and Deniz Yuret. 2022. Mukayese: Turkish NLP Strikes Back. In *Findings of the Association for Computational Linguistics: ACL 2022*, pages 846–863,

Dublin, Ireland. Association for Computational Linguistics.

Haşim Sak, Tunga Güngör, and Murat Saraçlar. 2007a. Morphological disambiguation of Turkish text with perceptron algorithm. In *Computational Linguistics and Intelligent Text Processing*, pages 107–118, Berlin, Heidelberg. Springer Berlin Heidelberg.

Haşim Sak, Tunga Güngör, and Murat Saraçlar. 2011. Resources for Turkish morphological processing. *Language Resources and Evaluation*, 45(2):249–261.

Haşim Sak, Tunga Güngör, and Murat Saraçlar. 2007b. Morphological Analyser. [Online; https://hdl.handle.net/20.500.12913/4; last accessed 19 July 2022].

Haşim Sak, Tunga Güngör, and Murat Saraçlar. 2007c. Morphological Disambiguator. [Online; https://hdl.handle.net/20.500.12913/8; last accessed 19 July 2022].

Haşim Sak, Tunga Güngör, and Murat Saraçlar. 2010. Web Corpus. [Online; https://hdl.handle.net/20.500.12913/16; last accessed 19 July 2022].

Pontus Stenetorp, Sampo Pyysalo, Goran Topić, Tomoko Ohta, Sophia Ananiadou, and Jun'ichi Tsujii. 2012. BRAT: a web-based tool for NLP-assisted text annotation. In *Proceedings of the Demonstrations at the 13th Conference of the European Chapter of the Association for Computational Linguistics*, pages 102–107.

Şerafettin Taşçı, A. Mustafa Güngör, and Tunga Güngör. 2006a. Compiling a Turkish-English bilingual corpus and developing an algorithm for sentence alignment. In *Proceedings of the Third International Bulgarian-Turkish Conference on ComputerScience*, pages 291–296, Istanbul.

Şerafettin Taşçı, Mustafa Güngör, and Tunga Güngör. 2006b. Turkish-English Parallel Corpus. [Online; https://hdl.handle.net/20.500.12913/19; last accessed 19 July 2022].

Utku Türk, Furkan Atmaca, Şaziye Betül Özateş, Gözde Berk, Seyyit Talha Bedir, Abdullatif Köksal, Balkız Öztürk Başaran, Tunga Güngör, and Arzucan Özgür. 2022. Resources for Turkish dependency parsing: Introducing the BOUN treebank and the BoAT annotation tool. *Language Resources and Evaluation*, 56(1):259–307.

Utku Türk, Furkan Atmaca, Şaziye Betül Özateş, Abdullatif Köksal, Balkiz Ozturk Basaran, Tunga Gungor, and Arzucan Özgür. 2019. Turkish treebanking: Unifying and constructing efforts. In *Proceedings of the 13th Linguistic Annotation Workshop*, pages 166–177.

Utku Türk, Furkan Atmaca, Şaziye Betül Özateş, Gözde Berk, Seyyit Talha Bedir, Abdullatif Köksal, Balkız Öztürk Başaran, Tunga Güngör, and Arzucan Özgür. 2021. BOUN Treebank. [Online; https://hdl.handle.net/20.500.12913/14; last accessed 19 July 2022].

UFAL. 2022. clarin-dspace digital repository. [Online; https://github.com/ufal/clarin-dspace; last accessed 31 July 2022].

Thomas Wolf, Lysandre Debut, Victor Sanh, Julien Chaumond, Clement Delangue, Anthony Moi, Pierric Cistac, Tim Rault, Remi Louf, Morgan Funtowicz, Joe Davison, Sam Shleifer, Patrick von Platen, Clara Ma, Yacine Jernite, Julien Plu, Canwen Xu, Teven Le Scao, Sylvain Gugger, Mariama Drame, Quentin Lhoest, and Alexander Rush. 2020. Transformers: State-of-the-art natural language processing. In *Proceedings of the 2020 Conference on Empirical Methods in Natural Language Processing: System Demonstrations*, pages 38–45, Online. Association for Computational Linguistics.

Zeynep Yirmibeşoğlu and Tunga Güngör. 2020a. ERMI at PARSEME shared task 2020: Embedding-rich multiword expression identification. In *Proceedings of the Joint Workshop on Multiword Expressions and Electronic Lexicons*, pages 130–135, online. Association for Computational Linguistics.

Zeynep Yirmibeşoğlu and Tunga Güngör. 2020b. Verbal MWE Identifier. [Online; https://hdl.handle.net/20.500.12913/10; last accessed 19 July 2022].

Şaziye Betül Özateş, Tunga Güngör, Arzucan Özgür, and Balkız Öztürk. 2018. A morphology-based representation model for lstm-based dependency parsing of agglutinative languages. In *Proceedings of the CoNLL 2018 Shared Task: Multilingual Parsing from Raw Text to Universal Dependencies*, pages 238–247.

Şaziye Betül Özateş, Tunga Güngör, Arzucan Özgür, and Balkız Öztürk. 2020. Dependency Parser. [Online; https://hdl.handle.net/20.500.12913/11; last accessed 19 July 2022].

Seçil Öztürk, Bülent Sankur, Tunga Güngör, Mustafa Berkay Yılmaz, Bilge Köroglu, Onur Ağın, Mustafa İşbilen, Çağdaş Ulaş, and Mehmet Ahat. 2014a. Scientific Abstracts Corpus. [Online; https://hdl.handle.net/20.500.12913/15; last accessed 19 July 2022].

Seçil Öztürk, Bülent Sankur, Tunga Güngör, Mustafa Berkay Yılmaz, Bilge Köroglu, Onur Ağın, Mustafa İşbilen, Çağdaş Ulaş, and Mehmet Ahat. 2014b. Turkish labeled text corpus. In *2014 22nd Signal Processing and Communications Applications Conference (SIU)*, pages 1395–1398.

ALANNO: An Active Learning Annotation System for Mortals

Josip Jukić[♠] **Fran Jelenić**[♠] **Miroslav Bićanić** **Jan Šnajder**
University of Zagreb, Faculty of Electrical Engineering and Computing
Text Analysis and Knowledge Engineering Lab
`{name.surname}@fer.hr`

Abstract

Supervised machine learning has become the cornerstone of today's data-driven society, increasing the need for labeled data. However, the process of acquiring labels is often expensive and tedious. One possible remedy is to use *active learning* (AL) – a special family of machine learning algorithms designed to reduce labeling costs. Although AL has been successful in practice, a number of practical challenges hinder its effectiveness and are often overlooked in existing AL annotation tools. To address these challenges, we developed ALANNO, an open-source annotation system for NLP tasks equipped with features to make AL effective in real-world annotation projects. ALANNO facilitates annotation management in a multi-annotator setup and supports a variety of AL methods and underlying models, which are easily configurable and extensible.

1 Introduction

We are witnessing an ever-growing demand for data along with the rapid development of machine learning and deep learning algorithms. In particular, we need an abundance of labeled data to develop well-performing models, which is not easy to obtain. For many natural language processing (NLP) tasks, the labeling process, i.e., annotation, is often the most expensive and time-consuming part of developing machine learning models. The cognitive exertion of human annotators can affect their judgment, which further affects label validity. Consequently, this manifests in poor *agreement* – a proxy for label reliability, which is a prerequisite for validity (Artstein and Poesio, 2008; Paun et al., 2022). Poor label reliability and validity negatively affect the machine learning algorithm, as it is only as good as the data it consumes.

Designed to alleviate labeling issues and reduce annotation cost, *active learning* (**AL**; Settles, 2009) is a special family of machine learning algorithms. In contrast to the standard random selection of instances for labeling, a typical AL method iteratively queries the most informative instances for the underlying model to achieve the best possible performance with the fewest possible labels. AL has been shown to reduce annotation effort across machine learning applications, e.g., (Beluch et al., 2018; Zhang and Chen, 2002), especially in NLP, e.g., (Chen et al., 2012; Settles and Craven, 2008; Ein-Dor et al., 2020).

Despite the demonstrated successes of AL, many challenges are involved in deploying AL in real-world scenarios (Lowell et al., 2019; Attenberg and Provost, 2011). Unfortunately, these challenges are often overlooked in both research and practice. In particular, annotation tools that support AL rarely address the problems of unbiased evaluation of AL, imbalanced data, and stopping criteria for AL. The lack of concrete solutions for these problems hinders the effectiveness of AL. Aside from the practical challenges in AL, managing annotation campaigns is often very cumbersome, especially in multi-annotator setups (when multiple annotators are assigned to a single instance). Specifically, assigning instances to multiple annotators can be painstaking, particularly if one aims to achieve balanced combinations of annotators across instances. While there are many serviceable frameworks for simulating AL in idealized scenarios, e.g., (Danka and Horvath, 2018; Tang et al., 2019; Schröder et al., 2021), there are only a few tools for running real-world AL annotation campaigns with multiple annotators, none of them explicitly addressing the practical AL challenges.

To facilitate the creation of high-quality NLP datasets at reduced annotation costs, we developed ALANNO (**A**ctive **L**earning **Anno**tation), an open-source annotation system with AL strategies for data sampling. ALANNO's is specifically designed to address the practical challenges of AL and fa-

[♠]Equal contribution

Proceedings of the 17th Conference of the European Chapter of the Association for Computational Linguistics
System Demonstrations, pages 228–235
May 2-4, 2023 ©2023 Association for Computational Linguistics

cilitate the management of multi-annotator annotation projects. In particular, ALANNO guides toward more quality labels with a novel method for the balanced assignment of unlabeled instances to annotators in a multi-annotator setup. We support building gold labels by monitoring the inter-annotator agreement with task-specific metrics and agreement-aware weighted aggregation of labels. Equally important, ALANNO incorporates many features to address the major challenges of using AL in practice. Namely, we support guided learning (Attenberg and Provost, 2010) for mitigating data imbalance, and we ensure trustworthy evaluation of the underlying model on an unbiased test set and a stopping criterion to maximize the effectiveness of AL. As an essential practical solution, we enable a project-specific stopping criterion with a novel performance forecasting method based on Bayesian regression. By estimating the performance of the underlying model with hypothetically enlarged labeled sets, we enable practitioners to determine on the spot whether further annotation will only have diminishing returns. Lastly, ALANNO supports a wide range of state-of-the-art AL methods from the literature, allowing seamless inclusion of new models or methods.

In summary, our main contribution is ALANNO, an open-source AL annotation system for NLP tasks, which features (1) practical strategies for applying AL to real-world problems with a range of AL methods and (2) annotation management facilitation in a multi-annotator setup with quality control. ALANNO enables non-experts in AL to reap its benefits by accounting for key practical issues in annotation management and AL. In two case studies, we demonstrate ALANNO's two key features – balanced data assignment and AL performance forecasting. We also provide a short video[1] demonstration and release the code[2] under the Apache 2.0 license. While ALANNO has been born out of several years of experience with NLP annotations for various tasks and has evolved with each new project, it remains highly configurable, allowing easy customization and extension.

2 System Overview

We briefly describe the key aspects of ALANNO, which include projects, data assignment, label management, and annotation.

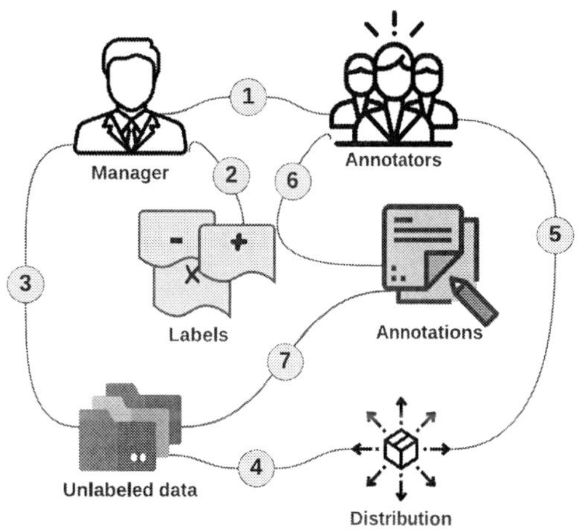

Figure 1: Organization of an ALANNO project. The lines between the icons indicate different lines of interaction, with the numbers denoting the temporal order. In brief, the project manager recruits annotators ①, creates labels ②, and imports the unlabeled data ③, which are then appointed to annotators via an assignment algorithm ④, ⑤. The annotators use the created labels ⑥ to annotate the data ⑦.

Projects. In ALANNO, the entire annotation process is encapsulated into a *project*, which handles the interactions between different parts of an annotation project, as depicted in Figure 1. A typical NLP annotation project is long-lasting and dynamic: annotators may be temporarily unavailable, new annotators may join an already-running project, and others may leave. ALANNO supports the managing of such a workforce dynamic. To separate the concerns and responsibilities, ALANNO defines two user roles: **project managers**, who are in charge of the annotation campaign, and **annotators**, whose task is to apply labels to the unlabeled data. At the moment, project managers can create three main types of projects: single- and multi-label classification, as well as sequence labeling tasks (e.g., named entity recognition).

Data assignment. Due to the dynamic nature of real-world annotation campaigns, it is convenient to separate the annotation process into smaller chunks. Moreover, annotation is an incremental process that often requires calibration in the initial phases. To meet these needs, the workload in ALANNO is divided into rounds, where each round can be configured independently. The project manager can specify the number of unlabeled instances to

[1] https://www.youtube.com/watch?v=hPcHPM8ttvE

[2] https://github.com/josipjukic/alanno

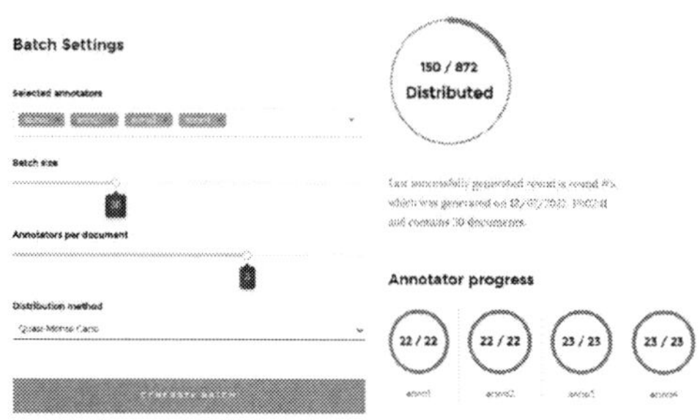

Figure 2: Data assignment interface

Figure 3: Annotation interface

be assigned, select annotators for the round, and the number of annotators per instance (Figure 2).

Annotation. The annotation interface (Figure 3) depends on the project type. For *classification* tasks, we support a single-label setup, where only one of the labels can be applied, and a multi-label setup with the possibility of applying multiple labels. In addition, we cover a large variety of *sequence labeling* tasks, where it is only necessary to define labels to fit the context of a specific use case. For example, one can define *organization*, *person name*, and *location* as labels for named entity recognition. Annotators can then select spans of text that fall into one of the defined categories.

Data management. The end product of an ALANNO project is the annotated dataset, which consists of labels gathered from annotators. ALANNO offers the user a choice between exporting an aggregated dataset, in which each instance appears precisely once with a single label obtained by aggregating the labels of different annotators, or a complete dataset, where each instance appears as many times as it has been annotated. The latter option is in line with recent recommendations to publish annotated datasets with the original labels rather than adjudicated labels (Kenyon-Dean et al., 2020), allowing for disagreement analysis, training of models that predict soft labels, e.g., (Pavlick and Kwiatkowski, 2019), or application of statistical label aggregation techniques, e.g., (Qing et al., 2014; Hovy and Yang, 2021; Gordon et al., 2021). Furthermore, to make it possible to follow up on earlier annotation projects, ALANNO supports partially annotated datasets where the annotations are specified as user-label pairs.

3 Features

Motivated by our experience in annotation projects and the practical challenges that emerge when deploying AL, we designed practical solutions that enable efficient labeling in real-world scenarios. We identified several key challenges, which, if not adequately addressed, may impair label quality and AL efficiency. Specifically, we focused on (1) label reliability, (2) unbiased evaluation of active learning models, (3) the stopping criterion for active learning, i.e., knowing when to terminate the active learning process, and (4) working with imbalanced data.

3.1 Annotation management

Annotation management in ALANNO is centered around the first critical challenge – label reliability. We support agreement-aware label aggregation and advanced data assignment to simultaneously promote label quality and make the management of annotation campaigns as seamless as possible.

Balanced assignment. Assigning unlabeled instances to annotators is an important aspect of the annotation process, in which combinations of annotators assigned to particular data points should be balanced to achieve more reliable labels. We have found that using uniform sampling based on pseudo-random numbers results in unbalanced combinations of annotators, with varying frequencies of different annotator tuples. To mitigate this and help improve label reliability, we developed a *Quasi-Monte Carlo* assignment method based on quasi-random numbers. In particular, we used Sobol sequences (Burhenne et al., 2011) to produce balanced combinations. In a scenario with n annotators and k annotators per data point, we draw n dimensional vectors generated from the Sobol sequence, where each element is in the $[0, 1]$ interval. We round the values to the nearest integer (0 or 1). If a particular vector has exactly k elements with value 1, we distribute the data point to the annotators at the corresponding indices of the vector. Otherwise, we discard the vector and draw a new one. The process is guaranteed to converge since all possible combinations are covered in the first 2^n vectors from the sequence. This procedure produces balanced combinations with uniform frequencies of annotator pairs, triplets, and up to k-tuples. We demonstrate its effects in a case study in Section 4.

Monitoring agreement. In a multi-annotator setup, annotator agreement is a strong indicator of label quality. ALANNO computes the inter-annotator agreement using metrics appropriate for the particular NLP task. Specifically, we use Cohen's κ coefficient (Cohen, 1960) to evaluate pairwise agreement for binary and multi-class annotation. For the joint measure that considers all annotators simultaneously, we use Fleiss' κ (Fleiss, 1971). On the other hand, for the multi-label setup, we use Krippendorff's α coefficient (Krippendorff, 2018) paired with MASI distance (Passonneau, 2006) for both pairwise and joint agreement.

Gold labels. Aggregating labels from multiple annotators is a critical component of creating high-quality datasets. In practice, different annotators often have different reliability levels due to differences in expertise. Such differences are exceptionally prominent with large groups of annotators. Therefore, ALANNO generates *gold labels* that consider an estimate of annotators' reliability. In particular, we aggregate the labels by assigning each annotator a weight proportional to how many times they assigned the majority label to a data point (Qing et al., 2014). For tasks with multiple labels, we chose to use the majority principle. The weighted aggregation leaves room for future improvement by incorporating systems such as Multi-Annotator Competence Estimation (MACE; Hovy et al., 2013).

3.2 AL acquisition models and functions

ALANNO supports AL as one of the key features. We incorporate practical solutions to mitigate the problems of deploying AL in real-world scenarios. We first describe what the system offers in terms of *acquisition models*, i.e., the underlying models used for AL, and *acquisition functions*, i.e., AL methods.

ALANNO offers a rich palette of acquisition models for AL. We include various approaches to preprocessing tailored for a specific language for the NLP task at hand, including TF-IDF, customizable n-gram models, and word embeddings, using English as the default language. Besides English, we currently also support Croatian. ALANNO provides many traditional models, including logistic regression, SVM, and random forest classifier. We also support deep models such as recurrent networks and Transformers (Vaswani et al., 2017).

ALANNO supports a wide range of active acquisition functions for both traditional and deep learning models. Starting from uncertainty sampling (Settles, 2009), a simple but powerful family of AL methods, ALANNO covers the *least confident*, *margin*, and *entropy* methods. All uncertainty-based methods are available for single- and multi-label problems. We have also incorporated acquisition functions that focus more on data diversity, such as the *informative density* method, which leverages information about the instances in the input space and gives higher weights to instances in high-density parts of the input space. From the family of AL methods specialized for deep neural networks, ALANNO provides the *core-set* method (Sener and Savarese, 2017) and BADGE (Ash et al., 2019).

3.3 AL challenges and solutions

We describe the aforementioned practical challenges in AL (unbiased evaluation, stopping criterion, and class imbalance) and our solutions that aim to preserve AL effectiveness.

Unbiased evaluation. Before starting the annotation process, ALANNO reserves a random sample of the imported data to be used later as a test set. In each round, managers can select how many test instances drawn from the reserved pool should be labeled out of the entire batch. In this way, one can adequately evaluate the model, as the reserved pool is not affected by the sampling bias (Prabhu et al., 2019). Since the acquisition functions often rely on the acquisition model's output, it is important to decouple evaluation and AL selection. A biased test set can lead to overestimating the model's performance, establishing a vicious cycle of uninformative queries in the early stages of acquisition. This often leads to redundant labels and, consequently, poorly performing models (Attenberg and Provost, 2011).

Stopping criterion. Although several stopping criteria for active learning have been proposed (Vlachos, 2008; Zhu et al., 2010; Laws and Schütze, 2008; Bloodgood and Vijay-Shanker, 2014), they

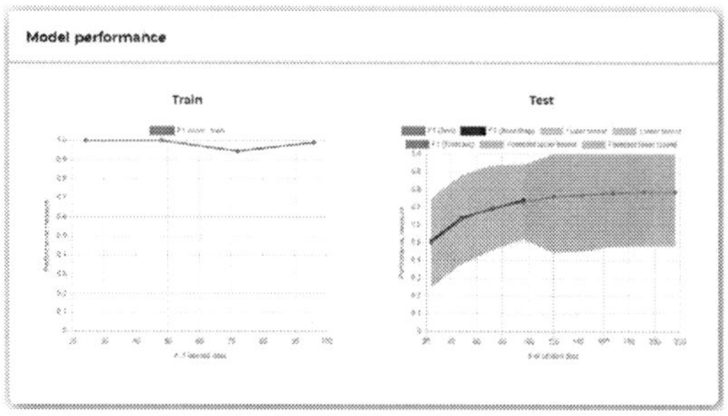

Figure 4: AL evaluation and performance forecasting. After each round, ALANNO re-trains the underlying AL model and plots the corresponding performance on the train set (the plot on the left-hand side). The performance is calculated on an unbiased test set reserved beforehand. We use F_1 score for the classification tasks, with confidence intervals approximated by bootstrapping. The plot on the right-hand side shows test performances on the data labeled so far (in green) and the forecast of performance increase with additional annotation effort (in gray).

are rarely employed in practice. We can save valuable resources by using a stopping criterion to identify when our model performs sufficiently well. Even more helpful would be the ability to forecast how much more data needs to be annotated to reach the desired model performance. To this end, we integrated a forecasting feature based on Bayesian regression, which we have implemented in Pyro (Bingham et al., 2019). The forecasting functionality is a practical solution for the stopping criterion, allowing annotation managers to gauge the trade-off between the expected boost in performance versus the additional annotation effort. Figure 4 shows an example of evaluating an active learning model and performance forecasting.

Class balancing through guided learning. AL often struggles with imbalanced data. Moreover, class balance is crucial for active learning strategies, especially in the early phases of the annotation process, as the model may have difficulty learning classes with low frequency. To address this, ALANNO supports *guided learning*, also known as *active search* (Attenberg and Provost, 2010). The main idea of guided learning in NLP is to use keywords to search for data points in the minority class. This way, users can annotate the retrieved data to make the class frequency distribution more uniform. We use BM25 (Robertson et al., 2009) as the retrieval algorithm for guided learning.

	$k=2$	$k=3$	$k=4$	$k=5$
UNIFORM	132.66	52.14	18.09	3.38
QMC	0.75	0.42	0.15	.03

Table 1: The average variance of k-tuple frequencies. UNIFORM denotes the standard uniform sampling of annotators, while QMC stands for our Quasi-Monte Carlo assignment method. We simulated the assignment of 1,000 unlabeled instances with ten annotators in total and five annotators per instance. We report the average variance of frequencies across 1,000 runs.

4 Case Studies

In the following case studies, we highlight the two essential features of ALANNO, namely balanced data assignment and AL performance forecasting.

Case study 1: Balanced assignment. To compare our Quasi-Monte Carlo assignment method with uniform annotators combinations, we ran simulations of distributing unlabeled instances to annotators. As Table 1 shows, our method achieves more balanced combinations compared to the standard uniform sampling, ranging from pairs and up to k-tuples, where k is the number of annotators per data point.

Case study 2: AL performance forecasting. To demonstrate the forecasting feature in ALANNO, we conducted a case study on the Stanford Sentiment Treebank (**SST;** Socher et al., 2013) and subjectivity (**SUBJ;** Pang and Lee, 2004) datasets. We used a simple logistic regression model with TF-IDF vectors and *least confident* sampling method for SST and BERT with BADGE sampling method for SUBJ. We then compared random sampling to AL and used our forecasting technique to predict the performance of AL. In each step, we sampled 200 data points for SST and 50 data points for SUBJ from the pool of unlabeled data, simulating the annotation process. We re-trained the models in each AL step and evaluated them on the test set. Figure 5 demonstrates the usefulness of performance forecasting, which provides a possibility to decide on the trade-off between the additional annotation cost and the expected increase in performance.

5 Related Work

As the popularity of machine learning and deep learning grows, so does the need for annotated data. Since high-quality data is imperative for high-quality machine learning models, data annotation

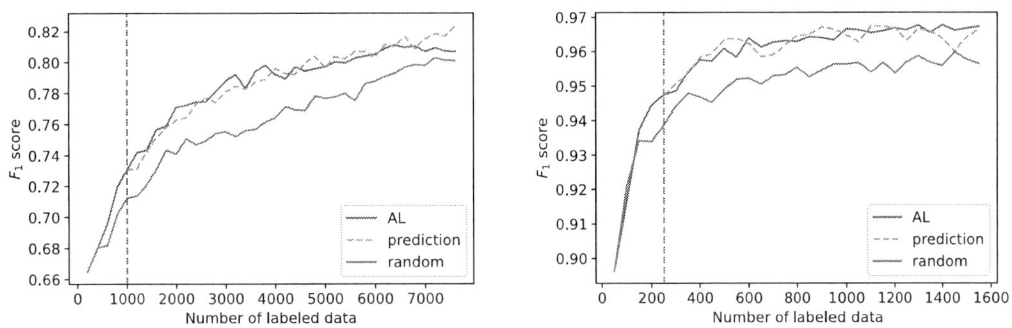

Figure 5: AL performance forecasting. The subfigures show the predictions of F_1 score gain with a hypothetical increase in the number of labeled data. The green line pertains to the random selection baseline, the blue one is the corresponding AL selection, and the dashed orange line is the forecast of F_1 score for AL selection. The dashed red line represents the boundary between the steps the forecast model was trained on (left of the line) and the steps whose values the forecast model was predicting (right of the line). The left subfigure shows the results for SST with logistic regression using uncertainty sampling as the AL method, while the right subfigure corresponds to SUBJ with BERT using BADGE for AL sampling.

has become a lucrative industry, and new tools are constantly emerging. There are commercial tools such as Prodigy,[3] V7,[4] and Hasty.[5] However, these tools hide their full functionality behind a paywall. In contrast to the mentioned commercial system, several open-source annotation tools have appeared recently, such as Label Sleuth (Shnarch et al., 2022), Label Studio,[6], INCEpTION (Klie et al., 2018), MATILDA (Cucurnia et al., 2021), and Paladin (Nghiem et al., 2021).

Label Sleuth is an elegant annotation system designed to make NLP accessible for non-experts. The system enables AL selection for labeling. However, it only supports simple binary classification with a single annotator per project.

Label Studio is offered as an open-source system and a paid enterprise version. While the paid version supports active learning, the free version is limited to random selection. The system supports multiple annotators but with minimal functionalities in managing the annotations.

INCEpTION is a highly configurable tool that supports AL and multi-annotator setups. However, the system is hard to use, as it requires external libraries to integrate a model for AL purposes.

MATILDA is a platform for dialogue annotation in a multi-annotator setup with support for multiple languages.

[3]https://prodi.gy/
[4]https://www.v7labs.com/
[5]https://hasty.ai/
[6]https://labelstud.io/

Paladin integrates active learning and supports multi-label classification.

To the best of our knowledge, ALANNO is the only AL annotation tool that explicitly addresses practical challenges in AL. ALANNO also differs from the above-mentioned systems in implementing practical solutions for managing multi-annotator annotation projects.

6 Conclusion

ALANNO is an open-source annotation system for natural language processing tasks powered by active learning. The system addresses the critical practical challenges of active learning in real-world annotation projects that have previously been overlooked. ALANNO enables non-experts in active learning to conduct effective annotation campaigns by supporting solutions for unbiased evaluation, stopping criterion for active learning, and class balancing. Additionally, the system facilitates annotation management in a multi-annotator setup, emphasizing label quality through agreement monitoring, agreement-aware label aggregation, and a novel method for the balanced assignment of unlabeled instances to annotators.

Acknowledgements

We thank the reviewers for their comments and interesting suggestions for future improvements. We also thank the people from TakeLab (Text Analysis and Knowledge Engineering Lab) who helped us in developing the system over the years.

References

Ron Artstein and Massimo Poesio. 2008. Inter-Coder Agreement for Computational Linguistics. *Computational Linguistics*, 34(4):555–596.

Jordan T. Ash, Chicheng Zhang, Akshay Krishnamurthy, John Langford, and Alekh Agarwal. 2019. Deep batch active learning by diverse, uncertain gradient lower bounds. *CoRR*, abs/1906.03671.

Josh Attenberg and Foster Provost. 2010. Why label when you can search? Alternatives to active learning for applying human resources to build classification models under extreme class imbalance. In *Proceedings of the 16th ACM SIGKDD international conference on Knowledge discovery and data mining*, pages 423–432.

Josh Attenberg and Foster Provost. 2011. Inactive learning? Difficulties employing active learning in practice. *ACM SIGKDD Explorations Newsletter*, 12(2):36–41.

William H Beluch, Tim Genewein, Andreas Nürnberger, and Jan M Köhler. 2018. The power of ensembles for active learning in image classification. In *Proceedings of the IEEE Conference on Computer Vision and Pattern Recognition*, pages 9368–9377.

Eli Bingham, Jonathan P Chen, Martin Jankowiak, Fritz Obermeyer, Neeraj Pradhan, Theofanis Karaletsos, Rohit Singh, Paul Szerlip, Paul Horsfall, and Noah D Goodman. 2019. Pyro: Deep universal probabilistic programming. *The Journal of Machine Learning Research*, 20(1):973–978.

Michael Bloodgood and K Vijay-Shanker. 2014. A method for stopping active learning based on stabilizing predictions and the need for user-adjustable stopping. *arXiv preprint arXiv:1409.5165*.

Sebastian Burhenne, Dirk Jacob, and Gregor Henze. 2011. Sampling based on Sobol' sequences for Monte Carlo techniques applied to building simulations. pages 1816–1823.

Yukun Chen, Subramani Mani, and Hua Xu. 2012. Applying active learning to assertion classification of concepts in clinical text. *Journal of biomedical informatics*, 45(2):265–272.

Jacob Cohen. 1960. A coefficient of agreement for nominal scales. *Educational and psychological measurement*, 20(1):37–46.

Davide Cucurnia, Nikolai Rozanov, Irene Sucameli, Augusto Ciuffoletti, and Maria Simi. 2021. MATILDA - multi-AnnoTator multi-language InteractiveLightweight dialogue annotator. In *Proceedings of the 16th Conference of the European Chapter of the Association for Computational Linguistics: System Demonstrations*, pages 32–39, Online. Association for Computational Linguistics.

Tivadar Danka and Peter Horvath. 2018. modal: A modular active learning framework for Python.

Liat Ein-Dor, Alon Halfon, Ariel Gera, Eyal Shnarch, Lena Dankin, Leshem Choshen, Marina Danilevsky, Ranit Aharonov, Yoav Katz, and Noam Slonim. 2020. Active Learning for BERT: An Empirical Study. In *Proceedings of the 2020 Conference on Empirical Methods in Natural Language Processing (EMNLP)*, pages 7949–7962, Online. Association for Computational Linguistics.

Joseph L Fleiss. 1971. Measuring nominal scale agreement among many raters. *Psychological bulletin*, 76(5):378.

Mitchell L Gordon, Kaitlyn Zhou, Kayur Patel, Tatsunori Hashimoto, and Michael S Bernstein. 2021. The disagreement deconvolution: Bringing machine learning performance metrics in line with reality. In *Proceedings of the 2021 CHI Conference on Human Factors in Computing Systems*, pages 1–14.

Dirk Hovy, Taylor Berg-Kirkpatrick, Ashish Vaswani, and Eduard Hovy. 2013. Learning whom to trust with MACE. In *Proceedings of the 2013 Conference of the North American Chapter of the Association for Computational Linguistics: Human Language Technologies*, pages 1120–1130, Atlanta, Georgia. Association for Computational Linguistics.

Dirk Hovy and Diyi Yang. 2021. The importance of modeling social factors of language: Theory and practice. In *Proceedings of the 2021 Conference of the North American Chapter of the Association for Computational Linguistics: Human Language Technologies*, pages 588–602, Online. Association for Computational Linguistics.

Kian Kenyon-Dean, Edward Newell, and Jackie Chi Kit Cheung. 2020. Deconstructing word embedding algorithms. In *Proceedings of the 2020 Conference on Empirical Methods in Natural Language Processing (EMNLP)*, pages 8479–8484, Online. Association for Computational Linguistics.

Jan-Christoph Klie, Michael Bugert, Beto Boullosa, Richard Eckart de Castilho, and Iryna Gurevych. 2018. The INCEpTION platform: Machine-assisted and knowledge-oriented interactive annotation. In *Proceedings of the 27th International Conference on Computational Linguistics: System Demonstrations*, pages 5–9, Santa Fe, New Mexico. Association for Computational Linguistics.

Klaus Krippendorff. 2018. *Content analysis: An introduction to its methodology*. Sage publications.

Florian Laws and Hinrich Schütze. 2008. Stopping criteria for active learning of named entity recognition. In *Proceedings of the 22nd International Conference on Computational Linguistics (Coling 2008)*, pages 465–472.

David Lowell, Zachary C. Lipton, and Byron C. Wallace. 2019. Practical obstacles to deploying active learning. In *Proceedings of the 2019 Conference on Empirical Methods in Natural Language Processing and the 9th International Joint Conference on Natural Language Processing (EMNLP-IJCNLP)*, pages 21–30, Hong Kong, China. Association for Computational Linguistics.

Minh-Quoc Nghiem, Paul Baylis, and Sophia Ananiadou. 2021. Paladin: an annotation tool based on active and proactive learning. In *Proceedings of the 16th Conference of the European Chapter of the Association for Computational Linguistics: System Demonstrations*, pages 238–243, Online. Association for Computational Linguistics.

Bo Pang and Lillian Lee. 2004. A sentimental education: Sentiment analysis using subjectivity summarization based on minimum cuts. In *Proceedings of the 42nd Annual Meeting of the Association for Computational Linguistics (ACL-04)*, pages 271–278, Barcelona, Spain.

Rebecca Passonneau. 2006. Measuring agreement on set-valued items (MASI) for semantic and pragmatic annotation. In *Proceedings of the Fifth International Conference on Language Resources and Evaluation (LREC'06)*, Genoa, Italy. European Language Resources Association (ELRA).

Silviu Paun, Ron Artstein, and Massimo Poesio. 2022. Statistical methods for annotation analysis. *Synthesis Lectures on Human Language Technologies*, 15(1):1–217.

Ellie Pavlick and Tom Kwiatkowski. 2019. Inherent disagreements in human textual inferences. *Transactions of the Association for Computational Linguistics*, 7:677–694.

Ameya Prabhu, Charles Dognin, and Maneesh Singh. 2019. Sampling bias in deep active classification: An empirical study. *arXiv preprint arXiv:1909.09389*.

Ciyang Qing, Ulle Endriss, Raquel Fernández, and Justin Kruger. 2014. Empirical analysis of aggregation methods for collective annotation.

Stephen Robertson, Hugo Zaragoza, et al. 2009. The probabilistic relevance framework: Bm25 and beyond. *Foundations and Trends® in Information Retrieval*, 3(4):333–389.

Christopher Schröder, Lydia Müller, Andreas Niekler, and Martin Potthast. 2021. Small-text: Active learning for text classification in python. *CoRR*, abs/2107.10314.

Ozan Sener and Silvio Savarese. 2017. Active learning for convolutional neural networks: A core-set approach. *arXiv preprint arXiv:1708.00489*.

Burr Settles. 2009. Active learning literature survey. Computer sciences technical report.

Burr Settles and Mark Craven. 2008. An analysis of active learning strategies for sequence labeling tasks. In *Proceedings of the 2008 Conference on Empirical Methods in Natural Language Processing*, pages 1070–1079, Honolulu, Hawaii. Association for Computational Linguistics.

Eyal Shnarch, Alon Halfon, Ariel Gera, Marina Danilevsky, Yannis Katsis, Leshem Choshen, Martin Santillan Cooper, Dina Epelboim, Zheng Zhang, Dakuo Wang, Lucy Yip, Liat Ein-Dor, Lena Dankin, Ilya Shnayderman, Ranit Aharonov, Yunyao Li, Naftali Liberman, Philip Levin Slesarev, Gwilym Newton, Shila Ofek-Koifman, Noam Slonim, and Yoav Katz. 2022. Label Sleuth: From unlabeled text to a classifier in a few hours.

Richard Socher, John Bauer, Christopher D. Manning, and Andrew Y. Ng. 2013. Parsing with compositional vector grammars. In *Proceedings of the 51st Annual Meeting of the Association for Computational Linguistics (Volume 1: Long Papers)*, pages 455–465, Sofia, Bulgaria. Association for Computational Linguistics.

Ying-Peng Tang, Guo-Xiang Li, and Sheng-Jun Huang. 2019. Alipy: Active learning in Python.

Ashish Vaswani, Noam Shazeer, Niki Parmar, Jakob Uszkoreit, Llion Jones, Aidan N Gomez, Łukasz Kaiser, and Illia Polosukhin. 2017. Attention is all you need. *Advances in neural information processing systems*, 30.

Andreas Vlachos. 2008. A stopping criterion for active learning. *Computer Speech & Language*, 22(3):295–312.

Cha Zhang and Tsuhan Chen. 2002. An active learning framework for content-based information retrieval. *IEEE transactions on multimedia*, 4(2):260–268.

Jingbo Zhu, Huizhen Wang, Eduard Hovy, and Matthew Ma. 2010. Confidence-based stopping criteria for active learning for data annotation. *ACM Transactions on Speech and Language Processing (TSLP)*, 6(3):1–24.

Automatically Summarizing Evidence from Clinical Trials: A Prototype Highlighting Current Challenges

Sanjana Ramprasad
Northeastern University
ramprasad.sa@northeastern.edu

Denis Jered McInerney
Northeastern University
mcinerney.de@northeastern.edu

Iain J. Marshall
King's College London
iainjmarshall@gmail.com

Byron C. Wallace
Northeastern University
b.wallace@northeastern.edu

Abstract

We present *TrialsSummarizer*, a system that aims to automatically summarize evidence presented in the set of randomized controlled trials most relevant to a given query. Building on prior work (Marshall et al., 2020), the system retrieves trial publications matching a query specifying a combination of condition, intervention(s), and outcome(s), and ranks these according to sample size and estimated study quality. The top-k such studies are passed through a neural multi-document summarization system, yielding a synopsis of these trials. We consider two architectures: A standard sequence-to-sequence model based on BART (Lewis et al., 2019), and a multi-headed architecture intended to provide greater transparency to end-users. Both models produce fluent and relevant summaries of evidence retrieved for queries, but their tendency to introduce unsupported statements render them inappropriate for use in this domain at present. The proposed architecture may help users verify outputs allowing users to trace generated tokens back to inputs. The demonstration video is available at: https://vimeo.com/735605060 The prototype, source code, and model weights are available at: https://sanjanaramprasad.github.io/trials-summarizer/.

1 Introduction

Patient treatment decisions would ideally be informed by all available relevant evidence. However, realizing this aim of evidence-based care has become increasingly difficult as the medical literature (already vast) has continued to rapidly expand (Bastian et al., 2010). Well over 100 new RCT reports are now published every day (Marshall et al., 2021). Language technologies — specifically automatic summarization methods — have the potential to provide concise overviews of all evidence relevant to a given clinical question, providing a kind of *systematic review* on demand (Wang et al., 2022; DeYoung et al., 2021; Wallace et al., 2021).

We describe a demonstration system, *TrialsSummarizer*, which combines retrieval over clinical trials literature with a summarization model to provide narrative overviews of current published evidence relevant to clinical questions. Figure 1 shows an illustrative query run in our system and the resultant output. A system capable of producing *accurate* summaries of the medical evidence on any given topic could dramatically improve the ability of caregivers to consult the whole of the evidence base to inform care.

However, current neural summarization systems are prone to inserting inaccuracies into outputs (Kryscinski et al., 2020; Maynez et al., 2020; Pagnoni et al., 2021; Ladhak et al., 2021; Choubey et al., 2021). This has been shown specifically to be a problem in the context of medical literature summarization (Wallace et al., 2021; Otmakhova et al., 2022), where there is a heightened need for factual accuracy. A system that produces plausible but often misleading summaries of comparative treatment efficacy is useless without an efficient means for users to assess the validity of outputs.

Motivated by this need for transparency when summarizing clinical trials, we implement a summarization architecture and interface designed to permit interactions that might instill trust in outputs. Specifically, the model associates each token in a generated summary with a particular source "aspect" extracted from inputs. This in turn allows one to trace output text back to (snippets of) inputs, permitting a form of verification. The architecture also provides functionality to "in-fill" pre-defined *template summaries*, providing a compromise between the control afforded by templates and the flexibility of abstractive summarization. We realize this functionality in our system demonstration.

2 Related Work

The (lack of) factuality of neural summarization systems is an active area of research (Chen et al.,

Proceedings of the 17th Conference of the European Chapter of the Association for Computational Linguistics System Demonstrations, pages 236–247
May 2-4, 2023 ©2023 Association for Computational Linguistics

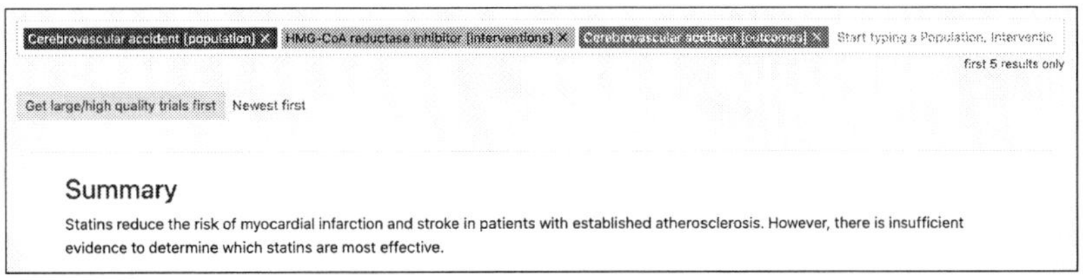

Figure 1: An example query (regarding use of *statins* to reduce risk of *stroke*) and output summary provided by the system. In this example, the summary accurately reflects the evidence, but this is not always the case.

2021; Cao et al., 2020; Dong et al., 2020; Liu et al., 2020; Goyal and Durrett, 2021; Zhang et al., 2021; Kryscinski et al., 2020; Xie et al., 2021). This demo paper considers this issue in the context of a specific domain and application. We also explored controllability to permit interaction, in part via templates. This follows prior work on hybrid template/neural summarization (Hua and Wang, 2020; Mishra et al., 2020; Wiseman et al., 2018).

We also note that this work draws upon prior work on visualizing summarization system outputs (Vig et al., 2021; Strobelt et al., 2018; Tenney et al., 2020) and biomedical literature summarization (Plaza and Carrillo-de Albornoz, 2013; Demner-Fushman and Lin, 2006; Mollá, 2010; Sarker et al., 2017; Wallace et al., 2021). However, to our knowledge this is the first working prototype to attempt to generate (draft) evidence reviews that are both interpretable and editable on demand.

3 System Overview

Our interface is built on top of Trialstreamer (Marshall et al., 2020), an automated system that identifies new reports of randomized controlled trials (RCTs) in humans and then extracts and stores salient information from these in a database of all published trial information. Our system works by identifying RCT reports relevant to a given query using a straightforward retrieval technique (Section 3.1), and then passing the top-k of these through a multi-document summarization model (Section 3.2). For the latter component we consider both a standard sequence-to-sequence approach and a *aspect structured* architecture (Section 3.3) intended to provide greater transparency.

3.1 Retrieving Articles

Trialstreamer (Marshall et al., 2020; Nye et al., 2020) monitors research databases — specifically, PubMed[1] and the World Health Organization International Clinical Trials Registry Platform — to automatically identify newly published reports of RCTs in humans using a previously validated classifier (Marshall et al., 2018).

Articles describing RCTs are then passed through a suite of machine learning models which extract key elements from trial reports, including: sample sizes; descriptions of trial populations, interventions, and outcomes; key results; and the reliability of the evidence reported (via an approximate risk of bias score; Higgins et al. 2019). This extracted (semi-)structured information is stored in the Trialstreamer relational database.

Extracted free-text snippets describing study populations, interventions, and outcomes (PICO elements) are also mapped onto MeSH terms,[2] using a re-implementation of MetaMap Lite (Demner-Fushman et al., 2017).

To facilitate search, users can enter MeSH terms for a subset of populations, interventions, and outcomes, which is used to search for matches over the articles and their corresponding extracted key data in the database. Matched studies are then ranked as a score function of sample size s and risk of bias score rob: score $= s/\text{rob}$; that is, we prioritize retrieval of large, high-quality trial reports.

The novelty on offer in this system demonstration is the inclusion of a *summarization* component, which consumes the top-k retrieved trials (we use k=5 here) and outputs a narrative summary of this evidence in the style of a systematic review abstract (Wallace et al., 2021). By combining this summarization module with the Trialstreamer database, we can provide real-time summarization of all trials that match a given query (Figure 1).

3.2 Summarizing Trials

We consider two realizations of the summarization module. We train both models on a dataset introduced in prior work which comprises collections

[1]https://pubmed.ncbi.nlm.nih.gov/

[2]MeSH — short for Medical Subject Headings — is a controlled vocabulary maintained by the National Library of Medicine (NLM).

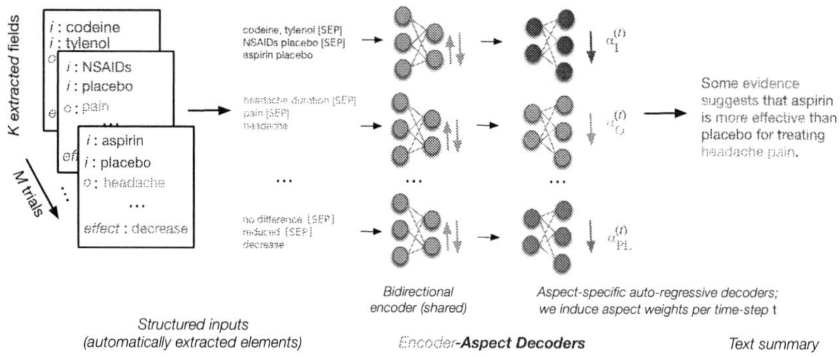

Figure 2: Our proposed structured summarization approach entails synthesizing individual aspects (automatically extracted in a pre-processing step), and conditionally generating text about each of these.

of RCT reports (PICO elements extracted from abstracts) as inputs and Authors' Conclusions sections of systematic review abstracts authored by members of the Cochrane Collaboration as targets (Wallace et al., 2021) (see Section 4).

As a first model, we adopt BART (Lewis et al., 2019) with a Longformer (Beltagy et al., 2020) encoder to accommodate the somewhat lengthy multi-document inputs. As inputs to the model we concatenate spans extracted from individual trials containing salient information, including populations, interventions, outcomes, and "punchlines." The latter refers to extracted snippets which seem to provide the main results or findings, e.g., "There was a significant increase in mortality ..."; see (Lehman et al., 2019) for more details. We enclose these spans in special tags. e.g., `<population>`Participants were diabetics ... `</population>`. As additional supervision we run the same extraction models over the targets and also demarcate these using the same set of tags.

An issue with standard sequence-to-sequence models for this task is that they provide no natural means to assess the provenance of tokens in outputs, which makes it difficult to verify the trustworthiness of generated summaries. Next we discuss an alternative architecture which is intended to provide greater transparency and controllability.

3.3 Proposed Aspect Structured Architecture to Increase Transparency

We adopt a multi-headed architecture similar to (Goyal et al., 2021), which explicitly generates tokens corresponding to the respective aspects (Figure 2). We assume inputs are segmented into texts corresponding to a set of K fields or aspects. Here these are descriptions of trial populations, interventions, and outcomes, and "punchline" snippets reporting the main study findings. We will denote inputs for each of the K aspects by $\{x^{a_1}, ..., x^{a_K}\}$, where x^{a_k} denotes the text for aspect k extracted from input x. Given that this is a multi-document setting (each input consists of multiple articles), x^{a_k} is formed by *concatenating aspect texts across all documents* using special tokens to delineate individual articles.

We encode aspect texts separately to obtain aspect-specific embeddings $x^{a_k}_{\text{enc}}$. We pass these (respectively) to aspect-specific decoders and a shared language model head to obtain vocabulary distributions $\hat{o}^{a_k}_t$. All model parameters are shared save for the last two decoder layers which comprise aspect-specific parameters. Importantly, the representation for a given aspect is *only based on the text associated with this aspect* (x^{a_k}).

We model the final output as a *mixture* over the respective aspect distributions: $\hat{o}_t = \sum_{k=1}^{K} z^{a_k}_t(\hat{o}^{a_k}_t)$. Mixture weights $z_t = z^{a_1}_t, \ldots, z^{a_K}_t$ encode a soft selection over aspects for timestep t and are obtained as a dot product between each penultimate representation of the decoder $y^{a_k}_t$ (prior to passing them through a language model head) and a learnable parameter, $W_z \in R^D$. The K logits $\tilde{z}^{a_k}_t$ are then normalized via a Softmax before multiplying with the aspect-specific vocabulary distributions $\hat{o}^{a_k}_t$

Tracing outputs to inputs This architecture permits one to inspect the mixture weights associated with individual tokens in a generated summary, which suggests which aspect (most) influenced the output. Further inspection of the corresponding snippets from studies for this aspect may facilitate verification of outputs, and/or help to resolve errors and where they may have been introduced.

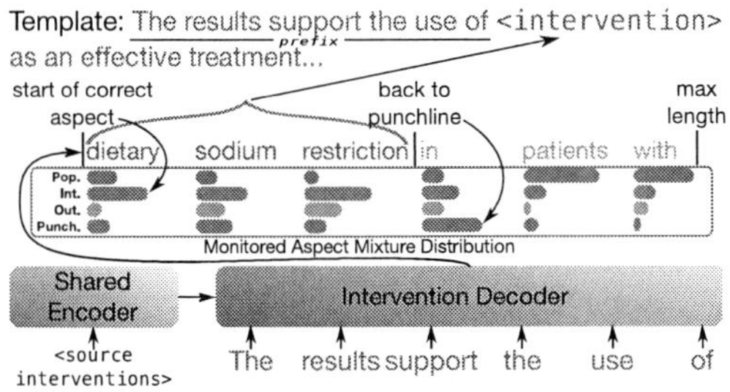

Figure 3: **Template generation.** To in-fill, we force generation from a specific head and monitor the model's mixture distribution to decide when to stop.

Controlled generation Neural summarization models often struggle to appropriately *synthesize* conflicting evidence to arrive at the correct overall determination concerning a particular intervention effectiveness. But while imperfect, summarization models may be useful nonetheless by providing a means to rapidly draft synopses of the evidence to be edited. The multi-headed architecture naturally permits template in-filling, because one can explicitly draw tokens from heads corresponding to aspects of interest. In our demo, we allow users to toggle between different templates which correspond to different conclusions regarding the overall effectiveness of the intervention in question. (It would be simple to extend this to allow users to specify their own templates to be in-filled.)

To in-fill templates we use template text preceding blanks as context and then generate text from the language head corresponding to the designated aspect. To determine span length dynamically we monitor the mixture distribution and stop when the it shifts to the another aspect (Figure 3).

3.4 User Interface

Figure 5 shows the interface we have built integrating the multi-headed architecture. Highlighted aspects in the summary provide a means of interpreting the source of output tokens by indicating the aspects that informed their production. One can in turn inspect the snippets associated with these aspects, which may help to identify unsupported content in the generated summary. To this end when users click on a token we display the subset of the input that most informed its production.

We provide additional context by displaying overviews (i.e., "punchlines") communicating the main findings of the trials. Because standard sequence-to-sequence models do not provide a mechanism to associate output tokens with input aspects, we display all aspects (and punchlines) for all trials alongside the summary for this model.

Capitalizing on the aforementioned in-filling abilities of our model, we also provide pre-defined templates for each possible "direction" of aggregate findings (significant vs. no effect). We discuss the interface along with examples in Section 5.

4 Dataset and Training Details

We aim to consume collections of titles and abstracts that describe RCTs addressing the same clinical question to abstractive summaries that synthesize the evidence presented in these. We train all models on an RCT summarization dataset (Wallace et al., 2021) where we extract clinically salient elements — i.e., our aspects — from each of the (unstructured) inputs as a pre-processing step using existing models (Marshall et al., 2020).

Training We use the Huggingface Transformers library (Wolf et al., 2020) to implement both models. We initalize both models to *bart-base* (Lewis et al., 2019). We fine-tune the models with a batch size of 2 for 3 epochs, using the Adam optimizer (Kingma and Ba, 2014) with a learning rate of 3e-5.

Inference We use beam search with a beam size of 3. We set the min and max length of generated text to be 10 and 300, respectively.

5 Case Study: Verification and Controllability

To demonstrate the potential usefulness of the interface (and the architecture which enables it), we walk through two case studies. We highlight the type of interpretability for verification our proposed approach provides, also demonstrate the ability to perform controllable summarization to show how this might be useful. The queries used in these case studies along with the investigation were performed by a co-author IJM, a medical doctor with substantial experience in evidence-based medicine. We also compare the models and report automatic scores for ROUGE and factuality in the Appendix section A and find that the two models perform comparably.

Model Interpretability As an example to highlight the potential of the proposed architecture and interface to permit verification, we consider a query regarding the effect of Oseltamivir as an intervention for patients infected with influenza. The standard architecture produces a summary of the top

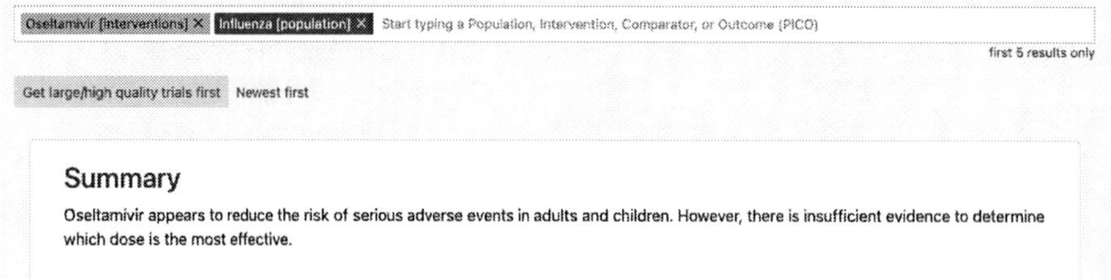

Figure 4: Example output and interface using a standard BART (Lewis et al., 2019) model.

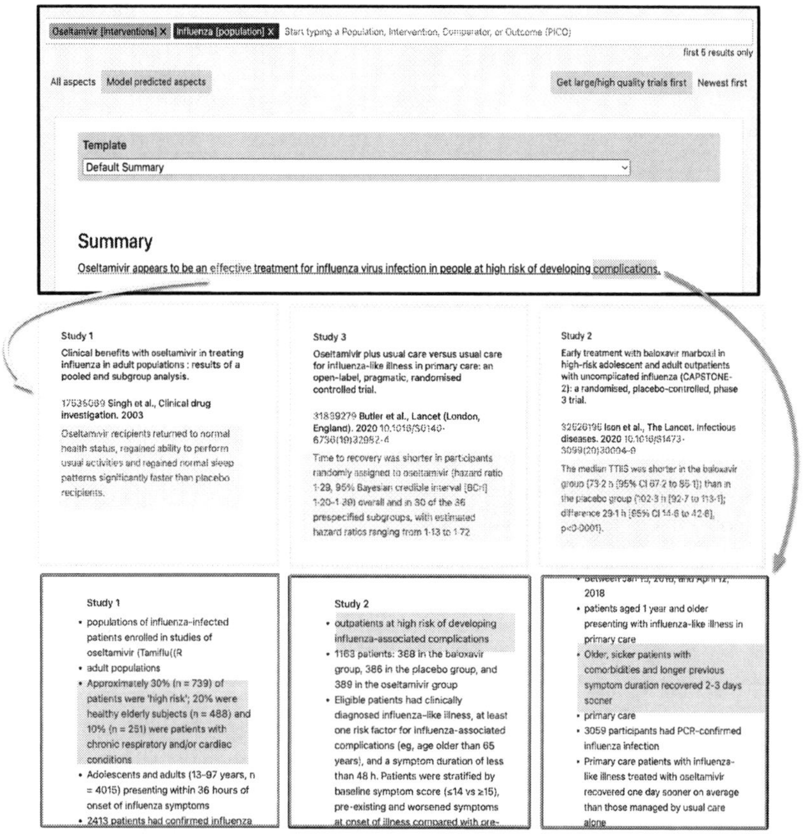

Figure 5: Qualitative example where the structured summarization model (and associated interface) permits token-level verification of the summary generated regarding the use of oseltamivir on influenza-infected patients. This approach readily indicates support for the claim that it is "effective" (top; yellow) and for the description of the population as individuals at risk of "complications" (bottom; purple).

most relevant RCTs to this query shown in Figure 4. This comprises two claims: (1) The intervention has been shown to reduce the risk of adverse events among adults and children, and, (2) There is no consensus as to the most effective dosage. One can inspect the inputs to attempt to verify these. Doing so, we find that reported results do tend to indicate a reduced risk of adverse events and that adolescents and adults were included in some of these studies, indicating that the first claim is accurate. The second claim is harder to verify on inspection; no such uncertainty regarding dosage is explicitly communicated in the inputs. Verifying these claims using the standard seq2seq architecture is onerous because the abstractive nature of such models makes it difficult to trace parts of the output back to inputs. Therefore, verification requires reading through entire inputs to verify different aspects.

The multi-headed architecture allows us to provide an interactive interface intended to permit easier verification. In particular, associating each output token with a particular aspect provides a natural

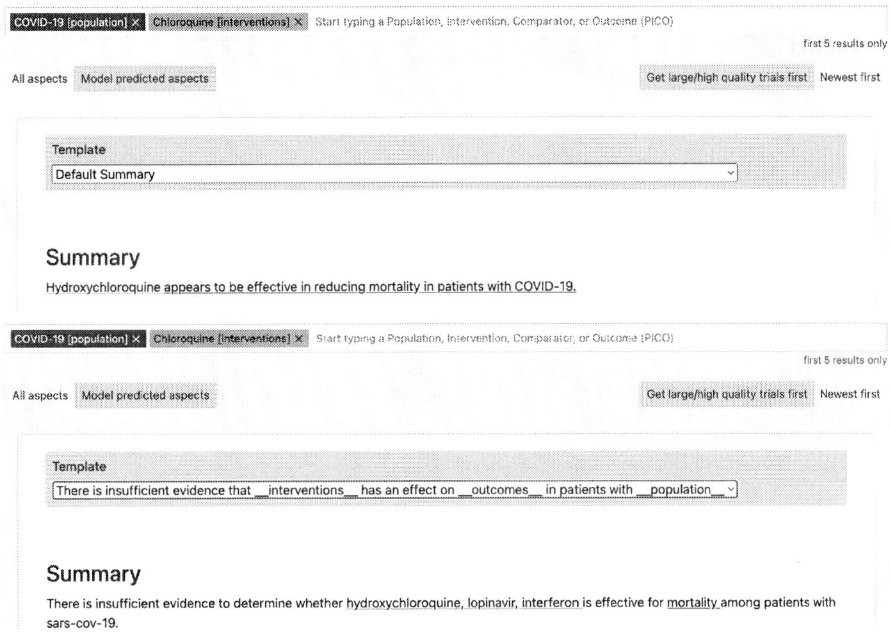

Figure 6: Inaccurate summaries generated by the structured model regarding the effect of Chloroquine on patients with COVID-19 (top). Template-controlled summary using the structured model (bottom).

mechanism for one to inspect snippets of the inputs that might support the generated text. Figure 5 illustrates this for the aforementioned Oseltamivir and flu example. Here we show how the "effective" token in the output can be clicked on to reveal the aspect that influenced its production (Figure 2), in this case tracing back to the extracted "punchlines" conveying main study findings. This readily reveals that the claim is supported. Similarly, we can verify the bit about the population being individuals at risk of complications by tracing back to the population snippets upon which this output was conditioned.

Controllability As mentioned above, another potential benefit of the proposed architecture is the ability to "in-fill" templates to imbue neural generative models with controllability. In particular, given that the overall (aggregate) treatment efficacy is of primary importance in this context, we pre-define templates which convey an effect direction. The idea is that if upon verification one finds that the model came to the wrong aggregate effect direction, they can use a pre-defined template corresponding to the correct direction to generate a more accurate summary on-demand.

We show an example of a summary generated by the structured model in the top part of Figure 6. By using the interpretability features for verification discussed above, we find that the model inaccurately communicates that the intervention Chloroquine is effective for treating COVID-19. However, with the interactive interface we are able to immediately generate a new summary featuring the corrected synthesis result (direction), as depicted in the bottom of Figure 6, without need for manual drafting.

We provide additional case studies in Appendix Section B.

6 Conclusions

We have described TrialsSummarizer, a prototype system for automatically summarizing RCTs relevant to a given query. Neural summarization models produce summaries that are readable and (mostly) relevant, but their tendency to introduce unsupported or incorrect information into outputs means they are not yet ready for use in this domain.

We implement a multi-headed architecture intended to provide greater transparency. We provided qualitative examples intended to highlight its potential to permit faster verification and controllable generation. Future work is needed to test the utility of this functionality in a user trial, and to inform new architectures that would further increase the accuracy and transparency of models for summarizing biomedical evidence.

Limitations and Ethical Issues

Limitations This work has several limitations. First, as stated above, while the prospect of automatic summarization of biomedical evidence is tantalizing, existing models are not yet fit for the task due to their tendency to introduce factual errors. Our working prototype serves in part to highlight this and motivate work toward resolving issues of reliability and trusworthiness.

In this demo paper we have also attempted to make some progress in mitigating such issues by way of the proposed structured summarization model and accompanying interface and provided qualitative examples highlighting its potential, but really a formal user study should be conducted to assess the utility of this. This is complicated by the difficulty of the task: To evaluate the factuality of automatic summaries requires deep domain expertise and considerable time to read through constituent inputs and determine the veracity of a generated summary.

Another limitation of this work is that we have made some ad-hoc design decisions in our current prototype system. For example, at present we (arbitrarily) pass only the top-5 (based on trial sample size and estimated reliability) articles retrieved for a given query through the summarization system. Future work might address this by considering better motivated methods to select which and how many studies ought to be included.

Ethics Accurate summaries of the biomedical evidence have the potential to ultimately improve patient care by supporting the practice of evidence-based medicine. However, at present such models bring inherent risks. In particular, one may be tempted to blindly trust model outputs; given the limitations of current summarization technologies, this would be ill-advised.

Our prototype demonstration system is designed in part to highlight existing challenges that must be solved in this space before any model might actually be adopted (and beyond this, we emphasize that need for verification of outputs, which has been the focus of the present effort). In the interface we indicate with a hard-to-miss warning message that this system should only be used for research purposes and these summaries are unreliable and *not to be trusted*.

Acknowledgements

This work was supported in part by the National Institutes of Health (NIH) under award R01LM012086, and by the National Science Foundation (NSF) awards 1901117 and 2211954. The content is solely the responsibility of the authors and does not necessarily represent the official views of the NIH or the NSF.

References

H Bastian, P Glasziou, and I Chalmers. 2010. Seventy-five trials and eleven systematic reviews a day: how will we ever keep up? *PLoS medicine*, 7(9).

Iz Beltagy, Matthew E Peters, and Arman Cohan. 2020. Longformer: The long-document transformer. *arXiv preprint arXiv:2004.05150*.

Meng Cao, Yue Dong, Jiapeng Wu, and Jackie Chi Kit Cheung. 2020. Factual error correction for abstractive summarization models. *arXiv preprint arXiv:2010.08712*.

Sihao Chen, Fan Zhang, Kazoo Sone, and Dan Roth. 2021. Improving faithfulness in abstractive summarization with contrast candidate generation and selection. *arXiv preprint arXiv:2104.09061*.

Prafulla Kumar Choubey, Jesse Vig, Wenhao Liu, and Nazneen Fatema Rajani. 2021. Mofe: Mixture of factual experts for controlling hallucinations in abstractive summarization. *arXiv preprint arXiv:2110.07166*.

Dina Demner-Fushman and Jimmy Lin. 2006. Answer extraction, semantic clustering, and extractive summarization for clinical question answering. In *Proceedings of the 21st International Conference on Computational Linguistics and 44th Annual Meeting of the Association for Computational Linguistics*, pages 841–848.

Dina Demner-Fushman, Willie J Rogers, and Alan R Aronson. 2017. Metamap lite: an evaluation of a new java implementation of metamap. *Journal of the American Medical Informatics Association*, 24(4):841–844.

Jay DeYoung, Iz Beltagy, Madeleine van Zuylen, Bailey Kuehl, and Lucy Lu Wang. 2021. Ms2: Multi-document summarization of medical studies. *arXiv preprint arXiv:2104.06486*.

Yue Dong, Shuohang Wang, Zhe Gan, Yu Cheng, Jackie Chi Kit Cheung, and Jingjing Liu. 2020. Multi-fact correction in abstractive text summarization. *arXiv preprint arXiv:2010.02443*.

Tanya Goyal and Greg Durrett. 2021. Annotating and modeling fine-grained factuality in summarization. *arXiv preprint arXiv:2104.04302*.

Tanya Goyal, Nazneen Fatema Rajani, Wenhao Liu, and Wojciech Kryściński. 2021. Hydrasum: Disentangling stylistic features in text summarization using multi-decoder models. *arXiv preprint arXiv:2110.04400*.

Julian PT Higgins, Jelena Savović, Matthew J Page, Roy G Elbers, and Jonathan AC Sterne. 2019. Assessing risk of bias in a randomized trial. *Cochrane handbook for systematic reviews of interventions*, pages 205–228.

Xinyu Hua and Lu Wang. 2020. Pair: Planning and iterative refinement in pre-trained transformers for long text generation. *arXiv preprint arXiv:2010.02301*.

Diederik P Kingma and Jimmy Ba. 2014. Adam: A method for stochastic optimization. *arXiv preprint arXiv:1412.6980*.

Wojciech Kryscinski, Bryan McCann, Caiming Xiong, and Richard Socher. 2020. Evaluating the factual consistency of abstractive text summarization. In *Proceedings of the 2020 Conference on Empirical Methods in Natural Language Processing (EMNLP)*, pages 9332–9346, Online. Association for Computational Linguistics.

Faisal Ladhak, Esin Durmus, He He, Claire Cardie, and Kathleen McKeown. 2021. Faithful or extractive? on mitigating the faithfulness-abstractiveness trade-off in abstractive summarization. *arXiv preprint arXiv:2108.13684*.

Eric Lehman, Jay DeYoung, Regina Barzilay, and Byron C Wallace. 2019. Inferring which medical treatments work from reports of clinical trials. *arXiv preprint arXiv:1904.01606*.

Mike Lewis, Yinhan Liu, Naman Goyal, Marjan Ghazvininejad, Abdelrahman Mohamed, Omer Levy, Ves Stoyanov, and Luke Zettlemoyer. 2019. Bart: Denoising sequence-to-sequence pre-training for natural language generation, translation, and comprehension. *arXiv preprint arXiv:1910.13461*.

Zhenghao Liu, Chenyan Xiong, Zhuyun Dai, Si Sun, Maosong Sun, and Zhiyuan Liu. 2020. Adapting open domain fact extraction and verification to covid-fact through in-domain language modeling. In *Findings of the Association for Computational Linguistics: EMNLP 2020*, pages 2395–2400.

Iain J Marshall, Anna Noel-Storr, Joël Kuiper, James Thomas, and Byron C Wallace. 2018. Machine learning for identifying randomized controlled trials: an evaluation and practitioner's guide. *Research synthesis methods*, 9(4):602–614.

Iain J Marshall, Benjamin Nye, Joël Kuiper, Anna Noel-Storr, Rachel Marshall, Rory Maclean, Frank Soboczenski, Ani Nenkova, James Thomas, and Byron C Wallace. 2020. Trialstreamer: A living, automatically updated database of clinical trial reports. *Journal of the American Medical Informatics Association*, 27(12):1903–1912.

Iain James Marshall, Veline L'Esperance, Rachel Marshall, James Thomas, Anna Noel-Storr, Frank Soboczenski, Benjamin Nye, Ani Nenkova, and Byron C Wallace. 2021. State of the evidence: a survey of global disparities in clinical trials. *BMJ Global Health*, 6(1):e004145.

Joshua Maynez, Shashi Narayan, Bernd Bohnet, and Ryan McDonald. 2020. On faithfulness and factuality in abstractive summarization. *arXiv preprint arXiv:2005.00661*.

Abhijit Mishra, Md Faisal Mahbub Chowdhury, Sagar Manohar, Dan Gutfreund, and Karthik Sankaranarayanan. 2020. Template controllable keywords-to-text generation. *arXiv preprint arXiv:2011.03722*.

Diego Mollá. 2010. A corpus for evidence based medicine summarisation. In *Proceedings of the Australasian Language Technology Association Workshop*, pages 76–80.

Benjamin E Nye, Ani Nenkova, Iain J Marshall, and Byron C Wallace. 2020. Trialstreamer: mapping and browsing medical evidence in real-time. In *Proceedings of the conference. Association for Computational Linguistics. North American Chapter. Meeting*, volume 2020, page 63. NIH Public Access.

Yulia Otmakhova, Karin Verspoor, Timothy Baldwin, and Jey Han Lau. 2022. The patient is more dead than alive: exploring the current state of the multi-document summarisation of the biomedical literature. In *Proceedings of the 60th Annual Meeting of the Association for Computational Linguistics (Volume 1: Long Papers)*, pages 5098–5111, Dublin, Ireland. Association for Computational Linguistics.

Artidoro Pagnoni, Vidhisha Balachandran, and Yulia Tsvetkov. 2021. Understanding factuality in abstractive summarization with frank: A benchmark for factuality metrics. *arXiv preprint arXiv:2104.13346*.

Laura Plaza and Jorge Carrillo-de Albornoz. 2013. Evaluating the use of different positional strategies for sentence selection in biomedical literature summarization. *BMC bioinformatics*, 14(1):1–11.

Abeed Sarker, Diego Molla, and Cecile Paris. 2017. Automated text summarisation and evidence-based medicine: A survey of two domains.

Hendrik Strobelt, Sebastian Gehrmann, Michael Behrisch, Adam Perer, Hanspeter Pfister, and Alexander M Rush. 2018. S eq 2s eq-v is: A visual debugging tool for sequence-to-sequence models. *IEEE transactions on visualization and computer graphics*, 25(1):353–363.

Ian Tenney, James Wexler, Jasmijn Bastings, Tolga Bolukbasi, Andy Coenen, Sebastian Gehrmann, Ellen Jiang, Mahima Pushkarna, Carey Radebaugh, Emily Reif, et al. 2020. The language interpretability tool: Extensible, interactive visualizations and analysis for nlp models. *arXiv preprint arXiv:2008.05122*.

Jesse Vig, Wojciech Kryściński, Karan Goel, and Nazneen Fatema Rajani. 2021. Summvis: Interactive visual analysis of models, data, and evaluation for text summarization. *arXiv preprint arXiv:2104.07605*.

Byron C Wallace, Sayantan Saha, Frank Soboczenski, and Iain J Marshall. 2021. Generating (factual?) narrative summaries of rcts: Experiments with neural multi-document summarization. In *AMIA Annual Symposium Proceedings*, volume 2021, page 605. American Medical Informatics Association.

Lucy Lu Wang, Jay DeYoung, and Byron Wallace. 2022. Overview of MSLR2022: A shared task on multi-document summarization for literature reviews. In *Proceedings of the Third Workshop on Scholarly Document Processing*, pages 175–180, Gyeongju, Republic of Korea. Association for Computational Linguistics.

Sam Wiseman, Stuart M Shieber, and Alexander M Rush. 2018. Learning neural templates for text generation. *arXiv preprint arXiv:1808.10122*.

Thomas Wolf, Lysandre Debut, Victor Sanh, Julien Chaumond, Clement Delangue, Anthony Moi, Pierric Cistac, Tim Rault, Rémi Louf, Morgan Funtowicz, et al. 2020. Transformers: State-of-the-art natural language processing. In *Proceedings of the 2020 conference on empirical methods in natural language processing: system demonstrations*, pages 38–45.

Yuexiang Xie, Fei Sun, Yang Deng, Yaliang Li, and Bolin Ding. 2021. Factual consistency evaluation for text summarization via counterfactual estimation. *arXiv preprint arXiv:2108.13134*.

Sen Zhang, Jianwei Niu, and Chuyuan Wei. 2021. Fine-grained factual consistency assessment for abstractive summarization models. In *Proceedings of the 2021 Conference on Empirical Methods in Natural Language Processing*, pages 107–116.

Appendix

A Automatic Evaluation

We report ROUGE scores with respect to the target (manually composed) Cochrane summaries, for both the development and test sets. We report scores for both the vanilla standard BART model along with our proposed multi-headed model intended to aid verifiability and controllability. The models perform about comparably with respect to this metric as can be seen in Table 1.

However ROUGE measures are based on (exact) n-gram overlap, and cannot measure the factuality of generated texts. Measuring factuality is in general an open problem, and evaluating the factual accuracy of biomedical reviews in particular is further complicated by the complexity of the domain and texts. Prior work has, however, proposed automated measures for this specific task (Wallace et al., 2021; DeYoung et al., 2021). These metrics are based on models which infer the reported *directionality* of the findings, e.g., whether or not a summary indicates that the treatment being described was effective. More specifically, we make binary predictions regarding whether generated and reference summaries report significant results (or not) and then calculate the F1 score of the former with respect to the latter.

Model	ROUGE-L (dev)	ROUGE-L(test)
BART	20.4	19.7
Multi-head	19.9	19.3

Table 1: ROUGE scores achieved by the standard BART model and our proposed multi-headed architecture on the dev and test sets.

Model	Direc (dev)	Direc(test)
BART	49.6	51.8
Multi-head	49.3	52.7

Table 2: Directionality scores on the vanilla BART model and our proposed multi-headed architecture on the dev and test sets.

B Additional Case Studies

In this section we highlight a few more use cases that demonstrate the need for interpretability and controllability.

Interpretability We first highlight a set of examples where verifying model generated summaries is difficult without an interface explicitly designed to provide interpretability capabilities. In Figure 7 (a) we show an example where the model generates a summary that accurately synthesized a summary on the effect of using Mirtazapine for patients with depression. However, the summary also includes a statement that states the need for adequate, well-designed trials. Because this statement is generic and does not point to discussing any of the PICO elements, it is unclear what element was responsible for the generation of the statement. A user would therefore need to review all (raw) input texts.

In the case of Figure 7 (b), the model generated summaries has two contradicting sentences. The first sentence indicates a reduction in hospital admission and death among COVID-19 patients

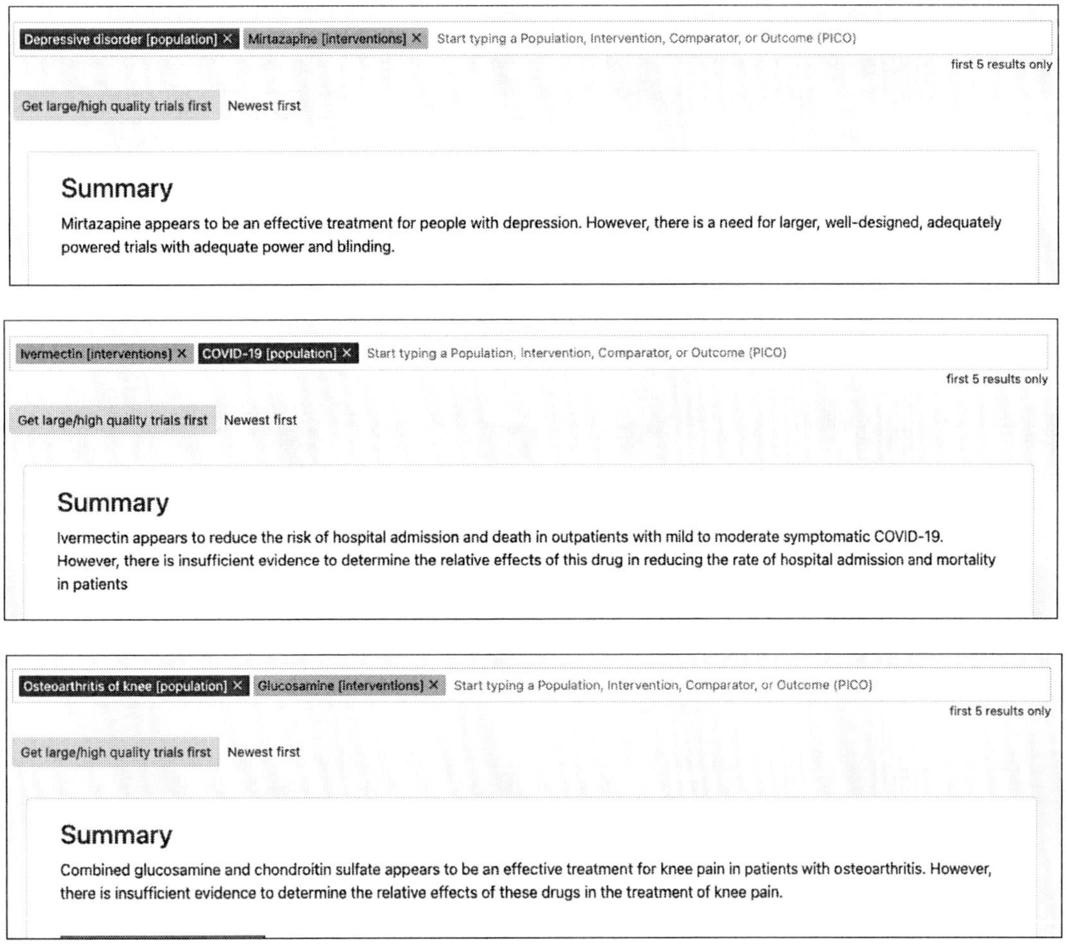

Figure 7: a) BART generated summary when queried about the use of *Mirtazapine* to treat *depression* b) BART generated summary when queried about the use of *Ivermectin* to treat *COVID-19*)

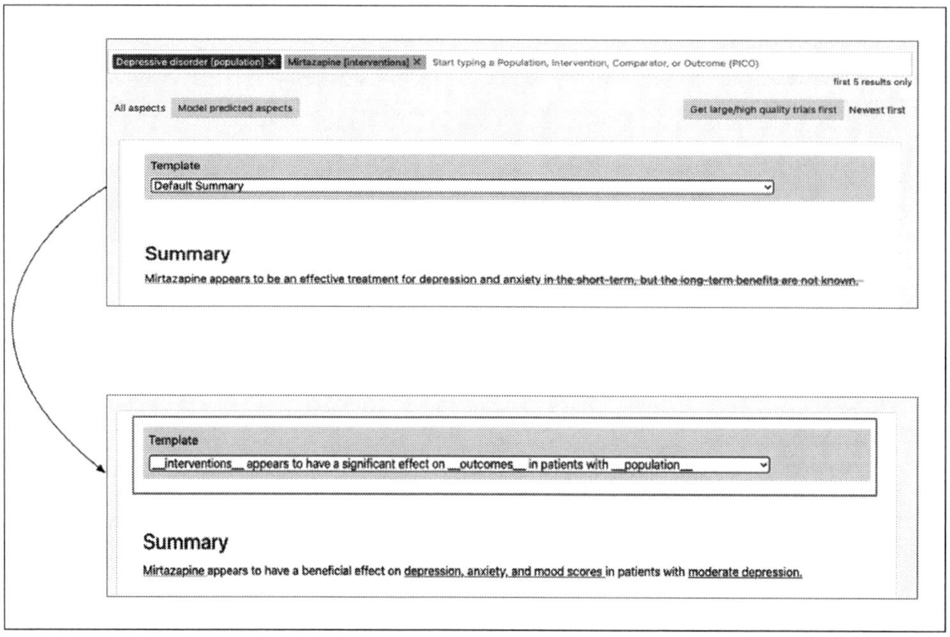

Figure 8: The summary on top shows the default summary generated by the multi-headed model when queried for the effect of *Mirtazapine* on *depression*. The bottom summary shows the controlled summary using a pre-defined template.

when Ivermectin was used and the second sentence claims there is insufficient evidence for the same. However without interpretability capabilities it is not possible to debug and verify if the same set of elements were responsible for contradicting statements or not.

The example in Figure 7 (c) shows a case where the model first accurately synthesizes the findings in the studies of the effect of glucosamine in combination of chondroitin sulfate on knee pain. However, the following statement talks about the relative effects of the two. Again, in this case it is is not intuitive which element led to the generation of the statement and verification requires careful reviewing of all the text and their implication in all elements.

Controllability We next highlight examples where one can effectively control the generation of summaries that would otherwise be incorrect using the template in-filling capabilities afforded by our model. While the interpretability features may permit efficient verification, models still struggle to consistently generate factual accurate summaries. We showcase instances where one can arrive at more accurate summaries quickly via the controllability (template in-filling) made possible by our model.

In the example shown in Figure 8 the default summary synthesizes the effect accurately. However, the model summary discusses the effect on short-term and long-term benefits generated from the punchlines of the studies. Reading through extracted 'punchlines', we find that the studies indicate issues upon withdrawal but do not necessarily provide information on long-term use of the medication. In-filling templates constrains the output, and can be used to produce more accurate summaries while still taking some advantage of the flexibility afforded by generation. For instance in this case we can see that the edited summary induced using the template is more accurate.

Similarly, in Figure 9 when the multi-headed model is queried for the effect of Glucosamine on Osteoarthritis of knee, we observe that the model on its own produces a summary conveying an incorrect aggregate effect of studies. We can verify this by inspecting the elements responsible for the generation, as discussed above. We then arrive at a more accurate summary using the template shown.

The example in Figure 10 is an interesting mistake made by the model. Because the outcomes can be presented with the same information but in a positive or negative direction (e.g., weight loss

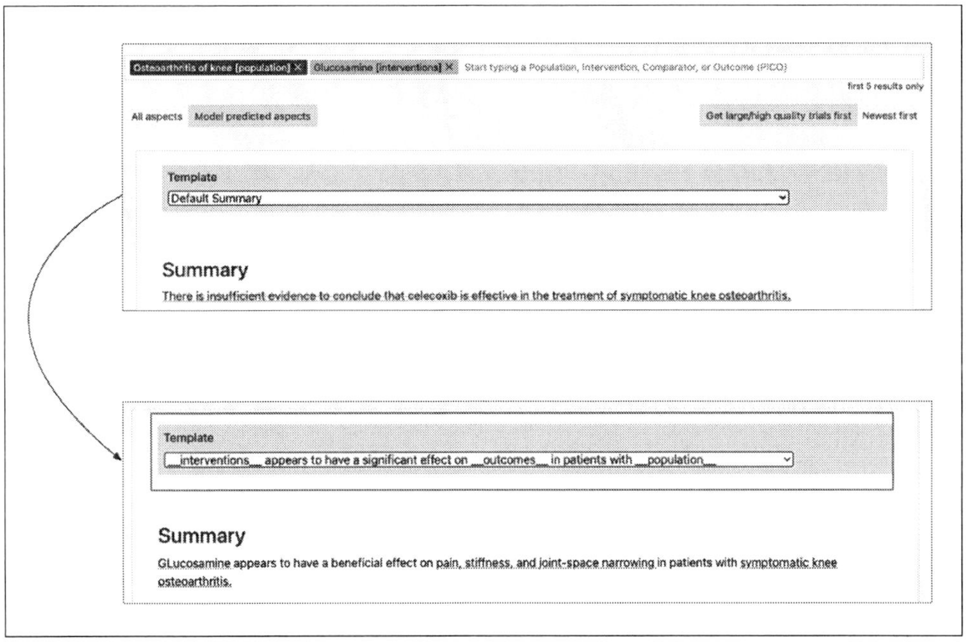

Figure 9: The summary on top shows the default summary generated by the multi-headed model when queried for the effect of *Glucosamine* on *Osteoarthritis of knee*. The bottom summary shows the edited summary using a pre-defined template

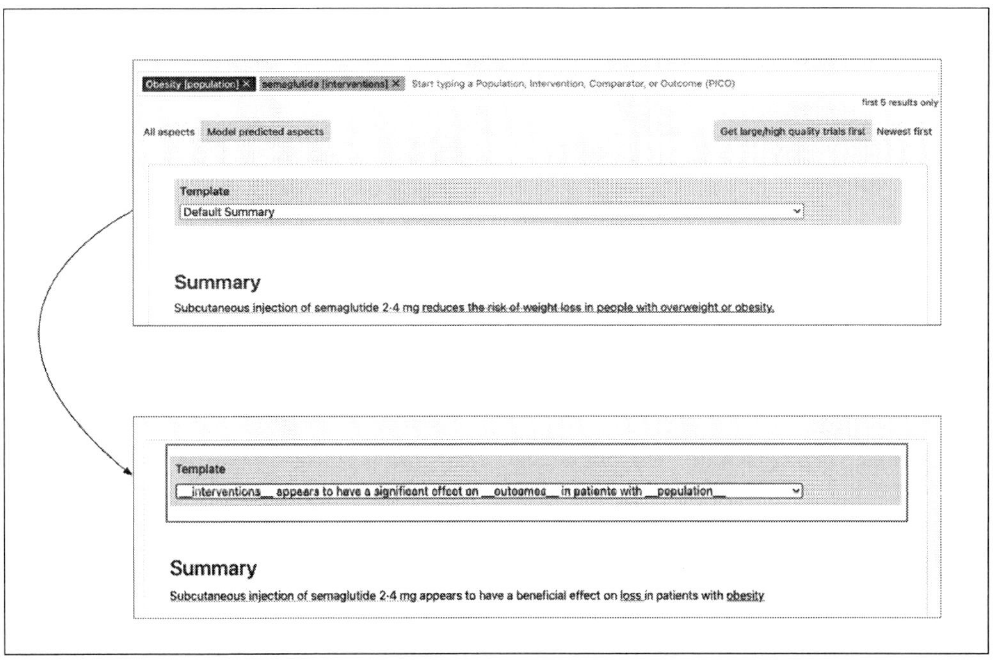

Figure 10: The summary on top shows the default summary generated by the multi-headed model when queried for the effect of *Semaglutide* on *obese* patients. The bottom summary shows the edited summary using a pre-defined template

vs weight gain), the model has to accurately infer the effect of all studies. In this case, the model generates a summary with the right effect but views weight loss as an undesirable effect. Here again we select a template and allow the model quickly in-fill, yielding a more accurate summary.

Corpus Annotation Graph Builder (CAG): An Architectural Framework to Create and Annotate a Multi-source Graph

Roxanne El Baff Tobias Hecking Andreas Hamm Jasper W. Korte Sabine Bartsch*
German Aerospace Center (DLR), Germany, `<first>.<last>@dlr.de`
* Technical University of Darmstadt, `sabine.bartsch@tu-darmstadt.de`

Abstract

Graphs are a natural representation of complex data as their structure allows users to discover (often implicit) relations among the nodes intuitively. Applications build graphs in an ad-hoc fashion, usually tailored to specific use cases, limiting their reusability. To account for this, we present the Corpus Annotation Graph (CAG) architectural framework based on a *create-and-annotate* pattern that enables users to build uniformly structured graphs from diverse data sources and extend them with automatically extracted annotations (e.g., named entities, topics). The resulting graphs can be used for further analyses across multiple downstream tasks (e.g., node classification). Code and resources are publicly available on GitHub[1, 2] and downloadable via PyPi[3] with the command `pip install cag`.

1 Introduction

In many areas of knowledge, facts are spread across a multitude of documents in various forms and modalities (e.g., texts, images, sound recordings, videos, and program code). It is of great interest to exploit explicit links between these documents and - even more so - to detect hidden (or implicit) connections — for knowledge extraction through searching, classifying, comparing, and analyzing.

The most explicit and efficient data structure for working with such interlinked document collections (corpora) is that of a graph whose nodes represent documents, entities, and annotations with edges representing relations between them. Graph databases can naturally manage these for efficient knowledge querying and storage. In particular, property graph databases like Neo4j[4] and ArangoDB[5] consider nodes as objects with attributes and are, therefore, appropriate for holding documents and metadata or more general objects of interest (OOI). OOIs can vary in scale and can be linked via containment relationships: e.g., a book series contains books, a book contains chapters, a chapter contains text, pictures, etc.

One central idea behind our framework is that graphs are not only the object of analysis but also containers for analysis results. More precisely, to unveil hidden connections, we suggest deriving a second type of nodes, which we call *annotation nodes* associated with the OOI nodes. They represent features extracted from the OOIs by methods like named entity recognition, topic discovery, sentiment analysis, image captioning, etc. Implicit links of OOIs can then be established via shared annotation nodes (e.g., common topics) that can be used for further analysis. In this way, with every analysis passed, the graph can get richer and possibly more connected. We call the resulting graph a *Corpus Annotation Graph.*

In this demo paper, we present an architectural framework that facilitates the application of the *create-and-annotate* pattern for creating such a graph: the **Corpus Annotation Graph Builder** (CAG). CAG is built on top of ArangoDB and its Python drivers. The *create-and-annotate* pattern consists of two phases (see Figure 1) that can be repeated multiple times: (1) OOI data can be collected from different sources (e.g., publication databases, online encyclopedias, news feeds, web portals, electronic libraries, repositories, media platforms) and pre-processed to build the core nodes. The component responsible for this phase is the **Graph-Creator**. (2) Annotations are extracted from the nodes, and corresponding annotation nodes are created and attached to the graph. The component dealing with this phase is the **Graph-Annotator**. At any time, new OOI nodes or new annotations can be added, introducing new information to enrich the graph with subsequent

[1] `https://github.com/DLR-SC/corpus-annotation-graph-builder`
[2] The README includes a link for the documentation.
[3] `https://pypi.org/project/cag/`
[4] `https://neo4j.com`
[5] `https://www.arangodb.com`

Proceedings of the 17th Conference of the European Chapter of the Association for Computational Linguistics System Demonstrations, pages 248–255
May 2-4, 2023 ©2023 Association for Computational Linguistics

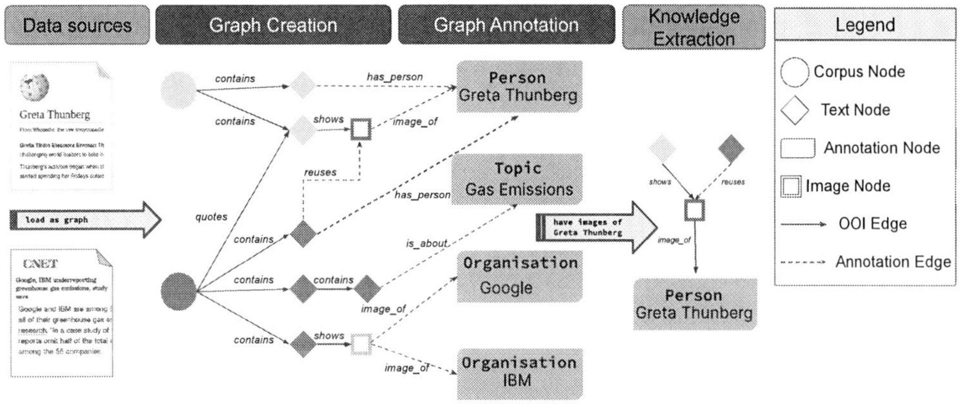

Figure 1: A simplified illustration of the framework: (1a) The data is collected from different data sources (e.g., scientific articles, Wikipedia. (1b) Then, the data is pre-processed and loaded into one common graph with core nodes and edges referred to as objects of interest (OOI). And (2) Annotations are added to the core nodes, which creates additional levels of abstraction and allows core components to be linked across different corpora. An example of a query is *Get all documents that contain images with the Person Of Interest; Greta Thunberg*. This results in getting *text a* from a datasource and *text b* from another datasource.

runs further.

The CAG architectural framework aims to offer researchers a flexible but unified way of organizing and maintaining their interlinked document collections in a reproducible way.

In the following sections, we go over related work (Section 2), then we present the architecture of CAG by describing the building blocks of our framework (Section 3). Last but not least, Section 4 exemplifies two applications, one as the backbone technology for searching scientific work and another one describing a knowledge graph construction using CAG.

2 Related Work

Existing research and tools related to graph data structures cover various topics, from database management systems for creating and maintaining graphs, over a formal framework for graph annotations, to task-oriented (e.g., information retrieval, node classification) approaches.

As we mentioned in the Introduction (Section 1), as the foundation of the architectural framework (CAG), we use a pattern of creating and annotating graphs. Currently, there exist powerful graph databases, such as Neo4j and ArangoDB.They offer a mature engine to build and persist property graphs. We base our architectural framework on ArangoDB because it allows saving attributes not only in the nodes but also in the edges of a graph. It is a valuable option for incorporating more information if needed.

Throughout the years, graphs are highly used to solve several downstream tasks, such as developing extended similarity metrics for documents embedded in graphs (Minkov et al., 2006), Named Entity Recognition (Yu et al., 2008), measuring the semantic distance between texts (Tsang and Stevenson, 2010), using a graph-based ranking algorithm (Demir et al., 2010), frame semantic parsing (Zheng et al., 2022) among many others ((Chen et al., 2022), (Colas et al., 2022), etc.). All these works demonstrate the importance of graphs and their multipurpose usage, making it essential to develop an architectural framework to create and annotate graphs so they can be (re)used later on for similar or different downstream tasks.

Regarding graph annotations, lately, Bikaun et al. (2022) introduced QuickGraph, a rapid annotation tool that allows users, via its web interface, to upload corpora and add annotations to it by selecting the annotation type from a predefined list (e.g., named entities). As mentioned above, CAG is not a tool but rather a more general programming framework that employs an architectural pattern for the goal of code centralization and reproducibility, giving users the flexibility to select their datasources and annotation types. CAG has predefined nodes (e.g., TextNode) and edges to encourage the unification of information from different sources, and it allows the addition of any annotation type to its predefined annotations.

Formerly, Bird and Liberman (1999, 2001) defined 'Linguistic annotation' as a descriptive or

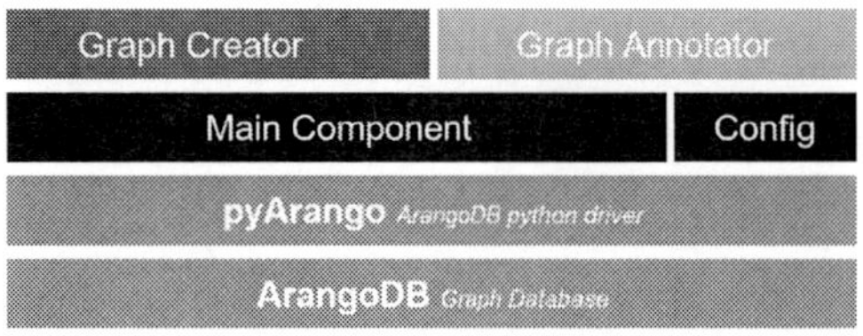

Figure 2: The building blocks of the CAG framework. The framework uses ArangoDB as a graph database with the Python driver *PyArango*. On top of that, CAG has a *Config* block responsible for establishing the connection to the database. Moreover, the *Main component* is the base component responsible for creating/updating the graph ontology, nodes, and edges. The top building blocks are *Graph-Creator* and *Graph-Annotator*.

analytical notation applied to raw language data of any form (e.g., textual, voice). The added notations may include annotations of all sorts (from phonetic features to discourse structures) (Bird and Liberman, 2001), which provides a formal framework for constructing, maintaining, and searching linguistic annotations while remaining consistent with many alternative data structures and formats. They focus on linguistic annotations regardless of the raw data from which they exploit the commonalities between them. Our work here adapts the same concept for *annotations*. Our annotation framework extends an existing graph with new node types holding a notation derived from any raw data. Maeda et al. (2002, 2006) present the Annotation Graph Toolkit, a formal framework to support the development of annotation tools of time series data based on Bird and Liberman (2001) framework; these tools allow users to annotate a data point manually. The main difference is that CAG is an architectural framework, not a toolkit. It allows the incorporation not only of time series data but any data. Most importantly, our framework supports automated bulk annotations instead of manual ones.

3 The Framework

In this section, we describe the technical framework of the Corpus Annotation Graph builder (CAG). As mentioned in Section 1, we create an architectural framework that employs the *create-and-annotate* pattern, which requires two main building blocks in CAG: Graph-Creator and Graph-Annotator. As shown in Figure 2, these two blocks are built on top of several other blocks. From the bottom up, CAG uses ArangoDB as a graph database to store graphs, which is accessed via the python library,

Function Name	Description
Main Component	`cag.framework.component.py`
Constructor	Establishes the connection to the database using the *Config* class, creates the graph ontology if it does not exist, or updates it.
get_document	Gets a node or an edge based on a key or set of attributes.
upsert_node	Updates or creates a new node instance. It uses the get_document function to fetch existing nodes.
get_edge_attributes	Gets the edge attributes based on Edge type and from and to nodes.
upsert_edge	Update or create a new edge instance.
Config `cag.utils.config.py`	
Constructor	Establishes the connection to the database using the database attributes: database URL, username, password, and port. It retries in case of connection failure.
configuration	Re-establishes a new connection and rewrites a previous one.

Table 1: Summary of the functions in the `Main Component` and the *Config*. These functions are used by CAG's Graph-Creator and -Annotator.

PyArango[6]. After that comes the **Main Component** block, which creates and updates the graph ontology by manipulating the graph elements. It uses the **Config** block to establish the connection to the database. Table 1 summarizes both components' methods, each a Python class.

The sections below delve deeper into the two main building blocks on top, Graph-Creator, and Graph-Annotator, where we explain the relation between them and between the lower blocks.

3.1 Graph-Creator

As mentioned in Section 1, a Graph-Creator (GC) creates objects of interest (OOI) from a datasource as nodes and edges where these OOIs are directly extracted without further analysis (e.g., text content, image). GC offers a unified layout, structuring the creation process of a graph from one or many datasources. **`GraphCreatorBase`**, CAG's primary GC class, allows the management of a datasource

[6] `https://pypi.org/project/pyArango/`

Function Name	Description
Constructor	Sets the path to the source data, sets the data configuration from *Config*, and calls the *initialization* method that should be implemented.
init_graph	An `abstract` method to initialize the nodes and edges by using pre-existing node/edge specific methods (e.g., `create_corpus_node`, `create_text_node`, `create_image_node`, `create_author_node`) or by using the *upsert_node* or `upsert_edge` from the **Component** class.
update_graph	An `abstract` method to update the nodes and edges by using pre-existing methods from the **Component** methods.

Table 2: Summary of the main functions in the `Graph Creator` abstract class.

Name	Attributes and Description
Nodes	
GenericOOSNode	timestamp. The generic node class from which all python class nodes inherit.
CorpusNode	name, type, description, created_on and timestamp.
TextNode	text, timestamp
AuthorNode	name and timestamp
ImageNode	URL and timestamp
WebResource	URL and timestamp
Edges	
BelongsTo	timestamp. For example a *TextNode* BelongsTo a *CorpusNode*
HasAuthor	timestamp. For example, *TextNode* HasAuthor an *AuthorNode*
RefersTo	timestamp. For example, *TextNode* RefersTo a *WebResource* node

Table 3: A sample of the predefined nodes and edges in CAG (`cag.graph_elements`).

within a graph. It is an abstract class that inherits all the functionalities of the "Main Component" (Table 1). As shown in Table 2, `GraphCreatorBase` enforces the implementation of two functions: one for *initializing* the graph from a datasource and one for *updating* it. Additionally, GC offers a predefined set of edges and nodes with their corresponding maintenance (inserting/updating) that can be optionally used (see Table 3). A project can have as many graph creators as is needed, usually one per datasource. A sample code is available on GitHub[7].

Another trait of GC is that it allows time propagation through linked nodes since each OOI node carries a timestamp of its creation. For example, if a set of content nodes (N) linked to a parent node (P) is updated/created, the latest timestamp of these nodes can be recursively propagated to P.

The CG creates a graph by loading raw data to it. This graph is enriched by using the Graph-Annotator.

3.2 Graph-Annotator

The Graph-Annotator (GA) enriches the graph by analyzing object of interest (OOI) nodes and linking them to newly created annotation nodes. For example, as shown in Figure 1, a textual node can be linked with a *has_person* edge to a named entity node of type PERSON and attribute "Greta Thunberg". Annotations can be applied on different levels: (1) a collection of nodes such as corpus level to extract corpus statistics, topics, etc., (2) a single node such as text nodes (e.g., keyphrases), image nodes (e.g., generated captions), etc.

Figure 3 shows the workflow of GA. A set of nodes, predefined by the user, is fed to a customizable **pipeline** where each **pipe** has three responsibilities:(1) accessing the node(s) and extracting a corresponding feature (e.g., named entities), (2) processing the features (e.g., count the number of times a named entity, e.g., ORGANIZATION: "Google", occurred), (3) updating the graph by saving the annotations corresponding to this pipe. For example, Figure 3 shows that all the text nodes were selected to be annotated. They are, then, fed to a pipeline that has three pipes: a *sentence divider*, a *named entity pipe*, and an *emotion* pipe. After running the pipeline, the graph is updated with the corresponding annotation nodes.

Pipe We define a CAG pipe as a set of objects that encapsulates several functionalities to deal with the technical part of annotation, the post-processing, and the persistency of the annotation nodes in the graph. A pipe is mainly defined in two steps: (1) defining its attributes in CAG's `registered pipes dictionary` and (2) and defining a `PipeOrchestrator`.

`registered pipes` is a Python dictionary that has one entry for each pipe, holding all at-

[7] `https://github.com/DLR-SC/corpus-annotation-graph-builder/blob/main/examples/1_create_graph.ipynb`

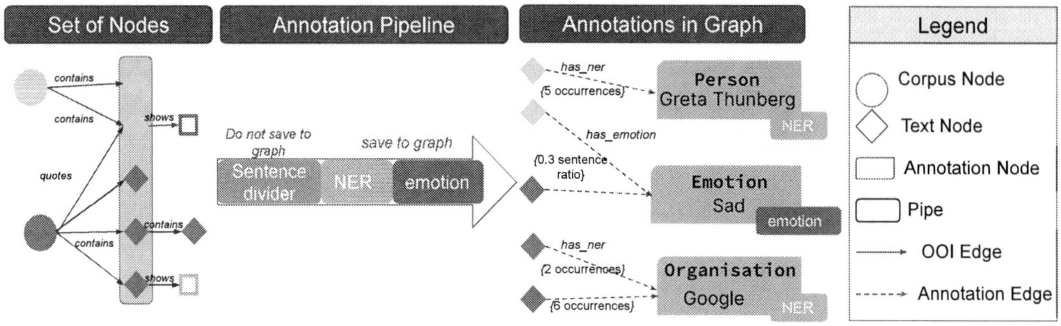

Figure 3: A simplified illustration of the Graph-Annotator. (1) The text node set is selected and fed to a pipeline. (2) The pipeline consists of three pipes: sentence divider (preprocessing), NER, and Emotion pipes. After annotating, (3) the annotation nodes are saved in the graph.

tributes (Table 4) needed for a pipe to tackle its responsibilities and distinguished by a unique key.
.

Attribute	Description
orchestrator_class	The path to the pipe's orchestrator class.
pipe_id_or_func	A *Spacy* predefined id (e.g., ner) or a customized function id that is implemented in the *pipe_path*.
pipe_path	The path to the customized function or empty in case of Spacy.
level	Annotation level whether it is on the level of a single node or a set of node.
data_type	Whether the annotated OOI is a text, image or URL.
annotated_node_name	the name of the OOI node being annotated.
node_class	The Path to the class of the annotation node.
edge_class	The Path to the class of the edge node.

Table 4: The attributes of a registered pipes. CAG's predefined pipes are under `cag.framework.annotator.registered_pipes`

The `PipeOrchestrator` is an abstract python class that loads the pipe components based on the attributes provided in the `registered pipes`. The orchestrator validates the attributes in Table 4 (e.g., ensures correct paths) and loads the required python modules, making them accessible later on for the **pipeline**. It also creates new annotation node/edge types by updating the graph ontology. Additionally, the PipeOrchestrator is an abstract class that enforces the implementation of three methods: `create_node`, `create_edge` and `save_annotations`. The latter method should loop over the annotations and use the other two methods to save the annotation nodes and edges.

After defining all the pipes, the **pipeline** manages them.

Pipeline GA offers a feature to unify the pipeline's definition. The **`pipeline`** manages pipes by using the pipe's information accessed from the `PipeOrchestrator`. It deals with enforcing the flow of the pipes (e.g., extract sentences before classifying them), executing the pipeline (using $pipe\_id\_or\_func$ in Table 4), which outputs the annotations, and saving to the graph (by calling the pipe's corresponding `save_annotations` mentioned previously). The Pipeline class supports the execution of customized pipes (a function call), Spacy (Honnibal et al., 2020) customized components, or Spacy native components (e.g., SentenceRecognizer for sentence segmentation). The pipeline only executes these functions based on information provided by the pipe, and it is not responsible for the logic within these pipes. A pipe is added as follows to a pipeline (sample on GitHub[8]):

```
add_annotation_pipe(
    name="MyPipeOrchestrator",
    save_output=True,
    is_spacy=True
    )
```

It is important to note that for provenance track-

[8]https://github.com/DLR-SC/corpus-annotation-graph-builder/blob/main/examples/2_annotate_graph.ipynb

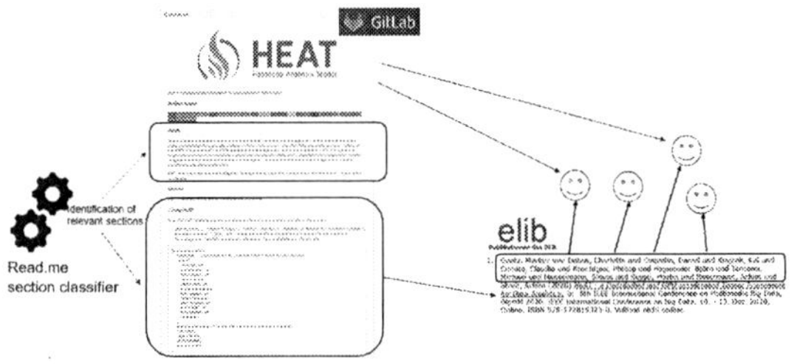

Figure 4: Linking Git repositories and publication entries through readme files and metadata.

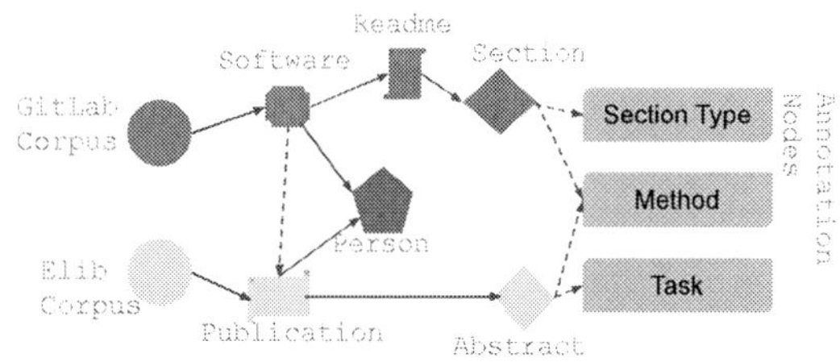

Figure 5: CAG structure for linking GitLab (blue) projects and publications (yellow). Graph creators create blue, yellow, and grey (common node) nodes and solid edges, and graph annotators add green nodes and dashed edges by analyzing the OOI nodes.

ing of annotations, an annotation node can be equipped with additional metadata about its creation timestamp, the component that created the annotation, and additional parameters needed for the analysis reproduction. An example is listed below:

```
{
  analysis_component: 'keyphrases,'
  parameters:
            {
              algorithm: text_rank,
              relevance_threshold: 0.75
            }
}
```

4 Use Cases

4.1 Linking Publications and Software

In many fields of science, it is common to use Git repositories hosting platforms such as GitHub and GitLab. Those repositories often have a "readme" file introducing the purpose of tools, dataset descriptions, or usage instructions. Thus, these files agglomerate valuable science and software knowledge (El Baff et al., 2021) that is worth exploring. Often one can also find references to associated traditional publications. We use the CAG to integrate search over fragmented information in publication outlets and Git repositories. More precisely, we build a graph that indirectly links repositories and papers via intermediate keywords and persons and directly by parsing paper references in repositories' "readme" files (Figure 4).

The German Aerospace Center (DLR), with a constantly growing corpus of publications and software tools, is interested in efficiently retrieving digital scientific information. Thus, as a backbone of an internal search application, the CAG framework is used to build an organizational knowledge graph linking publications in the DLR publication database elib[9] and repositories in its self-hosted GitLab instance[10].

Graph-Creator. The graph creator processes a dump of GitLab "readme" files and the associated project metadata (e.g., contributors, title, URL) retrieved through the GitLab API[11], as well as dumps of publication abstracts from the elib publication database along with titles, authors, institutes into the hierarchical structure of OOI nodes depicted in Figure 5 with colors blue for projects, yellow for publications and grey for common nodes between the datasources, linked via solid edges.

Graph Annotators. We implement a pipeline containing several pipes to annotate the graph by extracting information from the text nodes and saving the annotation nodes, as shown in Figure 5.

Readme section classifier: We use the Prana et al. (2019) readme classifier to extract sections labeled as a description (What/Why sections), reference, and acknowledgment. These labels are linked to the readme text nodes.

Reference parser: We developed a tool for parsing paper references in "readme" from raw form (e.g., APA, BibTeX) to items such as author, title, and venue. This annotator uses the extracted information to establish links to publication nodes where possible.

Concept extraction: For linking software repositories and publications, even if there is no direct reference or overlap in persons, we use the SPERT (Eberts and Ulges, 2020) information extraction model trained on scientific corpora SciERC (Luan et al., 2018) to extract concepts where we focus on "Method" and "Task" since these constitute the most relevant links between papers and software projects. Such concept annotations are attached

[9] https://elib.dlr.de/

[10] https://gitlab.dlr.de/

[11] https://docs.gitlab.com/ee/api/

to the text nodes of publication abstracts and the "readme" sections tagged as "description".

This use case is similar to the portal `https://paperswithcode.com/`, but our solution is automatized. The CAG framework eases processing large volumes of publications and repository corpora into a well-defined graph format.

4.2 Wikipedia Page Revisions

We present here a simple use case depicting the usage of the Graph-Creator and -Annotator from a widely known source, Wikipedia.

As a community-driven encyclopedia, Wikipedia has a lens on societal discourse. Since the entire revision history of each article is publicly available, Wikipedia constitutes a research dataset that allows tracing the evolution of themes over time. Using the CAG framework, we demonstrate how to create a graph from Wikipedia revisions for the two categories, *climate change* and *artificial intelligence*. We extract the revisions for two periods, October 2012 and -2022. The data is downloaded using our tool, `wikipedia-periodic-revisions`[12] which downloads Wikipedia revisions for a specific category and period. It, then, saves each Wikipedia Page as a file. The code is available on GitHub[13].

Graph-Creator. Figure 6 shows the nodes and edges predefined by CAG (in blue) and the ones the newly defined ones (in yellow). The Wikipedia graph creator loops over the pages to load the data into the graph. On top, it creates a Wikipedia corpus node as the most general OOI node, referenced by Wikipedia articles. Each article comprises of revision nodes, each linked to a text node. Additionally, the graph creator already establishes cross-article connections by parsing images and external references. Figure 6 shows the general scheme of our use case.

Graph-Annotators. We create an annotation pipeline utilizing the Spacy named entity recognition module[14] to extract named entities from revision texts. Text nodes containing common entities (e.g., referring to the same Organization) will be indirectly linked together through these entities. In this way, article relationships are also established

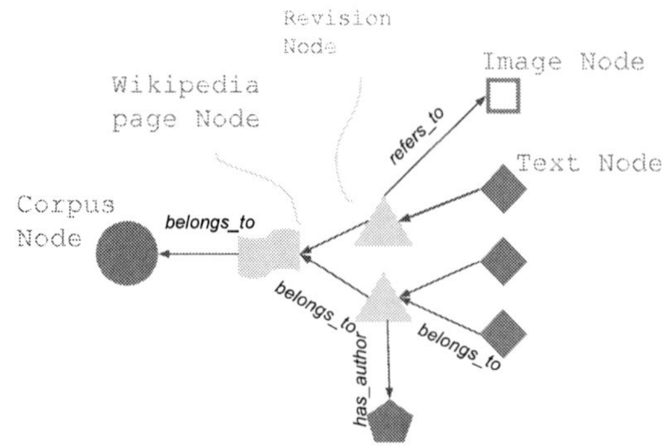

Figure 6: Wikipedia graph structure. CAG's predefined nodes are in blue, and newly defined nodes are in yellow.

based on common referencing (either explicit by containing, for example, common images (an OOI) or implicit by just mentioning common entities).

The resulting CAG structure (see Figure 6) allows interesting graph queries to analyze the co-evolution of Wikipedia articles through time. Examples are: "In which context a certain organization (named entity) is mentioned on Wikipedia?" or "Which articles reciprocally reference each other?".

5 Conclusion and Future Work

We presented CAG, a publicly available architectural framework aiming to employ unified and reproducible patterns in graph creation and extension via annotations. CAG allows users to concentrate on graph ontologies and pipelines while the framework takes the burden of handling repetitive and cumbersome tasks. We further aim to extend our framework to have an analysis component incorporating dynamic data analysis through time and space, exploiting the 'create-and-annotate' graph results.

6 Acknowledgment

This project is funded by the German Federal Ministry of Education (BMBF) under the InsightsNet[15] project. We want to thank Shahbaz Syed[16] for his valuable input, especially regarding the Figures presented in the paper. We also would like to thank the reviewers for their helpful comments.

[12] `https://github.com/DLR-SC/wikipedia-periodic-revisions`, also downloadable via PyPi `https://pypi.org/project/wikipedia_tools/`

[13] `https://github.com/roxanneelbaff/cag_wikipedia_usecase`

[14] `https://spacy.io/api/entityrecognizer`

[15] `http://insightsnet.org/`

[16] `https://scholar.google.com/citations?hl=en&user=eGe86TEAAAAJ`

References

Tyler Bikaun, Michael Stewart, and Wei Liu. 2022. QuickGraph: A rapid annotation tool for knowledge graph extraction from technical text. In *Proceedings of the 60th Annual Meeting of the Association for Computational Linguistics: System Demonstrations*, pages 270–278, Dublin, Ireland. Association for Computational Linguistics.

Steven Bird and Mark Liberman. 1999. Annotation graphs as a framework for multidimensional linguistic data analysis. In *Towards Standards and Tools for Discourse Tagging*.

Steven Bird and Mark Liberman. 2001. A formal framework for linguistic annotation. *Speech Communication*, 33(1):23–60. Speech Annotation and Corpus Tools.

Chen Chen, Yufei Wang, Bing Li, and Kwok-Yan Lam. 2022. Knowledge is flat: A Seq2Seq generative framework for various knowledge graph completion. In *Proceedings of the 29th International Conference on Computational Linguistics*, pages 4005–4017, Gyeongju, Republic of Korea. International Committee on Computational Linguistics.

Anthony Colas, Mehrdad Alvandipour, and Daisy Zhe Wang. 2022. GAP: A graph-aware language model framework for knowledge graph-to-text generation. In *Proceedings of the 29th International Conference on Computational Linguistics*, pages 5755–5769, Gyeongju, Republic of Korea. International Committee on Computational Linguistics.

Seniz Demir, Sandra Carberry, and Kathleen F. McCoy. 2010. A discourse-aware graph-based content-selection framework. In *Proceedings of the 6th International Natural Language Generation Conference*. Association for Computational Linguistics.

Markus Eberts and Adrian Ulges. 2020. Span-based joint entity and relation extraction with transformer pre-training. In *Proceedings of the 2020 European Conference on Artificial Intelligence*, pages 2006–2013. IOS Press.

Roxanne El Baff, Sivasurya Santhanam, and Tobias Hecking. 2021. Quantifying synergy between software projects using readme files only. In *Proceedings of the 33rd International Conference on Software Engineering and Knowledge Engineering*, volume 33. KSI Research Inc. and Knowledge Systems Institute Graduate School.

Matthew Honnibal, Ines Montani, Sofie Van Landeghem, and Adriane Boyd. 2020. spaCy: Industrial-strength Natural Language Processing in Python.

Yi Luan, Luheng He, Mari Ostendorf, and Hannaneh Hajishirzi. 2018. Multi-task identification of entities, relations, and coreference for scientific knowledge graph construction. In *Proceedings of the 2018 Conference on Empirical Methods in Natural Language Processing*, pages 3219–3232, Brussels, Belgium. Association for Computational Linguistics.

Kazauki Maeda, Steven Bird, Xiaoyi Ma, and Haejoong Lee. 2002. Creating annotation tools with the annotation graph toolkit. In *Proceedings of the Third International Conference on Language Resources and Evaluation (LREC'02)*, Las Palmas, Canary Islands - Spain. European Language Resources Association (ELRA).

Kazuaki Maeda, Haejoong Lee, Julie Medero, and Stephanie Strassel. 2006. A new phase in annotation tool development at the Linguistic Data Consortium: The evolution of the annotation graph toolkit. In *Proceedings of the Fifth International Conference on Language Resources and Evaluation (LREC'06)*, Genoa, Italy. European Language Resources Association (ELRA).

Einat Minkov, William Cohen, and Andrew Ng. 2006. A graphical framework for contextual search and name disambiguation in email. In *Proceedings of TextGraphs: the First Workshop on Graph Based Methods for Natural Language Processing*, pages 1–8, New York City. Association for Computational Linguistics.

Gede Artha Azriadi Prana, Christoph Treude, Ferdian Thung, Thushari Atapattu, and David Lo. 2019. Categorizing the content of github readme files. *Empirical Software Engineering*, 24(3):1296–1327.

Vivian Tsang and Suzanne Stevenson. 2010. A graph-theoretic framework for semantic distance. *Computational Linguistics*, 36(1):31–69.

Xiaofeng Yu, Wai Lam, and Shing-Kit Chan. 2008. A framework based on graphical models with logic for Chinese named entity recognition. In *Proceedings of the Third International Joint Conference on Natural Language Processing: Volume-I*.

Ce Zheng, Xudong Chen, Runxin Xu, and Baobao Chang. 2022. A double-graph based framework for frame semantic parsing. In *Proceedings of the 2022 Conference of the North American Chapter of the Association for Computational Linguistics: Human Language Technologies*, pages 4998–5011, Seattle, United States. Association for Computational Linguistics.

ferret: a Framework for Benchmarking Explainers on Transformers

Giuseppe Attanasio[♣], Eliana Pastor[◇], Chiara Di Bonaventura[♠], Debora Nozza[♣]

[♣]Bocconi University, Milan, Italy
[◇]Politecnico di Torino, Turin, Italy
[♠]King's College London, London, United Kingdom
{giuseppe.attanasio3,debora.nozza}@unibocconi.it
eliana.pastor@polito.it
chiara.di_bonaventura@kcl.ac.uk

Abstract

As Transformers are increasingly relied upon to solve complex NLP problems, there is an increased need for their decisions to be humanly interpretable. While several explainable AI (XAI) techniques for interpreting the outputs of transformer-based models have been proposed, there is still a lack of easy access to using and comparing them. We introduce *ferret*, a Python library to simplify the use and comparisons of XAI methods on transformer-based classifiers. With *ferret*, users can visualize and compare transformers-based models output explanations using state-of-the-art XAI methods on any free-text or existing XAI corpora. Moreover, users can also evaluate ad-hoc XAI metrics to select the most faithful and plausible explanations. To align with the recently consolidated process of sharing and using transformers-based models from Hugging Face, *ferret* interfaces directly with its Python library. In this paper, we showcase *ferret* to benchmark XAI methods used on transformers for sentiment analysis and hate speech detection. We show how specific methods provide consistently better explanations and are preferable in the context of transformer models.

1 Introduction

Transformers have revolutionized NLP applications in recent years due to their strong performance on various tasks; their black-box nature remains an obstacle for practitioners who need explanations about why specific predictions were made and what features drove them. The development of explainable AI (XAI) techniques on several NLP tasks (Madsen et al., 2022) has helped bridge this gap by providing insight into the inner workings of transformers and helping users gain trust in their decisions. Several XAI approaches have been proposed in the literature (Ribeiro et al., 2016; Lundberg and Lee, 2017; Simonyan et al., 2014a; Pastor and Baralis, 2019), also tailored to Transformer models (Wallace et al., 2019a; Li et al., 2016; Jin et al., 2019; Ross et al., 2021). Despite the importance of making XAI methods accessible to NLP experts and practitioners through practical tools, there is still a lack of accessibility for transformer models. XAI for transformers is mainly scattered and hard to operationalize. Methods come with independent implementations or framework-specific libraries that do not allow either evaluation or cross-method comparison. Further, existing implementations are not integrated with widespread transformers libraries (e.g., Hugging Face's *transformers* (Wolf et al., 2020)). The lack of standardization and weak interoperability leaves practitioners with unsolved questions, such as choosing the *best* method given a task and a model (Attanasio et al., 2022).

We introduce *ferret* (FramEwork foR benchmaRking Explainers on Transformers), an open-source Python library that drastically simplifies the use and comparison of XAI methods on transformers. The library stems from vertical scientific contributions and focused engineering efforts. On the one hand, *ferret* provides the first-of-its-kind API (see Figure 1) to use and compare explanation methods along the established criteria of faithfulness and plausibility (Jacovi and Goldberg, 2020). On the other hand, it integrates seamlessly with *transformers* (Wolf et al., 2020), making it an easy add-on to existing Transformer-based pipelines and NLP tasks. *ferret* permits to run four state-of-the-art XAI methods, compute six ad-hoc XAI evaluation metrics, and easily load four existing interpretability datasets. Further, it offers abstract interfaces to foster future integration of methods, metrics, and datasets.

We showcase *ferret* on sentiment analysis and

Proceedings of the 17th Conference of the European Chapter of the Association for Computational Linguistics System Demonstrations, pages 256–266
May 2-4, 2023 ©2023 Association for Computational Linguistics

hate speech detection case studies. Faithfulness and plausibility metrics highlight SHAP (Lundberg and Lee, 2017) as the most consistent explainer on single- and multiple-samples scenarios.

Contributions. We release *ferret*, the first-of-its-kind benchmarking framework for interpretability tightly integrated with Hugging Face's *transformers* library. We release our code and documentation,[1] an interactive demo,[2] and a video tutorial.[3]

2 Library Design

ferret builds on four core principles.

1. Built-in Post-hoc Interpretability We include four state-of-the-art post-hoc feature importance methods and three interpretability corpora. Ready-to-use methods allow users to explain any text with an arbitrary model. Annotated datasets provide valuable test cases for new interpretability methods and metrics. To the best of our knowledge, *ferret* is first in providing integrated access to XAI datasets, methods, and a full-fledged evaluation suite.

2. Unified Explanation Benchmarking We propose a unified API to evaluate explanations. We currently support six state-of-the metrics along the principles of faithfulness and plausibility (Jacovi and Goldberg, 2020).

3. Transformers-readiness *ferret* offers a direct interface with models from the Hugging Face Hub. Users can load models using standard naming conventions and explain them with the built-in methods effortlessly. Figure 1 shows the essential code to classify and explain a string with a pre-existing Hugging Face model and evaluate the resultıng explanations.

4. Modularity and Abstraction *ferret* counts three core modules, implementing Explainers, Evaluation, and Datasets APIs. Each module exposes an abstract interface to foster new development. For example, user can sub-class `BaseExplainer` or `BaseEvaluator` to include a new feature importance method or a new evaluation metric respectively.

[1] https://github.com/g8a9/ferret
[2] https://huggingface.co/spaces/g8a9/ferret
[3] https://youtu.be/kX0HcSah_M4

Feature	Category
Gradient	Saliency
Integrated Gradient	Saliency
LIME	Surrogate Model
SHAP	Shapley Values
Comprehensiveness	Faithfulness
Sufficiency	Faithfulness
Correlation with Leave-One-Out scores	Faithfulness
Intersection-Over-Union	Plausibility
Area Under Precision-Recall Curve	Plausibility
Token-level F1 score	Plausibility
HateXplain	Hate Speech
MovieReviews	Sentiment
SST	Sentiment
Thermostat	Generic

Table 1: *ferret* at a glance: built-in methods (top), metrics (middle), and datasets (bottom).

ferret builds on common choices from the interpretability community and good engineering practices. We report the most salient technical details (e.g., efficiency via GPU inference, visualization tools, etc.) in Appendix A.

2.1 Explainer API

We focus on the widely adopted family of post-hoc feature attribution methods (Danilevsky et al., 2020). I.e., given a model, a target class, and a prediction, *ferret* lets you measure *how much* each token contributed to that prediction. We integrate Gradient (Simonyan et al., 2014b) (also known as Saliency) and Integrated Gradient (Sundararajan et al., 2017); SHAP (Lundberg and Lee, 2017) as a Shapley value-based method, and LIME (Ribeiro et al., 2016) as representative of local surrogate methods.

We build on open-source libraries and streamline their interaction with Hugging Face models and paradigms. We report the supported configurations and functionalities in Appendix A.

2.2 Dataset API

Fostering a streamlined, accessible evaluation on independently released XAI datasets, we provide a convenient Dataset API. It enables users to load XAI datasets, explain individual or subsets of samples, and evaluate the resulting explanations.

```
from transformers import AutoModelForSequenceClassification, AutoTokenizer
from ferret import Benchmark

name = "cardiffnlp/twitter-xlm-roberta-base-sentiment"
model = AutoModelForSequenceClassification.from_pretrained(name)
tokenizer = AutoTokenizer.from_pretrained(name)

bench = Benchmark(model, tokenizer)
explanations = bench.explain("You look stunning!", target=1)
evaluations = bench.evaluate_explanations(explanations, target=1)
```

Figure 1: Essential code to benchmark explanations on an existing Hugging Face model using *ferret*.

Currently, *ferret* includes three classification-oriented datasets annotated with human rationales, i.e., annotations highlighting the most relevant words, phrases, or sentences a human annotator attributed to a given class label (DeYoung et al., 2020; Wiegreffe and Marasovic, 2021). Moreover, *ferret* API gives access to the Thermostat collection (Feldhus et al., 2021), a wide set of pre-computed feature attribution scores.

HateXplain (Mathew et al., 2021). It contains 20,148 English instances labeled along three axes: (i) hate (either hateful, offensive, normal or undecided), (ii) target group (either race, religion, gender, sexual orientation, or miscellaneous), and (iii) word-level human rationales (expressed only on hateful and offensive texts).[4]

MovieReviews (Zaidan and Eisner, 2008; DeYoung et al., 2020). The dataset contains 2,000 movie reviews annotated with positive and negative sentiment labels and phrase-level human rationales that support gold labels.

Stanford Sentiment Treebank (SST) (Socher et al., 2013). A sentiment classification dataset of 9,620 movie reviews annotated with binary sentiment labels, including human annotations for word phrases of the parse trees. We extract human rationales from annotations following the heuristic approach proposed in Carton et al. (2020).

Thermostat Datasets *Thermostat* (Feldhus et al., 2021) provides pre-computed feature attribution scores given a model, a dataset, and an explanation method. *ferret* currently provides built-in access to pre-computed attributions on the news topic classification and sentiment analysis tasks.

[4]If a model splits a relevant word into sub-words, we consider all of them relevant as well.

These datasets provide an *initial* example of what an integrated approach can offer to researchers and practitioners.

2.3 Evaluation API

We evaluate explanations on the faithfulness and plausibility properties (Jacovi and Goldberg, 2020; DeYoung et al., 2020). Specifically, *ferret* implements three state-of-the-art metrics to measure faithfulness and three for plausibility.

Faithfulness. Faithfulness evaluates how accurately the explanation reflects the inner working of the model (Jacovi and Goldberg, 2020).

ferret offers the following measures of faithfulness: comprehensiveness, sufficiency, (DeYoung et al., 2020) and correlations with 'leave-one-out' scores (Jain and Wallace, 2019).

Comprehensiveness (↑) evaluates whether the explanation captures the tokens the model used to make the prediction. We measure it by removing the tokens highlighted by the explainer and observing the change in probability as follows.

Let x be a sentence and let f_j be the prediction probability of the model f for a target class j. Let r_j be a discrete explanation or *rationale* indicating the set of tokens supporting the prediction f_j. Comprehensiveness is defined as $f(x)_j - f(x \backslash r_j)_j$ where $x \setminus r_j$ is the sentence x were tokens in r_j are removed. A high value of comprehensiveness indicates that the tokens in r_j are relevant for the prediction.

While comprehensiveness is defined for discrete explanations, feature attribution methods assign a continuous score to each token. We hence select identify r_j as follows. First, we filter out tokens with a negative contribution (i.e., they *pull* the prediction away from the chosen label). Then, we compute the metric multiple times, considering the $k\%$ most important tokens, with k ranging from

10% to 100% (step of 10%). Finally, we aggregate the comprehensiveness scores with the average, called Area Over the Perturbation Curve (AOPC) (DeYoung et al., 2020).

Sufficiency (↓) captures if the tokens in the explanation are sufficient for the model to make the prediction (DeYoung et al., 2020). It is measured as $f(x)_j - f(r_j)_j$. A low score indicates that tokens in r_j are indeed the ones driving the prediction. As for *Comprehensiveness*, we compute the AOPC by varying the number of the relevant tokens r_j.

Correlation with Leave-One-Out scores (↑). We first compute leave-one-out (LOO) scores by omitting tokens and measuring the difference in the model prediction. We do that for every token, once at a time. LOO scores represent a simple measure of individual feature importance under the linearity assumption (Jacovi and Goldberg, 2020). We then measure the Kendall rank correlation coefficient τ between the explanation and LOO importance (Jain and Wallace, 2019) ($taucorr\_loo$). $taucorr\_loo$ closer to 1 means higher faithfulness to LOO.

Plausibility. Plausibility reflects how explanations are aligned with human reasoning by comparing explanations with *human rationales* (DeYoung et al., 2020) .

We integrate into *ferret* three plausibility measures of the ERASER benchmark (DeYoung et al., 2020): Intersection-Over-Union (IOU) at the token level, token-level F1 scores, and Area Under the Precision-Recall curve (AUPRC).

The first two are defined for discrete explanations. Given the human and predicted rationale, *IOU* (↑) quantifies the overlap of the tokens they cover divided by the size of their union. *Token-level F1 scores* (↑) are derived by computing precision and recall at the token level. Following DeYoung et al. (2020) and Mathew et al. (2021), we derive discrete explanations by selecting the top K tokens with positive influence, where K is the average length of the human rationale for the dataset. While being intuitive, IOU and Token-level F1 are based only on a single threshold to derive rationales. Moreover, they do not consider tokens' relative ranking and degree of importance. We then also integrate the AUPRC (↑), defined for explanations with continuous scores (DeYoung et al., 2020). It is computed by varying a threshold over token importance scores, using the human rationale as ground truth.

2.4 Transformers-Ready Interface

ferret is deeply integrated with Hugging Face interfaces. Users working with their standard models and tokenizers can easily integrate it for diagnostic purposes. The contact point is the main `Benchmark` class. It receives any Hugging Face model and tokenizer and uses them to classify, run explanation methods and seamlessly evaluate the explanations. Similarly, our Dataset API leverages Hugging Face's *datasets*[5] to retrieve data and human rationales.

3 Case Studies

We showcase *ferret* in two real-world tasks, focusing on benchmarking explainers on individual samples or across multiple instances. In the following, we describe how *ferret* highlights the best explainers in sentiment analysis and hate speech detection tasks. Our running examples use an XLM-RoBERTa model fine-tuned for sentiment analysis (Barbieri et al., 2021) and a BERT model fine-tuned for hate speech detection (Mathew et al., 2021).

3.1 Faithfulness Metrics for Error Analysis

Explanations on individual instances are often used for model debugging and error analysis (Vig, 2019; Feng et al., 2018). However, different explanations can lead users to different conclusions, hindering a solid understanding of the model's flaws. We show how practitioners can alleviate this issue including *ferret* in their pipeline.

Figure 2 shows explanations and faithfulness metrics computed on the sentence "Great movie for a great nap!" for the "Positive" class label misclassified by the model as "Negative".

Faithfulness metrics show that SHAP adheres best to the model's inner workings since it returns the most comprehensive and relevant explanations. Indeed, SHAP retrieves the highest number of tokens the model used to make the prediction ($aopc\_compr(\uparrow) = 0.41$) that are relevant to drive the prediction ($aopc\_suff(\downarrow) = 0.09$). Further, $taucorr\_loo(\uparrow) = 0.43$ indicates that SHAP explanations capture the most important tokens for the prediction under the linearity assumption. Although Integrated Gradient (x Input) shows a higher $taucorr\_loo$, it does not provide comprehensive and sufficient explanations. Similarly, Gradient and Integrated Gradient show bad sufficiency and

[5]`https://github.com/huggingface/datasets`

```python
from transformers import
    AutoModelForSequenceClassification,
    AutoTokenizer
from ferret import Benchmark

name = "cardiffnlp/twitter-xlm-roberta-base
    -sentiment"
model = AutoModelForSequenceClassification.
    from_pretrained(name)
tokenizer = AutoTokenizer.
    from_pretrained(name)

bench = Benchmark(model, tokenizer)
query = "Great movie for a great nap!"

scores = bench.score(query)
print(scores)

# Run built-in explainers
explanations = bench.explain(
    query,
    target=2 # "Positive" label
)
bench.show_table(explanations)

# Evaluate explanations
evaluations = bench.evaluate_explanations(
    explanations, target=2
)
bench.show_evaluation_table(evaluations)

## Output
>> {'Negative': 0.013735532760620117,
>> 'Neutral': 0.06385018676519394,
>> 'Positive': 0.9224143028259277}
```

Token	_Great	_movie	_for	_a	_great	_nap	!
Partition SHAP	0.35	0.12	0.05	0.06	0.35	-0.00	0.05
LIME	-0.07	-0.08	0.03	-0.01	-0.24	0.17	0.06
Gradient	0.12	0.17	0.06	0.04	0.14	0.23	0.05
Gradient (x Input)	-0.11	-0.09	-0.08	0.03	0.03	0.11	-0.05
Integrated Gradient	-0.08	0.10	0.05	-0.06	0.00	0.03	-0.03
Integrated Gradient (x Input)	-0.09	-0.15	-0.17	-0.15	-0.10	-0.24	-0.10

	aopc_compr	aopc_suff	taucorr_loo
Partition SHAP	0.41	0.09	0.43
LIME	0.01	0.53	-0.33
Gradient	0.34	0.21	0.05
Gradient (x Input)	-0.01	0.44	-0.81
Integrated Gradient	0.05	0.50	-0.14
Integrated Gradient (x Input)	0.00	1.00	0.52

Figure 2: Code to explain and evaluate explanations on a sentiment classifier (top). Token attributions (middle): darker red (blue) show higher (lower) contribution to the prediction. Faithfulness metrics (bottom): darker colors show better performance.

comprehensiveness, respectively. LIME and Gradient (x Input) do not return trustworthy explanations according to all faithfulness metrics.

Once SHAP has been identified as the best explainer, its explanations enable researchers to investigate possible recurring patterns or detect model biases thoroughly. In this case, the explanations shed light on a type of lexical overfitting: the word "great" skews the prediction toward the positive label regardless of the context and semantics.

3.2 Multi-Instance Assessment

Instance-level analysis finds explainers that meet specific requirements locally. However, the best local explainer might be unsatisfactory across multiple instances. With *ferret*, users can easily produce and aggregate evaluation metrics across multiple dataset samples—or the entire corpus.

We describe how to choose the explainer that returns the most plausible and faithful explanations for the HateXplain dataset. For demonstration purposes, we focus only on a sample of the dataset.

Figure 3 (Appendix C) shows the metrics averaged across ten samples with the "hate speech" label. Results suggest again that SHAP yields the most faithful explanations. SHAP and Gradient achieve the best comprehensiveness and sufficiency scores, but SHAP outperforms all explainers for the τ correlation with LOO (*taucorr_loo* ($\uparrow$) = 0.41). Gradient provides the most plausible explanations, followed by SHAP.

4 Related Work

This section provides a review of tools and libraries that offer a subset of the *ferret*'s functionalities, namely the option to use multiple XAI methods and datasets, evaluation API, transformer-readiness, and built-in visualization. Table 2 summarizes them and compares *ferret* with similar frameworks.

Tools for Post-Hoc XAI. Toolkits for post-hoc interpretability offer built-in methods to explain model prediction, typically through a code interface. *ferret* builds on and extends this idea to a unified framework to generate explanations, *evaluate and compare* them, with support to several XAI datasets. Moreover, *ferret*'s explainers are integrated with transformers's (Wolf et al., 2020) principles and conventions.

PyTorch's Captum (Kokhlikyan et al., 2020) is a generic Python library supporting many interpretability methods. However, the library lacks integration with the Hugging Face Hub and offers no evaluation procedures. AllenNLP Interpret (Wallace et al., 2019b) provides interpretability methods based on gradients and adversarial attacks for AllenNLP models (Gardner et al., 2018). We borrow

	Multiple XAI approaches	Transformers-readiness	Evaluation APIs	XAI datasets	Built-in visualization
Captum	✓	✗	✗	✗	✓
AllenNLP Interpret	✓	✗	✗	✗	✗
Transformers-Interpret	✗	✓	✗	✗	✓
Thermostat	✓	✓	✗	✗	✓
ContrXT	✗	✗	✗	✗	✗
OpenXAI	✓	✗	✓	✗	✗
NLPVis	✗	✗	✗	✗	✓
Seq2Seq-Vis	✗	✗	✗	✗	✓
BertViz	✗	✓	✗	✗	✗
ELI5	✗	✗	✗	✗	✓
LIT	✓	✗	✗	✗	✓
ERASER	✗	✗	✓	✓	✗
Inseq	✓	✓	✗	✗	✓
ferret	✓	✓	✓	✓	✓

Table 2: Comparing off-the-shelf features across different XAI libraries. When assessing built-in visualization, we disregard tools that either do not provide a unified interface or provide single data-point visualizations.

the modular and extensible design and extend it to a wider set of explainers. Transformers-Interpret[6] leverages Captum to explain Transformer models, but it supports only a limited number of methods. Thermostat (Feldhus et al., 2021) exposes pre-computed feature attribution scores through the Hugging-Face Hub but no features oriented to implement or evaluate XAI. We support the Thermostat as a third-party add-on and let users test and benchmark pre-computed explanations. Unlike our study, Inseq (Sarti et al., 2023) focuses on post-hoc interpretability for sequence generation models. Although researchers can use the library to add interpretability evaluations to their models, the toolkit lacks built-in evaluation metrics.

Other related approaches enable global (rather than local) explainability (Malandri et al., 2022), or explanation interfaces for non-transformers models on non-NLP tasks (Agarwal et al., 2022). Other approaches study model behavior at the subgroup level (Wang et al., 2021; Goel et al., 2021; Pastor et al., 2021a,b), focusing more on model evaluation and robustness rather than its interpretation.

Visualization. Most studies that develop visualization tools to investigate the relationships among the input, the model, and the output focus either on specific NLP models - NLPVis (Liu et al., 2018), Seq2Seq-Vis (Strobelt et al., 2018), or explainers - BertViz (Vig, 2019), ELI5[7]. LIT (Tenney et al., 2020) streamlines exploration and analysis in different models. However, it acts mainly as a graphical browser interface. *ferret* provides a Python interface easy to integrate with pre-existing pipelines.

Evaluation. Although prior works introduced diagnostic properties for XAI techniques, evaluating them in practice remains challenging. Studies either concentrate on specific model architectures (Lertvittayakumjorn and Toni, 2019; Arras et al., 2019; DeYoung et al., 2020), individual datasets (Guan et al., 2019; Arras et al., 2019), or a single group of explainability methods (Robnik-Šikonja and Bohanec, 2018; Adebayo et al., 2018). Hence, providing a generally applicable and automated tool for choosing the most suitable method is crucial. To this end, Atanasova et al. (2020) present a comparative study of XAI techniques in three application tasks and model architectures. To the best of our knowledge, we are the first to present a user-friendly Python interface to interpret, visualize and empirically evaluate models directly from the Hugging Face Hub across several metrics. We extend previous work from DeYoung et al. (2020), who developed a benchmark for evaluating rationales on NLP models called ERASER by offering a unified interface for evaluation *and* visual comparison of the explanations at the instance- and dataset-level.

Closer to *ferret*, the OpenXAI framework (Agar-

[6]https://github.com/cdpierse/transformers-interpret

[7]https://github.com/TeamHG-Memex/eli5

wal et al., 2022) enables a systematic evaluation of feature attribution explanation, integrating multiple explainers and XAI structured datasets. OpenXAI supports tabular datasets while we focus on textual data and NLP models.

5 Conclusions

We introduced *ferret*, a novel Python framework to easily access XAI techniques on transformer models. With *ferret*, users can *explain* using state-of-the-art post-hoc explainability techniques, *evaluate* explanations on several metrics for faithfulness and plausibility, and easily *interact* with datasets annotated with human rationales.

We built *ferret* with modularity and abstraction in mind to facilitate future extensions and contributions from the community (see Appendix B for an overview of the ongoing development). As future work, we envision off-the-shelf support for new NLP tasks and scenarios. Building on the classification setup presented in this paper, we plan to add support to more NLP tasks that can be framed as classification, such as Mask Filling Prediction, Natural Language Inference, Zero-Shot Text Classification, Next Sentence Prediction, Token Classification, and Multiple-Choice QA. One further direction would be improving *ferret*'s interoperability with new libraries, e.g., Inseq (Sarti et al., 2023) for XAI on text generation tasks and models.

Ethics Statement

ferret's primary goal is to facilitate the comparison of methods that are instead frequently tested in isolation. Nonetheless, we cannot assume the metrics we currently implement provide a full, exhaustive picture, and we work towards enlarging this set accordingly.

Further, interpretability is much broader than post-hoc feature attribution. We focus on this family of approaches for their wide adoption and intuitiveness.

Similarly, the evaluation measures we integrate are based on removal-based criteria. Prior works pointed out their limitations, specifically the problem of erased inputs falling out of the model input distribution (Hooker et al., 2019).

Acknowledgments

This project has partially received funding from the European Research Council (ERC) under the European Union's Horizon 2020 research and innovation program (grant agreement No. 949944, INTEGRATOR), by Fondazione Cariplo (grant No. 2020-4288, MONICA), and by the grant "National Centre for HPC, Big Data and Quantum Computing", CN000013 (approved under the M42C Call for Proposals - Investment 1.4 - Notice "National Centers" - D.D. No. 3138, 16.12.2021, admitted for funding by MUR Decree No. 1031, 17.06.2022). DN and GA are members of the MilaNLP group and the Data and Marketing Insights Unit of the Bocconi Institute for Data Science and Analysis. EP did part of the work while at CENTAI and is currently a member of the DataBase and Data Mining Group (DBDMG) at Politecnico di Torino. CDB contributed to the work while at Bocconi University and is currently part of the UKRI Centre for Doctoral Training in Safe and Trusted Artificial Intelligence (www.safeandtrustedai.org).

References

Julius Adebayo, Justin Gilmer, Michael Muelly, Ian Goodfellow, Moritz Hardt, and Been Kim. 2018. Sanity checks for saliency maps. *Advances in neural information processing systems*, 31.

Chirag Agarwal, Satyapriya Krishna, Eshika Saxena, Martin Pawelczyk, Nari Johnson, Isha Puri, Marinka Zitnik, and Himabindu Lakkaraju. 2022. OpenXAI: Towards a transparent evaluation of model explanations. In *Thirty-sixth Conference on Neural Information Processing Systems Datasets and Benchmarks Track*.

Leila Arras, Ahmed Osman, Klaus-Robert Müller, and Wojciech Samek. 2019. Evaluating recurrent neural network explanations. In *Proceedings of the 2019 ACL Workshop BlackboxNLP: Analyzing and Interpreting Neural Networks for NLP*, pages 113–126, Florence, Italy. Association for Computational Linguistics.

Pepa Atanasova, Jakob Grue Simonsen, Christina Lioma, and Isabelle Augenstein. 2020. A diagnostic study of explainability techniques for text classification. In *Proceedings of the 2020 Conference on Empirical Methods in Natural Language Processing (EMNLP)*, pages 3256–3274, Online. Association for Computational Linguistics.

Giuseppe Attanasio, Debora Nozza, Eliana Pastor, and Dirk Hovy. 2022. Benchmarking post-hoc interpretability approaches for transformer-based misogyny detection. In *Proceedings of NLP Power! The First Workshop on Efficient Benchmarking in NLP*, pages 100–112, Dublin, Ireland. Association for Computational Linguistics.

Francesco Barbieri, Luis Espinosa Anke, and José Camacho-Collados. 2021. XLM-T: A multilingual language model toolkit for twitter. *CoRR*, abs/2104.12250.

Samuel Carton, Anirudh Rathore, and Chenhao Tan. 2020. Evaluating and characterizing human rationales. In *Proceedings of the 2020 Conference on Empirical Methods in Natural Language Processing (EMNLP)*, pages 9294–9307, Online. Association for Computational Linguistics.

Marina Danilevsky, Kun Qian, Ranit Aharonov, Yannis Katsis, Ban Kawas, and Prithviraj Sen. 2020. A survey of the state of explainable AI for natural language processing. In *Proceedings of the 1st Conference of the Asia-Pacific Chapter of the Association for Computational Linguistics and the 10th International Joint Conference on Natural Language Processing*, pages 447–459, Suzhou, China. Association for Computational Linguistics.

Jay DeYoung, Sarthak Jain, Nazneen Fatema Rajani, Eric Lehman, Caiming Xiong, Richard Socher, and Byron C. Wallace. 2020. ERASER: A benchmark to evaluate rationalized NLP models. In *Proceedings of the 58th Annual Meeting of the Association for Computational Linguistics*, pages 4443–4458, Online. Association for Computational Linguistics.

Nils Feldhus, Robert Schwarzenberg, and Sebastian Möller. 2021. Thermostat: A large collection of NLP model explanations and analysis tools. In *Proceedings of the 2021 Conference on Empirical Methods in Natural Language Processing: System Demonstrations*, pages 87–95, Online and Punta Cana, Dominican Republic. Association for Computational Linguistics.

Shi Feng, Eric Wallace, Alvin Grissom II, Mohit Iyyer, Pedro Rodriguez, and Jordan Boyd-Graber. 2018. Pathologies of neural models make interpretations difficult. In *Proceedings of the 2018 Conference on Empirical Methods in Natural Language Processing*, pages 3719–3728, Brussels, Belgium. Association for Computational Linguistics.

Matt Gardner, Joel Grus, Mark Neumann, Oyvind Tafjord, Pradeep Dasigi, Nelson F. Liu, Matthew Peters, Michael Schmitz, and Luke Zettlemoyer. 2018. AllenNLP: A deep semantic natural language processing platform. In *Proceedings of Workshop for NLP Open Source Software (NLP-OSS)*, pages 1–6, Melbourne, Australia. Association for Computational Linguistics.

Karan Goel, Nazneen Fatema Rajani, Jesse Vig, Zachary Taschdjian, Mohit Bansal, and Christopher Ré. 2021. Robustness gym: Unifying the NLP evaluation landscape. In *Proceedings of the 2021 Conference of the North American Chapter of the Association for Computational Linguistics: Human Language Technologies: Demonstrations*, pages 42–55, Online. Association for Computational Linguistics.

Chaoyu Guan, Xiting Wang, Quanshi Zhang, Runjin Chen, Di He, and Xing Xie. 2019. Towards a deep and unified understanding of deep neural models in nlp. In *International conference on machine learning*, pages 2454–2463. PMLR.

Sara Hooker, Dumitru Erhan, Pieter-Jan Kindermans, and Been Kim. 2019. A benchmark for interpretability methods in deep neural networks. In *Advances in Neural Information Processing Systems*, volume 32. Curran Associates, Inc.

Alon Jacovi and Yoav Goldberg. 2020. Towards faithfully interpretable NLP systems: How should we define and evaluate faithfulness? In *Proceedings of the 58th Annual Meeting of the Association for Computational Linguistics*, pages 4198–4205, Online. Association for Computational Linguistics.

Sarthak Jain and Byron C. Wallace. 2019. Attention is not Explanation. In *Proceedings of the 2019 Conference of the North American Chapter of the Association for Computational Linguistics: Human Language Technologies, Volume 1 (Long and Short Papers)*, pages 3543–3556, Minneapolis, Minnesota. Association for Computational Linguistics.

Xisen Jin, Zhongyu Wei, Junyi Du, Xiangyang Xue, and Xiang Ren. 2019. Towards hierarchical importance attribution: Explaining compositional semantics for neural sequence models. In *International Conference on Learning Representations*.

Narine Kokhlikyan, Vivek Miglani, Miguel Martin, Edward Wang, Bilal Alsallakh, Jonathan Reynolds, Alexander Melnikov, Natalia Kliushkina, Carlos Araya, Siqi Yan, et al. 2020. Captum: A unified and generic model interpretability library for pytorch. *arXiv preprint arXiv:2009.07896*.

Piyawat Lertvittayakumjorn and Francesca Toni. 2019. Human-grounded evaluations of explanation methods for text classification. In *Proceedings of the 2019 Conference on Empirical Methods in Natural Language Processing and the 9th International Joint Conference on Natural Language Processing (EMNLP-IJCNLP)*, pages 5195–5205, Hong Kong, China. Association for Computational Linguistics.

Jiwei Li, Will Monroe, and Dan Jurafsky. 2016. Understanding neural networks through representation erasure. *CoRR*, abs/1612.08220.

Shusen Liu, Tao Li, Zhimin Li, Vivek Srikumar, Valerio Pascucci, and Peer-Timo Bremer. 2018. Visual interrogation of attention-based models for natural language inference and machine comprehension. Technical report, Lawrence Livermore National Lab.(LLNL), Livermore, CA (United States).

Scott M Lundberg and Su-In Lee. 2017. A unified approach to interpreting model predictions. In *Advances in Neural Information Processing Systems*, volume 30. Curran Associates, Inc.

Andreas Madsen, Siva Reddy, and Sarath Chandar. 2022. Post-hoc interpretability for neural nlp: A survey. *ACM Comput. Surv.* Just Accepted.

Lorenzo Malandri, Fabio Mercorio, Mario Mezzanzanica, Navid Nobani, and Andrea Seveso. 2022. Contrastive explanations of text classifiers as a service. In *Proceedings of the 2022 Conference of the North American Chapter of the Association for Computational Linguistics: Human Language Technologies: System Demonstrations*, pages 46–53.

Binny Mathew, Punyajoy Saha, Seid Muhie Yimam, Chris Biemann, Pawan Goyal, and Animesh Mukherjee. 2021. Hatexplain: A benchmark dataset for explainable hate speech detection. *Proceedings of the AAAI Conference on Artificial Intelligence*, 35(17):14867–14875.

Eliana Pastor and Elena Baralis. 2019. Explaining black box models by means of local rules. In *Proceedings of the 34th ACM/SIGAPP Symposium on Applied Computing*, SAC '19, page 510–517, New York, NY, USA. Association for Computing Machinery.

Eliana Pastor, Luca de Alfaro, and Elena Baralis. 2021a. Looking for trouble: Analyzing classifier behavior via pattern divergence. In *Proceedings of the 2021 International Conference on Management of Data*, SIGMOD '21, page 1400–1412, New York, NY, USA. Association for Computing Machinery.

Eliana Pastor, Andrew Gavgavian, Elena Baralis, and Luca de Alfaro. 2021b. How divergent is your data? *Proc. VLDB Endow.*, 14(12):2835–2838.

Colin Raffel, Noam Shazeer, Adam Roberts, Katherine Lee, Sharan Narang, Michael Matena, Yanqi Zhou, Wei Li, Peter J Liu, et al. 2020. Exploring the limits of transfer learning with a unified text-to-text transformer. *J. Mach. Learn. Res.*, 21(140):1–67.

Marco Túlio Ribeiro, Sameer Singh, and Carlos Guestrin. 2016. "Why Should I Trust You?": Explaining the Predictions of Any Classifier. In *Proceedings of the 22nd ACM SIGKDD International Conference on Knowledge Discovery and Data Mining, San Francisco, CA, USA, August 13-17, 2016*, pages 1135–1144. ACM.

Marko Robnik-Šikonja and Marko Bohanec. 2018. Perturbation-based explanations of prediction models. In *Human and machine learning*, pages 159–175. Springer.

Alexis Ross, Ana Marasović, and Matthew Peters. 2021. Explaining NLP models via minimal contrastive editing (MiCE). In *Findings of the Association for Computational Linguistics: ACL-IJCNLP 2021*, pages 3840–3852, Online. Association for Computational Linguistics.

Soumya Sanyal and Xiang Ren. 2021. Discretized integrated gradients for explaining language models. In *Proceedings of the 2021 Conference on Empirical Methods in Natural Language Processing*, pages 10285–10299, Online and Punta Cana, Dominican Republic. Association for Computational Linguistics.

Gabriele Sarti, Nils Feldhus, Ludwig Sickert, and Oskar van der Wal. 2023. Inseq: An interpretability toolkit for sequence generation models. *ArXiv*, abs/2302.13942.

Karen Simonyan, Andrea Vedaldi, and Andrew Zisserman. 2014a. Deep inside convolutional networks: Visualising image classification models and saliency maps. In *2nd International Conference on Learning Representations, ICLR 2014, Banff, AB, Canada, April 14-16, 2014, Workshop Track Proceedings*.

Karen Simonyan, Andrea Vedaldi, and Andrew Zisserman. 2014b. Deep inside convolutional networks: Visualising image classification models and saliency maps. In *2nd International Conference on Learning Representations, ICLR 2014*.

Richard Socher, Alex Perelygin, Jean Wu, Jason Chuang, Christopher D Manning, Andrew Y Ng, and Christopher Potts. 2013. Recursive deep models for semantic compositionality over a sentiment treebank. In *Proceedings of the 2013 conference on empirical methods in natural language processing*, pages 1631–1642.

Hendrik Strobelt, Sebastian Gehrmann, Michael Behrisch, Adam Perer, Hanspeter Pfister, and Alexander M Rush. 2018. S eq 2s eq-v is: A visual debugging tool for sequence-to-sequence models. *IEEE transactions on visualization and computer graphics*, 25(1):353–363.

Mukund Sundararajan, Ankur Taly, and Qiqi Yan. 2017. Axiomatic attribution for deep networks. In *Proceedings of the 34th International Conference on Machine Learning - Volume 70*, ICML'17, page 3319–3328. JMLR.org.

Ian Tenney, James Wexler, Jasmijn Bastings, Tolga Bolukbasi, Andy Coenen, Sebastian Gehrmann, Ellen Jiang, Mahima Pushkarna, Carey Radebaugh, Emily Reif, and Ann Yuan. 2020. The language interpretability tool: Extensible, interactive visualizations and analysis for NLP models. In *Proceedings of the 2020 Conference on Empirical Methods in Natural Language Processing: System Demonstrations*, pages 107–118, Online. Association for Computational Linguistics.

Jesse Vig. 2019. Visualizing attention in transformer-based language representation models. *arXiv preprint arXiv:1904.02679*.

Eric Wallace, Shi Feng, Nikhil Kandpal, Matt Gardner, and Sameer Singh. 2019a. Universal adversarial triggers for attacking and analyzing NLP. In *Proceedings of the 2019 Conference on Empirical Methods in Natural Language Processing and the 9th International Joint Conference on Natural Language Processing (EMNLP-IJCNLP)*, pages 2153–2162, Hong Kong, China. Association for Computational Linguistics.

Eric Wallace, Jens Tuyls, Junlin Wang, Sanjay Subramanian, Matt Gardner, and Sameer Singh. 2019b. AllenNLP interpret: A framework for explaining predictions of NLP models. In *Proceedings of the 2019 Conference on Empirical Methods in Natural Language Processing and the 9th International Joint Conference on Natural Language Processing (EMNLP-IJCNLP): System Demonstrations*, pages 7–12, Hong Kong, China. Association for Computational Linguistics.

Xiao Wang, Qin Liu, Tao Gui, Qi Zhang, Yicheng Zou, Xin Zhou, Jiacheng Ye, Yongxin Zhang, Rui Zheng, Zexiong Pang, Qinzhuo Wu, Zhengyan Li, Chong Zhang, Ruotian Ma, Zichu Fei, Ruijian Cai, Jun Zhao, Xingwu Hu, Zhiheng Yan, Yiding Tan, Yuan Hu, Qiyuan Bian, Zhihua Liu, Shan Qin, Bolin Zhu, Xiaoyu Xing, Jinlan Fu, Yue Zhang, Minlong Peng, Xiaoqing Zheng, Yaqian Zhou, Zhongyu Wei, Xipeng Qiu, and Xuanjing Huang. 2021. TextFlint: Unified multilingual robustness evaluation toolkit for natural language processing. In *Proceedings of the 59th Annual Meeting of the Association for Computational Linguistics and the 11th International Joint Conference on Natural Language Processing: System Demonstrations*, pages 347–355, Online. Association for Computational Linguistics.

Sarah Wiegreffe and Ana Marasovic. 2021. Teach me to explain: A review of datasets for explainable natural language processing. In *Thirty-fifth Conference on Neural Information Processing Systems Datasets and Benchmarks Track (Round 1)*.

Thomas Wolf, Lysandre Debut, Victor Sanh, Julien Chaumond, Clement Delangue, Anthony Moi, Pierric Cistac, Tim Rault, Remi Louf, Morgan Funtowicz, Joe Davison, Sam Shleifer, Patrick von Platen, Clara Ma, Yacine Jernite, Julien Plu, Canwen Xu, Teven Le Scao, Sylvain Gugger, Mariama Drame, Quentin Lhoest, and Alexander Rush. 2020. Transformers: State-of-the-art natural language processing. In *Proceedings of the 2020 Conference on Empirical Methods in Natural Language Processing: System Demonstrations*, pages 38–45, Online. Association for Computational Linguistics.

Fan Yin, Zhouxing Shi, Cho-Jui Hsieh, and Kai-Wei Chang. 2022. On the sensitivity and stability of model interpretations in NLP. In *Proceedings of the 60th Annual Meeting of the Association for Computational Linguistics (Volume 1: Long Papers)*, pages 2631–2647, Dublin, Ireland. Association for Computational Linguistics.

Omar Zaidan and Jason Eisner. 2008. Modeling annotators: A generative approach to learning from annotator rationales. In *Proceedings of the 2008 conference on Empirical methods in natural language processing*, pages 31–40.

A Technical Details

A.1 Explainer API

Our implementation is built on top of original implementations (as for SHAP and LIME) and open-source libraries (as Captum (Kokhlikyan et al., 2020) for gradient-based explainers) to directly explain Transformer-based language models.

Currently, we integrate Gradient (G) (Simonyan et al., 2014b), Integrated Gradient (IG) (Sundararajan et al., 2017), SHAP (Lundberg and Lee, 2017), and LIME (Ribeiro et al., 2016). For G and IG, users can get explanations from plain gradients or multiply gradients by the input token embeddings. For SHAP, we use the Partition approximation to estimate Shapley values.[8]

A.1.1 Evaluation API

While human gold annotations are normally discrete, current explainers provide continuous token attribution scores. Following previous work, we hence go from continuous scores to a discrete set of *relevant* tokens (i.e., r_j in Section 2.3) as follows.

We consider only tokens with a positive contribution to the chosen label (i.e., they *push* the prediction towards the chosen label). For the AOPC comprehensiveness and sufficiency measures, the relevant tokens in the discrete rationale are the most $k\%$ important tokens with k ranging from 10% to 100% (step of 10%). For token-level IOU and F1 scores plausibility measure, we follow the DeYoung et al. (2020) and Mathew et al. (2021) approach, and we select the top k tokens where k is the average length of human rationales for the dataset.

The evaluation measures at the dataset level are the average scores across explanations. Differently than DeYoung et al. (2020) that use the F1 IOU score, we directly compute the average token-level IOU.

All human rationales are at the token level, indicating the most relevant tokens to a given class label.

A.2 Technical Features

ferret implements several functionalities to facilitate end users in using it.

- High-level interface. Most of *ferret*'s features, such as interpretability methods and evalua-

[8]https://shap.readthedocs.io/en/latest/generated/shap.explainers.Partition.html

Figure 3: Faithfulness and Plausibility metrics averaged across ten samples with the "hateful" label of HateXPlain. Darker colors mean better performance.

tion measures, are accessible via a single entry point, the `Benchmark` class.

- GPU-enabled batched inference. *ferret* requires running inference for certain executions. It uses batching and local GPUs transparently to the user whenever that happens.
- Visualization methods. The `Benchmark` class exposes several methods to visualize attribution scores and evaluation results in tabular format. These tables are plotted seamlessly on Jupyter Notebooks (see Figure 2 (bottom) for an example).

B Ongoing Development

ferret is under active development. We are extending the core modules as follows.

Explainers. We plan to integrate two recent interpretability methods that require training a complementary model. Sampling and Occlusion (SOC) (Jin et al., 2019) provides a hierarchical explanation to address compositional contributions. Minimal Contrastive Editing (MiCE) (Ross et al., 2021) trains a T5 (Raffel et al., 2020) model to implement contrastive edits to the input to change the model output. Finally, we are including a third gradient-based algorithm. Integrated Discretized Gradients (Sanyal and Ren, 2021) improve IG sampling intermediate steps close to actual words in the embedding space.

Evaluators. We plan to include additional evaluation measures such as sensitivity, stability (Yin et al., 2022), and Area Under the Threshold-Performance curve (AUC-TP) (Atanasova et al., 2020).

C Additional Results

Figure 3 shows a screenshot of dataset-level assessment from our demo web app. It reports the evaluation metrics averaged across ten samples with the "hate speech" label for the HateXplain dataset, discussed in Section 3.

The user specifies a model from the Hugging Face Hub (*HF Model* field), the target class (*Target*), and the set of samples of interest (*List of samples*). *ferret* web app directly computes explanation and their evaluation and visualizes the results.

Learn With Martian: A Tool For Creating Assignments That Can Write And Re-Write Themselves

Shriyash Upadhyay
Martian
yash@withmartian.com

Etan Ginsberg
Martian
etan@withmartian.com

Chris Callison-Burch
University of Pennsylvania
ccb@upenn.edu

Abstract

In this paper, we propose Learn, a unified, easy-to-use tool to apply question generation and selection in classrooms. The tool lets instructors and TAs create assignments that can write and re-write themselves. Given existing course materials, for example a reference textbook, Learn can generate questions, select the highest quality questions, show the questions to students, adapt question difficulty to student knowledge, and generate new questions based on how effectively old questions help students learn. The modular, composable nature of the tools for handling each sub-task allow instructors to use only the parts of the tool necessary to the course, allowing for integration in a large number of courses with varied teaching styles. We also report on the adoption of the tool in classes at the University of Pennsylvania with over 1000 students. Learn is publicly released at https://learn.withmartian.com.

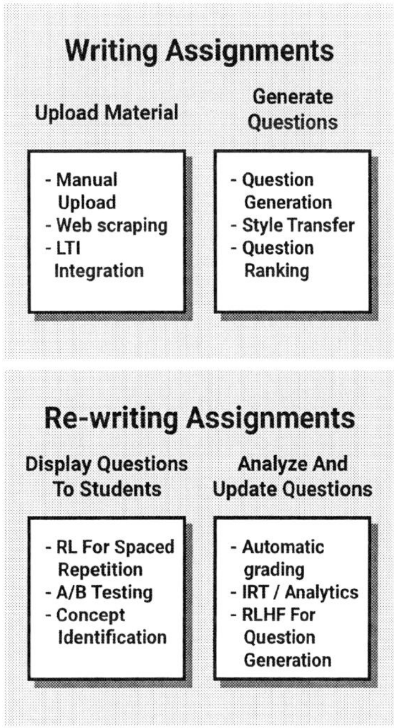

Figure 1: A diagram of steps, sub-steps, and features in Learn. Learn is a tool for creating assignments that write and re-write themselves. To write new assignments, users upload material and the platform generates questions. To re-write assignments and improve them, the questions are first shown to students, then the data from student interactions is analyzed to update the questions.

1 Introduction

Advances in natural language processing, particularly through large langauge models, will enable the creation of powerful applications in many fields (Bommasani et al., 2021). One of the most positive and most promising may be education, where rapid improvement has been achieved in fields like question generation (Dugan et al., 2022; Drori et al., 2022; Zhang et al., 2022).

In this paper, we propose Learn, a unified, easy-to-use tool to apply question generation in classrooms. The tool allows instructors to create assignments that can write and re-write themselves. Instructors provide existing course materials, and the platform is able to generate new questions, select the best questions, show those questions to students, provide analytics, and improve as it collects more data on student performance. We also report on a case study of the successful adoption of Learn in classes at the University of Pennsylvania.

We hope this tool can be used by course staff to save time and improve education, and that Learn can serve as an example of a high-quality social-good tool which inspires the development of further applications.

2 Tool Tour and Design

We begin with a brief tour. Generating questions is done simply by uploading the materials from which the questions should be generated.

Proceedings of the 17th Conference of the European Chapter of the Association for Computational Linguistics System Demonstrations, pages 267–276
May 2-4, 2023 ©2023 Association for Computational Linguistics

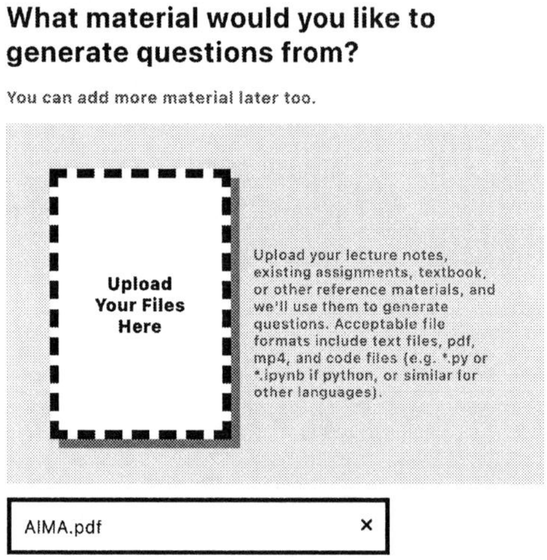

Figure 2: The interface for uploading material to Learn.

Uploaded materials can be text, code, pdf, or audio/video. In the case of PDF, they are converted to text through OCR. In the case of audio/video, they are converted to text through ASR.

Once the materials are uploaded and text is extracted, they are used to generate questions. The generated questions are then shown to the course staff.

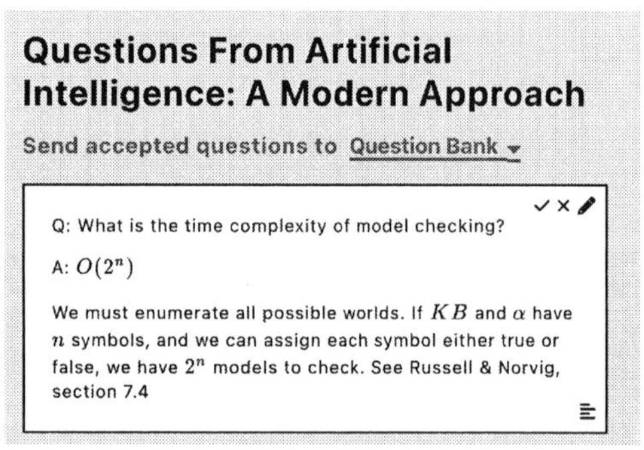

Figure 3: The interface which allows course staff to review questions. Users can accept, reject, or edit questions by clicking on the check, cross, and pencil buttons respectively.

Members of the course staff can accept, reject, or edit any question. Accepting a question adds it either to the general question bank for the course or to a particular assignment.

After questions are added to an assignment, the assignment can be released to students, who can then complete the assignment.

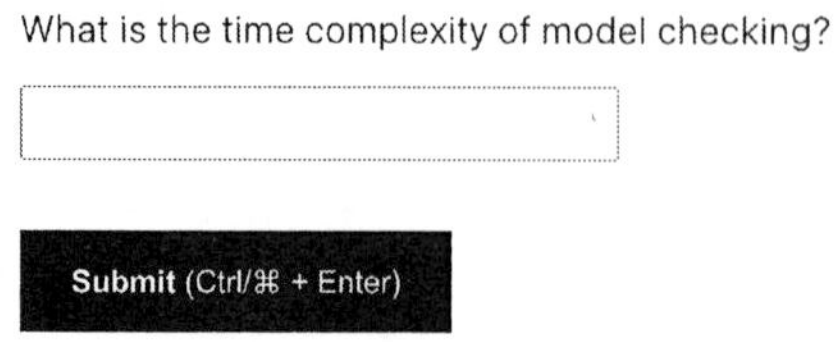

Figure 4: The interface through which a student completes assignments by answering questions.

When the student is completing the assignment, their answers are stored, alongside relevant metadata such as the amount of time to complete the question and whether the student got the question correct. Students can also mark questions as being "really good" for studying, or as "not helpful".

The data collected in this way is then analyzed, both to inform instructors and to improve future question generation. That data is used to provide suggestions to course staff.

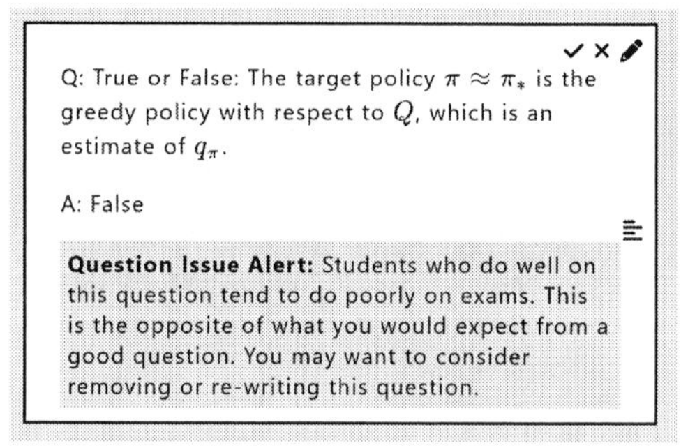

Figure 5: The interface alerting instructors about issues and potential improvement to existing questions.

Note 1: Uploading Material. Users have multiple means of uploading material to Learn. Although they can upload all their content manually, that is typically not necessary. Instead, if they have an existing course website, they can point a scraper built into the Learn tool at that website, and it will find the relevant material (e.g. the course textbook, lecture notes, youtube links, etc.) and only upload the material which cannot be found on their course website. We also have an LTI integration, allowing us to pull data from existing learning management systems (like Canvas and Moodle), as well as pushing data (like generated questions or student grades) to those systems. These alternative methods of uploading material decrease effort required to adopt the platform, making it something which can be used in minutes.

Note 2: Rich Question Formats. In most tools for creating assignments, questions are purely text. This is not the case for Learn. Instead, all questions are javascript functions of the type

```
() => ({question: HTML, answer: HTML})
```

If a user wants to create a question which acts like text, we provide an interface which lets them create such questions without writing any code, just as they would in a traditional assignment-creation software. However, we also give users access to a coding environment which they can use to create questions. This lets them – or our question generation models – generate questions in rich formats. That includes questions with images, Latex, or interactive components like coding challenges, animations, or full-fledged games (see figure 8).

Note 3: Composability. Courses can use the various parts of the tool independently. For example, if a course largely uses written assignments and does not want to switch to online assignments, the tool can be used purely for question generation by sending all questions to the question bank and then copying them into the physical exams. A course which has existing questions can bring them onto the platform, display them to students, then get analytics and have them re-written to be more effective. Courses with an LTI or which use other tools like gradescope can display all questions through those platforms, link them to Learn, and get analytics using their existing data. This allows many different kinds of courses to use the tool, and also for gradual adoption of those parts of the tool which are most useful to any given course.

Complete Flow An instructor uploads the material for their course, either manually, by pointing our scraper to their course website, or through an LTI integration. We then generate richly-formatted questions which can include interactive components through code. Those questions are placed into assignments which can be completed by students. Once students complete the assignments, the results are used to re-write the assignments and improve future question generation.

3 How Natural Language Processing Is Being Used To Augment Education

Although the most visible application of NLP in Learn is that questions are generated automatically, many aspects of writing and re-writing assignments are enhanced by NLP research. In this section, we detail the features of the platform enabled by NLP.

3.1 Question Generation

LLMs For Question Generation

Our platform uses multiple large langauge models, including GPT-3 (Brown et al., 2020), Codex (Chen et al., 2021), and a fine-tuned T5 (Raffel et al., 2019) variant to generate questions from material uploaded by course staff. Recent work has shown the ability of these models to generate questions for STEM subjects such as mathematics (Drori et al., 2022) and computer science (Zhang et al., 2022) at a college level. Our prior work (Dugan et al., 2022) showed that question quality can be greatly enhanced by summarizing input before using it to generate questions. Using that insight, we first extractively summarize the content using BERT (Devlin et al., 2018), before passing the summarized inputs to the larger models.

Prompting For Question Style Transfer

When generating questions for a course, there is a kind of cold-start problem. Courses use a wide variety of different questions, from multiple-choice to short-answer to long-form and proof-based. Courses may even prefer more fine-grained distinctions than those. How do we know what kind of question to generate, and how do we get our model to generate questions of that type?

Few-shot prompting, as in (Brown et al., 2020), allows us to solve this problem. In the materials which professors upload, there will often be examples of questions from assignments used in their class. We can then either generate question and then re-write them using an arbitrary style transfer method like that in (Reif et al.), or prepend a course's existing questions to our question generation prompt. This allows us to generate questions in a wide variety of styles, matching a wide variety of courses. As a demonstration, we can generate questions at all levels of Bloom's taxonomy (Bloom, 1956). Examples of questions at the different levels can be seen in appendix A (see table 1).

Over-generation & Ranking

Despite the successes of large language models, many of the questions which these models generate are still not acceptable according to human annotators. Our prior work established that even high-performing completely-automated methods only generate acceptable questions 50% of the time (Dugan et al., 2022). To mitigate this problem, we over-generate and rank questions using BERT. So, if a course needs 20 questions for an assignment, we might generate 200 questions and surface the top 20.

Course staff make the final decision about what questions should be shown to students. In particular, course staff are shown the generated questions, and either accept, reject, or edit questions. This has two advantages. First, it ensure that all questions which students see are of high quality. Second, it provides data to train a ranking model. Accepted questions are better than rejected questions, and edited questions are better after editing than before. As a result, our ranking model (and the quality of questions shown to users) improves over time.

3.2 Showing Questions To Students

Spaced Repetition & Reinforcement Learning

Not all orders of presenting material to students are equally effective. It is clear, for example, that showing a student material on calculus before they understand arithmetic is much less effective than the other way around.

A particularly effective method of ordering material to present it to students is spaced repetition (Tabibian et al., 2019). The core idea is that, instead of showing a piece of material to a student only once or cramming many reviews all at once, they should review that material multiple times at intervals to avoid forgetting it. This technique has been shown to improve student outcomes in subjects as varied as mathematics (Smith and Rothkopf, 1984; Mayfield and Chase, 2002; Patac and Patac JR, 2013), language learning (Cepeda et al., 2009), and medicine (Kerfoot and Brotschi, 2009; Kerfoot, 2009). (Donovan and Radosevich, 1999) find an overall mean weighted effect size of d=0.46 when evaluating the effectiveness of spaced repetition across 63 studies.

Learn implements spaced repetition to determine what questions should be shown to students. This improves student understanding without any additional effort for course instructors.

As noted in (Rafferty et al., 2016), the question of what material should be shown to students can be formulated as a Partially-Observable Markov Decision Process (POMDP). That means we can construct a schedule via reinforcement learning, as in (Reddy et al., 2017), to determine what material should be shown to a student in order to maximize their understanding of the material. This has the potential to significantly out-perform more traditional spaced-repetition algorithms.

A/B Testing Assignments

In addition to allowing the platform to select the questions shown to the students, we can test collections of questions by A/B testing assignments. This ability is also provided to instructors, who can assign different versions of an assignment to different students. This allows instructors to collect information about their assignments and get additional analytics (see section 3.3).

Automatically Identifying Course Concepts

A common criticism of spaced repetition is that it primarily aids in "rote memorization": if a student reviews the same question repeatedly, they may only remember the content of the question, as opposed to remembering the underlying concept.

A solution to this problem is to repeat a concept with multiple different questions, rather than a single question. For example, if asking questions about breadth-first search, the first repetition might ask about the running time, the second repetition about the implementation of the algorithm, the third repetition about a specific application, etc.

Learn implements both supervised and unsupervised methods to identify concepts. First, we use BERT to identify questions which are explicitly asking the same thing in different ways. Then, we cluster embedded vectors of the questions to identify groups of questions with high semantic similarity. By showing students questions selected from these groups, we can avoid the problem of memorization while still benefiting from spaced repetition.

3.3 Analytics & Improving Questions

Item Response Theory

Item response theory (IRT) is a statistical framework for analyzing the effectiveness of tests and of individual questions within those tests. An introduction to the theory can be found in (Partchev,

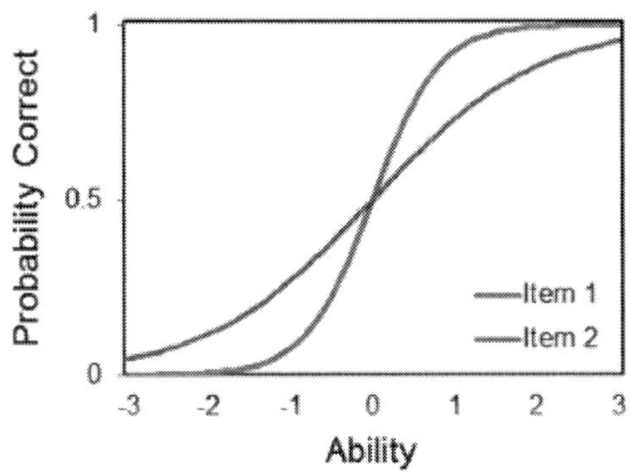

Figure 6: Examples of two IRT curves from Columbia Public Health. The x-axis represents a student's ability, as measured by standard deviations from average performance in the overall course. They y-axis represents the probability that a student gets the question correct. Both curves here are 3 parameter logistic regression models. Item 1 is a better question than item 2 because its IRT curve is steeper, are therefore distinguishes ability better. Both questions are of equal difficulty, as they are centered around the same point (ability=0).

2004).

At a basic level, we want questions to tell us what students know. A question is a good indicator of a student's knowledge if students who get that question correct tend to do well in the course overall. So, we can measure the quality of a question by seeing how strongly it correlates with overall performance on assignments (see figure 6).

By computing this correlation, we can inform course staff of particularly good or bad questions (see figure 5), and refine assignments over time.

Automating The Creation of Autograders

Some questions are easy to grade, and the act of creating them results in an auto-grader (e.g. multiple choice questions, or questions that are solved by invoking an algorithm such as linear algebra problems). Many questions are harder to grade, and in many classes a majority of TA time is spent grading such questions.

To reduce the burden on TAs, Learn can automatically construct auto-graders for questions using data collected when students complete the questions. There are multiple methods which Learn uses to do this. The first is that students or TAs can mark the questions as correct or incorrect, then the platform looks for exact strings matches in the future and is able to tell that those are certainly correct. We can also use a BERT model to classify the correctness of a new answer given previous answers. These can both be done in an automated manner, automatically reducing the grading burden for course staff. We also cluster the errors which students make, allowing TAs to grade the work of many students at once.

RLHF For Question Generation

The annotations we collect from TAs (accepting, rejecting, or editing questions) provides us with data about human feedback for question generation (see section 3.1). Following the methodology from (Ziegler et al., 2019), we can then use this data to improve our question generation models through the following process:

1. Starting with a supervised policy, in this case, our existing question generation model.
2. Training a reward model from the human feedback on question generation.
3. Optimizing a policy against the reward model using Proximal Policy Optimization (PPO). (Schulman et al., 2017)

This allows us to improve our question generation models over time as we collect additional usage data.

In the future, we will explore the use of other data we collect (for example, IRT metrics) as additional supervision signals; if analytics can improve questions that TAs have written, then they also express preferences which should be encoded in the reward model, potentially allowing for more rapid improvement.

4 Case Study

Learn has been integrated in multiple courses at the University of Pennsylvania, and over 1000 students have used the platform. The different classes used the tool in different ways, verifying its composability. In many of those classes, for example, Learn was a supplementary tool, whereas the Introduction to Artificial Intelligence class used it as a quizzing platform for reading quizzes. In the latter class, we were able to collect significant data on the efficacy of the platform, which we report here.

4.1 Methodology

We conducted a control trial in the Introduction to Artificial Intelligence course at the University of Pennsylvania. The course is divided into two sections of approximately 300 students each. We randomly assigned one section to use traditional reading quizzes (which had been used in the class during prior years), while the other section used the Learn platform. On both platforms, the quizzes were administered on a weekly basis. For the first three weeks of the class, all students used the traditional quizzes, then the section using Martian switched to using the new platform. The quizzes covered the required readings for that week (from the textbooks *Artificial Intelligence: A Modern Approach* and *Speech and Language Processing*). The students using Learn were also shown material from prior weeks due to the integration of spaced repetition (see section 3.2). Material on Learn was created through a combination of automatic generation and TA-written questions.

There is one notable confounder in the experiment, which is that one section of the class was entirely online, while the other had the option of both online and in-person classes. After random assignment, the online-only section used traditional reading quizzes, while the mixed section used Learn. However, from exams scores in previous semesters, we do not expect a difference in exam scores between the online and mixed sections.

We collected two evaluation metrics to determine the effectiveness of the platform. First, we collected the students' exam scores, which we could compare across sections. Second, as a more subjective metric, we asked the students who used both traditional reading quizzes and Learn which platform they preferred.

4.2 Results

The exam scores for students using Learn were higher than those using traditional reading quizzes. The students in the section that used Learn had exam scores which were 0.29σ higher on average. Among students who used Learn, every 15 minutes of additional studying led to a 0.08σ improvement in exam scores.

Similarly, Learn outperformed traditional reading quizzes according to the subjective evaluations of the students. 83% of students preferred Learn to traditional reading quizzes (see figure 7). 11% of students preferred traditional reading quizzes. 6% had no preference. We also received comments from students regarding the platform, overwhelmingly positive, some of which can be found in Appendix A.

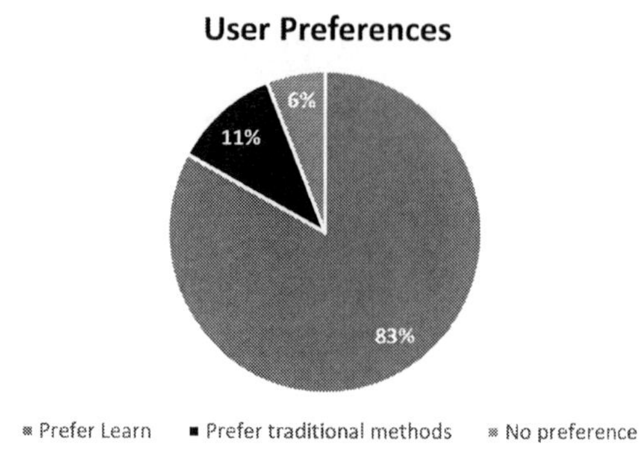

Figure 7: At the end of the semester, students were asked which section they preferred. A large majority of students preferred Learn to traditional methods.

5 Conclusion

Learn is a unified, easy-to-use tool to apply question generation in classrooms. The tool is able to create assignments which write and re-write themselves. It achieves this through a number of features enabled by recent advances in NLP. Having been tested in multiple classes with over 1000 students, it has been demonstrated to improve test scores and is prefered by students to traditional alternatives.

Limitations

While the platform is well-featured, we hope to be able to evaluate those features more thoroughly in the future. The limitations to evaluating the system so far stem from limits in how much the system has been used.

This is a direct limit in the case of testing certain features, like RLHF for question generation (see section 3.3), which require more data than we have currently collected. It is an indirect limit in the kinds of classes which the tool has been tested in. At the time of authorship, all the classes in which the tool has been tested are computer science classes. Although we see no reason why the tool should not generalize to other courses (we have tested the quesion generation outside of computer science), that should be verified through further expermentation.

Ethics Statement

If our platform works as intended and sees broader use in higher-ed, course staff and students can benefit.

For course staff, it can reduce the time taken in writing and grading assignments. It should also help to alleviate concerns around cheating, as new questions can be generated each semester, potentially even creating new questions for each individual student. By reducing this logistical burden, Learn will allow course staff to focus on the parts of teaching which are higher-leverage, and to improve their courses in ways that weren't before possible.

For students, the introduction of Learn into a classroom is an opportunity to use more effective methods for studying (such as spaced repetition), to see higher-quality study material, and to have many more questions with which to study. The ability to automatically generate questions provides an opportunity for students to get much more practice – an arbitrarily large quantities of practice question could be created, tailored to the topics in which any particular student is struggling. As the system improves over time we hope that students will have study materials of higher quality than they would without automated tools.

There are also large disparities in computer science, especially for certain underrepresented groups. These groups face structural issues which may lead to differences in achievement. For example, students in underrepresented groups may feel uncomfortable asking questions of or reaching out to course staff, and therefore may receive less attention and aid from instructors. We can help tackle those disparities by improving accessibility through more effective learning systems.

It is also important to note, however, the potential risks to privacy when building and using education applications. Given the sensitive nature of the data, such as grades, it is important to take proper privacy and security safeguards when deploying such systems. In order to minimize such risks, we went through thorough evaluation by the privacy office for the Computer and Information Science Department at the University of Pennsylvania. We also filled out the HECVAT lite security questionnaire, receiving an A rating.

As education is downstream of many important societal factors, such as economic growth and public welfare, we are optimistic about the positive impacts of new AI applications for education, like Learn.

Acknowledgements

This work would not be possible without Dr. Eleni Miltsakaki, Liam Dugan, Hannah Gonzalez, and Zhiqi "Tracy" Cui who helped do the fundamental question generation research underlying this work. We'd also like to express our thanks to Dylan Fields and the privacy team at the University of Pennsylvania for reviewing our application, and to Dr. Zachary Ives and Dr. Boon Thau Loo for their support in adopting Learn.

This research is based upon work supported in part by the the NSF (Award 1928631). Approved for Public Release, Distribution Unlimited. The views and conclusions contained herein are those of the authors and should not be interpreted as necessarily representing the official policies, either expressed or implied, of the NSF or the U.S. Government.

References

Benjamin Samuel Bloom. 1956. Taxonomy of educational objectives: The classification of educational goals. *Cognitive domain*.

Rishi Bommasani, Drew A Hudson, Ehsan Adeli, Russ Altman, Simran Arora, Sydney von Arx, Michael S Bernstein, Jeannette Bohg, Antoine Bosselut, Emma Brunskill, et al. 2021. On the opportunities and risks of foundation models. *arXiv preprint arXiv:2108.07258*.

Tom B. Brown, Benjamin Mann, Nick Ryder, Melanie Subbiah, Jared Kaplan, Prafulla Dhariwal, Arvind Neelakantan, Pranav Shyam, Girish Sastry, Amanda Askell, Sandhini Agarwal, Ariel Herbert-Voss, Gretchen Krueger, T. J. Henighan, Rewon Child, Aditya Ramesh, Daniel M. Ziegler, Jeff Wu, Clemens Winter, Christopher Hesse, Mark Chen, Eric Sigler, Mateusz Litwin, Scott Gray, Benjamin Chess, Jack Clark, Christopher Berner, Sam McCandlish, Alec Radford, Ilya Sutskever, and Dario Amodei. 2020. Language models are few-shot learners. *ArXiv*, abs/2005.14165.

Nicholas J Cepeda, Noriko Coburn, Doug Rohrer, John T Wixted, Michael C Mozer, and Harold Pashler. 2009. Optimizing distributed practice: theoretical analysis and practical implications. *Experimental psychology*, 56(4):236.

Mark Chen, Jerry Tworek, Heewoo Jun, Qiming Yuan, Henrique Ponde, Jared Kaplan, Harrison Edwards, Yura Burda, Nicholas Joseph, Greg Brockman, Alex Ray, Raul Puri, Gretchen Krueger, Michael Petrov, Heidy Khlaaf, Girish Sastry, Pamela Mishkin, Brooke Chan, Scott Gray, Nick Ryder, Mikhail

Pavlov, Alethea Power, Lukasz Kaiser, Mohammad Bavarian, Clemens Winter, Philippe Tillet, Felipe Petroski Such, David W. Cummings, Matthias Plappert, Fotios Chantzis, Elizabeth Barnes, Ariel Herbert-Voss, William H. Guss, Alex Nichol, Igor Babuschkin, S. Arun Balaji, Shantanu Jain, Andrew Carr, Jan Leike, Joshua Achiam, Vedant Misra, Evan Morikawa, Alec Radford, Matthew M. Knight, Miles Brundage, Mira Murati, Katie Mayer, Peter Welinder, Bob McGrew, Dario Amodei, Sam McCandlish, Ilya Sutskever, and Wojciech Zaremba. 2021. Evaluating large language models trained on code. *ArXiv*, abs/2107.03374.

Jacob Devlin, Ming-Wei Chang, Kenton Lee, and Kristina Toutanova. 2018. Bert: Pre-training of deep bidirectional transformers for language understanding.

John J Donovan and David J Radosevich. 1999. A meta-analytic review of the distribution of practice effect: Now you see it, now you don't. *Journal of Applied Psychology*, 84(5):795.

Iddo Drori, Sarah Zhang, Reece Shuttleworth, Leonard Tang, Albert Lu, Elizabeth Ke, Kevin Liu, Linda Chen, Sunny Tran, Newman Cheng, Roman Wang, Nikhil Singh, Taylor L. Patti, Jayson Lynch, Avi Shporer, Nakul Verma, Eugene Wu, and Gilbert Strang. 2022. A neural network solves, explains, and generates university math problems by program synthesis and few-shot learning at human level. *Proceedings of the National Academy of Sciences*, 119(32):e2123433119.

Liam Dugan, Eleni Miltsakaki, Shriyash Upadhyay, Etan Ginsberg, Hannah Gonzalez, DaHyeon Choi, Chuning Yuan, and Chris Callison-Burch. 2022. A feasibility study of answer-agnostic question generation for education. In *Findings of the Association for Computational Linguistics: ACL 2022*, pages 1919–1926, Dublin, Ireland. Association for Computational Linguistics.

B Price Kerfoot. 2009. Learning benefits of on-line spaced education persist for 2 years. *The Journal of urology*, 181(6):2671–2673.

B Price Kerfoot and Erica Brotschi. 2009. Online spaced education to teach urology to medical students: a multi-institutional randomized trial. *The American Journal of Surgery*, 197(1):89–95.

Kristin H Mayfield and Philip N Chase. 2002. The effects of cumulative practice on mathematics problem solving. *Journal of applied behavior analysis*, 35(2):105–123.

Ivailo Partchev. 2004. A visual guide to item response theory. *Retrieved November*, 9:2004.

Louida P Patac and Adriano V Patac JR. 2013. The analysis of two teaching programs: Massed and distributed. *IAMURE International Journal of Mathematics, Engineering & Technology*, 6:59.

Colin Raffel, Noam Shazeer, Adam Roberts, Katherine Lee, Sharan Narang, Michael Matena, Yanqi Zhou, Wei Li, and Peter J. Liu. 2019. Exploring the limits of transfer learning with a unified text-to-text transformer.

Anna N Rafferty, Emma Brunskill, Thomas L Griffiths, and Patrick Shafto. 2016. Faster teaching via pomdp planning. *Cognitive science*, 40(6):1290–1332.

Siddharth Reddy, Sergey Levine, and Anca Dragan. 2017. Accelerating human learning with deep reinforcement learning. In *NIPS'17 Workshop: Teaching Machines, Robots, and Humans*, pages 5–9.

Emily Reif, Daphne Ippolito, Ann Yuan, Andy Coenen, Chris Callison-Burch, and Jason Wei. A recipe for arbitrary text style transfer with large language models. In *Proceedings of the 60th Annual Meeting of the Association for Computational Linguistics (ACL 2022)*, Dublin, Ireland.

John Schulman, Filip Wolski, Prafulla Dhariwal, Alec Radford, and Oleg Klimov. 2017. Proximal policy optimization algorithms. *arXiv preprint arXiv:1707.06347*.

Steven M Smith and Ernst Z Rothkopf. 1984. Contextual enrichment and distribution of practice in the classroom. *Cognition and Instruction*, 1(3):341–358.

Behzad Tabibian, Utkarsh Upadhyay, Abir De, Ali Zarezade, Bernhard Schölkopf, and Manuel Gomez-Rodriguez. 2019. Enhancing human learning via spaced repetition optimization. *Proceedings of the National Academy of Sciences*, 116(10):3988–3993.

Sarah Zhang, Reece Shuttleworth, Derek Austin, Yann Hicke, Leonard Tang, Sathwik Karnik, Darnell Granberry, and Iddo Drori. 2022. A dataset and benchmark for automatically answering and generating machine learning final exams.

Daniel M Ziegler, Nisan Stiennon, Jeffrey Wu, Tom B Brown, Alec Radford, Dario Amodei, Paul Christiano, and Geoffrey Irving. 2019. Fine-tuning language models from human preferences. *arXiv preprint arXiv:1909.08593*.

A Select Comments From Students

1. "Thank you for making this! I really wasn't sure how much it would help me since I have established study techniques I've used throughout hs/college and didn't want to change. But this has actually been so immensely helpful and I now really believe in the proven science behind how tools like this can really help retain information."

2. "This is a great tool - amazing job overall!"

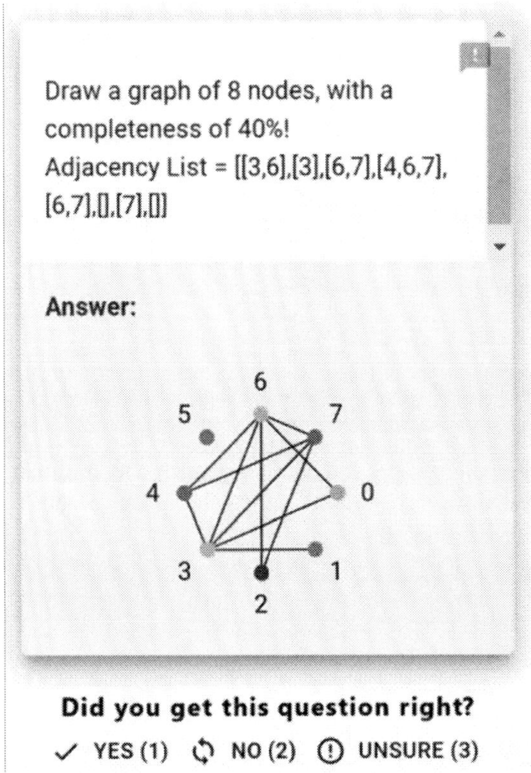

Figure 8: A question created using code which can randomly generate an graph from an adjacency list, and display an image of the generated graph.

3. "It was very helpful (the repetitive review of materials). The variety of some cards asking the same material helped a lot too."
4. "I thought [Learn] was [a] very helpful way to learn the material!"
5. "Thank you guys! This was really helpful!"

B Example Questions

Level	Question	Answer
Remember	What is the policy improvement theorem?	The policy improvement theorem is a theorem that says if we have two deterministic policies π and π' such that, for all $s \in \mathcal{S}$, $q_\pi(s, \pi'(s)) \geq v_\pi(s)$, then the policy π' must be as good as, or better than, π. That is, it must obtain greater or equal expected return from all states $s \in \mathcal{S}$: $v_{\pi'}(s) \geq v_\pi(s)$.
Understand	Why is policy evaluation guaranteed to converge?	Because the value function is a fixed point of the Bellman equation.
Apply	What is $v_\pi(15)$ for the equiprobable random policy in this case?	-1
Analyze	What is the difference between Synchronous DP and Asynchronous DP?	Synchronous DP updates state values in a deterministic order, e.g. from small to large. Asynchronous DP updates state values in a stochastic order.
Evaluate	What are the limitations of Dynamic Programming?	The limitations of Dynamic Programming are that it requires a perfect model of the environment and that it is computationally expensive.
Create	Draw a graph of 8 nodes, with a completeness of 40%! Adjacency List = [[3, 6], [3], [6, 7], [4, 6, 7], [6, 7], [], [7]]	Varies by response

Table 1: A collection of questions generated using Learn at each level of Bloom's taxonomy (Bloom, 1956). Bloom's taxonomy establishes a series of levels of that represent different cognitive goals. The cognitive goals become more difficult, going from remembering to creating.

EVALIGN: Visual Evaluation of Translation Alignment Models

Tariq Yousef † **Gerhard Heyer** † **Stefan Jänicke**‡

†Leipzig University ‡University of Southern Denmark

<tariq.yousef@uni-leipzig.de>

Abstract

This paper presents EVALIGN, a visual analytics framework for quantitative and qualitative evaluation of automatic translation alignment models. EVALIGN offers various visualization views enabling developers to visualize their models' predictions and compare the performance of their models with other baseline and state-of-the-art models. Through different search and filter functions, researchers and practitioners can also inspect the frequent alignment errors and their positions. EVALIGN hosts nine gold standard datasets and the predictions of multiple alignment models. The tool is extendable, and adding additional datasets and models is straightforward. EVALIGN can be deployed and used locally and is available on GitHub[1].

1 Introduction

Translation Alignment is the process of finding and linking translation equivalents between a text and its translations. It can be performed on different granularity levels. Word-level Translation Alignment plays a key role in several NLP and Digital Humanities tasks such as statistical machine translation (Brown et al., 1993; Koehn et al., 2003), cross-lingual transfer (Hinrichs et al., 2022; Jacqmin et al., 2021), classical language learning (Palladino et al., 2021; Palladino, 2020), dynamic dictionaries induction (Shi et al., 2021), Word Sense Disambiguation (Luan et al., 2020)and analyzing neural machine translation systems (Alkhouli et al., 2016).

The work on automatic translation alignment started 30 years ago when Brown et al. (1993) introduced the first statistical alignment models called IBM models. Later, several tools and models such as Giza++ (Och and Ney, 2003) and fast_align (Dyer et al., 2013) were developed based on Brown's models with different improvements and optimization additions. With the recent advances in neural machine translation systems and the emergence of pre-trained multilingual transformer models (Devlin et al., 2018; Conneau et al., 2019), it has been possible to develop neural alignment models that significantly outperform the statistical models without needing extensive training datasets.

Performance evaluation of alignment models is essential, and many ground truth datasets have been developed for this purpose. Precision, Recall, F1, and Alignment Error Rate (AER) are used as indicators of the alignment quality. Although they are widely used, quantitative metrics have their limitations (Ayan and Dorr, 2006; Vilar et al., 2006; Lambert et al., 2005). Thus, additional qualitative evaluation is required for a better understanding of the models behaviors.

For this purpose, we introduce EVALIGN, a tool for quantitative and qualitative evaluation of automatic alignment models that allows developers to estimate the quality of alignment models and get insights into their performance. With multiple visualization approaches and tailored views, the proposed framework helps researchers and developers working on automatic translation alignment models inspect their predictions with different gold standard data sets and compare their performance to other baseline and state-of-the-art models quantitatively and qualitatively. Further, it supports non-experts who want to employ alignment models in their research or business to explore different alignment models and their performance on texts in different languages to choose the suitable model for their purpose. EVALIGN is available online[2] and the online demo hosts nine benchmark datasets and five alignment methods combined with four different embeddings models (20 models in total); EVALIGN can be deployed locally, and users can add new datasets and import new models.

[1] https://github.com/TariqYousef/EVALign

[2] http://evalign.info/

Proceedings of the 17th Conference of the European Chapter of the Association for Computational Linguistics System Demonstrations, pages 277–297
May 2-4, 2023

2 Related Works

Employing visualization for exploring benchmark data sets, analyzing models' behaviour, and conducting qualitative evaluation is common practice in NLP. The Language Interpretability Tool *LIT* (Tenney et al., 2020) offers several interactive visualization techniques for a broad range of NLP tasks. *DeepCompare* (Murugesan et al., 2019) supports visual and interactive performance comparison of deep learning models. *SummVis* (Vig et al., 2021) and *Summary Explorer* (Syed et al., 2021) support qualitative evaluation for the summarization task. Paper with Code[3] platform allows to track state-of-the-art performance on benchmark datasets for different NLP tasks. *Vis-Eval* (Steele and Specia, 2018), *ASIYA* (Gonzàlez et al., 2012) and *MT-ComparEval* (Klejch et al., 2015) allow for systematic comparison and evaluation of various machine translation models.

Visualizing word-level alignments was the aim of many tools such as *Ugarit* (Yousef et al., 2022b) and *WA-Continuum* (Steele and Specia, 2015), which visualizes word alignment of automatically aligned sentences to facilitate their evaluation. ImaniGooghari et al. (2021) introduced the *Parallel Corpus Explorer* which supports exploring a word-aligned parallel corpus.

To our best knowledge, EVALIGN is the first system that allows researchers and practitioners to qualitatively evaluate the performance of alignment models on multiple gold standard datasets.

3 Automatic Alignment Models

Automatic translation alignment models can be categorized into three main categories: **Statistical models** such as Giza++, fast_align (Dyer et al., 2013), and eflomal (Östling and Tiedemann, 2016). They have been widely used and achieved state-of-the-art performance until recently and are currently used as a baseline. However, the performance of the statistical models is governed by the availability of training corpora in the form of parallel sentences. **Neural Models** utilize neural machine translation models or multilingual transformer models to capture word-level translation alignment. Different workflows are available. For instance, extracting alignment using embeddings-based semantic similarity by employing pre-trained and fine-tuned multilingual contextualized embeddings such as SIMALIGN (Jalili Sabet et al., 2020), AWEASOME (Dou and Neubig, 2021), XLM-ALIGN (Chi et al., 2021), and MirrorAlign(Wu et al., 2022). **Hybrid Models** combine statistical and neural models aiming for better performance, for instance, by using the output of statistical models as supervision to train neural models (Alkhouli et al., 2018).

[3] https://paperswithcode.com/

4 Evaluation

4.1 Alignment Gold Standards

Gold standards are the main components for evaluating the performance of NLP models. Developing alignment gold standards involves multiple domain experts (at least 2) to avoid any bias in the manual annotation process. Annotators must follow predefined guidelines to reduce disagreements and ensure consistency and quality of the manual alignments. Moreover, Inter-Annotator Agreement (IAA) can be computed to validate the reliability and quality of the alignment guidelines and gold standard. The gold standard dataset is a list of manually aligned sentences, each sentence has a list of translation pairs, and each translation pair is assigned one of two categories, SURE (S) or POSSIBLE (P).

Table 1 shows that most literature papers evaluated their models mainly on three alignment datasets, German-English, English-French (Och and Ney, 2003), and Romanian-English (Mihalcea and Pedersen, 2003). However, several datasets are available in various languages (Table 2), but they have not yet been used for performance evaluation. For this reason, EVALIGN hosts some of the "unused" datasets, and we generated the alignments of different alignment models for these datasets and made them available for users for further experiments.

4.2 Evaluation Metrics

In addition to the classical quantitative evaluation metrics Precision, Recall, and F1; researchers utilize the Alignment Error Rate (AER) (Och and Ney, 2003). These metrics are based on the overlap between the model's predictions A with the SURE (S), and POSSIBLE (P) alignment sets of the gold standards (Equation 1). Lambert et al. (2005) studied the influence of the amount of SURE and POSSIBLE alignments in the gold standard on AER and concluded that AER would be smaller when the S/P ratio is low, and vice versa. Figure 4 confirms this conclusion.

$$AER = 1 - \frac{|A \cap P| + |A \cap S|}{|A| + |S|} \quad (1)$$

4.3 Limitations

Evaluating the performance of translation alignment models is a complex task, even for humans. In many cases, it is challenging to tell if an alignment between two tokens/phrases is entirely correct because that relies on several factors, mainly the text genre, context, translation quality, and human annotator's knowledge.

AER is highly affected by the gold standard dataset, i.e., the selection of sure and possible translation pairs and their proportions of the whole dataset. And the gold standard alignments are subject to the alignment guidelines and annotators' agreement, which is also influenced by the characteristics of the selected corpus, the annotators' knowledge, and the target application. That means it might be possible to have correct alignments predicted by the models, but the gold standards do not consider them. Thus, AER will treat them as incorrect alignments. We encountered such cases repeatedly while inspecting the existing gold standard datasets.

AER is intolerant; it considers all tokens equally important and there is no distinction between function words and context words. In the example illustrated in Figures 5A and 5C, AER penalizes a missing alignment of the full-stop the same as missing alignment of $Madrid$.

Further, AER fails to capture phrase misalignments. In Figure 5B, the German word $auch$ must be aligned to the English phrase $aswell$, producing two sure alignments $auch - as$ and $auch - well$. Nevertheless, If an alignment model aligns only a part of the phrase, $auch - well$, this will be considered a correct alignment, while it is not because there is no constraint saying that the model must produce the two sure alignments together in order to count them as correct alignments. Also, AER does not consider null-alignments, i.e. tokens with no translation equivalents in the parallel sentence. Thus, quantitative evaluation gives an overview of models' performance, but it is limited and must be accompanied by qualitative evaluation.

All these reasons motivated us to develop EVALIGN. The framework allows users to explore quantitative evaluation metrics and also provides the ability to conduct an extensive qualitative evaluation using different interactive visualization views and filtering options. Additionally, we proposed two metrics to overcome the limitations above. The ALIGNMENT COVERAGE represents the portion of the aligned tokens out of all tokens in the dataset. It can computed for the gold standard dataset and for models' predictions. We compute *Coverage* as follows:

$$Coverage = 1 - \frac{|S_n| + |T_n|}{|S| + |T|} \quad (2)$$

Where S and T are the sets of all tokens in the source and target sentences, respectively, S_n and T_n are the sets of null-alignments in the source sentences and target sentences.

The PHRASE ALIGNMENT ACCURACY (PAC) measures the model's ability to align phrases. Phrase alignment appears when a token in one sentence is aligned to multiple tokens in the corresponding translation (one-to-many or many-to-one), or when multiple tokens in one sentence are aligned to multiple tokens in the corresponding sentence (many-to-many). Our definition of phrase does not constrain that the tokens must be consecutive. However, the phrase is correctly aligned if all its tokens are aligned with each other. For instance, the English phrase $public\ health\ policy$ and the German equivalent $Gesundheitspolitik$ are aligned correct if, and only if the model predicts $public - Gesundheitspolitik$, $health - Gesundheitspolitik$ and $policy - Gesundheitspolitik$ pairs. Because all tokens contribute to the meaning of the phrases, and missing any token changes the meaning or make it incomplete. We compute *PAC* as stated in Equation 3:

$$PAC = \frac{|P_m \cap P_{gs}|}{|P_{gs}|} \quad (3)$$

Where P_{gs} is the aligned phrases set of the gold standard, and P_m is the set of predicted aligned phrases by the model. Figure 14 compares the performance of the best five alignment models on the German-English dataset, the models use the fine-tuned mBERT embeddings.

5 Implementation Details

We surveyed the automatic alignment papers published after 2019 (Table 1). Most researchers evaluate their models performance on at least three benchmark datasets, mainly German-English, French-English, and Romanian-English. We used these three datasets in addition to six other datasets (English-French, English-Spanish, English-Portuguese, Spanish-French, Portuguese-Spanish, and Portuguese-French) that have not been used before for evaluation.

Regarding the alignment models, we selected embeddings-based $Softmax$, $Entmax$ (Dou and Neubig, 2021), $Argmax$, $Itermax$, and $Match$ (Jalili Sabet et al., 2020) with different contextualized embeddings, namely, mBERT, XLM-R, fine-tuned mBERT[4], and XLM-Align[5] (Chi et al., 2021). In addition to Giza++, fast_align, and EfLoMAl for the datasets DE-EN, EN-FR, and RO-EN. Our selection was subject to the implementation availability and reproducibility. We used the default implementations provided by authors in their GitHub repositories with the default parameters. The backend API is implemented using Django and Postgres database, while the visualization views are created with React JS and D3.js.

5.1 User Interface

Figure 1 illustrates EVALIGN usage workflow; users start navigating through the tool by selecting a dataset from the landing page, which lists all hosted benchmark datasets or selecting a model from the models page, which lists all hosted models or selecting a model or dataset from the aggregated overview. EVALIGN offers five main views:

Single Dataset vs Multiple Models (V1). This view provides a performance overview of the alignment models hosted on EVALIGN over the selected dataset using a *bar chart.* The overview allows users to select among different quantitative evaluation metrics, namely, Precision, Recall, F1, AER, Coverage, PAC, and the number of translation pairs. The view also visualizes all sentences of the selected dataset using a grid view allowing users to inspect the possible and sure alignments and assess their correctness and coverage (Figure 7A) . From this view, users can select a single model to inspect its performance on a specific dataset.

Single Model vs Multiple Datasets (V2). This view provides a summarized performance overview of the selected alignment model over different benchmark datasets using a *bar chart* that allows switching among different evaluation metrics. Selecting a dataset will forward the user to *Single Models vs Single Dataset* view.

Single Model vs Single Dataset (V3). This view offers various corpus-level and sentence level visualization views providing the user with all needed functions to inspect the the dataset sentences and explore the alignments predicted by the selected model. This view aggregate wrong alignments, missing alignments and correct alignments to facilitate the analysis of the model performance. Further it shows the relation of the different evaluation metrics with sentence lengths. The predicted alignments are visualized with *Grid*, *Side-by-side*, and *Table* views. Moreover, it offers various sorting, filtering and searching options to support qualitative evaluation (Figures 7B and 7C).

Two Models vs Single Dataset (V4). In this view, users can compare two models at sentence-level using the *Grid* and *Table* view which show the agreement and disagreement between the two models (figure 7D and 16).

All Models vs all Datasets (V5). In this aggregated view, all hosted datasets and models are presented in a table. Users can switch between different quantitative metrics with different sorting options (figure 13).

5.2 Visual Design

EVALIGN offers a variety of corpus and sentence level visualization views in addition to several searching and filtering functions. When designing EVALIGN, we consulted the text alignment visualization survey (Yousef and Jänicke, 2020) and adapted Schneiderman's Information Seeking Mantra (Shneiderman, 2003) "Overview first, zoom and filter, then details-on-demand" to facilitate interactive navigation through the benchmark datasets and alignment models.

5.2.1 Corpus-level Views

Corpus-level views provide comprehensive overviews of the compared models by visualizing aggregated statistics and evaluation metrics at the dataset level. A *bar chart* on the dataset page will be shown in the upper left corner, allowing users to compare available alignment models. A button bar is located above the bar chart, allowing users to switch between the evaluation metric. Each model is assigned a unique color (Figure 6A). A *bar chart* on the dataset page is placed in the upper

[4]https://github.com/neulab/awesome-align

[5]https://huggingface.co/microsoft/xlm-align-base

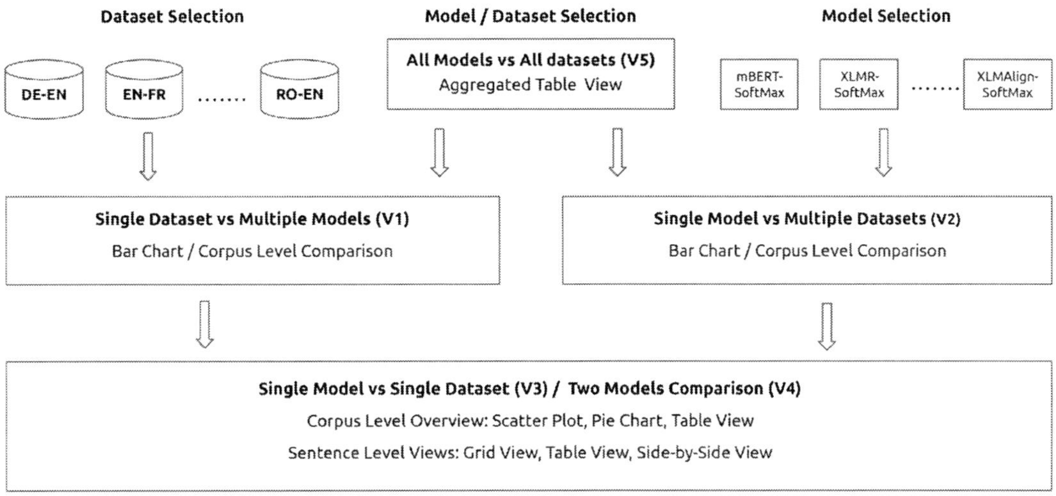

Figure 1: Overview of EVALIGN

left corner, allowing users to compare available alignment models. A button bar is located above the bar chart, allowing users to switch between seven evaluation metrics: AER, Precision, Recall, F1, Number of Translation Pairs, Coverage, and PAC. Each model is assigned a unique color (Figure 6A) and hovering a bar will show a tooltip with the corresponding information.

Selecting a model with a mouse click on the corresponding bar will load a *pie chart* that shows a comparison between the model predictions and the gold standard. We distinguish among three sets (Figure 3): i) *correct alignments*, where the model predictions match the gold standard, shown in green. ii) *wrong alignments*, where the model failed to align the translation pairs correctly, shown in red. iii) *missing alignments*, the pairs the model was supposed to align, shown in orange. Clicking on any of the three sets will load the corresponding translation pairs in the neighbouring table, which aggregates the translation pairs and shows them with their frequency. Moreover, the translation pairs are clickable, and the corresponding gold standard sentences with sentence-level views will be displayed when clicked.

Further, users can switch between the *pie chart* and the *scatter plot*, which displays the relation between the sentence length (x-axis) and the selected evaluation metric (y-axis) of the selected alignment model; each sentence is presented as one dot (Figure 6B). The *scatter plot* helps users detect outliers and interesting observations, such as the relation between the AER and the sentence length. Moreover, a range selector allows filtering of the dataset by selecting multiple sentences to be visualized at the sentence level for more detailed inspection. Further, the evaluation metrics will be calculated for the selected sentences and displayed under the scatter plot. This allows users to eliminate subsets (for example, short or long sentences) and see how these subsets affect the quantitative evaluation metrics. The selected sentences will be displayed as paginated list of sentence-level views. The tool provides sorting options according to the selected metric.

5.2.2 Sentence-level Views

The sentence-level views aim to show the alignment among words of the source and target sentences. The framework provides two sentence-level views, namely, *grid view* and *side-by-side view*. The views are accompanied with a *bar chart* showing the sentence-level evaluation metrics of the hosted models and enabling users to select a model to visualize its output for the corresponding sentence. The *grid view* places the two sentences as a grid. The source sentence tokens are placed vertically, and the target tokens are placed horizontally. The gold standard Sure and Possible alignments will be displayed in the corresponding cells as big and small dots, respectively. The *grid view* is suitable for visualizing the alignments of a single model by coloring the corresponding cells with the model's unique color. It is also appropriate to visualize the alignments of two models and their agreement (Figure 2).

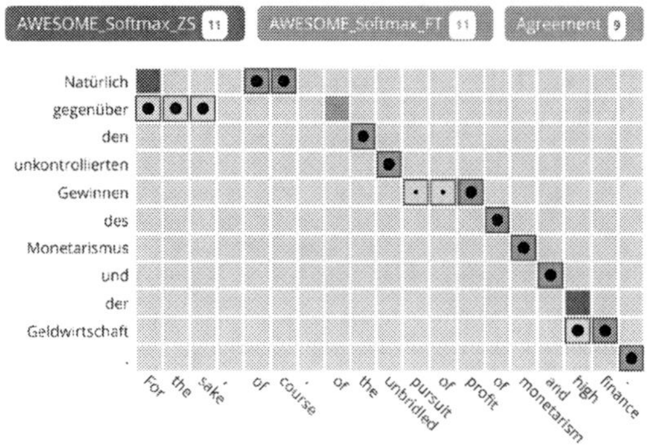

Figure 2: A Grid View to visualize the alignment at sentence level.

The *side-by-side view* places the two sentences alongside each other; it utilizes the mouse hover to highlight the hovered token and the aligned tokens in the parallel sentence. The current implementation of this view allows visualizing the alignment of a single model, and users can switch between models via a neighboring *bar chart.*

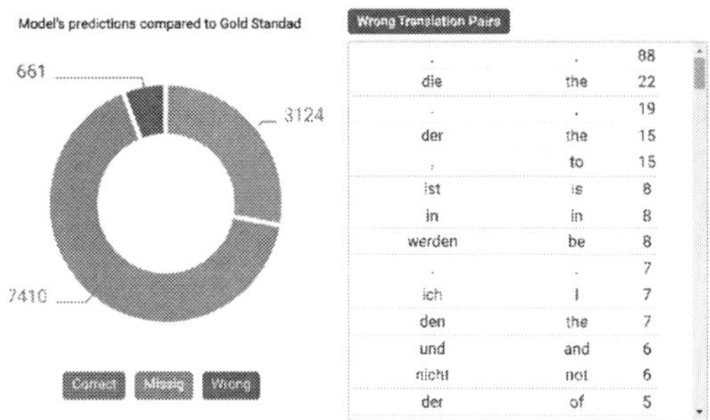

Figure 3: A Pie Chart shows the overlap between the model's predictions and the gold standard in three categories. The neighboring table shows the translation pairs with their frequency of a selected category.

6 Usage Scenarios

The framework offers a variety of usage scenarios that can be summarized as follows:

Gold standard quality control. Visualizing the gold standard datasets using the *Grid View* allowed us to inspect their accuracy and assess their quality. The analysis of the English-French (EN-FR) dataset showed that the dataset contains several single or two token sentences, for which the alignment will always be correct (figure 9C-D). Moreover, some sentences occur more than once in the dataset, and that would affect the evaluation process since they increase recall and precision and consequently reduce AER (figure 9B,C,E). The inspection showed that there are several sentences with plenty of *Possible* alignments and few or no *Sure* alignments (figure 9A,F).

Comparing datasets' characteristics. Users can see all hosted datasets on the datasets page with different statistics on the number of sentences, tokens, sure and possible alignments and their percentages. For instance, the English-French (EN-FR) dataset has significantly more possible alignments than sure alignments (figure 15). This explains why all alignment models have the lowest AER on this dataset compared to all other datasets. The same applies to the Romanian-English (RO-EN) dataset since it only has sure alignments, which explains why the AER is always higher than the other datasets.

Comparing model performance with different configurations. As an example, we compare the performance of $Softmax$ with two different embeddings models,namely, mBERT and a fine-tuned mBERT, to estimate the improvement achieved with the fine-tuning process. In addition to comparing all quantitative metrics, the framework allows filtering sentences where model *A* outperforms model *B*. Figure 2 shows that the fine-tuning enhanced the overall alignment accuracy and allowed to predict two more correct *Sure* alignments and eliminate two incorrect ones.

Comparing quantitative metrics. The framework provides different options to compare the models performance using different quantitative metrics at corpus and sentence levels using bar chart and table views. The aggregated results in the table view (V5) reveals that the fine-tuned mBert achieved the best results in all datasets regarding AER. While $Itermax$ achieved the best Recall on all datasets, $Argmax$ with fine-tuned mBert embeddings achieved best precision on 7 datasets and second best precision on 2 datasets. Further, $Itermax$ with the fine-tuned mBERT embeddings achieved the best Phrase Alignment Accuracy on all datasets. The $Match$ algorithm generates more translation pairs than all other algorithms, and $Entmax$ with XLM-RoBERTa embeddings generates always less translation pairs that all other algorithms.

Analyzing alignment errors. From the pie chart provided for the *Single Dataset – Single Model* view (figure 3), we can click on the red arc that represents the wrong alignment pairs to list all incorrect pairs produced by the model. Our analysis of $Itermax$ with the fine-tuned mBert model on the German-English (DE-EN) dataset revealed the following:

- The most frequent wrong pairs involve a punctuation mark in one or both languages. However, such issues can be avoided by adding constraints that prevent aligning punctuation to a word (Figure 18).

- Long sentences with repeated tokens are more likely to produce incorrect alignments despite that the pairs are correct translations, but their positions in the two sentences do not correspond (Figure 19).

- The majority of wrong pairs are function words, such as articles, pronouns, prepositions, and conjunctions, and most of them are semantically correct translations such as ($nicht$ - not) (Figure 12C).

- The German-English (DE-EN) dataset contains incorrect alignments. For instance, in sentence *10*, the model generated the correct pair *präzise - precise*. However, it is classified as wrong because the gold standard aligns *präzise* with $very$ and $sind$ with $precise$, which is incorrect. Moreover, some sentences are not entirely aligned, and many tokens are left. For example, in sentence *40* (Figure 8), there are many *correct* translation pairs predicted by the model such as $Soziale - social$ and $Sicherheit - security$, but they are not included in the gold standard. However, these errors are not model-specific but apply to different alignment models and datasets (Figure 11).

7 Conclusion

Evaluating translation alignment models is a non-trivial task. Qualitative evaluation is needed because quantitative evaluation metrics do not reflect the real quality of the alignment models due to many factors. For this purpose, we presented the framework EVALIGN that supports quantitative and qualitative evaluation of automatic alignment systems. EVALIGN hosts several evaluation datasets and various alignment models. It offers different visualization views and filtering functions to help users to investigate alignment datasets and models and conduct various quality analyses. Moreover, we presented different usage scenarios that showcase the use and effectiveness of the tool.

Our analyses revealed that gold standard datasets, especially the German-English (DE-EN) and French-English (FR-EN), which have been used almost in all related works on automatic alignment, contain plenty of errors and need to be revised and corrected by linguists and domain experts. In future work, we aim to incorporate morphological features such as POS, lemma and named entities to assess model performances and classify alignment errors.

Finally, we will keep the tool updated by adding new datasets and/or models, and we encourage researchers to send us the output of their new models to publish them on EVALIGN. A short video demonstrating the tool is available on youtube `https://youtu.be/hfii6x0bktw`

Limitations

Some literature papers do not share the source code or their models' output. Therefore, we could not host their models on EVALIGN. Also, not all datasets mentioned in the literature are accessible.

Regarding the visualization views, the current tool implementation allows for comparing two alignment models simultaneously at the sentence level. Also, the sentence-level side-by-side visualize only one model's alignments. The view does not allow comparing two or more models. The grid view is not suitable for long sentences.

Ethics Statement

The datasets hosted on EVALIGN are downloaded from their authors' websites. The datasets are well-known and have been used for evaluation in most literature papers. Model predictions are generated using the code published on developers' Github repositories. We have not retrained or fine-tuned any language models and used the publicly available language models on Huggingface. The tool offers visualization views to facilitate the performance evaluation to get a better understanding of models' behaviours.

References

Tamer Alkhouli, Gabriel Bretschner, and Hermann Ney. 2018. On the alignment problem in multi-head attention-based neural machine translation. In *Proceedings of the Third Conference on Machine Translation: Research Papers*, pages 177–185, Brussels, Belgium. Association for Computational Linguistics.

Tamer Alkhouli, Gabriel Bretschner, Jan-Thorsten Peter, Mohammed Hethnawi, Andreas Guta, and Hermann

Ney. 2016. Alignment-based neural machine translation. In *Proceedings of the First Conference on Machine Translation: Volume 1, Research Papers*, pages 54–65.

Necip Fazil Ayan and Bonnie Dorr. 2006. Going beyond aer: An extensive analysis of word alignments and their impact on mt. In *Proceedings of the 21st International Conference on Computational Linguistics and 44th Annual Meeting of the Association for Computational Linguistics*, pages 9–16.

Peter F. Brown, Stephen A. Della Pietra, Vincent J. Della Pietra, and Robert L. Mercer. 1993. The mathematics of statistical machine translation: Parameter estimation. *Computational Linguistics*, 19(2):263–311.

Chi Chen, Maosong Sun, and Yang Liu. 2021. Mask-align: Self-supervised neural word alignment. In *Proceedings of the 59th Annual Meeting of the Association for Computational Linguistics and the 11th International Joint Conference on Natural Language Processing (Volume 1: Long Papers)*, pages 4781–4791, Online. Association for Computational Linguistics.

Yun Chen, Yang Liu, Guanhua Chen, Xin Jiang, and Qun Liu. 2020. Accurate word alignment induction from neural machine translation. In *Proceedings of the 2020 Conference on Empirical Methods in Natural Language Processing (EMNLP)*, pages 566–576, Online. Association for Computational Linguistics.

Zewen Chi, Li Dong, Bo Zheng, Shaohan Huang, Xian-Ling Mao, He-Yan Huang, and Furu Wei. 2021. Improving pretrained cross-lingual language models via self-labeled word alignment. In *Proceedings of the 59th Annual Meeting of the Association for Computational Linguistics and the 11th International Joint Conference on Natural Language Processing (Volume 1: Long Papers)*, pages 3418–3430.

Alexis Conneau, Kartikay Khandelwal, Naman Goyal, Vishrav Chaudhary, Guillaume Wenzek, Francisco Guzmán, Edouard Grave, Myle Ott, Luke Zettlemoyer, and Veselin Stoyanov. 2019. Unsupervised cross-lingual representation learning at scale. *CoRR*, abs/1911.02116.

Jacob Devlin, Ming-Wei Chang, Kenton Lee, and Kristina Toutanova. 2018. BERT: pre-training of deep bidirectional transformers for language understanding. *CoRR*, abs/1810.04805.

Shuoyang Ding, Hainan Xu, and Philipp Koehn. 2019. Saliency-driven word alignment interpretation for neural machine translation. In *Proceedings of the Fourth Conference on Machine Translation (Volume 1: Research Papers)*, pages 1–12, Florence, Italy. Association for Computational Linguistics.

Zi-Yi Dou and Graham Neubig. 2021. Word alignment by fine-tuning embeddings on parallel corpora. In *Proceedings of the 16th Conference of the European Chapter of the Association for Computational Linguistics: Main Volume*, pages 2112–2128, Online. Association for Computational Linguistics.

Chris Dyer, Victor Chahuneau, and Noah A. Smith. 2013. A simple, fast, and effective reparameterization of IBM model 2. In *Proceedings of the 2013 Conference of the North American Chapter of the Association for Computational Linguistics: Human Language Technologies*, pages 644–648, Atlanta, Georgia. Association for Computational Linguistics.

Sarthak Garg, Stephan Peitz, Udhyakumar Nallasamy, and Matthias Paulik. 2019. Jointly learning to align and translate with transformer models. In *Proceedings of the 2019 Conference on Empirical Methods in Natural Language Processing and the 9th International Joint Conference on Natural Language Processing (EMNLP-IJCNLP)*, pages 4453–4462, Hong Kong, China. Association for Computational Linguistics.

Meritxell Gonzàlez, Jesús Giménez, and Lluís Màrquez. 2012. A graphical interface for MT evaluation and error analysis. In *Proceedings of the ACL 2012 System Demonstrations*, pages 139–144, Jeju Island, Korea. Association for Computational Linguistics.

Joao Graca, Joana Paulo Pardal, Luísa Coheur, and Diamantino Caseiro. 2008. Building a golden collection of parallel multi-language word alignment. In *Proceedings of the Sixth International Conference on Language Resources and Evaluation (LREC'08)*.

Nway Nway Han and Aye Thida. 2019. Annotated guidelines and building reference corpus for myanmar-english word alignment. *arXiv preprint arXiv:1909.11288*.

Nicolás Hinrichs, Maryam Foradi, Tariq Yousef, Elisa Hartmann, Susanne Triesch, Jan Kaßel, and Johannes Pein. 2022. Embodied metarepresentations. *Frontiers in neurorobotics*, 16.

Anh Khoa Ngo Ho and François Yvon. 2020. Generative latent neural models for automatic word alignment. *arXiv preprint arXiv:2009.13117*.

Maria Holmqvist and Lars Ahrenberg. 2011. A gold standard for English-Swedish word alignment. In *Proceedings of the 18th Nordic Conference of Computational Linguistics (NODALIDA 2011)*, pages 106–113, Riga, Latvia. Northern European Association for Language Technology (NEALT).

Ayyoob ImaniGooghari, Masoud Jalili Sabet, Philipp Dufter, Michael Cysou, and Hinrich Schütze. 2021. ParCourE: A parallel corpus explorer for a massively multilingual corpus. In *Proceedings of the 59th Annual Meeting of the Association for Computational Linguistics and the 11th International Joint Conference on Natural Language Processing: System Demonstrations*, pages 63–72, Online. Association for Computational Linguistics.

Léo Jacqmin, Gabriel Marzinotto, Justyna Gromada, Ewelina Szczekocka, Robert Kołodyński, and Géraldine Damnati. 2021. SpanAlign: Efficient sequence tagging annotation projection into translated data applied to cross-lingual opinion mining. In *Proceedings of the Seventh Workshop on Noisy User-generated Text (W-NUT 2021)*, pages 238–248, Online. Association for Computational Linguistics.

Masoud Jalili Sabet, Philipp Dufter, François Yvon, and Hinrich Schütze. 2020. SimAlign: High quality word alignments without parallel training data using static and contextualized embeddings. In *Findings of the Association for Computational Linguistics: EMNLP 2020*, pages 1627–1643, Online. Association for Computational Linguistics.

Ondrej Klejch, Eleftherios Avramidis, Aljoscha Burchardt, and Martin Popel. 2015. Mt-compareval: Graphical evaluation interface for machine translation development. *Prague Bull. Math. Linguistics*, 104:63–74.

Philipp Koehn, Franz J. Och, and Daniel Marcu. 2003. Statistical phrase-based translation. In *Proceedings of the 2003 Human Language Technology Conference of the North American Chapter of the Association for Computational Linguistics*, pages 127–133.

Ivana Kruijff-Korbayová, Klára Chvátalová, and Oana Postolache. 2006. Annotation guidelines for Czech-English word alignment. In *Proceedings of the Fifth International Conference on Language Resources and Evaluation (LREC'06)*, Genoa, Italy. European Language Resources Association (ELRA).

Patrik Lambert, Adria DE GISPERT, Rafael BANCHS, and José B MARINO. 2005. Guidelines for word alignment evaluation and manual alignment. *Language resources and evaluation*, 39(4):267–285.

Yixing Luan, Bradley Hauer, Lili Mou, and Grzegorz Kondrak. 2020. Improving word sense disambiguation with translations. In *Proceedings of the 2020 Conference on Empirical Methods in Natural Language Processing (EMNLP)*, pages 4055–4065.

Lieve Macken. 2010. An annotation scheme and gold standard for Dutch-English word alignment. In *Proceedings of the Seventh International Conference on Language Resources and Evaluation (LREC'10)*, Valletta, Malta. European Language Resources Association (ELRA).

Kelly Marchisio, Conghao Xiong, and Philipp Koehn. 2021. Embedding-enhanced giza++: Improving alignment in low-and high-resource scenarios using embedding space geometry. *arXiv preprint arXiv:2104.08721*.

Rada Mihalcea and Ted Pedersen. 2003. An evaluation exercise for word alignment. In *Proceedings of the HLT-NAACL 2003 Workshop on Building and using parallel texts: data driven machine translation and beyond*, pages 1–10.

Sugeerth Murugesan, Sana Malik, Fan Du, Eunyee Koh, and Tuan Manh Lai. 2019. Deepcompare: Visual and interactive comparison of deep learning model performance. *IEEE Computer Graphics and Applications*, 39(5):47–59.

Masaaki Nagata, Katsuki Chousa, and Masaaki Nishino. 2020. A supervised word alignment method based on cross-language span prediction using multilingual BERT. In *Proceedings of the 2020 Conference on Empirical Methods in Natural Language Processing (EMNLP)*, pages 555–565, Online. Association for Computational Linguistics.

Anh Khoa Ngo Ho and François Yvon. 2021. Optimizing word alignments with better subword tokenization. In *Proceedings of Machine Translation Summit XVIII: Research Track*, pages 256–269, Virtual. Association for Machine Translation in the Americas.

Franz Josef Och and Hermann Ney. 2000. A comparison of aligment models for statistical machine translation. In *Proceedings of the 18th International Conference on Computational Linguistics (COLING-ACL 2000)*.

Franz Josef Och and Hermann Ney. 2003. A systematic comparison of various statistical alignment models. *Computational Linguistics*, 29(1):19–51.

Robert Östling and Jörg Tiedemann. 2016. Efficient word alignment with Markov Chain Monte Carlo. *Prague Bulletin of Mathematical Linguistics*, 106:125–146.

Chiara Palladino. 2020. Reading texts in digital environments: Applications of translation alignment for classical language learning. *J. Interact. Technol. Pedagog*, 18:724–731.

Chiara Palladino, Maryam Foradi, and Tariq Yousef. 2021. Translation alignment for historical language learning: a case study. *Digital Humanities Quarterly*, 15(3).

Haoyue Shi, Luke Zettlemoyer, and Sida I. Wang. 2021. Bilingual lexicon induction via unsupervised bitext construction and word alignment. *CoRR*, abs/2101.00148.

Ben Shneiderman. 2003. The eyes have it: A task by data type taxonomy for information visualizations. In *The craft of information visualization*, pages 364–371. Elsevier.

David Steele and Lucia Specia. 2015. WA-continuum: Visualising word alignments across multiple parallel sentences simultaneously. In *Proceedings of ACL-IJCNLP 2015 System Demonstrations*, pages 121–126, Beijing, China. Association for Computational Linguistics and The Asian Federation of Natural Language Processing.

David Steele and Lucia Specia. 2018. Vis-eval metric viewer: A visualisation tool for inspecting and evaluating metric scores of machine translation output. In *Proceedings of the 2018 Conference of the North American Chapter of the Association for Computational Linguistics: Demonstrations*, pages 71–75, New Orleans, Louisiana. Association for Computational Linguistics.

Steinþór Steingrímsson, Hrafn Loftsson, and Andy Way. 2021. CombAlign: a tool for obtaining high-quality word alignments. In *Proceedings of the 23rd Nordic Conference on Computational Linguistics (NoDaLiDa)*, pages 64–73, Reykjavik, Iceland (Online). Linköping University Electronic Press, Sweden.

Elias Stengel-Eskin, Tzu-ray Su, Matt Post, and Benjamin Van Durme. 2019. A discriminative neural model for cross-lingual word alignment. In *Proceedings of the 2019 Conference on Empirical Methods in Natural Language Processing and the 9th International Joint Conference on Natural Language Processing (EMNLP-IJCNLP)*, pages 910–920, Hong Kong, China. Association for Computational Linguistics.

Shahbaz Syed, Tariq Yousef, Khalid Al Khatib, Stefan Jänicke, and Martin Potthast. 2021. Summary explorer: Visualizing the state of the art in text summarization. In *Proceedings of the 2021 Conference on Empirical Methods in Natural Language Processing: System Demonstrations*, pages 185–194, Online and Punta Cana, Dominican Republic. Association for Computational Linguistics.

Ian Tenney, James Wexler, Jasmijn Bastings, Tolga Bolukbasi, Andy Coenen, Sebastian Gehrmann, Ellen Jiang, Mahima Pushkarna, Carey Radebaugh, Emily Reif, and Ann Yuan. 2020. The language interpretability tool: Extensible, interactive visualizations and analysis for NLP models. In *Proceedings of the 2020 Conference on Empirical Methods in Natural Language Processing: System Demonstrations*, pages 107–118, Online. Association for Computational Linguistics.

Jesse Vig, Wojciech Kryscinski, Karan Goel, and Nazneen Rajani. 2021. SummVis: Interactive visual analysis of models, data, and evaluation for text summarization. In *Proceedings of the 59th Annual Meeting of the Association for Computational Linguistics and the 11th International Joint Conference on Natural Language Processing: System Demonstrations*, pages 150–158, Online. Association for Computational Linguistics.

David Vilar, Maja Popovic, and Hermann Ney. 2006. AER: do we need to "improve" our alignments? In *Proceedings of the Third International Workshop on Spoken Language Translation: Papers*, Kyoto, Japan.

Di Wu, Liang Ding, Shuo Yang, and Mingyang Li. 2022. MirrorAlign: A super lightweight unsupervised word alignment model via cross-lingual contrastive learning. In *Proceedings of the 19th International Conference on Spoken Language Translation (IWSLT 2022)*, pages 83–91, Dublin, Ireland (in-person and online). Association for Computational Linguistics.

Minhan Xu and Yu Hong. 2020. Improving word alignment with contextualized embedding and bilingual dictionary. In *CCF Conference on Big Data*, pages 180–194. Springer.

Tariq Yousef and Stefan Jänicke. 2020. A survey of text alignment visualization. *IEEE transactions on visualization and computer graphics*, 27(2):1149–1159.

Tariq Yousef, Chiara Palladino, Farnoosh Shamsian, Anise d'Orange Ferreira, and Michel Ferreira dos Reis. 2022a. An automatic model and gold standard for translation alignment of ancient greek. In *Proceedings of the Language Resources and Evaluation Conference*, pages 5894–5905, Marseille, France. European Language Resources Association.

Tariq Yousef, Chiara Palladino, Farnoosh Shamsian, and Maryam Foradi. 2022b. Translation alignment with ugarit. *Information*, 13(2).

Tariq Yousef, Chiara Palladino, David J. Wright, and Monica Berti. 2022c. Automatic translation alignment for ancient greek and latin. In *Proceedings of the Second Workshop on Language Technologies for Historical and Ancient Languages*, pages 101–107, Marseille, France. European Language Resources Association.

Thomas Zenkel, Joern Wuebker, and John DeNero. 2020. End-to-end neural word alignment outperforms GIZA++. In *Proceedings of the 58th Annual Meeting of the Association for Computational Linguistics*, pages 1605–1617, Online. Association for Computational Linguistics.

Vilém Zouhar and Daria Pylypenko. 2021. Leveraging neural machine translation for word alignment. *arXiv preprint arXiv:2103.17250*.

A Appendix

Paper	EN-CZ	EN-DE	EN-FR	EN-HI	EN-RO	EN-JA	EN-ZH	EN-IC	EN-VI	EN-FA	EN-AR
(Stengel-Eskin et al., 2019)							x				x
(Garg et al., 2019)		x	x		x						
(Ding et al., 2019)		x	x		x						
(Jalili Sabet et al., 2020)	x	x	x	x	x					x	
(Zenkel et al., 2020)		x	x		x						
(Chen et al., 2020)		x	x		x		x				
(Ho and Yvon, 2020)			x		x						
(Xu and Hong, 2020)			x	x	x						
(Nagata et al., 2020)		x	x		x	x	x				
(Dou and Neubig, 2021)		x	x		x	x	x				
(Zouhar and Pylypenko, 2021)	x	x									
(Steingrímsson et al., 2021)	x	x	x					x			
(Marchisio et al., 2021)		x	x		x						
(Ngo Ho and Yvon, 2021)	x	x	x		x	x			x		
(Chen et al., 2021)		x	x		x		x				
(Chi et al., 2021)		x	x	x	x						
(Wu et al., 2022)		x	x		x						

Table 1: An overview of gold standard datasets that have been used for performance evaluation in the literature papers.

Source	Language Pair	# Sentences	IAA	Text Type
(Och and Ney, 2000)	English-German	508		Verbmobil
(Mihalcea and Pedersen, 2003)	Romanian-English	248		
	English-French	447		Hansard
(Lambert et al., 2005)	English-Spanish	500		Europarl
(Kruijff-Korbayová et al., 2006)	Czech-English	2400	93%	Penn Treebank corpus (WSJ)
(Graca et al., 2008)	English-Portuguese	100	89.5 %	Europarl
	English-Spanish	100	86.7 %	Europarl
	English-French	100	90.8 %	Europarl
	Portuguese-Spanish	100	93.2 %	Europarl
	Portuguese-French	100	93.5 %	Europarl
	Spanish-French	100	96.5 %	Europarl
(Macken, 2010)	Dutch-English	1500	84-94 %	Journalistic texts, Newsletters, and Medical Reports
(Holmqvist and Ahrenberg, 2011)	English–Swedish	1164	91.3%	Europarl
(Steingrímsson et al., 2021)	Icelandic-English	604		ParIce Corpus[6] Project[7]
(Yousef et al., 2022a)	Ancient Greek-English	275	86.17%	Perseus Digital Library
	Ancient Greek-Portuguese	183	83.31%	Perseus Digital Library
(Yousef et al., 2022c)	Ancient Greek-Latin	100	90.50%	DFHG Project[8]
(Han and Thida, 2019)	Myanmar-English	500	91.56%	Myanmar- English ALT parallel corpus

Table 2: An overview of the existing alignment gold standard datasets.

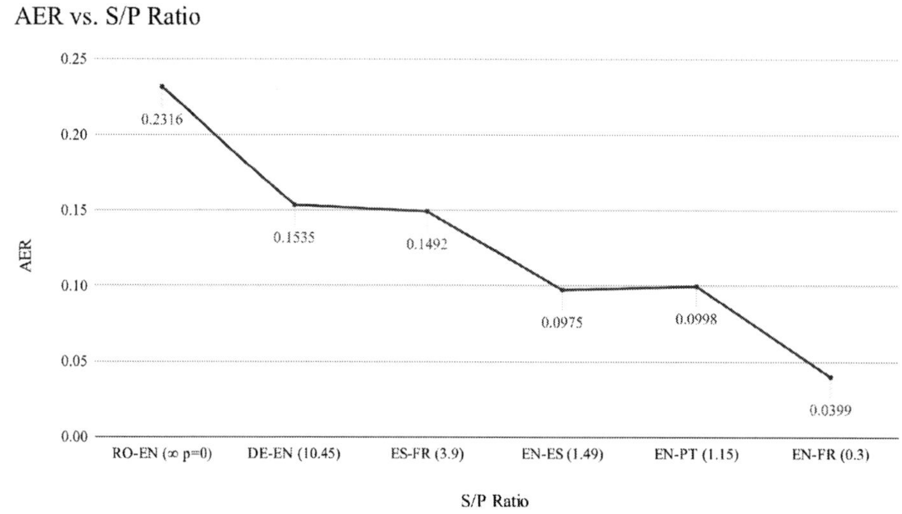

Figure 4: The correlation between AER and S/P Ratio. The alignment model used for this illustration uses Argmax method with fine-tuned mBERT Embeddings.

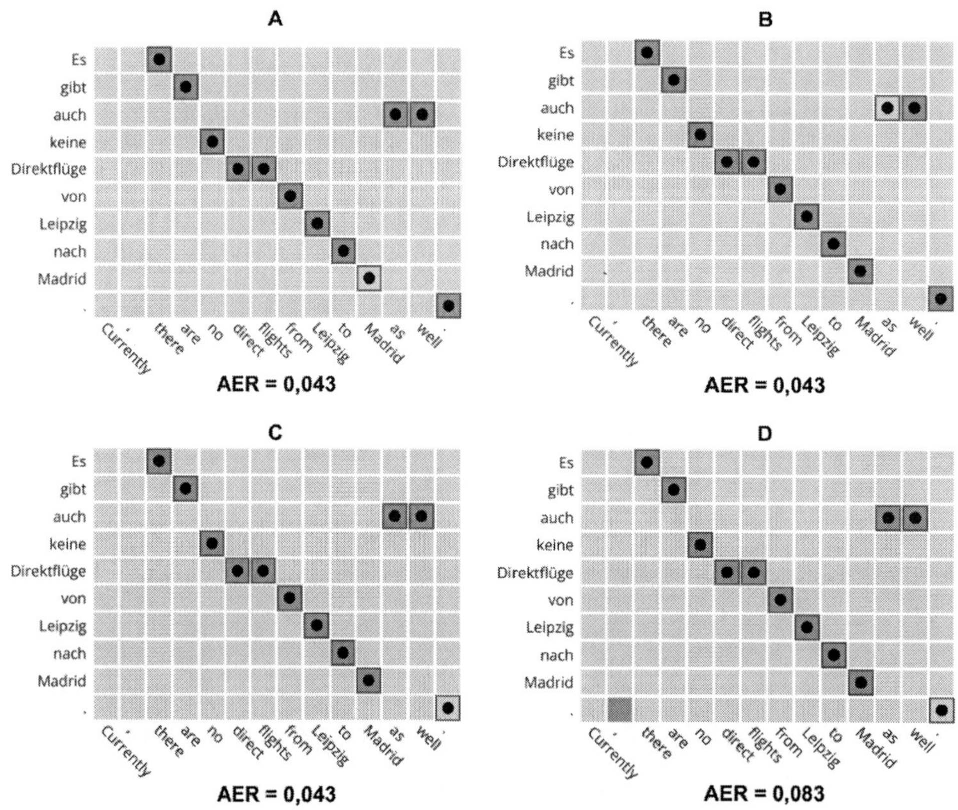

Figure 5: AER Limitations, the bold circles means gold standard sure alignments and colored cells represent model's output. A) The model failed to align *Madrid*. B) The model failed to align *auch* to *as well*. C) The model failed to align ".". D) The model aligned "." incorrectly.

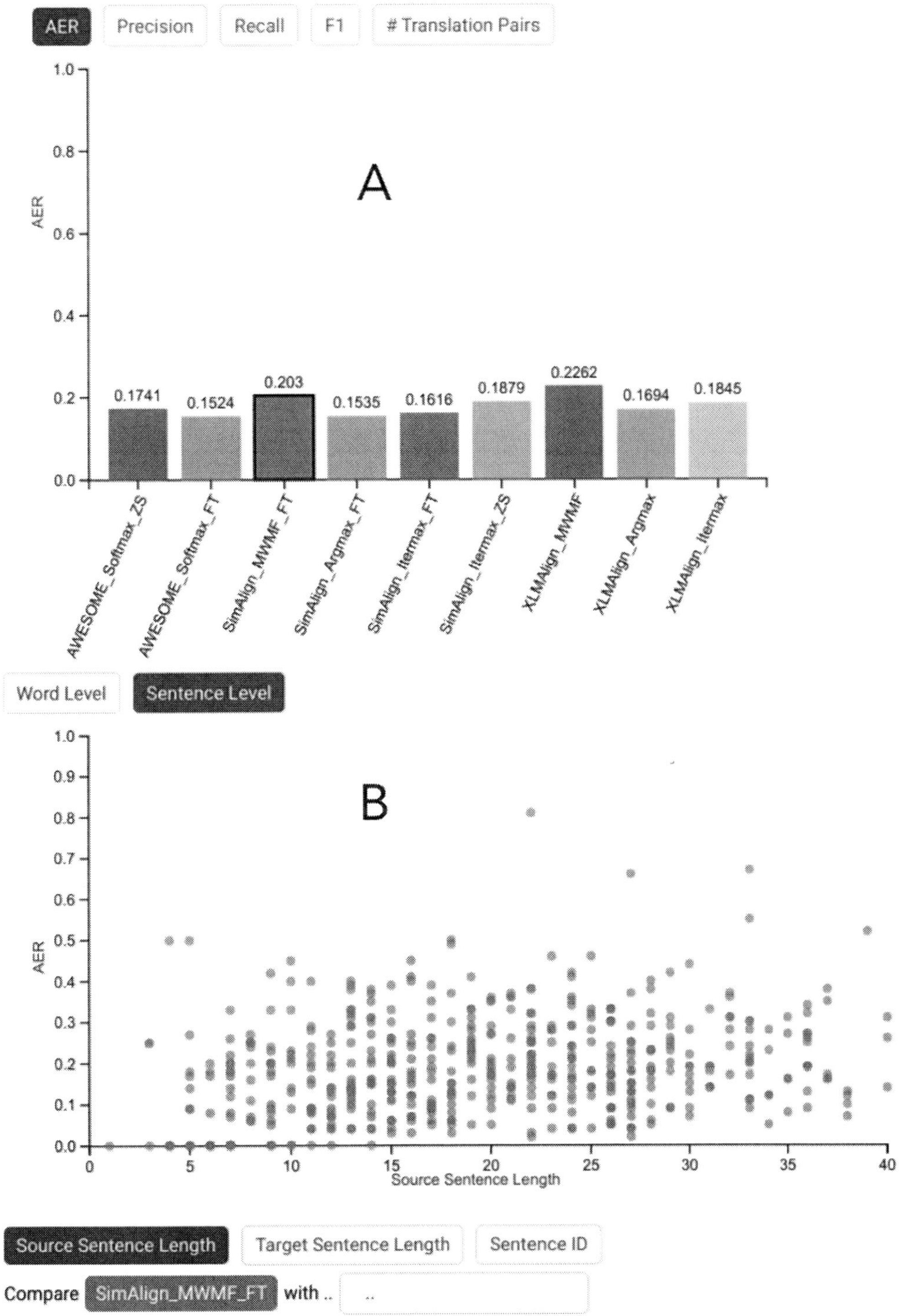

Figure 6: Single Dataset-Single Model view, A) Bar Char to compare the performance of different alignment models according to a selected metric. B) Scatter Plot shows the relation between sentences length and the selected metric.

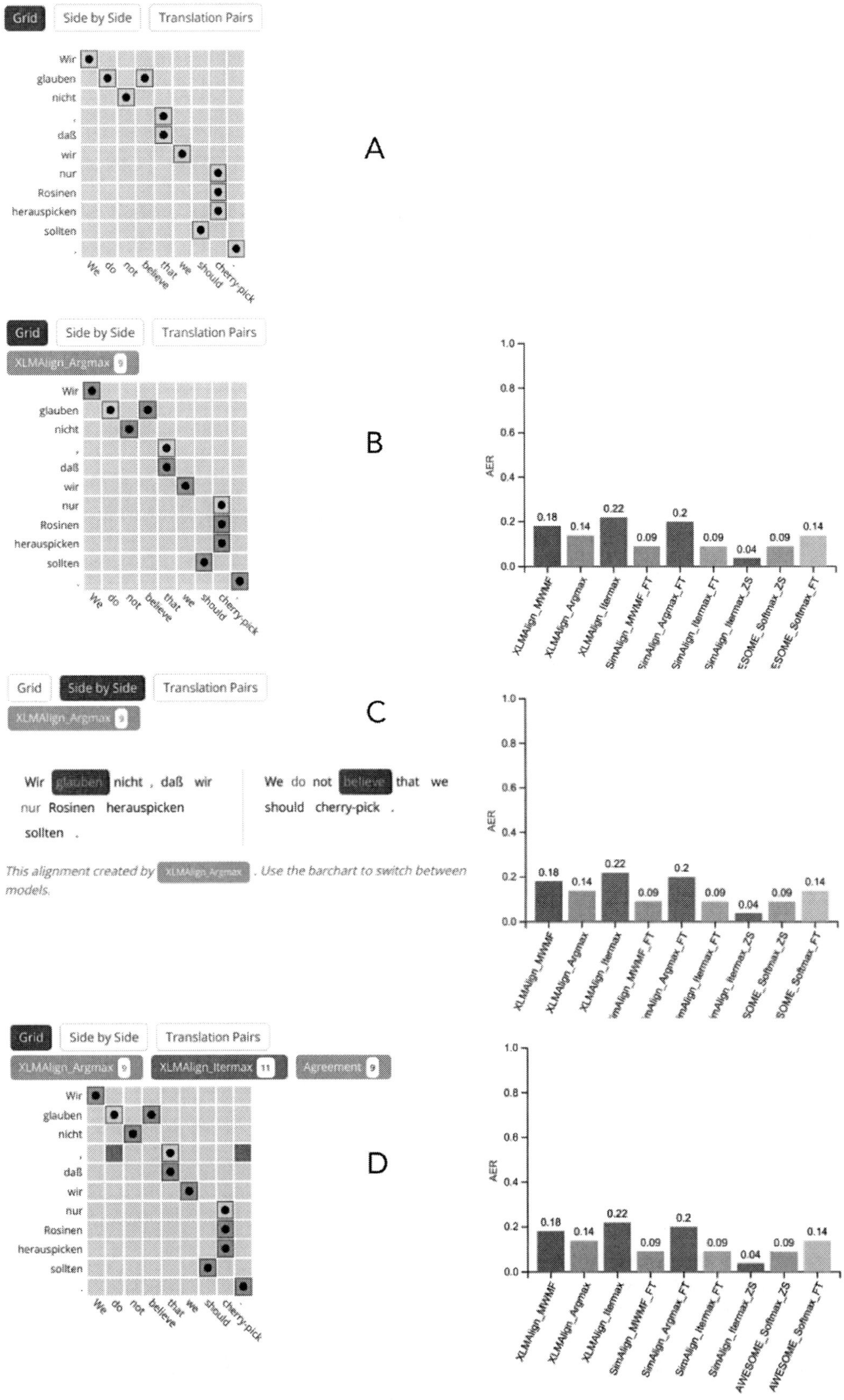

Figure 7: Sentence-level views, A) The default view when no model is selected, showing the sure (big dots) and possible (small dots) alignments. B) Visualizing the alignment of one model. C) the side-by-side view. D) the gird view visualizing the alignments of two models and their agreement.

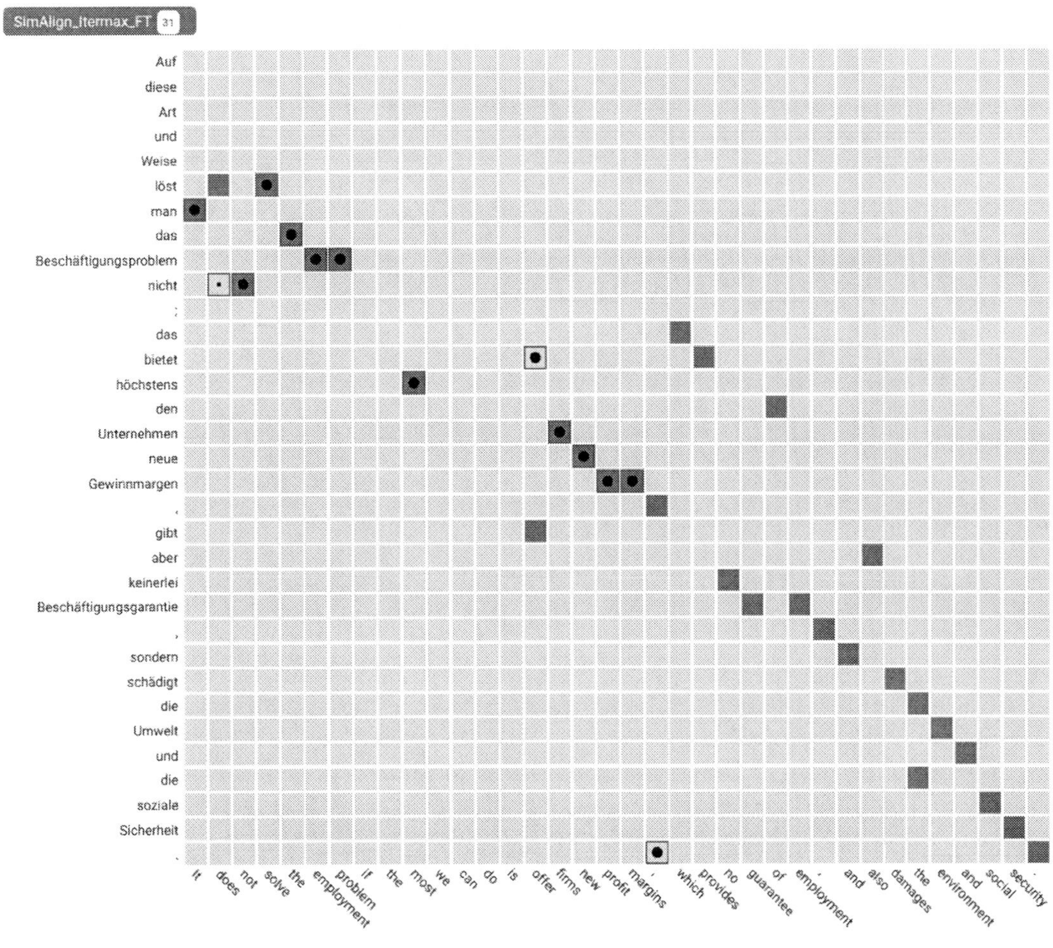

Figure 8: Sentence 40 in the DE-EN dataset, an example of incorrect/incomplete annotation of the gold standard sentence. The model predicts correct translation pairs but they are counted incorrect since they are not included in the gold standard.

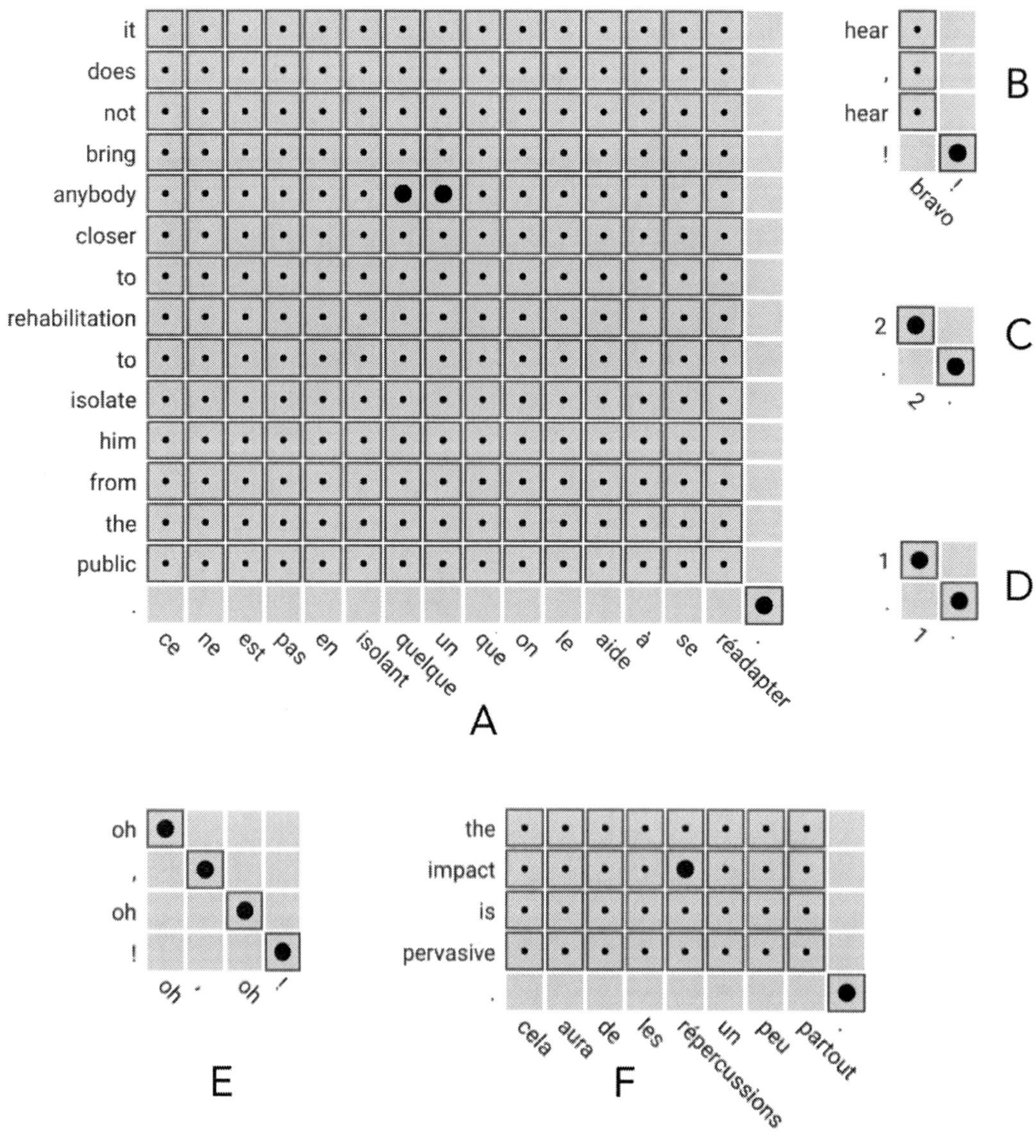

Figure 9: Examples from the EN-FR dataset. A) Sentence *0027* with too many possible links. B) This sentence is repeated 4 times in the datasets in sentences *0007*, *0008*, *0045*, and *0046*. C) This sentence is repeated twice in sentences *0001* and *0002*. D) Sentence *0011*, another example of short sentences with a number and a full stop. E) Short sentence with non-informative tokens repeated 3 times in sentences *0003*, *0004*, and *0005*. F) Sentence *0223*, another example of sentences with too many possible links.

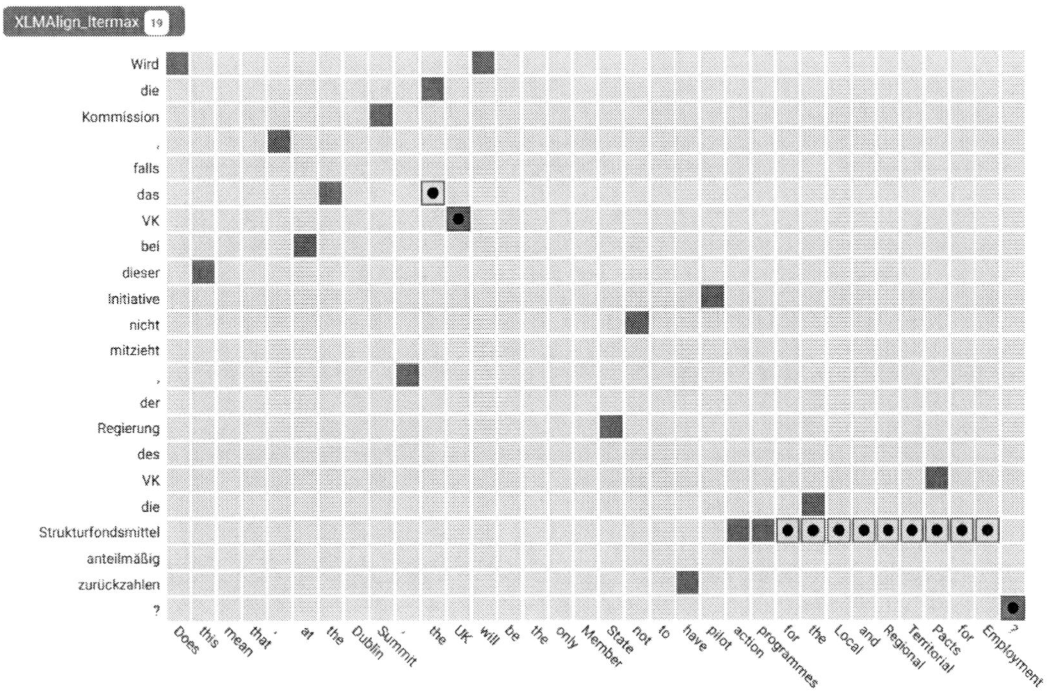

Figure 10: Sentence 202 in the DE-EN dataset, an example of incorrect/incomplete annotation of the gold standard sentence.

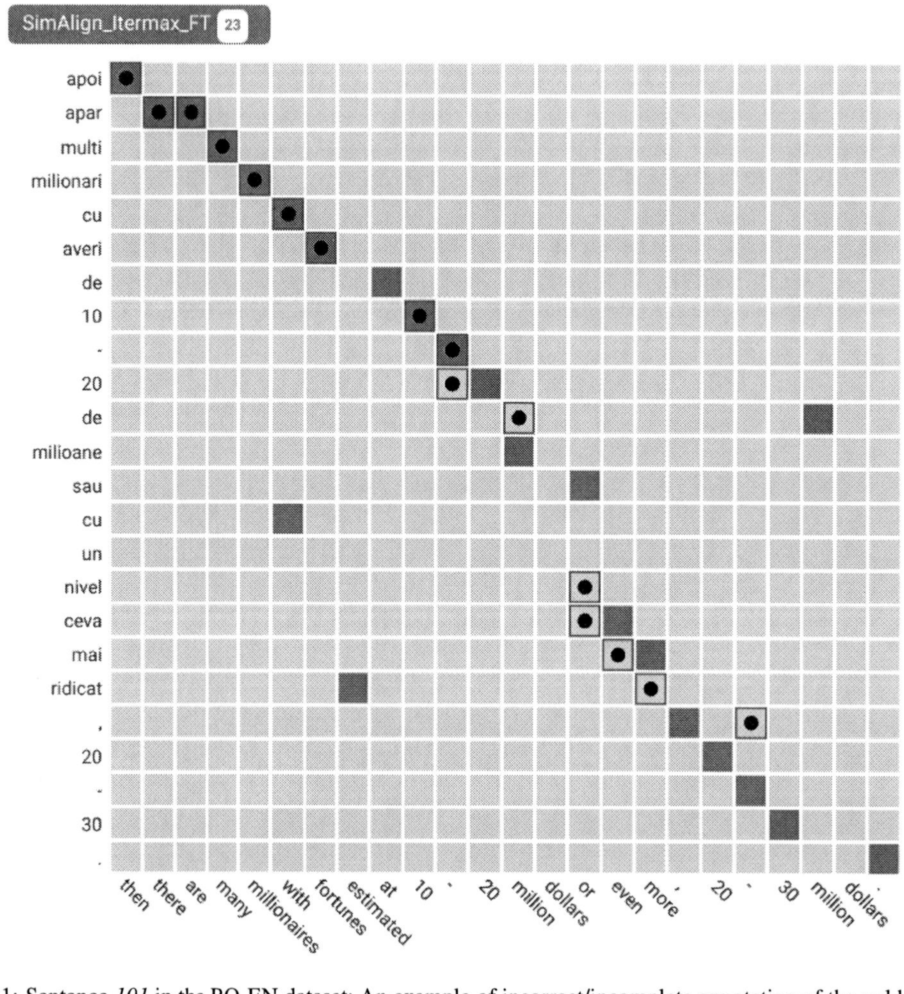

Figure 11: Sentence *101* in the RO-EN dataset; An example of incorrect/incomplete annotation of the gold standard sentence. The Romanian word *mollioane* is translated to *million* but the gold standard aligns the word *de* to *million* instead. Moreover, the sentence is not entirely aligned.

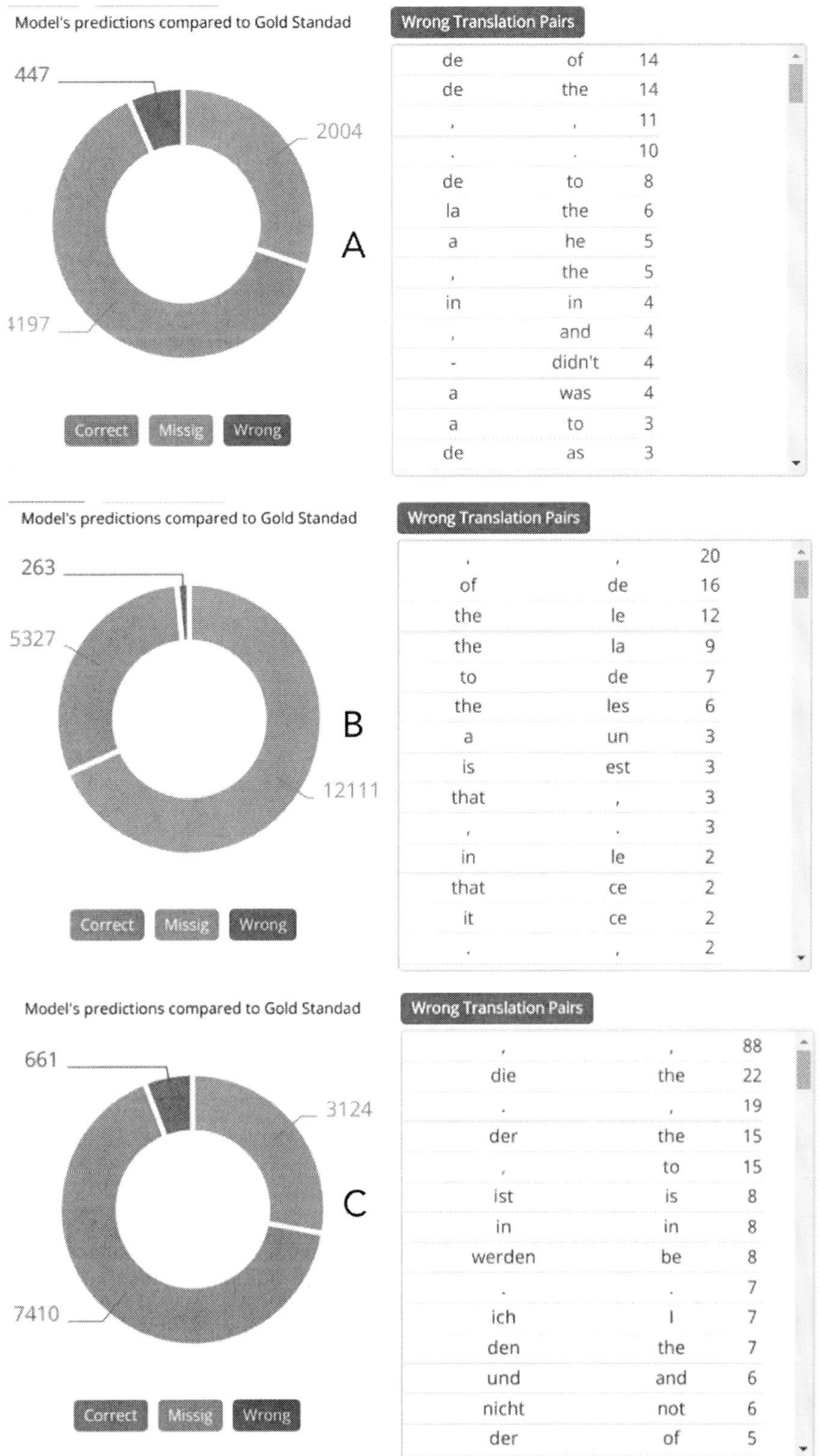

Figure 12: Frequent Alignment Errors, A) The alignment produced by *XLMAlign_Argmax* on RO-EN dataset. B) The alignment produced by *XLMAlign_Argmax* on EN-FR dataset. C) The alignment produced by XLMAlign_Argmax on DE-EN dataset.

AER | Precision | Recall | F1 | # Translation Pairs

Models/Datasets	EN-FR	EN-FR-100 ↑	EN-PT-100	ES-FR-100	PT-ES-100	PT-FR-100	DE-EN	EN-ES-100	RO-EN
Softmax_FT_mBERT	0.0407	**0.133**	0.1027	0.1403	0.0589	0.1564	0.1524	0.0958	0.226
Entmax_FT_mBERT	0.0392	**0.1354**	0.1013	0.1446	0.0611	0.1593	0.1539	0.0954	0.2293
Argmax_FT_mBERT	0.0399	**0.1359**	0.0998	0.1492	0.0659	0.16	0.1535	0.0975	0.2316
Itermax_FT_mBERT	0.067	**0.1362**	0.1207	0.1328	0.0739	0.1528	0.1616	0.109	0.221
Softmax_mBERT	0.0514	**0.1487**	0.1179	0.1478	0.0777	0.1595	0.1828	0.1093	0.2457
Entmax_mBERT	0.0511	**0.149**	0.1162	0.1533	0.0799	0.1686	0.1889	0.1107	0.2547
Argmax_mBERT	0.0519	**0.1579**	0.1245	0.1613	0.0797	0.1701	0.1971	0.1219	0.2645
Itermax_mBERT	0.0757	**0.1612**	0.1397	0.1559	0.0918	0.1747	0.1943	0.1292	0.2413
Argmax_XLMAlign	0.0569	**0.165**	0.1336	0.1721	0.0873	0.1937	0.1694	0.1165	0.2535
Softmax_XLMAlign	0.0792	**0.1697**	0.146	0.1637	0.0937	0.1944	0.1846	0.1272	0.2527
Entmax_XLMAlign	0.0736	**0.1714**	0.1407	0.172	0.0949	0.1974	0.1879	0.1221	0.2664
Itermax_XLMAlign	0.0903	**0.1753**	0.1631	0.1693	0.1109	0.2113	0.1845	0.1375	0.2473
Match_FT_mBERT	0.097	**0.1774**	0.1502	0.1831	0.1265	0.2187	0.203	0.1372	0.2493
Match_mBERT	0.1132	**0.1837**	0.1827	0.1887	0.1304	0.2233	0.2264	0.1499	0.2635
Argmax_XLMR	0.0655	**0.1924**	0.1324	0.1768	0.0743	0.2022	0.1923	0.1222	0.2591
Itermax_XLMR	0.0902	**0.1951**	0.1564	0.1784	0.1018	0.2204	0.1986	0.1418	0.2537
Softmax_XLMR	0.0918	**0.1953**	0.157	0.1771	0.0891	0.2162	0.2306	0.1406	0.2864
Entmax_XLMR	0.0901	**0.2115**	0.1693	0.1923	0.0925	0.2248	0.245	0.1463	0.302
Match_XLMAlign	0.1317	**0.2122**	0.1907	0.1976	0.1378	0.2523	0.2262	0.1711	0.2753
Match_XLMR	0.1357	**0.2192**	0.1864	0.2016	0.1329	0.2541	0.2369	0.1704	0.2781

Figure 13: Aggregated table view allows to compare the quantitative metrics of all models on all datasets.

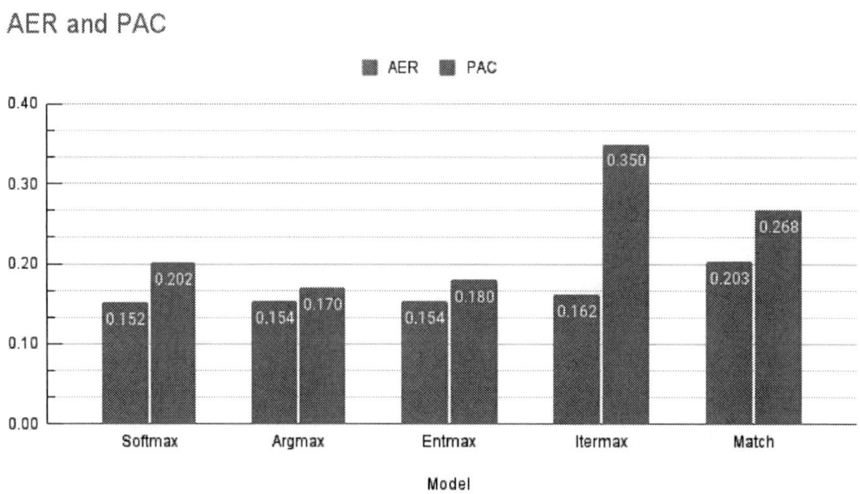

Figure 14: Comparison among five alignment models on the German-English dataset regarding AER and PAC.

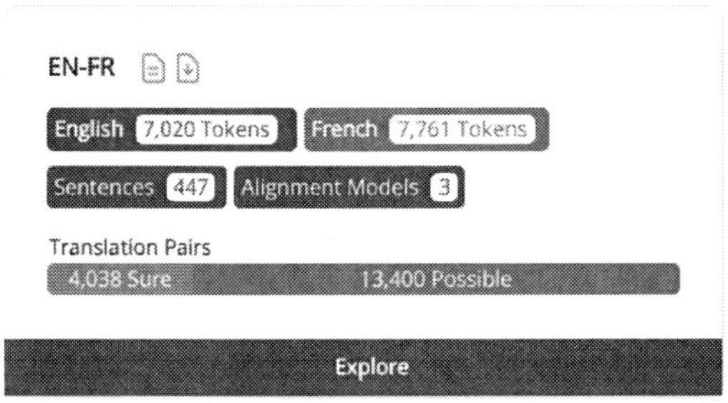

Figure 15: A dataset card contains all related information such as languages, number of tokens, sentences, Sure, and Possible pairs

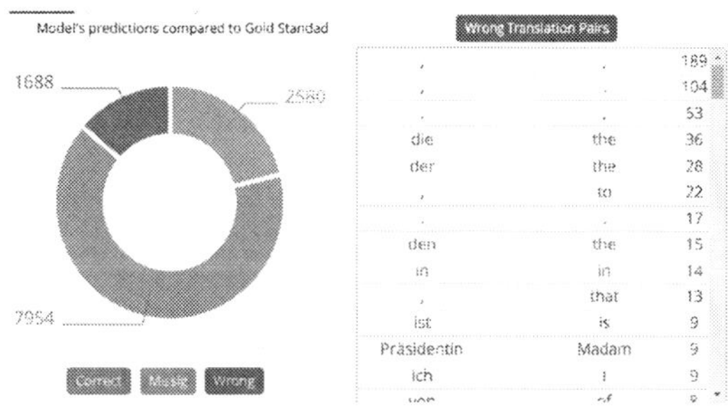

Figure 18: Frequent alignment errors produced *Itermax* model and fine-tuned mBert model on the DE-EN dataset.

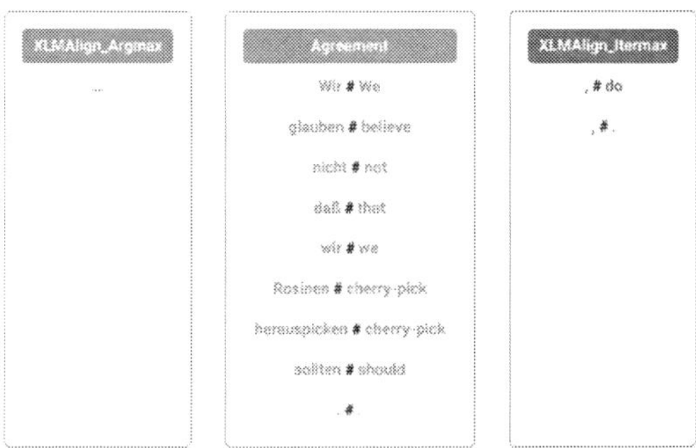

Figure 16: Table View shows the agreement of two models predictions at sentence level. Sentence 1 form DE-EN dataset

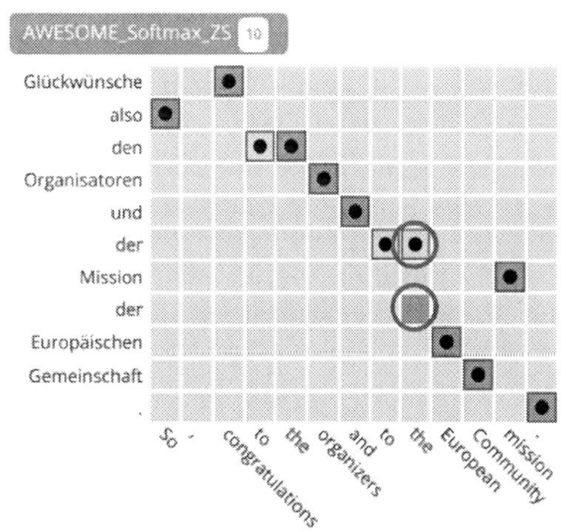

Figure 19: Sentence 127 from DE-EN, incorrect alignment of repeated tokens

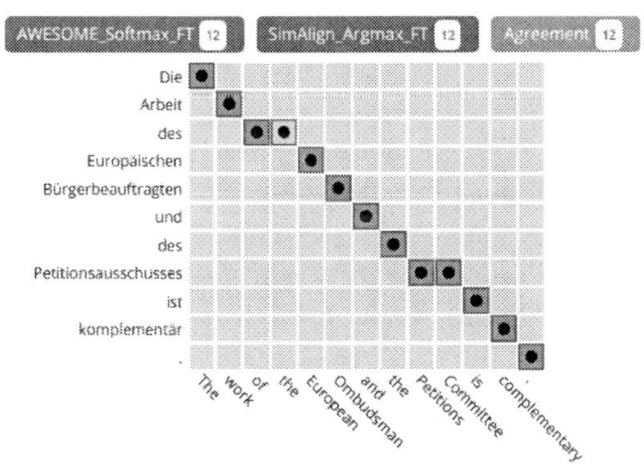

Figure 17: Sentence 46 from DE-EN, comparing two models at sentence level.

ALLECS: A Lightweight Language Error Correction System

Muhammad Reza Qorib, Geonsik Moon, and **Hwee Tou Ng**
Department of Computer Science, National University of Singapore
mrqorib@comp.nus.edu.sg, moon97@nus.edu.sg, nght@comp.nus.edu.sg

Abstract

In this paper, we present ALLECS, a lightweight web application to serve grammatical error correction (GEC) systems so that they can be easily used by the general public. We design ALLECS to be accessible to as many users as possible, including users who have a slow Internet connection and who use mobile phones as their main devices to connect to the Internet. ALLECS provides three state-of-the-art base GEC systems using two approaches (sequence-to-sequence generation and sequence tagging), as well as two state-of-the-art GEC system combination methods using two approaches (edit-based and text-based). ALLECS can be accessed at https://sterling8.d2.comp.nus.edu.sg/gec-demo/[1].

1 Introduction

English has become the *de facto* language for international discourse, spoken by approximately more than 1.4 billion speakers, with almost 75% of them being non-native speakers (Eberhard et al., 2022). As the number of English-as-a-second-language (ESL) and English-as-a-foreign-language (EFL) speakers keeps increasing, the need for automated tools to assist ESL and EFL speakers in learning and writing English also increases in tandem.

Grammatical Error Correction (GEC) is a task that aims to automatically detect and correct errors that are present in a text, including grammatical errors, orthographic errors, misspellings, word choice errors, etc. (Ng et al., 2014; Bryant et al., 2022). GEC tools have a wide range of applications, including helping native speakers to correct their occasional mistakes, assisting language learners (Knutsson et al., 2003; Chollampatt et al., 2016; Nadejde and Tetreault, 2019; Katinskaia and Yangarber, 2021), and improving the quality of other natural language processing (NLP) tasks (Yin et al., 2020; Liao et al., 2022).

GEC experienced significant progress in the last decade thanks to the HOO (Dale and Kilgarriff, 2011), CoNLL-2013 (Ng et al., 2013), CoNLL-2014 (Ng et al., 2014), and BEA-2019 (Bryant et al., 2019) shared tasks. Qorib and Ng (2022) reported that state-of-the-art GEC systems have exceeded human-level performance based on the standard evaluation metric, $F_{0.5}$ score. With the rapid progress in GEC, different approaches emerged to achieve state-of-the-art performance, including system combination (Qorib et al., 2022), sequence tagging (Lai et al., 2022), and sequence-to-sequence generation (Rothe et al., 2021). Even though many GEC systems publicly publish their source code along with their trained models, these systems can typically only be run through a command-line interface on a highly capable computing resource. Command-line interface is not easy to navigate for non-technical people and few people have access to a capable computing resource. These factors become a formidable barrier for the general public to benefit from the research progress of GEC.

In this paper, we present ALLECS (A Lightweight Language Error Correction System), a simple system to release GEC models to the general public with a lightweight web-based interface. Our web interface only requires 2.5 KB of data transfer overhead for each run. This means that ALLECS can be readily used by users in developing countries with slow Internet connections (Delaporte and Bahia, 2020). Furthermore, we use a responsive design for the web interface, allowing it to be run comfortably on devices with various screen dimensions and sizes. This allows users to use the system through a mobile phone, which is the dominant device type to connect to the Internet in developing countries (Glushkova et al., 2019). Usability is important for people living in developing countries, as they are the ones who can benefit the most from

[1]The source code and a video demonstration of ALLECS can be accessed at https://github.com/nusnlp/ALLECS.

Proceedings of the 17th Conference of the European Chapter of the Association for Computational Linguistics System Demonstrations, pages 298–306
May 2-4, 2023

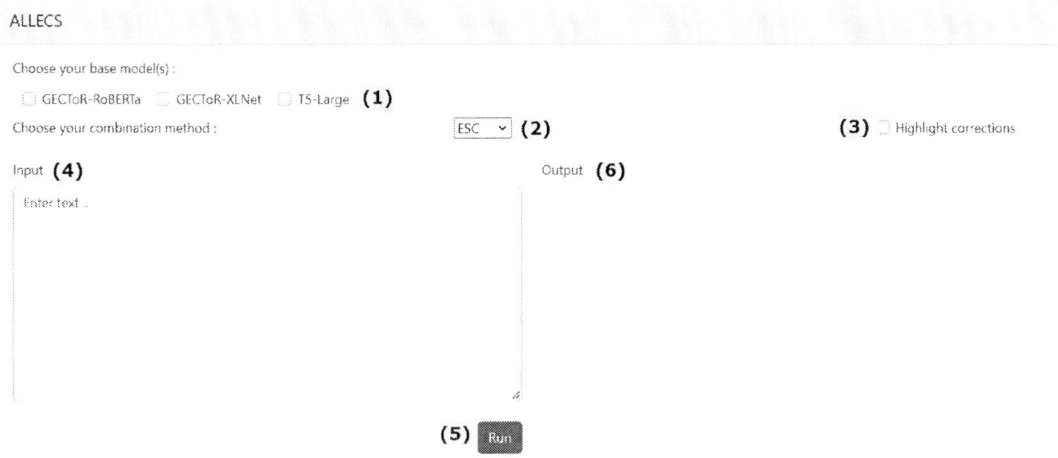

Figure 1: The user interface of ALLECS

a GEC system.

ALLECS can easily host GEC systems using different approaches, including system combination. Currently, ALLECS hosts two sequence-tagging base models, one sequence-to-sequence generation base model, and two combination methods. We briefly explain the base systems we use in ALLECS in Section 3. ALLECS also easily allows the addition of other base models. To the best of our knowledge, ALLECS is the first web application with a graphical user interface for GEC system combination methods.

2 System Overview

The interface of ALLECS consists of five components, which are base model selection, combination method selection, output mode, input text box, and output text box. The user interface of ALLECS is shown in Figure 1.

2.1 Base model selection

The user first needs to choose the base model(s). If the user chooses more than one base model, ALLECS will run a system combination method based on the combination method selected, as described in the next section. ALLECS includes three state-of-the-art GEC systems as the base models: GECToR Roberta (Omelianchuk et al., 2020), GECToR XLNet (Omelianchuk et al., 2020), and T5-Large (Rothe et al., 2021). We describe the base systems in more detail in Section 3.

2.2 Combination method selection

Next, the user needs to choose the combination method. If the user only chooses one base system, the selected combination method is ignored. ALLECS includes two state-of-the-art system combination methods, ESC (Qorib et al., 2022) and MEMT (Heafield and Lavie, 2010). We describe the system combination methods in more detail in Section 3.

2.3 Output mode

Users can choose to highlight the corrections by selecting the "Highlight corrections" box. If the user chooses to highlight the corrections, text spans in the output text that are different from the input text are highlighted in blue and a simple explanation of each correction can be displayed by clicking a highlighted text span. The appearance of highlighted corrections can be seen in Figure 2. Displaying corrections with simple explanations can help language learners to understand their mistakes better. We extracted the corrections with their edit types using ERRANT (Bryant et al., 2017).

2.4 Input text box

The user needs to put the text he wants to correct in the input text box and clicks the run button. The corrected text will then be displayed in the output text box. Most recent GEC base systems expect the input to be a single sentence tokenized with SpaCy (Honnibal et al., 2020) version 1.9, following the requirement from the BEA-2019 shared task. As such, an input text needs to be segmented into sentences and then tokenized with SpaCy before each

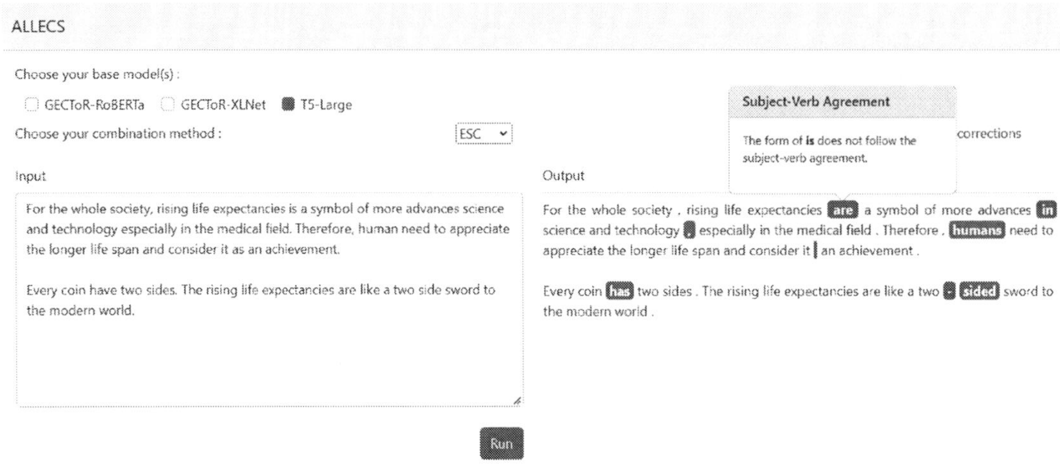

Figure 2: Text spans displayed in blue are the corrections made by the GEC system. A vertical blue bar without any text inside denotes text deletion. When a blue highlight or a blue bar is clicked, a simple explanation of the correction is shown.

sentence is given as the input to the GEC model. To retain the text structure, it is first split by line before segmented into sentences. This way, we can keep the information on which line a sentence should be printed. To segment a text into sentences, we follow the practice used in the NUCLE corpus (Dahlmeier et al., 2013) by using the nltk Punkt tokenizer (Bird and Loper, 2004; Kiss and Strunk, 2006).

2.5 Output text box

After a text is entered into the input text box and the "Run" button is clicked, the corrected text will appear in the output text box. As the base GEC systems are expected to work on tokenized input and output, the output text needs to be detokenized to look more natural. Since SpaCy does not have a detokenizer and the document context of the original input may no longer be relevant after a sentence is corrected, we use Moses (Koehn et al., 2007) to detokenize a sentence. We found that Moses can detokenize a sentence that is tokenized by SpaCy reasonably well, only missing some cases like the detokenization of "is n't" and "are n't" and removing spaces around hyphens. For these missed cases, we create simple rules to apply string replacement after Moses detokenization. Detokenization is not applied if the user chooses to highlight the corrections because the highlights need some room to make them clearly visible.

3 GEC Base Systems and Combination Methods

In ALLECS, we provide three base systems and two system combination methods. The base systems we provide come from two approaches, sequence-to-sequence generation (T5-Large) and sequence tagging (GECToR). The combination methods we provide also come from two approaches, edit-based (ESC) and text-based (MEMT) combination. The performance of the base systems and the combination methods on the BEA-2019 development set, CoNLL-2014 test set, and BEA-2019 test set is presented in Table 1. The scores of the base systems are presented in the top part of the table while the scores of the combination methods when combining the three base systems are presented in the bottom part.

3.1 T5-Large

T5 (Text-To-Text Transfer Transformer) (Raffel et al., 2020) is a large transformer model trained with a unified framework that converts all text-based language tasks into a text-to-text format. T5 is a sequence-to-sequence model with an architecture similar to the original Transformer (Vaswani et al., 2017).

Rothe et al. (2021) adapt T5 for grammatical error correction by fine-tuning the model on a new dataset they released, cLang-8. The cLang-8 dataset is made from re-labeling the Lang-8 dataset (Mizumoto et al., 2011; Tajiri et al., 2012), using a large model that is pre-trained with 50 billion doc-

Model	BEA-2019 Dev			CoNLL-2014			BEA-2019 Test		
	P	R	$F_{0.5}$	P	R	$F_{0.5}$	P	R	$F_{0.5}$
1. T5-Large	60.38	44.04	56.21	72.84	51.62	67.30	74.30	66.75	72.66
2. GECToR XLNet	66.00	34.14	55.62	77.49	40.15	65.34	79.20	53.90	72.40
3. GECToR Roberta	62.37	35.52	54.18	73.91	41.66	64.00	77.20	55.10	71.50
ESC	72.24	37.29	60.84	81.72	42.04	68.74	85.71	57.45	78.04
MEMT	61.82	44.02	57.19	70.64	50.20	65.32	75.41	66.44	73.42

Table 1: The top rows report the performance of the GEC systems that are provided as the base systems in ALLECS, while the bottom rows report the performance of the GEC system combination methods that are provided in ALLECS when combining the three base systems above.

uments from 101 languages and trained with the BEA-2019 training data. See (Rothe et al., 2021) for more details.

The T5 authors released the code[2] to train the GEC model but not their trained model. We use their original code to train the GEC base model using their hyper-parameter values[3].

3.2 GECToR

GECToR models GEC as a sequence tagging task by defining a set of token transformations. They defined two types of token transformations: basic transformations and g-transformations. The basic transformations include the keep, delete, and token-dependent append and replace transformations. The g-transformations are task-specific transformations such as merging two words, changing the verb form, changing the noun number, etc.

GECToR was built by fine-tuning a large pretrained model in three rounds of training. In the first round, they trained the model on 9M sentence pairs of synthetic data. In the last two rounds, the model is further trained on the BEA-2019 training data. At inference time, GECToR runs iteratively for a number of rounds. This helps to increase both precision and recall of the corrections. Despite running the inference multiple times, GECToR's inference speed is up to 10 times faster compared to models using the sequence-to-sequence approach. See (Omelianchuk et al., 2020) for more details.

In ALLECS, we use the XLNet and Roberta versions of GECToR, as the ensemble of these models produces the highest scores. We use the original source code and model weights[4] in ALLECS.

[2] https://github.com/google-research/text-to-text-transfer-transformer/

[3] https://github.com/google-research-datasets/clang8/issues/3#issuecomment-913682092

[4] https://github.com/grammarly/gector/tree/fea1532608

3.3 ESC

ESC is a system combination method that formulates the combination task as binary classification. ESC takes the union of all edits from the base systems and generates the features for each edit based on its edit type and inclusion in the base systems. ESC uses logistic regression to predict the probability that an edit is correct, and filters the edits based on a threshold and a greedy selection method.

At the time of writing, ESC is the highest-scoring GEC system on the CoNLL-2014 test set and the BEA-2019 test set, by combining T5-Large (Rothe et al., 2021), GECToR XLNet (Omelianchuk et al., 2020), GECToR Roberta (Omelianchuk et al., 2020), Riken & Tohoku (Kiyono et al., 2019), UEDIN-MS (Grundkiewicz et al., 2019), and Kakao&Bain (Choe et al., 2019). In ALLECS, for simplicity, we only provide the top three base systems since the performance of the ensemble of these three systems is still highly competitive with other state-of-the-art systems. We use ESC's original code[5] but slightly modify it to take inputs stored in memory rather than reading them from files. We then train the ensemble model for all possible base system configurations.

3.4 MEMT

MEMT is a system combination method that combines the base models' outputs by first aligning them and generating all possible candidate sentences based on the token alignment. Candidate generation has some constraints, such as no repetition, weak monotonicity, and completeness. For each candidate sentence, MEMT generates the features based on the language model score, n-gram similarity to each base model's output, and the sentence length. MEMT then learns the weights to score the features and uses the trained weights

[5] https://github.com/nusnlp/esc

to find the highest-scoring candidate sentence via beam search during inference.

MEMT was originally designed for combining machine translation models, but Susanto et al. (2014) have demonstrated that MEMT can effectively combine GEC models as well. In ALLECS, we use MEMT's original code[6] and train the ensemble model for all possible base system configurations.

4 System Design and Implementation

To make ALLECS more modular, we design it to have two parts: the web interface (front-end) and the base models' API (back-end). The web interface accepts a user's input text and handles the pre-processing and post-processing, while the base models' API focuses on generating a corrected sentence from the pre-processed input. This separation allows the base models' API to run on a GPU-powered server while the web interface runs on a CPU-focused server. However, both parts can also be run on the same server.

As Python has become the dominant programming language of choice for most NLP research projects, we develop ALLECS in Python. This makes ALLECS highly extensible such that it can be used to host new GEC systems in the future. The separation between the front-end and back-end parts also allows ALLECS to host other base models that are written in a different programming language or use different library dependencies. This also allows the web interface to work with other closed-source GEC models, as long as a GEC model provides an API to generate a corrected sentence.

We describe the process flow of ALLECS in Figure 3. All inputs are first split by line and segmented into sentences. The line index for each sentence is recorded to retain the text structure in the output. Then, the web interface tokenizes the sentences and combines them into mini-batches to be sent to the base models' API. If the user chooses to highlight the corrections or combine multiple base models with ESC, the web interface will also use ERRANT to parse the input sentences. After receiving the output sentences from each base model, the interface will then parse the base models' outputs using ERRANT if the user chooses to highlight corrections or use ESC. If not, the outputs are sent to MEMT if the user chooses to combine the models with MEMT. Otherwise, the output sentences are directly detokenized. Detokenization also applies to the combination method's output if the user selects more than one base model.

The correction speed of ALLECS is fast. Running on an NVIDIA Titan X GPU server with 12GB memory, GECToR Roberta can correct text at a speed of 723 words per second, GECToR XLNet at 640 words per second, and T5-Large at 37 words per second. Using ESC to combine base systems only adds a small amount of overhead. For example, using ESC to combine GECToR Roberta and T5-Large can correct text at a speed of 32 words per second, marginally slower than using T5-Large alone.

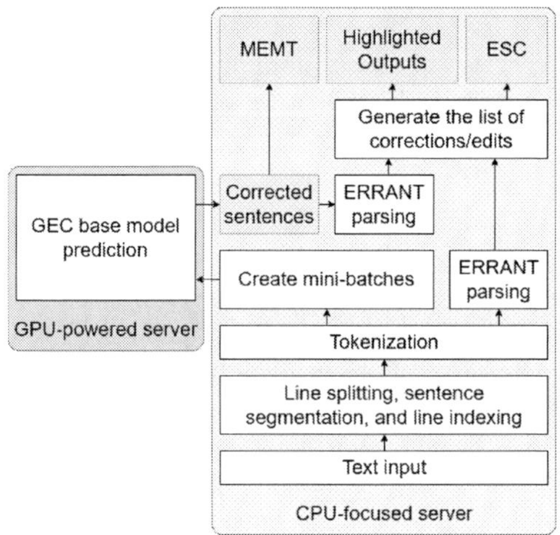

Figure 3: The process flow of ALLECS.

4.1 Web interface

We use flask version 2.0.3[7] and Bootstrap version 5[8] frameworks to develop the web interface. Bootstrap is a lightweight CSS and JavaScript framework that helps developers to design an interface with accessibility in mind, building a responsive layout and conforming with Web Content Accessibility Guideline (WCAG) 2.1. We design the web interface to only use colors with a contrast ratio above 4.5:1[9]. The web interface also works well when zoomed to 200%[10] and can be used with

[6] https://github.com/kpu/memt

[7] https://flask.palletsprojects.com/en/2.0.x/

[8] https://getbootstrap.com/docs/5.0/getting-started/introduction/

[9] Conforming to WCAG 2.1 minimum contrast recommendation https://w3.org/TR/WCAG/#contrast-minimum

[10] Conforming to WCAG 2.1 resize text recommendation https://www.w3.org/TR/WCAG/#resize-text

different screen dimensions and sizes[11]. With the responsive design, the position of the output box is moved to the bottom of the input box when opened from a screen with smaller size or with vertical orientation, such as on mobile phones, as shown in Figure 4.

Figure 4: The interface layout on a vertical screen such as a mobile phone.

4.2 Base models' API

The base models' API hosts all base systems in ALLECS. The base models' API first loads each base system on different GPUs at start time. This approach makes the application persistently uses a large amount of GPU memory but allows much faster inference. We build the base models' API using flask version 2.0.3 and flask RESTful version 0.3.9[12] frameworks. The base models' API serves an API with the HTTP POST request method, expecting a JSON that contains a list of sentences on the keyword "text_input_list", and returns a JSON that contains a list of corrected sentences with the same length as the input list, on the keyword "text_output_list". Adding new base systems to ALLECS only requires changing a few lines of code.

5 Related Work

There are some ready-to-use web services for correcting English text such as services from Grammarly[13] and John Snow Labs[14], but those web services are not open-source. Thus, they are not customizable for deploying different GEC systems. In this section, we will discuss the comparison of ALLECS to other open-source English correction tools, namely GECko+ (Calò et al., 2021) and MiSS (Li et al., 2021).

5.1 GECko+

GECko+ (Calò et al., 2021) is a grammatical and discourse correction tool that combines a sentence-level GEC model, GECToR XLNet, and a sentence ordering model (Prabhumoye et al., 2020). When a user inputs a text into the system, it segments the text into sentences and corrects the sentences with GECToR before re-ordering them by the sentence ordering model.

Compared to ALLECS, GECko+ lacks the options of choosing the GEC base models and using system combination methods. It is also unclear how easy it is to extend GECko+ to other GEC systems. ALLECS does not include a sentence re-ordering model because it focuses on grammatical error correction, and re-ordering sentences can confuse the user and makes it harder for the user to learn from the corrections.

5.2 MiSS

MiSS (Li et al., 2021) is a comprehensive tool for machine translation that includes grammatical error correction as a feature. The main machine translation features of MiSS include: basic machine translation, simultaneous machine translation, and back-translation for quality evaluation. For the GEC part, it uses GECToR XLNet for English GEC and GECToR with BERT-chinese and BERT-japanese models for Chinese and Japanese GEC respectively.

Compared to ALLECS, MiSS also lacks the options of choosing the GEC base models and using system combination methods. It is also unclear how easy it is to extend MiSS to other GEC systems.

6 Conclusion

We have presented ALLECS, a web-based application for GEC that can be easily used by the general public. We design ALLECS to be accessible to as many users as possible, including users who have a slow Internet connection and who use mobile

[11]Conforming to WCAG 2.1 orientation recommendation https://www.w3.org/TR/WCAG/#orientation

[12]https://flask-restful.readthedocs.io/en/latest/

[13]https://www.grammarly.com/

[14]https://demo.johnsnowlabs.com/public/T5_LINGUISTIC/

phones as their main devices to connect to the Internet. In ALLECS, we provide three base GEC systems using two types of approaches, sequence-to-sequence generation and sequence tagging, as well as two GEC system combination methods from two types of approaches, edit-based and text-based combination. ALLECS is separated into two parts to make the application modular and easily extensible to other base GEC systems.

Limitations

ALLECS is currently limited to English GEC systems, but it can be extended to other languages by incorporating base GEC models for other languages and modifying the pre-processing and post-processing steps.

Acknowledgements

This research is supported by the National Research Foundation, Singapore under its AI Singapore Programme (AISG Award No: AISG-RP-2019-014). The computational work for this article was partially performed on resources of the National Supercomputing Centre, Singapore (https://www.nscc.sg).

References

Steven Bird and Edward Loper. 2004. NLTK: The natural language toolkit. In *Proceedings of the ACL Interactive Poster and Demonstration Sessions*, pages 214–217.

Christopher Bryant, Mariano Felice, Øistein E. Andersen, and Ted Briscoe. 2019. The BEA-2019 shared task on grammatical error correction. In *Proceedings of the Fourteenth Workshop on Innovative Use of NLP for Building Educational Applications*, pages 52–75.

Christopher Bryant, Mariano Felice, and Ted Briscoe. 2017. Automatic annotation and evaluation of error types for grammatical error correction. In *Proceedings of the 55th Annual Meeting of the Association for Computational Linguistics (Volume 1: Long Papers)*, pages 793–805.

Christopher Bryant, Zheng Yuan, Muhammad Reza Qorib, Hannan Cao, Hwee Tou Ng, and Ted Briscoe. 2022. Grammatical error correction: A survey of the state of the art. arXiv. https://arxiv.org/abs/2211.05166.

Eduardo Calò, Léo Jacqmin, Thibo Rosemplatt, Maxime Amblard, Miguel Couceiro, and Ajinkya Kulkarni. 2021. GECko+: a grammatical and discourse error correction tool. In *Actes de la 28e Conférence sur le Traitement Automatique des Langues Naturelles. Volume 3 : Démonstrations*, pages 8–11. ATALA.

Yo Joong Choe, Jiyeon Ham, Kyubyong Park, and Yeoil Yoon. 2019. A neural grammatical error correction system built on better pre-training and sequential transfer learning. In *Proceedings of the Fourteenth Workshop on Innovative Use of NLP for Building Educational Applications*, pages 213–227.

Shamil Chollampatt, Duc Tam Hoang, and Hwee Tou Ng. 2016. Adapting grammatical error correction based on the native language of writers with neural network joint models. In *Proceedings of the 2016 Conference on Empirical Methods in Natural Language Processing*, pages 1901–1911.

Daniel Dahlmeier, Hwee Tou Ng, and Siew Mei Wu. 2013. Building a large annotated corpus of learner English: The NUS corpus of learner English. In *Proceedings of the Eighth Workshop on Innovative Use of NLP for Building Educational Applications*, pages 22–31.

Robert Dale and Adam Kilgarriff. 2011. Helping our own: The HOO 2011 pilot shared task. In *Proceedings of the 13th European Workshop on Natural Language Generation*, pages 242–249.

Anne Delaporte and Kalvin Bahia. 2020. The state of mobile internet connectivity 2022. Technical report, GSM Association.

David M. Eberhard, Gary F. Simons, and Charles D. Fennig. 2022. Ethnologue: Languages of the world.

Svetlana Glushkova, Denis Belotserkovich, Natalia Morgunova, and Yulia V. Yuzhakova. 2019. The role of smartphones and the internet in developing countries. *Revista ESPACIOS*, 40(27):10–18.

Roman Grundkiewicz, Marcin Junczys-Dowmunt, and Kenneth Heafield. 2019. Neural grammatical error correction systems with unsupervised pre-training on synthetic data. In *Proceedings of the Fourteenth Workshop on Innovative Use of NLP for Building Educational Applications*, pages 252–263.

Kenneth Heafield and Alon Lavie. 2010. CMU multi-engine machine translation for WMT 2010. In *Proceedings of the Joint Fifth Workshop on Statistical Machine Translation and MetricsMATR*, pages 301–306.

Matthew Honnibal, Ines Montani, Sofie Van Landeghem, and Adriane Boyd. 2020. spacy: Industrial-strength natural language processing in python.

Anisia Katinskaia and Roman Yangarber. 2021. Assessing grammatical correctness in language learning. In *Proceedings of the 16th Workshop on Innovative Use of NLP for Building Educational Applications*, pages 135–146.

Tibor Kiss and Jan Strunk. 2006. Unsupervised multilingual sentence boundary detection. *Computational Linguistics*, 32(4):485–525.

Shun Kiyono, Jun Suzuki, Masato Mita, Tomoya Mizumoto, and Kentaro Inui. 2019. An empirical study of incorporating pseudo data into grammatical error correction. In *Proceedings of the 2019 Conference on Empirical Methods in Natural Language Processing and the 9th International Joint Conference on Natural Language Processing (EMNLP-IJCNLP)*, pages 1236–1242.

Ola Knutsson, Teresa Cerrato Pargman, and Kerstin Severinson Eklundh. 2003. Transforming grammar checking technology into a learning environment for second language writing. In *Proceedings of the HLT-NAACL 03 Workshop on Building Educational Applications Using Natural Language Processing*, pages 38–45.

Philipp Koehn, Hieu Hoang, Alexandra Birch, Chris Callison-Burch, Marcello Federico, Nicola Bertoldi, Brooke Cowan, Wade Shen, Christine Moran, Richard Zens, Chris Dyer, Ondřej Bojar, Alexandra Constantin, and Evan Herbst. 2007. Moses: Open source toolkit for statistical machine translation. In *Proceedings of the 45th Annual Meeting of the Association for Computational Linguistics Companion Volume Proceedings of the Demo and Poster Sessions*, pages 177–180.

Shaopeng Lai, Qingyu Zhou, Jiali Zeng, Zhongli Li, Chao Li, Yunbo Cao, and Jinsong Su. 2022. Type-driven multi-turn corrections for grammatical error correction. In *Findings of the Association for Computational Linguistics: ACL 2022*, pages 3225–3236.

Zuchao Li, Kevin Parnow, Masao Utiyama, Eiichiro Sumita, and Hai Zhao. 2021. MiSS: An assistant for multi-style simultaneous translation. In *Proceedings of the 2021 Conference on Empirical Methods in Natural Language Processing: System Demonstrations*, pages 1–10.

Junwei Liao, Sefik Emre Eskimez, Liyang Lu, Yu Shi, Ming Gong, Linjun Shou, Hong Qu, and Michael Zeng. 2022. Improving readability for automatic speech recognition transcription. *ACM Transactions on Asian and Low-Resource Language Information Processing*.

Tomoya Mizumoto, Mamoru Komachi, Masaaki Nagata, and Yuji Matsumoto. 2011. Mining revision log of language learning SNS for automated Japanese error correction of second language learners. In *Proceedings of 5th International Joint Conference on Natural Language Processing*, pages 147–155.

Maria Nadejde and Joel Tetreault. 2019. Personalizing grammatical error correction: Adaptation to proficiency level and L1. In *Proceedings of the 5th Workshop on Noisy User-generated Text (W-NUT 2019)*, pages 27–33.

Hwee Tou Ng, Siew Mei Wu, Ted Briscoe, Christian Hadiwinoto, Raymond Hendy Susanto, and Christopher Bryant. 2014. The CoNLL-2014 shared task on grammatical error correction. In *Proceedings of the Eighteenth Conference on Computational Natural Language Learning: Shared Task*, pages 1–14.

Hwee Tou Ng, Siew Mei Wu, Yuanbin Wu, Christian Hadiwinoto, and Joel Tetreault. 2013. The CoNLL-2013 shared task on grammatical error correction. In *Proceedings of the Seventeenth Conference on Computational Natural Language Learning: Shared Task*, pages 1–12.

Kostiantyn Omelianchuk, Vitaliy Atrasevych, Artem Chernodub, and Oleksandr Skurzhanskyi. 2020. GECToR – grammatical error correction: Tag, not rewrite. In *Proceedings of the Fifteenth Workshop on Innovative Use of NLP for Building Educational Applications*, pages 163–170.

Shrimai Prabhumoye, Ruslan Salakhutdinov, and Alan W Black. 2020. Topological sort for sentence ordering. In *Proceedings of the 58th Annual Meeting of the Association for Computational Linguistics*, pages 2783–2792.

Muhammad Reza Qorib, Seung-Hoon Na, and Hwee Tou Ng. 2022. Frustratingly easy system combination for grammatical error correction. In *Proceedings of the 2022 Conference of the North American Chapter of the Association for Computational Linguistics: Human Language Technologies*, pages 1964–1974.

Muhammad Reza Qorib and Hwee Tou Ng. 2022. Grammatical error correction: Are we there yet? In *Proceedings of the 29th International Conference on Computational Linguistics*, pages 2794–2800.

Colin Raffel, Noam Shazeer, Adam Roberts, Katherine Lee, Sharan Narang, Michael Matena, Yanqi Zhou, Wei Li, and Peter J. Liu. 2020. Exploring the limits of transfer learning with a unified text-to-text transformer. *Journal of Machine Learning Research*, 21(140):1–67.

Sascha Rothe, Jonathan Mallinson, Eric Malmi, Sebastian Krause, and Aliaksei Severyn. 2021. A simple recipe for multilingual grammatical error correction. In *Proceedings of the 59th Annual Meeting of the Association for Computational Linguistics and the 11th International Joint Conference on Natural Language Processing (Volume 2: Short Papers)*, pages 702–707.

Raymond Hendy Susanto, Peter Phandi, and Hwee Tou Ng. 2014. System combination for grammatical error correction. In *Proceedings of the 2014 Conference on Empirical Methods in Natural Language Processing (EMNLP)*, pages 951–962.

Toshikazu Tajiri, Mamoru Komachi, and Yuji Matsumoto. 2012. Tense and aspect error correction for ESL learners using global context. In *Proceedings of the 50th Annual Meeting of the Association for Computational Linguistics (Volume 2: Short Papers)*, pages 198–202.

Ashish Vaswani, Noam Shazeer, Niki Parmar, Jakob Uszkoreit, Llion Jones, Aidan N Gomez, Ł ukasz Kaiser, and Illia Polosukhin. 2017. Attention is all you need. In *Advances in Neural Information Processing Systems*, volume 30. Curran Associates, Inc.

Fan Yin, Quanyu Long, Tao Meng, and Kai-Wei Chang. 2020. On the robustness of language encoders against grammatical errors. In *Proceedings of the 58th Annual Meeting of the Association for Computational Linguistics*, pages 3386–3403.

DAVE: Differential Diagnostic Analysis Automation and Visualization from Clinical Notes

Hadi Hamoud and **Chadi Abou Chakra** and **Mira Dankar** and **Fadi A. Zaraket**
Electrical and Computer Engineering Department, American University of Beirut
hkh21,cha21,mkd07@mail.aub.edu, fz11@aub.edu.lb

Abstract

Electronic Medical Records are integral parts of modern healthcare. Part of the records are *clinical notes* that healthcare providers take during encounters with patients. Notes are key to *differential analysis* which is the reasoning process leading to diagnosis and treatment. This paper presents DAVE, a *differential analysis automation and visualization* to assist healthcare professionals through the differential analysis process. DAVE takes as input clinical notes as they are being written by professionals and suggests candidate diagnostic algorithms. We digitized textbook diagnostic algorithms into directed acyclic graphs. We trained a distributional semantics model using an annotated corpora of electronic medical records and text from diagnostic algorithm descriptions. The model, boosted with PUBMed-based semantic similarity metrics, ranks the diagnostic algorithm graphs and suggests the top three. The model achieved 74.3% success rate and was highly accepted by multiple medical professionals for usability.

1 Introduction

Information reported in *electronic medical records* (EMRs) revolutionized medical language research. Healthcare providers follow specific procedures in the process of caring for and managing a patient. The clinical assessment starts by noting the *chief complaints* of the patient and the purpose of the visit. This step is followed by a review of family history and symptoms. The healthcare providers document the aforementioned information in *clinical notes* embedded in an EMR. They proceed with *differential analysis* leading to a diagnosis of the case on hand and a declaration of the future actions to be taken.

The adequate decision comes from following a specific set of evidence-based *diagnostic algorithms* that medical professionals learn during their education and training. These algorithms are decision diagrams whose top nodes are labeled with markers and identifiers that occur typically in the chief complaints.

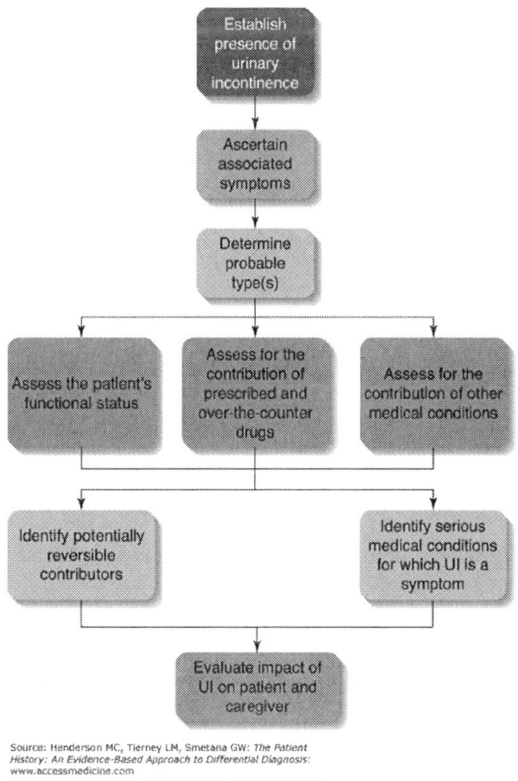

Figure 1: Diagnostic algorithm extracted from "Symptom to Diagnosis: An Evidence-based Guide"

The algorithms lead the healthcare providers with a series of choice nodes reaching to the leaves which typically dictate the diagnosis and the treatment plan. Intermediary nodes in the algorithms describe lab tests, medication prescriptions, special treatments, and life-style changes among other actions. The healthcare providers select the algorithms to follow after assessing the situation from discussions with the patient, initial clinical tests and documentation in the clinical notes and EMRs.

They select and follow the algorithm that best

Proceedings of the 17th Conference of the European Chapter of the Association for Computational Linguistics System Demonstrations, pages 307–314
May 2-4, 2023 ©2023 Association for Computational Linguistics

matches the encountered case. They traverse the decision diagram of the algorithm, come up with an adequate diagnosis, and declare further actions to be taken.

The healthcare provider documents the information collecting during the encounter with the patient in a clinical note summarizing the process from the initial complaint to the actual outcomes. Our aim is to assist the healthcare professionals in the process of coming up with adequate diagnosis by filtering out the top three diagnostic algorithms matching their notes and visualizing them.

In this paper, we present DAVE (Differential Analysis Visualizer for EMRs), a system that automates the selection and visualization process of the diagnostic algorithms. DAVE alleviates healthcare providers from the tedious tasks that require remembering and visualizing the graphs. It also simplifies the decision-making process involved in the *diagnostic differential analysis* (DDA) phase. DDA consists of analyzing in real time the input notes and selecting the most suitable algorithms.

We developed and fine-tuned DAVE via training on pre-existing curated datasets. We leveraged an annotated corpora of electronic medical records collected from AUBMC and the Hariri Medical Center in Beirut, Lebanon. The corpora consist of 151,930 total medical notes focused on family medicine. All the notes are annotated with diagnostic codes and treatment plans that annotate the whole record. A subset of 3,616 of the notes are richly annotated with textual annotations referring to textual elements in the note itself.

DAVE also leverages digitized clinical diagnostic algorithms extracted from medical books: "The Patient History: Evidence-Based Approach" (Henderson et al., 2012a) and "Symptom to Diagnosis: An Evidence-based Guide" (Stern et al., 2019). These textbook algorithms represent the steps that need to be taken to determine and treat a specific healthcare condition. Our method involves *cross-document* analysis based on cross-referencing electronic medical record entities. This aims at extracting diagnosis indicators from the notes using natural language processing (NLP) and computational linguistics (CL).

We presented DAVE to a number of medical professionals, physicians, and medical IT experts and received overwhelmingly positive feedback. We demonstrated the project to three physicians and interviewed them about usability and functionality. After using DAVE, they provided positive feedback and emphasized its usefulness, particularly for students, nurses, and young physicians. We also interviewed the head of IT at AUBMC, a well-established medical center, and her team. She also praised the software and encouraged its integration within the medical center for professional use.

2 Related Work

Information extraction (IE) from EMR has become a crucial tool to progress medical and clinical practice research since the emergence of digital records. The understanding gained from this data has a significant positive impact on current medical research. For this reason , a number of studies and initiatives have looked into the best ways of extracting data from medical records. Rule-based algorithms, machine learning (ML) models and keyword-based search are the major methodologies used in IE from EMRs, with rule-based models being the most accurate but most time consuming to build. This is due to the fact that the rules express accurately the direct knowledge and experience of healthcare professionals (Ford et al., 2016; Wang et al., 2018).

Several reviews discussed the different approaches used for IE in the medical field (Ford et al., 2016; Wang et al., 2018; Deléger et al., 2010). DAVE will be built using ML as its core. It will mimic the behavior of rule-based methods by capturing insight from clinical diagnostic books. It avoids the cost of rule-based approaches since healthcare professionals will not have to manually provide rules.

The work (B.Sharafeddin, 2020) introduced a model for the automation of the process of diagnostic extraction from clinical notes. It matches unstructured de-identified medical notes to medical diagnostic algorithms using a cross-document analysis method. The model uses the diagnostic algorithms (Henderson et al., 2012b) from medical books to build Bayesian Networks corresponding to every diagnosis case. In these networks, nodes are interrelated by informational dependencies.In other words, each node is given a conditional probability depending on the probability of its parent (Pearl, 2011).

Afterwards, it calculates the distributional similarity for the words in the electronic medical notes and United States Medical Licensing Examination (USMLE) questions using DISCO (extracting DIstributionally related words using CO-occurrences)

(Kolb, 2008).

This method allows the extraction of diagnosis indicators by retrieving the semantic similarity between words and phrases in large text fields to create sets of similar words for every word (B.Sharafeddin, 2020).

In order to compute *semantic similarity*, we also used DISCO, also known as the KOLB (after Peter Kolb) vector similarity. DISCO retrieves the most semantically similar words for an input word (Kolb, 2008). It is accompanied with the DISCO builder tool (DBuilder). The latter creates a database of contextually similar words, given a text corpus. Prior to the actual build, DBuilder recommends configuring the corpus to the given format to ensure the best possible outcome. DBuilder accepts lemmatized or tokenized input in single or multiple files. Larger contexts (or paragraphs as referred to by the documentation) should be specified using tags. DBuilder takes care of excluding stop-words from the context as they can contribute to noise. It is also important to specify the size of the context each word should be taken in when configuring the builder instance. (Kolb, 2008). Giving a ± 3 to the context window will check the surrounding three words from the right and left of each target term. Subsequently, DBuilder creates a matrix of co-occurrences in which each row describes a specific word.

The size of the resulting matrix would be $n \times m \times r$ where n denotes the number of words in the corpus, m denotes the number of words used as features and r is the window size.

Equation 1 is used to provide meaningful weights for the features in which w, and w' stand for words, r stands for the window size, $-$ within functional parameters stands for dependency relation and f is the frequency of occurrence.

$$\frac{\log(((f(w,r,w') - 0.95) * f(-,r,-))}{f(w,r,-) * f(-,r,w'))} \quad (1)$$

The information theory based Lin's measure is then used for the comparison of every word vector with all other word vectors to create a distributional similarity scheme between all the words (Kolb, 2008).

Negated words present in the medical notes lead to faulty results when matching them to the corresponding diagnostic algorithm in our work. The ConText algorithm provides an approach to deal with negated words by employing a specific scope of its trigger terms. Once medical conditions are indexed, the algorithm assigns three contextual properties to each condition being (i) Negation, (ii) Temporality and (iii) Experiencer. Negation can be either negated or affirmed. Temporality can be recent, historical, or hypothetical. Finally, experiencer can be either patient or other. A set of trigger words is assigned to each non-default status (Harkema et al., 2009).

The status of the contextual properties is updated when the indexed medical condition term falls within the scope of one of the trigger terms. Moreover, the algorithm contains pseudo-trigger words for each non-default status of the contextual properties. The scope of the trigger or pseudo-trigger terms includes all the clinical conditions following them till the termination word or till the end of the sentence if no termination word was present. The termination words are assembled in the algorithm following conceptual groups. In other words, the algorithm takes as input the sentence, indexes the clinical conditions, and assigns each of the contextual properties a default value. Then, it marks all the trigger, pseudo-trigger and termination words and iterates through them to determine the scope of each trigger term and update the corresponding contextual property of the indexed medical case.

3 Methods

This section discusses the preprocessing of EMR notes, building and utilising DISCO models, aggregating scores from different models, capturing user input, and visualizing the graphs.

3.1 Preprocessing

Since medical text contains a large amount of noise that affects the results of an NLP model we executed a series of preprocessing and data cleaning before inputting the data in our model.

3.1.1 Abbreviations

Medical doctors tend to use numerous abbreviations when documenting their clinical notes given the overloaded schedule, heavy workload, and overall workflow efficiency. In the aim of simulating a real medical note, a medical data set for abbreviations had to be included. This dataset was used to replace all the abbreviations in the medical corpora by their actual meaning. When processing the user's input, tokens are then matched with their full word if applicable.

3.1.2 Autocorrection

Apart from using abbreviations, potential spelling mistakes were accounted for in both the training and the user data. DAVE used Levenshtein's method of distance metrics for auto-correction through the PySpellChecker implementation. Theoretically, the Levenshtein distance is a metric for measuring the differences between two strings treated as two separate sequences (Yujian and Bo, 2007). This metric creates a matrix by looping over all the letters of the two input strings it takes according to the rule in figure 2 shown below.

$$\mathrm{lev}_{a,b}(i,j) = \begin{cases} \max(i,j) & \text{if } \min(i,j) = 0, \\ \min \begin{cases} \mathrm{lev}_{a,b}(i-1,j)+1 \\ \mathrm{lev}_{a,b}(i,j-1)+1 \\ \mathrm{lev}_{a,b}(i-1,j-1)+1_{(a_i \neq b_j)} \end{cases} & \text{otherwise.} \end{cases}$$

Figure 2: Levenshtein Distance Rule for Matrix Creation

The size of the matrix would be $(m+1)\times(n+1)$ where m and n are the sizes of the tested words, respectively. The matrix is filled from the upper left cell initialized to zero to the lower right entry with the actual distance between both words (Yujian and Bo, 2007).

This method proved to be the fastest for offline and dynamic performance. It uses the permutations within a 2 edit distance radius from the original word and returns the most likely correct result. However, in the case of medical autocorrection, many medical terms and abbreviations were treated as spelling mistakes and corrected accordingly. Therefore, a set of medical terms was included to be interpreted by PySpellChecker before making the decision to correct any given token. The process goes as follows:

1. The spell checker goes through the tokenized words and flags the included unknown words.

2. The unknown words are then filtered by the set of medical terms.

3. If not found to be medical terms, another pass is done to determine if the word is an abbreviation of a medical or an English term.

4. If the word is still not found, auto-correction is then applied.

For the training medical notes corpora, all of the tokenized words were checked in the described manner. However, for the dynamic user input, if the word is pre-computed and available in the model, it is automatically used for scoring and not passed for spell checking.

3.1.3 Negation Extraction

DAVE handled negated sentences featured in training medical notes by extracting and analyzing them on a context level rather than a token level by virtue of DISCO. However, negation can contribute to noise when analyzing the user's input. Therefore, DAVE adopted a conservative negation extraction technique. If an input token symbolizes negation, the following word is excluded from matching. For instance, in the sentence: "No Fever", the word "Fever" would be removed as it might lead to a faulty diagnosis conclusion if included(Mehrabi et al., 2015). The negation operators were identified within context from a precomputed NegSpaCy negation list.

Furthermore, we experimented with the ConText algorithm approach (Harkema et al., 2009), implemented as part of the MedSpacy library (Eyre et al., 2021) in the negation extraction scheme. The scheme returned good results in terms of accuracy and relevance. However, it is not yet implemented in the application and requires additional work to ensure optimization. The algorithm is in consideration for future work.

3.2 DISCO, PubMed word spaces

The DISCO (Kolb, 2008) linguistic tools compute the distributional similarity between given words in a left-right context array, given the start and the end of the context. DISCO takes input in tokenized or lemmatized format. The clinical notes corpora gathered from the Medical Institutes, is processed through DISCO Builder to create a word space out of the given lemmatized/tokenized documents. DBuilder relies on tags to determine the full corpora, and the seperate contexts at hand. We configured the medical corpora by lemmatizing the notes and seperating them into "contexts", where each note detail was considered to be one context. From there, every given word is analyzed based off a specific context window (i.e. words to its left and right). Word vectors are created based off contextual similarity. The weighting methods and the similarity measures are following Lin's measure and the KOLB methods respectively. The output of DBuilder is a word space, packaged through an indexing schema, ready to be loaded through the

DISCO java library to output scores. With a corpus size of $7,060,230$ feature words, $2,122,706$ after filtering, the output word space included a $136,145$ target feature words.

In order to provide better accuracy metrics, we also utilized a pre-computed word space from PubMed, with over 181 million tokens and feature words. This word space is built using approximately $100,000$ medical articles from the PubMed Open Access database.

3.3 Score Aggregation

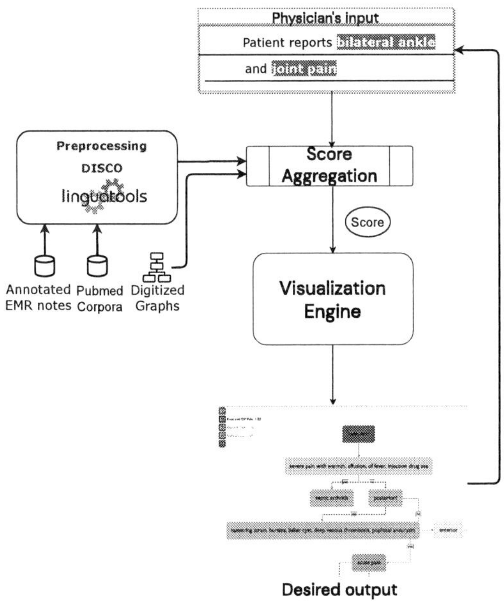

Figure 3: Illustration of DAVE's Pipeline

To generate diagnostic predictions, DAVE utilizes a map from the diagnostic algorithm nodes to the words present in these nodes featured. DAVE tokenizes the feature words and assigns the peak word score at 1. Every instance of a given term is stored accordingly, including repeated occurrences within the same graph.

The feature words are then augmented using the DISCO word space model. Each word featured originally in the map is passed through the indexed word space to retrieve the most semantically similar words within two collocation contexts.

1. The given word with the clinical note corpora word space.
2. The given word with the PubMed corpora word space.

The top three most semantically similar terms and their respective similarity scores are fed back into the model, and are matched with the same graphs as the original input term, but with the scores provided by DISCO.

To further refine the scores and reduce the noise caused by frequently occurring terms, DAVE applies a score modification scheme. The modified score considers the frequency of the term. This modified score assigns a lower weight to frequently occurring terms and a higher weight to less frequent terms, thus improving the accuracy of DAVE by giving more weight to terms specific to a particular diagnosis.

Finally, according to the user's input the score of each term is aggregated to provide a final score for each potential diagnosis. DAVE determines the score of each diagnostic graph by summing the scores of its nodes. This scoring aggregation scheme helps DAVE to accurately identify the most relevant diagnoses for a given clinical note.

3.4 Capturing User Input

DAVE takes the clinical notes written by the user as input, tokenizes them, and matches them with the feature words inside the computed DISCO models. With each tokenized input word w, if present, DAVE proceeds to score each diagnostic algorithm a based on the occurrences of w inside a. This leads to incrementing the scores of the involved algorithms, progressively forming a leaderboard of the top matching algorithms to the user's live input. The top matching algorithms are then transmitted to the user's interface graphing engine for display.

3.5 Graph Visualization

DAVE implemented the visualization of the graphs using Cytoscape.js(Franz et al., 2016), a powerful graph engine, and presented through a web interface. Cytoscape.js enabled us to achieve a fast and interactive experience for physicians.

It allowed us to customize our visualization schema by adding multiple extra features to enhance the user's experience. The user is prompted with the top three graphs along with their corresponding score and can issue a request for three more graphs. Furthermore, we implemented the displaying of the top matching node within a graph. The user is then free to accept or reject the given node. If rejected, the user is taken to the next top scoring node within the given graph. The Accept-Reject feature serves as a potential reinforcement learning model, to provide better results in the future.

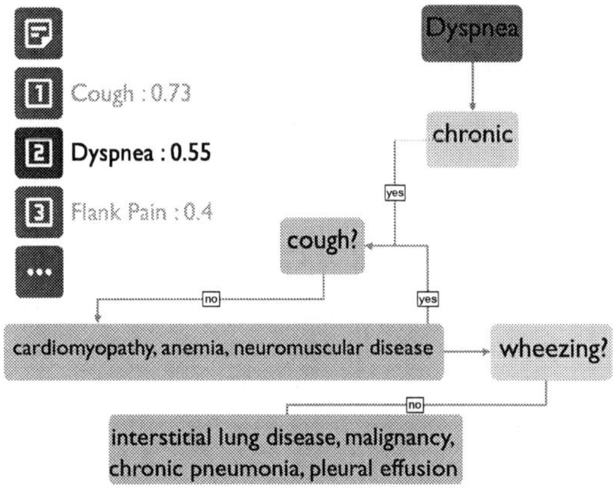

Figure 4: DAVE demo illustration

4 Testing

We tested the NLP model we built for DAVE on real medical notes from AUBMC and the Hariri Medical Center. The notes, in XML format, have the following standardized layout.

- The <text> tag represents the input of the medical doctor,
- The <DxDesc> represents the Diagnosis Description, which is the final diagnosis concluded by the MD.
- These two fields were the target for experimental testing.
- The remaining fields were anonymized if out of context.

We constructed a unit testing program that traverses the given notes and randomly picks out N notes for testing. One constraint forced on picking the target test note was the length of the text field after tokenization. We imposed a minimum length of 10 words, as notes shorter than that would prove inconclusive even to the medical doctor himself since they should be considered as poorly documented. After picking the N notes, the program pairs each text field with its diagnosis description field. Having gathered the test notes, the program stores the test notes for reference in future testing runs and requests the hash map model in question. The test program then compiles the given notes and passes them through the pipeline and outputs the top three results along with their scores.

The output is then dumped into a text file, where we check and calculate the given model and pipeline precision and accuracy. Even though the final diagnosis and considerations are included in the test notes, performance testing is reviewed manually since final note diagnoses are not standardized and show countless expressions for the same diagnosis across the dataset.

5 User Study and Feedback

During its development phases, Dr. Lama Sharafeddine and Dr. Rabiaa Algeboury provided valuable feedback on DAVE, praising its usability and effectiveness in its final version. As medical professionals themselves, they recommended the tool as a learning aid for up-and-coming physicians and a support tool for note completion during patient visits, as well as for the visualization of more complex cases. Additionally, they expressed interest in training DAVE with notes and algorithms in specialty medicine so that medical doctor residents may also benefit from its use.

We conducted two sets of interviews with medical IT experts, specifically the head of IT of AUBMC, Ms. Rola Antoun, and her team.

In the first round, we presented the idea of DAVE and our preliminary implementation plans. They commended our design and helped us brainstorm potential use cases among physicians. They also provided us with insight on what to avoid so that physicians don't refrain from using the software. For example, because it appears complex or requires any additional load like navigating through multiple pages and pressing multiple buttons. Finally, they showcased a few of the more popular software tools and applications among physicians, in hopes of providing further inspiration for DAVE. After completing the project, we met for a second round to demonstrate our work and get usability feedback. They praised the project, were fascinated by the results, and thought it was mature enough to be deployed in the EHR of the medical center for professional use. Furthermore, we had three physicians try out the software and discuss its usability and practicality. We first asked them if this software would benefit them. Two of three said they find the visualization very helpful and beneficiary and would assist the complex task of differential analysis visualization in memory. They also thought that expanding beyond the top three matches is helpful. When asked about user-friendliness, all physicians found the user experience to be simple, fast, and non-tasking. Finally, we received some ideas to make DAVE better. For example, adding specialty diagnostic books to target specific areas of medicine would make the software more useful for more experienced physicians.

6 Results

DAVE's model presented successful and promising results. Considering the difficulty and challenges of NLP in the medical field and case detection algorithms in general, DAVE's model achieved a fairly high accuracy while maintaining a small computation overhead since the results are required to be displayed instantaneously. It also has no problem supporting large text and does not require GPU resources. The best version of the model with all the processing and word augmentations achieved a 74.3% rate of displaying a related diagnosis in the top three scored algorithms. We opted for precision at the best three results to eliminate any chance of bias from headache and fatigue diagnoses which are very general making their symptoms usually present in all diagnoses. This accuracy increased significantly with the addition of PubMed medical corpora as shown in Table 1. The table presents different accuracy results after each step of the pipeline. The prediction rate improved significantly from the processing and the elimination of misleading scores and unnecessary words.

Text Corpus	Score
Notes + PubMed	57%
Notes + PubMed + stop words removed (SWR)	68%
Notes + PubMed + SWR + modification of scores (MS)	70%
Notes + PubMed + SWR + MS + correction (CORR)	73%
Notes + PubMed + SWR + MS + CORR + negation	74.3%

Table 1: Summary of the experimental results throughout multiple stages of the DAVE's pipeline

To further understand the performance of DAVE we also conducted a precision@k test where the evaluation metric is predicting a correct diagnosis in one of the top k-matched graphs, with k ranging from 1 to 5. Table 2 presents the results. The results reinforce that displaying the *top three* scored algorithms for the medical professionals is the best practical choice.

K	1	2	3	4	5
Precision (%)	31.25	53.125	74.3	78.125	78.125

Table 2: Precision obtained when a correct diagnosis is in the top k-matched algorithms.

To conclude, DAVE achieved accurate results and was deemed user-friendly and very convenient for professional use. It offloads a tedious task from physicians and supports their decision-making during patient visits. It was also regarded as ready for professional use by medical professionals and medical IT experts. Several medical information outlets such as hospitals, and medical insurance companies provide text to diagnosis portals. However, they do not attempt to fully automate the differential diagnosis process. Up to our knowledge no DAVE alternative systems exist so that we can perform a one to one comparison.

7 Limitations

The main limitation of DAVE is testing it in real time situations. Since the involvement of physicians is required to test DAVE in different note-taking stages, exhaustive realtime testing proved to be difficult. DAVE's objective is to guide and support the physician during the diagnosis process, hence we are interested in the accuracy of the program during different stages of completion of the clinical note. We tested DAVE with volunteer physicians, however, we consider the sample tests as initial and we think that full deployment requires more systematic testing.

8 Conclusion

This paper details a novel model that can suggest diagnostic algorithms to medical professionals based on their clinical notes in real-time. The model uses directed acyclic graphs and semantic similarity metrics to rank diagnostic algorithm graphs taken from digitized medical textbooks and suggests the top three for consideration. The model achieves 74.3% success rate and high acceptance for usability. This model is a significant step forward in improving the accuracy and efficiency of the differential analysis process, which is crucial in making timely and accurate diagnoses and developing effective treatment plans for patients. You can find DAVE online: www.davemr.com. The following is a DAVE system demonstration video. You could also find DAVE's source code on Github

References

B.Sharafeddin. 2020. Cross-document analysis for diagnosis extraction from electronic medical records.

Louise Deléger, Cyril Grouin, and Pierre Zweigenbaum. 2010. Extracting medical information from narrative patient records: the case of medication-related information. *Journal of the American Medical Informatics Association*, 17(5):555–558.

H. Eyre, A. B. Chapman, K. S. Peterson, J. Shi, P. R. Alba, M. M. Jones, T. L. Box, S. L. DuVall, and O. V. Patterson. 2021. Launching into clinical space with medspaCy: a new clinical text processing toolkit in Python. *AMIA Annu Symp Proc*, 2021:438–447.

Elizabeth Ford, John A Carroll, Helen E Smith, Donia Scott, and Jackie A Cassell. 2016. Extracting information from the text of electronic medical records to improve case detection: a systematic review. *Journal of the American Medical Informatics Association*, 23(5):1007–1015.

Max Franz, Christian T Lopes, Gerardo Huck, Yue Dong, Onur Sumer, and Gary D Bader. 2016. Cytoscape. js: a graph theory library for visualisation and analysis. *Bioinformatics*, 32(2):309–311.

Henk Harkema, John N Dowling, Tyler Thornblade, and Wendy W Chapman. 2009. Context: an algorithm for determining negation, experiencer, and temporal status from clinical reports. *Journal of biomedical informatics*, 42(5):839–851.

Mark Henderson, Lawrence M Tierney, and Gerald W Smetana. 2012a. *The patient history: Evidence-based approach*. McGraw Hill Professional.

Mark Richard Henderson, Lawrence M Tierney, and Gerald W Smetana. 2012b. *The patient history: an evidence-based approach to differential diagnosis*. Ph.D. thesis, Univerza v Ljubljani, Medicinska fakulteta.

Peter Kolb. 2008. Disco: A multilingual database of distributionally similar words. *Proceedings of KONVENS-2008, Berlin*, 156.

Saeed Mehrabi, Anand Krishnan, Sunghwan Sohn, Alexandra M Roch, Heidi Schmidt, Joe Kesterson, Chris Beesley, Paul Dexter, C Max Schmidt, Hongfang Liu, et al. 2015. Deepen: A negation detection system for clinical text incorporating dependency relation into negex. *Journal of biomedical informatics*, 54:213–219.

Judea Pearl. 2011. Bayesian networks.

Scott DC Stern, Adam S Cifu, and Diane Altkorn. 2019. *Symptom to Diagnosis An Evidence Based Guide*. McGraw Hill Professional.

Yanshan Wang, Liwei Wang, Majid Rastegar-Mojarad, Sungrim Moon, Feichen Shen, Naveed Afzal, Sijia Liu, Yuqun Zeng, Saeed Mehrabi, Sunghwan Sohn, et al. 2018. Clinical information extraction applications: a literature review. *Journal of biomedical informatics*, 77:34–49.

Li Yujian and Liu Bo. 2007. A normalized levenshtein distance metric. *IEEE transactions on pattern analysis and machine intelligence*, 29(6):1091–1095.

Author Index

Abbas, Ummar, 75
Abou Chakra, Chadi, 307
Akkurt, Furkan, 219
Albalak, Alon, 1
Amplayo, Reinald Kim, 105
Arana-catania, Miguel, 67
Arenas-garcía, Jerónimo, 43
Attanasio, Giuseppe, 256

Barbosa, Denilson, 18
Bartsch, Sabine, 248
Biemann, Chris, 11
Bićanić, Miroslav, 228
Bontcheva, Kalina, 145
Bosselut, Antoine, 96

Callison-burch, Chris, 267
Calvo Bartolomé, Lorena, 43
Chae, Hyungjoo, 195
Chiang, Yi-shyuan, 50
Cote, Marc-alexandre, 169

Dalvi, Fahim, 75
Dankar, Mira, 307
Das, Dipanjan, 105
De Stefani, Jacopo, 117
Di Bonaventura, Chiara, 256
Do, Truong, 35
Durrani, Nadir, 75

Einarsson, Hafsteinn, 152
El Baff, Roxanne, 248
Espinosa Melchor, José Antonio, 43

Finlayson, Mark, 27

Ganchev, Kuzman, 105
Ginsberg, Etan, 267
Grace, Marie, 209
Gudmundsson, Breki, 152
Gui, Lin, 67
Gungor, Onur, 219
Guzhva, Kostyantyn, 18
Güngör, Tunga, 219
Gürbüz, Merve, 219

Hamm, Andreas, 248
Hamoud, Hadi, 307
He, Yulan, 67
Hecking, Tobias, 248
Hervieux, Natalie, 18
Heyer, Gerhard, 277
Hou, Jue, 136
Huang, Ta-wei, 50
Huang, Yu-shiang, 50
Hummer, Jared, 27
Huot, Fantine, 105
Husaini, Mus'ab, 75

Ismayilzada, Mete, 96

Jaban, Tamim, 75
Jang, Yul, 195
Jansen, Peter, 169
Jelenić, Fran, 228
Joo, Se June, 195
Ju, Jia-huei, 50
Jukić, Josip, 228
Jänicke, Stefan, 277

Karmakharm, Twin, 145
Katinskaia, Anisia, 136
Khan, Abuzar, 152
Kim, Seungone, 195
Kleinen-von Konigslow, Katharina, 11
Kochkina, Elena, 67
Kogkalidis, Konstantinos, 128
Korte, Jasper W., 248
Kosmajac, Matej, 18

Lapata, Mirella, 105
Larusdottir, Marta Kristin, 152
Lenaerts, Tom, 117
Levy, Sharon, 1
Liakata, Maria, 67
Lin, Cheng-wei, 50
Loftsson, Hrafn, 152
Louis, Annie Priyadarshini, 105

Ma, Jingkun, 57
Marciniak, Malgorzata, 178
Marshall, Iain, 236
Matsumoto, Yuji, 35
Maynez, Joshua, 105
Mcinerney, Jered, 236
Moon, Geonsik, 298

Moortgat, Michael, 128
Moot, Richard, 128
Mujadia, Vandan, 161
Mykowiecka, Agnieszka, 178
Müller, Lydia, 84

Nachtegael, Charlotte, 117
Narayan, Shashi, 105
Ng, Hwee Tou, 298
Nguyen, Chau, 35
Nguyen, Minh, 35
Niekler, Andreas, 84
Nozza, Debora, 256
Nyberg, Eric, 152

Ocal, Mustafa, 27
Özgür, Arzucan, 219

Palmer, Alexis, 209
Pastor, Eliana, 256
Petersen-frey, Fynn, 11
Potthast, Martin, 84
Procter, Rob, 67

Qorib, Muhammad Reza, 298

Radas, Antonela, 27
Ramprasad, Sanjana, 236
Ribeiro, Bruno, 187
Roberts, Ian, 145
Rolla, Vitor, 187
Rychlik, Piotr, 178

Sajjad, Hassan, 75
Sandholm, Anders, 105
Santos, Ricardo, 187
Satoh, Ken, 35
Schneider, Florian, 11
Schröder, Christopher, 84
Seabrum, Jay, 209
Sharma, Dipti, 161
Singh, Akul, 27
Skarphedinsson, Njall, 152
Smari, Steinar, 152
Snajder, Jan, 228
Song, Xingyi, 145
Srinivas, Dananjay, 209
Şen, Muhammet, 219

Tran, Vu, 35

Upadhyay, Shriyash, 267
Uskudarli, Susan, 219

Von Nordheim, Gerret, 11
Vu, Anh-duc, 136

Waheed, Abeer, 18
Wallace, Byron, 236
Wang, Chuan-ju, 50
Wang, William Yang, 1
Wilby, David, 145
Wong, Derek F., 57

Yangarber, Roman, 136
Yao, Peiran, 18
Yeo, Jinyoung, 195
Yimam, Seid Muhie, 11
Yousef, Tariq, 277

Zaraket, Fadi, 307
Zhan, Runzhe, 57
Zhao, Runcong, 67
Zhu, Lixing, 67
Zubiaga, Arkaitz, 67

Association for Computational Linguistics
209 N. Eighth Street
Stroudsburg, Pennsylvania 18360

ISBN 978-1-7138-7377-8

CURRAN ASSOCIATES INC.
proceedings.com